COLLECTED WORKS OF

BERNARD LONERGAN

VOLUME 22

EARLY WORKS ON THEOLOGICAL METHOD 1

D1605639

GENERAL EDITORS

Frederick E. Crowe and Robert M. Doran

COLLECTED WORKS
OF BERNARD

LONERGAN

*EARLY WORKS ON
THEOLOGICAL METHOD 1*

*edited by
Robert M. Doran and
Robert C. Croken*

Published for Lonergan Research Institute
of Regis College, Toronto
by University of Toronto Press
Toronto Buffalo London

ISBN 978-1-4426-4086-3 (cloth)
ISBN 978-1-4426-1020-0 (paper)

Printed on acid-free, 100% post-consumer recycled paper with vegetable-based inks.

Library and Archives Canada Cataloguing in Publication

Lonergan, Bernard J.F. (Bernard Joseph Francis), 1904–1984
Collected works of Bernard Lonergan

Partial contents: v. 22. Early works on theological method I / edited by Robert M. Doran and Robert C. Croken
Includes bibliographical references and index.
ISBN 978-1-4426-4086-3 (bound)   ISBN 978-1-4426-1020-0 (pbk.)

1. Theology – 20th century.   2. Catholic Church.   I. Croken, Robert C., 1933–
II. Doran, Robert M., 1939–   III. Lonergan Research Institute   IV. Title.

BX891.L595 1988   230   c880-933283

The Lonergan Research institute gratefully acknowledges the generous contribution of the Malliner Charitable Foundation, which has made possible the production of this entire series.

The Lonergan Reseach Institute gratefully acknowledges the contribution of Ronald C. Chochol toward publication of this volume.

University of Toronto Press acknowledges the financial assistance to its publishing program of the Canada Council for the Arts and Ontario Arts Council.

University of Toronto Press acknowledges the financial support for its publishing activities of the Government of Canada through the Canada Book Fund.

Contents

General Editors' Preface, ROBERT M. DORAN / xiii

PART ONE: REGIS COLLEGE INSTITUTE 'ON THE
METHOD OF THEOLOGY,' 9–20 JULY 1962 / 1

1962-1 Operations, the Subject, Objects, Method / 3
  1 Method and Operations / 4
    1.1 Piaget, Operations, and Habits / 5
    1.2 Three Types of Mediation / 8
    1.3 The Brevity of Methodical Analysis / 9
    1.4 Experiencing the Operations / 10
    1.5 Fundamental Cognitional Operations / 11
  2 The Subject / 12
    2.1 Horizon / 13
    2.2 Conversion / 14
    2.3 Inauthenticity / 15
  3 Objects / 19
    3.1 Formal and Material Objects / 19
    3.2 Contexts and Development / 20
    3.3 A Note on Method / 23
  4 Consideration of Method / 24
    *4.1 Method Immediately about Operations, Mediately about
       Subjects and Objects /* 24
    4.2 Comparative, Genetic, and Dialectical Methods / 24

**1962-2 The Human Good, Meaning, and Differentiations
of Consciousness** / 30

1 Summary of Previous Lecture / 30

2 The Human Good / 34

    2.1 The Structure / 34

    2.2 The Particular Good / 35

    2.3 The Good of Order / 36

    2.4 Terminal Values / 38

    2.5 Progress and Decline / 40

3 Meaning / 40

4 Classifications of Development / 42

    4.1 An Alternative Basis of Development / 42

    4.2 The Sacred and the Profane / 43

    4.3 The Subject and the Object / 46

    4.4 Common Sense and Theory / 49

    4.5 Consciousness as Foundation of These Distinctions / 52

    4.6 Mediation / 53

**1962-3 Integration of Worlds and Contemporary
Theological Problems** / 56

1 Limits and Development / 56

2 Worlds / 60

3 Integration of the Different Worlds / 64

4 Contemporary Theological Problems / 67

    4.1 The Aristotelian-Augustinian Controversy / 68

    4.2 Aristotelian Science / 70

    4.3 Modern Science / 71

    4.4 Historical Consciousness / 73

    4.5 New Tendencies and the Eclipse of the World of Theory / 76

1962-4 Elements of Theology / 81

1 Theory / 81

2 The Scientific Model / 88

    2.1 The Greek Ideal and the Modern Notion / 88

    2.2 Certainty versus Probability / 88

    2.3 The Universal versus the Concrete / 89

    2.4 Immutability versus Process / 89

    2.5 Necessity versus Empirical Intelligibility / 90

    2.6 Complementing the Old with the New / 90

3 Intelligibility and Truth / 92

    3.1 Empirical Intelligibility / 92

3.2 *Judgment* / 95

3.3 *Logic, Method, Esprit de finesse, Illative Sense* / 100

3.4 *Wisdom* / 102

1962-5 Beyond Extrinsicism and Immanentism / 103

1 Theology and Wisdom: Concluding Remarks / 103

2 Extrinsicism / 108

2.1 *Extrinsicism Defined* / 108

2.2 *Deductivist Extrinsicism* / 109

2.3 *Operational Extrinsicism* / 113

2.4 *Metaphysical Extrinsicism* / 116

2.5 *Intuitionist Extrinsicism* / 118

3 Immanentism / 123

3.1 *The Root of Immanentism* / 123

3.2 *Breaking Immanentism* / 124

3.3 *Contemporary Immanentisms* / 125

1962-6 Knowing, Believing, and Theology / 128

1 Clarifications of Cognitional Theory / 128

1.1 *The Preconceptual and the Unity of the Ancient and Modern Ideals of Science* / 128

1.2 *Thomist and Scotist Analysis* / 129

1.3 *Notion, Concept, Knowledge, and Idea of Being* / 131

1.4 *Knowing Is a Compound* / 132

1.5 *Self-consciousness and Self-knowledge* / 132

1.6 *The Unity of Human Knowledge* / 133

1.7 *The Compound Notion of Human Knowing and Metaphysics* / 134

2 Assembling the Elements / 136

2.1 *The Systematic Exigence and the World of Theory* / 136

2.2 *The Critical Exigence and the World of Interiority* / 138

2.3 *The Methodical Exigence* / 138

2.4 *The Genetic Circle* / 140

2.5 *Aberrations and Deviations* / 140

3 Knowledge and Belief / 141

3.1 *The Effects of Belief* / 142

3.2 *Elements of Belief* / 143

3.2.1 Object / 143

3.2.2 Motive / 143

3.2.3 The Act of Faith / 143

3.2.4 The Act of Will / 144

3.2.5 Grasping the Unconditioned / 144

      3.3 Human and Divine Faith / 145
      3.4 The Light of Faith / 147
      3.5 A New Interiority / 150
   4 Theology, Faith, and Knowledge / 150
      4.1 The Vatican Decree / 151
      4.2 Human Intellect and Natural Knowledge / 151
      4.3 Faith and Theology / 152
   5 From Faith to Theology / 153

1962-7 Transitions and Thematizations / 156
   1 From Faith to Theology / 156
   2 An Illustration / 158
   3 Modes of the Transition / 161
   4 Three Instances of Thematizing / 162
   5 Symbolic, Classical, and Historical Consciousness / 164
   6 A Concrete Example of the Transition from Scripture to
     Theological Assertion / 166
   7 Thematization, Summation, Integration / 170
   8 Thematization and Dogmatic Theology / 175

1962-8 Positive and Systematic Theology, and Meaning / 182
   1 Positive Theology / 182
      1.1 Truth and Thematization / 182
      1.2 Comparative Method / 185
      1.3 Understanding the Doctrine and Understanding the History
        of the Doctrine / 188
      1.4 Genetic Method / 191
      1.5 Dialectical Method / 192
   2 Systematic Theology / 194
   3 Meaning / 197
      3.1 Intersubjective Meaning / 198
      3.2 Aesthetic Meaning / 201
      3.3 Symbolic Meaning / 204

1962-9 Hermeneutics / 208
   1 Applying a Cognitional Theory / 209
   2 Interpreting a Text / 211
      2.1 Understanding the Text / 211
         2.1.1 Understanding the Thing or Object / 211
         2.1.2 Understanding the Words / 214

2.1.3 Understanding the Author / 216

2.1.4 Romantic Hermeneutics / 218

2.1.5 Development of the Interpreter / 220

2.2 *Judging the Correctness of One's Understanding* / 221

2.3 *Stating the Meaning of the Text* / 225

2.3.1 Commonsense Communication / 227

2.3.2 Scientific Communication / 227

2.3.3 Foundations of Communication / 228

2.3.4 Philosophy and Theology in Communication / 230

2.3.5 Basic Context / 232

1962-10 History / 234

1 The Notion of Time / 235

2 History and Time / 235

3 Existential and Narrative History / 236

4 Critical History / 238

5 Historismus / 240

5.1 Historical Consciousness / 241

5.2 Historical Relativism / 242

5.3 Historical Method / 244

6 Methodical Classification of Historical Studies / 249

6.1 Common Historical Research / 249

6.2 The Historical Essay / 250

6.3 History and Science / 251

6.4 History and Philosophy / 252

6.5 History and Tradition / 253

6.6 History and Religion / 256

6.7 History and Apologetics / 257

6.8 Theological Mediation of History / 258

1962 Discussion 1 / 260

1962 Discussion 2 / 282

1962 Discussion 3 / 303

1962 Discussion 4 / 326

1962 Discussion 5 / 339

1962 Discussion 6 / 354

1962 Discussion 7 / 366

PART TWO: AVERY CARDINAL DULLES'S NOTES
FOR LONERGAN'S 'A FIVE-DAY INSTITUTE:
THE METHOD IN THEOLOGY,' 13–17 JULY 1964,
GEORGETOWN UNIVERSITY / 375

1964-1 The Contemporary Problem / 377
    Morning Lecture: Factors External to Theology / 377
        1 Shift in Model of Science / 377
        2 Notion of Meaning / 379
        Questions / 382
    Afternoon Lecture, part 1: Factors External to Theology
    (continued) / 383
        Notion of Meaning (continued) / 383
        3 Historical Consciousness / 384
        Afternoon Lecture, part 2: The Internal Situation / 385
        Questions / 387

1964-2 Reason Illumined by Faith / 388
    Morning Lecture: Human Knowing as Operational Structure / 388
        1 Knowing / 388
        2 Objectivity / 389
        3 Consciousness / 390
    Afternoon Lecture: Transformation of Reason by Faith / 391
        1 This Transformation Affects the Levels of Data,
            Understanding, and Judgment / 391
        2 Mediation / 392
        Responses to Questions / 393

1964-3 Differentiation of Methods I / 395
    Morning Lecture: Foundations / 395
        Responses to Questions / 399
    Afternoon Lecture: Positive Theology / 401
        Questions and Responses / 404

1964-4 Differentiation of Methods II / 406
    Morning Lecture, Part 1: Positive Theology (continued) / 406
    Morning Lecture, Part 2: Dogmatic Method / 408
    [Questions?] / 410
    Afternoon Lecture: Systematic Theology / 410
    Questions / 413

1964-5 Special Questions / 415
    Morning Lecture: Development of Dogma / 415
    Afternoon Lecture: The Argument from Scripture / 418

PART THREE: 'TRANSCENDENTAL PHILOSOPHY AND
THE STUDY OF RELIGION,' 3–12 JULY 1968, BOSTON
COLLEGE / 421

1968-1 **Method** / 423
    1 A Preliminary Notion / 425
    2 The Basic Pattern of Operations / 426
    3 Transcendental Method / 435

1968-2 **Method (continued), Functional Specialties, and an Introduction
    to Horizons and Categories** / 441
    1 The Functions of Transcendental Method / 442
    2 Functional Specialties / 446
        2.1 Three Types of Specialization / 446
        2.2 An Eightfold Division / 449
        2.3 Grounds of the Division / 453
        2.4 The Need for the Division / 455
        2.5 A Dynamic Unity / 457
    3 Horizons and Categories, Introduction / 466

1968-3 **Horizons and Categories** / 473
    1 Horizons (continued) / 473
    2 Categories / 477
    3 General Categories / 478
    4 Special Categories / 482
    5 Use of the Categories / 486
    6 Theologians and Scientists / 487
    7 Pluralism / 492

1968-4 **The Human Good and Values** / 494
    1 The Human Good / 494
    2 Development as Operational / 500
    3 The Development of Feelings / 504
    4 Progress and Decline / 506
    5 The Notion of Value / 508
    6 Judgments of Value / 510

1968-5 **Beliefs and Carriers of Meaning** / 513
    1 Beliefs / 513
    2 Carriers of Meaning / 517
        2.1 Intersubjectivity / 517
        2.2 Art / 520
        2.3 Symbols / 523
        2.4 Linguistic Meaning / 529

1968-6 Analysis of Meaning and Introduction to Religion / 534
  1 Elements of Meaning / 534
  2 Exigences / 537
  3 Functions of Meaning / 541
  4 Meaning in History / 542
  5 The Question of God / 543
  6 Religious Values / 549

1968-7 Religious Expression, Faith, Conversion / 553
  1 Religious Expression / 553
  2 Faith / 558
  3 Conversions and Breakdowns / 562

1968 Discussion 1 / 569

1968 Discussion 2 / 580

1968 Discussion 3 / 594

1968 Discussion 4 / 605

1968 Discussion 5 / 617

1968 Discussion 6 / 626

  Appendix: Hermeneutics / 635

  Lexicon of Latin and Greek Words and Phrases / 655

  Index / 661

General Editors' Preface

This volume and volume 23 record Bernard Lonergan's classes and some of his institutes on theological method, and in doing so present much of the data on his development between the publication of *Insight* and the completion of *Method in Theology*.

The material has been divided according to language. The present volume contains a record of his English lectures on method delivered at institutes in 1962 (Regis College, Toronto), 1964 (Georgetown University), and 1968 (Boston College), while volume 23 contains a record of Latin courses on method offered at the Gregorian University between 1958 and 1962.

These two volumes do not, of course, exhaust the data available on the composition of *Method in Theology*, for (1) there are in the Lonergan Archives handwritten schematic notes on other courses offered at the Gregorian in 1963 and 1964 that could not conveniently be transcribed into book form, (2) there are lectures on other topics that contain valuable information on Lonergan's development during these years, and (3) there are recordings of the major institutes on the book *Method in Theology* from 1969 (Regis), 1970 (Boston College), and 1971 (Milltown Park, Dublin). These additional sources can and must all be consulted if one wishes to assemble a relatively complete record of the available data. And that presents little difficulty, since (1) and (3) will be available online by the time this volume is published, and the lectures in (2) can be found scattered in several volumes (mainly 6 and 18) of Lonergan's Collected Works.

The accessibility of relevant online material, however, does not stop with (1) and (3). The present volume is the most 'interactive' yet published in the Collected Works series. Not only are the audio recordings from which the lectures of 1962 and 1968 were transcribed now available on the website www.bernardlonergan.com, in work done by Greg Lauzon, but also PDF files available on the same website represent the autograph of some of the lectures in the 1964 institute at Georgetown. Assistance in identifying these items was provided by Ivo Coelho, whose book *Hermeneutics and Method* presents, among other things, a remarkably clear and accurate account of this complex period of Lonergan's development.[1]

The present volume, even when read on its own without consulting either what will be volume 23 or the archival material, enables the reader to sketch in at least broad outline the development of Lonergan's ideas on such key notions as horizon, conversion, and meaning, as well as the movement from the division of theology into positive, dogmatic, and systematic (parts 1 and 2) to the division in terms of operational or functional specialization (part 3). Much of the material to be discussed in later chapters on the functional specialties of interpretation and history was already in place in 1962, as is clear especially from the appendix (a manuscript on hermeneutics distributed at the Regis institute), but the structure of functional specialization clearly had not yet emerged; we know from other data that it emerged only in February 1965.

As I have indicated, parts 1 and 3 of the present volume are transcripts made from the digital audio restoration done by Greg Lauzon, who worked from the original tapes. The first footnote in each chapter provides the call number on www.bernardlonergan.com for the recorded lectures.

As for part 2, we are extremely grateful to the late Avery Cardinal Dulles, s.j., for allowing us to publish in this volume his notes from the Georgetown lectures, and to Patrick Brown of Seattle University for alerting us to the existence of these notes and for supplying me with a copy and a digital transcription. Prior to the discovery of these notes, interested scholars were able to rely on the notes of Sister Rose St Mary Wilker, which have been available for some time in the library of the Lonergan Research Institute in Toronto. Sr Wilker's notes are now available online on the same website (www.bernardlonergan.com). Cardinal Dulles's notes provide yet another source to help us fill a lacuna regarding the precise order and content of the lectures that Lonergan delivered at Georgetown University in 1964. Moreover, the information provided by Ivo Coelho allows us to correlate large segments of these notes with archival material to which the reader now has direct access through the website.

Recordings were made in 1962 and 1968 not only of the lectures but also of question-and-answer sessions, here referred to as 'Discussions.' In many

1 Ivo Coelho, *Hermeneutics and Method: The 'Universal Viewpoint' in Bernard Lonergan* (Toronto: University of Toronto Press, 2001).

instances the questions were based on the lectures either of the same day or of earlier days, but they were not restricted to these contents.

The appendix, 'Hermeneutics,' is an extremely valuable document in that it fills another gap; namely, it shows more clearly than does the chapter on interpretation in *Method in Theology* the relation between the hermeneutic theory of chapter 17 of *Insight* and that which is presented in *Method*; or perhaps more precisely, it contains toward the end the materials from chapter 17 of *Insight* that were later differentiated into the functional specialties of history and dialectic, but, if I may speculate for a moment, it also offers, precisely because of its connection with the hermeneutics of *Insight*, perhaps a more hopeful view of the possibility of a moment of explanation in historical studies themselves than is found in the two chapters on history in *Method in Theology*.

As is customary in many of the volumes of the Collected Works, we conclude the book with a Lexicon of Latin and Greek Words and Phrases. The editorial conventions (*Chicago Manual of Style, Oxford American Dictionary*, etc.) with which readers of the Collected Works are familiar remain in place in the present volume. I wish to thank Robert Croken for his careful and repeated reading of the manuscript and for the many suggestions that have helped in the editing. Fr Croken has since retired from many years of work at the Lonergan Research Institute, and I wish to thank him for his dedication to promoting the Lonergan legacy. I wish to thank also my fellow General Editor Frederick Crowe for his continued inspiration, which lies behind the entire series of volumes in the Collected Works. Terrance Quinn provided invaluable advice on a complex mathematical formula, for which I am very grateful. Finally, I cannot write a preface such as this without mentioning once again the contribution, tangible and intangible, that Marquette University has made to my work as General Editor.

ROBERT M. DORAN
Marquette University

PART ONE

Regis College Institute 'On the Method of Theology,' 9–20 July 1962

Collected Works of Bernard Lonergan

1962-1

Operations, the Subject, Objects, Method[1]

I wish to thank you all for coming. I shall try to do what I can with this subject, method in theology, which is not on the beaten track. There is no
article in the *Dictionnaire de théologie catholique* that is expressly on the topic
'method in theology,' although Fr Congar's article 'Théologie' has a section that does treat explicitly of method.[2]

Making a topic of method is, of course, first of all, not to try to provide a
recipe on how to do theology, or to provide you with a cookbook. Again, it is
not a question of an introduction to theology; it presupposes that you all

1 Monday, 9 July 1962, Lauzon CD/MP3 301 (www.bernardlonergan.com
30100A0E060) and 302 (30200A0E060). Lonergan had been introduced
by the Rector of Regis College, Fr Edward F. Sheridan, sj. His opening words
were, 'Thank you, Fr Rector.'
2 Yves Congar, 'Théologie,' *Dictionnaire de théologie catholique* 15:1 (Paris:
Letouzey et Amé, 1946) cols. 462–72. Lonergan indicated that the relevant
columns began at 462. See Congar, *A History of Theology*, trans. Hunter
Guthrie (Garden City, ny: Doubleday & Co., 1968) 147–50. Lonergan had
distributed a set of Latin notes created by students from his course 'De
methodo theologiae' at the Gregorian University during the second
semester of the 1961–62 academic year. These notes will be mentioned on a
number of occasions in the course of the present lectures. The bibliographical information on Congar's article is the first item in the notes. The
autograph of Lonergan's notes for that Latin course will appear as part of
cwl 23, *Early Works on Theological Method* 2, both in Latin and in an English
translation by Michael G. Shields. In the present volume, references to the
student notes, which correspond quite closely to the autograph, will be
given, where this is necessary, by indicating the section or sections to which
Lonergan is referring. This first lecture corresponds to and expands on
chapter 1 (*caput primum*) of the notes 'De methodo theologiae.'

know theology. It is concerned with a further dimension in the field of theology, a dimension that has always existed, because whenever anything was done, it was done in a certain way. But reflecting on the way in which it is done, and doing so explicitly, is the consideration of method in theology.

The reasons for a consideration of method in theology can be given, but I think they are better treated later on after we have developed some precise notions in connection with method.[3] Very briefly, Charles Journet, in his *Introduction à la théologie*, claimed that what we have to do is to add the dimension of time to medieval theology.[4] Adding the dimension of time to medieval theology is a somewhat complex matter. Diagramatically or schematically, there is the external world, the world of common sense, in which there is the birth of our Lord, the preaching of the gospel, and the life of the church. There is the world of theory, which came into prominence in Catholic thought mainly in the medieval period. The world of theory has quite different characteristics from the world as apprehended by common sense, by ordinary religious living. The world of theory tends to be atemporal, free from the dimension of time. How is one to connect the external world, the world of common sense that develops through the ages, with the world of theory? The approach through method adds a third consideration, the consideration of the subject, the world of interiority. Since the subject is involved both in the external world of common sense and in the world of theory, it is through the subject that one can bring these two into relation. And as everything ultimately is for God, and religion is what is concerned with the ultimate, all three are referred ultimately to God, and so all three have a reference to theology.

1   Method and Operations

The consideration of method, then, is not directly the consideration of objects. According to St Thomas in *Summa theologiae*, 1, q. 1, a.7, ad 2m, 'theologia tractat de Deo et de aliis quae ad Deum ordinantur.'[5] That is the object of theology. But consideration of method is concerned directly not with the object, not with God, with scripture, with the councils, with the Fathers, with the liturgy, or with the Scholastics, but with me and my operations. It

---

3 See below, section 4, pp. 24–29.
4 Charles Journet, *Introduction à la théologie* (Paris: Desclée de Brouwer, 1947) 137–43.
5 'Theology treats of God and of other things that are ordered to God.'

is concerned with the theologian and what the theologian does. It does not imply a total neglect of the object. That is impossible. If you eliminate the object you eliminate operation, and if you eliminate operation the subject reverts to the state of sleep, and there are no operations at all. But it is not directly concerned with the objects, and insofar as it considers objects it considers them through the operations. Similarly, it considers the subject not purely as subject without any operations, but as operating.

Accordingly, while it is necessary to begin from objects, still objects are considered simply as a means to pin down the operations that are involved. It considers objects not for their own sake, but as discriminants of operations.

1.1 Piaget, Operations, and Habits

On consideration of operations, we have the numerous works of Jean Piaget on childhood psychology.[6] He treated the psychology of children from the day of birth to about the age of fifteen. He did this in a series of about twenty or thirty volumes from about 1926 to 1950. Before that he had been a biologist, and in 1951 he set to work on what had been his aim in his biology and in his child psychology. He wrote three volumes entitled *Introduction à l'épistémologie génétique.*[7] By that time he had attracted Rockefeller money. He has at Geneva an institute to which he brings four top men a year to work with him on various further questions, and he publishes a volume at the end of every year, at least from about 1957 on. Then, at the end of the year, he is able to bring about twelve more men to discuss the results of their work during the year. He has been translated into English, though perhaps not all his works.

His fundamental idea concerns operations. It is useful for us briefly to consider Piaget's work because it throws a new light on the notion of the habit. Any science, according to Scholasticism, is a habit. What precisely is a habit? We are familiar with our general definitions, but it will help us to bring them down into the concrete if we briefly consider what Piaget did.

He conceived the whole development of the child as a series of cumulative adaptations. Once one adaptation is made, another is added onto it. He

6 Lonergan had treated Piaget in some detail in the lectures on the philosophy of education in 1959. See Bernard Lonergan, *Topics in Education*, vol. 10 in Collected Works of Bernard Lonergan, ed. Robert M. Doran and Frederick E. Crowe (Toronto: University of Toronto Press, 1993), esp. chapter 8. The notes distributed for the present lectures provide a brief bibliography of Piaget's works (*caput primum*, § 2).
7 Jean Piaget, *Introduction à l'épistémologie génétique*, 3 vols. (Paris: Presses Universitaires de France, 1950).

found an adaptation to involve two elements: an element of assimilation, making use of operations, skills, and facilities that one already has; and an element of accommodation, which is more or less a fitting onto, a change in, existing operations, operations that one is already familiar with, so as to be able to deal with this particular object. He starts off from the child short-ly after birth. He had three children of his own, and he watched them close-ly day after day; he analyzed the developments in their ability. He noticed, for example, that they were much better at feeding at the breast at the end of the second day than the first time they tried. The first time they tried to feed at the breast they were digging about rather aimlessly with their heads, but by the end of the second day, by the feel of the breast they would know which way to move the head to arrive at the nipple.

He found throughout the operations in boys and girls up to the age of fif-teen that it was always the same thing: making use of the operations for which there is a natural spontaneity, the *habitus naturalis*, or simply the potency. The *habitus naturalis* or the mere natural potency grounds the possibility of some operation, but that operation is not efficacious, it is not economical, it doesn't hit the bull's-eye on the first shot; it is approximative; it comes more or less near what is wanted; and the development consists in starting from these natural, spontaneous, inefficacious, uneconomical operations and changing them to fit right onto whatever object happens to be given. There is the ele-ment, then, of adaptation of natural, spontaneous operations.

These adaptations result in differentiations of the operations. Because there are several different objects and different adaptations for each one, the natural operation becomes a series of different operations adapted each to particular types of objects.

In the third place, there are combinations of differentiated operations. For example, when you are learning to type you are differentiating the movements of your fingers, and then you combine these differentiated operations. So from natural operations one proceeds to the differentiation of these natural operations for different objects, and then to the combina-tion of differentiated operations.

The fourth step[8] is the group of combinations. Now that word 'group' is used on the analogy of a very fundamental mathematical theorem. I don't think we had better go into it. Fundamentally, it is simple: it means the to-tality of operations that are related to one another, that form a whole. Piaget

---

8 Lonergan said 'the third step,' but he had already designated combinations
   'in the third place.'

found that a toddler who is just about able to walk will toddle from his mother's chair over to his father's chair and back again. He devised experiments to show that the child did not realize that he was going back – it was just more walking for him. In other words, the child did not have any organization of space. Piaget fixed an approximate period in the child's life in which one would pass from the stage in which one performed operations more or less aimlessly, without any control of the totality, to a further stage when the totality would be under control and the child would be aware that he was going back. That idea of relating operations to one another to form a closed group is an ultimate step of a certain line of development.

The two volumes on the birth of intelligence in the child, covering the period from birth to the age of two, are frightfully interesting.[9] He shows how the child first develops oral movements, movements of the head, adding on movements of the hand, and then combining movements of the hand with movements of the mouth, and joining the hand with movements of the eye, distinguishing objects; at that point, everything the child sees he tries to grab and put in his mouth. So Piaget works through all the corporal movements, and he does this in a steady study of children up to the age of fifteen.

Now in that case we are dealing with what Aristotle and the Scholastics called the *habitus acquisitus*. But it is not habits broken up according to the potencies. If one reads the *Secunda secundae* one finds a terrific list of virtues, and one wonders how one gets them all together into one man. Piaget's type of analysis is based strictly empirically. It does not deal with isolated habits in the intellect, in the senses, in the sensitive appetites, in the will, and so on. These operations are total operations of the whole child, and the development of the operations amounts to a unified development of habits. So, instead of comparing habit and operation as *actus primus* and *actus secundus*, in Piaget's analysis what one has are habits and groups of operations. The set of habits corresponds to a group of operations, that is, a totality of combinations of differentiated operations; and beyond the group there is the group of groups. In other words, as the child goes on he combines the lower groups into the new totalities that involve differentiations in the lower groups.

9 Lonergan may be referring to Jean Piaget, *La naissance de l'intelligence chez l'enfant* (Neuchâtel, Paris: Delacheux et Niestlé, 1936); in English, *The Origins of Intelligence in Children*, trans. Margaret Cook (New York: International Universities Press, 1952); and *La construction du réel chez l'enfant* (Neuchâtel, Paris: Delacheux et Niestlé, 1937); in English, *The Constitution of Reality in the Child*, trans. Margaret Cook (New York: Basic Books, 1954). These are the first two volumes mentioned in the brief Piaget bibliography in the notes.

That is one aspect of analyzing operations, and Piaget's work has resulted in changes and new ideas in elementary education. I was told by a psychologist at Weston[10] that in the States Piaget is a little too speculative for them, but they have taken his experiments and put the whole thing on a good solid positivist basis. They know he is right, but they don't want his theoretical superstructure. It is fantastic the experiments he was able to devise to show just at what age a child was able to do this or that, when the child was able to use logic, when one was able to solve problems of certain types, and so on.

1.2   *Three Types of Mediation*

Now there is another aspect to the matter that also appears in Piaget's work. The objects that he studies in the infant are sensible objects that are seen with the eye, grabbed with the hand, put in the mouth, related to movements of the body, and so on. They are immediate objects. He studies the stage at which the child begins to deal with mediated objects, objects that the child cannot see, feel, touch, and so on, but can only imagine or talk about – the mediation of imagination and language. That gives a new world, a terrific extension to what had been the infant's prior world; it is a move from a purely immediate world to a world mediated by images and words.

Now, as long as we are on that level, we are still in the external world. But when one starts using a technical language – the technical language of mathematics, natural science, human science, philosophy, theology – one is at a second mediation. It is not merely the mediation of imagination and language; it is the mediation of a technical language. There comes a point in any subject where ordinary language is not sufficient and one has to introduce technical terms. Then one is moving to a new level and to a far greater enlargement of the field of possible operations.

There is a final level, and in that case one is dealing neither with the immediate sensible, nor with the imagined as expressed in ordinary language, nor even with what is properly the technically defined object, but with the operations that may be dealing with any of the preceding. It is on that level that one is considering method. In method the mediation is by the experience of the operation itself. It is the last level that one can reach: not the sensible, not the ordinary description, not the scientifically explained, but the operations involved on any of these levels. Those operations, while they

10 Lonergan is referring to the theologate of the New England Jesuit Province, then located at Weston, MA. It has since become Weston Jesuit School of Theology, first in Cambridge, MA, and more recently at Boston College.

may be illustrated concretely by performing them, by their external results, or their written-down results as in the case of theoretical things, also occur in consciousness. Then we get the mediation of interiority.

Now, just as the world of imagination and language is far larger than the world of immediate sensitive apprehension, as the world of science and theory is far larger than the world of imagination and language, so the world of interiority, including all possibilities of operation, puts together these different worlds and envisages them at the most radical point, namely, how you go about it.

1.3 The Brevity of Methodical Analysis

The power of methodical analysis is illustrated by its brevity. Anyone can hit a key upon a piano, but to hit the right number of keys at the right time in the right series with the right pressure is to become a pianist. The difference between a person who is not a pianist and one who is is the difference between natural, spontaneous, undifferentiated, approximative operations and, on the other hand, differentiated operations adapted to very precise demands. There are combinations of differentiated operations and the grouping of all these combinations. One is able to strike any chord with either hand according to how one looks at the score, and so one is able to play a page of Chopin that is practically black with notes. The process there is from the undifferentiated to the group of combinations, the totality of combinations of differentiated operations.

That is a concrete example. One can apply the same analysis to such a thing as Euclid's geometry, and of course one has to know the geometry inside out. If one applies an operational analysis, one shortly discovers that Euclid has a set of tricks that he keeps applying over and over again, with slight adaptations and changes.

Another example is St Thomas's *Summa contra Gentiles*. The chapters run along, and there will be thirty-four arguments for this and thirty-eight for that, and on the next point there may be fourteen, and so on. If one compares one chapter with the next, one finds that St Thomas is not doing totally different things; he doesn't discover thirty-six arguments in this case entirely different from the thirty-eight he had in the preceding chapter. All the arguments here are fundamentally similar to all the arguments in the preceding chapter. There are slight adaptations because the subject matter is different. He adapts them. He has a fundamental group of combinations of differentiated operations, and as each topic comes along he selects out of that group of combinations of differentiated operations the ones that bear on the point, and he lists them.

1.4 Experiencing the Operations

So much for a general idea of what is meant by method. It is concerned primarily with operations, and the operations are considered. To reach the operations, one has to have familiarity on the level of immediate sense, on the level of imagination and ordinary language, and on the level of theory. But the immediate approach to the operations is the inner experience of them while you are performing them.

That inner experience is quite easily reached in the field of sensation. I can look out the window and see the library wing, and close my eyes and see nothing, and while the obvious difference is between the library seen and unseen, there is also a difference in my experience as I open and close my eyes. It is quite easy to pin down the experience of seeing or hearing or touching or feeling, and so on.

Things are a little more difficult when it comes to the experience of understanding. No one will say that never in his life did he ever understand anything whatever, but if you start talking to him about the act of understanding and his experience of understanding, he is apt to be nonplussed. You cannot turn understanding off and on the way you can turn seeing off and on. To come to understand the point, you have to study, you have to puzzle a thing out; that process of puzzling things out takes time, and at the end of it you get one act of understanding. Perhaps you will have a bit of a thrill if you really worked hard to get it, but to get another act you have to start this process of studying over again.

People are apt to think that the syllogism is just silly, that there is no point to it. The reason is that the syllogism is illustrated by examples in which one has nothing to learn, in which one is not understanding anything for the first time but is merely using one's habitual understanding. Because one is learning nothing, one finds nothing in it. If one uses the syllogism to express something that one is learning for the first time, it begins to have a meaning.

The difficulty of that type of illustration is that the person has to be learning something for the first time. It may be hard to find instances. The instances that are helpful for some people will not be helpful for others. However, to take a simple example, Aristotle has the argument that the moon must be spherical because of its phases. 'If the moon goes through these phases it must be a sphere. But the moon goes through these phases.

Therefore it is a sphere.' Now that argument has a meaning for you insofar as either you imagine or perform an experiment. If you set a disc and shine a flashlight on it, the whole disc is illuminated, or not at all. If you have the flashlight behind it the disc will not be illuminated, but from any angle in front the whole disc is illuminated. If you set up a rugby ball in a dark room and turn the flashlight on it, as you move the flashlight around and the person stays in the same position he will see different shapes as the lighting changes. However, the different shapes will not be the shapes of the phases of the moon. It is only when you illuminate a sphere and walk around it with the light that you get the different phases of the moon. That is the meaning of this argument: if the moon goes through these phases it must be a sphere. And it is insofar as this grasp of intelligibility in the concrete is communicated through the syllogism that one is using the syllogism to express an act of learning.

1.5 Fundamental Cognitional Operations

Our next topic treats of the fundamental cognitional operations. In Thomist analysis, as I happen to understand it, there are an *intellectus agens*, external sense, imagination, a possible intellect in which nothing is written at the start – like a *tabula rasa* – on which there are impressed *species intelligibiles*; and there occur acts of understanding which are expressed in *verba incomplexa*, definitions. When you arrive at a definition you wonder whether it is so, whether anything corresponding to the definition exists. There is reflective understanding, the *reductio in principia*, and that is expressed in the *verbum complexum*. One has external sense. *Intellectus agens* with respect to imagination is the spirit of inquiry. When you are imagining, and your imagining is inquisitive, intellectual, wondering why, your phantasm is illuminated. When the image falls into a proper perspective – when you are imagining the light falling not on a rugby ball or on a disc but on a sphere – there is impressed on possible intellect the *species intelligibilis*, the intelligible form that fits that image. This *species intelligibilis* is not conscious; it is a metaphysical condition for the limitation of this act of understanding. This act of understanding is not *ipsum intelligere*, rather it is a limited *intelligere* – it understands merely this, why the moon must be a sphere. This is expressed in the correlation between phases of the moon and sphericity. One can then ask whether that correlation really is so, and then proceed to try out all the other instances one can think of, and then come to the conclusion that it is so.

One can read the text of St Thomas under other influences and come to a different analysis that eliminates the act of understanding and replaces it by a scheme in which you have the *species intelligibilis* and then the *verbum*. *Intelligere* is the producing of the *verbum*, the *species* is the *intellectus in actu*, and first it produces the *verbum* and then it looks at it. There is no difference between *conversio ad phantasma*, in which this *intelligere* is grasping the intelligible in the phantasm, and, on the other hand, the *reflexio supra phantasma* that conjoins the universal *verbum* with the image to make it particular. And so on. You will find this analysis in John of St Thomas. It gives you a psychology that is entirely similar to Scotist psychology. The act of understanding is eliminated. What you have are sensations, images, concepts, and when you get more than one concept you compare them and see the nexus.

However, St Thomas does not talk about seeing the nexus. He talks about forms. When you understand you are grasping the form in the image. That is what you know. However, that is a long, disputed question. I wrote on *verbum* in *Theological Studies* (1946–49) to present Thomas's account of psychology and cognitional theory,[11] and I found that the main difficulty was that people were not ready to talk about the act of understanding. They would not say that St Thomas never understood anything, or that he never had the experience of understanding anything, but they did not see that it fitted in. So I wrote *Insight* to show that understanding is something that exists and is relevant and cannot be avoided.

Those are fundamental cognitional operations. Common sense and science are different ways of using that fundamental structure.

So much on operations in general.

2   The Subject

The operations are connected with the subject. There is the Scholastic axiom, *Quidquid recipitur ad modum recipientis recipitur*. It means that we all have acquired habits, and whatever is simply a matter of using our acquired habits is something that we do promptly, with facility, and with pleasure. It is as easy as rolling off a log, once you have the habit. Those habits regard matters of skill, matters of apprehension, matters of appetite, of willing,

---

11 Bernard Lonergan, 'The Concept of *Verbum* in the Writings of St Thomas Aquinas,' *Theological Studies* 7 (1946) 349–92; 8 (1947) 35–79, 404–44; 10 (1949) 3–40, 359–93; now available as *Verbum: Word and Idea in Aquinas*, vol. 2 in Collected Works of Bernard Lonergan, ed. Frederick E. Crowe and Robert M. Doran (Toronto: University of Toronto Press, 1997).

and of choosing. Our acquired habits give to all of us a field in which we operate with the greatest ease and joy and pleasure.

However, we do not get outside that field without further development. We have to effect further differentiations in our operations, further combinations of differentiated operations, further integrations of combinations of differentiated operations, to enlarge our little world, the world that corresponds to our acquired habits. The result is that the older each of us gets the more we become prisoners of our past achievements. If we had the time we could acquire further habits, but we are so busy that we fail to do so. We become crystallized, so to speak. So we arrive at the notion of horizon, which is a fundamental notion, particularly in existentialist thought.

2.1 Horizon

By the horizon, my horizon, I shall mean the world, the totality of objects, with which I can promptly deal in virtue of my acquired habits. I am master of whatever lies within that field. I can do it at once, and I enjoy doing it. But what is beyond that field is something that I do not advert to. It may be there, but I do not see it. It may be important, but I couldn't care less. It is beyond my horizon. That horizon isn't absolute. Intellect extends to *ens*, and *ens* includes absolutely everything; will extends to the *bonum*, and *omne ens est bonum*; the adequate objects of man's intellect and will are unlimited. But that lack of limitation regards basic potency. It does not regard what I am able to do here and now without acquiring any further skill, without understanding or learning anything more, without being persuaded or persuading myself to do something that I have always avoided doing. To do that I have to acquire new habits, and to acquire new habits takes time. I have to take time out to develop myself further. So while the horizon is not an absolute limit, still it is a de facto limit that is there until I take time out to acquire a further skill, to learn something more, to be persuaded or to persuade myself to do something more.

Now, one can broaden or enlarge one's horizon by dealing with new immediate objects, for example, by acquiring an interest in the arts; by operating on new mediated objects, objects that are mediated by imagination and symbols, or objects that are mediated by ordinary language – even if I cannot read a book on pure mathematics, still there are lots of books I can read – and by further developing one's theoretical knowledge, one's scientific, philosophic, and theological knowledge. The third and radical way of broadening one's horizon is through the mediation of the operations with which one deals with anything. Fr Eric O'Connor, who is quite a mathematician, remarked to me that he would never have gotten anywhere in mathematics if he had not stopped and asked himself just what he was doing.[12] I think that is true in any subject. Unless one gets down and faces the fundamental questions – What am I doing? What am I trying to do? How precisely is the best way to go about it? – one does not become a master of that subject.

2.2 *Conversion*

I have spoken of the topic of horizon, and it is a correlative to the notion of habits. A second point is the conversion of the subject. Not only can horizons be broadened, but also the subject can undergo an upheaval, a turnover, a conversion. A conversion is a reorganization of the subject, of his operations, of the world with which he is familiar. It can imply a broadening of the horizon, but principally it is that change in the subject himself.

Fundamentally, there are three kinds of conversion: moral conversion, intellectual conversion, and religious conversion.

Moral conversion is from the objects of desire and fear as ultimate, to the normative, to what ought to be so whether one likes it or not. One can go a very long way on the basis of desire and fear, if one includes the beatific vision among the objects of desire, and hell and purgatory among the objects of fear. However, there is a radical change in the subject when basic motivation shifts from objects of desire and fear to the 'what ought to be.'

The second type of conversion is intellectual. Up to the age of seven years we are not reputed to have yet reached the age of reason. Before the age of seven years we have pretty good ideas about what is really real. We can distinguish waking and dreaming, what is just a story, and what is a fib. The child, before reaching the age of reason, has arrived at certain criteria of the real. Those criteria can remain with one for all of one's life without being revised or corrected, even though one becomes a philosopher or a professor of philosophy. One can argue the thing out philosophically with a great deal of skill and subtlety, but when one gets down to the fine points, what does one appeal to? One appeals to what was the really real before one had reached the age of reason. Intellectual conversion, fundamentally, is

---

12 R. Eric O'Connor, SJ, a long-time friend of Bernard Lonergan's, was professor of mathematics at Loyola College, Montreal, and one of the founding members of the Thomas More Institute for Adult Education, where Lonergan gave some of his most important lectures, including the course 'Thought and Reality' (1945–46), in which he expressed some of the basic points of what was to become the book *Insight.*

the shift from prerational criteria of childhood to ultimate reliance upon rational criteria. It is the shift from the real as the 'already out there now' that one can put one's paw on, to the real as *id quod est*, where *id quod est* is what is rationally affirmed. The two are not exactly the same!

In the third place, there is religious conversion, where the ultimate ceases to be oneself and becomes God, and indeed not God as naturally known or knowable, but as revealed in the Catholic faith.

In each case what occurs is fundamentally a reorganization of the subject. What before had been taught ceases to be taught, and what before had been unimportant becomes all-important.

2.3 Inauthenticity[13]

Besides the horizon of the subject and the conversion of the subject, there is the inauthentic subject. Inauthenticity, of course, is a very popular term at the present time. One may distinguish between a relative and an absolute inauthenticity. The notion of relative inauthenticity is developed rather fully by Karl Jaspers in his *Psychologie der Weltanschauungen*.[14] A relative inauthenticity is a divergence between what the subject really experiences, really understands, really judges to be true and, on the other hand, the characteristic mode of experiencing, understanding, and judging of a given group or of a given doctrine. In the authentic subject, his personal experience, understanding, judgment and the characteristic modes of the doctrines, be it Buddhism, Confucianism, Christianity, or Thomism, Kantianism, Hegelianism, coincide. But in the unauthentic subject there is a divergence. The divergence is not complete: the unauthentic Thomist or Kantian or Hegelian coincides with Thomist, Kantian, or Hegelian views on a whole series of points, and because of that coincidence he feels

13 In the present lectures, Lonergan alternates indiscriminately between 'inauthenticity' and 'unauthenticity.' In *Method in Theology*, the latter term is used exclusively. An effort has been made here to use either term, in accord with Lonergan's usage in his lecture. It is interesting as well to note the relation between what here are called relative and absolute authenticity and inauthenticity and what later would be called minor and major authenticity and unauthenticity. See, for example, Bernard Lonergan, *Method in Theology* (latest printing, Toronto: University of Toronto Press, 2007) 80.

14 Karl Jaspers, *Psychologie der Weltanschauungen* (Berlin: J. Springer, 1925). Lonergan commented, 'He wrote it before he wrote any works on philosophy, in 1925. His *Philosophie* is about 1931.' Actually, the book was first published in 1919 (Berlin: J. Springer); a second edition, unaltered, was published in 1925. *Philosophie* (three volumes) dates from 1932 (Berlin: J. Springer).

at home in those doctrines. He thinks of himself as a Thomist or a Kantian or a Hegelian, and at the same time the points of divergence, the lack of total coincidence, is something to which he does not advert; it is beyond his horizon. So there is the person who thinks of himself, and lives his life, as if he were a Buddhist, Confucian, Christian, Catholic, Lutheran, and so on, but at the same time he really is not; there are whole elements in those positions to which he is blind. He is unaware of these differences, and it is very difficult for him to get over these differences, simply because the differences themselves lie beyond his horizon. He uses the language, the technical terms, the principles, the theorems, not in their proper, quasi-objective sense, but in the sense that accrues to them from his own mentality, orientation, and way of living. There results a sort of systematic simplification, devalorization, devaluation, deformation of the doctrine or the mode of life. I say 'a sort of systematic'; in other words, what is systematic is not what the Scholastics called *per accidens, praeter intentionem*, but here, with him, it is *praeter intentionem*; he has no apprehension that this is what he is doing. However, it is quasi-systematic since it results spontaneously and inevitably because of the divergence between his apprehension and what is to be apprehended. He will believe himself completely authentic, a most faithful disciple of Kant or St Thomas, completely free from any originality or personal opinions of his own, but that happens not to be so.

Such relative inauthenticity can occur in single individuals, but it is not restricted to them. The unauthentic person can preach, direct others, teach publicly, write books, and be held in very high esteem by others who have exactly the same deviation. So schools will split into parts, or a whole school of thought can go into decadence. When such inauthenticity arises and spreads and becomes endemic, the only thing to do is to lay the axe to the root. However, laying the axe to the root is a tricky business. One is apt to find, as St John the Baptist did, that one's head is chopped off and put on a platter.

Fr Congar, in his article 'Théologie,' in *Dictionnaire de théologie catholique*, lists the defects of fifteenth-century Scholasticism.[15] In column 410, he says there is a Scholasticism in the narrow and pejorative sense of the word, when, instead of feeling for the profound meaning of questions, one treats them in a purely academic fashion; instead of living one's own life on the basis of principles, one merely discusses other people's opinions or opinions held by a

15 See Congar, 'Théologie,' cols. 407–10. See also Congar, *A History of Theology* 137–43.

group or a school, with all the bitterness and narrowness, the formalism and the impossibility of assimilating other persons' views which are the order of the day in such a situation. About the middle of the fifteenth century, theology had become a matter of convents and houses specialized in that type of thought, a question of rival schools, of disputes between systems. It is with regard to schools of this type, and in particular in speaking of Thomism and Scotism, that M. Gilson was able to write that on both sides one made the mistake of philosophizing on philosophers instead of philosophizing upon problems.[16]

Now, of course, that description of the fifteenth century is something with which we are all more or less familiar, something we know about as a fact. Theology had declined in the fifteenth century. However, to quote Gilson (to whom Congar refers) in his recent book, *Le philosophe et la théologie* (1960): 'At the beginning of the twentieth century, in Western Europe, in the teaching of Catholic schools and among Scholastics who considered themselves Thomists, the true meaning of the Christian philosophy of Saint Thomas had been lost.'[17] That is Gilson's opinion, but whether it is true or not, it is the meaning of what I am talking about when I speak of this relative inauthenticity. The real meaning of statements can be missed, and the reason why it is missed is not that the statements are not clear or exact. No matter how many statements are put out, they will all be assimilated to the viewpoint, and given the interpretation, that fits in with the inauthentic subject. That is the fundamental problem of inauthenticity.[18]

Relative inauthenticity regards any doctrine, any mode of life, any culture. But in Heidegger's *Sein und Zeit*,[19] inauthenticity is considered in a

16 'On both sides they committed the fault of philosophizing on philosophies instead of philosophizing on problems.' Étienne Gilson as quoted by Congar, *The History of Theology* 143. The Gilson reference is to *L'esprit de la philosophie médiévale*, vol. 2 (Paris: J. Vrin, 1932) 267. In this paragraph Lonergan has been translating Congar's text. See Congar, *A History of Theology* 142–43 for another translation of the same material.

17 Étienne Gilson, *The Philosopher and Theology*, trans. Cécile Gilson (New York: Random House, 1962) 157. Lonergan gave the bibliographical information for the French original, published by A. Fayard (Paris), where this material appears on p. 172.

18 A break was taken at this point. After the break Lonergan began, 'I've been speaking of operations, the subject, horizon, conversion, and inauthenticity. And first of relative inauthenticity.' The new material is recorded on Lauzon CD/MP3 302 (30200A0E060).

19 Martin Heidegger, *Sein und Zeit* (Tübingen: Neomarius, 1949; first published in 1927). There are two English translations: *Being and Time*, trans. John Macquarrie and Edward Robinson (London: SCM, 1962) and *Being and Time*,

more absolute way. It is not relative to any doctrine, but, if I may use a term that Heidegger would not use, it is relative to the nature of man. Heidegger speaks of the unauthentic man as one who refuses to accept his personal responsibility for his own living and thinking. He does what everyone else does, and everyone else carries on in the same fashion. He says what everyone else says, and everyone else talks in the same fashion. They are all saying what everyone else says too. He thinks and chooses what everyone else thinks and chooses, and everyone else is thinking and choosing for the same reason, because everyone else does so. In the lot, there is no one who is on his own, who is thinking and judging and choosing and talking and acting on his own responsibility. There is an evasion of personal responsibility, of being oneself, all along the line, and the society just drifts. Heidegger gives a devastating description of man in modern industrialized society.

I will not enlarge upon Heidegger's views here. They can be found in A. de Waelhens's *La philosophie de Martin Heidegger* (1942).[20] The book does not go into the later developments in Heidegger, which are more complex, but it is a very satisfactory study that brings very forcibly to one's attention just what it was that made *Sein und Zeit* one of the most influential books of the century. Heidegger has penetrated depth psychology in the existential psychologists, chiefly through Binswanger; he has penetrated, as you know, scriptural studies, as well as general theories of hermeneutics in people like Gadamer. In countless fields, his thought in one way or another has been extremely important on the continent of Europe.

While Heidegger is useful from the viewpoint of considering people of our present time, more fundamentally, from a Scholastic viewpoint, the unauthentic man is the one who falls short of rationality. Man is a rational animal, and insofar as that rationality merely means the potency to be rational, that is something common to infants, morons, and lunatics, as well as to the rest of us. Insofar as rationality is something that is to be actuated and should be actuated according to the stage of one's development, then one has a criterion for an absolute inauthenticity, a failing to be what one ought to be. That aspect of inauthenticity is developed in *Insight* in chapter 7 on common sense as object, in chapter 18 on ethics, and in chapter 20 on the problem of apologetics.

trans. Joan Stambaugh (Albany: State University of New York, 1996).
20 Alphonse de Waelhens, *La philosophie de Martin Heidegger* (Louvain: Institut supérieur de philosophie, 1942; fifth ed., Louvain: Publications universitaires de Louvain; Paris, B. Nauwelaerts, 1967).

3 Objects

3.1 Formal and Material Objects

We have spoken of operations and their subjects, and now we have to say something about objects from the methodological viewpoint. One is apt to think simply of objects and forget the subject entirely. The methodological viewpoint considers objects only through the operations.

Objects commonly are divided into material and formal. The material object is the thing with which one is concerned, the *res de qua agitur.* Theology is about God, and God is the material object. The formal object is the *ratio sub qua res attingitur,* and so natural theology is concerned with God as first principle and last end; the beatific vision is concerned with God as known immediately by his own essence; and in dogmatic theology the formal object is God as revealed, God as the author of the supernatural life.

Now, formal objects can be considered in two ways: de iure and de facto. De iure, the formal object is the object as defined, or if it is related to the habit and conceived in terms of operations, then it is concerned with the ideal group of operations: the most perfect mathematician, the most perfect theologian, the most perfect philosopher. It is something of an ideal entity. If one considers the formal object concretely, the object as it is de facto reached, then it is the object as reached through such and such a group of combinations of differentiated operations. That concrete, de facto consideration of the formal object is the methodological way of viewing things.

What is theology? Theology is the science of God, *quae tractat de Deo et de aliis quae ad Deum referuntur.* But that definition does not distinguish between the different stages in the development of theology. It does not distinguish directly between proper developments and aberrations in the history of theology. It is a concept of theology that prescinds from time. When one conceives the formal object as the material object inasmuch as it is reached by such and such a group of combinations of differentiated operations, then one can distinguish all the stages in the development of theology, because at each stage in the development the group of operations differs, is larger; there have been elements that have dropped out, elements that have been developed, elements that have been introduced in new combinations, and so on – if there has been a development. Consequently, the methodological consideration of the formal object, the formal object as de facto it is reached by these theologians, makes room for a historical consideration. In such a historical consideration, one will speak not so much of theology as of the dogmatic-theological context.[21]

3.2 Contexts and Development

What does that mean? A context is a remainder concept; it is the rest. The rest is not very well defined when people are ready to say, 'Your interpretation is all out of context,' or 'This objection disregards the context of the remark.' If you ask them, 'Well, what is the context?' they are inevitably going to be at a loss. Context is not something that is sharply defined. It is all the rest that is relevant to understanding correctly what I am saying. If a person makes any statement that regards either dogma or theology, there is a whole circle of other statements that are relevant to the exploration of exactly what each word means, to the defense of that proposition, to the solution to all the objections that can be brought against it. There is an immediate and rather large circle that goes around any particular dogmatic or theological statement, and it forms the context of that statement. But all these other statements each have their own circle, and so one goes out to a circle of circles. But the thing does not go off to infinity. There is such a thing as the dogmatic-theological context at any given time. It is what is taught and learnt in seminaries and theological schools. It is what is assumed by all Catholics. It is not all of one piece: there are elements that are *de fide definita*, others that are *doctrina catholica*, others that are *theologice certa*, and others that are theological opinions with more or less certainty. It is a nuanced whole. It is taken for granted when any Catholic speaks on theological or dogmatic matters that he is talking in that context. What's wrong with the heretics? Well, they disregard the context. What they say may be something true, but it is outside that dogmatic-theological context; it is implicitly or explicitly denying elements that pertain to that context. What are we trying to do in a theological course? We are trying to communicate that context. What is it that corresponds in the subject to that context? It is the group of combinations of differentiated operations that are involved in making any of the statements belonging to the context and being able to explain all the terms, give the adversaries, prove the thesis, and answer the objections, and so move on to some further element in the context. Teaching theology is communicating the dogmatic-theological context. No

---

21 Lonergan alternates between 'dogmatic-theological context' and 'dogmatico-theological context.' The former expression is used throughout this text.

one will attempt to define what it is exactly in all its details, but it is something that belongs to the community and is passed on.

Theology as that context is recognized not only by all theologians but
also by the church. In Romans 12.5, things are to be understood according
to the analogy of faith, and the same expression, 'the analogy of faith,' occurs in the oath against Modernism.[22] What is the analogy of faith? It is
taking things in the proper Catholic context. They all hang together. The
precise way in which they hang together may be a matter of opinion, or it
may be a matter of certitude; and which it is you know from knowing the
context, the whole totality of truths and understanding of the truths and
grasping of the meanings.

Again, when we speak of the *sensus ecclesiae*, the *consensus theologorum*, and
the *consensus Patrum*, we are talking about statements as belonging to a certain context, as understood correctly within that context. That is why we are
able to say that what this Father says at this time does not count, but that
what he says somewhere else proves the thesis; on this point the Fathers
have been morally unanimous, and on that they are not, and so on.

That context is something that is not too closely defined. It develops:
there is the history of theology and the history of dogma. And the development is also a development in operations: further differentiations of operations, new combinations, and larger groupings of the operations.

From a methodological viewpoint, then, one can define a science, its formal object, by defining the group of operations by which the object of that
science is reached. In that fashion, one can define logic, mathematics, physics, chemistry, and any given science by specifying the relevant operations.
That mode of division is necessary insofar as sciences are developing. As

22 Romans 12.3–8: 'For by the grace given to me I say to everyone among you
    not to think of yourself more highly than you ought to think, but to think
    with sober judgment, *each according to the measure of faith that God has assigned.*
    For as in one body we have many members, and not all the members have
    the same function, so we, who are many, are one body in Christ, and
    individually we are members one of another. We have gifts that differ
    according to the grace given to us: prophecy, in proportion to faith;
    ministry, in ministering; the teacher, in teaching; the exhorter, in exhorta-
    tion; the giver, in generosity; the leader, in diligence; the compassionate,
    in cheerfulness.' From the oath against modernism (DB 2146, DS 3546):
    'I reject that method of judging and interpreting Sacred Scripture which,
    departing from the tradition of the Church, the analogy of faith, and the
    norms of the Apostolic See, embraces the misrepresentations of the
    rationalists and with no prudence or restraint adopts textual criticism as
    the one and supreme norm.'

long as a science is not something *in facto esse* but *in fieri*, it is only by the succession of the developments in the groups of operations that one can say what the science is. One can assign its history.

That definition of methodological consideration as a consideration of the objects from the viewpoint of the operations extends beyond the scientific field. Just as Piaget used the idea of groups of operations to distinguish stages in the development of the child, so groups of operations can be used to distinguish stages in the development of civilizations, in the movement from the primitive to the ancient high civilizations represented by Egypt, Babylon, Mesopotamia, Crete, India, and China. In those civilizations, there were certain characteristic groups of operations, and there were other types of operations that were totally missing. Similarly, individuals or national groups can be distinguished by modes of operations. The Russians have a very different common sense from us, but they have a common sense that is their own. It is fundamentally the same type of development of intellect, but it develops in a different way. As that distinguishing of groups of operations can be applied to the development of the child and to the development of a science, so it can be applied to the development of humanity, of a civilization or a culture. And it is in that fashion, de facto, that we do characterize, *grosso modo*, writers, members of schools, and so on. For example, one can say of the value of a piece of exegesis that it was done by an Englishman in about 1910, that he was an Anglican, that he belonged to a rather idealist school of philosophy, that he studied at such a school and such a university, that he belonged to such a milieu, that he was writing on this or that book of the Old Testament which was his main object. One forms an idea of the writer and of his tendencies simply by indicating in a general way the type of operations and combinations of operations that can be expected of him.

Now, while Piaget was able to use groups of operations to distinguish stages in the development of the child, and while theoretically that is possible in the fields we are discussing, still, practically, we will have to develop later on a different way of classifying development.[23] One of the chief problems in putting the dimension of time into theology is to be able to work out some sort of a classification of development. We come to that later. The type of analysis based on Piaget's analysis of the development of the child, which is closely related to the Aristotelian and Thomist development of the

23 See below, pp. 42–55.

habits, is very concrete, but when you start dealing with rather large developments, it becomes an unwieldy instrument.

3.3 A Note on Method

At this point I would like to make a note on the general idea of method.
Method is not a matter of having one single track on which your train moves
at high speed, always the same track and always the same train. Rather, it is
a matter of getting hold of a great variety of modes of conceiving and being
able to select the one that suits the particular problem with which one is
dealing. Pierre Boutroux wrote a book about 1924 – it was reissued about
1954 by Presses Universitaires de France – on *L'idéal scientifique des
mathématiciens*, the scientific ideal of the mathematicians.[24] He distinguished three scientific ideals. There was the Greek ideal, which imposed
upon mathematics aesthetic limitations: geometry is Euclidean if you can
do it with a ruler and a compass, but when you introduce further mechanical means, then you are not solving problems in the Euclidean manner. His
second class was the deductivist type of mathematics, the systematic deduction of the whole field, which he placed as coming into prominence with
Descartes and Leibniz and reaching its ultimate stage in deductivist attempts such as Whitehead and Russell's *Principia Mathematica*.[25] The third
type of mathematics, which he claimed developed largely in the nineteenth
century, was to think of a mathematical object that is somehow independent of the mathematician, and not completely within the grasp, the domination, of the mathematician. The mathematician's job is to develop different techniques, different methods that will handle this aspect of the subject
and that aspect of the subject and a third aspect and a fourth and a fifth.
And the mathematician is the one who can use whichever one of the methods or techniques or developments enables him to deal with the problem
in hand.

I have considered development, which is a fundamental matter for a theologian particularly at the present time, in terms of Piaget's development of
groups of operations, which is very closely related to the Aristotelian-Thomist

24 Pierre Boutroux, *L'idéal scientifique des mathématiciens dans l'Antiquité et les
    Temps modernes*, new ed. (Paris: Presses Universitaires de France, 1955;
    Sceaux: Éditions Jacques Gabay, 1992).
25 Alfred North Whitehead and Bertrand Russell, *Principia Mathematica*, 3 vols.
    (Cambridge: Cambridge University Press, first ed., 1910–13; 2nd., 1925–27;
    regularly reprinted).

development of habits. In chapter 15 of *Insight,* on the elements of metaphysics, there is an account of organic development, psychic development, human development, and that is another approach to the question of development.[26] And shortly, I hope to be able to introduce another mode of classifying developments that will be more practical in handling the problems we have to deal with.[27]

So much for the consideration of operations, subject, objects. There is a final section[28] on the nature of methodological consideration. It is a reflection in a way on what we have done, but it also helps to bring together what we have said.

4 Consideration of Method[29]

4.1 Method Immediately about Operations, Mediately about Subjects and Objects

First of all, consideration of method is immediately of operations: of seeing, inquiring, understanding, defining, reflecting, weighing the evidence, judging, and so on: all the operations that people perform. And mediately, through the operations, it classifies subjects as with such and such a horizon, as authentic or unauthentic, with the authenticity as relative or absolute, and as converted or unconverted intellectually, morally, religiously. It classifies the objects in terms of the operations that deal with them. Consequently, while objects may remain unchanged, still the development in the operations gives development in the science, and a fuller apprehension of the object as the science develops. The value of a methodological consideration is that it can take into account intrinsically the development of a science.

4.2 Comparative, Genetic, and Dialectical Methods

Insofar as it considers the objects, method is comparative, genetic, and dialectical.

26 Bernard Lonergan, *Insight: A Study of Human Understanding,* vol. 3 in Collected Works of Bernard Lonergan, ed. Frederick E. Crowe and Robert M. Doran (Toronto: University of Toronto Press, 1992) 488–504.
27 See below, pp. 42–55.
28 Lonergan is referring to the notes, caput primum, §5, 'De Ipsa Consideratione Methodologica.'
29 See above, p. 4 at note 3.

It is comparative. The point to comparison is not that it answers the questions, but that it is always the preliminary clearing of the ground. It opens the way to picking out the key issues. In any question that is urgent, interesting, and pressing, there is going to be a key issue involved. It is a matter of starting from the data as they are given; and through a process of comparison one can pick out where the turning points are, where the key points are, where the key differences are. To illustrate that is not something that is possible in a short period of time. The examples with which I happen to be familiar because of the work I did myself can be found in *De Deo trino*.[30] Pages 15–113 deal with the pre-Nicene movement, and the things that I pick out are differences that stick out a mile.[31] In Daniélou's *Théologie du judéo-christianisme*, the early Jewish Christians illustrated symbolic thinking. They thought of the Son and the Holy Ghost as the two angels that in the vision of Isaiah shouted, 'Holy, holy, holy.' By angels they did not mean creatures; they were thinking of the Trinity within the categories, the modes of apprehension, of the Old Testament.[32] Another type of trinitarian thought that is after the New Testament comes with the Gnostics. They have their own oddities, and are totally different from the Jewish Christians. A third type is illustrated by Tertullian, and it is a mixed type. On the one hand, he can talk about the Son as God and the Son as Son, just as any good Scholastic would. But at the same time, he thinks of the Son as divine because he is made out of the right stuff. He is made out of spiritual matter, and not merely spiritual matter, but divine matter, and it is because of that that he is God. That is what is meant by really being God. And because that is what is meant by really being God, it makes no difference if the Son comes into existence in time; it makes no difference if he is subordinate to the Father; it makes no difference if the Father gives the orders and the Son carries them out. If he is made of the right stuff, that is all that counts. It is

30 Lonergan is referring to the 'Praemittenda' of his *De Deo trino: Pars analytica* (Rome: Gregorian University Press, 1961). This was to become the *pars dogmatica* of his 1964 *De Deo trino*, where some changes were made in the 'Praemittenda.' The work is now available as *The Triune God: Doctrines*, vol. 11 in Collected Works of Bernard Lonergan, trans. Michael G. Shields, ed. Robert M. Doran and H. Daniel Monsour (Toronto: University of Toronto Press, 2009).
31 In *The Triune God: Doctrines*, this material is found on pp. 28–255. The page numbers given in the lecture are those from *De Deo trino: Pars analytica*.
32 Jean Daniélou, *Théologie du judéo-christianisme* (Tournai-Paris: Desclée & Cie, 1958). In English: *The Theology of Jewish Christianity*, trans. and ed. John A. Baker (London: Darton, Longman & Todd, and Chicago: The Henry Regnery Company, 1964).

not predicates about the Son that count; it is the reality that the Son is that makes him God.[33]

Another completely different way of apprehending the issue appears in Origen. The criterion of reality, the idea of the divinity, or what can be truly said about the Son, as opposed to the merely symbolic thinking of the Jewish Christians and the Gnostics, was in Platonist terms. There is an entirely new view of the divinity of the Son. The Son is divine by participation: only the Father is *autotheos*; the Son is *theos*; the Father is goodness itself, the Son is good; the Son is truth itself and wisdom itself, but the Father is far better than that. It is a subordinationism of a totally different type from Tertullian's.[34]

With the council of Nicea, one arrives at the consubstantial, the *homoousion*, not in the earlier sense that can be found in Tertullian, *unius substantiae*, made of the same stuff, but as having the same predicates, as we say in the Preface: 'Quod enim de tua gloria, revelante te, credimus, hoc de Filio tuo, hoc de Spiritu sancto, sine differentia discretionis sentimus.'[35] And Athanasius says, 'Omnia de Filio quae de Patre dicuntur, excepto Patris nomine.'[36]

Just by considering the facts, then, one arrives at a series of different ways of apprehending the Son, and they are all found in the Christian milieu after the New Testament period. Comparison is the fundamental step. By the comparisons, by seeing the difference between the Jewish Christians and the Gnostics, the Gnostics and Tertullian, Tertullian and Origen, and between any of those and Athanasius or Alexander of Alexandria, and the discussions with the Arians, one comes across differences simply by comparing the texts. They will not be noticed by someone specializing only in Tertullian or only in Origen. It is a level of consideration above purely historical study, especially highly specialist historical study: a level of comparison. Origen probably did not think much of Tertullian, and Tertullian did not think much of Origen. They were not related. They belonged to different worlds. But they both belonged to the Catholic milieu, and comparison between them reveals differences.

The second stage is to understand the differences, and that understanding of the differences always reduces to two things. There is the genetic ele-

---

33 On Tertullian, see Lonergan, *The Triune God: Doctrines* 94–107.

34 On Origen, see ibid. 116–37.

35 'For what we believe through your revelation about your glory, we hold the same about your Son and the same about the Holy Spirit without any difference or discrimination.' As translated by Michael G. Shields in *The Triune God: Doctrines*, 43.

36 'The same things are said of the Son as are said of the Father, except that the Son is not the Father.'

ment, development, genesis: one is making explicit what was implicit, according to the classical formulation. And on the other hand, there is the dialectical element, the lack of moral conversion, intellectual conversion, religious conversion. The heretics represent a lack in religious conversion, but there are orthodox thinkers who are lacking in intellectual conversion. Tertullian's idea of the reality of the Son as being made of the right stuff is a lack in that intellectual conversion, at least in my opinion. Method as fundamentally comparative gets the process from one to the next, and as genetic makes explicit what already had been taken for granted in what was implicit in the tradition. Besides the genetic element, the element of development, in Christian doctrine, there is also always the dialectical element. There is always somebody there to contradict, and you have a choice between them. All the possibilities in the development of dogma usually are fully explored. All the discussion and all the councils that were held between AD 325 and AD 360, and all the views that were put forward about the divinity of the Son, covered completely the field of possibilities. But they could not all be right; they were opposed to one another. Dialectical analysis, insofar as it introduces a normative element, effects the transition from the history of the doctrine to the doctrine itself. This is a fundamental point in theological method, namely, the possibility of a transition from the history of a doctrine to the doctrine itself, the transition from positive to systematic theology. That possibility arises insofar as the history is understood, and indeed understood normatively, in terms of what should be and what should not be, in terms of being on the right track and on the wrong track. Insofar as that normative element can be introduced, one can effect a transition from the mere history of the doctrine, what de facto was held, to the doctrine itself.

Again, consideration from the methodological viewpoint is *one*: it considers everything from the viewpoint of operations. It is *synthetic*, that is, putting things together and understanding them, insofar as it arrives at a genetic-dialectical understanding of the situation. It is *concrete* because this analysis, just as it can be applied to the development of the infant and the child, so too it can be applied to the writing of a poem, the interpretation of a poem, the considerations of style, and many other matters. Finally, it is *transcendental*. It is transcendental in the Scholastic sense. In other words, any horizon falls short of *ens* and *bonum*, but *ens* and *bonum* include absolutely everything, they run through or over all the categories. The object of the intellect is *ens*, and of the will is *bonum*, and so among human operations there is a transcendental element in the Scholastic sense. It is transcendental also in another sense. The important point usually is not the precise operation, but the combination of operations. Now if there is a combination of operations, there is also going to be a combination, a structure, in the object, in the product. If a house is built by combining operations in such and such a manner, there is a structure in the house itself that corresponds to the order and arrangement of the operations that made it. To take another example, there is a similarity in structure between the notes in the musical score and the movement of the pianist's fingers or the singer's vocal cords, the relations between the indentations in the gramophone record and the sound waves in the air and the vibrations in the ear. The same pattern will be found in all of them; otherwise it would not be the same piece of music.

Insofar as we arrive either at natural combinations of operations, or at hypothetically necessary combinations of operations, then we have two types of conclusion that are possible: one that regards the relation between the subject and the object, the other that regards the relation between this subject who is thinking of someone else's thinking, and that other thinking.

On the relation between the subject and the object, St Thomas states that the proportionate object of human intellect is *quidditas sive natura in materia corporali existens.*[37] How does he know this? He does not tell us. How can one know that any human intellect is going to have that object? If human knowing has the structure that I have indicated today, then any example of human knowing is going to involve some act of understanding. And insofar as there is some act of understanding, there is something that is understood, there is an element corresponding to understanding as such, and that is *quidditas,* the *to ti ēn einai,* the *morphē,* the *eidos.* We understand only insofar as there is something to be understood. We do not just understand, but always understand something, and that something is sensibly given or represented linguistically. So, if there is an *eidos,* a *morphē,* there is also sensibility, and what corresponds to sensibility or imagination will be *in materia corporali.*

But if you experience with your senses and understand with your mind, this does not mean that you know anything. Bright ideas are a dime a dozen: they are not all right, they are usually all wrong. Besides sensibility and understanding, you also have to have judgment. You will decide whether this understanding fits the data completely. You judge by saying *est* or *non est,* it exists or it does not exist. So you reach the other element in the object, *ex-*

---

37 Thomas Aquinas, *Summa theologiae,* 1, q. 84, a. 7 c. '... the quiddity or nature existing in corporeal matter.'

istens: quidditas sive natura in materia corporali existens. You can deduce the proportionate object of human intellect from the structure of human knowing. Since this is the natural combination of operations in any human knowing, you have a transcendental element in the methodological approach.

There is another sense, namely, using the analysis of the structure of the operations to understand someone else. Did Matthew, Mark, Luke, and John have any idea of *ens*, or was it the Scholastics who discovered that? Is the *homoousion* of Nicea something totally extraneous to the Gospels, the importation of Hellenistic culture into a religion that developed in the religious soil of Palestine, as Harnack said? If inquiry and reflection, the *intellectus agens*, promote the process from sensibility to understanding, and from understanding to judging, if they are the *intentio intendens* of everything you are ever going to know or can know, and if that is the intention of being, then either Matthew, Mark, Luke, and John were completely stupid and completely nonrational, or else they had that *intentio* of being, and the *intentio* of being was not something totally alien to them. This is a second type of the use of a transcendental method.[38]

---

38 Lonergan added, 'Whether that is Kantian or not, there are further notes on that.' He is referring to the notes, caput primum, §5e: 'Estne haec methodus transcendentalis Kantiana?' ('Is this transcendental method Kantian?')

1962-2

The Human Good, Meaning, and Differentiations of Consciousness[1]

1 Summary of Previous Lecture

What we had to say yesterday may be summed up under the five headings of object, operations, habits, subject, and the characteristic of the method as transcendental.

With regard to objects, we can distinguish between final objects (what you know) and terminal objects (the inner words by which it is known, the judgments).

The final object is being, which is the same as the good: everything about everything that is, insofar as it is. Consequently, it is completely universal and completely concrete at once. Again, since knowledge is of opposites, the final object is also all that is not, insofar as it is not. That is the object of human operations generally, because among the human operations there are operations of intellect, which regards *ens*, everything. St Thomas proves that the object of intellect is *ens* because *intellectus* is *potens omnia facere et fieri*, so that *ens* and *omnia* are equivalent.

The terminal object, in general, is the universe affirmed in true propositions, that is, everything that can be truly affirmed. In theology, it is the dogmatic-theological context, in other words, the remainder of all that is presupposed or assumed or implied whenever one makes any theological statement. That context has developed. The [First] Vatican Council, in the

1 Tuesday, 10 July 1962, part 1, Lauzon CD/MP3 303 (30300A0E060) and 304 (30400A0E060).

chapter on faith and reason (DB 1800 [DS 3020, ND 136]), says the church prays that there continue to be an increase of understanding, knowledge, and wisdom with regard to revealed doctrine, and the fact that there also are future developments is attested to in *Humani generis* (DB 2314 [DS 3886, ND 859]), where it is stated that the sources of revelation never will be exhausted.

That development has not been pure development, simply and always to something that is a statement of what is truly implicit[2] in the original revelation; there also have been heresies. There are not only true theological opinions, but also mistaken opinions. Consequently, in the development, there is a dialectical element, and by 'dialectical' is meant that truth develops in opposition to error. It is commonly said, though not universally true, that the definitions of the faith are occasioned by the heresies; the heresies force developments of doctrine that otherwise would not occur.

Now that concept of theology is not the concept of some ideal; it is the concept of the theology that has existed and exists. It is entirely concrete; it is in terms of the dogmatic-theological context that is handed down in theological schools and that has developed down the ages.

So much from the viewpoint of the object, a reality apprehended through true propositions. What are those true propositions? They are not easily enumerated, but they form a context. If a person makes a theological statement, you can force that person to a circle of other statements, and that circle will force him to further circles. And the thing does not go off to infinity.

Next, there are operations, and the operations differentiate. There is a great difference between St Thomas and the theologians who wrote even shortly before him. There is a point of maximum development in Catholic theology. There is a differentiation of prior operations, and new combinations of the differentiated operations, and grouping of the combinations. Just as in Piaget's analysis of child development, there are operations that occur. To specify them is a further task.

The operations presuppose the development of habits. They occur promptly, easily, with satisfaction, and with respect to any combination of differentiated operations, in the person who has learnt theology, who knows theology. Theology is fundamentally a habit, in Scholastic analysis.

Next, there is the subject. The subject potentially is unlimited in the sense that the object of intellect is being and the object of will is the good.

2 Compare Method *in Theology* 353: '... the shift from a predominately logical to a basically methodical viewpoint may involve a revision of the view that doctrinal developments were "implicitly" revealed.'

Being and the good include everything. But actually there always is a horizon. A person has so much in the way of acquired habits, and for one to acquire more means practice, learning, being persuaded. Consequently, at any given moment there is a limitation, a dividing line, between what one can do right away, and what one could do if one took the time out or were able to take the time out to acquire further skills, to learn more, and to be persuaded to more.

Again, the subject is either in need of conversion or converted, and in three ways. There is the moral conversion from the egocentric life, in which everything is considered from the viewpoint of desire and fear, to the rational life, in which the fundamental viewpoint is what ought to be in the order of the universe established by God. There is the intellectual conversion from views on reality and truth that are developed prior to attaining the age of reason, to the critical viewpoint that is attained insofar as there occurs, in philosophy, a conversion. One knows exactly what it is if one has been through it, and, like anything else, one does not know it very well if one has not. Finally, there is religious conversion; and with us, it is conversion to the Catholic faith.[3]

Next, there is the unauthentic and the authentic subject. The unauthentic subject is the person who feels that he knows all about it when in fact he does not; and not only does he not but it is beyond his horizon that he does not. There are fundamental tasks of learning and of being persuaded that he has to meet before he can discover that he does not.

Those limitations of the subject – his horizon, his need of conversion, his lack of authenticity – are the proximate sources of the deviations, the dialectical element, in the development of the theological context. Because they are the source of error, they also are the reason for correction. You can say, 'This particular opinion, at this particular time, in the thought of this man or group, is due to a lack of authenticity, a lack of intellectual conversion, a lack of religious conversion, a horizon in that man or at his time.' On that ground, one can say that what is right is not what he is saying, but the opposite of what he is saying.

So, for example, in Tertullian's view on the divinity of the Son, one can say that what is right about Tertullian is found in the passages in which he says

3 The statement that religious conversion is conversion to the Catholic faith is, of course, one that, by the time he wrote *Method in Theology*, Lonergan would not make. Authenticity is self-transcendence, and religious authenticity is religious self-transcendence. Catholics have no premium on that. Lonergan would insist on this, despite describing himself, correctly, as 'a Roman Catholic with quite conservative views on religious and church doctrines.' Lonergan, *Method in Theology* 332.

that the Son and the Father are two as Father and Son, but not two as God; where he is using that little word 'as,' *qua*, which reoccurs continuously in Scholastic thought. On the other hand, insofar as Tertullian thinks of the divinity, not as what is known by truth, but as what is imagined as made out of the divine matter, there he is revealing a lack of intellectual conversion. He is a naive realist, or, as historians would put it, he is under Stoic influence. That part of Tertullian, simply because it is that part and has that source, is treated dialectically: what is to be done with it is to say the opposite.

The point to such dialectical consideration not only is that it gives a reason for our taking some passages from the Fathers as being their witness to the Catholic tradition, and saying of other passages, 'Well, these are queer sorts of things, and we don't know just how the Fathers happened to say that, but it is not what we hold.' It can seem arbitrary in some presentations of arguments of the Fathers that we do that, but the use of dialectic in the analysis of the development reveals why some statements are set aside and others are accepted. Moreover, that introduction of a normative element effects the transition from understanding the history of a doctrine to understanding the doctrine itself. By adding the normative element it builds the bridge from a positive theology that investigates what was said to what is true. That reconciliation of positive and systematic theology is, of course, a fundamental problem at our time.

Finally, these considerations regard method in general. I have thrown in points that are particularly relevant to theology, but in its basic structure that conception of method is transcendental. It spreads over the whole field, every field, it holds for every subject, and it holds for every object.

It holds for every subject, for all human subjects, that is. Either the subject experiences, or he does not; either he experiences this or that, or he does not; either he understands, or he does not; either he understands this or that, or he does not; either he judges, affirms or denies, or he does not. Those are the fundamental cognitive operations.

Similarly, it holds for every proper object of human knowledge. The proper object of human knowledge is the *quidditas sive natura in materia corporali existens.* We know it as existing insofar as we judge; we know it as *quidditas sive natura,* or form, insofar as we understand; and we know it as *in materia corporali* insofar as we experience externally with our senses.

Not only does it hold for proportionate objects, but also it presents proportionate objects in the way in which we proceed analogously to the total object of human knowledge. The Thomist conception of the angels is a compound, not of potency, form, and act as in man or in the material order, but of form and act. The Thomist concept of God is pure act. If our thinking, our notion, of the reality of material things is in terms of potency, form, and act, where potency corresponds to experiencing, form to understanding, and act to judging, then one proceeds to the purely spiritual order of God and the angels by dropping off potency in the case of the angels, and identifying form and act in the case of God.

One could go on and discuss whether this transcendental method is transcendental in the Kantian sense, but this involves a rather large digression, devoted mainly to explaining what Kant held. And it is not, I believe, a real problem. There is something on it in the notes at the end of the first section, pp. 6 and 7, and there is something more on p. 32.[4] We shall move ahead, for the time being at least.

The analysis of development in terms of the differentiation of operations is a very minute thing. The differentiation of operations into all their types and forms and the modes in which they can be grouped and described in detail would lead to an enormous catalogue and would be extremely cumbersome. We need to put the matter on a new basis, as it were, to be able to distinguish and classify fundamental developments in a way that will satisfy our needs in a method of theology. In that direction, there is in the notes a discussion of the sacred and profane, the subject and object, and common sense and theory.[5] Perhaps it will make that discussion more concrete, and so more helpful, if I begin from a brief scheme that expresses what the human good is.

2   The Human Good

2.1   The Structure

According to St Thomas and Aristotle, *verum et falsum sunt in mente, bonum et malum sunt in rebus,* true and false are in the mind, while good and evil are in things. Consequently, when you ask about the good, you are asking about

4 Lonergan is referring again to the notes based on his lectures at the Gregorian, 'De methodo theologiae.' There is a section at the end of the first chapter of those notes, corresponding to what here is referred to as pp. 6 and 7, 'Estne haec methodus transcendentalis Kantiana?' ('Is this transcendental method Kantian?') and another mention of the question, corresponding to what here is referred to as p. 32, in the section on intuitive extrinsicism. For a correspondence in these lectures to the latter reference, see below, pp. 118–23.
5 The discussion to which Lonergan is referring appeared near the beginning of 'Caput II' in the Latin course 'De methodo theologiae.' In the present lectures it occurs after the treatment of the human good which Lonergan is entering upon now. See below, pp. 42–52.

the concrete. The good can be considered in its total range, or one can limit oneself simply to the human good. It is with regard to the human good that development occurs fundamentally. Consequently, we have to ask ourselves what the human good is.

We get to that, not by some abstract definition, but by a general analysis that fits every instance of the human good. I will give first of all a scheme,[6] and then a few notes on various elements in the scheme.[7]

Potency of subject	Act	Social mediation	Object
Need and ability	Operation	Cooperation	Particular good
Capacity for development	Acquired habit	Institutions	Good of order
Freedom	Orientation in life	Interpersonal relations	Terminal values

The potency of the subject may be considered on three levels. There is need and ability, there is capacity for development, and there is freedom. The act resulting from need and ability is some operation. The act of capacity for development, the first act, is acquired habit. The act of freedom is an orientation in life and in one's existential being.

In virtue of the social mediation of the human good, operation becomes cooperation, acquired habits are matched by institutions, and orientations are matched by personal or interpersonal relations. The object of the operation or cooperation is a particular good, the object of acquired habits and institutions is the good of order, and the objects of orientation and personal relations are terminal values. The orientation of liberty is the originating value.

Now for some notes on each one of those elements.

2.2 The Particular Good

This analysis of the concrete human good is relevant to any stage of human development, from the primitive fruit gatherers to the present time and beyond. To need (hunger and thirst) is conjoined ability (the capacity of

6 Compare the slightly more complex scheme in Lonergan, *Method in Theology* 48.
7 At this point, Lonergan takes several minutes to put the scheme on the board.

getting food somehow or other). Regarding operation and cooperation, we may say that Robinson Crusoe operated, while the rest of us spend most of our lives cooperating in some way or other. Regarding the particular good, we may say that any good is particular insofar as it responds to, or is the good of, this particular appetite. This apple, this dinner, this instance of the beatific vision, are all instances of the particular good. They are the objects of an appetite, a desire.

2.3 The Good of Order

One moves from the first line to the second insofar as the instances of the particular good within this world are not eternal like the beatific vision, and the need for them is recurrent. One does not merely want breakfast; one wants breakfast every day. And so on for everything else: the need is recurrent.

The good of order not merely regards the particular goods. It also regards the totality of needs and abilities, the totality of dreams that they can give rise to for attaining particular goods, and the combination of the lot in such a way that breakfast happens not just today but every day, that you not merely have a class but a university course and the continuity of the university courses that keep on supplying education to an endless number of individuals. The good of order is what gives rise to the constant, regular, rhythmic occurrence of the particular goods.

The most striking example of the significance of the good of order was the great Depression of the 1930s. The Depression did not mean any shortage of natural resources. It did not mean that workers were unwilling to work – there was nothing they wanted more than work. It did not mean that the capitalists were unwilling to invest – they were longing for opportunities to invest. It did not mean that there was any lack of entrepreneurs – they were all eager for any opportunity they could find to start something going. It did not mean any opposition on the part of the government – the government was eager to prime the pumps. The whole trouble was that when they primed the pumps all that happened was that the machine gave one spurt, and they had to prime it again to get it going and do another turn. The thing did not just flow along on its own. The good of order was lacking.

The good of order can be found on all sorts of levels. The family is an instance, in the concrete, of a good of order: it provides for the good of the parents, of husband and wife, and for the good of the children. The good of order attained in each family is something peculiar to that family; it is the way they live. There is the good of order in the state. There is the good of order in international relations. That good of order is not some ideal, something that ought to be but is not; it is something concrete, actually functioning. If it were not concrete and actually functioning, then the breakfast would not recur, and so on for every other particular good. It is not a matter of the theoretical conception of that good of order. It is not what the economist thinks the good of order is, but what the economist is approximately trying to get to know. It is something that is objective and realized. The ideal is, of course, something real, something essential to man and intrinsic to man and what leads to his development, but if you conceive the good simply in terms of the ideal, then you are never talking about the good that really is. The good that really is is the only good that is *in rebus*; and the good of order is *in rebus, non tantum in mente.*

A friend of mine, teaching in the Gregorian at the Social Institute, Fr Kevin Quinn, an Irishman, had great difficulty expounding the English cooperative movement to people from Latin countries, from Portugal, Spain, and so on. The cooperative movement in England has an annual turnover of millions and millions of pounds. He explained the legal foundation of the movement. It consisted in a law to the following effect: let there be non-profit organizations named cooperatives. This was simply incomprehensible to these people from an entirely different background in which, if something were to be done in the social order, you drew up a code of laws foreseeing every possible eventuality and provided for it, and when that was finished there was no more to be done. It was attention to the good as ideal, and an incapacity to apprehend the good as it really is, as something that functions in the society. It is that which functions in the society actually and which can be improved (by slow stages usually) that is the real good of order.

Institutions in the good of order are the family, society, education, morals, the state, the law, the economy, and the technology. They are not to be identified with the good of order. They are instruments for it, or ordered to it, not necessarily subordinate to it. They are, in the objective social milieu, what the acquired habit is in the individual. If people are going to cooperate, there have to be a number of things that are taken for granted, that they understand; and so they know what you mean. If all the presuppositions of a cooperation had to be worked out every time there was a cooperation, we would never get around to cooperating on anything. There has to be that broad field of common understanding and common consent: what it means to get married, what it means to be the citizens of a state, what it means to be educated, and so on. The institutions embody that gradually developing common knowledge and common consent that is the presupposition of the cooperations and the presupposition of the functioning of the good of order. Such elements of common knowledge and common consent become institutionalized, something permanent in a society. Thus there is what a marriage is in that society. Again, what is a state? An abstract definition of the state may be given, and it will hold for every state from the most simple to the most modern and complicated forms. But states, concretely, are very different from one another. The English notion of a state is not the same as the French, and both differ from the German, and all three differ from the Russian, and there is a difference between them and the Italian and the American, and so forth. The state concretely is what the people in the state understand the state to be, and it is the state in that sense that we are speaking of as the functioning institution. And so on for the other elements.

Acquired habits develop through exercise, through practice – practice makes perfect – and through the self-correcting process of learning. One gets an insight, one catches on to something, and then finds that it is not quite the whole story, and catches on to something more, and gradually builds up a whole circle of insights that yield one a certain mastery of the situation. Finally, there is becoming persuaded. One does not have to be persuaded to eat one's dinner, but one wants good reasons for fasting, and has to be persuaded almost on each occasion. And so on all along the line. When one has the acquired habit, one does not have to persuade oneself, one does not have to learn, and one does not have to practice, as one has to do with things beyond one's horizon.

Acquired habits ground the possibility of specializations. One specializes insofar as one's acquired habits are heading towards and fulfilling a very precise function within the social mediation of the good. Such specialization is partly from nature, for example, the difference between male and female or between people with or without special gifts and natural aptitudes, as well as from acquired habits.

2.4 Terminal Values

One moves from the second line to the third insofar as one reflects that no good of order, no institution or set of institutions, is the only one possible. The family can be patriarchial or matriarchial, polygamous or monogamous, and there can be perpetual monogamy or, as in Hollywood, serial monogamy. Education can be classical or philological, modern, scientific, or technical; there can be many different kinds of education. The law can be the law of custom, as in the English common law, in which the law gradually develops through the decisions made by judges, who have considerable discretionary powers; or the law can be entirely contained in a code, and all that the judge has to do is apply the code. The organization of society, the differences between capitalism and socialism, democracy and totalitarianism, are different possibilities in the institutions of the society. In general, children fight about particular goods but adults fight about the good of order. The good of order is a manifold of possibilities, and the fundamental profane divisions among people regard that good of order; they will say, for example, that democratic countries are the good countries and the others are the bad countries.

The existence of a manifold of possibilities for the good of order and the institutions that underpin them gives rise to, reveals, and brings to light the notion of value. Why is this order better than that? It opens the way to values, or it contains in itself a value that the other does not have. What do you mean by a value? Reductionists will say that the more particular goods you get out of it, the greatest happiness of the greatest number, is the criterion of value. Those at the opposite pole set down absolute norms, either aesthetic norms or ethical norms or religious norms, which state that which should be, what ought to be, and they want the order of society and the good of order determined by those norms.

By orientation is meant the direction in which the use of liberty heads. That orientation is closely connected with authenticity and inauthenticity, with conversion – intellectual, moral, and religious – and the lack of such conversion. We spoke of terminal values, but the orientation is the originating value. As Kant remarked, the only thing that is simply good is a good will. In that sense, the orientation of the person or personality is what is simply good, because it is insofar as there is good will that this whole process will function.

Finally, there are interpersonal relations. Interpersonal relations may arise from the institutions, from one's role in society: one is father of the family or son, one is professor or student, one is a pastor or belongs to the people, one is the boss or a worker, and so on all along the line: there are interpersonal relations that arise from institutional roles. Insofar as interpersonal relations arise from family conflicts, represented for example by the family of Laius, whose son was Oedipus and whose wife was Jocasta, they are studied at some length in Freudian depth psychology. But there is also the well-known dialectic between the master and the slave in Hegel's *Phenomenology of Mind,* and Fr Fessard's transposition of that in the dialectic of the unconverted Jew and the converted pagan in their relations to Christ.[8]

With that, one has an analysis, a concrete notion of the human good, that can be specified and adapted to any particular situation: it is the good in that situation. It mediates an apprehension of what in the concrete the human good is, and while it leads to an enormous description at any particular stage, it makes things more concrete than otherwise they would be.

2.5 *Progress and Decline*

According to St Paul in the opening three chapters of Romans, all men have sinned, and sin introduces the irrational, the surd, into the human good. The effects of that introduction can be found outlined in chapter 7 and chapter 18 in *Insight.* What sin heads for is the breakdown and reduction of all this process of the human good to a mere equilibrium of forces, to wars, to class struggles, and so on. On the other hand, the body of Christ is inserted in the order of the human good, and it operates by introducing the supernatural gifts of faith, hope, and charity that not only head us towards eternal life, insofar as grace is elevating, but also, as *gratia sanans,* counteract the influence of sin in that social order. That aspect of the matter can be found in chapter 20 of *Insight.*

3   Meaning

If one adds one brief reflection to the foregoing outline, one comes upon the fundamental problem of theology at the present time.

This whole structure of the human good is based on nature, on man's needs and abilities, his capacity for development, his native freedom. But the development is constituted on the formal level, one might almost say, by meaning.[9] Without meaning there is no human cooperation, except in the most elementary forms, especially if you take meaning in its full sense: not merely linguistic meaning, but also symbolic meaning, aesthetic meaning – the meaning of a work of art – and intersubjective meaning – the look on

---

8   Gaston Fessard, *De l'actualité historique,* vol. 1 (Paris: Desclée de Brouwer, 1960).
9   These statements perhaps illuminate how Lonergan conceived the relation between what became chapter 2 ('The Human Good') and chapter 3 ('Meaning') in *Method in Theology.*

a person's face that modifies a situation. For example, if someone knocks at your door, if you are interrupted while struggling with a problem, there is a certain amount of inadaptation to the other's presence, and both of you will become embarrassed, whereas he may be greeted by another man with a broad smile and delight. The interpersonal situations are entirely different, not because of anything said, but because of the intersubjective meaning that is involved.

To enlarge on each of those types of meaning would take us a little far afield. But meaning in its full extent is what is understood in the concrete situation and actions of the person, from frowns to long speeches, and as such is the formal element in this process of the human good. All the institutions involve meaning. The law courts and the prisons apart from meaning are sound and fury, the sound in the law courts and the fury in the prisons. It is insofar as you give meaning to, and know the meaning of, human actions and human institutions that there is something there.

Further, meaning develops. I have said that the state in England or France or Germany is what the people there understand the state to be. That is a main determinant in what their state is. And so on in other countries. Meanings develop. When one moves to the point where one considers that human activity is constituted formally by the intentional, by the *esse intentionale*, by meaning, that the meanings develop, and that the understanding of human activities is the understanding of these developing meanings, one arrives at the viewpoint called historical consciousness. It is that viewpoint, which developed mainly in Germany with Hegelianism and the Historical School (Savigny, Grimm, Ranke), with Dilthey's *Geisteswissenschaften*, and later with Husserl and Heidegger, that has a terrific importance in any effort to deal fundamentally with the problems of contemporary theology. We are inundated with historical studies. Theology is becoming more and more penetrated with historical and psychological studies of all kinds, and it is insofar as we can get hold of precisely what the meaning and import of that movement is that we will know what it is that has been disturbing theology and getting us into all sorts of difficulties, particularly over the past fifty or sixty years.

I have given an indication of the human good and its formal constitution by meaning, in any of the senses of the word 'meaning,' and I might add a word on revelation. What is revelation? It is a new meaning added into human life. By bringing a new meaning into this process of the human good, you transform something that is formally constitutive of that human good. What is the body of Christ? It is an order. Just as the family, the state, the economy, and the law express an order, so too is the body of Christ an order, and it is a redemptive order that counteracts the evil of sin in that social mediation of the human good.

4 Classifications of Development

4.1 An Alternative Basis of Development

I have introduced the foregoing considerations as a background to a consideration and classification of development that will suit our purposes in the way that Piaget's use of groups of operations suited his purposes in understanding the development of children. The analysis of development that concerns us turns upon three fundamental antitheses: between the sacred and the profane, the subject and the object, common sense and theory.[10] We have to clarify those distinctions. We have to have some understanding of the process from the undifferentiated to the differentiated consciousness. And finally, we have to grasp the existence and nature of a problem of integration.

Piaget, in his account of development, speaks of operations, their differentiation, the combination of differentiated operations, and the grouping of these combinations. But there comes a point where the grouping of groups comes upon a block. You cannot simply group all operations. There are fundamental antitheses, and they are not met by trying to put them together, but basically (generally at least) by leaving them apart and shifting from one to the other. The operations that one performs during one's meditation, Mass, thanksgiving, and the recitation of the breviary form a circle, a group that does not mix easily with the group of operations one performs in having meals, recreation, going to class, or teaching. They are entirely different groups of operations. St Teresa was able, after many years of progress, to carry on her work of founding convents all over Spain, and at the same time to be in a profound mystical state; but she found herself, as it were, cut in two. They don't mix easily.

Consequently, integration with groups of operations of that type is – to use Toynbee's phrase – by withdrawal and return.[11] There is a time for praying

---

10 See above, note 5.
11 Arnold J. Toynbee, *A Study of History*, 12 vols. (London: Oxford University Press, 1934–61). For his treatment of withdrawal and return, see the indices in vol. 3, *The Growth of Civilizations* (1934), vol. 6, *The*

and a time for resting and a time for this and a time for that. One is an all-round person insofar as one moves from one to the other. But one cannot make them interpenetrate, and there are fundamental reasons for that difficulty or impossibility of interpenetration. That fact, finally, enables us to give a fundamental classification of development. It is insofar as this process of grouping runs up against a brick wall and we discover an impossibility or an extreme difficulty of grouping that we come upon a new possibility of classifying development.

4.2   The Sacred and the Profane

The first of these antitheses is between the sacred and the profane. All our knowledge of God in this life is analogous and mediated. We know God on the analogy of creatures. We know that God exists because we know that creatures exist. Immediate knowledge of God is the beatific vision, and that is not had in this life. Again, St Thomas in the *Pars prima*, q. 44, a. 4, ad 3m, insists that all desire – natural, sensitive, and intellectual – is ultimately desire of God: *omnia Deum appetunt ut finem*, because every good is a good insofar as it is a similitude of God. But again, that reveals that we reach God mediately; our desires are directly for the finite, and it is ultimately that God is the object of desire.

There is, then, a fundamental division between the immediate and the ultimate, or the proximate and the ultimate, and that opposition grounds the distinction between the sacred and the profane. There is the field in which we can be the masters, in which a spade is just a spade; but there is also what is mediated by that field, what is beyond it, above it, before it, at the beginning, or in the world to come, after it. It is obscure. We do not know it properly, but it is the ultimate end of all our desiring, and not only of sensitive desire, but also of intellectual desire, the natural desire for the vision of God according to St Thomas, the natural desire for beatitude, the need for having an ultimate foundation for values.

And finally, there is the preformation, the preparation, of these ultimate tendencies of the soul that occurs upon the psychic level. The depth psychologists have been drawing out, discovering, that the preconscious is something that is very religious.

Now those two can be differentiated. In the profane world, the spade is just a spade, and that's all there is to it. And on the other hand, the world

---

Disintegration of Civilizations, Part Two (1939), and vol. 10, *The Inspiration of Historians* (1954).

of the sacred is completely distinct. But that is the result of a differentiation. Among the primitives, there is not that differentiation of the sacred and the profane. For the primitive, there is a sacralization of the profane and a secularization of the sacred, and for him that is the only way to conceive things. In Wordsworth's 'Ode on the Intimations of Immortality':

> There was a time when meadow, grove, and stream
> The earth, and every common sight,
>   To me did seem
> Apparelled in a celestial light,
> The glory and the freshness of a dream.

In that stage, the spade is not just a spade. It has a plus, and so on for everything else. And for the primitive, for the undifferentiated consciousness, there is always that plus to everything. The sacred interpenetrates with the profane, and the profane with the sacred.

What Jung, particularly, has brought to light is that symbols are of the same type as the undifferentiated primitive consciousness. In the symbols of the dream, or of free association, the waking dream as it is called, one has the type of consciousness in which the sacred and profane are not differentiated. There is a sacred meaning in the symbol as well as a profane meaning, and the two interpenetrate. On that subject, on Jung in particular, there is a very fine note in the appendix to Mircea Eliade's *The Forge and the Crucible* in which he accurately pulls out the defects in Jung's presentation, while he agrees with Jung's real discovery, namely, that the symbol is of the type of primitive undifferentiated consciousness, that it is at once religious and secular. There is also a very vivid description of this interpenetration of the sacred and the profane.[12]

That differentiation of consciousness is not merely a matter of a logical distinction, knowing what the sacred is and knowing what the profane is. Rather, it is a matter of the subject's consciousness. Insofar as one's consciousness is symbolic, the two are going to merge into one. On the other hand, insofar as consciousness develops, insofar as operations become

---

12 Mircea Eliade, *Forgerons et alchemistes* (Paris: Flammarion, 1956) 151–56 and 221–24, note N; in English, *The Forge and the Crucible*, trans. Stephen Corrin (London: Rider & Company, 1962) 148–52 and 221–26, note N. In the lecture, Lonergan cited the page references from the French edition.

A break was taken at this point. The second part of the lecture is recorded on Lauzon CD/MP3 (30400AOE060).

differentiated and specialized, and the huge combinations of differentiated operations combine into groups, the two are going to separate. That
is something fundamental simply because the sacred is what is beyond,
what is known only mediately and analogously. It is what is desired ultimately. That's the way we are built.

A concrete illustration of the process of differentiation can be had from
Congar's account of the difference between Augustinian thought, as represented by Augustine and Bonaventure, and, on the other hand, Thomism.
In his article on 'Théologie' in *Dictionnaire de théologie catholique* 15, column
388, he presents very neatly the difference between the Augustinian attitude
and the Thomist. I will give you a free translation of a French passage.

> As the sciences and philosophy for the Augustinian had no value
> except insofar as they refer to God, it followed that the sciences and
> philosophy did not bring to Christian wisdom any knowledge of the
> nature of things in themselves, but merely examples and illustra-
> tions. All our knowledge of the created world had only one function.
> It was not to know something more, it was not to know further truth
> about them, but to provide illustrations, examples, that would
> further one's knowledge of God. It had a symbolic value, to aid one
> to an understanding of the true revelation, and that true revelation
> came from above and was in a purely spiritual order. This enables
> one to grasp in what sense the Augustinians spoke of philosophy as
> the *ancilla theologiae*. Sciences exist only to serve, and one does not
> ask them more than to serve. They have no function of contributing
> any truth of their own, and that is the meaning of the expression
> *ancilla theologiae* in the letters of Gregory ix and Alexander iv to the
> University of Paris.[13]

What Thomism meant was a break from that Augustinian distinction of
the *ratio superior* and *inferior*. In the medieval unfolding of the Augustinian
view, the sciences were purely ancillary, they provided illustrations and
examples for knowledge of the divine, but they were not a separate department of knowledge, they did not possess a truth in their own right. There
is an incompleteness in the differentiation between the sacred and the
profane. On the other hand, Thomism, with its acceptance of Aristotelian

13 Congar, 'Théologie,' col. 388. For another translation see Congar, *A History
of Theology* 107.

science, involved an acceptance of a full differentiation between the sacred and the profane.

4.3 The Subject and the Object

Our second antithesis is between the inner and outer, the subject and the object, the external world and the world of interiority. The objective world includes everything that we apprehend as object, everything we desire, everything we choose. It includes the subject insofar as the subject is objectified, insofar as the subject is apprehended as object in a concept or a judgment, insofar as the subject's desires are explicitly willed. But besides that purely objective world, there is also the subject as subject: the subject as experiencing, inquiring, understanding, thinking, weighing the evidence, judging, desiring, willing, choosing. That subject as subject is presence. That presence of the subject to himself was put down in a rather clear fashion by Augustine in *De Trinitate*, book 10 (IX, 12), where he brings out the notion of the subject by a series of contrasts: '... non ita dicitur menti: Cognosce te ipsam sicut dicitur: "Cognosce cherubim et seraphim"; de absentibus enim illis credimus secundum quod caelestes quaedam potestates esse praedicantur.'[14] He is bringing us the notion of the subject by the phrase 'know yourself,' the precept of the sage, and you do not know yourself the way you know the cherubim and seraphim; they are far away, and we know that they are *caelestes potestates*. 'Neque sicut dicitur: "Cognosce voluntatem illius hominis," quae nobis nec ad sentiendum ullo modo nec ad intelligendum praesto est nisi corporalibus signis editis, et hoc ita ut magis credamus quam intelligamus.'[15] We do not know ourselves the way we know another's will. We know another's will by the signs he makes, and the signs may be made to take us in just as well as to reveal what he really wants, what he's really up to. 'Neque ita ut dicitur homini: "Vide faciem tuam," quod nisi in speculo fieri non potest. Nam et ipsa nostra facies absens ab aspectu

14   '["Know yourself"] is not said to the mind as is "Know the cherubim and the seraphim": for they are absent, and we believe concerning them, and according to that belief they are declared to be certain celestial powers.' Augustine, *On the Trinity*, as translated by Arthur West Haddan and W.G.T. Shedd, in vol. 3 of *Nicene and Post-Nicene Fathers*, ed. Philip Schaff (Grand Rapids, MI: Eerdmans, 1980) 140.
15   'Nor yet again as it is said, Know the will of that man; for this is not within our reach to perceive at all, either by sense or by understanding, unless by corporeal signs actually set forth; and this in such a way that we rather believe than understand.' Ibid.

nostro est quia non ibi est quo ille dirigi potest.'[16] To look at our face we need a mirror. Our face is physically present to everyone of us, but we can't see it. We can see other people's faces, not our own, unless we have a mirror. It is present physically, but it is not present in the intentional order. 'Sed cum dicitur menti: "Cognosce te ipsam, eo ictu quo intelligit quod dictum est te ipsam cognoscit se ipsam, nec ob aliud quam eo quod sibi praesens est.'[17] The *anima*, the *mens*, is present to itself if it is dreaming or if it is awake, but not if you're sound asleep. Whenever you are operating you are present to yourself, and this is not the material presence by which a table is in the room or my face is present to me. That is a physical presence. It is not the intentional presence of an object, in the way that the cherubim and seraphim can be apprehended by me through a true judgment (*verum est medium in quo ens cognoscitur*) nor in the way in which others are present to me as objects. But for anything to be present to me I have to be present to myself at the same time. If I am not present to myself, there is no one to whom the objects are present – we have just the spectacle and no spectator. The spectator is present to himself not as spectacle but as spectator. That subject is present, and that subject is the field of interiority. There is not only the seen but the seer, and the seer is not seeing his presence to himself by the third presence that is the condition of anything being present to him. There is not only the understood, but the understander, and he is present to himself as understanding, not as understood; to understand himself is a further task. There is the presence of the judge to himself as judging. It is not the presence of what is judged about, the presence of the object. It is not something that is added on by an afterthought, as though he were absent from himself, sound asleep, while judging, and only in turning back, in reflection, did he discover that there was something that did the judgment, discover it as an object.

There is, then, just as radical as the opposition between the proximate and the ultimate, the opposition between the subject and the object. The subject as present to himself is not present as an object, and when he objectifies himself he is not only present to himself as object but also as subject.

---

16 'Nor again as it is said to a man, Behold thy own face; which he can only do in a looking-glass. For even our own face itself is out of the reach of our seeing it; because it is not there where our look can be directed.' Ibid.
17 'But when it is said to the mind, Know thyself; then it knows itself by that very act by which it understands the word "thyself"; and this for no other reason than that it is present to itself.' Ibid.

Now that distinction between subject and object, between inner and outer, between interiority and the external world, is a fundamental distinction. Thomas à Kempis remarks that it is better to feel compunction than to define it, and the difference there is between interiority and the object. When you feel compunction you are not talking about compunction or thinking about compunction; you are before God, aware of your sins and of God's goodness and his right. Defining compunction takes the compunction from the side of the subject, the one who is innerly present to himself, and makes an object of it, transferring it to the objective world. Similarly the person who goes around saying that we should not define compunction, we should feel it, is talking about compunction, dealing with compunction as object. He is not feeling it when he is talking about it; the feeling of compunction is the prior thing. It's on the side of the subject.

Life is fundamentally something we know by being alive. Such expressions as 'That's life' or 'I might as well be dead' reveal that inner experience of being alive. Being in love is not simply an act of will, or a combination of acts of will, or habits of acts of will, but the total orientation of one's interiority. Similarly the presence of God is not thinking of an object, but rather the presence of the absent. The presence of the absent, like all desire, is the presence of what one does not have, and since all desire is ultimately for God, the presence of God is, as it were, the ultimate presence of the absent.

The world of interiority was explored in modern philosophy by Hegel in his youthful writings. At the beginning of this century a new era started in Hegelian studies with Dilthey's *Die Jugendgeschichte Hegels.*[18] And since then there have been endless studies on the subject. I put in the notes the last one, published at Louvain by Asveld.[19] Kantianism confined Hegel to the inner world, and Hegelian theory has its origins in the study of that interiority.

The historical process that brings out the opposition between subject and object is the emergence of individualism. For the primitive, the object is, as it were, personalized – everything is thought of personally – and at the same time the subject is objectified; it is the community that thinks, discusses, decides, acts, and the individual is simply a member of the community. The ancient high civilizations of Egypt, Mesopotamia, India, China, as also, in all probability, the Mayas and Incas of Central America, had terrific achievements

18 Wilhelm Dilthey, *Gesammelte Schriften*, vol. 4, *Die Jugendgeschichte Hegels und andere Abhandlungen zur Geschichte des deutschen Idealismus* (Stuttgart: Teubner, 1957).
19 Paul Asveld, *La pensée religieuse du jeune Hegel, Liberté et Aliénation* (Louvain: Publications Universitaires, 1953).

in the whole order of external techniques – in architecture, agriculture, irriga-
tion – and in the control of men in economics and politics, but there was no
individualism in the modern sense of the word. Karl Jaspers, in *Vom Ursprung
und Ziel der Geschichte, The Origin and Goal of History*,[20] places what he calls the
axis of history between the years 800 BC and 200 BC, when the old empires
broke down and men had to think and act and do for themselves. Before that
they were just parts in these enormous states; individualism arose when those
states fell apart and the individual had to act on his own. There occurred then,
with the emergence of that individualism, a flowering of the subject, the subject becoming aware of himself as subject. There can be individualism at any
stage of human development – the shaman and the Indian mystic are individualists – but the type of individualism that results depends upon the prior development of the society.

4.4 Common Sense and Theory

The final antithesis is between the world of common sense and the world of
theory. It is just as fundamental as the other two. The difference between
reality as known through theory and reality as known through common
sense is not, as commonly conceived, that one is abstract and the other is
concrete: both can be equally concrete. But they differ in other aspects that
are of fundamental moment.

   Theoretical inquiry aims at truth in its total extent and for itself.
Commonsense inquiry is limited by practicality. It does not inquire beyond
what can be put into practice: 'What's the use of it?' There is a difference,
then, in end.

   There is a difference in the object. Common sense considers things in
their relations to us, in their relations to human senses and human appetites. Its foundation, its starting point, is the *priora quoad nos*. Theory is concerned with things in their relations to one another; it is concerned with
the *priora quoad se*, fundamentally. One can proceed from the *priora quoad se*
to the objects of common sense, just as from the *priora quoad nos* one can
proceed to theory, but the two are antithetical.

   The New Testament, fundamentally, is a document on soteriology, on
salvation. Cerfaux, in his work on the Christology of St Paul, starts with the
doctrine of the redemption, and only later goes on to the incarnation: it is

20 Karl Jaspers, *The Origin and Goal of History*, trans. Michael Bullock (London:
   Routledge & Kegan Paul, 1953).

the presentation of the Christian revelation according to the *priora quoad nos*.[21] But you can't write a *De Verbo incarnato* by starting from the redemption, because the whole meaning of the redemption to us is that it was performed by the God-Man. The mere fact that you move to a theoretical presentation means that you are going to start with something that is not first for us but that is logically first, that is presupposed by the rest and has no presuppositions of its own, at least in that order. There is that inversion. Similarly, the New Testament talks about the missions of the divine persons, the sending of the Son by the Father, the sending of the Holy Ghost by the Father and the Son. Trinitarian doctrine in the New Testament is contained in those missions. In the *Summa theologiae*, the first part, St Thomas discusses the Trinity from questions 27 to 43, and he does not start with the missions. He ends with the missions, in question 43. It is after he developed his whole account of the Trinity that he comes down to what they did. But from the viewpoint of the *priora quoad nos*, one starts from what they did and moves back towards what fundamentally they are.

Thirdly, the world of theory and the world of common sense speak different languages. Common sense uses ordinary language, and the world of theory is forced to develop a technical language. And the point to the technical language is that you say in a word what otherwise requires a paragraph, a chapter, or a book.

Finally, the basic difference between the world of common sense and the world of theory lies in the structure of consciousness. In the structure of the consciousness of the theoretic subject qua theoretic subject, there is a domination by intellect, by the desire to understand and know the truth. Everything else is subordinated. A mathematician's consciousness, when he is doing mathematics, eliminates all elements of affectivity and aggressivity. He is concerned simply with writing down symbols and transforming the symbols he has written down, and writing down more symbols. That is the flow of his consciousness on the sensitive level, and there are also the acts of understanding and judgment rising up from that level. It is a consciousness dominated by intellectual concern. The only activity of will is to exclude other concerns, and not let the will itself interfere with the purely intellectual process. On the other hand, in commonsense consciousness, intellect is just part of the whole. There is no indifference to truth involved in that, but still intellect functions as a part of the whole man. There is not this restriction of consciousness simply to intellectual ends.

21 Lucien Cerfaux, *Le Christ dans la théologie de saint Paul* (Paris: Éditions du Cerf, 1951); in English, *Christ in the Theology of St Paul*, trans. Geoffrey Webb and Adrian Walker (New York: Herder & Herder, 1958).

That differentiation between the theoretic and the commonsense subject
has its classical illustrations. There is the story of Thales and the milkmaid.
Thales, gazing at the stars, tumbled into the well, and the milkmaid said,
'How can he know anything about the stars when he couldn't even see a
well at his feet?' He could not see the well at his feet because he was absorbed in his intellectual pursuit, and if the milkmaid had become interested in the stars she would not have seen the well either. Newton, when he
was working out the theory of gravitation, spent weeks in his room; meals
were brought to him and he paid very little attention to them. It took a terrific and prolonged concentration to work out that theory.

The story of Thales and the milkmaid illustrates the difference on the
side of the subject and the structure of consciousness. On the side of the
object, there is the example of Socrates and the Athenians. Socrates was
asking what fortitude, temperance, justice, knowledge, etc., were. The
Athenians knew perfectly well what was meant by such expressions, but they
could not arrive at what, according to Aristotle in Book M [XIII] of the
Metaphysics, had not been attempted before in any systematic fashion: universal definitions. You can know perfectly well what it is to be a brave man
in any concrete instance and be unable to give a definition that holds universally for bravery, and the reason for this is that when you attempt the
universal definition, you have to shift from the *priora quoad nos* to the *priora
quoad se* and obtain a fundamental circle of terms that are defined by their
relations to one another, and use them to pick out just what bravery or the
other virtues are. Aristotle was able to do this with his theory of habits –
good operative habits and entitative habits – but he had to have a whole
theoretic structure to be able to define the virtues. The Athenians did not
have that theoretic structure and did not know about the need for it, so
Socrates was able to make fools of them every time. The transition from the
world of common sense to the world of theory is illustrated abundantly in
all its aspects in Plato's early dialogues.

The distinction between the world of common sense and the world
of theory tends to be obliterated by culture, by the organized transmission of
the achievements of the past. The teacher has to deal, not with a group of
men like Socrates, but with a group of Athenians. His effort to make intelligible to them what he is saying will involve a certain amount of pouring it
back from the world of theory to the world of common sense, a watering
down, a devaluation, a simplification. That will come to be mistaken for all
that is any good in theory, and it is not theory at all. It just misses the edge
that makes theory something worth while. There is to culture a tendency to

praise the theorists of the past, the great men that are no longer around. There is the greatest admiration for Aristotle or St Thomas, and so on, according to one's predilections, but as for theorists at the present time, well, 'They're just queer.' The apprehension of theory tends to be an apprehension, not of theory, but of some *haute vulgarisation* of theory. In the modern world, at the present time, theory is developed to an extraordinary degree. In modern mathematics, modern physics, modern chemistry, theory is just pushed to the limit. Similarly modern philosophy is systematic, transcendental, methodic, and so on. It has all sorts of exigences that are pushed to the limit, and the simplest way out, of course, is to suppose that it does not count. One can be blocked to a real apprehension of the world of theory simply because one has never come up against it, and that blocking occurs insofar as culture becomes an unauthentic apprehension of theory.

4.5 *Consciousness as Foundation of These Distinctions*

Those fundamental distinctions between the sacred and the profane, the inner and the outer, the theoretic and the commonsense, have their foundation in the very nature of human consciousness. The distinction between the sacred and the profane is founded on the dynamism of human consciousness. Insofar as there is always something beyond whatever we achieve, there is that distinction between the sacred and the profane. Insofar as there is not only the object that is presented but the person present to himself to whom it is presented, there is the opposition between subject and object. Insofar as there is the radical opposition between two quite different structures of consciousness, the theoretic subject and the commonsense subject, we have another fundamental opposition. One can switch over from one to the other, but they are something like oil and water: they do not mix without a violent process of emulsion.[22]

By taking those ultimate differences, breaking them down, and combining them, one has the world of interiority, the world of community (that is, the visible universe, the external world), the world of theory, and the object of religion, God.[23] The differentiation between these occurs in time. Regressivity can block out the differentiation as between the world of theory

---

22 Lonergan said, '... unless you introduce some violent process of – I don't know what the word for it is, emulsion or something.'
23 These correspond to some of what would become the realms of meaning in *Method in Theology*: common sense, theory, interiority, and transcendence. See Lonergan, *Method in Theology* 81–85.

and the world of common sense, of community; the subject can be lost; and so on. But those are the fundamental differentiations. Developments are canalized, as it were, into one of those fields. Piaget speaks of the grouping of groups to ever higher groups, but that ultimately is not true; it is only insofar as the study is of the secularized child that that simple type of development as worked out by Piaget applies.

4.6 Mediation

At this point we can introduce the idea of mediation as a means of classifying developments. It is a type of classification that is somewhat algebraic: it deals with x's and y's. But it is helpful.

What is meant by mediation? Hegel conceived religion as something that was sublated by philosophy. Religion was an imaginative stage in human development that was superior to art, but philosophy retains all that is good in religion and also provides something better. Fr Coreth, in his *Metaphysik*, says that philosophy mediates religion,[24] and that statement will give us an idea of the meaning of that word 'mediate.' A Catholic can be a very good Catholic, performing the same religious operations of attending Mass, meditating, prayer, and so on, whether he knows philosophy or not, but there will be a difference between the religiosity of one and that of another in view of the fact that one has studied philosophy and the other has not. There will be a precision, a clarity, an exactness, a lack of fuzziness, to the religious life of someone who has studied philosophy that is not found in the religious life of one who has not. The former will know much better what he is doing and why he is doing it in an explicit fashion, not because he does any philosophic thinking or has any philosophic preoccupations in his religious life, but simply from the presence of this other development. One development, by its co-presence with another, produces a modification in the other.

Let me take another example. Rostovtseff wrote *The Social and Economic History of the Roman Empire*.[25] It is possible at the present time, with modern scientific knowledge of economics, to understand the economics in the Roman Empire in a way the Romans could not do, simply because there is now an economic science that then did not exist. At the present time one

24 Emerich Coreth, *Metaphysik: Eine methodisch-systematische Grundlegung* (Innsbruck: Tyrolia-Verlag, 2nd ed., 1964) 537–40.
25 Michael Rostovtseff, *The Social and Economic History of the Roman Empire* (Oxford: The Clarendon Press, 1926).

can understand cycles, depressions, and crises in a way that was not possible twenty centuries ago or even one century ago. Writing history is the commonsense type of understanding. By common sense I mean a specialization of intelligence that deals with the particular, the concrete, and the present-to-hand. History, insofar as it is history, uses that type of understanding. But if a man knows economics he will be able to understand the historical data, and see points and elements in the historical data that otherwise he would not. In reading an economic history of a historical period, the understanding one has is quite different if one understands the economics or the social science involved. Again we have a case of a type of concrete commonsense knowledge that is mediated by a theoretical type of knowledge. The knowledge of history becomes something different, more full, more exact, more comprehensive, simply by the co-presence of another development.

That is a fundamental meaning of the word 'mediation,' and the most significant.

Now we have the world of community, and one can know the world of community, of common sense, the visible world, by living it, and that is the way everyone does. But insofar as one knows the human sciences and philosophy, one can have one's knowledge of community mediated by theory. One understands the life of community in a fuller, more exact way by virtue of the presence of this other development. Again, theory always pushes one's ultimate questions. And one can mediate theory by interiority reaching down to the fundamental operations involved in knowing anything: experiencing, understanding, judging, making acts of faith; doing theology presupposes the other four. Insofar as one moves to interiority, one is mediating theory by the development in interiority.

Similarly, the function of the lay retreat movement is a development in interiority. One is improving one's parish, and the life of one's parish, insofar as one has individuals in the parish who have developed in the interior life. One is mediating community by a development in interiority.

Finally, in this life, the ultimate is always God, always religion. Religion can be mediated by community, by the church. But one knows the church better, and its ultimate aim, God, if one mediates it by theory, through theology. If the question of what one is trying to do in doing theology, in trying to make a proof, in speaking from scripture, etc., leads to a difficulty, one can mediate one's theory by interiority, and then one is raising the question of method in theology.

The notion of mediation goes back to Aristotle, who distinguished immediate principles, which had no middle term and were self-evident, from mediated conclusions that were established by introducing a middle term.[26] Mediation is a notion proper to the Christian religion. St Paul in 1 Timothy 2 speaks of the one mediator: there is one God and one mediator, the man Jesus Christ. Hegel gave a peculiar sense to mediation, both in his earlier studies of interiority and later in his more fully developed dialectic. On Hegel's use of the word 'mediation,' there is a book by Henri Niel, *De la médiation dans la philosophie de Hegel*. It has a bibliography.[27] We do not want to use the word 'mediation' with any peculiar Hegelian implications. On the other hand, it is a term that enables us to express the effects of related developments, such as the effect that knowing theology makes in the religious life of a person. Knowledge of theology mediates the religious life. And the other instances of mediation that I have given have a meaning, and they enable us to find some way of classifying, at least roughly, the developments that occur in the course of history.[28]

26 See the slightly later paper by Lonergan, 'The Mediation of Christ in Prayer,' *Philosophical and Theological Papers 1958–1964*, vol. 6 in Collected Works of Bernard Lonergan, ed. Robert C. Croken, Frederick E. Crowe, and Robert M. Doran (Toronto: University of Toronto Press, 1996) 160–61.
27 Henri Niel, *De la médiation dans la philosophie de Hegel* (Paris: Aubier, 1945). The bibliography is on pp. 7–11.
28 The first question–and–answer session was held later this day. See below, pp. 260–81.

1962-3

Integration of Worlds and Contemporary Theological Problems[1]

1 Limits and Development

We begin by summarizing what we said yesterday. The first and fundamental point was that the analysis of human development in terms of
spontaneous operations that become differentiated, combinations of differentiated operations, the grouping of combinations of differentiated
operations, and finally the grouping of groups, runs into a limit. The
dynamism of consciousness leads to a differentiation between operations
that regard the ultimate – religious acts, the activities we perform when we
say Mass, meditate, recite the breviary – and on the other hand the activities of studying and teaching, of eating and recreation. They tend to form
– and the more they develop the more they tend to form – two separated
fields of development, to give a distinction between the sacred and the
profane. Again, the structure of consciousness leads to a differentiation of
the inner and the outer, the world of interiority and the visible universe,
the world of community, the world of common sense. Thirdly, there is the
specialization of consciousness in which intellect dominates. Purely intellectual ends become the total end of the activity of the person as long as
he is in the intellectual pattern of consciousness, and this sets up an opposition between a world of theory and on the other hand a world of common sense.

---

1 Wednesday, 11 July 1962, Lauzon CD/MP3 (30500A0E060) and 306
(30600A0E060).

Now, whenever one runs into limits one has a tool for a further advance. This has frequently been the experience of mathematicians. They discover new fields simply because they find that nothing more can be done in the field in which they are. Galois's celebrated discoveries at the beginning of the last century were due to the realization that certain types of equations cannot be solved. You can solve second-, third-, and fourth-degree equations, but you cannot solve fifth-degree equations. Using that limit he proceeded to develop a whole new field of mathematics. Similarly here, the fact that the sacred and the profane, the inner and the outer, and the theoretical and the commonsense fields of development cannot be grouped together to form as it were a single homogeneous piece provides a basis for a logical division of development.

We have to distinguish between a logical division and a historical division. A logical division gives, first of all, the opposition between common sense and theory, the difference between the milkmaid and Thales, between the Athenians and Socrates. There is a difference in the subject, and a difference in the mode in which the objects are apprehended, in their language, in the societies they form, in the way they apprehend the world. Eddington spoke of his two tables. One was just like this one: light brown, hard, heavy, solid, and so on, while the other consisted mostly of empty space, with here and there a little electron and proton that he could not imagine.[2] The worlds of theory and common sense yielded two apprehensions of the same table. Both the world of theory and the world of common sense first consist of objects, but there is always the subject that does the apprehending, and the subject as subject is never an object; so we get a third world, that of interiority. Finally, all three are proximate, and they mediate an ultimate: the religious world and, in our language, God.

Now, that logical division of fields of development provides a clue, a tool, for distinguishing developments generally. If one tackles the question of trying to describe medieval thought, Greek thought, Hebrew thought, either one can become so specialized in one area that one knows very little about anything else, and then one is not able to compare, or one doesn't become a specialist and one uses a few vague descriptive terms like 'Hebraism,' 'Paulinism,' 'Hellenism,' and so on. If one is to conceive those things in an explanatory fashion, with some exactitude, one has to move from mere description to explanation, and one does that insofar as one proceeds from a

2   Sir Arthur Eddington, *The Nature of the Physical World* (Cambridge: Cambridge University Press, 1928) xi–xv; also *New Pathways in Science* (Cambridge: Cambridge University Press, 1947) 1.

basic common root of undifferentiated consciousness in which the four worlds exist but are not distinguished. The primitive, as a starting point, does not distinguish between the sacred and the profane. The profane is sacralized, and the sacred is secularized. But that is just our way of putting the thing. For him there is just no distinction at all: a spade is not just a spade, but is open towards infinity; and the same for everything else. Eliade will tell you that it is impossible for a person of the modern world to achieve that lack of differentiation. He gives you descriptions of the way the world appears to the primitive, in which the most ordinary actions are just as liturgical as his rites, his liturgy, and the sacred actions, while, on the other hand, the liturgy and the sacred actions are just as practical as anything else. The distinction does not exist. It has not yet been thought out.

At the same time, there is an objectivation of the subject. The subject is not an individualist, but thinks, decides, and acts as part of the group. Along with the objectivation of the subject, there is a subjectivation of the object: everything is thought of in personal terms, on the analogy of the person. This is described rather well by Frankfort in his *Before Philosophy*.[3] He is describing the type of thinking that precedes the development of philosophy, the distinction between the theoretical and the commonsense worlds, and between the subject and the object.

Finally, in the primitive mind theoretical questions are raised. They have their own idea of causality, and their questions regarding origins and ends. The philosophic questions somehow are raised, but they are not raised in any philosophic manner, and they are answered not in the technical terms of any philosophy but symbolically. Because the answers are symbolic, they easily move into myth and magic.

On that development there is Ernst Cassirer's three-volume work, *The Philosophy of Symbolic Forms* (1923–29),[4] somewhat summarized in *An Essay on Man* (1944);[5] Eric Voegelin's work *Order and History* (1956–57), particularly the first three chapters of volume 1, *Israel and Revelation* (1956),[6] in which he

3 Henri Frankfort, Henriette Antonia Frankfort, et al., *Before Philosophy: The Intellectual Adventure of Ancient Man* (Harmondsworth, Middlesex: Penguin, 1949, 1963).
4 Ernst Cassirer, *The Philosophy of Symbolic Forms*, trans. Ralph Mannheim, vol. 1: *Language*, vol. 2: *Mythical Thought*, vol. 3: *The Phenomenology of Knowledge* (New Haven: Yale University Press, 1955, 1957).
5 Ernst Cassirer, *An Essay on Man: An Introduction to a Philosophy of Culture* (New Haven: Yale University Press, 1944).
6 Eric Voegelin, *Israel and Revelation* (Baton Rouge: Louisiana State University Press, 1956).

draws the distinction between the ideas in Israel due to the revelation and on the other hand the ultimately mythical conceptions of the ancient high civilizations in Egypt and Babylonia; finally, Malinowski's *Magic, Science and Religion* (1954).[7] That type of book enables one to get some apprehension of man's initial undifferentiated consciousness, in which these four – interiority, the world of theory, the world of community, and the ultimate – merge in a fundamental, not exactly confusion, but an initial undifferentiation.

Proceeding from that base, one sees that a development in any field will have implications with regard to the other fields. The ancient high civilizations were a development in community, in the human good, in making and producing an objective good of order. In the civilizations of Egypt, Crete, Babylonia, India, China, and the Mayas and Incas in America, everything that regarded the external world was developed to an extremely high point, but ultimately the cosmological, political, and religious theories were simply symbolic and mythical. However, the mere occurrence of that development in community implied that when the social structure broke down, the individuals that necessarily emerged had a basis on which to start to differentiate, and to bring about the development of theory such as occurred in Greek culture.

So the notion of mediation has a fundamental meaning insofar as any type of development or differentiation has repercussions on the whole setup. If you bring any one of the circles into focus, you get it somehow separated from the others. You have opened the way to differentiating the others and developing them in their proper distinction from the others.

'Mediation' is used in a very general sense. Any prior development mediates a later development. Before you can have a written literature you have to have the development of writing, which originally occurred, I think, in bookkeeping in Babylonia and Egypt. Any development in one field, in one world, affects the other fields. It reduces the initial confusion in differentiation. Any development mediates the subject. It enables him to develop along that line. There is a development of the subject mediated by community. It makes all the difference in the world whether you were born in London or New York or, on the other hand, in central Africa or central Asia. Your possibilities of development are quite different. The subject is mediated also by theory. You have a concrete, immediate experience and apprehension of your own acts simply by having them, but you cannot define, distinguish,

7 Bronislaw Malinowski, *Magic, Science and Religion and Other Essays* (New York: The Free Press, 1948; repr. Westport, CT: Greenwood Press, 1984).

and relate them unless they are objectified, and their objectification is a theory of the subject: the subject is mediated by theory. Again, the subject is developed religiously and mediated by his religious activities: he reveals what he is, his ultimate destiny, in and through his religious activities, his manifested relationship to God. It is insofar as our acts produce and manifest ourselves that we can know ourselves.

All development, then, mediates the subject, and just as all desire ultimately is desire of God, so similarly all development, including the development of the subject, ultimately opens the way to development in religion.

2 Worlds

Now on page 11 and following in the notes we have a set of reflections on this notion of worlds, the distinctions of worlds, of fields.[8] A world, for example the world of community or the world of theory, is not some one object. It is a field of possible objects. Again, the differentiation of worlds is not a matter of laying down the properties of each, comparing them, pointing to the differences between the world of theory and the world of common sense and the world of interiority, and assigning them properties. The differentiation rests on the mode of operation of the subject. God is what we do not reach immediately. All our knowledge of God is mediated. We do not know God immediately in this life. And that is the definition of the world of the sacred: what is never immediate. The world of the subject is what is always immediate. Insofar as the theory of the subject is grasped, there is a mediation of that immediacy; still, the theory has a meaning insofar as it points to and distinguishes elements of immediate experience. Consequently, the differentiation of the worlds rests upon differentiations in the subject. The *dynamism* of consciousness leads to the opposition between the ultimate and the proximate; the *structure* of consciousness leads to the opposition between subject and object; the subject is never conscious unless he is dealing with some object, but the subject as subject never is an object; and finally, the *specialization* of consciousness leads to the movement from the milkmaid to Thales, from the Athenians to Socrates.

The religious world of one person is not the same as that of another. The religious world of the shaman is not the religious world of St Teresa of Avila. They are analogous, and the analogy does not lie in comparing the properties

---

8 The section to which Lonergan refers is entitled in the notes 'Reflexio super praecedentia' ('Reflection on the foregoing').

of the two worlds. It is an analogy not of attribution but of proportion: what is ultimate for the shaman is his religious world, and what is ultimate for St Teresa of Avila is her religious world.

Because they are defined and conceived in terms of an analogy of proportion, those worlds are conceived concretely. And that is an important point. How is it that metaphysics can be knowledge of being if being is the concrete? Metaphysics seems to be extremely abstract. Matter and form are known and have a quasi-definition by their mutual relation, their mutual proportion. If one considers that proportion as such, then one is dealing with an abstraction. But one can consider the concrete entities that stand in that proportion, and then one is thinking of matter and form concretely. What are matter and form? They are the concrete entities that are related to one another as, say, imaginative representation to insight, or if you want other examples, as the eye to sight, as the ear to the faculty of hearing, as the palate to the faculty of tasting, and so on.

Because they are concrete, they are historical; when we are talking about these worlds we are talking about them concretely, and so also historically. All determinations are included implicitly and can be added on. We are not talking about some abstract religion or some world of theory that no one ever thought of, but always of concrete theories, these precise theories conceived by these precise people. Although we are not always assigning all the determinations, still the reference is to the historically concrete. Why? Because we are not prescinding from anything. Just as we define matter and form as the concrete entities that stand in a given type of proportion, and do not consider proportion abstractly as such, so we can conceive the worlds of religion, of interiority, and so on, in their concreteness, and consequently in their changes, in their movements. Movement is had only in the concrete, and unless the mode of apprehension is concrete one does not include their movements.

All these worlds are mobile; they change. It is of course true that a culture can go on for centuries and even millennia without practically any noticeable change. Writing their history is very simple: the way it was at any time is the way it is at all times. It is insofar as cultures and civilizations are on the move that they become objects of interest and study. That mobility rests ultimately on the pure desire to know: man asks questions. It rests on the fact that will follows intellect. And it rests on the possibility of openness. Insofar as one becomes closed, one becomes unauthentic; one ceases to be acting according to one's nature, which is ever open to further skill, further learning, and further willingness.

Similarly, a society can be open, and if any given society is not open, developments can occur elsewhere and force themselves upon that society. Modern science developed in Western civilization, but it is imposing itself upon the whole world at the present time. I remember discussing once with an Indian whether Scholastic philosophy and theology fits in any way into Indian thought. He said that just as the Indians have no difficulty in learning Western physics and mathematics, they would have no difficulty in learning philosophy and theology. I would not like to say whether that is a complete answer to the question or not, but it illustrates the fact that there is no watering down of Western science when the Eastern nations proceed to develop.

There is, then, a general mobility in these worlds, but the mobility is not necessarily for the better. As there is progress, so also there is decline, deviation. We list at the bottom of page 12 various forms of deviation.[9]

There is inauthenticity insofar as the apprehension, the way of living, is simplified, watered down, devaluated, or made into something that everyone can easily understand, resulting in something else that is not quite as good.

Again, there is formalism. The great attack on formalism in recent years is Edmund Husserl's posthumously published work *The Crisis of European Sciences and Transcendental Phenomenology.*[10] The part about transcendental phenomenology is not so important, but his account of the crisis of European science is extremely interesting. It illustrates formalism, performing the proper things: no more can be asked of anyone than to perform what is considered the proper thing. According to Husserl, at the present time the more the sciences become specialized and subdivided, the more there ceases to be any interest or concern for any scientific ideal. It becomes a matter of observing the conventions, a matter of a small group who write articles and praise one another's articles and meet in congresses and say how good each other is; and they're the scientists. And what science is, any ultimate question like that, is simply omitted. If anyone wants to ask what really is a science, well that is another specialty, and he is quite free to go along and

9 The list to which Lonergan refers can be found later in the same section of the notes: 'Non solum evolvendo sed etiam regrediendo mutantur mundi' ('Worlds change not only by developing but also by regressing').
10 Edmund Husserl, *Die Krisis der europäischen Wissenschaften und die transzendentale Phänomenologie: Eine Einleitung in die phänomenologische Philosophie,* ed. Walter Biemel (The Hague: Martinus Nijhoff, 1954); in English, *The Crisis of European Sciences and Transcendental Phenomenology: An Introduction to Phenomenological Philosophy,* trans. David Carr (Evanston, IL: Northwestern University Press, 1970).

work at his special field, but he must not expect the other specialists to pay any more attention to him than they do to the other specialists – and that is no attention at all. There is no general acknowledgment of an architectonic of the sciences, no one particular field that decides what is scientific and what is not, laying down the law universally. Last summer at Seattle University, a doctor of engineering was saying to me that as far as he could see, good work in his field is a matter of making an investigation that opens the way to a large number of other investigations. If you do that, well, you're doing good work and everyone thinks you're pretty good; you're an important person. There is no theoretical control on what the idea of science is. Husserl's ultimate question was, Is Western man just another anthropological type, no better and no worse than any other anthropological type, or does Western civilization and culture include an absolute ideal, an expression of what humanity should be, and does science include the expression of such an ideal? Is there an absolute somewhere or not? Of course, that was Husserl's concern all through his life and in all his writing, to arrive at an absolute value that provided foundations for science.

What is formalism? Formalism is being correct with regard to all the details, having a magnificently thorough bibliography at the end of your book, having complete footnotes, quoting all the people that it is important to quote on the subject, and so on and so forth. The introduction of ultimate criteria in judging your work is just going off onto some point that anyone can dispute about indefinitely; it is irrelevant. You can get that in all sorts of forms and in all sorts of ways. We will have more to say on that later when we discuss the subject of extrinsicism.

Just as there can be complete competence of the formalist, so there can be the man who really gets hold of the problems and really has felt his way towards their solution, but cannot give any theoretically or technically competent account or expression of his findings. For example, Scheeben was a man who certainly got hold of a large number of fertile ideas in theology that are still exerting an influence and fructifying in the field, but his theoretical expression of his findings, such as the quasi-formal causality by which the Holy Ghost inhabits the soul, runs into endless theoretical difficulties. People do not want to accept his theoretical expression, but at the same time they find him very suggestive, very stimulating.[11]

11 For more on Matthias Scheeben, see Lonergan, 'Theology and Understanding,' *Collection*, vol. 4 in Collected Works of Bernard Lonergan, ed. Frederick E. Crowe and Robert M. Doran (Toronto: University of Toronto Press, 1988) 115, 121.

Intellectualism and anti-intellectualism are two instances of the same defect. For the anti-intellectualist there must not be any world of theory at all, and for the intellectualist there is only the world of theory.

There are also archaism and anachronism: the archaist wants everything in the church today to be the way it was in the New Testament – 'Back to the scriptures!' – while the anachronist finds the definitions of Nicea, Chalcedon, Trent, and the Vatican Council already right down there in the scriptures. Both of them are getting away from the fact of development.

Finally, there is regressivity: 'Things are far too complex now; what we have to do is go back to some earlier period when they were simpler, and then everything would be ever so much easier.' Just as in the individual, when psychic problems become too complex, there is a regression to infantile or childish attitudes, so too in the culture or civilization, whenever things become very complex, there is a tendency to get back to something that is simpler, to what used to be: things were quite satisfactory then; let's go back. The trouble is that one cannot go back, and one is only kidding oneself if one tries.

3 Integration of the Different Worlds

The simplest form of integration of the different worlds is by omission. If one drops out the world of theory, the world of interiority, and the world of religion, of the ultimate, one is left with the world of everyday common sense, the profane world, the visible world, the external world, the world of the newspaper.

Again, instead of eliminating half the problem, one can eliminate the oppositions between them. Against Hegel's unification by sublation, Kierkegaard insisted upon the *aut/aut*, either/or. It is a matter of having both without confusing them. The world of common sense is not the world of theory, and you cannot sublate the two into something higher or different; you have to keep both and acknowledge their distinctions.

There can be a simplification of the problem. This is illustrated by a very rough outline of Brahmanism. In Brahmanism, there is not an elimination of any part of the problem, but there is an identification of interiority, the world of theory, and the world of religion in the Atman, the absolute subject, and on the other hand, an identification of the external, the profane, and the commonsense world in *Maya*, the field of *metempsychosis* and of karma.

A third possibility of integration is oscillation. According to the book of Ecclesiasticus, there is a time for weeping and a time for rejoicing, a time for being born and a time for dying, and so on. There is Toynbee's withdrawal-and-return: he spends almost endless pages on the great men who spent part of their lives in retirement and who, upon coming back, left their mark upon history. The Chinese *Tao* is the snaky line that alternates between the symbols of heaven and earth, day and night, male and female, dry and wet; it alternates from one to the other, and acknowledges that any one at its climax is the beginning of the opposite.

Instead of oscillation, there can be transposition. Transposition is a difficult notion to illustrate. I take it in terms of symbols. The account of symbols is based upon Gilbert Durand's *Les structures anthropologiques de l'imaginaire*, with the subtitle *Introduction à l'archétypologie générale*.[12] He studies symbols in a very thorough fashion, omitting the Freudian type because he thinks that pertains to a certain type of civilization.

His first set of symbols includes all the symbols of fear. His second set deals with the mastering of fear, as in the compound symbol of St George and the Dragon. In the dragon there are combined in a single fantastic monster practically all the symbols of fear. St George on his horse slaying the dragon shows man's overcoming his fear; that symbol expresses the ascensional attitude connected with the dominant reflex by which we maintain our balance. If there is a danger of slipping, everything else stops until balance is recovered: it is a dominant reflex. That is one attitude towards objects of fear: overcoming the fear by slaying the dragon.

Another attitude towards objects of fear is represented by the symbol of Jonah and the whale. The whale is just as much a monster as the dragon. However, instead of killing the whale, Jonah is swallowed by it, and when he comes out after three days he is just as well off as ever. The objects of fear are euphemized. They aren't so terrible after all. The dominant reflex involved there is that of swallowing, not of falling. If St George did not kill the dragon, he would fall and be killed, but in the Jonah symbol you do not fall, you descend lightly in the way that food goes down the gullet. The twilight and the darkness are not so terrible after all. It is a totally different attitude towards objects of fear.

One can combine those two attitudes towards objects of fear, and then one has oscillation from one to the other, as in the Tao and in general in synthetic symbols that combine the two attitudes towards objects of fear.

12 Gilbert Durand, *Les structures anthropologiques de l'imaginaire: Introduction à l'archétypologie générale* (Paris: Presses universitaires de France, 1960). The second edition (1963) is mentioned in *Method in Theology* 69, but here and in other references prior to 1963 Lonergan had to be working from the first edition (Lonergan says, 'published at Grenoble, 1960').

So far we have not dealt with the notion of any transposition or sublimation. But if we introduce the Christian attitude – 'the only evil is sin, there is nothing to be afraid of except sin, and sin depends upon me' – then we have the attitude of *caritas foras expellit timorem, et qui timet non est perfectus in caritate*, as St John says in his epistle, because the person who is *perfectus in caritate* does not sin and does not fear anything except sin; fear is eliminated. And so one effects a transposition away from both the St George attitude and the Jonah attitude. One neither dominates fear nor euphemizes it; one just changes the whole field of application. However, when one does that, one does not eliminate the problem; one simply transposes it. No doubt, charity is afraid of nothing except sin. But am I really charitable, have I charity? It may be all right for the saints, but is it any good for me? The problem then is transposed to the field of interiority, to my relations with God, to the attitudes of prayer, and it is only within prayer, in one's converse with God, that that problem admits anything in the way of a solution.

I have given this as an illustration of what is meant by a transposition. Toynbee gives a similar illustration of a transposition of a simpler sort: the problem of transportation. The motorcar is a magnificent solution to the problem of transportation, but if everyone had one, the roads would not be large enough to handle the traffic. If the problem is to be solved, the question, Do we have to move around that much after all? must be raised. The problem is transposed to a moral level.

Just as the worlds are mobile, move along, and develop for good or bad, so the integrations have to change. The integrations achieved at any time will no longer be satisfactory integrations when what is integrated has changed.

Finally, there is the locus of the integration, and that is perhaps the fundamental point to be made. It is the fundamental problem in theology at the present time. A perfect theological doctrine or theory is just within the world of theory; it is not an integration. It may integrate everything within the world of theory, but when it does so all it does is integrate objects, and indeed objects as theoretically apprehended by their relations to one another. Integration in the sense we are speaking of is integration of the worlds, and it is not located within any one world such as the world of theory. If one demands of theory that it be integration, then one is demanding what it cannot do. Integration is a matter of being able to move coherently from one world to another, of being able to give each its due. I am not saying that this is *necessarily* the only way of achieving integration, namely, moving from one to the other. There may be better possibilities. But it is the only way I know, and it is important not to expect more than that. To expect more than that is to expect something that is beyond the limitations of human nature. God is perfectly integrated. By one and the same act he comprehends himself and in that comprehension of himself comprehends everything he can do, and consequently knows all the possibles, and comprehends everything he does, and so knows all the actuals. That is the perfect integration within a single act. But that is not a possible human achievment. Man moves towards the infinite but he cannot get it all into a single package, and he should not expect to.

So much for introductory considerations on method. What is method? Fundamentally, it is the mediation of the world of theory and the world of community by interiority. It is concerned with the operations performed. By knowing the operations, one can fix, clarify, and eliminate the confusions that are involved in theoretical objects, and the theory throws light on the world of community. Again, understanding yourself gives you a fundamental analogy for understanding all the members in the community at the whole series of stages of their historical development.

4 Contemporary Theological Problems

Our next step is to ask, What are we going to use method for? In other words, what are the theological problems at the present time?

First of all, the problem is not a problem of the Catholic religion. The Catholic religion, within itself, unites the different worlds. It is a sacralization of the profane world. The Word became flesh, the church is the body of Christ, and the church lives under the direction, and with the inhabitation, of the Holy Spirit. That sacralization of the profane world penetrates the interiority of the Catholic: there is repentance for one's sins; there is the perpetual process of conversion by prayer and fasting; there are the theological virtues of faith, hope, and charity that unite the subject to God, to the church, and to one's neighbor. It takes its place in the external world with the hierarchy, the apostolic succession, the kerygma, preaching and missions, with sacrifice and sacrament in liturgy. It transforms human institutions such as the family and education, society and state, the law and the economy. It has its transition from the world of community to the world of theory. There is an evolution of dogma and an evolution of theology, and they are products of the Catholic religion.

The problem, then, is not a problem of the Catholic religion. The problem is theological, and that problem goes back a long way.

4.1 The Aristotelian-Augustinian Controversy

A fundamental element of the problem is in the Aristotelian-Augustinian controversy that exploded at the end of the thirteenth century. In Congar's presentation of medieval thought, it is not too difficult to discern what de facto was the method employed in, and that produced, medieval theology. It starts from Abelard's *Sic et non*. Abelard listed about 158 propositions, if I remember correctly, and quoted the Fathers and canons in favor of both sides of the contradiction: *sic et non*. He could quote authorities on either side, and he did it for 158 propositions; you could prove both sides of the contradictions from the Fathers, or canons, or reason.

The next step was the definition of the *quaestio*. Gilbert de la Porrée defined the *quaestio* as existing if and only if authorities or solid reasons could be adduced for both sides of a contradiction, following right out of Abelard's *Sic et non*; and so you have in the *quaestio*, first of all, *Videtur quod non*, the authorities or reasons on one side, and then *Sed contra est*, the authorities or reasons on the other. In the *Summa theologiae* of St Thomas, that technique of the *quaestio* has become something rather formal. However, if you want to see the technique of the *quaestio* at work, read *De veritate*, q. 24, a. 12, and compare the answer to the second book of the commentary on the *Sentences*, d. 28, q. 1 or 2 – anyway, the question is whether the sinner can avoid further sin.[13] In the *Sentences*, St Thomas says that he can, but in *De veritate*, he says that he cannot. In the *De veritate*, where he changes his mind, he has about twenty-four authorities on the one side and eleven on the other – the *sic et non* are at work. His answer runs through a number of columns in the Vivès edition, and then he draws the distinctions with regard to the authorities and reasons adduced on both sides. There you see the *quaestio* as a functioning technique in the development of theology.

The *quaestio* was a theoretical development from Abelard, but there was also the positive development on Abelard in the books of *Sentences*, of which the most celebrated was Peter Lombard's (but there were several others). Peter Lombard was for the medieval period what for the theologian today is his Denzinger, Rouët de Journel,[14] and biblical concordance. When he collected all the passages that he thought relevant to a series of points, it was a collection of the positive theological material. Just as Abelard had used positive material to prove both sides of 158 contradictions, Peter

---

13 Thomas Aquinas, *Scriptum super Sententias*, 2, d. 28, q. 1, a. 2, Utrum homo sine gratia posit vitare peccatum.
14 M.J. Rouët de Journel, *Enchiridion Patristicum* (Barcelona: Herder, 1962).

Lombard and the others who wrote books of *Sentences* provided materials, with a little less point to them. They were not out to establish that the authorities contradicted one another, but to set the problem: 'Here is what they say, what are you going to do about it?' The *quaestio* was the technique of handling that material; it was the pursuit of an ideal of coherence. Commentaries on the *Sentences* were written for four and a half centuries, 1150–1600; the last was that of Estius about 1607.

The fundamental element was theology developing on a positive basis – the Fathers and scripture – and seeking coherence. They sought coherence by drawing distinctions, but the distinctions have to be coherent; otherwise you're just giving rise to a new set of problems. And so there came the further development of the *Summa*. What is the *Summa*? The *Summa* is the effort of the theologian to provide a fundamental set of coherent terms and distinctions such that he will be able to solve the problems set by the authorities in a coherent fashion, in answers that stand together and do not give rise to more problems.

Now the Augustinian-Aristotelian controversy had to do with that development of the *Summa*. Where does the theologian get his coherent set of basic terms? What St Thomas had done was to take over Aristotle, who had a magnificent set of such terms, and make the necessary adjustments for the Christian religion. In contemporary jargon, the fundamental set of terms with which all answers are conceived is called the *Begrifflichkeit*. Bultmann got a *Begrifflichkeit* from Heidegger for the interpretation of the New Testament; Aquinas got a *Begrifflichkeit* from Aristotle for handling theological problems. The objection raised against this procedure was, What does this pagan Aristotle have to do with Christian revelation and Christian truth? Roger Marston, in his *Quaestiones disputatae*, is trying to solve problems by using as his *Begrifflichkeit*, his fundamental set of terms, the language of St Augustine, a Christian Father, to avoid dependence on the pagan Aristotle.

Without a *Begrifflichkeit*, without a set of fundamental coherent terms, you cannot have a science in any sense of the word 'science.' You will be confined necessarily to commonsense terms, to ordinary language. You can't have something that you can manage in scientific fashion. Any movement towards science in any field is forced, as soon as it reaches the explanatory level, to develop a language of its own, and it needs a language of its own because it has a new set of concepts of its own. Chemistry is in terms of the periodic table, and the periodic table is the fundamental set of concepts in chemistry. Physics has had a succession of sets of fundamental concepts and theorems, but this was necessary if it is to be technical. Without that technical element, you are not doing science seriously.

That was the fundamental methodological question raised in the Middle Ages, and the verdict, eventually, has been in favor of Thomas, acknowledging the necessity of the *Begrifflichkeit.*

However, there is a further question about the limitations of the Aristotelian approach, and indeed on the level of the notions of science involved.[15]

4.2 *Aristotelian Science*

The second element in the problem is that there are limitations to the Aristotelian basis. Aristotelianism involves an integration of the world of common sense and the world of theory. Hylomorphism is, as it were, a compenetration of the two worlds. The two are separate in Platonism. For Plato the Ideas are *ta ontōs onta,* what really is, and the world of shadows, the world of common sense, is *ta mē onta,* the things that are not: not *ta ouk onta,* the things that are not at all, but *ta mē onta* – there is a slight difference between *ouk* and *mē.* The Aristotelian theory acknowledges *substantiae separatae, ta chōrista,* and they are substances and not just ideas, not merely something to be known but also knowers: *in his quae sunt sine materia idem est intelligens et intellectum.* In the Platonist theory, there are just Ideas; the gods that look at the Ideas are in a second order. (That is not quite Plato, but it is Platonist.)

Again, there is an integration of the interior and the exterior. Aristotelian logic and psychology is an objectification of the subject. Aristotle has his logic, his *principia per se nota,* his psychology, his metaphysical analysis of the subject as of everything else, his ethics and politics and rhetoric and poetry. But there is in that objectification of the subject a danger of forgetting the subject, and when that occurs the Aristotelian analysis can become sounding brass and tinkling cymbal, not through any fault of Aristotle's but through the fault of those who consider only the objectification and not what it means.

The *corpus Aristotelicum* of course is a great achievement, but despite that achievement there are limitations that come to light when one examines the *obvious* Aristotelian ideal of science. By that I mean the points that in Aristotle are so stressed that no one can miss them, as in the *Posterior*

15 A break was taken at this point. The remainder of the lecture is recorded on Lauzon CD/MP3 306 (30600A0E060).

Analytics. Scattered throughout Aristotle's work, here and there, all sorts of qualifications upon that somewhat rigid ideal of science can be found, but they are easily overlooked. They are the sort of thing that must be argued for and explained to convince people that they are really Aristotelian. But prescinding from those finer points, those qualifications that a student of Aristotle will know about and introduce, and taking the Aristotle of obvious and common interpretation, one finds that Aristotelian science is certain, concerned with the unchangeable, the unmovable, the *per se*, the necessary, and the universal.

4.3 Modern Science

In contrast with the Aristotelian ideal, *certa rerum cognitio per causas,* modern science is not certain and never claims to be more than probable. The periodic table has open spaces for new elements, and it has been added to steadily ever since it was discovered by Mendeleev, but no chemist will tell you that it is certain, that it is impossible that there should ever be any revision of it. He does not know how such a revision could come about. He knows that there are 300,000 different compounds (not mixtures) that are explained accurately by about 100 elements, and 300,000 compounds is quite a lot; and he knows that any new theory would have to account equally well for all the data covered by that, but still he is not certain; still less are the physicists and biologists. Science is probable.

Again, modern science is not of the unchangeable. It discovers the intelligibility in the change itself. The differential calculus is change at the instant. For Aristotle, *motus intelligitur ex termino,* the standard Scholastic dictum. One understands all the stages in the development of the organ, the eye, from the embryo through the fetus to the animal, by thinking of the eye that is the terminus of the development. Modern science wants to understand the development itself, not just the end. And so on for everything else. It is genetic. It is concerned with the development itself. It finds its intelligibility in the development itself. In the *Metaphysics,* book E, Aristotle says that there is no science of the *per accidens*: there can be a science of trombone players, and there can be a science of red hair, but there cannot be a science that deals with red-haired trombone players. And this seems to make perfectly good sense. But modern science is statistical; it studies trends, and the statistics and trends are concerned with an intelligibility found in the *per accidens.*

Modern science does not seek necessary intelligibility, what must be so and cannot be otherwise; it seeks the intelligibility that de facto is found in things, an empirical intelligibility. 'Bodies fall proportionately to the square of the time of their fall' – this is intelligible and true, but it is not necessary, and the same holds for all other physical, chemical, and biological laws. They have a de facto intelligibility, not an absolutely necessary intelligibility. They could be otherwise. If bodies fell proportionately to the cube of the time, it would still be just as intelligible as the fact that they fall at the square of the time, but the square of the time is the proportion that has been veri-fied directly and indirectly for four centuries. Modern science is empirical science. It seeks not a necessary intelligibility but a de facto intelligibility.

Because modern science deals with the *per accidens*, with change, with empirical intelligibility, it has an understanding of the particular. It does not understand the particular as such: Aristotle is perfectly right about that. The principle of individuation is matter. However, simply because consider-ation is genetic, one is understanding the particulars within the genesis. There are various theories about the genesis of the planetary system, asking how it came about that in our planetary system the planets are moving with these particular velocities at these particular distances from the sun. There are theories about the genesis of this world: was it an initial explosion? Similarly, in a theory of the evolution of species, the species are understood in some fashion.

There is, then, a type of science that de facto has developed and that has not the properties of the ideal of science developed by Aristotle. Moreover, that modern differentiation of science is applied to man. There are empir-ical human sciences. In the empirical human sciences the object is not *nat-ura pura*, man as he would be if he were not given grace and there were no original sin; they do not study man as a hypothetical entity. What is studied is man as he actually is, with original sin, with a need of grace, with the gift of grace and its acceptance or rejection. Man de facto is involved within a theological context. They are concerned with the men who have been, who are, who will be. They are concerned not with the ideal family, the ideal society, the ideal morality, the ideal education, but with the family, the soci-ety, the morality, the education that de facto exist. Can you make them bet-ter, and how do you go about it? These are concrete questions. Augustine is concerned with man not as he is *sed prout sempiternis rationibus esse debeat.* Modern human science does not know anything about those *sempiternae rationes.* It seeks the empirical intelligibility, the de facto intelligibility, of things human as de facto they occur. The result is that we have all about us an enormous development of human science that does not fit into the medieval synthesis in its general outline. The medieval synthesis took over

Aristotle as philosophy, which was in perfect coherence with Aristotle as science; within the Aristotelian corpus a large number of sciences are developed. It effected adaptations in the philosophy and in the science and put theology on top, and there was a synthesis of the whole field of human knowing. But empirical human science deals with man not as he can be philosophically known; it deals with man as he de facto is, in a fallen world, who has been redeemed. This sets up a new problem of integration.

4.4 Historical Consciousness

Further, there has developed in the last century and a half, perhaps a little more, what is called historical consciousness. Historical consciousness is in opposition to classical culture. Classical culture is concerned with the ideal, the norm, the exemplar, the precept, the law, the rule, the 'what ought to be.' While it acknowledges temporal contingencies and their complexity and the existence of the bizarre, the irrational, the spontaneous, the original, still they are just temporal contingencies. *Plus ça change, plus c'est la même chose.* It is not important. What you apprehend is the universal, the norm, the ideal. Of course, classical culture is not something to be sniffed at; it ran the world from the fifth century BC to the French Revolution. But historical consciousness effects the shift from man as substance, in which St Thomas and a drunkard, Einstein and a lunatic, are equally men; within the meaning of the definition they are all rational animals. But when you think of man as subject, you are thinking of man as conscious, as at least dreaming and preferably awake, as possibly and actually intelligent and manifesting his intelligence, his rationality, and his virtue. When you think of man as subject, you are decreasing the generality of your consideration, but you are concentrating on what is important in human living.

Moreover, historical consciousness effects the transition from an ideal order, what the family, the state, the law, education, the economy should be, to what de facto is, the good of order that de facto concretely functions here and now in this society.

Again, it effects the transition from the proper meaning, the right meaning, what the words really mean, an ideal meaning that is settled by argument, to the de facto meaning that informs human minds, human wills, human intentions, human operations, human goals.

The development of historical consciousness has not occurred within the Catholic context. To a certain extent it has, but to a great extent it has occurred outside it and against it. The development of that historical consciousness occurs first of all within the world of community: there were the voyages and the discovery of new lands and the development of the vernacular tongues and literatures. In the seventeenth century they disputed on the relative merits of the ancients and the moderns, the classical literatures and the modern literatures; the question no longer exists. There was the development of new forms in the plastic and representative arts, in architecture, and particularly in music. There were new political forms, new economic systems, new industry and commerce and technics, new types of education, new moralities, new types of the family, new religions.

In that development, the element of historical consciousness that made it something new was that throughout that development questions, whether theoretical or practical, were not settled, and at the present time are not settled, by asking, 'What used to be?' 'What used to be done?' Tradition has ceased to be the norm, and increasingly so since the Renaissance. There have been great individuals effecting great changes. Modern man was on his own. That development of historical consciousness, that awareness that man in the past created his societies, his families, his economies, and his states, and that we can do the same, do it better, profit from their experience and eliminate the old mistakes, is the first aspect of historical consciousness.

That first aspect is coupled with other aspects. There has occurred an invasion by historical consciousness of the sources of theology. The scriptures, the writings of the Fathers, of the medieval theologians, of the orthodox and the heretics, have been studied in accord with historical-critical methods. Classics in the Renaissance had been, as in Jesuit education, integrated and expurgated to give rise to a Christian classicism. The historical type of thought was concerned to reveal that the ancient authors (Plato, Aristotle, Cicero, Tacitus, and so on) were all pagans. That was knowing the past as it really was, knowing the classical authors as they really were. The scriptures were taken out of the context of interpretation provided by dogmatic development and placed within the context of the history of religions and studied just as any other historical document is studied.

The question arises, Is our study of the documents to be carried on in the same (scientific) fashion? You will find the question discussed in *Sacra Pagina*, the two-volume product of a congress of Catholic biblical scholars at Louvain in 1958, published in 1959.[16] Descamps (now a bishop) has an article on the notion, the method, of biblical theology; and he says that we must not have some sort of hybrid method that is partly historical and partly theological. The main job of the biblical theologian is to apply honestly, objectively, without theological preoccupations, the literary-historical method that is known and accepted by everyone, and he argues the point out. Peinador offers in the following article an entirely different viewpoint on the method of biblical theology, in which, to understand the scriptures, you need the definition of the Assumption: you really begin to understand the scripture when you read it in the light of the dogmas. There you have a question: what is the proper method? It is a question that exists. Historical consciousness has invaded the sources of theology. And what is done with the scriptures is done with the Fathers, and so on all along the line.

Theological doctrine itself has been invaded by historical consciousness. In the good old days one laid down the definition of what a person is and proceeded from that. There was no discussion of definitions. But if you are teaching in a historically-minded milieu, you explain the evolution of the definition of the person. The term probably came from the Greek literary critics talking about Homer speaking in his own person and speaking in the person of Achilles or Diamede or someone else. And it was taken up by Origen in his commentary on the Psalms: sometimes the psalmist was speaking in his own person, sometimes in the person of the wicked man, sometimes in the person of God; and sometimes it was very hard to tell in whose person he was talking. In Hippolytus's account of the Trinity there are two persons: the Father and the Son. These persons talk. And there is also the grace of the Holy Spirit. In Tertullian, there are three persons. The Holy Ghost speaks through the prophets. Is this the origin of the notion of person? The historical inquiry can go on indefinitely. You can always get further developments. There is the Augustinian notion of the person. What do you mean by person? Well, Father and Son and Holy Ghost are three; three what? are they three Gods? three Fathers? three Sons? three Holy Ghosts? no; what three, then? We have to answer that question, and the answer we arrive at is 'person.' This is the heuristic notion of person. Boethius gave a

16 *Sacra Pagina: Miscellanea Biblica Congressus Internationalis Catholici de Re Biblica*, 2 vols., ed. J. Coppens, A. Descamps, and E. Massaux (Gembloux: Éditions J. Duculot, 1959). The paper by Albert Descamps is 'Reflexions sur la méthode en théologie biblique,' pp. 132–57, and that by Maximo Peinador 'La integración de la exégesis en la teología,' pp. 158–79. Both papers are in vol. 1.

definition of the person. Richard of St Victor gave a definition of the person. St Thomas gave a third definition of the person: *subsistens distinctum in natura intellectuali*. After the business of the definition of the person was settled, they went on to the metaphysical constitution of the person. One has the theory of Scotus and of Tiphanus and of Suarez and of Capreolus and of Cajetan. And the metaphysics did not get people very far, so they went into the psychology. The person is the conscious subject, and you have psychological theories of the person. Finally, you come to the *ego-tu*: Martin Buber and other people, the phenomenological account of the person: the person is the one who says 'I.'

This is true not only of 'person' but of every other theological notion. By the time you have gone through them, where are you? Not only that but, according to canon law, we teach theology according to the principles, the doctrine, and the procedures, the *ratio*, of St Thomas; but if you take up any text of St Thomas, a proper interpretation puts him in his historical milieu, and to understand St Thomas you have to know Aristotelian physics pretty well, or you will not understand his illustrations. And to know why he is discussing this question, you have to know a lot more of medieval theory. And so on all along the line. Your teaching of St Thomas, if it is aware of contemporary discussions and publications on St Thomas, very easily ceases to be a presentation of the doctrine of St Thomas and is driven to become a critical-historical account of the doctrine of St Thomas in its medieval setting. This is the problem raised by historical consciousness.

4.5 New Tendencies and the Eclipse of the World of Theory

In the fifth place, there have emerged new tendencies: phenomenology, existentialism, personalism. And the tendency of all three is an eclipse of the world of theory. You have the ultimate, the world of theory, the world of community and common sense, and the world of interiority. Those tendencies unite the world of interiority and the external world of common sense to skip all this theoretical junk that no one understands anyway. All it does is lead to endless disputed questions. But then one proceeds from the immediate, the concrete that is given in the external world, directly to the world of interiority. All abstract considerations can be omitted. What is merely theoretical, speculative, systematic can be dropped out.

Phenomenology, fundamentally, is considering the data and expressing an insight into the data. However, it has various developments, takes various turns, in Husserl, Max Scheler, Heidegger, and others. But the emphasis on the personal, the existential, the phenomenological, what is immediately understood in the data – 'Let the object reveal itself' – is the eclipse of the world of theory, and that includes the eclipse of the dogmas. Dogmas are all right, but they are not as important as the dogmatic theologians think. I have a quotation of Gabriel Marcel from Troisfontaine's book *De l'existence à l'être.* 'The more it is a matter of what I am and not what I have, the more all this business of questions and answers – think of the *Summa theologiae: utrum, utrum, utrum* – loses all meaning. When I ask myself what I believe, I cannot be content to line up a series of propositions to which I subscribe. Those formulae, manifestly, express a more profound reality, a more intimate reality: the fact of being in open circuit, of having intercourse with Transcendent Reality recognized as a Thou.'[17]

The move from the world of community to the world of prayer, interiority, that is what has meaning, that is what has a concrete influence on one's living, and all this business of questions and answers, of formulas to which one subscribes, does not count for much. So one finds in Hans Urs von Balthasar praise for a theology that gets on its knees and prays, not that speculates and disputes and argues.[18] Or there is mention of kerygmatic theology, of *Verkündigungstheologie*, that speaks in a manner that everyone can understand, that announces the word of God, that preaches rather than attempts to teach.

The personalist movement, the existentialist movement, the phenomenological movement, spontaneously tend to an insistence on the concrete, the immediate, the real, the affective, that immediately proceeds from the world of common sense to the world of interiority; and the world of theory, of dogmatic and theological development – well, it's all right, but it doesn't fit in with this scheme of things.

On the other hand, if one accepts that eclipse of theory, one finds oneself in rather queer company. First of all, there is Ernst Troeltsch. He was an out-and-out liberal theologian. He was a Christian because he was a European. He felt that the inhabitants of more primitive tribes in Africa should be converted to one of the great religions, but he did not see any point to converting people of high culture, such as the Indians and Chinese, to Christianity. He was an ultimate product of the Dilthey school. And as he

---

17 Roger Troisfontaines, *De l'existence à l'être: La philosophie de Gabriel Marcel*, vol. 2 (Louvain: Nauwelaerts, and Paris: Vrin, 1953) 352. A more precise translation is given in CWL 18, *Phenomenology and Logic*, ed. Philip J. McShane (Toronto: University of Toronto Press, 2001) 228.

18 For references, see Edward T. Oakes, *Pattern of Redemption: The Theology of Hans Urs von Balthasar* (New York: Continuum, 1994) index, 'kneeling theology of Balthasar.'

remarked, 'Dogmatics is a piece of practical theology and no real science.'[19] And certainly, if you omit the whole theoretical world and theoretical interests, you cannot call it a genuine science. It is just a practical bit of religious knowledge to get people into heaven.

Henry Duméry took dogmatic theology as just a practical science. But, of course, there is need for critical reason, and that critical reason is exercised by the philosopher of religion. He undertook to set about the critical philosophy not merely of religion in general but of the Catholic religion from a strictly philosophical, critical viewpoint. The theologians did not want theory; and if the theologians do not want theory, someone else will provide them with their theory. Duméry's books were promptly put on the Index. But if you drop out all theory, you have no reason why Duméry should be on the Index.[20]

The third consequence is that the Catholic religion is left intellectually unarmed. I just quoted to you a passage from Gabriel Marcel, and I do not want to imply in any way that Gabriel Marcel is a Modernist. But I want you to reflect and ask yourself just where the difference between the two lies. The Modernists know all about inner experience. They explicitly state that dogmas are simply symbolic expressions of this inner experience, useful for a certain type of mentality. But it is in the inner experience that God is known, that what counts is found. Gabriel Marcel does not say that; he does not draw the Modernist consequences. But has he anything that would prevent you from drawing them? He has: he distinguishes between what he is and what he has; and he has the dogmas, but he is not them; they do not count for what he is but for what he has; he can draw distinctions, and so on. But there is a danger in that sort of position: if you renounce theory, where are you when theoretical difficulties arise?

There further arises the question whether theology, if it is not a science, pertains to the field of the sociology of knowledge. The sociology of knowledge was a notion developed first of all, I think, by Max Scheler in his *Die Wissensformen und Die Gesellschaft* (*Forms of Knowledge and Society*)

19 Lonergan's notes quote Troeltsch: 'So ist die Dogmatik ein Stuck der praktischen Theologie und keine eigentliche Wissenschaft.' The reference given is *Gessamelte Schriften* 2 (Tübingen: Mohr, 1932) 515.
20 See Henry Duméry, *Le problème de Dieu en philosophie de la religion* (Paris: Desclée de Brouwer, 1957); in English, *The Problem of God in Philosophy of Religion*, trans. Charles Courtenay (Evanston, IL: Northwestern University Press, 1964).

and, again, *Sociologie des Wissens.*[21] It is taken up by Karl Mannheim mainly as a generalization of the Marxian view of ideology. Marxians call everyone else's views ideology; but their own is the truth. In any case, Mannheim generalized Marx: if everything is ideology, what do you have? You have sociology of knowledge. You get the approach in *Ideology and Utopia*; there is a bibliography in it, but it regards what is before 1935.[22] In later writings, Mannheim further developed the notion of the sociology of knowledge,[23] and he was very keenly aware that he had to avoid a relativism because he was a Jew who had been bounced out of Germany under the Nazis, and he did not want to accept anything at all of pure relativism, but he had some difficulty getting around it. It was his problem. Similarly for Werner Stark, who teaches in England and wrote *The Sociology of Knowledge* (ca. 1957).[24] In Robert Merton's *Social Theory and Social Structure*,[25] which is something of a classic in contemporary sociology, there is a chapter with bibliography on the sociology of knowledge. The sociology of knowledge is what people think because of their social milieu and influences. Is Catholic doctrine that kind of thing? Or is it a matter of truth? If it is a matter of truth, you are driven into the theoretical field.

Again, I believe that Catholic metaphysics was developed in the Greek councils. St Thomas, in *Summa theologiae*, 1, q. 3, a. 4, in one of the responses, is talking about the *esse* of God, and he distinguishes between the *esse* of the being and the *esse* in the proposition, the *esse* of truth. And he says that we know the divine *esse* insofar as we know that the proposition *Deus est* is true. Similarly, we know the divinity of Christ insofar as we know that the proposition 'Jesus Christ is God' is true. But such a statement presupposes a whole metaphysics and a whole epistemology. And if you want to see what happens when you do not have this metaphysics and this epistemology, read J.S.

21 Max Scheler, *Die Wissensformen und Die Gesellschaft* (Bern: Francke, 1960); *Problems of a Sociology of Knowledge*, trans. Manfred S. Frings; ed. Kenneth W. Stikkers (London: Routledge & Kegan Paul, 1980). The latter is a translation of an essay which originally appeared as the introduction to the anthology *Versuche zu einer Soziologie des Wissens*, ed. Max Scheler (Munich and Leipzig: Duncker & Humblot, 1924).
22 Karl Mannheim, *Ideology and Utopia: An Introduction to the Sociology of Knowledge*, trans. Louis Wirth and Edward Shils (New York: Harcourt, Brace, 1949).
23 Karl Mannheim, *Essays on the Sociology of Knowledge*, ed. Paul Kecskemeti (London: Routledge & Kegan Paul, 1952).
24 Werner Stark, *The Sociology of Knowledge: Toward a Deeper Understanding of the History of Ideas* (London: Routledge & Kegan Paul, 1958).
25 Robert K. Merton, *Social Theory and Social Structure* (Glencoe, IL: The Free Press, 1957).

Lawton, an Anglican, *Conflict in Christology*, who describes what happened to Anglican theology between *Lux Mundi* and *Foundations*, roughly about 1886 and 1914.[26] Christology went out the window. The situation became one in which no one could understand what on earth was meant by belief in the divinity of Christ. As Bultmann said, when he was asked by the ecumenical movement what he thought of their formula that acknowledged Jesus Christ as God, 'What on earth can that mean?' So they settled on calling Jesus Christ 'Lord.' He is called 'Lord' a lot in the New Testament. Thus, without some metaphysical, theoretical background, the dogmas will disappear.

So much, then, for an outline of the problematic of theology at the present time.[27]

26 John S. Lawton, *Conflict in Christology: A Study of British and American Christology from 1889 to 1914* (London: Society for Promoting Christian Knowledge, 1947). For more on Lawton, see Lonergan, 'Theology as Christian Phenomenon,' in *Philosophical and Theological Papers 1958–1964* 266–67, 269.
27 The second question-and-answer session was held later this day. See below, pp. 282–302.

1962-4

Elements of Theology[1]

We ended yesterday's lecture by outlining certain fundamental problems that confront the contemporary theologian. Today we start trying to pick out elements that can be determined.

1 Theory

Our first question will be, Does theology contain a theoretic element? By that I mean, Is it, at least in part, within the world of theory in the strict sense of that term? Does it involve the psychological differences illustrated by the story about Thales and the milkmaid? Does it involve the concern for rigor that is illustrated by Plato's early dialogues, in which Socrates shows the Athenians that they do not know what they certainly feel they do know? Does it involve turning away from the concrete world of community as illustrated by Eddington's two tables? Does theology go off to things like the table that you cannot see, the real table that consists of electrons and protons? Does it involve a technical language? Is it a matter of questions and answers – and not simply, as Gabriel Marcel would prefer, the question, What am I? as opposed to, What do I have? (Questions and answers are matters that are very foreign to him.) In brief, does it involve the continuance of the Scholastic tradition?

To take concrete illustrations: does it bother about the psychological analogy of the Trinity and its implications? about the *unicum esse* in Christ?

---

1 Thursday, 12 July 1962, Lauzon CD/MP3 307 (30700A0E060) and 308 (30800A0E060).

about the supernatural order, as a theorem and not just as an epithet to praise? Does it pay attention to the complex questions concerned with grace and liberty, predestination and reprobation, the analysis of the act of faith, and in general the question about 'the nature of ...'?

That is an issue that is quite real at the present time – perhaps not as much on this side of the ocean as in Europe. I found it, and I was surprised to find it, a very real problem for students in Europe. And it is important, I think, to make clear the things we are not arguing for when we say that theology does include a theoretic element, because most of the objections against Scholasticism, against a rigorously scientific element in theology, are directed not against systematic theology but against bad systematic theology.

I am not arguing, then, for perpetually disputed questions. We have had them, and they have been disputed for centuries. I am not arguing for their continuance. On the contrary, I am concerned with the method of theology because I believe it is possible to eliminate them in methodical fashion.

Again, I am not arguing for a theology that prescinds from time, one that works in the abstract and necessary and universal. Rigorous science does not necessarily imply that.

I will admit that such scientific theology cannot be taught to everyone. You cannot teach relativity and quantum theory in high school – you can hardly do it in college! – but that is not an argument against the existence of that part of modern physics. And I am not arguing that this theoretic element is something that should be taught to everyone. On the contrary, I would admit that it cannot be taught to everyone.

I am not maintaining that it cannot be eclipsed, omitted. The Catholic Church began, and flourished for centuries, before any systematic theology was developed. And what causes the movement away from Scholasticism at the present time is the discovery of other areas, the world of community, the world of interiority, which are quite distinct from the world of theory, which are accessible to everyone, and which are more immediately relevant to Christian and Catholic living and the propagation of the faith. The world of theory can be eclipsed; that is not an impossibility. And we would not cease being Catholics immediately if that were to happen.

I said the question was, Does theology include a theoretic element? This means I am not asking for a theology that is exclusively theoretic, that is solely systematic, that cannot find any room for the personalist, existentialist, phenomenological trends that are in the ascendancy at the present time or for the positive theology that has been developing over the centuries and that has flowered and fructified in biblical and patristic and other departments of theology.

Again, by the systematic element in theology, I do not mean that it is the integration of everything from every point of view. It is not. We have spent some time on this talk about worlds and horizons, and so on, simply to make clear that integration is not found within one world, not even the world of theory. The world of theory will integrate everything by making everything a theoretical object, but that is not the only way in which objects are apprehended. They are apprehended in the world of interiority; they are apprehended in the world of community as well. The theoretic element in theology does make a contribution to integration, to the possibility of continuous movement from one world to the other. It enables one to understand what one is doing. But the integration itself is something different. It is the ability of the subject to move smoothly from one world to the other. The integration does not lie within the single world of theory. If you try to situate the integration within the single world of theory, then you have the dilemma: either the one or the other. It was to bring out the need for an adequate concept of integration that we spent so much time on this business of different worlds.

Finally, I am not arguing for the Aristotelian ideal of science. Whether we are to have the Aristotelian ideal of science or to complement it with the contribution of the modern achievement of science is a further question. But we are asking the fundamental question, Is theology to include a theoretic element in the sense that was indicated earlier?

The problem is not difficult as a yes or no question. The church has committed herself to the theoretic element. When Athanasius argued against the Arians for the *homoousion*, he believed he was arguing for an exception that was necessary in this particular case. If one was going to deal with these confounded Arians, then the only satisfactory way of doing it was to stand by the definition of Nicea and to affirm that the Son is consubstantial with the Father. If one did not want to say that, one's motives ultimately were under suspicion. De facto, the stand taken at Nicea and put across mainly by Athanasius was a precedent. The *homoousion* introduced into the formulas of faith a term that was not found in scripture, and it was defended in the fourth century on the grounds of a particular necessity against this group or set of groups of heretics. Still, de facto it turned out to be a precedent. At Chalcedon we have the one person and the two natures of Christ defined. In the Third Council of Constantinople, after a lot of wavering about (illustrated by Constantinople II and Lateran I, in which Neo-Chalcedonism came to the fore – they were using both Cyril's formulae and the formulae of Chalcedon), we have defined not only two natures and two properties as at Chalcedon but also two natural operations and two natural wills. The church in the Greek councils committed itself to that movement towards the theoretical realm. Scholasticism generalized the process. It asked, What is it? about everything involved in Catholic living. The [First] Vatican Council gave a permanent status to the theoretical element in theology in its decree *De fide et ratione.* 'Ratio quidem humana cum pie, sobrie, sedulo quaerit, aliquam intelligentiam eamque fructuosissimam mysteriorum attingere potest.'[2] You cannot agree with the Vatican Council and either deny the possibility of some imperfect understanding of the mysteries or deny that the understanding is fruitful. The code of canon law and the apostolic constitution *Deus Scientiarum Dominus* want theology taught according to the principles, the procedure, and the doctrine of St Thomas. Attacks on Scholasticism have regularly been reproved by the Holy Office. And so on. The church is in it, and that is a fact.

Moreover, it pertains to the perfection of the church, to the perfection of divine revelation, to its full expansion, that it dominate not only the interior world of each individual and the world of community but also the world of theory.

Now that is a very general argument, but it is a sound argument. All power was given to Christ in heaven and on earth, and the Catholic fact naturally expands into all realms of human activity. One cannot put a wall around theory and say Catholics do not bother their heads about that.

Besides such arguments from authority and general considerations, one can assign intrinsic reasons in the matter. According to Pius IX and Pius XII the most noble task of the theologian is to show that the dogmas in the sense in which they were defined are contained in the sources of revelation. And to show that they are so contained is to study the process by which the church proceeded from what is in the sources of revelation to the conciliar definitions, which, in their strict tenor, employ terms and concepts that are not found in the sources. Something was developing; there was something in process of becoming in that movement. What was it? You cannot say what it was unless you acknowledge it to be a movement towards theoretical conception and definition of the contents of revelation.

2 Lonergan is not quoting exactly. A translation of the exact statement is, 'Reason illumined by faith, when it inquires diligently, reverently, and judiciously, with God's help attains some understanding of the mysteries, and that a highly fruitful one ...' (DB 1796, DS 3016, ND 132).

In other words, systematic and positive theology go hand in hand. One cannot drop the one without being in endless difficulties with regard to the other. You can do endless history about the process, but to show that there is continuity, that there is the same doctrine, that the one is an explicitation of the other, you must give a precise content to the idea of development. What is developing? How can it be the same truth in the councils and in the New Testament if they are using different languages and different concepts? It can be understood insofar as it is conceived as a transposition from the world of community and the world of interiority to the world of theory. The same truth can be stated from the viewpoint of the different worlds. But if your account of the development is a movement towards theory, a *Wendung zur Idee*,[3] then you are acknowledging as a term the existence of a systematic theology.

To consider the point from another angle, which is negative, the key element in the movement towards the elimination of the systematic element in theology (in other words, the possibility of dispensing with this theoretical theology) comes from phenomenology. I mean, of course, not just the normal, natural reaction of the sound man of common sense who wonders what all this theory is about: it cannot be very important because he himself and men just as good as himself have gotten along very well all their lives without paying much attention to it. That sort of thing is never going to be eliminated. But a serious attempt at eliminating the theory or brushing it aside comes from phenomenology.

Phenomenology is an instrument that can begin from the most concrete of human experiences and occurrences and proceed towards a quite profound grasp of elements in the interior life, in Christian living, and so on. You can study the phenomenology of a meeting between two persons, or of a smile, and go right on through all aspects of Christian life. It is easy, and it is enlightening, and it is helpful, and it can be universally applied. But it is not ultimately satisfactory, and that point has to be grasped, I think.

What is phenomenology? It is simply a matter of exploiting the fact that man understands in sensible data: insight occurs with respect to sensible data. To take the type of instance that the phenomenologist works upon in his interpretation, in his letting the object appear, in letting the object reveal its essence, its significance, would involve a rather long process. But the fundamental idea in it I am going to attempt to illustrate by using the first proposition in the first book of Euclid's *Elements*. It is something that need

3 See below, p. 260 and note 3.

frighten no one, no matter how great one's distaste for or horror of mathematics, because it is the first proposition in the first book.

The problem was: on a given base *AB* in the plane of the blackboard, construct an equilateral triangle. And Euclid said: take center *A* and radius *AB* and draw a circle. Take center *B* and radius *BA* and draw a circle. Call the point of intersection *C*. Join *CA* and *CB*. Then you will have an equilateral triangle, because *AC* and *AB* are radii of the same circle and all radii of the same circle are equal; *BA* and *BC* are radii of another identical circle, and all radii of the same circle are equal; and things equal to the same are equal to one another; and therefore *CA* and *CB* are equal – *quod erat faciendum*: we have constructed an equilateral triangle.[4]

Modern geometers note that, while what Euclid says is true in its way, still he does not prove it. And he does not prove it because he does not prove that those two circles will intersect. If you have two circles in the same plane, you can have one inside the other or one outside the other; in either case there is no intersection. How did Euclid know that these two circles will intersect? Well, you can see that they must intersect: if you draw a circle and then take a point on the circumference and draw another circle, they have to intersect. It's obvious. They must.

Well, is that an axiom or a postulate or a definition? It is neither one of Euclid's axioms, nor one of his postulates, nor one of his definitions. Nor is it possible in Euclidean terms to state that necessity as a postulate, axiom, or definition. You can see that it is so, and that is insight into sensible data. But for 2,000 years there was no conceptualization of that.[5]

Now, Euclid's *Elements* involves a dependence on nonrigorously formulated insights. Phenomenology very easily does the same thing: everybody understands it; it is obvious; you can see it cannot be otherwise; but you do not have things pinned down accurately.

With regard to phenomenology, I have a quotation from Heinrich Fries.[6] He published in 1949 at Heidelberg *The Catholic Philosophy of Religion at the Present Time*,[7] and he goes through a long list of Catholic philosophers of

---

4 For the relevant diagram, see Bernard Lonergan, *Understanding and Being*, vol. 5 in Collected Works of Bernard Lonergan, ed. Elizabeth A. Morelli and Mark D. Morelli (Toronto: University of Toronto Press, 1990) 23; also Lonergan, *Topics in Education* 111.

5 Lonergan proceeded to give another example. For the example and the relevant diagram, see Lonergan, *Understanding and Being* 25 and *Topics in Education* 112.

6 Lonergan refers to p. 20 in the notes he had distributed for these lectures.

7 Heinrich Fries, *Die katholische Religionsphilosophie der Gegenwart: Der Einfluss*

religion and shows that the vast majority of them depend upon Max Scheler. Max Scheler was a great exponent of phenomenology of a particular type. Then he takes the others who do not depend on Scheler and a few who were a bit in reaction. And he says that Scheler himself is an example of how easily and frequently the danger of arbitrariness breaks out and how one can use exactly the same phenomenological method to reach contradictory 'evident' results. In other words, when you are dealing with concrete human affairs and getting insight into them and seeing what is obvious, one man can apply the phenomenological method to bring out something and make it very evident, and someone else can apply the same method to get contrary results. Phenomenology gives insights. It is illuminating. It is helpful. It opens up windows. But it has to be submitted to the further test of rational judgment, and that is the element that gets eclipsed. As Fries says, however genial and fruitful the grasp of essence may be, it needs the control of rational criticism. Then he goes on to the other limitation of phenomenology: because phenomenology operates on the level of sense and understanding without paying attention to the critical control of rational judgment, all it can do about the question of existence is, as Husserl did, to put it in brackets. Husserl prescinds systematically from questions of existence. And, as Fries remarks, that is the only way that the phenomenologist can proceed. It means that he cannot deal with the existential in an adequate fashion. And if he cannot do that, whether he is dealing merely with bright ideas or with something that is true is something that he cannot determine.

Consequently, while it would be a mistake to turn one's back on phenomenology, one also has to acknowledge its limitations. And if one proposes to effect the eclipse of theoretical theology on the grounds that you can make people understand everything, that is perfectly all right from a pedagogical point of view; but by this you are not preparing your students against ultimate difficulties that may very well arise later on, and in any case you are not doing a scientific, rigorous study of your subject matter.

In brief, then, with regard to our first question, I would say that we have to acknowledge the value, the utility, the help that comes to us from all the new fields and developments in theology. But all development is a matter of differentiation and integration. One combines the new with the old, and then one progresses. If one wants to substitute the new for the old, one is not progressing, one is just introducing big changes.

Max Schelers auf ihre Formen und Gestalten: Eine problemgeschichtliche Studie (Heidelberg: F.H. Kerle, 1949).

2 The Scientific Model

2.1 The Greek Ideal and the Modern Notion

Given that theology includes a theoretic element, the next question is whether that theoretic element is to be modeled on the Greek ideal of science. The Greeks did not achieve too much in science, but they did achieve a formulation, a conception, of science, an expression of the ideal. But is that Greek expression of the ideal of science to be considered definitive, so that when we say that theology is analogously a science we mean that it stands in an analogy to the Greek ideal of science? Or are we to say that theology is a science in the sense in which modern inquiries are scientific?

The two statements have quite different meanings. There are two possible analogies. To which science is the theoretic component in theology analogous? Our statement involves two elements: we have to admit, make room for, science of the modern type; but we have to do so in a way in which it is a coherent prolongation of the ancient type.

First of all, we have to make room for the modern concept or notion of science because, in many different ways, it fits in better with the Catholic fact, the dogmatic-theological context, than does the ancient Greek ideal.

2.2 Certainty versus Probability

According to the ancient ideal, science is certain: *certa rerum per causas cognitio*. But it is a fact that theology in its systematic part presents theses that for the most part are probable. There are elements that are *de fide definita* and *de fide divina et catholica* and *theologice certa*. But if you have only those elements, you do not have anything that fits together, you have no way of grasping systematically just what it means. As soon as a theologian goes on to meeting the ultimate questions – what do you mean when you say that God the Father had a Son? is it just some vague sort of nonsense? or has it a real meaning? and what is that real meaning? can you state it exactly in a way that answers every objection that anyone can think up? – when you try to answer questions like that, you do not come up with answers that are certain or that are universally accepted as certain. You find theologians dividing up. The answers are probable, and that happens all along the line.

The elements in theology that have been defined by the church, that are settled by the universal consent, the moral unanimity, of the Fathers, of the theologians, and so on, go along fine. But not everything is settled in that

:30

way. And when you come to questions of meaning, of *quid sit?* of 'what on earth are you trying to say?' and the fundamental questions of that order, then things are usually probable. It would help theology to acknowledge that the probable also is scientific. And insofar as de facto theology has parts that are just probable, it is de facto like the modern science and not like the Greek ideal.

2.3 The Universal versus the Concrete

Again, science is of the universal, according to the Greek ideal. But our Lord Jesus Christ was not a universal. The facts narrated in the scriptures were not universals. The Catholic tradition is not a universal: it is a concrete historical fact. What are called the *facta dogmatica* – that this council occurred, and that it defined that – are not universals. And one cannot say that these particulars, these singular persons and events, pertain to theology by way of examples. St Thomas puts the question in *Summa theologiae*, 1, q. 1, a. 2, ad 2, and he says that Abraham, Isaac, and Jacob pertain to *sacra doctrina* by way of examples. But Jesus Christ does not pertain to the Christian revelation by way of an example, and he is singular.

De facto, Catholic theology deals with the singular, and an idea of science that reveals that possibility is more consonant with Catholic theology than an idea of science that does not.

2.4 Immutability versus Process

Again, the Greek ideal of science deals with the changeless. But the history of salvation, the *Heilsgeschichte*, is not something changeless. It is a historical event and a historical process. It consists in a movement, in the movement narrated in the Old Testament, in the movement begun according to the narrations of the New Testament and the history of the church.

There is the fact of evolution. Revelation develops throughout the Old Testament. There occurs a development of revelation within the New Testament. And after the canon of scriptures was closed, there was the development of the dogmas and the development of theology. Those movements, those developments, are objects of theological understanding. It is true that such developments have only recently become objects of theological understanding. There was little concern with history in the Middle Ages, and subsequent theology followed more the medieval pattern than the developing contemporary sciences. But it remains that those problems at the present time cannot be ignored. We have to understand not only eternal, immutable truths, but also developments in the field of truth. They are part of the problem of a contemporary theology. And insofar as that problem is intrinsic to our theology, we have to have a science that is more like contemporary science than like Greek science.

2.5 Necessity versus Empirical Intelligibility

Science, for the Greek ideal, is of the necessary. But the central elements in Catholic truth are not necessary elements. The incarnation need not have occurred. The redemption need not have occurred. And if they did occur, they need not have occurred in the precise way that they did. There need not have been inspired scriptures. And if there were, they need not have been precisely the inspired scriptures that we have. The church is not a matter of absolute metaphysical necessity; it is a fact that God chose to institute, but God could have saved men in other ways. Everything that does not involve a contradiction is something that God could have done, and it is not demonstrable to the point that a contradiction is involved.

Again, why is the problem of nature and grace such a problem? It is because it is assumed that the only type of intelligibility is absolute necessity. If the only type of intelligibility is absolute necessity, then the relations of nature to grace cannot be intelligible; otherwise grace would not be gratuitous. There is an intrinsic contingency to the relations between nature and grace. Otherwise you destroy grace as gratuitous. But that does not mean that those relations are unintelligible. Besides the intelligibility of absolute necessity, there is also the intelligibility that is empirical, such as the law of gravity and so on, as is illustrated continuously in the modern sciences. They present intelligibilities that de facto are true. But things could be understood if they were otherwise.

Again, then, in a fundamental manner Catholic theology is more at home in a contemporary notion of science than in the Greek ideal of science.

2.6 Complementing the Old with the New

For those reasons we have to make room for science in the modern meaning of the term, the meaning of the term in which there is an intelligibility within movement itself, within the *per accidens*. That intelligibility is not an absolute necessity but an empirical fact, and it extends to the particular, to the singular.

However, that making room for notions on science that are cognate to modern science is not to be accepted in any manner whatsoever. It has to be taken as a prolongation of what has been regarded as science of the past. It is a matter of enriching the Greek ideal, not of simply eliminating and replacing it.

The reasons for this are clear enough. While it is true that there is an intelligibility that is empirical, it is also true that there are absolute necessities. While it is true that there are elements in theology that are just probable, it also is true that there are elements that are certain. While it is true that there is an intelligibility in movement, it remains that there is intelligibility in what is changeless. And while there is intelligibility in what is *per accidens*, there also is intelligibility in what is *per se*. One is not to accept the new as something that eliminates the old. It has to be something that complements, that fills out the old.

Further, one is not to go to the modern scientist and learn from him what he thinks his science is. Einstein made the remark, when an epistemologist asked him how he should go about finding out just what the theory of knowledge implicit in physics was, 'Well, you watch what the scientists do, but you don't pay any attention to what they say.' That is very sound and profound. The scientist knows his physics, but knowing physics is not knowing knowing physics. That is something quite different. And to that something quite different the scientist probably has paid very little attention and certainly no professional attention. He is an amateur on that subject. Moreover, he will hand out what has been the philosophy of science in the scientific tradition, and that will be a mechanist determinism, or a positivism, or a pragmatism, or something else. It will not be a rounded satisfactory philosophy. Consequently, anything one takes from the modern scientist has to be criticized. You have to understand what he is doing, be able to account for all that he does. But you need not pay any attention to what he says about cognitional theory. Without that criticism of modern science, any acceptance of it within theology would just be asking for trouble.

Finally, how does one effect this critique, this purification, of modern science so that room can be made for it within theology? It is a matter of understanding what we already have. Leo XIII has something about *vetera novis augere et perficere*, and I have long been convinced that our fundamental problem is to know what the *vetera* really are, really to understand them. It is insofar as we understand them adequately, fully, exactly, with their full depth and not according to the simplifications that make them fit more easily into one's own horizon, that one gets into a position to meet fundamental problems. It is insofar, then, as we really grasp what the *vetera* are saying that we reach the point where we are able to prolong their work and perfect it by including the new contributions that come from the achievements of modern science.

In other words, while Aristotle and St Thomas did not anticipate or explicitly formulate the points that can be established from reflecting on modern science, still they laid foundations that enable one to understand what is going on in modern science and moreover to criticize it from a more fundamental viewpoint.[8]

3 Intelligibility and Truth

3.1 Empirical Intelligibility

With regard to the question, *Quid sit?* (the question for intelligence), making room for the modern type of science within the theological tradition essentially involves two points, one that regards the intelligibility in the thing, the intelligibility to be known, and the other that regards knowing it. I take the example of the process from the New Testament to Nicea. That process is not something of absolute necessity. One cannot establish that the procedure from the New Testament to Nicea was of absolute necessity, that it must have occurred just that way and that it could not have occurred any other way. What one can understand about that process is the intelligibility that de facto is found there.

Again, one finds that intelligibility not in abstract speculation on the nature of the evolution of dogma, such as in the position on the homogeneous evolution of dogma.[9] In such a position, there is an evolution of dogma insofar as there is a metaphysical nexus between the truths of revelation and the doctrine defined. But this is proceeding by abstract speculation on the nature of what an evolution of dogma can be. And the evolution of dogma is not that at all. It is something to be understood in the historical process, in the movement of thought that one can ascertain to have existed de facto during those three centuries. It is something to be

8 The last five minutes of this part of the lecture are unavailable because of a defective portion of the original tape. The second part of the lecture of Thursday, 12 July, begins with the next section. It is recorded on Lauzon CD/MP3 308 (30800A0E060).

9 Lonergan was groping for the name of a certain proponent of this position. It is not clear from the lecture just who is meant.

reached by understanding the concrete, by an insight into the data and not by a deduction from abstract principles.

In the third place, when one reaches in the data that intelligibility that could be otherwise but still de facto is intelligible, one does not have a universal premise from which one can deduce what all other evolutions of dogma must have been. Just as there was the evolution from the New Testament to Nicea, so too there was the evolution from Nicea to the First Council of Constantinople, and from First Constantinople to Ephesus, and so on. The evolution in the different cases can very well be different. It is to be found by further examination of the data, so that the development of dogma can itself be something that develops.

In other words, what we are moving *from* is intelligibility that is of absolute necessity, such as the principle of contradiction or the principle of identity or the principle of sufficient reason, and we are moving *to* the intelligibility that rises from the data, that is grasped in the data and that develops in time, that changes in time.

Further, with regard to knowledge of that intelligibility, it is not something that is discovered by a stroke of genius. It is something that is gradually discovered, that gradually comes to light. The question of the ante-Nicene Fathers is something that has been investigated since the days of Petavius.[10] Countless people have been over the ground. Petavius discovered the problem. Further investigators isolated various elements, made this point clear and that point clear, and so on. One followed after the other, and each successive investigator corrected something in the previous man's work; gradually one moves towards an understanding of what took place. But it is a long process of gradually coming to apprehend what exactly was the thought of the various Christian writers involved and of their opposite numbers and of coming to understand what precisely was the difficulty that led to incorrect statements about the divinity of the Son and how a different view was forced upon Catholic thought.

In other words, we are within the concrete field of historical study, though it is historical study of a particular type. To say anything more about it at the

---

10 Dionysius Petavius (1582–1652), Denis Pétau, a Jesuit historian and theology, was one of the first to accept the idea of doctrinal development. Lonergan acknowledges this when he opens the lengthy Prolegomena to his study of the doctrine of the Trinity by saying: 'Beginning with Petavius, the question has been asked why the very earliest Christian writers so failed to anticipate the Nicene and subsequent decrees that they seem at times to have entertained opinions quite at variance with them.' Lonergan, *The Triune God: Doctrines* 29.

present time would be to involve ourselves in methodological difficulties. Later I shall attempt to say something on the subject of history and the difference between history and positive theology. But at the present time I use that instance. Many other instances could be used to indicate the field or the type of intelligibility that is introduced and is given a status within theological science when one enlarges the notion of science to include the modern type of science and gets questions of the type, Why? to be answered in terms of an empirical de facto intelligibility that in the course of time comes to be grasped ever more fully.

Now such acts of understanding and judgment are not something alien to the Aristotelian-Thomist type of thought. Both Aristotle and St Thomas were perfectly well aware of the existence of the act of understanding, and of the act of understanding in sensible data. St Thomas explicitly states that intellect not only abstracts species from phantasm but also sees species in phantasm. Intellect grasps intelligibility in the sensible data. He says that anyone can know by experience that when he tries to understand anything, he forms images in which, as it were, he inspects what he is trying to understand.[11] That type of understanding was quite well known both to Aristotle and to Aquinas. They were perfectly well aware that one learns. The Aristotelian dialectic is running though the opinions of people who discussed the matter before one and gleaning from them the elements of truth one finds there. They were well aware that no one understands things so perfectly that nothing can be left to be discovered by posterity, and they stated this explicitly. They were aware that understanding of an object develops gradually. Aristotle compares the discovery of the universal to a rally. The army is defeated, and the troops are in rout. But one man followed by only one other turns around and stops and makes a stand against his pursuers, and he is joined by another, and a third comes along. Finally, the people who are being chased, because there are fewer against them, are able to stand up against the men that are pursuing them, and so there begins the rally in the rout. And Aristotle says that understanding a thing is like that rally in the rout; one gets hold of one point, and then adds on another and a third and a fourth and a fifth, and finally one has got hold of the whole issue.

What can be said to be lacking to some extent in the thought of Aristotle and Aquinas was the idea of organized scientific collaboration. Modern science is the work not so much of individuals. It has outstanding individuals, but the work is carried on in a more or less not quite anonymous but

---

11 Thomas Aquinas, *Summa theologiae*, 1, q. 84, a. 7.

quasi-anonymous fashion by thousands of people scattered over the world. With regard to historical tasks, as with the question that has been developing since Petavius, for example, the question of the ante-Nicene Fathers, that type of collaboration over time to reach the solution to a single problem is something that is new. But it is not something that is essentially new. It does not introduce some new type of knowledge. It introduces the element of human collaboration in a systematic fashion.

In other words, I think that the acknowledgment of empirical intelligibility, of an intelligibility that de facto is so, is something for which there is ample provision in the Aristotelian and Thomist tradition.

3.2 Judgment

With regard to the second question, *An sit?* we have a more complex problem. It is easy enough to be certain when you are deducing necessary conclusions from necessary and universal premises. When you are certain of the premises, you can be certain of the conclusions. But the fundamental difficulty about making room for the modern notion of science within theology is the problem of certitude. If one were to announce that theology was only probable, one would promptly be in difficulties. And how is one to arrive at certitude when modern science professes merely to be probable – it doesn't give two hoots about the question of certitude – when from the nature of the case one has a developing understanding with regard to an intelligibility that de facto is so but is not necessary? One has a very nice problem of judgment there. And the fundamental problem with regard to making room for a modern type of science within theology is the problem of judgment, getting an exact grasp of what is meant by judgment and what is meant by wisdom.

What is a judgment? One can determine a judgment by determining the type of question it answers. The question for intelligence – what is it? why is it so? – is a question that cannot be answered by a yes or no. If someone asks you what is the logarithm of the square root of minus 1, you will not make sense by answering either yes or no. This is a question for intelligence.

On the other hand, there are questions to which the proper answer is either yes or no. For instance: does such a logarithm exist? One makes sense either if one says yes or if one says no. One answer would be wrong and the other would be right; but in either case one is answering the question. Judgment is the act that answers questions of that second type: it says yes or no.

Again, one can determine what is meant by judgment by comparing judgment with statements. If I write out notes, I not merely consider what they are saying, I also implicitly affirm them to be true, to state what I think is true. But when you read them, you do not do that. You read them and say, 'Well, I wonder what he's saying.' And if you understand them you go on to say, 'I wonder whether it's true.'

In the first instance, you merely consider. You perform operations of the first type, operations of understanding and conceiving, of grasping the meaning, of understanding what is said. Whether it is true or not is a further question to be considered later on. We may agree or disagree, or simply not know.

When one's attitude toward statements is simply consideration, effort to understand, to comprehend, to grasp exactly what is meant, one is not judging. It is when one says, 'He's wrong' or 'He's right' or 'I agree with him' or 'I reject it entirely or in part or draw distinctions' that one is making a judgment.

This act of judgment is not a *compositio vel divisio*. It is not a matter of putting concepts together or of separating them. It is an absolute positing. When you simply consider a statement, you put concepts together. You understand how it all hangs together. You can read the whole of Newton's mechanics and understand it perfectly but neither affirm nor deny it. There is no judgment about it. But if you understand it, you put it all together. This is synthesis. Synthesis is not judgment. Synthesis pertains to the act of understanding. Judgment adds something to the synthesis. It posits it or rejects it. It says, 'That's so; yes,' or, 'It's not so; no.'

That aspect of judgment as absolute positing is something that has not been too clear in the Aristotelian-Thomist tradition. And it is totally missing, as far as I can see, with the possible exception of Kant, from the German philosophic tradition.[12] And it is a matter of essential importance. Aristotle took over from Plato the combination of the forms, and he spoke of judgment as a synthesis. This is a logical account of the judgment; it does not draw attention to the absolute element in any judgment. St Thomas commonly spoke as did Aristotle. The judgment is *compositio vel divisio*. Occasionally he qualifies it: *per affirmationem vel negationem*. But this element of the absolute, of the positing, of absolutely positing, is the key element in any sound epistemology, and it is the outstanding feature of

12 In *Method in Theology* Lonergan does not seem to grant 'the possible exception of Kant.' See p. 335.

the act of faith: to agree, to say it is so. What is so? Well, a lot of the objects of faith can be merely implicit, but you have no act of faith without that absolute positing. And similarly, you have no judgment without that absolute positing.

When this element of absolute positing is missed, what happens? One proceeds in one's analysis from understanding to an act of will. Consider Bultmann's collection of essays under the title *Glauben und Verstehen*.[13] You understand, and beyond understanding there is the *Entscheidung*: you make a decision. But between the act of will that decides and the act of understanding that grasps the object in all its details and in all its ramifications, there is no intervening element of judgment that absolutely posits.

That absolute positing is not an act of will. It does not regard the good as does the act of will. It regards the true, and it is a purely intellectual act. When it is missed, one is left with some form of immanentism: the idealism of Hegel, or the phenomenology of Husserl, or the existentialism of Heidegger, or something like that. They cannot get out of the subject because they do not have the judgment that posits absolutely what is so. It is in that act that knowledge becomes transcendent. When that act is skipped, you cannot have an account of knowledge that is transcendent. You are boxed up somehow or other in immanence, and you have no way out.

This absolute positing is a personal act, an act of one's personal intellectual probity. It is not strictly moral, because 'moral' involves the will. But there is a type of morality of the intellect itself, and that is involved in the judgment.

The point was made by de la Rochefoucauld in one of his maxims, to the effect that everyone complains about his memory but no one about his judgment.[14] People have not only poor memories, but also poor judgments, but while everyone will complain about his poor memory no one complains about 'my poor judgment.' Why? Because memory is not something over which we are personally masters. But we do not have to judge. We not only have the alternatives yes and no; we can also say we do not know. We can make a modal judgment: probably it is so; perhaps it is so; it might be so. We can change the question, turn it around, and say, 'At least I am certain of this; I am not certain of the whole thing.' The act of judgment offers all sorts of alternatives. And it is *we* that judge. There is an element of personal responsibility, of personal commitment, in the judgment.

13 Rudolf Bultmann, *Glauben und Verstehen: Gesammelte Aufsätze* (Tubingen: J.C.B. Mohr, 1954, 1961).
14 See John Bartlett, *Familiar Quotations* (Boston, Toronto: Little, Brown & Co., 1955) 265.

Because of that element of personal commitment in the judgment, a merely automatic method, a mechanical method, never can be equal to the task of knowing, because a mechanical or an automatic method cannot involve personal responsibility; you just follow the instructions. But to reach truth, to make a judgment, there is needed something more. There is a personal element of responsibility, of self-commitment to the exigences of truth, that is involved in every judgment. That element of self-commitment is not something that is settled merely by any extrinsicist approach to the problems of knowledge or science.

A judgment, next, is a rational act. It has to be preceded by a grasp of the sufficiency of the evidence. But that is a vague statement. How much evidence is sufficient? How do you know you have sufficient evidence, and what do you mean when you say you have sufficient evidence?

To answer that question, we consider a schematic syllogism: If A, then B; but A; therefore B. A and B may stand for one or more propositions. A and B may also stand for elements in knowledge that are pre-propositional, pre-predicative. If they are propositional, one has the explicit syllogism. If pre-propositional, pre-predicative elements are represented by the A and B, then the syllogism is implicit.

Now there are two ways of interpreting the syllogism. One can consider the syllogism as the beginning of an infinite regress. You prove B if the major and the minor are true. And the major will be true if you have another syllogism that proves it; and the minor will be true if you have another syllogism that proves it. However, those syllogisms will be true if you have another major to prove two more majors and two more minors in each case, and so on, off to 2^n. You go off to infinity in the search for further prosyllogisms.

But one can analyze or interpret the syllogism intrinsically. The function of the syllogism is to exhibit the conclusion as unconditioned, as absolute. The unconditioned can be thought of formally or virtually. Formally, the unconditioned has no conditions whatever. God is the one and only instance of the formally unconditioned. But there is the virtually unconditioned. It is the conditioned that has its conditions fulfilled. And B in the syllogism is exhibited as virtually unconditioned. The major exhibits B as conditioned: if A, then B. The minor offers the fulfillment of the conditions, A. It follows that B is virtually unconditioned.

Now 'the virtually unconditioned' is, I would say, an exact statement of what is meant by the sufficiency of the evidence. If your prospective judgment is a virtually unconditioned, then you are rationally necessitated to affirm it.

It is outside the realm of what might be or might not be: it is. It has gotten beyond the level where it still has conditions to be fulfilled. On the other hand, if one has not the virtually unconditioned, if one has not sufficient evidence, one does not know whether or not some condition is fulfilled. And if one does not know that and nonetheless judges, then the judgment is temerarious. One is affirming what may not be so as far as one knows.

I think, then – and I develop the point at greater length in chapter 10 of *Insight* by applying it to a whole series of examples – that in any case in which one has sufficient evidence one has grasped a virtually unconditioned. The virtually unconditioned may be such that the premises stand in explicit propositions. But the premises also may be such that they are found in the pre-propositional, pre-predicative order. And that is the case that arises with regard to judgments that in their line are ultimate.

To take an example of the latter type, how do you make an elementary judgment of fact such as 'The microphone is here?'

There is the process of knowing, in which you begin from sensible data. You reach some act of understanding and formulation. You have the reflective act of understanding, in which you grasp the unconditioned. And as a result you say yes or no, it is or it is not. This is the general case of the process of human knowing: sensible data, understanding and conception, reflection and judgment.

When one considers the implicit syllogism, namely, where the *A* and *B* are not formulated propositions but elements within the cognitional process to which one must reduce judgments that are in their line ultimate, then the *A*, the fulfillment of the conditions, is the occurrence of the relevant experiences. When I look at the microphone, I see something. There is a definite visual pattern produced. One proceeds from the data to a conception – 'This is a microphone' – as a conception, as a hypothesis. There is, then, a process. Because of *intellectus agens*, intellectual light, this process does not occur blindly. It occurs intelligently. It occurs in accord with the norms and exigences of human intelligence. There is de facto a link between the experience and the conception 'a microphone.' And that process is guided by one's intelligence, one's intellectual light. Insofar as that process fulfills the norms and the exigences of one's intelligence, one has not only the data as given (*A*) but also one's conception, the link between the *A* and the *B*: if *A*, then *B*.

The reflective act of understanding puts together the link 'if *A*, then *B*' and the givenness of the data *A*, to reach *B* as unconditioned and to affirm it in the judgment.

That analysis in chapter 10 of *Insight* I apply to a series of instances. That is the fundamental case of the emergence of a judgment as a virtually unconditioned. There are different kinds of judgments, and I line them up in the tenth chapter and apply the same analysis to each case.

In that analysis, one can distinguish three elements in objectivity. There is an experiential element: the data are given. There is a normative element: the process from the data to the conception, the role of intellectual light, of intelligence, of the native light of intelligence or whatever else you want to call it. It is that normative element that is the ultimate ground of the major, 'If *A*, if these data, then a microphone.' Finally, there is the absolute element, the virtually unconditioned. Objectivity results from the combination of three different components.

I can illustrate what I mean by objectivity by considering its opposite. If you look at my hand and say, 'It's white,' well, is it? Is it white? It is not the same color as the sheet of paper, at least. That is the experiential element. It is just the presentation and the contrast. Next, if I make a postulate that no proposition that regards all classes is valid, someone can say, 'Well, your postulate is a proposition, and it regards all classes; therefore it is not valid.' There one is appealing to the normative element, to what is characterized generally as contradictory. In one type of objectivity one appeals to the data and compares the color of the hand with the color of the sheet: objectivity of the statement 'It is white.' Another type appeals to norms. If a person postulates that no proposition regarding all classes is valid, his proposition apparently regards all classes, and therefore, on its own showing, it cannot be valid. There is a normative element in objectivity. Or again, you are walking alone through the woods, and you meet one of these enormous hounds, and you say, 'Well, this is a particular type of hound.' And the fellow beside you says, 'Are you sure it isn't a wolf?' Are you sure? That element of certitude illustrates the absolute element in objectivity.

Now those three elements combine to give objectivity with a capital 'O,' just one. You need all three to have one objectivity in the full sense of the term. You need the experiential element of the data, the normative element of the link from the data to the conception, and the putting the two together that gives you what is meant by sufficient evidence.

3.3 *Logic, Method,* Esprit de finesse, *Illative Sense*

So much for what is judgment and what is sufficient evidence. We have to ask another question: what is logic, methodology, Pascal's *esprit de finesse,* Newman's illative sense?

We have already spoken of the native light of intelligence controlling the process from the data to the conception. Insofar as one is simply using the native light of intelligence, it is something on the side of the subject. It is not some object that one formulates and looks at. But one can objectify that light of intelligence, and one can do so in two ways.

The first way is with regard to knowledge *in facto esse*, as expressed in propositions that are definitive; definitive, that is, as far as the becoming of the proposition is concerned. And in that case, if one attends to the very general rules that are absolutely evident to anybody at all, one arrives at logic.

What does logic do? It expresses the normativeness and the exigences of intellectual light with regard to their implications in propositions. Propositions are logical if they meet certain fundamental exigences and norms that proceed from our created participation of uncreated light.

Method regards the genesis of the propositions. It regards knowledge *in fieri*. It lays down either general rules with regard to the acquisition of knowledge in any scientific field or more special rules that regard the special methodologies in different fields.

But any such objectification in the propositions and rules of a logic and in the theorems and assertions of a method is an objectification that does not exhaust all the resources of the light of intelligence. The light of intelligence is capable of much more, and it does much more. But to attempt to objectify it in its fuller employment, when it is dealing with extremely complex matters – the judgment of the expert – is in itself an extremely complex matter. Professor Albright, for example, received from Palestine a few of the jars found at Qumrân, and one of the jars was broken. He picked up the clay between his forefinger and thumb, moved it around, and was able to tell in what century and what part of what century the jar had been made. There is the acquisition, the development, of the special knowledge of the expert in the field. Well, how could he be certain? Well, if you are going to try to objectify the process by which he acquired the possibility of arriving at a high probability or a certitude in such matters, you will have more or less to recount Albright's autobiography in great part and in a far greater analysis than Albright himself would be ready to attempt.

The potentialities of intellectual light go way beyond what can be catalogued in a logic or a method. It is that function of intellectual light that Pascal spoke of when he spoke of the *esprit de finesse* and that Newman was feeling around for when he spoke of his illative sense. If theology is to introduce into its science this field in which the intelligibility is not an absolute necessity but de facto so, in which the grasp of that intelligibility is something that gradually develops over time, then one cannot restrict one's judgment to the type of judgment that can be made on the basis of a logic or a formulated method. One has to be ready to commit oneself to judgment on the basis of the light of intelligence that God gave each of us. In other words, we have to make room for Pascal's *esprit de finesse* or Newman's illative sense.

3.4 Wisdom

The next point is wisdom, and the fundamental point about wisdom is this: to reach the unconditioned, you must be able to say at least in some implicit fashion, 'If *A*, then *B*'; and to do that you have to know what the totality of the conditions for B are. To be able to make a judgment, one has to have some view of the whole. Without that view of the whole, one's judgments are not going to be sound. One has to have some ordering of the totality before one is able to judge. One has to have that ordering of the totality if one is going to pay attention to all the conditions of B that are necessary for asserting B. And that is the necessity of wisdom: *sapientis est ordinare*, and *summa sapientia ordinat omnia*. Wisdom is the intellectual habit that regards judgment, and its necessity is intrinsic to good judgment. Why is it that children up to the age of seven are said not to have reached the use of reason? It's because, while they have intellectual light and are asking questions from morning to night till they drive their parents crazy and are very eager to learn, still as yet they have no view of the whole that makes their judgments reliable. Why is it that minors are only minors, that they do not have full responsibility before the law? It is not because they do not have intellectual light; they can be a lot more intelligent than their elders. And it is not because they do not have the use of reason; they have passed the age of seven years. But to have full responsibility before the law, they have to have a fuller ordering of the matters on which they can pass judgment than is commonly attained at that age. And similarly with regard to Aristotle's remark that young people cannot study ethics. And his expression 'young people' means something beyond what we call minors.

1962-5

Beyond Extrinsicism
and Immanentism[1]

1 Theology and Wisdom: Concluding Remarks

Yesterday we reached the problem of certitude of judgment that is raised
when one attempts to integrate the modern notion or fact of science with
the ancient ideal. And we had something to say about the nature of the act
of judgment, the nature of sufficient evidence, the objectifications of intellectual light, of the light of intelligence, in logic and method, and the remainder that never succeeds in being objectified. In other words, intelligence
is something more than simply what can be objectified in logic or a method,
no matter how elaborate. Not all problems are the same, and yet there are
always the normativeness and the exigences of intelligence and rationality
that are guiding intellectual operations. Consequently, there is beyond logic
and method what Pascal named the *esprit de finesse* as opposed to the *esprit de
géométrie* – the spirit of geometry is always able to objectify every element in
its process, though Euclid did not succeed in doing so – or what Newman
called the illative sense in his *Grammar of Assent*.

So we are brought to the question of wisdom. And it is important to note
that wisdom is ultimate. Its significance is basic. Science, according to the
Aristotelian classification, has to do with conclusions, which are deduced
from principles. Intellect, the Aristotelian *nous,* has to do with principles,
and you know principles *statim, cognitis terminis.* But the question arises,

---

1 Friday, 13 July 1962, part 1, Lauzon CD/MP3 309 (30900A0E060) and 310
(31000A0E060).

Which terms do you select? There is an operation of selection in setting up principles, and there are radical difficulties. Every principle or every interpretation of every principle presupposes some notion of being, and there are all sorts of notions of being. There is Parmenides' notion and Plato's and Aristotle's and Plotinus's and Avicenna's and Averroes's and Aquinas's and Scotus's and Hegel's and Heidegger's; and they do not mean the same thing by 'being.' You cannot select which is the right notion of being by appealing to principles, because the principles are a manifold according to the different notions of being that you choose. How do you know which are the right fundamental notions? St Thomas says that it is by wisdom. *Summa theologiae*, 1-2, q. 66, a. 5, ad 4m: 'Sapientia iudicat de ente et non ente, et de iis quae per se sunt entis.'

So wisdom is something ultimate. The epistemological problem is ultimately a problem of wisdom. And wisdom is not something we are born with. It is something that has to be acquired. It is not simply an intellectual light, but intellectual light as applied, intellectual light as ordering everything: *sapientis est ordinare.* There is the necessity of that ordering of a totality to make a correct judgment. Every judgment occurs within a context. When one makes a judgment, one can be led on to expound, 'Just precisely what do you mean?' That will involve further judgments that qualify and complement the particular judgment one made. The original judgment has its presuppositions, and it has its consequences. And there are the reasons one will allege that account for one's making that judgment. One cannot allege always all the reasons; the judgment depends upon the illative sense, the *esprit de finesse.* A judgment occurs within a context, and a judgment is going to be correct or mistaken insofar as it proceeds out of the context of a mind that has a grasp of the whole matter in hand.

For that reason it is true that children do not reach the age of reason for something like seven years. Why? Because they haven't got that view of the whole even for elementary judgments. It is for the same reason that minors are minors. They haven't got a sufficient view of the whole to be completely responsible before the law. It is the reason Aristotle wanted people of mature age to study ethics. When they are younger, they haven't got sufficient experience of human affairs to be competent moralists. And so on for every change in our occupations. Shift a man from one job to another, from one environment to another; start studying a new subject, and you will find that there is a period in which you do not judge but wait and see, size up the situation, get the feel of things. If one steps into a new situation with which one isn't familiar and starts making snap judgments, they are mostly blunders.

One has to get a view of the whole and of the way things fit together before one can judge accurately.

How is it that one moves towards this view of the whole if one hasn't got it at the start? There is a paradox to the thing. One does not become wise, acquire wisdom, by deducing from one's prior lack of wisdom. It is not a deductive process. It is the self-correcting process of learning: one gets one insight, complements it with another, and gradually builds up to familiarity with the situation or familiarity with the subject. There is, then, that genesis of wisdom.

Finally, there are the divisions of wisdom, viewing wisdom in all its different cases. The supreme wisdom is, of course, divine wisdom. To be a perfect judge of everything, you need divine wisdom. St Thomas in *Summa theologiae*, 1, q. 25, a. 5, maintains that the possibles are not a set of isolated monads. They occur within orders. *Divina sapientia totum posse potentiae comprehendit.*[2] For that reason anything that God can do he also can do wisely. The possibles are already within an order determined by infinite wisdom. There is the totality of possible world orders; and any world order can exist, but the possibles occur only within infinitely wise orders. Consequently, anything that does not involve a contradiction not only can God do but he can do it wisely in accord with infinite wisdom, because divine wisdom is entitatively exactly the same thing as divine power. They are both really identical with the infinite act, and consequently divine wisdom comprehends the whole of divine power.

That divine wisdom has its proximate participation in the beatific vision, and that is the greatest wisdom a creature can attain.

There are further participations of that divine wisdom on a lower scale, namely, in divine revelation and inspiration, which are directly under the measure, the guidance, of divine wisdom.

Again, in negative form, there is the assistance that God gives the church and the bishops and the pope to save them from error in matters of faith and morals when the church defines. And again we have something directly dependent upon, guaranteed by, divine wisdom.

The wisdom of the theologian is not divine wisdom, not the wisdom of the blessed, not the wisdom of divine revelation or inspiration, not the wisdom of the infallibility of the church, but something that has to be learned. And since the matter treated by the theologian (the mysteries hidden in God and revealed to the church) are to be judged by a proportionate principle, only

2 '... divine wisdom comprehends everything that is possible for [divine] power.'

by divine wisdom, the theologian knows always that he is beyond his depth. The proportionate principle for passing judgment on the mysteries is not any human acquisition; it is divine wisdom. And it is only insofar as the theologian obtains wisdom through revelation, through the virtue of faith and the gifts of the Holy Spirit, that he can venture to make theological judgments. And because his participation in divine wisdom, which alone is proportionate to passing judgment on the object, is an imperfect participation, the theologian is always ready to submit his judgment to the judgment of the church.

Imperfect as it is, still the wisdom of the theologian is human wisdom in the actual order of the universe. If man had been created *in statu naturae purae*, then the proper wisdom of man would have been the wisdom of the philosopher, as it was for Aristotle. But philosophic wisdom is only hypothetically wisdom, and the hypothesis is not verified. It is theological wisdom that judges all things in the actual order of the universe. It replaces the wisdom of the philosopher, because the wisdom of the philosopher is commensurate not to the actual order but to an order that is purely hypothetical, the order of *natura pura*.

If theological wisdom in the actual order replaces the wisdom of the philosopher, still it is a wisdom that has to be complemented by particular wisdoms. It is a general wisdom that views the whole, but a view of the whole has to be complemented by more precise views of lesser totalities. The cobbler is an expert as long as he is dealing with shoes. He can give you sound judgment on anything that regards shoes: that is his field, he knows about shoes from every viewpoint. Similarly, every other specialist is the one to rely on in his field.

Insofar as theology attempts to step into the field of the contingent, the changeable, the historical, the *per accidens*, the empirical intelligibility, it needs to be complemented by the particular types of wisdom that are proper to the experts in the various fields. While the theologian can replace the philosopher in the actual universe, theology as a general subject has to complement itself with the particular wisdoms that are wisdom only within particular fields. It is true that the cobbler is an expert at his last, but it is also true: *ne, sutor, ultra crepidam* – cobbler, cobbler, stick to your last. While his judgment is excellent on the matter of shoes, it is not excellent on anything else. You don't consult him about changing the bank rate. Similarly, every specialist can be expected to move towards good judgment in his field, but that does not mean he will have good judgment outside his field. In general, when experts in physics or chemistry or economics attempt to pronounce on general issues, they are very likely to talk nonsense.

There has to be, then, a collaboration of the general wisdom of the theologian with the specialized, particularized wisdoms of experts in particular fields. And that is a peculiar problem that arises in theology as a result of passing beyond the Greek ideal of science and attempting to incorporate the modern achievement of science.

The same point can be put in another fashion. There is in Aristotle and St Thomas a general tendency to confine science to the universal, the necessary, the certain, the per se, the changeless. This is speaking roughly, for they have a lot of crude assertions that qualify the general statement; for example, Aristotle in Book M (I think chapter 10) states that knowledge of the universal is knowledge in potency, knowledge of the particular is knowledge in act;[3] he wasn't confined to a world of universals by any manner of means; but there still is that general tendency. And the result is that they have a practical virtue named prudence that deals with the particular, the contingent, the *per accidens*, the changeable. They developed it at great length. See *Summa theologiae*, 2-2, qq. 47–56, where ten questions are devoted to prudence in its various aspects. Prudence is not the same as wisdom. Wisdom is speculative; prudence is practical. In other words, prudence is limited to judgments on what I am to say and on what I am to do in this particular concrete situation. Prudence is the *recta ratio agibilium*.

However, human history is the work either of prudent or of imprudent men. Everything that is said and done is raw material for human history. And everything that is said and done either follows the precepts of prudence or it does not. It is in the field of the particular, the concrete, the contingent, the *per accidens*.

Insofar as the modern achievement of science is integrated into the older conception, the Greek conception of science, and becomes part of the science to which theology is analogous, there is a need for a transposition of the ancient prudence to a wisdom. Good historical judgment is not a matter of saying what Churchill or Caesar or Alexander the Great ought to have said or ought to have done, but it is a matter of making true judgments about particular facts that are contingent, have a contingent intelligibility, an empirical intelligibility, that are in the field of the *per accidens*, and so on.

3 'For knowledge, like the verb "to know," means two things, of which one is potential and one actual. The potency, being, as matter, universal and indefinite, deals with the universal and indefinite; but the actuality, being definite, deals with a definite object – being a "this," it deals with a "this."' Aristotle, *Metaphysics*, XIII (M), 10, 1087a 15–18.

There is a need, then, for a transformation of prudence, a comple-
menting of the ancient ideal of wisdom, which was purely speculative
(where 'speculative' means the universal and the necessary), a comple-
menting of that idea of wisdom with a transformation of prudence from
the practical to the speculative order, in other words, from the order of
what is to be said and done to the order of what is true. That is achieved
practically when the judgment of the experts in particular fields complements the judgment of the overall wisdom of the dogmatic theologian
and, inversely, when the judgment of the overall wisdom of the dogmatic
theologian links together the particular wisdoms of the specialists in the
various fields.

That is a fundamental problem that arises, and it is perhaps the ultimate
form of the problem of answering the question, *An sit?* is it so? when one
complements the ancient ideal of science with the modern achievement.

2   Extrinsicism

The fourth assertion on page 28 is, as it were, a corollary: *Quibus excluduntur
tum extrinsecismus tum immanentismus, omnesque quaestiones ad duo fundamen-
talia reducuntur, nempe, quid sit et an sit.*[4]

The medieval controversy had mainly to do with the question of universals, but that is not the key problem at the present time. The key problems
at the present time, the two excesses between which the Catholic mean is
found, are extrinsicism, on the one hand, and immanentism, on the other.
If one falls into either of the extremes, then one is blocked at any effort
towards a serious method of theology.

2.1 Extrinsicism Defined

First of all, then, what is meant by extrinsicism? In general, it is forgetting
oneself, forgetting that one has a mind and that one is using it. That forgetting of oneself, forgetting of one's mind, forgetting of the possibility that
one may be unauthentic, in need of conversion, and in need of a broader
horizon, has its motivation, which usually is secret, namely, the fear of
understanding and the flight from the responsibility of judging. People will

---

4 Another reference to the distributed notes. 'There are to be excluded both
extrinsicism and immanentism, and all questions are reduced to two
fundamental questions, namely, What is it? and Is it?'

agree with Augustine: *valde ama intellectum*.[5] But when they are put with all the questions that push them to the limit on any particular point, they are very likely to tell you, 'Well, you mustn't go too far, you must not want too much, you have to take this with moderation,' and so on and so forth. And similarly with regard to the flight from the responsibility of judging, an awful lot of the interest in and insistence on method is a desire to free oneself from one's responsibility of judging. One wants to put the task of judgment in some type of extrinsic process or mechanical device or common consent or democratic counting of noses, or anything at all as long as I don't have to take the responsibility of making a judgment. This is the root of extrinsicism.

It has many manifestations, and I enumerate four: deductivist extrinsicism, operational extrinsicism, metaphysical extrinsicism, and intuitionist extrinsicism.

2.2 Deductivist Extrinsicism

By deductivist extrinsicism is not meant the fact that a theologian or a philosopher or anyone else uses deduction, or that he uses very long and very subtle deduction, that he goes on for pages and pages rigorously deducing one thing from another. That is not what is meant by deductivism as extrinsic.

Deductivism becomes extrinsic when there is acknowledged the external process *and nothing else*, when it is assumed or supposed, or things are so conceived, that the existence of any mind operating in a manner corresponding to the deduction that is down in a book is regarded as something *per accidens*, something one can prescind from. There is the objective process, and we attend only to that, and the fact that any minds are operating with respect to it is beside the point. Then one arrives at a deductivist extrinsicism.

I indicate two examples in the notes. The first is the critical reader or student who, every time he hears a proof of anything whatever, given by anyone, reacts with, 'That doesn't prove.' What he really means is that he thinks a proof is a sort of *gratia gratis data* that produces conviction in him without any intellectual or rational effort on his part. In the fourteenth century, as the century proceeded, it was concluded that one divine attribute after another could not be demonstrated. They were all top-notch logicians; and the more

5 Augustine, 'Epistola cxx. Consentio ad quaestiones de Trinitate sibi propositas,' c. 3, §13: '... Intellectum vero valde ama.' 'Love understanding very much.' *The Works of Saint Augustine*, vol. 2/2, *Letters 100–155*, trans. Roland Teske (Hyde Park, NY: New City Press, 2003) 136.

they used their logic, the more they were brought to the conclusion that you cannot prove this and you cannot prove that, and so on right along the line. See Vignaux's article in *Dictionnaire de théologie catholique*, 'Nominalisme.' Towards the end of the article, summing things up, he says, 'Everything goes forward as if the theologian had only one instrument, his reason, his rational powers, his deductive powers; and what those powers were was something that was settled by rules of logic.'[6] You get away from the mind. Logic becomes a tool. You put the propositions down. There is an oversight of intelligence. Unless understanding develops, one does not see the nexus between terms that can be seen if intelligence does develop. And if one is interested simply in manipulating propositions, there is no effort to develop one's understanding. Consequently, as the century proceeded, as less and less attention was paid to the development of intelligence, fewer and fewer necessary nexus could be grasped, because they were not trying to understand. They were concerned with an objective process of proof.

The fundamental error in that fourteenth-century decadence, as in the lad who finds that nothing ever proves anything, is that they do not grasp the meaning of syllogism. Syllogism is an objectification, an expression in terms and propositions, either of a process of learning or of a judgment. But if you consider only the objectification, only the external manifestation, and prescind entirely from the mind that could be learning, that could be grasping the unconditioned, then what have you got? Sounding brass and tinkling cymbal.

I have in the notes an illustration of syllogism as a process of learning, one that I have already used: namely, because the moon goes through these phases, it must be a sphere. The truth of the major is something you can grasp by insight. But unless you make experiments or imagine experiments, you will not know what this proposition means. It will be meaningless for you; and when something is meaningless for you, it does not prove anything to you. It is not an instrument for the development of understanding.

That is one aspect of the syllogism. There are two aspects of the Aristotelian syllogism. Aristotle is very interested in the *syllogismos epistēmonikos*, the *syllogismus faciens scire*, as the medieval authors named it. It is the syllogism that makes you understand the necessity of a conclusion. It is a syllogism that expresses a process of learning. This is one aspect of the syllogism, the syllogism as supplying the answer to the question, *Quid sit?* How do you know that the moon must be a sphere? Because of its phases: the *causa cognoscendi*.

6 P. Vignaux, 'Nominalisme,' *Dictionnaire de théologie catholique* xi (21) 779.

Or, inversely, why must the moon go through these phases? Because it is a sphere: the *causa essendi.*

The syllogism also is the expression of the virtually unconditioned to be grasped in a judgment. But that grasp of the virtually unconditioned is an act of reflective intelligence. The syllogism itself is not evidence formally but simply materially. It puts into compact form the materials in which one can grasp the unconditioned. But unless there is a mind that grasps the unconditioned, there is no mind that is going to make a certain judgment as a result of that. And if one prescinds from any mind at all grasping the unconditioned and making a judgment in virtue of that grasp, if one expects the purely objective deductive process to mean something, one is overlooking the mind; one is in an extrinsicism.

That is the radical appearance of deductivist extrinsicism. But deductivist extrinsicism has a whole series of manifestations. In the earlier decades of this century a distinction was drawn by a number of theologians between faith of authority and scientific faith. There is faith that is a supernatural virtue, in which you assent to the mysteries on the authority of God. But there is also another faith you can demonstrate. What God has revealed is true. And the major premise is established in natural theology: God neither can deceive nor be deceived; he is infinitely perfect. The major is absolutely certain to natural human reason. God has revealed this: the Blessed Trinity, the Incarnation, whatever mystery you please. And the fact of revelation is settled in fundamental theology, prior to faith: the proof from the substantial accuracy of the scriptures, through the divine legate and the role of the church, is established from reason. Therefore, there is a rational proof that the mysteries are true. *Quod Deus revelat est verum. Deus hoc revelavit:* the Trinity, the Incarnation, whatever mystery you please. *Ergo hoc est verum.*[7] You have it demonstrated that the mysteries are true. And so there is a scientific faith as well as the faith of authority that you have with a religious act in which you accept the mysteries not because you have demonstrated that they must be true but because you assent to the authority of God.

Now this demonstration of the mysteries is simply an example of extrinsicism. The argument as it stands presupposes that besides the truths that are in minds there is also a truth that is objective: it is out there in the air. *Quod Deus revelat est verum: verum* – it is objectively true. And if one agrees with St Thomas that *bonum et malum sunt in rebus et verum et falsum sunt in mente,*[8]

7 'What God reveals is true. God has revealed this. Therefore this is true.'
8 'Good and evil are in things, true and false are in the mind.'

well you've distinguished that major premise, *quod Deus revelat est verum in mente divina, concedo; in mente humana, subdistinguo; credentis, concedo; non credentis, nego.*[9] If a person does not believe them, they are not truths in his mind. *Concedo minorem:* you do not have to appeal to the lack of evidence of the fact of revelation. This is one way to get around scientific faith: affirming the lack of evidence of the fact of revelation. *Concedo minorem: Deus hoc revelavit. Ergo, hoc est verum: in mente divina, concedo; in mente credentis, concedo; in mente non credentis, nego.*[10] When you make those distinctions, your scientific faith vanishes.

That argument is an illustration of extrinsicism. It is another form of it. The truths are out there. They are not in anybody's mind at all. In such a view, Thomas was all wrong when he said *verum et falsum sunt in mente.* They are objective, and objective means 'out there.'

Similarly, besides objective truths there are objective concepts. The right concept is not in anybody's mind; it is the right concept; it is the proper meaning of the word. When you get these right concepts, there is no room for evolution there: they do not move. So you have quite a problem with the development of dogma or the development of theology. It can only arise insofar as people are not forming the objective concepts that are out there and do not change.

Similarly, there is eliminated the more accurate enunciation of principles. If concepts are expressions of acts of understanding, then, as understanding develops, the concepts will become more precise, be more accurately conceived, and so on; and there is room for a historical development of ideas. As ideas develop, principles will be enunciated more fully, more accurately, with greater nuance. There is room for a historical development in the enunciation of principles; and similarly, there is room for a historical development in the conclusions that are drawn from the principles. But if the principles are objective and the concepts are objective, they are not in any minds that can move, and there is no room for them improving. This is a further illustration of extrinsicism. It makes the very possibility of the conception of a development of doctrine, of a positive theology, an impossibility.

Further, not only does the extrinsicist do himself harm, but he thinks that unless you hold, acknowledge, these concepts and truths and principles

---

9 'What God reveals is true: in the divine mind, yes; as for the human mind, well, yes, in the mind of the believer, but not in the mind of the unbeliever.'
10 'I concede the minor: God has revealed this. Therefore, this is true: in the divine mind, yes; in the mind of the believer, yes; in the mind of the unbeliever, no.'

and conclusions that are free from any development, unless you hold that they are the right ones as out there, you must be a relativist. And that view not only does not refute relativism – the relativists are not talking about concepts in nobody's mind; they are talking about the concepts that are in human minds and the principles that are in human minds, so it is no refutation of relativism to talk about these things that do not change – it also prevents any possibility of refuting relativism. To refute relativism, you have to talk about the things the relativists are talking about, namely, concepts that are in people's minds. And if you start doing that, the extrinsicist will say, 'You are a relativist, you are thinking about concepts that are in people's minds.' They do not do it quite as crudely as that, but that is there.

Another aspect of this extrinsicism is *the* proof. What is *the* proof for the existence of God? There is one right proof that is objective – or five of them. And they are out there. They are not in anybody's mind. They cannot improve. They cannot be understood more or less adequately, and so on.

But there are no concepts except in minds, no principles except in minds, no proofs except in minds, and so on. And it is extrinsicism to think of anything else.

2.3 *Operational Extrinsicism*

Besides the logical type of extrinsicism that is one way of evading the existence of my mind, of making out that it is of no importance, that my operations are of no importance, there is an operational extrinsicism. It is the same sort of thing, only instead of being based upon a knowledge of traditional logic, it has found new ways of evading the fact that I have a mind (where 'I' means not only my mind but everybody's).

To start talking about the processes of the mind to the operational extrinsicist is to obscure, to impede, to block, to destroy the objectivity of science. Science is not something that is in the particular mind of any man. It is the objective historical process. It develops. It is science with a capital *S*.

At the Philosophic Congress at Brussels in 1953, there was held a colloquy of logicians, people who are concerned with the foundations of mathematics, the foundations of science, symbolic logic. This particular meeting was not reported in the Acts, but it was reported the following year in the *Revue internationale de philosophie*. There are three main movements concerning the foundations of mathematics at the present time: (1) the axiomatic formalists, the Bourbaki school, centered more or less in Paris; (2) the intuitionist school, which is very small, led by Brouwer and centered in Holland; and

(3) the *Dialectica* group, around Gonseth, centered in Zürich. And at this meeting Gonseth was setting forth his view, namely, mathematics is something that develops by its interaction with general cultural movements; mathematics develops with developments in scientific fields, in philosophic fields, and so on. And Alfred Tarski, who has done rather brilliant work in symbolic logic and is quite a name in the field, got up and said that he could not find anything reasonable whatever in what Gonseth was saying – period. Gonseth got up and explained that Tarski might understand him this way and that, and there would be this answer, or this way and that, and there would be another answer, and so on – he was able to walk all around the matter – and Tarski got up again and said he could not see anything rational in what Gonseth was saying. And why couldn't he? Because for him 'rational' meant the objective manipulation of the symbols in symbolic logic. That is what rationality was for him. He was not articulate enough to say that, but to my mind that is the interpretation of his position.[11]

I gave another illustration of that the other night, talking about what they call material and formal implication.[12] Symbolic logic, in its fundamental form, has nothing equivalent to the proposition 'If ... then.' If A, then B: that just does not exist. It is a matter of mathematical combinations: either they are together or they are not together, and so on. It is based upon simply that. They call that formal implication. The nearest they have to 'If P, then Q' is 'Not P without Q.' If bananas grow on telegraph poles, Eisenhower is President of the United States. You cannot have the antecedent without the consequent. It is not a proper 'if ... then' proposition, but it is a proper CPQ type of proposition, to use the Polish notation.

Now there are symbolic logicians that will say that this meaning 'if ... then' that does not appear in their symbolism, since it does not appear in their symbolism, is something like the old conviction of a flat earth or the sun moving around the earth. It is just an ancient myth. It has nothing to do with logic as a science. What counts is the objective process; and in the objective process, in the symbolic logic that is most effective, you just have combinations. Therefore, 'if ... then' goes out of the picture. Logic is not something that has a norm in the nature of human intelligence and rationality. It is on its own.

11 Lonergan discusses this interchange in his 1957 lectures on mathematical logic. See Lonergan, *Phenomenology and Logic: The Boston College Lectures on Mathematical Logic and Existentialism*, ed. Philip J. McShane (Toronto: University of Toronto Press, 2001) 99–100. Note 20, p. 90, gives sources.
12 See the first discussion session, below, at p. 267.

Similarly, natural science often is conceived in a similar pragmatic fashion. I think I have already illustrated that. And at a further step, human science is scientific insofar as its methods are the same as those of natural science. So you study everything about man that you can measure or count. And anything that is specifically human is simply beyond the possibility of science. That is the naturalist tendency in human science.

Moreover, while the traditional German school of *Geisteswissenschaften* is not involved in that error, it can be involved in other errors. There is a recent quite profound book by Gadamer, *Wahrheit und Methode*.[13] It is mainly on hermeneutics, and he acknowledges the function of tradition in interpreting authors. I will have more to say about him later. But he points out that nineteenth-century history had such reliance upon objective techniques and methods that the historian could disregard his own historicity, his own development, his own background, and consequently head history into a relativism. Insofar as all historians forget their own role and rely entirely on an objective method that settles what is right and what is wrong – all objective criteria – the subjectivity of the historian is overlooked; and there is no means of dealing with that subjectivity. There are many histories of the same thing, and what is the right history? Well, there is no means of telling. Unless you have criteria that judge different subjectivities, your history cannot be objective; it is bound to be driven to a relativism.

The importance of such extrinsicism is that it exaggerates the point that science of the modern type is not certain but only probable. It is true that the positive achievements of modern science, whether natural or human,[14] are verified possibilities, not what must necessarily be so. But in fact, extrinsicism ignores not only the mind but also the judgment of the investigator; and if judgment is ignored then not only certitude but even known probability is eliminated. If, however, extrinsicism is rejected and the personal act in which we judge is restored to its place of honor, it becomes clear that not only probable judgments but also in many areas certain judgments can be made in the empirical sciences. First of all, outdated or superseded hypotheses and theories are rejected, not merely with probability but with certitude. It is quite certain that Aristotle's four elements are wrong. That is not probable. Again, it is certain that any future development has to take

---

13 Hans-Georg Gadamer, *Wahrheit und Methode: Grundzüge einer philosophischen Hermeneutik* (Tübingen: Mohr, 1960).
14 There is a brief break in the tape at this point. The material from here to 'It is quite certain' a few lines later is supplied mainly by reference to the notes that Lonergan distributed for these lectures.

into account present achievement; take, for example, chemistry, with its about 100 elements and about 300,000 compounds. They are linked and locked together through the most accurate measurements and weighing imaginable. It may be that the basic theory of the periodic table can be profoundly modified by developments in nuclear physics, studies of the atom, and so on, but any change in that periodic table will have to leave untouched the verified results of the relations between the elements and the compounds and of the compounds with one another – and there are an awful lot of relations between 300,000 compounds. There is a mass there that you may be able to modify here and there on particular points, but any future theory has to be able to cover that. And while you have to be a chemist to be able to say just what could be modified and what could not, there is room for judgment, for the exercise of wisdom, in that field, and those judgments can be certain.

When Einsteinian relativity replaced Newton's mechanics, it did not take long to arrive at the conclusion that there was no need to do their measurements again. There was nothing in relativity that would lead them to perform over again the experiments they had already performed. Relativity was simply a change in the theoretical structure. There is no difficulty about that judgment being certain. The experts in a field can make a number of judgments that are certain or of extremely high probability even though the status of the positive, dominant theory is ultimately one of probability. But to make those judgments is not a matter of appealing to objectified norms of a logic, a method, or anything like that. It is a matter of using native intelligence and rationality that have developed into a particular wisdom in that field.[15]

2.4 Metaphysical Extrinsicism

The third type of extrinsicism is metaphysical, and it is concerned with the 'thing in itself.' By common sense we know things in their relations to us, as they are related to our senses, to our appetites, to our feelings, to our interests, to our purposes. By science we know things in their relations to one another. For example, Aristotle has two definitions of the soul. One relates the soul to the body; the other relates the soul to vital activities. *Anima est actus primus corporis potentia vitam habentis*[16] defines the soul as form of the body. The

---

15 A break was taken at this point. The remainder of the lecture is recorded on Lauzon CD/MP3 310 (31000A0E060).

16 'The soul is the first act of a body that potentially has life.'

other one is *Anima est primum quo vivimus, sentimus, intelligimus.*[17] It defines the soul by its relation to operations. But the 'thing in itself' is related neither to us nor to other things; and it seems to be at best just an abstraction, and often an illegitimate abstraction. The soul, according to the Fifth Lateran Council, is essentially the form of the body. If you remove an essential property from your notion of something, you are talking about a contradiction in terms. But there is a type of extrinsicism that wants to be concerned solely with things in themselves: all the rest, that's of no importance; let's get the reality itself.

The same type of thing crops up when you start talking about distinctions. According to a very widespread definition, the real distinction is *ante omnem operationem mentis.*[18] It is not something you know with your mind: *ante omnem operationem mentis.* And if you do not know it, what are you talking about? You are talking about something you do not know when you are talking about a real distinction. It is the idea that the real is something out there all by itself, quite apart from any knower, and knowers know it without knowing it, somehow. It is a phenomenon that does not make sense when you reflect upon it. But it has an appeal to an extrinsicist tendency that wants to get away from the fact that we have minds and use them. That is the way to become objective: forget about having a mind.

The celebrated illustration of that notion of the real distinction is Scotus's proof of the *distinctio formalis* or the *nonidentitas formalis a parte rei.* Down the centuries it has been very difficult to find out what on earth that distinction that is neither real nor notional could be. But Scotus's proof of it is perfectly simple and completely cogent if you admit his premises. There is God the Father, and, *a parte rei, ante omnem mentis operationem,* there is some nonidentity – he distinguishes between paternity and divinity – and that distinction that is *a parte rei ante omnem mentis operationem* is the formal nonidentity *a parte rei,* the formal distinction *a parte rei.* And what is the proof that there has to be that formal nonidentity or that formal distinction? Well, if you do not have it, then when God the Father knows the Son, either the Son is God, and then he is seen as identical not only with divinity but also with paternity because *a parte rei* there is no distinction, or else he is seen as distinct from paternity, and then he cannot be God. On Scotus's presuppositions, that argument is unanswerable, whether it makes sense or not.

The only answer a Thomist can give is that there is no distinction whatever between the *divinum esse* and the *divinum intelligere.* The knowing and

17 'The soul is the principle by which we live, sense, understand.'
18 'before every operation of the mind'

the being are identical. They are one and the same. In *Summa theologiae*, 1, q. 16, a. 5, ad 2m, St Thomas says that truth is a similarity between the knowing and the object, except in God where, if you prescind from the trinitarian processions, where there is a certain similarity between the Son and the Father, and proceed only on the ordinary level upon which this discussion is being conducted, there is only an absence of dissimilarity.[19] Similarity would imply some duality, some distinction between the *esse* and the *intelligere;* and there is none. And because there is none, there is no possibility of having the *esse ante omnem mentis operationem.* Consequently, the presuppositions of this argument are eliminated.

The proper definition of a distinction is: *distincta sunt quorum unum non est aliud;* of a real distinction: *realiter distincta sunt quorum unum qua reale non est aliud qua reale;* of a notional distinction: *quorum conceptio unius non est conceptio alterius.*[20] Distinction is what is known through the negative comparative judgment. It is not a matter of looking now at this and then at that and seeing what is distinct *ante omnem mentis operationem.* Just as you know being by the true judgment *est,* so you know distinction by knowing the true judgments: *A est; B est; A non est B.* But you get away from true judgment into an extrinsicist metaphysics that wants to think about things in themselves in a manner that properly is simply an abstraction, prescinding from the relations both to us and to one another, and that can frequently be an illegitimate abstraction because it destroys the essence of a thing: those relations can be essential. There are a lot of fallacies connected with that, and they are indicated at the end of that section.[21]

2.5 *Intuitionist Extrinsicism*

There is an intuitionist extrinsicism, and its foundation is epistemological. Intuitionist extrinsicism meets the critical question, How can it be that an

19 'Et similiter dici potest similitudo principii veritas divina, inquantum eius esse non est suo intellectui dissimile.' Thomas Aquinas, *Summa theologiae*, 1, q. 16, a. 5, ad 2m.
20 'distinct: one is not the other ... really distinct: one as real is not the other as real ... notionally distinct: the conception of one is not the conception of the other.'
21 This is a reference again to the notes. The fallacies include confusing things with respect to themselves with things in themselves; falsely praising science because it knows things in themselves; falling into idealism when one realizes that things in themselves cannot be known and do not even exist; attempting to validate realism on the basis of arguing that things in themselves do exist and can be known; and conceiving metaphysics as the science of things in themselves.

object is known? What is the possibility of knowing an object? by saying that we know objects because we see them, perceive them, inspect them, intuit them, and unless we have something like seeing, perceiving, intuiting, inspecting, then there is no possibility of knowing an object. That is self-evident; that is the basic possibility of knowing an object.

What is meant by seeing, perceiving, inspecting, intuiting, gazing upon, contemplating? It is not using 'seeing' in the proper sense of ocular vision. It is using it in an analogous sense. The analogous sense is not based upon any psychological investigation to find out how much tasting is like seeing and how much it is different, how much judgment is like seeing and how much it is different. There is no need to bother about the psychological facts at all: this is an epistemological necessity. Either knowing is something like seeing or it cannot be knowing at all, because knowing, of its nature, is transcendent and the only possibility of transcendence is some type of seeing. Consequently, every cognitional act, if it is cognitional in the proper sense, if it is transcendent, must have some similarity to seeing, whether you can find out in what that similarity consists or not. The necessity that all knowing be something like seeing is an epistemological necessity.

Now, from that premise one can go in different directions. One can go with M. Gilson to an intuitive realism. I have a series of quotes at the bottom of p. 32 of the notes from his *Réalisme thomiste et critique de la connaissance*: 'The only realist answer to the question, at any level whatever you put it, "How does one know a thing exists?" is "by perceiving it"' (p. 208). On page 215 he comes back to the theme: Intellect sees the content of the concept of being in any sensible data whatever. You see the stick straight, and you see being in the straightness when it is out of the water, and you see being in the bentness when you see it in the water. 'By our senses we perceive the sensible, but intellect can *see* (italics his) being in the sensible' (p. 225). It is an application of the fundamental epistemological principle that if you know anything, then your knowing is some type of seeing. And, of course, what Gilson sees is reality.[22]

---

22 Lonergan read the quotations in French and then either translated them or commented on them. Here only his translations or comments are reported. For an extended discussion of Gilson's position in *Réalisme thomiste et critique de la connaissance* (Paris: Vrin, 1939; in English, San Francisco: Ignatius Press, 1987) see Bernard Lonergan, 'Metaphysics as Horizon,' in *Collection*, vol. 4 in Collected Works of Bernard Lonergan, ed. Frederick E. Crowe and Robert M. Doran (Toronto: University of Toronto Press, 1988) 192–203. The Kantian position discussed in the next several paragraphs is also addressed in these same sections from 'Metaphysics as Horizon.'

Now in Kant, you have exactly the same principle, except that what Kant sees is appearance. In his Transcendental Aesthetic, 'In whatever manner and by whatever means an act of knowledge can be related to objects, still the manner in which it is related immediately to objects and the goal towards which all thinking as a mere means tends is *Anschauung*, taking a look.' *Anschauungen und Begriffen*, acts of looking and concepts, are the elements in all our knowing. All our knowing reduces to looks and to concepts. The thoughts, the concepts, without the content obtained from the look, are empty. Looking without the concepts is blind. But this is incidental. It just makes his enumeration complete. There are concepts and there are acts of looking. Judgment is not immediate knowledge of any object. If it is conjoined with an *Anschauung*, with a looking, then it mediately is referred to an object, namely, by adding on the look. Of itself, it is just thinking; it is in a purely logical order. Of itself, it is a representation of a representation. Your primary representation is given in the looking. And you get a secondary, mediated representation of the thing when you move to the judgment. It is the looking by which you are immediately related to the object. The judgment is related to the object only mediately.

What Kant calls the ideas of reason are at a further remove. Of themselves they have no relation to objects whatever. They are related to objects insofar as their field of application is the understanding with its concepts and judgments. The concepts and judgments, when used empirically, are conjoined with acts of looking.

The conclusion Kant draws is that, since the objects of our looking are appearances, then our judgments, even when valid, can have only a phenomenal validity. Further, the idea of reason, the native tendency of the mind by which it is *potens omnia facere et fieri*, the soul – *anima est quodammodo omnia* – that basic tendency of all intelligence and rationality towards everything, not merely towards appearance but also towards reality, must be a transcendental illusion.

You can proceed, then, from the basic assumption that knowing, to be knowing, must be looking, either to Gilson's position, in which you look at being, you see reality, or to Kant's, in which you look at appearance and your operations, even when valid, have no more than a phenomenal validity. There is a common premise to both positions, namely, the epistemological position that knowing essentially is a matter of taking a look.

Now what is the value of that common premise? It is this: knowing, if it is going to be imagined as transcendent, has to be *imagined* as a sort of looking. That is true. You cannot imagine knowing as transcendent without introducing some similarity to looking. If knowledge is transcendent, the knowing and the known are distinct: one is not the other. And how are you going to imagine the knowing being distinct from the known and yet knowing it? You will imagine something like looking.

But the necessity of imagination is just the necessity of mythic thinking, and nothing more than that. There is no necessity of transcendence being imagined. Transcendence can be something purely rational, and de facto that is what it is. How is it that our knowing is of the distinct? Fundamentally, because our knowing attains an absolute, because it attains an unconditioned. The judgment rests upon an unconditioned, a virtually unconditioned, that is, a conditioned that has all its conditions fulfilled. You attain an absolute when you affirm truly of anything, 'It is.'

Because you attain an unconditioned you attain what has no conditions in the subject. When you say that something is, you do not mean: that is the way it appears to be; that is what I think; that is what seems to me; that is what probably is so; that is the way I feel about it. When you say, 'It is,' you exclude all of those. You have entered into an absolute realm, the absolute realm of being. And you arrive at a real distinction by affirming the existence of A and the existence of B and by denying: A is not B. The microphone is; I am; I am not the microphone. The real distinction between subject and object is a matter of rational judgment. And because it is a matter of rational judgment, and because rational judgment is not something to be imagined, transcendence is not something to be imagined.

The difference between a discursive and an intuitive realism is that the intuitive realist accepts Kant's major premise and denies his minor premise while the discursive realist rejects both Kant's major premise and his minor premise. The intuitive realist agrees with Kant that there cannot be an immediate relation to an object except by an intuition in some meaning of the word 'intuition' that is analogous to ocular vision. But he disagrees with Kant's premise that what we see, what we look at, are appearances. The discursive realist rejects this notion that what we see are appearances. This is something that Kant took over from the tradition stemming from Galileo. The objects of experience are data; they are given. They are not appearances. They become appearances only by adding on the judgment, 'It seems,' 'It is not, but it seems.' You get the notion of appearance on the level of judgment, not on the level of sense. The discursive realist also rejects Kant's major premise: knowing essentially and fundamentally is a matter of looking. The discursive realist does not see any necessity that for God the Father to know Himself he has to be the object *ante omnem operationem mentis,* at least insofar as we consider it, and then have an act that takes the look. If you want to imagine knowledge and to imagine transcendence, then no doubt you have to do that. But the only necessity of doing that is mythic consciousness, which not merely uses symbols but in the symbols finds the essences of things, the essence of knowing. When I look at my hand, I see something distinct that is out there. The distance between my hand and my eye is obvious. There is an obvious representation of transcendence. If the essence of transcendence is to be found in that representation, then necessarily every cognitional act has to be something like taking a look. But there is no necessity of that being the essence of transcendence, and there is no proof that it is. Transcendence de facto arises: we are in immediate relation to objects when we make true judgments. And there is no proof that making a true judgment is something like taking a look. It is a rational act, rationally necessitated by grasping the sufficiency of the evidence, grasping the unconditioned. If you have grasped the unconditioned, you have reached what is independent of everything else, and therefore independent of the subject. The unconditioned has no outstanding conditions; and because it has no outstanding conditions, it has no outstanding conditions in the subject. If it has no outstanding conditions in the subject, it is independent of the subject.

The importance of rejecting that intuitive realism from the viewpoint of a methodology is paramount. If your epistemology at its root is myth, you have to go into all sorts of fictions and fabrications to make everything else coherent with your myth. You cannot think of human intellect as one and the same thing as human intelligence because there is very little similarity between intelligence and looking. Seeing an object does not develop the way understanding an object develops. There are all sorts of dissimilarities. If you try to assimilate intellect to seeing, you will be left with an intellect that is not intelligent. If you try to assimilate rationality to seeing, your assimilation will be a fabrication; and you will have missed out on what rationality really is. And when you have substituted a set of fabrications for the mind God gave you, you will not be able to proceed methodically, where 'method' means knowing exactly what your operations are and what they imply.

So much for extrinsicism. The dividing line lies in the true judgment. And one can get away from the middle position either by falling over into an extrinsicism that forgets about the mind and precludes the possibility of correct method or by falling on the other side of the line. In the latter case, one is in an immanentism.

3 Immanentism

3.1 The Root of Immanentism

The door to immanentism is, of course, the critical exigence. Philosophical and theological theories are built up, and disputes are endless. The critical exigence is an attempt to cut them short by demanding that people do not talk about what they cannot know. If you are talking about something you cannot know, well, you are talking about something you do not know. If you are talking about something you do not know, you are wasting not only your own time but other peoples'. You eliminate an extremely large area of controversy and obscurity by confining yourself to issues the answers to which can be known. That is a very rational and apparently very simple proposal, and very efficacious, too. But it can land one into a set of problems where the probability that one will solve them is extremely slight.

To say what one can know and can't know, and so to meet the critical exigence, involves both psychological knowledge and epistemological knowledge. It involves psychological knowledge: what are the facts concerning human cognitional activities? And it involves epistemological knowledge: how can facts of such a kind result in one's knowing anything whatever?

Now those two questions are interdependent. If you go about the business, you will want to be able to know something. And it is very difficult to accept the psychological facts unless one knows what the real epistemological solution is and one is convinced of its truth. If one has hold of the epistemological solution, one is not afraid to face the facts in all their details and in all their implications because one still sees how that can be knowing. However, if one does not know yet what the epistemological solution is, one will be afraid all the time one is making one's psychological investigation, and one will be pushing things to one's imperfect epistemological solution. It will be extremely difficult to arrive at a knowledge of what the cognitional facts are. To arrive at the psychology, one really needs to have the epistemological solution beforehand.

But the opposite is also true. To arrive at the epistemological solution, you have to know what the psychological facts are. The epistemological solution is not something that stands all by itself and that you can grasp and get hold of without knowing exactly what the facts are, because the epistemological solution emerges from adequate knowledge of the facts.

So one is faced with the type of problem that either one solves the whole thing in one giant stride, which cannot be done very well, or else one is boxed in. And that is at the root of immanentism.

For example, insofar as Kant accepted the epistemological principle that our knowledge is related directly to objects only through *Anschauung*, it was extremely difficult for him to get beyond an immanentism, because the more you study human intelligence the less similarity you find in it to anything like seeing. And the more you know about human rationality still less is it like seeing. And since they are not like seeing, then they are immanent. It is something that goes on in the subject. Kant did not have a very good knowledge of the psychological facts. He conceived judgment as an operation of understanding, for example. And there are other things that are wrong with his psychology. But still, you can improve on Kant's psychology, but unless you remove that fundamental 'jigger' on the possibility of objectivity, you are not going to get beyond his position. Karl Jaspers knows a lot more psychology than Kant, but he is not an inch beyond Kant. Although he calls himself an existentialist, he is fundamentally Kantian.

3.2 *Breaking Immanentism*

To break immanentism, the fundamental step is grasping the nature of judgment as an absolute positing and the significance of judgment as resting on an unconditioned. Once judgment rests upon an unconditioned, then it rests upon something that is not conditioned by the subject, something that is independent of the subject, something that is in an absolute order. And that is what transcendence means, fundamentally; that is the basic meaning of transcendence. Transcendence in terms of knowing an object distinct from the subject is a type of transcendence that is not had in God's knowledge of himself. God's knowledge of himself is not knowing something distinct from the knowing. The knowing and the being are one and the same. But in any other instance of knowledge there is the distinction, but that distinction is known just as any other distinction is known: *A* and *B* are really distinct if *A* as real is not *B* as real, if the reality of *A* is not the reality of *B*. Knowing real distinction is on the level of judgment. And, of course, it is the discursive realist that conceives the real distinction in terms of the comparative negative judgment. The intuitive realist, if he wants to talk about real distinctions, talks about something that is there *ante omnem operationem mentis.*

Moreover, I have said that the difficulty of meeting the critical exigence is that epistemology and psychology are interdependent. You can know one only if you already know the other. And it is true both ways. It makes it a particularly nasty sort of problem. But it is also true that metaphysics has to be simultaneous with the other two. What you really need to meet the critical exigence is the simultaneous achievement of a psychology, an epistemology, and a metaphysics.

That significance of judgment as an act of rationality, not an act of understanding (a point missed by Kant), is totally missing in the idealist tradition such as is represented by Hegel. For Hegel, judgment is simply the compounding of concepts, putting them together, synthesis. That Hegel and Kant are immanentists there is no doubt.

3.3 Contemporary Immanentisms

There are at the present time two different streams, both of which are immanentist but have the false appearance of being realist.

The first consists in the appeal to experience. What is the reality of religion, the reality of God? It is that my religious experience is just as real to me as my experience in eating my meal. It is on the level of experience. And most people will spontaneously feel, 'Well, at least he's a realist.' But it does not follow at all. What follows most directly from that is Modernism. For this position judgments are just symbols, and you can change those symbols when they are not evoking the proper feelings, the proper experiences.

H.D. Lewis in 1959 published *Our Experience of God.*[23] The question is whether we in some fashion experience God, not whether the judgment 'God exists' is true. People very easily feel that if you talk about the truth of the judgment 'God exists,' you are quite unhelpful. You are interested in some sort of medieval metaphysical debate. But if you talk about our experience of God, you are really helping souls and bringing them to God. Well, there is a sense in which that is true, but that sense is not a sense that will provide a basis for a sound theology. It is a sense that will provide a basis for the destruction of all theology, as was the case in modernism.

The second type of immanentism that can be easily mistaken for a realism is the existentialist-phenomenological trend. The phenomenologist, the existentialist, is concerned to let the object appear, let the object reveal itself, let the object make itself known; and he does an awful lot of talking about that. And everyone will say, 'He's a realist.' When Husserl's books were first coming to attention, it was thought he was realist. Heidegger, by raising the metaphysical question, a question that had not been raised for a considerable time, was again thought to be heading towards realism. Well,

23 H.D. Lewis, *Our Experience of God* (New York: Macmillan, 1959).

he still is heading, and maybe towards realism. But insofar as people are basing their thought, their theology, their exegesis on letting the object reveal itself, they want experience and they want understanding, too. They are a step ahead of the purely experiential, empiricist type of thinking. They include the activity of intelligence. But Heidegger's attempt towards a *Fundamentalontologie* and any similar attempt is never more than a transcendence within immanence, if there is no acknowledgment of the significance of true judgment and the basing of metaphysics on true judgment in any part of the strictly phenomenological or existential movement. They talk about ontology, but what they mean by an ontology is the thing as revealing itself and especially the thing as revealing to me a possibility of my being a man, of human existence. And while they talk about the ontic and the ontological, it is an ontic and an ontological that has not escaped from within the limitations of immanence.

The fundamental division, then, as I see it, is between extrinsicism on the one hand and immanentism on the other. And the central line is along the words of the Sermon on the Mount: 'Sit sermo vester "Est, est et non, non,"'[24] and the classical formula of the councils of the church: 'Si quis dixerit ..., anathema sit.'[25] What counts is the true judgment, and to maintain that central line, the dogmatic line and the evangelical line, one can almost say, one has to be between extrinsicism on the one hand and immanentism on the other.

With those deviations excluded, we have a unity in all human knowledge, because human knowledge is a matter of answering questions. Saying 'est, est' or 'non, non' is answering a question, whether it is so. St Thomas spent an awful lot of time and covered a very large number of pages answering *utrum.* What is human knowing and, in particular, what is theological knowing? It is answering the questions, *quid sit?* what do you mean? and *utrum sit?* is it so? And the whole of human knowing, if human knowing is achieved in the act of judgment, is the activity that leads to the answers to questions. Raising and answering questions is not the verbalism that Scholasticism usually appears to be to the English-speaking mind. It is expressing in its most direct form human cognitional activity.

By that reduction of everything to the answering of questions, since the question *quid sit?* does not settle a priori whether the answer is going to be an absolute necessity or an empirical intelligibility, whether that intelligibility is

24 Matthew 5.36: 'Let your word be "Yes, yes, and No, no."'
25 'If anyone says ..., let him be anathema.'

found in the unchangeable or in the changing, whether it is like a classical law and the per se or a statistical law and the *per accidens*, one has a fundamental approach that is capable of including along with the ancient ideal of science also what can be learned from the modern achievement of science. One brings together both types of science by proceeding to something that is preconceptual, namely, the questions that arise and lead to the acts of understanding and the formation of concepts. To put together the changing and the changeless within a single view, one must go behind both – they are contradictory. And similarly, the absolute necessity and the empirical intelligibility come together insofar as one is asking for any intelligibility; and that is at the level of the question.[26]

26 Lonergan concluded with, 'There is a final point I want to make, but I'm afraid I haven't got time.' The material in the 'Review' at the beginning of the next lecture may be what he intended to add at the end of this one. The third question-and-answer session was held later on this day. See below, pp. 303–25.

1962-6

Knowing, Believing, and Theology[1]

1 Clarifications of Cognitional Theory

1.1 The Preconceptual and the Unity of the Ancient and Modern Ideals of Science

We begin with a twofold point.[2] We can handle within the same science the necessary and the empirically intelligible, the universal and the imaginative scheme which approaches the singular, the changeable and the unchanging, the *per se* and the *per accidens*, insofar as we go behind the conceptual order. Within the conceptual order those terms are contradictory. But prior to conceiving, there is the act of understanding, and prior to the act of understanding, there is the state of mind that is expressed in the question. When it is expressed in the question, one has concepts. But the prior state of mind itself is not a set of words or a set of concepts. It is the *admiratio* of which Aristotle speaks, the *thaumazein* that is the beginning of all science and philosophy. Consequently, one can unify the ancient ideal of science with elements from the modern achievement insofar as one simply takes a step back from the conceptual to the preconceptual. And, of course, there

1 Monday, 16 July 1962, Lauzon CD/MP3 311 (31100A0E060) and 312 (31200A0E060). Lonergan began by referring to pages in the notes that corresponded to the material he is addressing in this review, indicating that it is a summary of what has already been covered.
2 The twofold point would seem to be (1) the need to go behind the conceptual to the preconceptual order and (2) the integration that this allows of the ancient and modern ideals of science.

is plenty of room for that within the Thomist theory of knowledge, which acknowledges an *intellectus agens*, sense, phantasm, possible intellect in which there are impressed species, acts of understanding which are expressed in *verba incomplexa*, definitions, and are followed up by reflective acts of understanding which are expressed in *verba complexa, compositio vel divisio per affirmationem vel negationem.*

The elements that have a psychological meaning, elements immediately given in consciousness are (1) states of inquiry and reflection – one is wondering what it is, one is reflecting whether it is so; (2) images and sensible data; (3) acts of understanding – when you understand something you feel a bit of a thrill if it is something big, and the feeling is very slight if it is not; (4) conceptions; (5) reflective acts of understanding, grasping the unconditioned; and (6) judgments. They all occur in consciousness. They are immediate data of consciousness.

There are the *species intelligibilis*, the *species qua*, and in a later terminology the *species impressa*. St Thomas does not explicitly distinguish between *species impressa* and *expressa*. The *species impressa* he calls *species intelligibilis*; and the *species expressa* he calls *verbum*. The *species impressa* is known only by metaphysical analysis. Acts of understanding, insights, are not understanding everything about everything. They are limited, a limited *actus, de se delimitatus*. It requires a specific limitation to be understanding this sort of thing: understanding mathematics, understanding the first proposition in Euclid's *Elements*. And again, the *intellectus possibilis* is the possibility, the potency, for the genus of all intellectual acts. The *species intelligibilis* and the *intellectus possibilis* are not data of consciousness but conclusions from data of consciousness, just as the capacity to imagine, the existence of a sense as distinct from sensation, are conclusions from data.

1.2 Thomist and Scotist Analysis

I was asked to contrast the Thomist with the Scotist analysis. The Scotist analysis is understood if you begin from a book on logic in which the first chapter deals with terms or concepts, the second with propositions or judgments, and the third with syllogisms or reasoning. If you simply consider that, then what is the mind? Scotus distinguishes the *potentia intellectiva* from sense and from imagination. As far as I know, he does not want to distinguish between the *potentia intellectiva* as *agens vel patiens* – at least there is the *potentia intellectiva*. From the phantasm there is impressed upon intellect what he calls the *species intelligibilis*; and that is a meaning, a content of meaning that corresponds to the content of a concept as does Thomas's *verbum*. The *species intelligibilis* corresponds for Scotus to a concept, to a word, to the meaning of a word in Thomas.

The act of understanding is grasp of a form. For example, the people who for centuries knew that Euclid's first proposition was right but had no formulation of why it was right had the act of understanding but did not have any adequate conceptualization. That act of understanding that is prior to the concept is not grasp of a concept. It is an act of understanding of an intelligibility in sensible data, of the form that fits in those data. But for Scotus there is produced in the intellect the *species impressa*, the *species intelligibilis*, which is not the Thomist *species impressa* but *expressa*, the *verbum*. And then there follows the act of seeing the *species*, knowing the *species*, and that is produced concurrently by the object (the *species*) and by the faculty. He has his *concausae*. Scotus solves the difficulty of the question, Is it the object or the faculty that produces the act? Scotus says it is both. If the object is extremely excellent, as in the beatific vision, then the object causes most of the act, and the faculty hardly causes anything. On the other hand, if the object is a very minor thing, then the faculty is more of a cause than the object. Then phantasm can produce another *species*, and you will see that. The act is produced partly by the object and partly by the faculty. And you can have a further act that compares the two *species*, and then you get the grasp of nexus, of compossibility or incompossibility.

On that analysis the preconceptual part of the Thomist analysis is dropped out. It is preconceptual, and so it does not fit into the picture. However, it is an extremely simple analysis, and Thomas can be interpreted as though his psychology were the same as Scotus's. You have sense, agent intellect, phantasm, possible intellect. There is impressed a *species intelligibilis*, which produces a concept. First, there is *intelligere* as producing: while the concept has not yet been produced, *intelligere* is production. Once it is produced, then it is looking at the concept. There tends to be a confusion between *conversio ad phantasma* and *reflexio ad phantasma*. The two have quite different meanings in Thomas. *Reflexio ad phantasma* is to know the singularity of what you already know as universal. *Conversio ad phantasma* is the necessity of any faculty being applied to its object. Unless sight converts to color you see nothing; you see nothing unless you open your eyes. Similarly, unless possible intellect is directed towards the phantasm, you have no possibility of understanding anything whatsoever – not merely knowing the singularity of a universal you already know, which is a *reflexio ad phantasma*; you cannot understand anything at all without the *conversio ad phantasma*. In this case, the *species intelligibilis* is the form that makes the *intellectus possibilis* an *intellectus in actu*. And when the *intellectus possibilis* is informed by the *species*, in *actu*, in act, it acts, it produces the *verbum* and then looks at it. In that way you get a psychology that is the same as Scotus's, and the difference between Thomas and Scotus is in the metaphysical analysis.

Also, you will note that this proceeding of the *verbum* from the *species* is something that is unconscious. You have no intellectual act whatever until you have a concept, nothing conscious in intellect until you have a concept. Consequently, the *emanatio intelligibilis* of the *verbum* from the intellect in act cannot be an intelligent process, a rational process. There can be no psychological analogy for the Trinity. It can only be metaphysical. And so, you can arrive at Billot's view that the imagination is just as good an illustration of the trinitarian processions as is the intellect.[3] If it is just as good an illustration there is no reason for saying with St Thomas that the *imago Dei* is found only in man and only in the rational part of man.

From that comparison we come back to our material.

1.3 Notion, Concept, Knowledge, and Idea of Being

The principle of all inquiry and reflection is the agent intellect. It is the fundamental *intentio entis intendens*. There is a distinction between *intentio intendens* and *intentio intenta*. Your *verba* can be *intentiones intentae*, but the *intentio intendens*, the *pensée pensante*, is something different. Since one asks questions about absolutely everything without limit, the goal of the agent intellect is *ens*. What is about everything is about being. That is what I call the notion of being in *Insight*.[4]

Every concept is at least implicitly a concept of being. Concept is not the same as notion. Notion is the universal drive, the universal desire of intellect heading for everything and, consequently, intending *ens*. The concept of being is any concept whatever insofar as it is referred to the judgment and through the judgment to being as known. You conceive, define, form a hypothesis, in order to make a judgment. Intellect spontaneously by its rationality goes beyond every concept and heads towards a judgment about the concept: is it so? Every concept is related to *esse*. Insofar as every concept is related to *esse*, it is a concept of *ens*: *ens est id cui suo modo competit esse*. Everything that is conceived is somehow related to *esse* because everything

3 See Lonergan, *Verbum* 11, note 11.
4 See Lonergan, *Insight*, chapter 12.

that is conceived is conceived in order to be judged, and what is known in the judgment is *esse*. The judgment is absolute positing: *est/non est*. It's the point where being becomes known. So, we have notion of being, concept of being, knowledge of being in the judgment and, finally, the idea of being: understanding everything about everything is the divine act of understanding. The divine essence is *eminenter*, containing absolutely everything possible and actual.

1.4 Knowing Is a Compound

There is an ambiguity in the word 'know.' You can say that the dog knows his master – animal knowing. You can use the word 'know' as expressing the common element in every cognitional act: seeing is knowing; imagining is knowing; understanding is knowing; conceiving is knowing; grasping the unconditioned is knowing; making a judgment is knowing. There is something common to all of them, and that common element is called knowing. And that usage of the word 'know' is the favorite usage of the word 'know' when you have as your epistemological theorem: every act if it is cognitional must be like taking a look. The common element in every cognitional act is that is has some similarity to taking a look.

The third meaning of the word 'know' is knowing in the proper human sense. And in that case knowing is a compound. The proper object of human knowledge in this life is *quidditas sive natura in materia corporali existens*. But you know the corporeal matter by sense, the *quidditas sive natura* by understanding, and the *existens* by judgment. All three – experience, understanding, and judgment – combine to give one act of knowing; and that is knowing in the strong sense. Knowing is composite.

In that case you use the word 'know' the way the word 'thing' is used in metaphysics. Prime matter is not a thing; it is an *ens quo*. Material substantial form is not a thing; it is an *ens quo*. *Esse*, existence, is not a thing; it is an *ens quo*. When you have all three, you have one thing. And that one thing is not compounded of three things but of three components. Similarly, 'know' in that strong sense, that last sense, is not sensing, not understanding, not judging. It is only when all three are combined that you have one instance of knowing.

1.5 Self-consciousness and Self-knowledge

Now that composite, that strong sense of 'know,' brings out the difference between self-consciousness and self-knowledge. We are conscious of ourselves in all our activities. But that consciousness is merely on the level of experience. It is a matter of data. There is empirical consciousness insofar as we sense; intellectual consciousness insofar as we try to understand and do understand and conceive; rational consciousness insofar as we reflect, grasp the unconditioned, judge; rational self-consciousness insofar as the judgment is a judgment of value, and we deliberate and choose and act.

Consciousness has its levels, but they are all on the level of experience. It is the experience of the subject, the subject's presence to himself; and everyone has that presence to himself. But not everyone understands himself. Not everyone knows himself. To understand oneself, one has to go beyond the data of consciousness, perform acts of understanding with respect to them, line them up, relate them to one another as in this metaphysical-psychological scheme in the writings of St Thomas, or some other; the scheme is purely psychological as in *Insight*, at least until we get to metaphysics about chapter 15. Finally, one has to make the judgment, 'I am a knower,' or whatever judgments there are to be made about oneself.

That difference between self-consciousness and self-knowledge comes out clearly when one thinks of knowing in the third sense: human knowing as something compounded. Similarly, an immanentist philosophy can be fully aware of all the data of consciousness and understand them; but insofar as it does not grasp the significance of judgment and the fact that metaphysics depends upon the judgment, that transcendence comes with the judgment, it will be locked inside; it will be immanentist. There will be an awful lot of knowledge of the subject. It can be extended more or less illegitimately to other subjects, as in absolute idealism. It can be completely understood. But if the significance of judgment is lacking, one is locked in an immanentist philosophy whether of the idealist or the existentialist type.

1.6 The Unity of Human Knowledge

The mere fact that one says that the goal of all effort to understand, the goal of all reflection, is being, that every concept by the mere fact that it is related to a judgment – we form concepts in order to judge – is also related to *esse* and, consequently, is at least implicitly a concept of being, that mere fact gives a basic unity to the whole of human knowledge. While that basic unity may seem very small, not to have it is disastrous. The illustration of that is Max Scheler and the numerous people who more or less consciously or almost unconsciously depend upon Scheler. Scheler worked out specialized forms of knowing with regard to values, with regard to religion, with regard to persons, with regard to reality, with regard to science. Insofar as

you consider in each case what is specific to those different forms of knowledge, you get different fields. And insofar as those different fields are not
united by the common element that they are all concerned with being, the
fields are unrelated and incapable of any unification. When people say,
'God is not an object,' they are talking Scheler.

What is the apprehension of value for Scheler? It is the intentional element in an affective act. Positive values are apprehended insofar as you are
loving; negative insofar as you are hating. And it is the intentional element
in love and in hate that grounds the apprehension of value. He worked this
out in beautiful detail.

The religious object is known by considering the religious acts, liturgical
acts, acts of prayer. By a detailed phenomenological study of those acts, he
presents the field of the religious.

The field of the personal is the field of cooperation. One knows another
person by working with him, by collaborating with him, by carrying on the
same task with him. Insofar as two or many gather together and are engaged in the same task, they come to know one another. Personal knowledge is of that type. God is a person. We know God insofar as we are
collaborating with God in the work of the universe, and it makes much
more specific and concrete our knowledge of God to attend to that.

The difficulty with Scheler is not his detailed additions. It is the lack of
any unifying principle, and the result in Scheler was that while he was a
Catholic, or almost a Catholic, when he wrote for example *Vom Ewigen im
Menschen*,[5] still in the last ten years or so of his life he dropped any acknowledgment of Catholicism whatever and ended up with a radical dualism, an
irrationality, the first principle and ground of irrationality. And the root of
that difficulty lay in multiple spheres unrelated to one another in any fundamental way. I refer you to a study of Scheler and his influence on Catholic
philosophy of religion by Heinrich Fries.[6]

1.7 The Compound Notion of Human Knowing and Metaphysics

The compound notion of human knowledge reveals the analogy between
human knowledge and metaphysics. As the knowing is compounded of

---

5 Max Scheler, *Vom Ewigen im Menschen* (Bern: Francke, 1954).
6 Lonergan's exact words were, 'I note that study of Scheler ...,' referring to
   his notes, p. 37. The book to which he refers is Heinrich Fries, *Die katholische
   Religionsphilosophie der Gegenwart* (see above, p. 86 note 7).

experiencing, understanding, and judging, so the proportionate object is a compound of potency, form, and act: in the substantial order, prime matter, substantial form, existence; and in the accidental order, eye, sight, seeing; possible intellect, *species intelligibilis*, act of understanding; the will as a faculty, the will as habit, the will as act; will, willingness, willing.

That triadic division in the object corresponds to, is analogous to, is isomorphic with, the triadic division in the knowing, and necessarily so. When science reaches its ultimate goal of explaining all phenomena, what will it consist in? It will be a theory verified in endless instances. Because there are endless instances, you have matter, potency. Because you have a theory, something corresponding to understanding, you have form. Insofar as you have verification, you have judgment and existence of what is known by the theory.

It is also important to grasp that the difference between Aristotle and Plato in proceeding beyond this world is precisely that Plato proceeded fundamentally in terms of concepts, of objects, while Aristotle proceeded in terms not only of the object but also of the subject. The Aristotelian *substantia separata* is reached from the act of insight. We cannot understand anything without having at least an image that we ask about, that we try to understand, and in which we grasp intelligible form, intelligible species. But the *substantia separata* has no senses. Its proper object is not a material object. Its understanding cannot be of that type. Because it has no senses, it cannot be grasping intelligibility in the sensible. How can there then be a *substantia separata?* You have Aristotle's fundamental remark: *in his quae sunt sine materia idem est intelligens et intellectum;* in the immaterial order one and the same is what understands and what is understood. It is because our intellects need conversion to sense that they are understanding of forms in imaginable or sensible matter. And, on the other hand, because the *substantia separata* or the Thomist angel has no body, no senses, and deals with other spirits, its understanding not only is identical with itself but it is also its own object.

That is something quite different from the Platonic procedure from the concept to the idea. The Platonic ideas are just objects or perhaps just norms; they are not knowing. According to Plato, knowing is a *passio,* and the first cannot be suffering from something prior to it. Consequently, the celestial or intelligible order for Plato is just of objects, just ideas. Aristotle proceeds, and St Thomas too, not only from the side of the object, but also from the side of the subject. In St Thomas, God is *ipsum esse,* but he is also *ipsum intelligere,* and the two are the same. And the Aristotelian identity of understander and understood is insisted upon; see, for example, *Summa theologiae,* 1, q. 14, a. 2.

The fact that one proceeds in that fashion eliminates certain difficulties that are raised about the analogy of *ens* in proving the existence of God. Have you got an analogy when, starting from a compound of essence and existence, you proceed to the infinite point where there is no distinction between essence and existence? Do you not eliminate your analogy? You have difficulties, I think, in that procedure if you merely think of the object. But if you are proceeding from the finite act of understanding to the infinite act of understanding, those difficulties are eliminated However, that's a rather complex question.

2   Assembling the Elements

We now have to start again, putting together the elements we have seen.[7] We started off from the notion of operations and grouping of operations, and we found that the grouping hit limits. We had to distinguish the world of community (common sense, the visible universe), the world of theory, the world of interiority, and what they all mediate, the ultimate, the sacred, God. Now, having done something about the problem of what science theology is analogous to, we want to put this together and distinguish theological operations from all other operations.

2.1   The Systematic Exigence and the World of Theory

The first distinction is between the world of community and the world of theory.

The world of community is the world of common sense, and common sense is the specialization of human intelligence with regard to the concrete, the practical, the immediate, the tasks of human living. It is characterized by an absence of any drive to universal definitions. According to Aristotle's *Metaphysics*, in Book M, while Democritus and the Pythagoreans introduced a few definitions, still Socrates was the first one to make a business of it, to want universal definitions of everything. And of course, or at

---

7 Lonergan reads in Latin a statement on p. 38 of the notes that can be translated as follows: 'Given the unity both metaphysical on the side of the object and methodological on the side of cognitive operations, we proceed now to distinctions within this unity, distinguishing between common sense (= ordinary understanding), natural sciences, philosophy, faith, theology, positive theology, and systematic theology.'

least it appears, he did not know them. But he convinced the Athenians also that they did not know what fortitude was, what cowardice was, and so on. That is, they knew perfectly well what they were, but they were not able to give universal definitions. There is the systematic exigence that moves from the world of common sense to the world of theory. One can define the virtues when one sets up a system, as Aristotle did, distinguishing potencies and habits, habits that are entitative and operative, operative habits that are good and bad. The good operative habits are the virtues, and the bad ones are the vices. But you need a whole systematic analysis of human psychology and human activity to do that. That is just what the Athenians did not have when Socrates was asking them what the virtues are.

That seeking of universal definitions drives one towards setting up a system. If the man of common sense goes to work or is driven to work by an inquirer such as Socrates was, then sooner or later he finds himself with a system. It is the only way in which he can give coherent answers to all the questions that are raised. If you ask just about one virtue, you may get away with some sort of a satisfactory definition, but it will be with difficulty. And there is no reason why questions about the others should not be put. The total range of questions is met only by a systematic basis that provides the possibility of definition and distinction and theorem with regard to the total set of questions. That is the exigence for system, moving from the world of community, common sense, the visible universe, to the world of theory. That process from the world of common sense to the world of theory involves the reversal from the *priora quoad nos* to the *priora quoad se*, to the systematically conceived basic terms.

In that process there are effected several differences. There is the differentiation of the scientist from the man of common sense: the scientist stands to the man of common sense as Thales to the milkmaid. In his consciousness knowing is not just a part, not just a human function. It takes over, and everything else in consciousness is subordinated to the end of knowing. It is a new technique of consciousness on the side of the subject. It is a new language, a new set of concepts, on the side of the object. And because you have new subjects and new objects, you also have a new world: the difference between Eddington's two tables, the table he saw and could put his hands on and rest on, found solid, and the table compounded of a very large number of invisible electrons and protons that, if they were put side by side, would not fill a small part in a matchbox – the world of common sense and the world of theory.

2.2   *The Critical Exigence and the World of Interiority*

Besides the systematic exigence that moves from the world of common sense to the world of theory, there is the critical exigence that moves from the world of theory to the world of interiority.

The critical exigence is: don't talk about what you don't know, and much less don't talk about what you can't know. It raises the question of knowledge for a specific purpose: to clear out from the world of theory the bluffers and the guessers. The critical exigence as such is irrefutable. On the other hand, to meet the critical exigence adequately, as we have said, involves doing, in a single leap as it were, psychology, epistemology, and metaphysics. You have to meet all three coherently and more or less at once. Meeting that critical exigence is to come to awareness of one's operations. As soon as one begins to describe those operations, to relate them to one another, to say that insight is into phantasm, to say that the reflective act of understanding grasps the virtually unconditioned, and so on, one is doing the opposite process: one is objectifying the world of interiority in the world of theory.

2.3   *The Methodical Exigence*

Insofar as there is the self-appropriation of the subject, insofar as he becomes clearly and distinctly aware of his operations, there arises method. The operations of the subject are guided by his awareness of what they can do and what they cannot do. The guidance of operations in the light of what they are and what they can do gives rise to methodical operations, so that method proceeds from interiority back to the world of common sense and the world of theory, and also it is concerned to relate these two worlds to one another.

Through that self-appropriation of the subject one sets up a new realm distinct from theory in the ordinary sense: what are things? what is the physical order? the chemical order? the biological order? the sensitive order? the intellectual order? And what is God beyond all these orders? In that case one is dealing with science of particular types of objects. But the reversal from the world of theory to interiority and the self-appropriation of the self as grounding all method is, in its most general form, philosophy: philosophy as reflecting on all departments of science and, in that sense, metaphysics coming after the sciences of the nature of this and that.

The importance of this reversal to interiority is that it overcomes the break in the object and the break in the subject that arise from the differentiation of the world of theory and the world of common sense. That differentiation is something that is very palpable to people who know modern physics. They are fully conscious that they live in two quite different worlds. Insofar as they are dealing with the world through relativity and quantum theory, they are in a purely intellectual pattern of experience, and they have no way of relating the objects they deal with then with the objects of their ordinary lives when they go home to their wives and children or when they talk with their friends. They see no connection, no way of relating the two. The world of theory and the world of common sense are quite separate.

And not only is there the break on the side of the object, there is also the break on the side of the subject. A man as he is when he deals with his friends and discusses his life insurance and eats his meals and plays with his children is a different subject from the purely intellectual subject who deals with highly abstruse theories. There is a fission in the subject and a fission in the object, and that double hiatus is overcome insofar as the subject accomplishes his self-appropriation, reaches his own interiority, and understands precisely in what the break in the subject consists. It consists in specializing the subject into purely cognitional activities or using cognitional activities just as part of the operation of the whole man – understanding the difference between the theoretic subject and the commonsense subject. The two worlds are related to one another insofar as both are cases of knowing *ens* and, indeed, in principle, of knowing the same beings. It is one and the same being that is known by common sense and dealt with in a commonsense fashion and, on the other hand, is analyzed into its elements by the scientist. They begin from different ends. Common sense begins and stops with the thing as for us. The scientist has his foundations in the realm of what is *priora quoad se*, the elements which are defined and known only theoretically. But it is possible to proceed from the world of immediacy to the world of theory. Otherwise there never would have arisen scientific theories. And similarly it is possible to proceed back from the world of theory to the world of common sense. Otherwise there would not be scientific applications. There would not be the utility of science.

To put those two worlds together, to show in what sense they are identical and what are the differences in the two apprehensions, is the task of a third approach, and that is the philosophic approach, which rests ultimately on interiority. From an understanding of the subject and his knowing, you can set up a metaphysics, and so forth.

What is known in the world of common sense also can be understood scientifically. The object in the world of common sense is usually a horribly complex thing that the scientist does not particularly care to analyze. The chemical composition of this piece of chalk, for example, would take a chemist some time to work out in detail. And he does not care to make his studies on ordinary objects. He wants to get pure materials. But it is possible to carry out such operations. One can work from one to the other and back again by the applications of science. There is the structural similarity. There is the possibility of a material correspondence, of going from one to the other.

Moreover, the world of community, by the systematic exigence, goes into the world of theory. And one can say the world of community is the medium, the mediation, by which one proceeds to the world of theory. Both of them together lead one back into interiority, and interiority is the ground of method.

2.4 *The Genetic Circle*

That circle – the systematic exigence, the critical exigence, and the methodical exigence – is also a genetic process. One lives first of all in the world of community and then learns a bit of science and then reflects, is driven towards interiority to understand precisely what one is doing in science and how it stands to one's operations in the world of community. And that genetic process does not occur once. It occurs over and over again. One gets a certain grasp of science and is led on to certain points in the world of interiority. One finds that one has not got hold of everything, gets hold of something more, and so on. It is a process of spiraling upwards to an ever fuller view. That circle – systematic, critical, and methodical exigence – does not occur just once. It occurs over and over again in the self-correcting process of learning.

2.5 *Aberrations and Deviations*

Moreover, that process as described, this matter of continually progressing in learning, is an ideal process. In the concrete there are the aberrations of extrinsicism and immanentism. Those aberrations result in falsifications or deviations of the development. Insofar as those deviations occur, they occur within the historical development of man. The existence of deviation gives rise to a criticism in a much fuller and much more fundamental sense.

One's study of history reveals that there has been development. There is the genetic process from the world of community to the world of theory, from the New Testament to the Greek Councils. The Greek Councils are the *Wendung zur Idee*, the movement from the world of common sense towards its systematizing. And there is the further move to a much fuller systematizing in the Middle Ages. But that process was not merely the formulation of dogmas but also the formulation of heresies. And in the medieval period there was not only the ideal theologian St Thomas but also lots of others with contrary views. One accounts for the array of opinions that arose historically by reducing some simply to development but others to aberration. And the aberration is either by the excess of extrinsicism or the defect of immanentism, according to the analysis already covered, made on the side of the object. On the side of the subject, there is lack of intellectual, moral, and religious conversion, and what we say in the discussion of horizon and authenticity.

The possibility of a fundamental criticism provides the practical canons of further developing the positions – what results simply from development: what has been developed can be developed further – and of reversing the counterpositions, what has resulted from deviation. By eliminating the element of deviation, the lack of conversion, the lack of authenticity, the excessive limitations of horizon, by removing those, one transforms the counterposition into a position. On that technique as a philosophic technique, you can see *Insight*. The same admits its application in the field of theology.

3 Knowledge and Belief

So far we have been speaking simply of knowledge. We now introduce a new type of operation, belief, and, first of all, human belief.

There are no truths outside minds. When St Thomas asks whether there are any eternal truths, he says that any truth is in some mind, and the only way you can have an eternal truth is by having an eternal mind. And consequently the only eternal truths are the truths in the divine mind. Any other truth, being in a temporal mind, is not eternal: *verum et falsum sunt in mente.*[8]

However, the *verum* can be in the mind in two ways: as known and as believed. It is known insofar as the knowledge results from *my* experience, *my* understanding, *my* judgment, insofar as the known is something that is simply the achievement of the subject. But we do not experience everything. Or, of the things we experience, we do not understand everything. Insofar as we do understand we are not always certain. There is the possibility of the

8 See Thomas Aquinas, *Summa theologiae*, 1, q. 16, a. 7.

knowledge of the truth not being in our mind but in someone else's mind. Belief generalizes from the one knowing subject: it carries the truth from that single mind in which it is known or from the several minds in which it is known to the minds of others who do not know, who do not arrive at the truth by their personal experience and their adequate understanding and their certain judgment. They rely on the fact that the process has been carried out by someone else. I have never been to Asia. I do not know a number of things by experience, but I can have that experience vicariously insofar as others tell me about it. I can understand Einstein's proof that energy is equal to the mass by the square of the time of the velocity of light. But if I do not see the proof myself I can accept the fact that all the physicists agree with Einstein on that point. It is not my understanding but someone else's. Someone else has understood it, and that can be good enough for me. In that case I have the truth in my mind, but I am not knowing it; I am believing it.

3.1 The Effects of Belief

So the first effect of belief is that it increases the extension of truth. It increases the number of minds in which truths can be found.

In the second place, belief doubles the meaning of the word 'true.' There is one truth that is known. It is in the mind of the knower. But there is also truth as believed in the mind of the believer. Both are true, but they are true as in a mind since all truth is in some mind, but the truth can be differently in different minds. It can be known in one and believed in others. And the belief is the subordinate type. If there was no mind in which it is known, there would be no one to be believed and, consequently, there could not be other minds that have it by believing.

In the third place, the process of faith is from the truth that is known by John to the truth that is believed by James. The principle, the starting point of the process is the one who knows and utters a truth. And the term is the person who hears and believes a truth. And between the *terminus a quo* and the *terminus ad quem*, there is the process, the mediation between the principle and the term.

That mediation can be considered abstractly, and then it lies in truth as an intellectual good: it is good for my intellect to have the truth on the matter, even though I do not know it. That's the abstract mediation. The concrete mediation consists in the operations of the believer. He apprehends the truth known by somebody else as at least a good for himself, while not known as true for him. Someone else has worked out the logarithmic tables with a terrific amount of labor. The prospective believer does not know that they are true. He would have to work just as hard as the man who drew up the tables or the slide rule. But he can believe. It would be a good thing for him to consider them true. It would be a good thing if he believed them: he would be able to solve all sorts of problems. Or it would be good for him to believe the computer. He sees the intellectual value of that truth for him. That apprehension of a value grounds an act of will, and the act of will commands the act of assent to that truth.

There is a mediation, then, of apprehension of value, willing of value, and the act of belief. And because the will comes in, there is no need for a lack of evidence in the object to make the act of belief an act of belief. In the case of mathematical tables, very few mathematicians know the truth of mathematical tables. The horrible labor of working out those tables was done once by somebody they trust. That's enough. But it is still a case of belief.[9]

3.2   Elements of Belief

The key act in the process of coming to believe is the reflective act of understanding. To see that, one just has to enumerate the various elements in an act of belief.

3.2.1   Object

The object of belief is what is believed: the logarithmic tables are true.

3.2.2   Motive

The motive of belief is why one believes. One believes because the man who made the tables neither was deceived nor was deceiving.

3.2.3   The Act of Faith

The act of faith is the assent of intellect. It is the same as a judgment except that it differs in the way in which it arises. It is an absolute positing of *est* or *non est* just as a judgment is, but it differs insofar as the judgment of

---

9   A break was taken at this point. The second part of the lecture is recorded on Lauzon CD/MP3 312 (31200A0E060).

knowledge proceeds directly from a grasp of the sufficiency of the evidence, from a grasp of the unconditioned, while the act of belief proceeds directly from an act of will.

3.2.4 The Act of Will

The *pius credulitatis affectus*, the act of will, is the 'I will to believe that the mathematical tables are true.' The act of belief: they are true. The act of will: I want to believe that they are true.

The act of will depends upon a judgment, in traditional language, of 'credibility and credendity': I can and I should will to believe that the tables are true.

3.2.5 Grasping the Unconditioned

That judgment, that judgment of possibility and value, of credibility and credendity, as all judgments, depends upon a grasp of the virtually unconditioned. One grasps the sufficiency of the evidence for affirming that I can and ought to will to believe that the tables are true. That reflective act of understanding is preceded by the *praeambula fidei*, the major and minor premise, implicit or explicit, in which one grasps the unconditioned as unconditioned, the judgment of possibility, and the value of willing to believe.

Now the act of belief follows naturally from the will to believe. If I will to believe, the act of believing follows. The will to believe follows in a man of good will from the judgment of value: it's worth while believing that the tables are true; it's intellectually possible; it's an intellectual good to affirm that the tables are true. That judgment of value follows rationally from grasping the sufficiency of the evidence. But grasping the sufficiency of the evidence is not in the same way precontained in the preambles, in the evidence. It's one thing to have the evidence, and that's a matter of experience and acts of understanding and the process from the experience to the acts of understanding. It's another thing, a new emergence on a higher level, when one grasps the sufficiency of the evidence. Evidence is one thing; grasping the sufficiency of the evidence is another. The existence of that originating act on a new level, which is the reflective act of understanding, is missed out if one just puts down the two premises and supposes that the conclusion follows automatically in some objective order quite apart from any mind. If you take the mind into account, then the element of rational reflection and grasping the sufficiency of the evidence is the starting point that heads rationally and morally into the act of believing.

The reflective act of understanding is not precontained in the preambles the way the subsequent acts are precontained in the reflective act of understanding. In the reflective act of understanding one names all the subsequent acts. It is anticipative. It looks forward to the act of belief. I grasp the sufficiency of the evidence for affirming that it is possible and right to will to believe that the mathematical tables are true. All the subsequent acts are precontained in that reflective act of understanding. The subsequent acts, however, are not similarly precontained in the preambles. The preambles stand as form to act, as matter to form, when compared with the reflective act of understanding.

We've gone through this business on belief within the human order to have a basis for discussing faith. That was the purpose of it. But we also wanted to draw attention to the fact that it is not possible for anyone to separate in his own mind what he knows from what he believes. If we examine closely enough anything that we think we know, we'll find that there is a large number of elements about which we'll say, 'Well, really I don't know that; it's not something generated in virtue of my knowledge; there's a certain amount of believing what other people have said.' Especially in the world of common sense is that true. All we know through the newspapers and the radio and everyday conversation, and here in class, without making a personal investigation of the matter, is belief. The human mind is a matter of a symbiosis of believing and knowing, and it's not possible to separate the two. That is the point to Newman's remark that if he had to choose between doubting everything with Descartes and believing everything, he would prefer to believe everything. If you doubted everything, you would have nothing to go by to arrive at some truth. If you believed everything, you could knock out the errors one by one and be left with the truth. And since a large part of what everyone knows is not a matter of knowledge, since the truths to which one assents are not a result of one's personal experience, understanding, and judgment but to a great extent, to an indeterminable extent, depend on what one has learned from others, what others have told one, in one way or another, when one introduces universal doubt, one might be able to restore the elements that one knows, but one is not going to restore the elements that one believes.

3.3 Human and Divine Faith

If we compare *fides humana* and *fides divina*, human belief and divine faith, we find first of all that in divine faith there recur the elements that are found in human belief; and, on the other hand, in each recurrence there is also an element of fundamental difference.

The main features of divine faith are presupposed. You can get them from the [First] Vatican Council and, further, in the treatise *de actu fidei*. There is faith that is divine not only because of the motive but also because of the object. But we are skipping faith that is divine because of the motive but not because of the object, faith in what could be naturally known but de facto is believed. There are also truths of that type.

Similarly, there are truths that are a matter of human belief because of both the motive and the object, or that may be a matter of human belief because of the motive but not because of the object. If a child believes the truths of faith merely because of his parents, his motive is human while his object is divine. In other words, there can be mixtures. But we will consider two pure cases: faith that is divine because of both motive and object and faith that is human because of both motive and object. In the latter case one believes relativity to be true, and in the former case one believes the Trinity to be true.

If we consider those two cases, first of all, we find the extension. We said that belief increased the number of minds that know what is true. In one case there is the knower, and the increase is an increase of people believing it to be true. The same occurs with divine revelation. What only God knew now is also held to be true in virtue of faith. Consequently, there is a numerical increase of minds holding things to be true in virtue of faith.

However, there is a difference between the two cases. By human belief you can only believe natural truths, in the restrictive sense in which we are using the two terms of object and motive, but divine faith introduces a whole new order of truths that are supernatural, that cannot naturally be known, as the [First] Vatican Council says.

In the second place, there is the distinction between two ways in which the word 'true' or the expression 'held to be true' are employed. One can hold something to be true because one knows it or because one believes it. The same is true in terms of divine faith. One can hold things to be true because one knows them and because one believes. But in this second case the mediation that grounds the believing is indeed an intellectual value, it is in the order of the good, but that good is not a natural good for man. It's a supernatural good. So we have supernatural truths, the mediation of a supernatural good in which one has the process of belief. One does not believe the mysteries revealed by God because it is a natural good of human intellect. It's supernatural, something beyond the nature of man.

In the third place, the reflective act of understanding, when divine faith occurs, has to be a supernatural act of understanding. There has to be a supernatural light in it. And the reason for that is because the object is supernatural. One believes not the mathematical tables, but the mysteries. To believe the mysteries is to perform an act with a supernatural object. But if to believe the mysteries is a supernatural act, to will to believe the mysteries is a supernatural act. The mysteries are still the specifying object for the act of will.

Similarly, for the judgment of credibility and credendity, the object is again the mysteries. 'I can and should will to believe that the mysteries are true.' The mysteries again specify the object of what you are judging. And as the judgment is supernatural, so the reflective act of understanding will be supernatural. 'I grasp the sufficiency of the evidence for affirming that I can and should will to believe that the mysteries are true.' The whole sentence has a specific meaning insofar as you introduce the mysteries. The mysteries are supernatural, and consequently the series of acts is supernatural.

Now I made the point that the key element in the process of belief exists in that reflective act of understanding because, when one makes that statement and goes on to the order of divine faith, then one sees the point at which per se the supernatural enters into belief. It is at the point of the specification of the act by a supernatural object that per se, that is, in every case, one is having a supernatural act.

In the *praeambula fidei* it is not necessary that there occur any supernatural act. De facto, because there is need of *gratia sanans* and so on, and because of the way in which grace is granted in this order, there will normally be supernatural acts before one reaches the reflective act of understanding. Still, the objects prior to that reflective act of understanding need not be supernatural. The reason for this is that even if God revealed in this order only natural truths, he could have done so through the type of prophecy and miracles and so on that are appealed to in the *praeambula fidei*. But in that case those *praeambula* would not be heading to the mysteries. There would be nothing supernatural *quoad se, quoad substantiam*, in any of the acts and, consequently, not in the *praeambula*.

3.4   The Light of Faith

Accordingly, the light of faith, in the sense in which the light of faith is the light involved in the reflective act of understanding grounding the judgment of credibility and credendity, is the per se pivot in the genesis of divine faith.

It is the point at which there is effected per se the transition from a natural to a supernatural order.

Further, the light of faith in that sense regards the question, *An sit?* It heads to a judgment. Is it so or is it not so? Is believing the mysteries an intellectual value or is it not? The question regards *an sit?* not *quid sit?*

Consequently, when I speak of the *lumen fidei*, I do not mean something like Rousselot's *les yeux de la foi*.[10] Rousselot has not got the sharp distinction between *an sit* and *quid sit* when he speaks of *les yeux de la foi*. And consequently, there have been raised objections against Rousselot: that faith doesn't involve any infused species and so that there must be something wrong with his theory. Faith doesn't involve understanding anything. We believe not because we understand but because of the authority of God. The act of faith is a supernatural light in the reflective act of understanding, grounding the *quid sit*, the judgment of credendity, which grounds the act of will and throws back the event of faith. The light of faith is not a new *species intelligibilis* grounding a new type of understanding that leads to explanation, inner words, in the sense of definition and hypothesis. What is true in Rousselot's theory is, I believe, that the reflective act of understanding is supernatural because its object is supernatural. But he speaks about *les yeux de la foi* as discerning the miracles as signs of a divine intervention. That's *understanding* the miracles as signs. It regards understanding and not the level of judgment, of the *an sit*.

Because the light of faith introduces us to the supernatural good of believing, and to supernatural truth, the truths that are believed, it effects a transition from human truth, from anything that can be known, in the proper sense of knowing, by the human mind. That whole field is transcended when one adds on the supernatural truth that is accessible to us only through the light of faith. And precisely because it brings us to this supernatural field of truth, it cannot be based upon human truth. It cannot be a conclusion from the field of human truth. Human truth leads only to further human truth. There has to be a movement upwards to a new field. And that is the point ultimately of saying that the motive of faith is believed in the act of faith. I believe in the knowledge and veracity of God. I believe in God's knowing, not according to the measure of my natural knowledge of God's knowledge, but in virtue of what I believe God to know.

10 Pierre Rousselot, 'Les yeux de la foi,' *Recherches de science religieuse* 1 (1910), 241–59, 444–75; 4 (1913) 1–36; 5 (1914) 57–69, 453–58; now in English, *The Eyes of Faith*, trans. Joseph Donceel (New York: Fordham University Press, 1990).

In other words, what one can naturally know about God is analogous. Insofar as it is analogous, it is not only knowing but also a twofold ignorance. It is ignorance insofar as the object is not only similar but also dissimilar to the medium that we use as the means of our analogy. And it is an ignorance, further, insofar as we do not know just how important that dissimilarity is, how far it extends. The Fourth Lateran Council says that so great is the difference between creature and creator that no similarity can be noted without a greater dissimilarity being noted. But insofar as God is dissimilar, we don't know. That's the limitation to analogy. And because we don't know what that dissimilarity is, we have no way of saying how it compares with what is similar. There is a twofold ignorance involved in all analogous knowledge. By the light of faith we go beyond what can be humanly known, and we rely upon God's knowledge of what alone is divinely known. We are entering the field that from the viewpoint of natural knowledge is for us something we cannot know.

The light of faith, the light that comes in that reflective act of understanding, is directly opposed to rationalism. For the rationalist it cannot be a good for the human intellect to hold as true something that no man can possibly know to be true. That's the fundamental meaning and basis of rationalism. The mysteries are not to be believed; God is not to be believed when he reveals to us something that lies simply outside the human field of possible knowledge. The light of faith is the contradictory to that rationalist position, and it's one way of defining what the light of faith gives.

But while the light of faith is radically opposed to rationalism, it is not similarly opposed to what I have called the critical exigence. The critical exigence can be taken in a Kantian sense, and then of course it is opposed because Kant was also a rationalist. But there is not the intrinsic opposition between the two, because the critical exigence demands that one not talk about something one does not know as if one knew it. The critical exigence is not a critique of belief. The believer does not claim that he knows the mysteries by ordinary human procedures without any belief. He claims simply that he believes them. And similarly, there is the possibility of a critical justification of believing the mysteries, because man naturally desires to know more than he naturally can attain. Because of the fact that the formal object of any intellect is being, while the proper object of human intellect is *quidditas sive natura in materia corporali existens*, there is a difference between the two. There is a difference between what man naturally desires to know by his intellect, insofar as in his intellect he naturally desires to know everything, and what he naturally can attain, which is limited to the *quidditas sive natura in materia corporali existens* plus analogous knowledge of other things. The disparity between the proper and the formal objects of human intellect creates an opening, an openness, for accepting a divine revelation beyond what man can naturally attain.

3.5 A New Interiority

The result of introducing divine faith is that it gives us a new interiority. Hitherto, we have been considering interiority in terms of natural operations. Now we have to add in the operating subject not only human faith but also divine faith. Interiority is not merely a matter of what you experience, understand, and judge in virtue of your experience and understanding. It is also a matter of what you believe, the interiority of the act of faith. Insofar as there is the community that is the body of Christ and the movement to system that is contained in dogmatic and theological development, then the relevant interiority is a believing interiority. And that believing interiority is the source of method in theology and in reflections on community.

4 Theology, Faith, and Knowledge

We have now to introduce the notion of theology. There are three types.

In general, theology is concerned with God. There is natural theology, in which the means, the medium, is *per res creatas. E rebus creatis Deus Dominus principium et finis certo cognosci potest,* according to the definition of the [First] Vatican [Council]. Natural theology is knowledge of God by the natural light of reason through the things that have been created.

Theologia patriae has no medium. Or you can say that the medium is the divine essence itself, not creatures but God Himself. And the principle is human intellect elevated, perfected, by the light of glory, the *lumen gloriae.*

Between those two theologies there is theology in the sense with which we are concerned. And in that case the medium is the word of God and the order of the church, the order of the body of Christ. The mediation of our knowing in theology is, not God as in the beatific vision, not creatures as in natural theology, but the word of God and the order of the mystical body, a meaning and an order. The subjective principle is not just unaided reason, and it is not the light of glory. It is reason illuminated by faith. When I say reason illuminated by faith, I mean that the principle in theology is interiority, not just the operation of faith apart from natural operations of experiencing, understanding, and judging, but the natural operations as transformed by faith.

The *ratio per fidem illustrata* spoken of in the Vatican Council (DB 1796) is not to be confused with *fides per rationem adiuta*. There are those who want a complete separation: if something sounds philosophical, it has nothing to do with theology. Why? Because theology is simply faith. Well, theology is not simply faith, and it is not simply faith on which you tack a few rational conclusions. It is the human subject with all his natural powers plus a further transformation that is the principle in theology: *ratio per fidem illustrata*, not just *fides per rationem adiuta*.

4.1   The Vatican Decree

The comparison of natural knowledge with faith and theology one can put together from the Vatican decrees. In DB 1795 it is stated that the Catholic Church has always held and holds that there are two orders distinct both by their principle and by their object. By their principle: in one, one knows by the natural light of reason, and in the other, one knows by divine faith. By their object: in the one, one knows the objects at which human reason can naturally arrive, and in the other, one knows the mysteries hidden in God, which we could not know unless God chose to reveal them to us. The contrast between natural human knowledge and, on the other hand, divine faith is drawn clearly in DB 1795 of the Vatican Council.

Theology receives a fundamental charter in the next paragraph of the Vatican Council when it states that reason illumined by faith, when it inquires diligently, reverently, and judiciously, with God's help attains some understanding of the mysteries, and that a highly fruitful one, both from the analogy of what we naturally know and from the interconnection of the mysteries with one another and with our last end.[11] What is theology? Its principle is not just reason and not just faith. It is *ratio per fidem illustrata*. And its object is not just believing the mysteries. It presupposes believing the mysteries, it presupposes faith, and it adds some understanding of the mysteries.

4.2   Human Intellect and Natural Knowledge

It is important to note that human intellect and natural knowledge are not to be confused. Faith is above natural human knowledge. It is something supernatural and so opposed to natural human knowledge. But faith is not

---

11 Lonergan read or recited the passage in Latin.

similarly opposed to human intellect. It is an operation of human intellect. Similarly, theology is something distinct from what man naturally can know; its object is distinct from that; but it isn't similarly opposed to human intellect. Theology is an operation, or a group of operations, of human intellect. Faith exceeds natural knowledge both in its principle – it is a supernatural virtue – and in its object – it is concerned with mysteries that we could not know unless they were revealed by God. There is a clear opposition there. But faith is an assent of human intellect: *non est caecus animae motus*, as the Vatican Council also states. It is an operation of intellect, and because it is an operation of intellect, it does not simply stand beyond human intellect, it is an operation within human intellect, and it is an operation for which there is room in human intellect because human intellect naturally desires more than it can naturally attain. Its formal object is broader than its proper object; and faith is filling in to some extent that gap between the proper and the formal object.

Similarly, on the side of the object, the formal object of human intellect is the transcendental *ens*. And the supernatural is not something beyond *ens*, some *non ens* beyond *ens* or some *super ens*. It is within *ens*. It is a being. It is not a being that we can understand *viribus naturalibus*; but still it is a being. It lies within the transcendental object of intellect.

4.3 Faith and Theology

We have been comparing both faith and theology with human intellect. There is a comparison as well between faith and theology. Faith simply believes. It holds to be true all that the Catholic Church believes and teaches. Theology is not simply more believing. It presupposes belief and moves toward some understanding of what is believed. There is a celebrated passage in St Thomas in the *Quodlibetum* 4, a. 18, in which he distinguishes between the *disputatio* that is ordered to attaining certitude and the *disputatio magistralis*. It was a fundamental text with regard to theological method. The theologian is concerned to attain an understanding, not a false understanding but a true understanding. And so he has not only the question *quid sit?* but also the question *an sit?* Still, the two questions are not handled in the same manner. There are the problems of certitude. The problems of certitude in theology are solved by quoting the authorities: scripture, the councils, and so on: matters with which you are all familiar. But there is also the problem of understanding, knowing what is meant, reaching some understanding, however inadequate, of the doctrines of faith. And that is a different type of operation. St Thomas expresses himself rather clearly on the point: *Quaedam vero disputatio est magistralis in scholis non ad removendum errorem sed ad instruendum auditores ut inducantur ad intellectum veritatis quam intendit: et tunc oportet rationibus inniti investigantibus veritatis radicem, et facientibus scire* – Aristotle's *syllogismos epistēmonikos, syllogismus faciens scire* – *quomodo sit verum quod dicitur: alioquin si nudis auctoritatibus magister quaestionem determinet, certificabitur quidem auditor quod ita est, sed nihil scientiae vel intellectus acquiret, et vacuus abscedet*.[12] That's fairly strong. If you merely teach your pupils in theology that it's so – that's so, God has revealed it – well, they will be perfectly certain that that's so, that God has revealed it, that the Church teaches it, but if you do no more than that, then according to St Thomas, *nihil scientiae vel intellectus acquiret et vacuus abscedet*. Theology is something more. It is a matter of arriving at some understanding of the truths of faith.

It follows that a pure *Denzingertheologie*, a pure Christian positivism, does not satisfy such a notion of theology. It is not enough to establish that things are so and everything else is all guesswork. If that is one's attitude towards theology, then one is helpless when confronted with all the problems, and one just sets up a brick wall with regard to all problems: we don't understand, well, what of that? we are not worried about understanding anything anyway. So there's no reason to worry if there are special problems in scripture, patristics, development of dogma, and so on and so forth. It is insofar as there is some effort to understand that, there can be some mastery of difficulties.

5   From Faith to Theology

So far we have just been engaged in analysis, distinguishing different operations. Method is concerned with operations, and we have distinguished common sense, natural science, philosophy, belief, divine faith, theology. Now we want to consider the same operations when something is happening.

12 '... another kind of argument is that of the teacher in the schools. It seeks not to remove error but to instruct the students so that they understand the truth that the teacher hopes to convey. In such cases it is important to base one's argument on reasons that go to the root of the truth in question, that make hearers understand how what is said is true. Otherwise, if the teacher settles a question simply by an appeal to authorities, the students will have their certitude that the facts are indeed as stated; but they will acquire no knowledge or understanding, and they will go away empty.' Translation by Michael G. Shields, as in Bernard Lonergan, *The Triune God: Systematics*, trans. Michael G. Shields, ed. Robert M. Doran and H. Daniel Monsour, vol. 12 in Collected Works of Bernard Lonergan (Toronto: University of Toronto Press, 2007) 9.

We have marked off a field, and now we start considering movements between different elements in the field.

The transition from divine faith to theology is the process from the world of community to the world of theory. It is meeting the systematic exigence in the case where the community is the church, the body of Christ, and the theory is the field, the context, the dogmatic-theological context on which we had something to say earlier, and which we have gotten back to again.

Now we consider that transition, first of all generically, and in the second place in a particular instance.[13]

Generically, there is the *terminus a quo*, the *terminus ad quem*, the principle of the transition, the end of the transition, and the return, the application from the world of theory back to the world of community.

The transition from the *terminus a quo* – the world of community, the visible universe, the church, the world of the church, the hierarchy and the lay people – the transition from that world to the dogmatic-theological context is like the comparison of the implicit and the explicit, the *actus exercitus* and the *actus signatus*: we all understand, but it is something further to pick out and say, 'That's what the act of understanding contributes to the process; that's what's lacking here and what's added there.' This is the difference between the *actus exercitus* (I move my hand) and the *actus signatus* (I talk about moving my hand), the difference between *le vécu* and *le thématique*, which is fundamental in Husserl's *Investigations*; it is another way of putting the same thing. The French have the neatest expression of it. *Le vécu*: it is life as it is lived, without any worrying about theory, and things are fine; and thematizing: it is picking out some element and starting to think about that, ask questions about that. The liturgical movement thematizes the cult of the church which was going on for centuries before the liturgical movement began. This is the transition from doing something to starting to talk about and ask questions about it. One makes it an explicit thema, an explicit object of consideration, analysis, discussion. That is the process from the *vécu* to the *thématique*. Dilthey distinguished *Verstehen und Erklären*. Dilthey was concerned to distinguish the *Naturwissenshaften* and the *Geisteswissenshaften*, sciences of nature and the human sciences or, in positivist circles, the behavioral sciences. And he found the fundamental distinction to be between what he called *Verstehen*, understanding, and *Erklären*,

---

13 Because of time constraints, Lonergan ended the lecture in the middle of the generic consideration of the transition without getting to the specific consideration. The latter is presented in the next lecture. See below, p. 158, note 3.

explaining. What does that mean? It means this, that when you are dealing with electrons or hydrogen atoms or plants or animals, before you understand anything you have a whole series of observations, and you draw up graphs and so on, and finally you get out a little bit of understanding which you pin down in a formula that you verify. But when you are dealing with human things, the understanding comes first. In anything that any man does, you have a pretty good understanding of what he is up to. Simply from the mere fact of the man there is an immediate understanding. Now the real basis of that distinction between *Verstehen* and *Erklären* is the difference between the world of community and the world of theory. In the world of theory one starts systematic explaining. In the world of common sense it is enough to understand and then do it. The artist understands, but his expression of his understanding is the work of art. It is not a conceptual system. It is simply *Verstehen*. And it is that understanding that is unformulated, that is not systematically expressed, that is fundamental in all the human sciences. The distinctive mark of the human sciences is that you have that understanding of human life, and you have to presuppose it before you can go on to do any sort of scientific investigation of human affairs. If you go into a law court as a sociologist and you start off making measurements of the number of decibels of the sound made by this orator and so on, well, you are just wasting your time. You have to understand what it means, to know that it is a law court. It is just commonsense understanding, but that type of understanding comes first all along the line.

The transition from the world of community to the world of theory is from an understanding that is implicit, given with human living, to an understanding that expresses itself systematically.[14]

14 The fourth question-and-answer session was held later this same day. See below, pp. 326–38.

1962-7

Transitions and Thematizations[1]

1 From Faith to Theology

After distinguishing types and groups of operations under the names of common sense, natural science, philosophy, belief, divine faith, and theology, we want to examine more closely the transition, the movement, from faith to theology. It is the type of movement that occurs from the world of common sense, community, the visible universe, to the world of theory.

The *terminus a quo* and the *terminus ad quem* can be compared as the implicit and the explicit, the *actus exercitus* and the *actus signatus*, the *vécu* and the *thématique*, *Verstehen* and *Erklären*. *Erklären* means explaining, that is, giving a scientifically formulated and systematic explanation as opposed to simply understanding the way everyone understood that Euclid's first proposition in his first book was right although they did not have the scientific concepts that would be necessary to show that that was right – what we already have shown about Euclid's solution to the problem of how to construct an equilateral triangle. He has the right solution; his answer is true, but it does not follow logically from his definitions, axioms, and postulates, and it cannot follow logically. New concepts and new axioms are required. But people understood, and they understood correctly. Understanding proceeds similarly in ordinary human living. We understand what someone means, but we could not answer questions that would explain just the precise nature of that meaning. You know what I mean;

1 17 July 1962, Lauzon CD/MP3 313 (31300A0E060) and 314 (31400A0E060).

I know what I mean; what more do you want? That's the way everything goes on normally.

Again, the *existenziell* and the *existenzial* is a distinction introduced by Heidegger. The *existenziell* is the understanding, the consciousness or the understanding of human life, that is given along with living. It is common-sense understanding. The *existenzial* is the reflective categorization, explicitation, of that spontaneous understanding of human life.

Again, there is the difference between life and theory: let's live; let's not waste our time doing any theory. The opposition is clear. There is also experience and experiment: the man of experience need never have performed any experiments. He knows by experience an awful lot about men and about things, but he has not performed experiments. Experiment is a thematized experience. In the experiment one wants to know just where the needle stands on the dial: is it at 5.67, or is it someplace else, yes or no? You take a look. Any one can take a look. Anyone who can count can say where the needle stands, on up to two decimal places. That looking, however, is experiment insofar as there is a large conceptual construction that puts a precise question, and that question is answered yes or no when one looks at the dial. It is not the looking that answers the question. It is the looking as put within the context. Modern physics is supposed to have arrived at the point where the man that can manipulate the instruments, set up the experimental apparatus, know how to use it, know enough about the materials, has not got a ghost of a notion of what this speculative mathematical construction is or means; whereas on the other hand, the man that understands the mathematics and puts the questions could not do the experiment. The two Chinese who recently got the Nobel Prize for work on parity did not do the experiment.[2] Some friend of theirs knew someone running a laboratory somewhere, and they persuaded him to perform the experiment: and their theory was found out to be right. The theoretical work and the experimental work can become so specialized, and in each field so complex, that two different sets of people carry on the different parts of the task. We live by experience. We learn by experience. And in doing so it is only slightly that we thematize our experiencing. On the other hand, the sciences are built up not by the vague experience, the unthematized experiences of ordinary living, but by getting insights, formulating hypotheses, deducing all the conclusions from the hypotheses, and confronting all

2 Lonergan is probably referring to T.D. Lee and C.N. Yang, whose paper 'Question of Parity Conservation in Weak Interactions,' which appeared in the 1 October 1956 issue of *The Physical Review*, led to a series of experiments that challenged some fundamental convictions in physics.

these possible conclusions with precise data produced under controlled conditions, where the requisite conditions are determined by the hypothesis.

There is the dramatico-practical subject, that is, the subject living with people and doing things, the man of common sense, the man in whom intellectual operations are only a part and an integrated part within the totality of his living. This subject is opposed to the theoretical subject in whom intellectual operations are an end in themselves – he's out for the truth, and nothing must interfere with the norms and exigences of pure intelligence; it is a quite different pattern of consciousness. And, finally, corresponding to the two subjects, there is the world of theory on the one hand and, on the other, the world of the visible universe.

The process from the objects of faith to theology is a process, then, that illustrates that set of opposites, the nine contrasts that we have given. It is something very common, very familiar; it is formulated in different ways by different people, but fundamentally they are all talking about the same thing. The basis, the principle, of the transition is Aristotle's wonder, the beginning of all science and philosophy. The term of the movement is when one arrives at the explicit, the *signatum*, the thematized, the explained, the *existenzial*, the theory, the experiment, the theoretical subject, the intelligible universe. And one arrives there in two steps: *quid sit?* and *an sit?*

However, note: one moves from one world to the other not because of one single question. The movement is effected and becomes noticeable only when there is a whole series of questions. It is in the task of meeting the whole series of questions on a single basis, in a coherent manner, in providing one coherent set of basic statements with which one can deal with the whole lot, that in an appreciable fashion one has the movement from the world of faith to the dogmatic-theological context. Our upper circle represents the dogmatic-theological context, the lower circle the world of faith, from revelation, the kerygma, up to the present-day believers in the Catholic Church. Theologians are also believers; they belong to both worlds.

2 An Illustration[3]

An illustration of that is found in Landgraf's book or his articles on grace, the doctrine of grace in the earlier medieval period.[4] The book is published

---

3 This is the specific consideration that Lonergan mentioned toward the end of the previous lecture but did not have time to discuss then.
4 Artur M. Landgraf, *Dogmengeschichte der Frühscholastik*, Erster Teil, *Die Gnadenlehre*, Band 1 (Regensburg: Verlag Friedrich Pustet, 1952).

by Pustet at Regensberg. Before putting out this series of volumes on the history of dogma in early Scholasticism, he had done endless articles scattered through all sorts of reviews. In general, the articles are more enlightening and more helpful, because the books compress the work done in the articles. In this final series of volumes he summarizes. He also introduces improvements and gives more mature judgments, but to get the detailed expositions and the full quotations, one goes to the articles written earlier and scattered all over in a series of reviews.

He has a series of articles dealing with various aspects of the doctrine of grace, and for any later theologian it's amusing the problems they were just baffled by in the twelfth and at the beginning of the thirteenth century. Grace – well, it's not natural. They distinguished the *gratuita* and the *naturalia*. But what is there that is not *gratuitum*? What is it that we have not got as a free gift of God? Well, we have nothing. Everything is *gratuitum*. And how do you get around it? Well, they had no way of getting around it; but they gave a series of more or less guesswork solutions. And they were all explored in detail. They were working directly with Augustine, trying to reconcile, fit together, all the different statements of Augustine. You can see in those articles of Landgraf – and he is working mainly from manuscript sources – the process, the transition, from the world of faith to the world of theory. About 1230 the whole thing bangs into perspective. They get the idea of two entitative orders, one natural and one supernatural, distinct and related. They formulate the idea of the supernatural habit, and theology is away, so to speak.

Lottin has done a parallel investigation of the theories of freedom from Anselm to St Thomas, and so simultaneously with the developments on grace.[5] Lottin says that treatises on freedom start in 1230. Before, they had been trying to define freedom. At Peter Lombard's time they had two definitions of freedom: the philosophers' – that by which one is *immunis a necessitate* – and the theologians' – that by which one does right when one has God's grace and does wrong when one has not got God's grace. It was impossible for the theologian to give a definition of freedom that did not seem to be denying grace. Why was it so? Because he had no distinction between two orders: freedom, something that belonged to the natural order, and grace coming in in a way that didn't destroy freedom – and fundamentally it could do so because it belonged to another order. All the

5 Dom Odon Lottin, *La théorie du libre arbitre depuis s. Anselme jusqu'à saint Thomas d'Aquin* (Saint-Maximum, France: École de Théologie, and Louvain: Abbaye du Mont-César, 1929).

problems in grace were all there, and they had no solution to any of them. Then they got the key about 1230. It is a very clear instance of this *transitus* from faith to theology.

Of course, when they got the idea of the supernatural habit, they tried to explain absolutely everything in terms of it. St Thomas in his commentary on the *Sentences* has no acknowledgment of the reality that we refer to as actual grace, as something from divine providence. That's particularly clear in Book 2, dist. 28, where he holds that the sinner without grace cannot have his sins forgiven but he can keep on avoiding sin. He has answers to all the arguments you can put to the contrary: he can avoid some but not all. If he can avoid some, he becomes more capable of resisting; he advances in virtue and, consequently, he is more capable. He develops an increasing capacity to avoid sin as time goes on. Read Book 2, dist. 28, art. 2: *utrum peccator possit evitare peccatum.*[6] Peter Lombard, who was prior to this, had said: *homo non potest non peccare etiam damnabiliter.* But when they got to the supernatural habit, they thought they had the explanation of everything. It was similar with the preparation for grace: there is no habit prior to the habit; and if there is no habit prior to the habit, then there is no question of a prior grace. In St Thomas the term 'actual grace' never occurs, but the reality gradually develops from the *Sentences* on, illustrating the process from the world of faith to the world of theory.

This process can be a major or a minor operation. It can be something that is done by one man within his lifetime, and it can be the sort of thing that occurs only through a large number of workers and over a long time. Christological theory was in movement from Apollinaris (ca. 380) to the Third Council of Constantinople (ca. 680), and the issues were becoming clearer as time went on. There were all sorts of various complications involved. Similarly, this problem of grace in all its aspects was a problem that Anselm tried to handle only speculatively, without a mastery of the data; and it occupied the theologians right up to Thomas's death. Thomas arrives at a fully satisfactory theory of actual grace only in his later works.

There are, then, the major movements. And there are the minor movements that any one man, if he is a very good theologian, can perform.

6 Thomas Aquinas, *Scriptum super Sententias,* 2, d. 28, q. 1, a. 2, 'Utrum homo sine gratia possit vitare peccatum' (whether man can avoid sin without grace).

3 Modes of the Transition

Besides the distinction between major and minor movements or studies, there also is a distinction between the modes of the transition. The transition from the implicit to the explicit, from the world of faith to the world of theory, can be either explicit or itself only implicit. It was very definitely implicit when Athanasius was defending the *homoousion*. He had no intention of laying down the foundation stone for dogmatic and theological development. He defended the word *homoousion* as an exception. The formulae of faith should be expressed in scriptural terms. He defended the word *homoousion* simply because of the extraordinary necessities of his day: it was the one and only way of dealing satisfactorily with the Arian heresy. If you did not introduce that term, then there was no way of distinguishing between people who really acknowledged the divinity of Christ and people who did not.

However, what the Council of Nicea, followed by Athanasius, put across in one instance did become the rule. When the Council of Chalcedon defined the existence of two natures in Christ, they were unaware of the fact that they were using the word 'nature' in a sense quite different from its usage in Athanasius, Basil, the two Gregories, and Cyril of Alexandria. These theologians used 'nature' in the same sense as subsistent being, a concrete, total existent being. And if there are two natures in Christ in that sense, there would have to be two persons too. It was later in the Byzantine Scholasticism, something less than a century later, that they introduced the distinction between two kinds of natures: the *physis enhypostatos* and the *physis anhypostatos*. They had the distinction between hypostasis and nature in such a way that two natures did not necessarily imply two persons. But the Council of Chalcedon proceeded simply from the dogmatic data. The human nature is not the divine; there is some real distinction there: the two natures, *etiam post Incarnationem*, against the Monophysites.

So the process of moving from the world of faith to the world of theology, of divine dogmas in theology, can go on implicitly. Thematizing the process is discovering the development of dogma. And discovering the development of dogma occurred after the development of dogma. The two are distinct. In other words, the process of thematizing what is said in scripture about the Son and arriving at the *homoousion* is one thing, and it is a second thing to thematize that process, to be aware that that process is going on; and that was not something of which the Fathers or the medieval Scholastics were adequately aware. Full awareness of it comes when one knows precisely what the development of dogma is and how it occurs. At the same time, one is working towards a development of dogma.

4 Three Instances of Thematizing

The precise nature of that process of thematizing is illustrated by comparing the patient and the doctor, the witness and the judge, or anyone arriving at what he means when he uses the word 'I.'[7]

The patient is not feeling well and goes to see the doctor and gives him certain generalities which enable the doctor to ask further questions, some of which the patient might have anticipated, others of which he did not. And what is the doctor doing all this time? He is transposing what the patient says. The patient has the experience of the illness, and the doctor transposes the patient's account of his ills into diagnostic symptoms that will separate one malady from another. There is a transposition from the categories of common sense to the categories of medicine. By this transposition the doctor knows something from the patient's words that the patient does not know. He knows the patient better than the patient knows himself from the viewpoint of medicine. From the viewpoint of experiencing a heart attack or something like that, the patient may know more about it than the doctor; the doctor needn't have had a heart attack himself. But from the viewpoint of experiment, of asking precise questions to which the patient answers yes or no, the doctor knows more about the patient than the patient does himself. There are the two contexts. There is the systematic context learned by the doctor in his medical studies, and there is the commonsense, experiential context of the man who is ill. He knows how he feels in the morning, how he feels at noon, and so on throughout the day, and he is able to recount the symptoms, but by the questioning of the doctor he is able to describe more accurately than he would be without that questioning. The doctor will ask, 'Is it this or is it that? Pick between the two.' The doctor is always asking leading questions.

Again, the judge and the witness. The witness sees a crime committed, and he is terribly upset. He has all sorts of emotional experiences. But the judge is not interested in his emotional experiences. Nor is he interested in the human tragedy of the crime or anything like that. He wants simply to subsume what went on under legal categories. Was a crime committed, or

7 Lonergan referred again to the notes he had distributed.

was it not? Was it committed with intent, or was it accidental? And so on – all the questions the judge has to have the answers to in order to be able to pronounce a just sentence. The judge reconceives the whole thing from a different point of view. Still, his total source of information lies in the witness or the witnesses. There is, then, a process from the world of ordinary experience, the witness to a crime, to the world of law and its categories: what is a crime? what are the different kinds? what is the degree of guilt acknowledged by the law?

Similarly, from a fairly early age we all say 'I.' Very small children will talk about themselves in the third person – 'John wants this' – but fairly early we get on to using the word 'I.' What do we mean? You can give a purely grammatical answer to the question: 'I' is a personal pronoun, first person singular. You can give a metaphysical answer: 'I' refers to the substance when he is awake – or, at least, the subject uses 'I' to refer to himself when he is awake; he need not be awake insofar as he is referred to. I can say that I was dead to the world, in a dreamless sleep. I was that way. 'I' names the substance. Or you can push the question further: the I when he says 'I.' And then you are brought to the notion of the subject, the psychological subject. We are all subjects in potency but not always subjects in act. When we are in dreamless sleep we are subjects only in potency. We are dead to the world, and we are not there to have the world dead to us: you are not a subject when you are in dreamless sleep.

The thing can be worked out in terms of cognitional theory. How is it that I know the I? There are the experiences of the subject. The subject is given along with his acts, and the subject is always the same though the acts vary. One is conscious of that enduring identity. Insofar as one is simply conscious, insofar as it is simply given, it is on the level of experience; and experience alone is not yet knowledge. There has to be understanding of the experiences and their conceptualization and a judgment that the conceptions are right, to arrive at knowledge. By that process the 'I' that is always given as subject also is objectified, and you have the subject as object.

Again, those three instances are given to illustrate the fact that one and the same reality and one and the same truth about the same reality can be transposed from the context and the mode of apprehension of common sense, of community, to the mode of apprehension of theory. The transposition is not a falsification. Because the judge subsumes the case under legal categories, it does not mean he is getting away from the truth, from the facts. He is knowing the facts more accurately from his own particular viewpoint, namely, the juridical viewpoint. Similarly, because the doctor understands your illness in terms of categories he learned in medical school that have no meaning for you, this does not mean he is misconceiving your malady. It means he is knowing your malady better than you know it. It is simply on the basis of your knowledge that the doctor decides just what the illness is. One can use another type of knowledge to attain a more accurate type of knowledge in a different world.

5 Symbolic, Classical, and Historical Consciousness

Next, there is a distinction to be made between symbolic, classical, and historical consciousness.

In symbolic consciousness the world of theory is more or less nonexistent. The questions that lead to the world of theory are there. Even primitives wonder about what we call the first cause and man's destiny and all these questions. But they handle them not in theoretical fashion by defining their terms and proving their conclusions from principles. They do so symbolically. It is a symbolic mode of apprehension. The image carries the meaning, and the meaning carried by the image is not systematically determined by a theoretical structure. And because those questions are handled symbolically, they very easily head into mythical answers.

Secondly, classical culture results from the Greek discovery of the *logos*, the expulsion of *mythos* by *logos*, the achievement of Greek culture. Its limitation, insofar as one goes beyond the big men to its systematic diffusion through systems of education, teaching, schools, books, popularizations, and so on, is that the strictly theoretical element tends to vanish. One gets the *haute vulgarisation* instead of science, theory, in its rigorous sense. Newton may have had to spend weeks in this very rigorous intellectual pattern of experience to work out the theory of universal gravitation, but all the people that have talked about it for over two centuries did not go through that same experience. Most people talk about Newton's discovery of universal gravitation without any notion whatever of what a theory is or what it is to be a theoretical subject. The element of pure intellectual achievement in it is something beyond their horizon. The classicist tendency lives on theory, but the purely theoretical element tends to vanish. If the theorist lived a few centuries ago, he is regarded as a great man, but if he is living with you, well, he is just a bit queer, isn't he?

Again, on the other hand, just as there is a certain blind spot towards the apprehension of theory in what is called classicist mentality, similarly there is a blind spot with regard to concrete human living. Concrete human living is apprehended through ideals, norms, precepts, laws, universals. It is recognized, of course, that in the concrete there are a lot more very complicated further determinations, that there is spontaneity and originality and personality and irrationality and all the rest of it – that's the way human life is. But still that does not matter; that is just a matter of temporal contingencies. The classicist wants to be satisfied with the eternal verities. He does not want a detailed, patient investigation of all the precise, minute differences that are to be found in persons, in literary movements, in social movements, and so on. All that is just a superfluous sort of junk. What you need is a man who has a firm grasp of the principles. With regard to these details, *plus ça change, plus c'est la même chose.* Human nature is ever the same, and they hang on to whatever is the same: it is ever so much easier to learn and know about. There is a certain blindness with regard to the concrete in its developments, its changes, its variations, its peculiarities. And that is why we went along so peacefully for centuries without any acknowledgment whatever of the existence of a development of dogma. To a certain extent the question was raised by Petavius a number of centuries ago. The question was raised by Catholics. But what really drove us to acknowledging it was the work of the German liberal Protestants writing their *Dogmengeschichte.* More and more we were forced to acknowledge that at least the words were not the same in scripture and the councils, then that there was some difference between them, some sort of progress of some kind. But there still exist in decreasing numbers what may be referred to as the anachronists, who want to find in the scriptures exactly all the valid concepts of theology. The word *homoousion* is not there, but the meaning has to be there in the sense defined. Just how it is there is left to someone else to work out, but that is what has to be. It is not an attempt to understand how truth can be transposed from one context to the other.

There were, for example, not so long ago, interpretations in which people were asking questions about the meaning of the New Testament author in terms of presupposing the definition of Chalcedon. If you presuppose Chalcedon, you can draw the distinction between *Christus ut Deus et Christus ut homo.* But when you ask whether Mark or Luke or John or Paul is talking about *Christus ut Deus* or *Christus ut homo,* you are asking a question that is an anachronism. That distinction was provided with its basis about the year 450. Prior patristic modes of thinking of Christ were in the two schemes: the Alexandrian scheme of the *Verbum-caro* and the Antiochene scheme of the *homo-Deus,* which do not mean the same thing as *Christus ut Deus* and *Christus ut homo,* if you are using terms accurately. Those two schemes have their basis in more complex and more concrete schemes that are to be found in the New Testament, and if you are discussing what the New Testament means, you have to go back to those earlier schemes and not ask questions about the text of the sort, Does John mean this or does John mean that? when you are using categories that arose several centuries later. You cannot be faithful either to the later categories or to the earlier position without drawing that temporal distinction.

The same difficulty arises in the opposite fashion. Just as there is a tendency to anachronism among Catholics, so there is a tendency to archaism among non-Catholics. If the later formulations are not to be found in scripture, then they are later corruptions. On both sides there is no room for development. There is no room for development because of the classicists' prescinding from the concrete, the particular, the determinate, the variable, and so on. And one gets two types of difficulties: one forcing later categories upon the interpretation of scripture, and the other demanding that the later categories cannot in any way be justified if they are not already present in scripture. This is just one illustration.

Historical consciousness is interested in all the multiplicity and manifoldness of human living from the most primitive tribes to the most cultivated nations and civilizations. And it wants to understand man, to arrive at an understanding of man, through those data. You know human nature by understanding the data on man provided by history and provided by contemporary sociological investigations. Just as you understand other things by proceeding from the data to your insights, to your hypotheses, similarly such is your understanding of man.

6   A Concrete Example of the Transition from Scripture to Theological Assertion

Those are generalities on the transition from the world of community, faith, common sense, the visible universe to the world of theory, doctrine, theology. We want to take now a concrete example of the way in which a theologian moves from scripture to a theological assertion, and we take an example from contemporary Catholic thought because that simplifies matters. If one was to take a medieval or a patristic example, one might have a more conspicuous member of the Catholic tradition than the person I am quoting, but one would have enormous historical problems of determining what exactly was the situation when this man raised the question and what exactly was his contribution to its solution. And to recreate the situation, the mental, the intellectual situation of the fourth or the fifth or the sixth or the seventh century, or of the twelfth or the thirteenth, is a major operation on which, in any given instance, endless amounts of material can be written and endless questions can be asked. We eliminate all that complexity by taking a question that is new to theology and considering an answer that has been given recently, in 1960. I refer to Fr Gutwenger's book on the consciousness and knowledge of Christ.[8]

First of all, we have a logical sketch of his argument. In chapter 3 of the first part he considers the passages in the Gospels in which Christ is reported to have used the word 'I.' In the fourth chapter he considers one's ordinary human psychological experience and, in particular, differentiates the experience on which use is made of the word 'I' as distinct from the word 'you,' 'Thou.' And in the fifth chapter he comes to his conclusion about Christ's human experience of an 'I.'

The logical scheme is as follows. The third chapter gives the minor premise: Christ said 'I' in precisely this sense on several occasions. The major premise: if Christ said 'I' in this sense on a number of occasions, then such and such a conclusion is to be drawn about Christ's self-consciousness. Gutwenger belongs to Galtier's school, with a difference. Both of them follow Tiphanus on the metaphysical analysis of the hypostatic union. Galtier held that the hypostatic union was in the ontological order, and simply in the ontological order, and therefore that there was nothing psychological about it. There was to be no consciousness of the divine ego in the human experience of Christ. If the person is something simply ontological, not a datum of consciousness, then there is no conscious experience of the ego in Christ's human consciousness. Gutwenger agrees with Galtier on the metaphysical analysis of the hypostatic union, but from his reading of scripture and the fact that Christ said 'I' and 'I' has to mean the person, there must have been some consciousness, apprehension, awareness of the person in Christ's humanity. That roughly is his line of thought.

What we have to understand is what precisely is the nature of the argument. First of all, we note that the passages cited by Gutwenger have been known to Christians for 2000 years approximately, and they have been thematized time and again by the Fathers and by the theologians. They are quite familiar passages. Everyone knows that Christ said 'I' countless times. Very elaborate arguments have been drawn from such passages as 'I and the

8 Engelbert Gutwenger, s.j., *Bewusstsein und Wissen Christi: Eine dogmatische Studie* (Innsbruck: Verlag Felizian Rauch, 1960).

Father are one,' and so on. All these passages used by Gutwenger have been handled over and over again.

Secondly, the question that Gutwenger is asking is a new question that despite all the earlier handling of these texts was not attended to, namely, the question of the psychological subject in the sense of the one who consciously says 'I.' If you say 'I,' you don't mean me. That question arose in Protestant theology in the last century, and it was introduced to Catholic theology by Déodat de Basly and then by Galtier in 1939 in his work on the unity of Christ.[9] And it has been discussed rather vigorously for the last twenty years. But earlier in Catholic theology that precise question was not raised. Scriptures were not thematized in that manner. Further – and this is the reason why we take this particular example – there is no prehistory of that precise type of thematization.

Gutwenger's major premise: if Christ said 'I' and in a sense in which you refer to the person – for example, when Christ on the cross says, 'I thirst' – is he referring to the person? Well, for Gutwenger, that is not certain. It may be simply a spontaneous expression of the suffering psyche. It need not refer to the person. There is that possibility there. He limits his texts precisely to the texts in which 'I' occurs in a context of interpersonal relations – that is one of his main considerations, at least – so that it is quite clear that when the 'I' is used it is referring to a person.

But to go from that premise to his conclusion he has an enormous structure of presuppositions. He has all the Christological dogmas. He has the theological discussions of the hypostatic union, and in particular Tiphanus's solution to that question. He has the problem of determining what precisely is meant by the psychological subject. He has the problem of relating the psychological subject to the metaphysical subsistent, the *id quod est*. And he has the problem of proceeding analogously from the ordinary psychological subject with its metaphysical presuppositions to the case of the God-man in which one has a particular instance. Therefore, the problem has a heap of presuppositions that reside in the already established dogmatic-theological context. He goes to the scriptures and picks out, as though he were doing an experiment, a very large series of passages in which the word 'I' is uttered by Christ and means indubitably the person. This is the key element from the scriptures that he wants answered, and to determine the nature of the psychological subject, Gutwenger appeals to the difference between the 'I' that is always subject and the 'you,' the difference between

9 Paul Galtier, *L'unité du Christ* (Paris: Beauchesne, 1939).

experiencing 'I' and 'you.' They are never the same; there is an obvious contrast. When one says 'you,' one is speaking of an object. When one says 'I,' one is speaking of the speaker. There is a clear-cut opposition between the two types. The subject as subject is never object, and the 'I' is an objectification of that subject. That is his fourth chapter, his theoretical part insofar as he has a theoretical part.

Because of that difference, then, he has to leave Galtier's position in which Christ knew the divine person only as an object through the beatific vision. If Christ as man knew the divine person that he was only as an object through the beatific vision, then he could not have referred to that object as 'I' because the 'I' is never simply an object in that fashion. That's his argument.

Because he gets these data from scripture within his dogmatic, theological, psychological, and analogous context – that enormous set of presuppositions – he argues from the text taken not as experience, not as trying to understand everything in the context around the 'I.' He refers you back to the exegetes for everything in the passage except the use of the word 'I.' It makes no difference to his question. The one thing he presupposes is that there is some substantial identity between the words attributed to Christ in the gospel and the words that Christ uttered. If Christ spoke in some such fashion, if he used the pronoun 'I,' then that is all he wants. All the questions about the history of the synoptic tradition, the composition of the Gospels, the precise context in each case under which Christ happened to use the word 'I,' that is all irrelevant. The one thing that counts in a physical experiment is: where does the needle stand? does it stand right there or somewhere else? Similarly, in the argument, when Christ says 'I,' does he mean the person or does he not? Does he mean some merely psychic subject such as might be the case when he says, 'I thirst?' He decides that the meaning of the Gospels is that he means the person. 'I' refers to the person. But 'I' does not refer to an object. Therefore, there is some consciousness in Christ of the person. Such is his argument.

The point I want to make, of course, is not that Gutwenger's position is true. I do not agree with it. (I agree well enough with what I'm saying, but his position ultimately I don't agree with.) But the point is to grasp the nature of the use of scripture in theology. We have taken theology in a highly developed context, a highly developed dogmatic-theological context, in which the Christological dogmas are presupposed, a special theory of the hypostatic union is presupposed, and the question is raised as to the nature of the psychological subject and given an answer in terms of the contrast between the experience of 'I' and the experience of 'you.' There are further problems regarding the subsistent and the analogous transition from an ordinary man to the case of the consciousness of Christ. In that very large and complex dogmatic, theological, psychological, metaphysical context, there is raised a precise question: did Christ use the word 'I' in the sense of the person – and there is only one person in Christ, the divine person – or did he not? And an answer is sought from the scriptures. This is not an attempt to understand just how Christ felt when he said, 'The ancients said, it was said of old, but I say unto you,' the series of passages in the Sermon on the Mount. There is no investigation of just why Christ did that, and just what he said and all the rest of it. The one and only question that counts is, Did he say 'I' and mean the person or did he not?

I want to stress that there is something entirely different between the approach of the dogmatic theologian to scripture and the approach of the exegete. The exegete does not get his questions from this later dogmatic-theological context. He gets his questions from the scriptures themselves. And he is out to understand not problems on how we should conceive the consciousness of Christ but as much as St John or St Matthew or St Mark or St Luke have to tell us about our Lord. The questions are entirely different, and the mode of answering them is entirely different. The exegete's purpose is to remain within the world in which the text was written and tell us about that as much as possible in the terms of the text itself. But when you are transposing from one world to another, then your questions come out of the world you are heading for, and the criteria of what an answer is come out of that theoretical world. Your appeal to scriptures is an appeal to what may be very fragmentary and minute points in the scriptures, but it has to be decisive. And the decisive point is not in terms of experience – something that gradually builds up as you gradually understand St John's way of talking better and better after reading endless commentaries, and so on – but is the word 'I' there, or is it not? Does it mean a person, or does it not? If you get the two answers 'yes,' then you have your dogmatic-theological conclusion.[10]

7   Thematization, Summation, Integration

We have been saying that the process from the world of common sense, community, faith, to the dogmatic-theological context is a process of thematization. Just as there is a process from what the patient tells about his illness

10 A break was taken at this point. The remainder of the lecture is recorded on Lauzon CD/MP3 314 (31400A0E060).

to the doctor's interpretation of his words to arrive at symptoms and so pick out just what the malady is in a totally new context in which the doctor is operating in the light of his medical knowledge, presupposing his medical categories, asking questions of the patient in the light of these medical categories and principles and correlations, and taking the patient's answers out of the context of the patient's experience and the context of the patient's words and transposing them into this other context, and so arriving at what the illness of the patient really is; or similarly, just as with the witness and the judge there is a transposition from the world of experience to the world of law; so too, there is a transposition of the same type that poses questions from a dogmatic-theological context that has gradually been built up in the church, that is taken for granted by all Catholics, that is handed on, communicated in seminaries, theological schools, and theological writings. That context is something that exists in the church. It is acknowledged by all Catholics. From that context questions arise. The precise nature of the questions and the definition of all the terms come from the contemporary context. The criteria that are employed come from the contemporary context. But the answer is sought in the sources of revelation, and it is sought in the sources of revelation not in an attempt to reenact the experiences, the thoughts, the sensibility, the affectivity, and so on, that lie behind the words of the scriptures, but in taking the scriptures as true and finding in them precise elements that settle one way or another the questions arising in the dogmatic-theological context.

We now have to take a leap. We have been talking about a single transition. The single transition we chose as our example was this discussion, this argument of Gutwenger's, his particular way of handling the problem of the consciousness of Christ and departing from Fr Galtier to a theory that acknowledged the ego, the divine subject, as somehow given in Christ's human consciousness. And the reason why he acknowledged that was because Christ as man said 'I' and meant the person, and there is only one divine person in Christ, who is both God and man, one person in two natures. That was given simply as an example.

Now, our leap is the leap of summation-integration. The simplest example is the mathematical example. You have a pair of coordinate axes. With reference to that, you have some curve. And a person may ask, 'What is the area under that curve from the point $x = 0$ to the point a?' We will suppose that the equation of the curve is $f(x) = y$, where y is equal to any function you please of x, where y is the distance vertically, and x the distance horizontally. Now $f(x) = y$ simply means any function of x, any algebraic function of x: $y = x^3 + 4x^2 + 3x + 10$, or anything of that type, or any trigono-metric function, or any exponential or logarithmic function of x, and so on: any function that you can think of; let that be the curve. The visual way the thing can be imagined is to take tiny little slices in the area and find the area of each one, which will be approximated by drawing a line that elimin-ates the curve, makes the ends flat; and one has a series of rectangles to find. To make the thing more certain, the nearer those downward lines are together, then the more accurate one's calculation of the area will be. When you get that distance between the lines as an infinitesimal, a number small-er than any number that can be assigned, then you are heading for absolute accuracy. And it will be written down: the area is equal to the integral $\int_0^a f(x)\ dx$, which is the infinitesmal. And this integral is a summation. Now that is just an illustration.

Where does the dogmatic-theological context come from? It is a matter of summing up, putting together, all the little transitions that have occurred for the last 1900 and some years. We said that Gutwenger was presupposing a dogmatic-theological context in the light of which he put his questions, from which he got his criteria. Using that total apparatus he went to scrip-ture and found, not experience, not reenacting experience, but experi-ment. Singling out precise points and getting a yes or no answer, he got the answer to his question.

Now that has occurred not only on one occasion; it has occurred again and again down the centuries. In all their debates with heretics, the Fathers appealed to scripture. Similarly, the theologians settle their questions by appealing to scripture, directly by quoting scripture or indirectly by appeal-ing to the Fathers. And the later theologians appeal to the earlier theolo-gians. The context has gradually built up. That gradual building up of the dogmatic-theological context is the development of dogma, the develop-ment of theology. Each step in that development is a transition. The dog-matic-theological context at any time is the point where you are summing up the area up to now. Let this point be such and such a year, e.g. 1000, and you add on a further area: the dogmatic-theological context is increasing. And it will continue to increase. *Humani Generis* says the sources of revela-tion never will be exhausted (DB 2314 [DS 3886, ND 859]). The [First] Vatican Council asks us to pray that there always continue to be in the church the increase of understanding, knowledge, and wisdom with respect to the doctrine of faith. As the development has existed in the past so it will continue in the future. The point I want to make is that that development is a summation, a continual addition of little points, each one of which is a transition from the world of faith to the world of theory; and it is precisely the dogmatic-theological context.

The second point is that the best way to understand the dogmatic-theological context and its development is to study questions at the time at which they were new. The place to handle any question is in terms of the historical situation and context when the question first arose. People want an argument from tradition. But prior to the time when the thing was formulated, it was not treated any more explicitly than in scripture. And after the time in which the issue was settled, we have simply the repetition in a manner adapted to a certain group of students of the point already made. The ideal time to study the crucial point in any theological or dogmatic question is the time at which the new element was added. You study the consubstantiality of the divine persons by understanding what went on in the fourth century. Everyone since has been talking about the consubstantiality of the divine persons, but one sees that question in its precise meaning, in all its difficulties, by considering all the various Arian doctrines and their antecedents and Athanasius's and later the Cappodocians' answers and their antecedents. Similarly, with regard to Christology, the whole question was set by Apollinaris, who affirmed one person, one nature, one operation, one will. And the subsequent task was to save what was correct in Apollinaris and to eliminate what was wrong. And you have the whole movement after Apollinaris: Cyril of Alexandria with his dependence upon the *fraudes Apollinistarum*; and the Antiochenes: first of all, Theodorus of Tarsus and Theodore of Mopsuestia insisting on the two natures against Apollinaris's affirmation of one nature; Nestorius's exaggeration of their position; and Cyril's intervention in a way that was compromised by using the Apollinarist formula: *mia physis tou theou logou sesarkōmenē*; the problems of the formula of union in 433, leading up to Chalcedon. If one understands just what was going on then, what the difficulties were, what the arguments were, one understands that development of the dogma. One sees how they are relying upon the earlier tradition at Ephesus. What was the criterion? It was the symbol of Nicea. Cyril, in his part of the Council, had the decree of Nicea read; and then Cyril had his letter read to them, and asked, 'Is my doctrine in agreement with Nicea?' And they said, 'Yes.' And he read Nestorius's letter. 'Is Nestorius's letter in agreement with Nicea?' And they said, 'No.' The problem raised by Nestorius – the immortal is not the mortal, the unchangeable is not the changeable, and so on – was very clear in the definition of Nicea. They took the Apostles' Creed and added in the 'consubstantial': *Deum de Deo, Lumen de Lumine,* and so on. Nestorius's contradictions were clearly contained in Nicea. His will to have two persons and two natures somehow brought together by a name or in the various Nestorian fashions was rejected. Cyril insisted that it is one and the same that is both God and man, and that was his point, whatever the defects in his formulation.

In going through the thing historically, studying the time at which the transition was made from the world of faith to the world of theory is the best way to understand what exactly is the world of theory, what precisely is contained in it, what is the exact content of the dogma, and what were the problems left over for the theologians later to solve.

By gradually building up the dogmatic-theological context as de facto historically it was built up, one arrives at an understanding of the development, one sees very concretely why it did occur, and one sees as well the further problems to which it gives rise.

So much in general.

More specifically, there is always presupposed a context. The New Testament presupposes the Old Testament. It has been claimed that the New Testament writers had at their disposition sets of *testimonia* collected from the Old Testament and that the dependence in the New Testament as well as in the primitive Christian community was upon the Old Testament. The New Testament presupposes the Old. Similarly the later discussions: there was not only presupposed the New Testament but also the traditions of the Apostles, the teaching of the Apostles contained in the continuity of the churches. On that basis, theologizing began. It presupposed only the tradition and the Old and New Testaments. But later theologizing presupposed the earlier, as Ephesus presupposed Nicea. There has always been the context from which the Catholic proceeded back to scripture, in which he formulated his questions, and in the light of which he sought answers from the scriptures.

The concrete illustration of that development is from reading Tertullian against Praxeas, Athanasius against the Arians, Basil on the Holy Ghost, Cyril against the Nestorians, Augustine against the Pelagians, Leontius of Byzantium against the Monophysites, Maximus the Confessor against the Monothelites, and so on. For the development of the doctrine of grace in the medieval period, read Landgraf and the material he has collected.

There is, then, that constant presence of a developing context from which questions that are put to scripture constitute the thematizing of scripture.

8 Thematization and Dogmatic Theology

With regard to the mode in which the thematizing occurs, the fundamental point is that the dogmatic theologian thematizes scripture as the expression of a truth.

Scripture can be taken in a large number of ways. It is an instrument for the study of *koinē* Greek in the first century. It is an instrument for the study of grammar and, further on, of comparative grammar. It can be taken in less extrinsic fashion as an event and as narrating about events, and in that case one gets the history of the composition of the various books in the canon and the history that is related in the scriptural books. It can be taken as an expression, an *Ausdruck*. In that case one is interested in the precise nature or way in which the book arose. One is concerned with the mentality, the affectivity, the imagination, the feeling, the style of a writer and considering it as a manifestation of him. It is a manner of interpretation that began with Winckelmann's study on the interpretation, the art criticism, and the study of works of art.[11] And in the work of art it is a very obvious way to proceed: conceive the work of art as an expression, a manifestation, an objectification of the artist. The better you understand the artist, the better will you understand the work of art, for the work of art is a manifestation of the artist.

That study of a text or a book as expression, as manifestation, is something quite distinct from considering it as true. You can study the classics even though you don't agree with Cicero or Plato or with Thucydides or Herodotus; you study them as expressions of a time, a mentality. It can be taken as a meeting, an *occursus*, and then one has a double psychological consideration: the one speaking and the one spoken to and the interactions between the two.

Somewhat more profoundly, one can consider the scriptures as a source of recurrent meetings: in other words, scripture as the ground of a tradition. There are the scriptures as the source, the people, the meeting effected by the scriptures with a first generation. The first generation forms a second, which is influenced by the scriptures both directly insofar as they study the scriptures but also indirectly insomuch as their formation has been through

11 Johann Joachim Winckelmann, *Geschichte der Kunst der Altertums* (Dresden, 1764). There is an E-book edition of this book (Berlin, 2003) available through Google. An English translation by G. Henry Lodge was published in 1872 (Boston: Houghton Mifflin).

a generation already acquainted with and guided by the scriptures. There is the gradual building up of a tradition, a culture that has its source in the scriptures, just as classical culture has its source in the classical authors.

All these considerations are perfectly legitimate. There is nothing wrong about studying the New Testament from the viewpoint of Palestinian geography in the first century and, similarly, studying it as expression, studying it as historical text, and so on. But those are not the viewpoints of the dogmatic theologian. You learn an awful lot about scripture and an awful lot, too, that can be of use to the dogmatic theologian. But his precise viewpoint is scripture as canonical, as true, as containing the word of God, as saying that which a Catholic cannot contradict. It grounds the classical dogmatic utterance: *si quis dixerit, anathema sit*. The dogmatic concern with scriptures, then, is concern with scriptures as the word of God and, indeed, as the word of God which cannot be contradicted, as something that is true.

With regard to that mode of thematization, proceeding from scriptures as the word of God and, indeed, as the word of God which is true, which cannot be contradicted, certain observations are to be made. The first is that the process of thematizing may or may not itself be thematized.

St Paul is talking about his preaching to the Galatians when in the Epistle to the Galatians he says: *sed licet nos aut angelus de coelo evangelizet vobis praeterquam quod evangelizavimus vobis, anathema sit.*[12] St Paul is saying something about the gospel he preached there. There is a certain thematizing of the gospel that was preached. But it is only implicit in that statement that Paul is thematizing the gospel he preached as true. He puts it concretely: 'If an angel from heaven were to teach you another gospel, let him be anathema if it is different from the gospel I preached.' If you want to explain Paul's expression, you will appeal to the notion of truth, to the immutability of truth, to the fact that Paul's gospel was true, to the point that a contradictory gospel cannot be true. And in that way you will be explaining what Paul said. But Paul did not do that explicitly. One can say it is implicit in his defense of his gospel, but his statement was much more concrete, much more direct. It is a minimum thematizing, in which thematizing the gospel insofar as it is true is only implicit. From that minimum type of thematizing one can go on to the arguments, for example, in the Council of Carthage against the Pelagians, who argued that the saints when they said, 'Dimitte nobis debita nostra,' said it 'humiliter non veraciter.' The Fathers at Carthage said that if anyone says

---

12 Galatians 1.8: 'Even if we or an angel from heaven should proclaim to you a gospel contrary to what we proclaimed to you, let that one be accursed.'

that in reciting the Our Father we say, 'Dimitte nobis debita nostra non veraciter sed humiliter,' anathema sit.[13] They were appealing to the truth of the
words of our Lord in assigning us the Our Father as our mode of prayer. We
say, 'Dimitte nobis debita nostra,' because we have sins to be forgiven. And
that is even true of the *iusti*, of the holy people in the church. No exception
is made for them. They pray that way, too. They are insisting on the truth of
scripture. It is coming out a little more clearly.

In reading the Fathers, you find they use the scriptures a great deal. If
you want to understand the argument, scripture is something that has to be
accepted. It is thematized in the way it would be thematized if it were being
thematized as true, but still that element of truth is implicit. And from the
implicit thematizing of scripture as true, one can move on to ever more
explicit uses of the process of thematizing.

The second point is that when one thematizes scripture as true, one is
determining what can be transferred from one context to another. Truth is
an unconditioned. It is independent of the subject that utters it. It is independent of any subject, and in virtue of that independence, that absoluteness, it is not dependent on some particular historical context. It is because
truth is transcendent, an absolute, an unconditioned, that it is possible to
transfer truths from one context to another, from one world to another.
And the point to note there above all is the radical difference between the
matizing a text as true and thereby grounding the possibility of a transference from one context to another, from one world to another, and, on the
other hand, the procedure of Romantic hermeneutics.

Romantic hermeneutics attempts to eliminate difference of context. The
ideal interpreter by a process of empathy (*Einfühlung*) enters into the affectivity, the mode of imagination, the way of understanding, the way of feeling,
the way of writing, of the author. By that intimacy with the author he reaches
the point where he can explain just why the author expressed himself in this
particular passage in this precise way. He will be able to say that the author
might have put it this way and might have put it that way and might have put
it some third way; but at the same time he will give the reasons why he chose
this particular way because this was precisely what he wanted to convey. That
ideal of interpretation, of hermeneutics, aims at eliminating any difference
of context between the interpreter and the text he is interpreting. One enters into another's mentality. The ideal interpreter from the viewpoint of

13 'Dimitte nobis debita nostra': 'Forgive us our sins'; 'humiliter non veraciter':
    'humbly not truly.'

Romantic hermeneutics understands the text better than the author himself did. The author is not able to give you the reasons why he used precisely those words; he uses them but he is not able to do all the literary analysis that an expert at that sort of thing can do. In Romantic hermeneutics one takes on the whole viewpoint and mentality and mode of expression of the author and comes to understand perfectly just why he wrote what he wrote in the way in which he wrote it.

That Romantic hermeneutics is not the mode of procedure of dogmatic theology down the centuries. It is something entirely different from the thematizing a text as true that I believe to be the real way in which theologians after the Fathers have proceeded.

Insofar as a text is taken as true, thematized qua true, something is found that can be transposed from one context to another simply because truth is transcendent. The other procedure no doubt can reveal an awful lot about the text, but it is the sort of thing that you can arrive at only after a lifetime of study. Kierkegaard in his *Concluding Unscientific Postscript* describes the man who spent his life studying the New Testament. At the moment he has a book going through the press that throws light on the whole aspect of the New Testament canon. Unfortunately he dies, and, simply studying the New Testament so far, he never got down to the question of whether he should believe it or not. Now that problem is a very real problem. Scripture studies can be endless. They are not finished yet. The scripture scholars at the present time represent the best opinion available at the present time. They cannot prove, and they do not claim, that future scriptural scholarship won't arrive at fuller and more accurate results. As in all empirical science, so in the work of interpretation, the procedure is through hypothesis and verification. You study the text; you reach an understanding of it; you pass judgment on the accuracy of your understanding; and your judgment usually is, 'This is probably what is meant.' And it is through a process in which more probable views are correcting less probable views that studies advance.

The dogmatic theologian is not waiting until scriptural studies are finished and have reached their ultimate results. If dogmatic theology rested upon a Romantic hermeneutics of scripture, it would not be able to begin yet. And, moreover, there is no hope of dogmatic theologians ever having the expertise in interpreting the scriptures that specialists have who devote their whole lives to one particular author, to St John or to the major epistles of St Paul. They are never going to arrive at that knowledge of St Paul, and dogmatic theology does not rest upon that. It takes the scriptures as true. It is content with a very minor determination of the meaning, a point we will have something more to say about later. But the point to be made now is that it rests on finding what was said as true and transposing that to another context. It does not rest upon the ideal of Romantic hermeneutics, which eliminates ,the necessity for a transposition from one context to another, and wants to refashion a man of the present day until he acquires purely and simply not merely the mentality of the first century AD but the mentality of this particular man Paul, who wrote these epistles, or something similar.

The third point is that it is something entirely different to take a text as a datum and thematize that and to take a text as an expression of truth and thematize that truth.

When a text is taken as a datum, the next step is to understand the datum. If one takes the gospels as data, one has before one the synoptic problem: why is it that they say so many things that are similar, yet there are differences? Some omit totally a whole series of passages. And when they do say the same thing, well, they don't say it in exactly the same way. There is a very complex problem called the synoptic problem. There have been a lot of theories towards its solution. When one proceeds in that fashion, one first of all determines just what the data are. In the second place, one arrives at some understanding of how the data could be what they are. And in the third place, one arrives at a judgment of how the synoptic gospels arose, what was their mode of composition, and so on – a theory on the synoptic problem which will be probable or true, as the case may be.

But in that case, when one begins from a text as a datum, there occurs between the datum and some knowledge of truth a process of understanding. And, in general, such processes of understanding yield probable results that probably will be improved upon by another scholar coming along and taking advantage of previous work and going a little further.

When, however, a text is taken as a truth, thematized qua *verum,* then one has truth right from the start. One's concern is to assimilate that truth, to understand what precisely it is, and insofar as one's understanding is really an understanding of that truth, one is not bringing truth into existence for the first time, as occurs when you begin from data and then understand and then judge. One is beginning from true judgments and making those true judgments one's own by understanding what precisely their meaning is. It is an entirely different type of process, and it is the proper process of dogmatic theology. Dogmatic theology does not begin from scriptures as a set of data but as a communication of truth. Thematizing what is true has a problem of understanding, but it is a problem of understanding the meaning of that truth. Truth is not something that is going to be added to the statements according to my judgment. Truth is already had from the start, and my judgment is limited to the manner in which I reach the meaning of the text.

In the third place, something is to be said more precisely about taking the text not from the viewpoint of a Romantic hermeneutics but as a truth that can be transposed into another context: thus, about taking the text not as data to be understood and leading to new judgments, for example, on the synoptic problem – neither Matthew, Mark, Luke, nor John tells us anything about the synoptic problem; they merely give evidence of the existence of the problem – but about taking what they said as true and understanding that. Something more determinate is to be added on the way the dogmatic theologian gets the truths in scripture that he uses to transpose into other contexts.

I think I have already made clearly enough the point that he uses the scripture not experientially but experimentally. Experience occurs in all of us all the time. On the basis of that experience, without any particular attention to it, our acts of understanding emerge, and it is by our experience that we judge. But when the scientist makes his measurements and performs his experiments, he is seeking a very precise experience as an answer to a theoretical question. That is what is meant by the experimental procedure. And the analogous procedure that I am talking about is something totally distinct from the exegete's total task, which is arriving at the meaning of the authors in the sense of the authors. Moreover, to a notable extent, it presupposes the exegetical task as performed, at least to a certain extent. Exegesis is a distinct type of task from the use of scriptures by the dogmatic theologian.

What precisely is that use by the dogmatic theologian? First of all, it makes use of heuristic definitions. What is meant precisely by a heuristic definition? It is a definition that is fixed, constituted, by a question, more or less, or algebraically by saying, 'Let the unknown be x.' For example, there is the theory of fire that is found in Aristotle: fire is a substance, one of the four elements. There is a theory of fire of the chemists prior to Lavoisier according to which fire is some entity called phlogiston. And there is the later theory of fire as a process of oxidization. The three theories are totally distinct and mutually opposed to one another, and it is not in terms of any one of the theories that one says they are all about fire. What is this fire they are all about? You have some notion of fire that is distinct from Aristotle's notion, Lavoisier's predecessors' notion, and the present chemical notion of what fire is. That prior notion, common to all three, presupposed by all three, the means by which one can say that the third is correct and the other two are wrong, the reason a man holding the second theory could say that Aristotle's was wrong, the reason we can say that all three are about the same thing, is taking the sensible data of fire and asking, What is it? It is the heuristic notion. It is something determined by the data and the state of inquiry of the subject. And that type of heuristic notion can be expressed most neatly by using an algebraic symbol: it's x.

For example, in the prologue of St John, there occurs the word *logos*, about four times. What is the *logos*? Well, if you ask yourself that question, you can start running through pretty well everything. The literature is endless. How can one go about it most simply and most expeditiously? Well, the *logos* is x, and it is an x that we know something about. That x was in the beginning. That x was with God. That x was God, *theos* if not *ho theos*. By him all things were made, and without him nothing was made, and so on. One can run through the series of assertions that occur in the prologue about the *logos*, and by attributing all those assertions to this x, one has, from St John himself, a considerable determination of what he meant by the word *logos*.

The advantage of that heuristic type of procedure is, first of all, it escapes revision by the future developments of biblical scholarship. Unless the prologue is argued to not belong to St John's gospel for some reason or other, then any future student of what St John meant by the *logos* in any future century will have to find a *logos* that satisfies what John says the *logos* is; otherwise he is not talking about St John's *logos*. So there is a fundamental advantage to that heuristic definition of the *logos*: you take precisely those points as determining what you mean by the *logos* that are given by St John and that cannot be eliminated by any future student or theory about what St John meant. They are part of the data.

Moreover, there occurs a reduction of the obscure to the clear. We may not be very clear about what is meant by the *logos*, but we do have more precise notions on *erat in principio, erat apud Deum, erat Deus, sine ipso factum est nihil, per ipsum omnia facta sunt*,[14] and so on. All these assertions about the *logos* are much clearer than the name *logos* itself.

This is an example of one technique that can be used by the dogmatic theologian, taking the scriptures as something true, arriving at an element that can be transposed from the scriptural context into the dogmatic-theological context. Similar examples are offered in the notes, a collection of similar statements, and the use, a certain type of use, of the development of ideas and doctrines.[15]

14 '... was in the beginning, was with God, was God, without him nothing was made, through him all were made ...'
15 The passage to which Lonergan refers asks who is Jesus, and provides a number of indications from the New Testament that any answer must satisfy. The fifth question-and-answer session was held later this day. See below, pp. 339–53.

1962-8

Positive and Systematic Theology, and Meaning[1]

I shall this morning attempt something on positive and systematic theology, which will serve as a summary, and then go on to the topic of meaning and the different levels of meaning. Tomorrow I shall say something on hermeneutics, on interpretation, and on Friday something on history.

1 Positive Theology

1.1 Truth and Thematization

We began from theology as a dogmatic-theological context, where context is a remainder concept. It denotes the rest. In other words, when any theological or dogmatic statement is made, there is a somewhat indeterminate set of other statements that complement, qualify, explain, defend the statement that is made. No statement stands by itself in splendid isolation. It always has to be clarified. There are always objections to be made, questions that can be asked. The context is that remainder. This dogmatic-theological context is the context of the present time: what is taken for granted among Catholics, what is taught and learned in seminaries and theological schools, what is discussed in theological periodicals and set forth in theological books.

Positive theology is concerned with the relation between the contemporary context and the sources of revelation. According to Pius XII, repeating

1 Wednesday, 18 July 1962, Lauzon CD/MP3 315 (31500A0E060) and 316 (31600A0E060). Lonergan began by indicating that he was now moving beyond the notes that he had distributed.

Pius IX, the noblest task of the theologian is to show how the doctrine defined by the church is contained in the sources of revelation and, indeed, contained in the sources of revelation in the same sense as it was defined. In that case, one is concerned with the justification of the contemporary context. But there is another relation between the contemporary context and the sources, and that regards the further development of the contemporary context. According to the [First] Vatican Council the church hopes and prays that the increase of understanding, knowledge, and wisdom with regard to the doctrine of faith will ever continue in the church. *Humani generis* (DB 2314 [DS 3886, ND 859]) states that the sources of revelation never will be exhausted: *numquam exhauriantur.* So there are those two aspects to positive theology, and the more fundamental one, the one that engages our attention principally, is the one of justification, which is also the work of communicating the contemporary context.

The ground or level on which that justification and communication moves is the level of truth. The scriptures and tradition can be considered in many different ways, and the theologian is concerned with them as true, as God's word, as something not to be contradicted. Truth, as we saw, is based on an absolute, an unconditioned. It proceeds from a grasp of the unconditioned, and for that reason it is independent of the subject. It is transcendent. Because of that transcendence, the same truth can be known by different subjects. Again, because of that transcendence, a truth known by one person can be believed by another on the authority of the person who knows. And the truth in the believer has its motive not in his knowledge of the other's knowledge but in the other person's knowledge. Divine faith rests ultimately not on our knowledge of God's knowledge of the mysteries but on God's knowledge of God's knowledge of the mysteries. Because it rests on God's knowledge of God's knowledge of the mysteries, it is a knowledge, a certitude, that is *super omnia.*

Besides the independence of the subject that pertains to truth as transcendent, as independent, as an absolute that grounds both the fact that the same truth may be known by many and that the same truth may be known by some and believed by others, there also results from that transcendence of truth its independence of the particular context in which it first was uttered. When one says that the truth of a statement is independent of the context in which it was uttered, one does not mean that one can determine its meaning independently of that context: meaning is always to be determined by the context in which it is uttered. But once you have determined the meaning of the truth in that context, it does not follow that the truth can be stated, can be apprehended, can be uttered, only in that context. There is a possibility of transferring the same meaning, the same truth, to other contexts, and that is the fundamental possibility of the development of dogma.

In other words, the development of dogma does not rest on Romantic hermeneutics, which eliminates the diversity of contexts, and in which one takes on the exact mentality, affectivity, imagination, and mode of expression of another and comes to understand how the other wrote just what he did in precisely the way he did. Rather, the development of dogma is based on the possibility of a transference, of a transposition, of a movement that takes truths in the sense they have in one context and expresses the same truth, the same meaning, in another context. In other words, as is clear from the example of the doctor, the judge, the psychologist, in each case they listen to what the other person says, and then they know better in their own categories precisely what the other person means.

That process of thematization is a universal human phenomenon. Men not only found families and belong to societies and have morals and systems of education and states and laws and economies and technologies, they also think about them. And this thinking about them is a thematization of them. We not only have a state, we not only have democracies, we also have a lot of talk about democracy. There is a movement towards doctrine, a movement towards theory, because there is not only the human fact with its meaning, but there is also the clarification of the meaning. And that clarification develops in time. It brings about a transposition from the world of common sense, community, the visible universe, the more obvious, to the world of doctrine, theory, system. That occurs in all the human sciences. It occurs too in men of religion, since they think about religion and work out religious doctrines and religious theories, theories of religion. That process is a universal process in human affairs, and it also occurs and has occurred in the past in the Christian religion.

That process of thematization of itself neither changes the thing that is known nor changes one's knowledge of the thing, but it adds a further knowledge. It uses the prior knowledge of the thing to attain a further, clearer, distinct type of apprehension of the same thing. It is the same malady that is known by the patient and known by the doctor who diagnoses the malady. It is the same crime that is known by the witness and is known by the judge who finds out what legal categories the crime comes under. It is the same psychological experience that is undergone by the patient and is analyzed by the therapist.

Per se the process of thematization is a transference from one type of apprehension of a truth to another type of apprehension of the same truth. But *per accidens* that process can go awry. Insofar as there is a movement to system, the system may be inadequate. It may fit the facts roughly but not accurately. It may fit some of them but not all. Again, insofar as the process to system is incomplete, the system may be incoherent. The application of logical procedures to the systematization brings to light its defects: 'If you say this, you ought to say that; but that's nonsense, and, therefore, this initial statement has to be corrected.'

A more fundamental difficulty arises from the subjects who carry out the thematization. Insofar as the subject who does the thematizing is unauthentic, his results will also be unauthentic. His horizon will reappear in his results. His lack of conversion, intellectual, moral, or religious, will reappear in his results. And so the process of thematization is not only a genetic process, a matter of pure development; it can be accompanied in other subjects by inadequate developments, failures to reach a coherent, adequate system, or, more fundamentally, by the deviations that the subject as lacking conversion, as possessing a horizon that is unauthentic, may bring about in the thematization.

Such are general reflections that hold for any process of thematization, whether in the secular world of studying societies, states, systems of law, systems of education, systems of morals, and so on, or in our particular field of the development of dogma and the development of theology.

1.2 Comparative Method

How is the theologian to go about the task of justifying, of reducing to the sources, the contemporary dogmatic-theological context? We said that the first rule is to concentrate on the turning points, on the moments of development, on the elements of change. Insofar as one studies all the changes, one is able to complete the movement from the initial formulations of the faith, of the original revelation, to the formulations employed in the contemporary dogmatic-theological context. The final result is a summation of all the changes. By concentrating on the points of change, one simplifies one's task a great deal. Instead of studying each question over the course of 2000 years and finding that in the first 400 years people were just about saying the same thing, and then from 600 to the present day they were saying again what had been developed, by concentrating on the points of change, one gets right down to the center, to where the real issues lie in their original and basic formulation. One reaches those points of change, those genetic moments, the fields in which the developing is occurring, as distinct from the periods in which the development was yet to occur or in which the development had already occurred, by employing a comparative method. Comparative method is a fundamental tool. It is not a complete method, but it does serve to isolate the points of interest.

To take a concrete instance, the term 'consubstantiality' became Catholic dogma with the Council of Nicea in 325. You can find the term 'consubstantiality' used in all the subsequent Fathers, in all the Scholastic writers, in all the subsequent theologians. They all know about it, and they are saying substantially the same thing as was meant at Nicea and was crystallized for the Western church in the preface of the Most Holy Trinity: *quod enim de tua gloria revelante te credimus, hoc de Filio tuo, hoc de Spiritu Sancto sine differentia discretionis sentimus.*[2] Prior to 325 you have different meanings of the *homoousion*. In the Council of Nicea itself, there were five bishops who refused to accept the symbol because, they said, consubstantiality can be said of the Son only by presupposing that the Son and the Father are material. There was a sense of consubstantiality that was in more common use prior to Nicea, a sense that was simply material: the Son is consubstantial to his Father because he comes out of the matter supplied by his Father; there is a community of matter. That was one of the meanings of the term, and it was the only meaning known by the five bishops who refused the formula, at least according to their allegations.

Again, the term 'supernatural,' while it was used as a laudatory epithet long before 1230, became at that period, through the instrumentality principally of Philip the Chancellor at the University of Paris, a highly technical, theoretical term. You get the meaning of the term in understanding the movement that culminated with the solution put forward by Philip the Chancellor. You will find the supernatural in subsequent writers in approximately the same sense, and it is no novelty and no problem. The way it is used prior to that is not the strict technical sense of the theorem that, once it was put forward by Philip the Chancellor, solved endless problems. You get, in the genetic moment, the point of change, the place in which your positive studies most fruitfully are concentrated; and you find those points by using comparative method when the differences arise.

Comparative method is – again, a point to be insisted upon – not the whole of method, but it is the initial and fundamental task of finding and

2 See above, p. 26, note 35.

collecting the relevant data. There is the comparative method in selecting the genetic moments. It is used in two ways. One way is exclusion, what we need not study particularly, namely, all the subsequent repetitions of the development. Again, it can be used to eliminate all the prior statements that are simply repetitions of the original revelation in scripture. One concentrates on that precise slice of thought in which the development is occurring. Again, comparative method is applied within that slice because, in general, a development is not just a leap. It involves all sorts of little steps; there are preparatory steps. And by studying all the differences within that process, one comes to possess the data on which a further method is to be applied.

For example, with regard to the consubstantiality of the Son: (1) there is the symbolic thinking of the Jewish Christians and the quasi-symbolic thinking, the pseudo-mythical thinking, of the Gnostics. This is one type. (2) Again, there are the heresies of the Adoptionists and the Patripassians. (3) There is the mode of conceiving the divinity of the Son in Tertullian, which is approximately that the Son is made of the right matter, and therefore he can be temporal and subordinate; he is divine if he is made of the right divine stuff. (4) There are the ideas of Origen, which are Platonist. The Son is truth itself and wisdom itself and redemption itself, but he is not goodness itself or divinity itself. The Father alone is divinity itself and goodness itself, and the Son is a participation of these. (5) There is the recasting of the issue by Arius. The Son is either a creature or a creator. He is not the creator. He is *ab alio*. He is a Son. Therefore, he must be a creature. One has there several different modes in which the question might have been put, the gradual developing of the question.

Similarly, with regard to Christology, where the fundamental element is Nicea, which predicates of one and the same – 'and in Jesus Christ, His only Son, our Lord' – both divine attributes and human attributes. He is God of God and Light of Light, true God of true God, consubstantial with the Father, *natum non factum* – all these statements that occur in Nicea. At the same time, he is conceived of the Holy Spirit and born of the Virgin Mary, he suffered under Pontius Pilate, and so on; these other human statements are made about him. The basic step was Apollinaris's, in his conceiving the Son as one nature, one person, with one natural operation, one natural will. Apollinaris is attacked by the Antiochenes who insisted on the two natures: Diodore of Tarsus, principally, and Theodore of Mopsuestia. There was an extension, an exaggeration, of their position by Nestorius and a reaction by Cyril of Alexandria, who insisted on the unity of the Son and who, without being aware of it, was quoting Apollinarist writings under the impression that they were Athanasius's. And there is the further development between the two, the quasi-settlement at Chalcedon, with the objections of the Egyptians, who wanted to stick closer to Cyril, Cyril's mistakes in terminology, and so on.

But that is the field in which that development occurs. One selects that field. One understands what exactly all the terms meant to each of the writers, where the problems really lay, and what they thought the problems were. By a comparative method one gets the data of that development.

1.3   Understanding the Doctrine and Understanding the History of the Doctrine

One comes closer to one's task of justification, showing that it was the same after and before – there was a development, but it was a proper thematization, not an aberration – by the point that understanding the history of a doctrine is intimately related to understanding the doctrine itself. It is intimately related in two ways. If you understand the history of the doctrine, you will understand the doctrine. And, inversely, if you understand the doctrine, you will be able to pick out the key points in the development of the doctrine.

If, for example, a man is a medical doctor, he will be able to write a history of medicine. He will know just what was significant. Consider two men, for example: one is not a medical doctor, and the other is; and they both attempt to write a history of medicine. Well, both can collect all the documents that regard the history of medicine. But the fellow who is not a medical doctor, who does not know the contemporary science, will be able to pick out the documents that obviously bear upon medicine, but he may easily miss things that have a real and perhaps very significant bearing upon medicine, simply because he does not know enough medicine. There may be lacunae. He may collect things that are of no great importance. The man who is a doctor, merely in selecting, in gathering his materials, will spot the things that bear on the questions that one who is not a doctor will overlook. He will be able to evaluate significance and blocks in the development in a way one who does not understand medicine will not be able to do. The same is true in the history of any science. Unless you are a mathematician, you are wasting your time trying to write the history of mathematics. Unless you are a physicist, you are wasting your time trying to write the history of physics. Unless you are a chemist, you are wasting your time trying to write the history of chemistry. And unless you are a theologian, you are wasting your time trying to write the history of dogma and of theology. The understanding of the contemporary context is what enables one to understand just where the key points were in the process of development. Inversely, if you understand the history, you will arrive at a very accurate and precise and adequate understanding of the doctrine itself.

Now, by understanding the history I do not mean that one understands the doctrine and throws it back on the history. You have to be able to read a text, and de facto that is a rare gift. The number of people that cannot read a text is extraordinary. I will give you a simple instance from personal experience. You will find in my *Divinarum Personarum Conceptio Analogica*, on page 248, a series of quotations from St Thomas in which St Thomas states in every possible manner conceivable that the act of sensation itself is passive and that it is caused by the object.[3] Every one of the passages that I quote directly contradicts the doctrine of vital act that has been attributed by Thomist commentators and everyone else to St Thomas for 650 years. I first published that series of quotations at least thirteen, probably fifteen years ago, and as far as I know it has made very little impression on anyone. They still keep interpreting St Thomas in terms of vital act, and if you simply read those texts there is no way of reconciling that position with what St Thomas is explicitly stating. And if you investigate the foundations in St Thomas, where on earth do they find the doctrine of vital act? Well, 'It is always implicit. It is never anything St Thomas says explicitly. But it is what St Thomas must obviously mean.'

I have given a particularly clear example from St Thomas, but there are countless other instances of the difficulty of reading a text, of seeing just what is said. That is a particularly clear one. Take Bouillard's *Conversion et grâce chez s. Thomas*, published some years earlier.[4] In it, he holds that St Thomas has not got our notion of actual grace, that there is a basic difference. He does not mean the same thing as we do because he has no elevation of the faculty prior to justification. According to all the later theologians there is required some sort of elevation of the faculty for a supernatural act prior to justification. Why must there be this elevation of the faculty? Because the faculty produces the act; it is a vital act. But if St Thomas does not hold vital act, there is no sense in saying he does not hold the same

---

3 For these texts, see Bernard Lonergan, *The Triune God: Systematics* (see above, p. 153, note 12) 546–52.
4 Henri Bouillard, *Conversion et grâce chez s. Thomas d'Aquin, étude historique* (Paris: Aubier, 1944).

doctrine regarding actual grace. What is true is he does not accept the principle of vital act in that particular meaning. I do not mean St Thomas does not admit the existence of living beings and the specific difference between living beings and non-living beings. That is not the point. It is a precise theory of what a vital act is. According to Aristotle, *quidquid movetur ab alio movetur*. According to Plato, the soul moves itself. According to 13th-century Augustinians, when they were forced to acknowledge a real distinction between substance and accidents, substance and potencies, there are vital potencies, potencies that move themselves. That the potency moves itself is the doctrine of vital act. It is the opposite of *quidquid movetur ab alio movetur*. If you hold that view of vital act, then you have to have an elevation of a faculty to be able to produce its own supernatural act if it has not yet got the habit. But because you don't find that elevation of the faculty in St Thomas's discussion of acts prior to justification, it does not mean one does not find actual grace there. Of course, if you read St Thomas through the notion of vital act, you just do not get to the text at all.

When I say, 'Understand the history of the doctrine; understand the doctrine,' I mean you have to read the text and see what is said. Don't interpret it by what is implicit. What is implicit is a hypothetical thematization of the text. If your author did not carry out that thematization, then it is not in the text. It may be a conclusion that someone else can legitimately draw, but it isn't in the text. Studying the history of a doctrine is studying what is explicit in the texts. Attend to that. What is implicit will come out in subsequent thematizations. To understand the history of the doctrine, you first of all have to get the relevant texts. You find them by comparative method. You have to read them and consider what is explicitly stated. Do not qualify what is explicitly stated by what would be implicit for you. What is implicit for you is a further thematization. What you have to do is get back to the stage prior to the thematization. You cannot get back to the stage prior to the thematization if every text you read contains a number of things that are there implicitly. And the number of things that are there implicitly – what are they? They are the contemporary dogmatic-theological context.

To justify the development you have to be able to see objectively what the thought was prior to the development. How did they conceive it? You can come to know how they conceive it by reading what they say and taking it at its face value and not adding to it what is implicit there, in some vague sense of the word 'implicit,' but is never explicit. Before you can attempt to understand the history of the doctrine, you have to be able to read the texts in their explicit obvious meaning.

1.4 Genetic Method

Next, the comparative method reveals differences within the process. The comparative method becomes genetic when you account for the differences.

Now, such differences may be between different authors, or they may be in a single author. If you have a highly intelligent author, such as Aquinas, you will find an array of differences, of sequences of differences, that otherwise you would only find in a few centuries of sequences of different authors. Both are understood in general in the same way. There is always a reason why the change was made, and one has to read enough around the place where one has found the difference to spot why the change occurred. If it is a change in theology in St Thomas, the best thing to look for is his quotations from St Augustine. They usually account for why Thomas changed on this point or that. Look for his quotations from St Augustine in the objections, in the *videtur quod non*, in the *sed contra est*, and you will be able to pin the thing down pretty well.

Again, differences do not occur in an isolated fashion. My doctoral work was on *gratia operans* in St Thomas, and there was a whole series of fronts on which the development took place: in the doctrine of grace, in his conception of Pelagianism, in his doctrine on operation in general, in his doctrine on divine operation, in his doctrine on will, and in his doctrine on liberty. The whole set was moving forward, from the *Sentences* to the *Prima Secundae*, and you could spot the reason why he changed right along the line. When St Thomas says the same thing one hundred times or any author says the same thing one hundred times, it gets you no further than if he said it once. You understand it or you don't. But when he says different things, a series of different things on the same topic, and concomitantly a series of other different things on a related topic, and another series of different things on a third related topic, and a number of different things on yet a fourth related topic, then the *libertas errandi* is cut down. It is much harder to misinterpret that whole movement than it is to misinterpret one text or one statement that is repeated over and over again. And the more you pinpoint just why the change occurred, what would account for the change, it becomes still harder. In other words, when a study of a development begins to pin things down in all its correlations and interrelations, the possibility of misinterpretation is cut down and down and down with every stroke. The more detailed and fuller one's study of the process becomes, the more ingenious one has to be to misinterpret it. And there is a limit to human ingenuity, even at making mistakes. That is the application of genetic method.

1.5   Dialectical Method

But the study of a development does not limit itself to the developing process. Along with it there will occur opposite movements. Usually there are not definitions of dogmas without there also being condemnations of heretics. And they form part of the study of history.

To illustrate the different ways of development, take the question of the procession of the Holy Ghost. Gregory Nazianzen attempted to meet the argument of Eunomius. If the Holy Ghost is not a Son, well, what on earth is he? He is not the Father. He is not the Son. What on earth do you mean by saying that he proceeds? How can he be distinct from the Father and not another Son? Or perhaps a daughter or a grandson? And Gregory, to meet the issue, appealed to the early chapters in Genesis and said Seth, the son of Adam, was related to Adam as God the Son to God the Father. But Eve also had the same nature. Eve was not a son and Eve was not a daughter. Yet Eve was consubstantial with Adam. She was taken out of his side. And that became a rather popular image. It recurs frequently right down to John Damascene: that the Holy Spirit is like Eve, the Son like Seth, and God the Father like Adam. Adam, Eve, and Seth have the same human nature, but they are also distinct, and the way in which Eve arises from the father is not the same as the way in which Seth arises from the father. Seth was generated, but Eve was not generated.

That mode of conception, of course, ties right in with Photius's doctrine that the Holy Spirit does not proceed from the Son but only from the Father. Eve does not proceed from Seth. She is quite independent of Seth, in fact prior to Seth.

Gregory of Nyssa started from the traditional doctrine, the traditional defense of the Trinity in terms of the *monarchia*. There is one principle. Consequently for Gregory, both the Son and the Holy Spirit are *principiata, aitiatoi*. And the difference between the Son and the Holy Spirit is that the Son is *principiatum immediate* while the Holy Spirit is *principiatum mediate*.

A third mode of conception is in Augustine. He accepted the doctrine of *monarchia*: the Father is the origin of everything. But he quoted St John: *principium, qui et loquor vobiscum.*[5] The Son also is a principle. According to Augustine not only the Father is a principle but also the Son. The Father is *principium in principiatum*; the Son *principium principiatum*. And Augustine is saying something about the Son that was not said either by Gregory of Nazianzus or Gregory of Nyssa. The Son is a principle.

---

5   The reference is to a reading of John 8.25.

You get the difference, then, between the Greek theology and the Western. Following Gregory of Nyssa, only the Father is principle. The Son is not principle. He is *principiatum*, but *immediate*. In the Western teaching, both the Father and the Son are the one principle of the Holy Spirit. There one can see how one will get two equivalent theories, Gregory of Nyssa and Augustine, saying the same thing but in different ways. For Augustine the Son is a principle. For Gregory of Nyssa, he is not. But one will also get this image of Adam, Seth, and Eve that kept being repeated in popular fashion right down to St John Damascene. One will also find it in Photius. Whether it has any bearing on Photius's doctrine I have not been able to establish, but at least it is coherent with Photius's position. There is the possibility of different developments occurring. Gregory Nazianzen is very careful to state that, of course, this image merely provides some remote explanation of the matter, and he is not venturing to scrutinize the mystery in any way. If one reads Gregory at all, one will not venture to transfer any of the differences between Seth and Eve to the differences between the Son and the Holy Spirit. Gregory Nazianzen takes all precautions about it, but the precautions were forgotten later on, and they were not insisted on in the same respect. One cannot argue from Gregory Nazianzen to Photius, but one can get some understanding of Photius from Gregory Nazianzen and the repetition of that analogy: thought on the level of an image, thought on the level of two modes of analysis. This gives one a basic understanding of the quarrel between the East and West on the procession of the Holy Spirit.[6]

The dialectical element enters in insofar as developments which are equivalent are not seen to be equivalent because of horizon, because of unauthenticity, because of a lack of conversion. Or, when one development is correct and another mode is not, then again one has the opposition. Insofar as one side can be reduced to an unauthenticity, a lack of conversion, a lack of an adequate horizon, one has in the history itself a norm that enables one to say, 'This development is the true development and that is an aberration.' Insofar as in the history itself there is a manifestation of elements of aberration in opposition to what goes forward as a pure thematization, the history itself provides a norm, a principle of judgment. And insofar as it provides a norm, a principle of judgment, one has from history, as understood, the transition to doctrine, to the statement, 'This is correct; the other is the opposite.'

That possibility of the transition from understanding history to determining which is the correct doctrine seems to me to be the fundamental key or tool in

6 Lonergan goes into much greater detail on these questions in thesis 4 of *The Triune God: Doctrines*, (see above. p. 25, note 30).

positive theology. We know by the authority of the church, by the divine assistance granted the magisterium, that later developments that are defined of faith and defined as revealed are contained in the deposit of faith. But the church is not content with authority, however much the theologian may want to be content with authority and tell the boys, 'Fall down and adore – that's what has been determined by the magisterium.' The church, in the words of Pius IX and Pius XII, wants the theologian to show how the defined doctrine is contained in the original source, not simply to agree with the church defining but to take the further step of showing how what is defined is found in the sources. One meets that task insofar as the study of history reveals its own immanent norms, insofar as the dialectical element, the element of opposition, can be traced to some type of aberration. Consequently, the opposition between opposed developments or the opposition between development and reaction reveals an element of aberration and provides an objective criterion of judgment for saying, 'This is correct and that is mistaken.' Insofar as from the history itself one can arrive at a judgment, 'This is true and that is not,' positive theology can fulfill the task of justifying, of showing how the formulas employed in definitions have their basis in the original sources.

As positive theology relates the contemporary context to its origins either in a process of justification of the contemporary context or to fill out the present context, to fill out the current development of theology based upon contemporary scriptural studies, patristic studies, conciliar studies, and so on, positive theology also makes a contribution to the further development of theology.

2 Systematic Theology

As, then, positive theology relates the context to its origins, systematic theology relates the contemporary context, the developments that have occurred, to their end.

Why should there be any development? The answer is what is stated in the [First] Vatican Council: that reason illumined by faith can arrive at some understanding, and that a most fruitful understanding, of the mysteries. What is the point to the developments that have occurred in the past? They give us some understanding of the mysteries. Now that is true of the dogmatic developments, and it is true further of the theological developments.

Insofar as method concerns systematic theology, the fundamental point it makes is that each one of us in doing theology is using the mind God gave us and the gift of faith God gave us. And insofar as one's theology is to be methodical, one has to know exactly what that mind is and what its faith is. The basic unauthenticity in all thinking is, on the one hand, to use the mind

God gave one and, at the same time, to suppose and think and judge and speak as though it were something else. The outstanding illustration of that is Hume. Hume's account of the human mind is in terms of impressions related to one another by custom and habit. But if you read Hume, you will find that he is as intelligent and as sharp as anything. If his mind were just a set of impressions related by habits, he would not have been able to write his *Enquiry concerning Human Understanding*. He would have just poured forth what everyone else was saying. He would have merely given his impressions related by habits. He would have talked like a moron. The fundamental refutation of Hume is the opposition between the mind Hume used and what Hume said the mind was. And that opposition is not confined to Hume. All conceptualism ignores human intelligence, human rationality, human acts of understanding, and puts in their place a metaphysical machine in which concepts pop out and are looked at and compared. A great deal of Scholastic theology has been done on that basis. What is insight or understanding? Well, it is something that is very new and very vague. One can read an awful lot of Thomist literature without coming across any great advertence to the fact that St Thomas said, '... *anima humana cognoscit seipsam per suum intelligere, quod est actus proprius eius, perfecte demonstrans virtutem eius et naturam.*'[7] Instead of appealing to the *intelligere*, to the act of understanding, to demonstrate perfectly the nature and the powers of the soul, what do you find in most textbooks? They appeal to the universal concept to demonstrate the spirituality of the soul, the spirituality of intellect, and so forth. The act of understanding is something beyond the horizon.

Secondly, the structure of knowing is isomorphic with the structure of the proportionate known. Theory of knowledge leads to, grounds, a metaphysics of proportionate being. Our knowing in the strong sense is a compound of activities that occur on three levels: a level of experiencing, a level of understanding, a level of judging. But it is one knowing that occurs through the three sets of activities. Experiencing is not the same as understanding. Neither experiencing nor understanding is the same as judging. They are three quite distinct levels; yet all three are needed to have one knowing in the full, strong sense of the word 'know.'

Because there are three levels of activity, three types of act, there are three types of partial objects. If experiencing is different from understanding, the object of experiencing is different from the object of understanding. You are not experiencing again when you understand. Just as there are partial

7 'The human soul knows itself through its own act of understanding, which is its proper act, perfectly demonstrating its power and its nature.' Thomas Aquinas, *Summa theologiae*, 1, q. 88, a. 2, ad 3m.

components in one knowing, so there are partial components in one known. If there is one knowing, there is one known. But that one known has to be a compound of three partial objects. Accordingly, if knowing builds up on three levels, the known similarly has to build up on three levels. And so an object proportionate to human knowing is going to be a compound of object of experience, object of understanding, object of judgment. And in traditional terms, object of judgment, what is known insofar as you judge *est*, is act. Object of understanding, what is known insofar as you understand, is form, intelligibility in the strong sense of intelligibility. And object of experience, what is known insofar as you experience, what never is made intelligible, the material or empirical residue, is, in traditional language, potency. Any proportionate object of human knowing is a compound of potency, form, and act. It is *quidditas sive natura* (form) *in materia corporali* (potency) *existens* (act).

If one knows one's knowing, one knows one's proportionate object. One has fundamental, basic definitions for fundamental, basic terms, and one has the proportion of matter to form, potency to form, settled as clearly as one has the proportion of sense to understanding determined. One has the proportion of form to act as clearly determined as one has the proportion of understanding to judgment, known in one's experience of oneself.

Once one gets some basic terms that are clearly defined, one has a basis on which one can work. Metaphysics is obscure when there is nothing clear about it, when that is the common difficulty. When one gets certain basic terms clear as crystal, one has a starting point and one can go on.

According to the [First] Vatican Council, the theologian reaches his imperfect but fruitful understanding of the mysteries *ex analogia eorum quae naturaliter cognoscuntur*.[8] The great difficulty with these analogies, as far as I can see, is that the theologians tend to say, 'Well, this natural knowledge, that's a matter for psychologists or metaphysicians or physicists, and so on and so forth; I needn't bother about it.' There have been disputes about the consciousness of Christ for roughly twenty years. And as far as I can see, the fundamental difficulty is that the majority of people who have written on the topic will not take the trouble to find out what exactly consciousness is in the ordinary, everyday human being. If that were clarified, 98 per cent of the difficulties would be eliminated. Another example is the trinitarian processions. According to St Thomas there is an analogy to the trinitarian processions only in man, in the rational creature, and in the rational creature only considered according to his rational part. The vast majority of accounts of the psychological analogy that have been put forth since St Thomas, as far

8 '… from the analogy of what is naturally known.'

as I have been able to see, have not paid any attention to that psychological process. We have had metaphysical theories of various kinds, but that psychological theory has, in my opinion, been neglected. You cannot have an understanding of the mysteries based on the analogy of natural knowledge if you don't want to take the trouble to acquire the natural knowledge. Unless that natural knowledge is acquired accurately and fully, you are building a house on sand, and you are destroying the confidence of your students in speculative theology, in the existence of an end to this development.

Finally, all analogy involves a twofold ignorance. It knows something similar, and it knows that there also is something dissimilar, but it does not know what that is. That is one element of ignorance. The second is that it does not know how important, how significant, that unknown is. That element of ignorance involved in all analogy tends to be systematically overlooked. St Thomas repeatedly states that we do not know *quid sit Deus*. We only know God analogously. There is a type of knowledge that we have to be able to talk about that is not analogous knowledge, in order to say the knowledge we have not got. St Thomas's expression for it is saying we do not know *quid sit Deus*. Now I can quote you endless theologians who assert we do know *quid sit Deus*, that one is agnostic if one says we do not know *quid sit Deus*. Well, they are not meaning the same thing as St Thomas, but it is important to know what that *quid sit* means. You know *quid sit* when you understand a thing properly, when the form or species that limits your act of understanding is proportionate to the form or species that constitutes the thing. And so, the only way one can have an understanding of God is by the beatific vision.

3 Meaning[9]

We are all more or less familiar with linguistic meaning, the meaning of words. But it is not the only form of meaning. And to understand the meaning of words in everything except a strictly scientific treatise, it is important to know about other types of meaning which come in and interfere with the purely logical process that, outside the treatise, is an unrealized ideal.

In *Insight*, in chapter 17, I have a section on the limitations of the treatise;[10] and by a treatise I mean a text in which every term is defined

9 The break was taken at the end of the preceding paragraph. The recording after the break begins in mid-sentence: '... varieties, significance, moments, and go on to the determination of what other people mean. Hermeneutics tomorrow, and then the historical movement of meanings on Friday. It's a fundamental topic.' The second part of the lecture is recorded on Lauzon CD/MP3 316 (31600AOE060).

10 Lonergan, *Insight* 595–600.

exactly and used univocally, in one sense and only one sense, in which all relations between terms are either postulated or syllogistically derived, and in which the whole statement consists solely in that. There are very few fields of inquiry in which the treatise is something established. It is the ideal of symbolic logic, how to put treatises together; but symbolic logic has limited fields of application.

Besides linguistic meaning there are intersubjective, aesthetic, and symbolic meaning. And in the fourth place I will add something about their influence on linguistic meaning.

3.1   Intersubjective Meaning

St Thomas speaks of hands rising spontaneously to defend the head: if the head is threatened, the arm will go up to protect it. He extends this to the body social. There is an intersubjectivity, a spontaneous relationship between different human beings, that seems in a way to antecede, to precede, the distinction between the I and Thou.

To give an example: I was walking up the ramp that leads into the Borghese Gardens, and there was a mother and little child coming out, and the child was running and took a tumble. Spontaneously, although I was fifteen feet away from the child, I found myself moving forward to try and prevent its fall. There is an intersubjective field in which we are spontaneously, as it were, in communication, that somehow is prior to the distinction between I and Thou.

The fundamental investigation of this field is Max Scheler's *Wesen und Formen der Sympathie*; and that has been translated certainly into French, probably into English – literally, *The Nature and Forms of Sympathy*.[11]

As there is this intersubjectivity, so there also is intersubjective meaning. Intersubjective meaning is something we perceive. We perceive it in a person's countenance, in the movements of his eyes, of his lips, of his facial muscles, of his head, his fingers, hands, arms, torso, legs. Meaning can be communicated in a manner that, as it were, escapes notice. You go into another's room, and there is a spontaneous reaction on his part that is met by another spontaneous reaction on your part, and it more or less settles the basis from which communication will start out. If you go in to ask a superior for permission and you have a big permission to ask, and you see the look on his face, you may change your inquiry. Or you go in to ask a ques-

---

11 Max Scheler, *Wesen und Formen der Sympathie* (Bern: Francks, 1953); in English, *The Nature of Sympathy*, trans. Peter Heath (London: Routledge & Kegan Paul 1954).

tion and you find the professor highly disturbed or something like that, well, you'll cut it short. It's the sort of thing one has to watch and observe in oneself to discover what it really is. All I can give you are a few clues to note the reality of this intersubjective level of meaning. We will take as an example a smile.

First of all, a smile has a meaning. It is not simply a movement of the lips and the facial muscles and the eyes. Beyond that there is a form, in the sense of a meaning conveyed by the smile. And that is the reason why we do not walk around the street smiling at everyone we meet. We would be misunderstood if we did. There is a meaning in the smile, whatever it is. Moreover, that meaning is highly perceptible. The slightest trace of an incipient smile may give a person away. And the reason it is highly perceptible is precisely because it has a meaning. What has a meaning is easily perceived. You can be walking along the street with someone, carrying on a conversation in a rather low voice. The traffic is roaring by, exhaust is bursting, and all sorts of street noises are coming on; and you don't hear them. You just hear that voice. If the person were talking gibberish, it would not be selected out from all the sounds that are going on. Precisely because it has a meaning, it is selected out. You hear that and listen to it, and all the rest is somehow blocked out. It is going on; it is there, but it is not successfully, significantly passing the threshold of consciousness unless there is a sudden explosion of some sort that makes you jump. And the reason why what has a meaning is easily perceived is that our psychic flow of consciousness, our flow of apprehensions, is not something that is determined solely by light waves and sound waves and other impressions upon us. There occur the impressions, but there is also the selectivity of the subject. And what the subject selects is what has a meaning. The rest passes unnoticed.

That apprehension of meaning is immediate. It is not a conclusion. We don't see the movements of the facial muscles and say, 'If these movements occur, there is a smile, and this kind of smile with this kind of meaning.' It is insight into the sensible data. Just as the intelligent subject communicates himself by these spontaneous movements, so the spontaneous movements are understood.

The meaning contained in the smile is not a conventional meaning. It is natural, spontaneous. We have to learn to walk, we have to learn to talk, we have to learn to swim. But we do not learn to smile. We do not practice smiling and gradually reach the point where we are able to smile well – unless perhaps one is a movie actor.

Again, the meaning of the smile is not something that is taught to us. We catch on. And if we did not catch on, we would never know the meaning, unless we find it out for ourselves. No one has to have explained to him the meaning of the smile. One understands at once. That meaning is not reducible to some other meaning. It is not elucidated by putting it in words. One is effecting a thematization, moving off into another field in which one can have something that corresponds; but one cannot reproduce that type of meaning in the smile within the conceptual field. Just as in listening to a symphony, there is a meaning to the symphony, but that meaning is communicable only through the symphony. There can be a music critic who will explain the symphony to you, but he is operating on another level, and he is not giving you the equivalent of hearing the symphony.

There is a set of divergences between the type of meaning in the intersubjective field, illustrated by the smile, and the type of meaning in the conceptual order. Conceptual meaning always aims at univocity. It tries to have one meaning for one word. It does not get there, but it has an aim at it. But a smile expresses all sorts of quite different things. There can be a smile of recognition, a smile of welcome, a smile of friendship, a smile of love, a smile of joy, a smile of pleasure, a smile of satisfaction, a smile of contentment, a smile of ridicule, a smile that is ironic, a smile that is resigned, a smile that simply means one is fagged out, tired: 'Don't bother me any more.' It can run through all sorts of meanings.

Again, a conceptual meaning may be truth or lying, truth as opposed to lying, saying what one does not mean. And it may be true as opposed to false. One is saying what one thinks is true, but one is mistaken. Intersubjective meaning may be true in the sense opposed to mendacity, in the sense opposed to deception. And again, it can be an intended deception: one can smile and smile and be a villain. But it is not properly the type of meaning that is true or false. A smile is not true or false in the manner in which a conceptual meaning is true or false. It is truth in the sense in which one can say that a person is true, a thing is true. But it is usually not true in the sense in which a proposition is true or false.

Meaning on the intersubjective level is at a lower stage of differentiation than meaning on the level of language, of concepts and language. In language, endless differentiation is possible. We distinguish what we feel, what we desire, what we fear, what we think, what we know, what we will, what we command, what we intend, what we will as our end. But those distinctions are not drawn on the intersubjective level. One can understand them, the better one understands the smile, but they are not determinate, differentiated on that level.

The conceptual meaning refers to something else, to a meant. But the intersubjective meaning is part of the constitution of the intersubjective situation. It presupposes the situation, the meeting, the presence, the previous relations one has had with another. It acknowledges the interpersonal situation. It determines the situation. It rather betrays the subject than describes the subject. One reveals oneself in a spontaneous fashion by these intersubjective manifestations of meaning. It is, as it were, a transparency of the person. The meaning of the smile is antecedent to any distinction between soul and body. It is a manifestation of the other person in which the other person is, as it were, immediately manifested, manifesting, self-revealing to the other.

Now, that is just a set of hints on intersubjective meaning. One knows what intersubjective meaning is in the measure in which one attends to one's apprehension of intersubjective meanings in the way others behave and deal with us, and one attends to one's own self-revelation intersubjectively.

3.2 Aesthetic Meaning

Another type of meaning is the aesthetic meaning. In this I am indebted mainly to Susanne Langer. She is quite a brilliant woman, and she has, to my mind, a very fine study of the nature of art in her book *Feeling and Form*.[12]

Art may be conceived as the objectification of a purely experiential pattern. And we will take the terms one by one.

Pattern; first of all, what is meant by pattern? One can think of an abstract pattern. There is a pattern in the musical score. There is a pattern in the indentations on a gramophone record. There is a pattern in the sound waves. In each case one has something that is in a one-to-one correspondence with the concrete pattern that is realized in colors that are seen, in sounds that are heard. The concrete pattern is in the acts of perceiving, in the movements of the body, in hearing sounds, in seeing colors. That pattern is an experiential pattern when it is concrete, when it is occurring in one's acts of perceiving. We said already in speaking of hearing another's voice that, because it has a meaning, it is perceptible. And the reason why what has a meaning is perceptible is that our perceptions are not determined by the objective light waves and sound waves that are impinging upon us but by a meaningful selection of them. Because the

---

12 Susanne Langer, *Feeling and Form: A Theory of Art* (New York: Charles Scribner's Sons, 1953).

experience in the case of art is put in a pattern and the pattern has some sort of meaning, is meaning on some level, somewhat similar to the intersubjective meaning, because that experience is patterned, it is already, as it were, predigested, it already is meaningful. It would be quite an achievement to listen to the street noises and then give some sort of reproduction of them. They are not perceptible except in a very vague fashion – there is a lot of noise going on – simply because they are not patterned. On the other hand, if we hear a tune, a melody, it is easy to apprehend it and to repeat it if one has any musical talent at all. It is easy to learn verses by heart precisely because they are patterned. A decorated surface is a surface that is easily seen. One does not attend to a blank surface. And in general, the decorated surface is built up on some organic motif. There is the basic movement of the trunk and the spreading of the branches in various types of ways, but the eye can catch a basic line and follow through all the ramifications and developments and see the thing as a whole. The thing is patterned.

It is a purely experiential pattern that I wish to speak about. And by that is meant a pattern in experiencing that is native, proper to the experiencing. Our senses can be simply an apparatus in which we exercise automatic behavior in a ready-made world. The light shifts from red to green, and the foot gets off the brake and presses the accelerator without any notable thought process occurring. Our senses respond to signals and result in actions that are automatic. We become adjusted, and we behave. Our senses in that case are not performing according to any native pattern, any native scheme. They become mere instruments for adjusting, producing the automatic expected behavior of this human animal in this environment.

Again, our senses can become mere instruments of scientific inquiry. One sees what is of intellectual concern, and one sees nothing else. One attends to that. One can draw all sorts of distinctions along that line. One's seeing is guided by an already constructed conceptual scheme. One sees every element that is found in that conceptual scheme. One does not notice anything else. The operations of sense in that case are not according to any spontaneity of sense. They are in accord with the exigences of intellect, of intelligence and rationality.

But besides being mere instruments utilized solely for extraneous purposes, the senses and perceptions can have and do have a life of their own. And the purely experiential pattern is the pattern that is in conformity with the spontaneity of sensitivity, of perceptivity, in its own realm. Moreover, that spontaneity as not interfered with by any physiological or psychological theory of perception is human sensitivity in its native openness to its object and to its fundamental finality.

Such a purely experiential pattern, native to sense, is a liberation of sense, of perceptivity, from ulterior purposes of adjustment to our industrialized civilization, of subservience to scientific pursuits or anything else. When sensitivity is so liberated, its spontaneity, its vitality, comes to life. It manifests itself in its native experiential patterns in all their possible varieties. And there there is found the field of aesthetic meaning.

Langer speaks about artists. When they find something good they say it's alive. They look at a picture by Matisse, and it's a picture of a room with a stove in it and everything – it's all alive. She quotes all sorts of artists, and they all say the same sort of thing. What do they mean? Well, obviously the stove is not alive, and all the other things. What do they mean? It is a type, she says, of mythical thought. It is a type of approximation to what they mean that further analysis will clarify and say exactly what they mean. That element of finding the object alive is reducible to the fact that the purely experiential pattern is sensitive living in its native form.

Because sensitivity is liberated from other influences, from sheer instrumentalization, it also involves a transformation of the objective world. People will find the world of art, of artistic forms, either an illusory world or a world that is more real than the world of everyday life. But at least it is a different world. It is the world that corresponds to sensitivity, to perceptivity in its native expansion. Art reveals a world that is other, different, unaccustomed, strange, new, remote, and still very intimate.

The artist seeks the objectification of purely experiential patterns. Of itself, a purely experiential pattern is merely experienced. But unless it is objectified, unless it proceeds from the conscious subject experiencing it and is given some sort of objective form in colors, in sounds, in architecture, and so forth, then it is not something that can be looked at, scrutinized, appreciated, contemplated. The artist objectifies the purely experiential pattern that he may reveal what has got hold of him, that he may look at it, that he may do so repeatedly, that he may enjoy it.

In Langer you can find various applications of this type of analysis to all the different fields of art. All I want to do is point out that there is a level of aesthetic meaning that is something different from intersubjective meaning yet differs from conceptual meaning, linguistic meaning, in much the same way as does intersubjective meaning. It differs from intersubjective meaning insofar as intersubjective meaning is entirely spontaneous and to a great extent not consciously noted. You have to be told about intersubject-

ive meaning to note it and study it. Artistic meaning includes an objectification. It is a step beyond intersubjective meaning.

3.3 Symbolic Meaning

Symbolic meaning is a third type. It is not without its relation to Newman's
cor ad cor loquitur or Pascal's *le coeur a ses raisons que la raison ne connaît pas.*
Symbolic meaning is, basically, in the field of affectivity. But by our affectivity and aggressivity we are related to our world. We are orientated in it. We
are disposed to certain types of actions, to certain attitudes towards life, towards persons, to the things that threaten us or the things we hope for.

The symbol itself is an image, an image that induces and educes an affect
of a certain kind or a certain pattern of affects or, inversely, that is originated by the affects, expresses them, reveals them.

It induces the affect. Just as the real object [does], so also the image of
the real object excites our affectivity, our fears, our desires. It may do so in
an expected manner. You tell a person, 'Well, you're afraid, but you have
something to be afraid of.' But it may do so in a manner that is unexpected.
The child is afraid of the dark. Why should the child be afraid of the dark?
It is because the visible universe has been blotted out, but the audible universe is still there. The audible universe is not something that is mastered
without being correlated with the things you see. And everything the child
hears is something that, unless he can connect it with something that he
knows familiarly, is a cause of fear. At least that is one explanation of why
children are afraid of the dark. The images call forth the affects either in an
expected manner or in an unexpected manner.

Inversely, the spontaneously formed image can manifest the affective
state of the subject, his affective dispositions, his affective habits, his affective capacities, his affective needs, his affective drive, and his affective finality; so that in the symbols, in the images, there is provided a revelation of
the world of one's affectivity, of the way in which one is orientated in life
towards other persons, towards human ends. In everyone there is some affective life at a certain stage of development with a certain degree of maturity. And because affectivity provides a profound revelation of the orientation
of the subject, it is a key to knowing persons. Still further, because all desire
is ultimately desire of God, there is in symbolism and in the symbol ultimately a profound religious significance.

On the other hand, just as affective living can go awry, so there are sym-
bolizations of such aberration. Freudian depth psychology studies affectiv-

ity mainly from the viewpoint of interpersonal relations. The interesting interpersonal relations are those that are contained in the Theban legend, the *Oedipus Rex* and the *Seven Against Thebes*: that beautiful family of Laius in which all types of crime were committed.

In Durand – I have already quoted him: *Les structures anthropologiques de l'imaginaire*[13] – there is a thoroughgoing, systematic study of all types of symbols and all types of combinations of symbols, and a revelation, to a certain extent, of their meaning and development, that prescinds throughout from the Freudian type of symbol. He says the latter is not fundamental. It is a type of symbolization that arises in a certain type of human society.

This symbolic type of meaning, perhaps more than the aesthetic and the intersubjective, exerts an influence upon style, upon one's mode of expression. It is perhaps the main determinant of the pull away from a purely logical communication of meanings.

The influence of affectivity, of symbolic meaning, in linguistic discourse appears insofar as class names, universals, give place to representative figures; insofar as univocity gives place to a plurality of different meanings all of which are meant; insofar as proof gives place to reiteration and variation on the same theme. Or as in the remark, 'Mr Belloc says so three times; therefore it is true,' where the principle of the excluded middle – either A or B, either you have stopped beating your wife or you have not – gives place to a superdetermination that combines opposites: both bitter and sweet, both love and hate; where negation – it's not so – gives place to a sort of positing and then an overwhelming of what is posited; where the single line, one theme that is gradually developed, is replaced by the simultaneous development of different themes called condensation. Insofar as language slips from the universal to the representative figure, from univocity to a plurality of things meant at the same time, from proof to reiteration, variation on the same theme, and similar rhetorical devices, from the principle of excluded middle to the combination of opposites or contradictories, from negation to the overwhelming, to a positing of something that then is overwhelmed, to condensation, that is, the simultaneous development of different themes, one has the influence of the laws of imagination and affectivity in linguistic discourse.

Linguistic discourse or the theoretical ideal is something that is purely logical. You predicate the attribute of the subject affirmatively or negatively. You do so either assertorically (it is so) or problematically (it may or could

13 See above, p. 65, note 14.

be so) or necessarily (it must be so) – all the logical analyses of discourse. But most human talking is not of that kind. Nor are all our documents of that kind. There is a combination, an interference, of the two modes.

Now let us illustrate. I am borrowing again from Langer. Those contrasts, are derived from Freud's dream analysis. He was discussing the laws of dreams, and those oppositions I have given are from there. But that type of analysis has gone into literary study. A lot of the works quoted by Durand are literary studies, Victor Hugo and the rest. An example of symbolic negation in which one posits the opposite and obliterates it comes from Swinburne's 'The Garden of Proserpine,' cited by Langer on page 243.

> Then star nor sun shall waken,
> Nor any change of light:
> Nor sound of waters shaken,
> Nor any sound or sight:
> Nor wintry leaves nor vernal;
> Nor days nor things diurnal
> Only the sleep eternal
> In an eternal night.

There are posited sun, star, light, water, sound, sight, leaves, wintry and vernal, days, things. And they are all just posited to be denied. What is affirmed is only the sleep eternal in an eternal night: an illustration of the substitution of overcoming for a simple negation.

Condensation – and Shakespeare is full of condensation – is illustrated in this passage from Macbeth:

> And pity, like a naked newborn babe,
> Striding the blast, or heaven's cherubin, hors'd
> Upon the sightless couriers of the air,
> Shall blow the horrid deed in every eye,
> That tears shall drown the wind.[14]

One has pity related to a naked newborn babe, and then one has to imagine a naked newborn babe striding the blast. And then, just how tears drown the wind is not too clear, but it is magnificent poetry. Shakespeare is full of condensation, the combination of quite different themes, communicating the horror that will be occasioned by disseminating, bringing to light,

14 Act 1, scene 7, lines 21–25.

Macbeth's misdeeds. But it is an illustration of condensation.

Now you can read St Paul in his more impassioned passages, and you will find liberal use of representative figures, multiple meanings, and reiterations. Human expression, literary expression, is not merely logical. It has its logic, but it also has the logic proper to imagination and affectivity, and that is something different. To properly grasp linguistic meaning one has to be aware and take into account these other levels of meaning.[15]

15 The sixth question-and-answer session was held later this day. See below, pp. 354–65.

1962-9

Hermeneutics[1]

Hermeneutics and exegesis are concerned with the interpretation of the meaning of texts. A distinction is drawn between the two. Hermeneutics is concerned with general principles, and exegesis with their application to particular cases.

In general, exegesis is learned in practice, in a seminar. The four articles I wrote on *gratia operans* in *Theological Studies* in 1941–1942[2] represent the exegesis of an article in St Thomas, *Summa theologiae*, 1-2, q. 111, a. 2. What does this article mean? Well, you can easily write four articles and refer to all sorts of elements in St Thomas's thought to set forth the meaning of that one article.

We are not dealing with exegesis this morning, with the concrete task of interpreting a text. We could very easily spend two weeks on a job like that. But we are concerned with the general question of hermeneutics.

The first point to be made – I have already made it[3] – is that hermeneutics is not a primary field of inquiry. That fact is shown by the impossibility of

---

1 Thursday, 19 July 1962, Lauzon CD/MP3 317 (31700A0E060) and 318 (31800A0E060). Lonergan distributed a 16-page typescript on hermeneutics that appears below as appendix 1. See note 1 there, p. 635, for further details.
2 Bernard Lonergan, 'St Thomas' Thought on *Gratia Operans*,' *Theological Studies* 2 (1941) 289–324, 3 (1942) 69–88, 375–402, 533–78; now in *Grace and Freedom*, vol. 1 in Collected Works of Bernard Lonergan, ed. Frederick E. Crowe and Robert M. Doran (Toronto: University of Toronto Press, 2000), part 1.
3 See below, pp. 354–55, in the discussion of the previous evening.

offering an exegesis of everything. To offer an exegesis of everything would be to offer an exegesis of your exegesis, and so on ad infinitum. There have to be a certain number of cases in which the meaning of the text is plain and stands in no need of exegesis.

The primary field of inquiry that lies behind hermeneutics is cognitional theory, which deals with knowledge in all cases. The particular case of knowing what an author means is a particular case of knowing, and it is a particular application of a general cognitional theory. Consequently, the only satisfactory treatment of hermeneutics is by applying a cognitional theory.

1 Applying a Cognitional Theory

Traditionally, that application was something fairly simple. Aristotle was commonly received as the philosopher. He wrote *Peri hermeneias*, On Interpretation; and Aristotle's work has remained down the centuries the fundamental work on hermeneutics. It is still universally received, but at the present time further questions are raised. What Aristotle taught about interpreting texts is still basic practice universally. Further refinements have been added, but the substance of the subject is there, and it is not a matter of any difficulty.

However, contemporary hermeneutics is complicated by four factors.

First of all, an emphasis has been placed upon the particular, upon development. There has been a movement from a classicism that disregarded details to a historical consciousness that wants to interpret, to understand, everything human in all its determinations. That understanding is an understanding of human development, of progress and decline.

Secondly, in the approach to the human sciences as conceived in the German tradition, not as behavioral sciences or as moral sciences but as *Geisteswissenschaften*, the fundamental category is meaning. Because hermeneutics deals with meaning, hermeneutics is a fundamental discipline in the human sciences, given that approach.

In the third place, the lack of a commonly accepted cognitional theory has had two results. On the one hand, there have been imported into the interpretation of texts mistaken philosophies. For example, there was the importation of Hegelianism into the early Tübingen school of the interpretation of scripture, so that scripture had to satisfy the processes of the Hegelian dialectic. Inversely, there is the attitude of the plain man, who wants to brush aside all such theoretical conceptions to follow good plain common sense. And while he does good work as long as he is following good plain common sense, he is apt to complicate his procedures by following the more superficial catch-phrases disseminated by the theorists of the subject, with the result of a certain amount of complacent chaos.

In the fourth place, modern man has been busy creating a modern world, in freeing himself from reliance on tradition and authority. Modernity has increasingly meant, from the sixteenth century on, settling no question, settling no issue, by appealing to the wisdom of one's ancestors. That wisdom was probably wrong. One must settle questions afresh for oneself, and, of course, modern man has done a lot. He has created new languages and new literatures, discovered new lands, developed new arts, a new industry, new commerce, new philosophies, new religions. All things have been made new. Part of that process involved a reinterpretation of everything that had been handed down previously by tradition or development. In a Christian humanism up to fairly recently, up to somewhere in the nineteenth century, the Greek and Latin authors were conceived as ideals, humanistic ideals; but they were understood in a more or less Christian context. The hermeneutic problem of the philologists was to strip away from the interpretation of the understanding of the Greek and Latin authors all this Christian environment and mode of thought and reveal these authors simply as what they were, namely, pagans. Similarly, in the field of the scriptures, their task was to eliminate the interpretation of scriptures in the light of a subsequent doctrinal development and place the scriptures in the context of the history of religions. And thirdly, another great field of interpretation is, of course, the law – literature, the scriptures, and the law. The effort was to remove the law from any Christian philosophy of law or concept of law, and reinterpret it in a new context of some more acceptable modern philosophy. There has been going forward systematically or automatically a reinterpretation of the past in the light of modernity.

To a great extent, consequently, the problem of hermeneutics coincides with the problems of a Catholic theology. It is once more the problem of distinguishing between what is good and what is bad, what is true and what is false, what we can take over from modernity and what we have to reject.

So much for a general introduction of the question of hermeneutics at the present time. Its background, its theoretical basis, lies in cognitional theory. It is a peculiar problem at the present time because of the emergence of historical consciousness, because of the significance of meaning in the *Geisteswissenschaften*, because of either the application of mistaken philosophies to hermeneutics or the desire to do it without any philosophy at all, with the result that one is guided largely by catch-phrases, and because of a wholesale reinterpretation of the past that has been conducted by the modern mind.

2 Interpreting a Text

On the operation of interpreting a text, I distinguish three main points. The first is understanding the text. The second is judging how correct one's understanding of the text is. And the third is stating what one considers the correct interpretation of the text. So there are three points. The first is to understand the text. The second is to judge whether and to what extent one's understanding is correct: how much of it is certain? how much of it is probable? how much is doubtful? And in the third place, after one has understood the text and reflected critically on one's understanding, one aims to communicate, to state, what one understands the meaning of the text to be.

2.1 Understanding the Text

The first point may be considered on four successive levels: understanding the thing, understanding the words, understanding the author, and developing one's own capacity for understanding.

Sometimes the whole problem lies just on the first level, understanding the thing. Sometimes one has the double problem of understanding the thing and understanding the words. In further cases the question of understanding the author arises. And in still further cases one oneself has to develop, undergo a conversion or revolution, before one is going to understand the text.

We will take those four points in turn. Sometimes all four are needed. Sometimes the problem of interpretation varies from text to text, from reader to reader.

2.1.1 Understanding the Thing or Object

The first point is understanding the thing or object, *die Sache*, what the text is about. The basic step in understanding a text or the basic phenomenon, so to speak, what the Germans call the *Urphänomen*, is not understanding the words but understanding the thing. When you are listening to me, you are understanding what I am talking about: hermeneutics. You are not paying any great attention to my words. The normal procedure in conversation, in a lecture, in reading a book, is to understand what the book is talking about. One understands the thing by the words, but there is no great attention to the words. The words, according to St Thomas, mean the concepts, and the concepts mean the thing. Understanding heads directly towards the thing. And so the first step in understanding a text is to understand the thing.

In general, understanding a text or an author or the words is a matter of utilizing potential knowledge we already possess. One has certain habits of understanding, knowledge, and wisdom, and in reading an author one simply actuates one's acquired habits. Those acquired habits regard things, objects, what people talk about, what people write about. The first point, then, in any exegetical task is to understand the thing.

This does not mean that, if I understand the thing, the author is going to understand it the same way, or that a true understanding of the thing is going to be understanding what the author meant. The point to this first requirement is that if you do not understand the thing you are not going to understand the author. If you do not know mathematics, you are wasting your time in reading an advanced treatise on some queer sort of space. A blind man is not going to understand an account of pictorial art. He does not know the thing. A person who never adverted to the occurrence in himself of acts of understanding is not going to understand a discussion of understanding. He has to know the thing.

So again the first requirement is that the interpreter has to have his own understanding of the thing and know what that understanding is and distinguish it from the author's understanding of the thing and not leap to the conclusion that the author is going to understand it in exactly the same way. He may, and he may not. But the first thing is to understand the thing.

That claim, that the first task of the exegete is to know the thing, the object, whether in the visible universe or in the world of theory or in the world of interiority or in the world of the sacred, the claim that the fundamental requirement is to understand that object, is opposed to what I would refer to as the Principle of the Empty Head.

The Principle of the Empty Head is to the effect that if one is to be objective, if one is not to drag in one's own notions, if one is not to settle in a priori fashion what the text must mean no matter what it says, if one is not to read into the text what is not there, if one is not to project one's own ideas on the text, then one must have an empty head. And if it isn't empty, then one must do one's best to empty it. That is a widespread view of interpretation in positivist circles and in Catholic circles. It is based upon the epistemological idea that you know by taking a look. If you know by taking a look, then to know, all you have to do is look. The only possible method is to look often, and that's all there is to it. There is no problem of understanding anything or judging whether your understanding is correct. That's all superfluous. What you have to do is look. And the only thing that can interfere with your looking and seeing what is there is the fact that you already know something. So the less you know, the better off you will be.

In fact, what is there is just black on white in certain shapes and in a certain order. Anything the interpreter does beyond reissuing, giving a new edition of the textual datum, results from the use of his own experience, his own intelligence, and his own judgment. The more the interpreter has – the more fully his sensibility and affectivity is developed, the more fully his understanding is developed, the more profound and wise his judgment is – the better will be his position to understand exactly what the author is talking about. And the less the development of his sensitivity and affectivity, of his intelligence and judgment, then the less the likelihood that he is going to arrive at an understanding of what the text is about. The fully developed interpreter can, is in potency to, select any of the possible meanings of the text and pick out the one that fits on to it. The man with a minimum development has to acquire at least the development that the author had, and usually authors are not people who know nothing. They have spent an awful lot of time developing, and they have reached the point where they think they have something to say. The interpreter has to pull himself at least up to that level. If he is there already, then he is better equipped to interpret the text than the man who has to get up there. The ideal interpreter is not a baby of one day.

Now that point is fairly widely recognized at the present time. To quote our great adversary Bultmann, 'The requirement that the interpreter has to silence his own subjectivity, that he has to extinguish his individuality to arrive at an objective knowledge of what the text is saying, is the most nonsensical idea that can be imagined.'[4] One can get the same thing from Ebeling or Gadamer or any of the other people who are discussing hermeneutics at the present time.

The first task, then, is to understand the thing insofar as one can. If one understands the thing, it does not follow that the author is going to

---

4 This is a slightly different translation of a passage from Bultmann that Lonergan refers to in *Method in Theology* 158, note 2. See below, p. 639, note 2. The source is given there: 'Das Problem der Hermeneutik,' *Zeitschrift für Theologie und Kirche* 47 (1950) 64.

understand it in the same way. But at least one is one step advanced towards understanding what the author says. And if one does not understand the thing, one will not understand what the author is driving at.

2.1.2 Understanding the Words

In the second place, there arises the question of understanding the words. Insofar as it happens that the way the interpreter understands the thing and the way the author understands the thing coincide, there is no difficulty. That coincidence accounts for the cases in which the meaning of the text is plain. However, as in conversation, so also in reading, it can very well happen that one man is talking about A and the listener is understanding him to be talking about B. Things may go along for a while on the basis of that misunderstanding, but sooner or later it will appear to the listener that what the speaker has to say is just nonsense: A and B have not got the same predicates. Jones is talking about A, and Smith thinks he is talking about B. Sooner or later Smith is going to feel that Jones is talking nonsense, that he is saying things that are patently false.

That raises the problem of understanding the words. There are two alternatives. If Smith is a controversialist, he has all that he wants. All that he has to do is to show what nonsense Jones is talking, making these statements about B which any fool can see are sheer nonsense. However, if Smith wants to understand what Jones is really writing about, he will read further. He will read again what he has said, and sooner or later he will get the light. 'Perhaps he wasn't talking about B at all; perhaps he was talking about A, and in that case Jones isn't the fool I thought he was. If I suppose he is talking about A, then all along the line what he is saying is something I agree with, something I find to be perfectly normal.'

Now that confusion of A and B can occur in all sorts of ways and in all sorts of manners. For instance, they may be really in agreement on the fundamental issue but not be coinciding on the aspect of the issue that is being considered. This just shows the complications and the multiplicity of possibilities where the reader is thinking of one thing and the writer is thinking of another. A vast number of possibilities arise for confusion, and the correction of them is the problem of understanding the words.

The process of correction is simply the self-correcting process of learning. One sees that what the author is saying does not make sense the way one is interpreting him. Well, let us not suppose immediately that he's a fool. Let us go back, read again, exercise a bit of ingenuity, try and figure out what he's talking about, what way he's viewing things. That can recur over and over again. It occurs particularly when one is interpreting texts that were written centuries ago. If you want to understand St Thomas, you have to understand a lot of things that were familiar to every writer in the thirteenth century and have become decreasingly familiar to readers and writers since. And if you are not familiar with that medieval context, then you come to see the necessity of learning it insofar as the statements made do not hang together, that is, insofar as you don't understand. Note every time you don't understand, and investigate further, and you will find the author is saying something that may not seem very clear but at least makes sense.

Now this self-correcting process of learning is a matter of adding insight to insight until finally one gets the rounded view that fits, that gets the wavelength and locks on to the station. It is described in *Insight* in the first part of chapter 6, and it comes up again in the section on commonsense judgments in chapter 10.

One must not confuse this coming to understand the words, getting the author's drift, seeing what he is talking about, with judgment on the correctness of one's understanding or the statement of one's understanding. Those are further issues that come up later. We are still concerned with the original problem of the text making sense. And first it makes sense insofar as one understands the thing; secondly, insofar as one understands the words, comes to grasp what precisely is meant by those words.

That development, that self-correcting process of learning, that gradual accumulation of more and more insights into the meaning of the author's words, matches what is called the hermeneutic circle. It is a puzzling fact. In interpreting a text one reaches the whole only through the parts. One understands the sentence by understanding each word. One understands the paragraph by understanding each sentence. One understands the chapter by understanding each paragraph. And one understands the book by understanding each chapter. But the opposite is also true. You cannot understand the chapter without understanding the book. The book determines the meaning of the chapter. The chapter determines the meaning of the paragraphs. The paragraphs determine the meaning of the sentences. And the sentences determine the meaning of the words. There is a vicious circle, and it is called the hermeneutic circle. The reason for its existence is something fairly simple. A meaning is an *esse intentionale*. It is intentional. The meaning, one meaning, unfolds itself through chapters, paragraphs, sentences, words. The one meaning intended by the book is, as it were, differentiated and organized, sorted out and separated, brought down into details by, as it were, the organicity of language, of self-expression. The whole selects and determines the parts, and the parts are the means through which the whole is communicated. Just as it is said of the soul that it is *tota in singulis partibus et tota in toto corpore*,[5] similarly a meaning is not something that is localized. It is in the whole and in all the parts. The meaning of the whole has a determining influence on the meaning of the parts, and inversely, it is only through the parts that one arrives at the whole.

Now that apparent vicious circle is called the hermeneutic circle. And what matches it? How is it that the hermeneutic circle is not a block to understanding anything? Well, it is only a block in a logical order, in an order of concepts. But insight, understanding, is the same sort of thing. The gradual development of understanding is a development that understands the parts and corrects, qualifies, complements the acts of understanding with regard to each part as one moves through the whole discourse, from the words to the sentence, from the sentence to the paragraph, from the paragraphs to the chapter, from the chapters to the book. It is by the self-correcting process of learning that we gradually spiral into what the author is really saying.

That primacy of understanding adds an important qualification to rules of hermeneutics. You can get rules of hermeneutics, and they are well known. One has to analyze the composition of the text, determine the author's purpose, determine who are the people to whom he wrote, determine what was the occasion on which he wrote; one must characterize the means he employed: the linguistic means, the grammatical means, the stylistic means, and so on. A whole, long, beautiful table of rules for interpreting can be drawn up, and they are all useful. But one does not understand the text because one observes the rules. One observes the rules in order to understand the text. The rules are never foolproof. If one is stupid, they are no help. Observing the rules can be mere pedantry, and observing the rules can be inefficacious. The one thing necessary, the one thing that counts, is that development of understanding that gets the author's meaning, in which there occurs the correcting of all my lack of understanding, the development of my understanding on all the points so that I come to understand just what the author means.

2.1.3 Understanding the Author

In the third step or element in understanding a text, besides understanding the thing and understanding the words, one comes to the level of

---

5 'entirely in each part and entirely in the whole body'

understanding the author. When the meaning of a text is plain, then by the words, with the author, one immediately understands the thing. When a simple misunderstanding arises, when one is thinking the author is talking about *A* when in fact he is talking about *B*, a fairly simple, though maybe prolonged, exercise of inventiveness and ingenuity will enable one to overcome the difficulties. But there are texts one can read, and they give just a glimmer of understanding and a host of puzzles. There is an extremely long and an extremely arduous self-correcting process of learning that is required to arrive at understanding. Then the problem is not so much understanding the thing or understanding the words, but understanding the author himself. He is somebody so different from me. He belongs to another nation, another time, another language, another culture, another way of life, another cast of mind. To come to understand him is a big job.

In that case one is developing one's understanding not so much of the thing that he is talking about, not of his language, but of the author himself. In what does that understanding consist? It is similar in structure to our understanding of the common sense of the people we live with. People will say, 'That's just like him' or 'That's just like you.' And we know what it means: it's the way this person would act in that situation. It's the sort of thing you would expect of him though one would not think of doing it oneself. One understands by one's common sense not only the objects one deals with but also the persons. One understands their common sense, and one understands it to be different from one's own.

That understanding of another's common sense is not the cognitional theorist's answer to the question, What is common sense? But by our common sense we know what to say and what to do in any of a very large range of commonly occurring situations. When we understand another person's common sense, we know what he would say or would do in any of those situations. We have to have that knowledge of other people to live with them. It is what we know we can expect from other people and what we can count on from them that enables us to live and operate with them. One has to have some understanding of one's boss to get along well with him and some understanding of one's subordinates to get along with them. There is, then, in ordinary living an understanding not only of things and words but of people.

Now, the business of understanding people of a very different common sense from our own, when they write books or supply us with texts to be interpreted, is a development of that third component in everyday common sense. One develops a certain aspect of the common sense current in the eighth century BC among the Hebrews, in the fifth century BC among the Athenians, and so on. One has some idea of the way they expressed themselves, the sort of things they would do. It is a development of one's commonsense knowledge of other people. What one knows by one's commonsense knowledge of other people is the way their common sense operates. It is not a theoretical knowledge of what common sense is but, as it were, a schedule of concrete anticipations. Imagine him in this situation. What would he do? What would he say? We have a pretty good idea of the way other people would behave.

2.1.4   Romantic Hermeneutics

This understanding of another's common sense is something that was expressed in Romantic hermeneutics, though somewhat inadequately and inaccurately. Romantic hermeneutics derives mainly from Winckelmann.[6] It was further developed by Schleiermacher and then by Dilthey. Winckelmann was concerned with art, but Schleiermacher was concerned with hermeneutics, and so was Dilthey. Schleiermacher's *Hermeneutik* was first published in 1838, and was reissued in 1911 in a four-volume selection.[7] Dilthey's 'Die Enstehung der Hermeneutik,' ('The Development of Hermeneutics'), 1900, is in his Complete Works, volume 5, pp. 317–38.[8] They are fundamental contributions to the problems of hermeneutics, and they are in the line of Romantic hermeneutics.

Romantic hermeneutics is a matter of three terms: *Ausdruck* (expression); *Einfühlen* (empathy), and *Reproduzieren* (reproduction).

The text is an expression. It is a concretization of the subjectivity, sensitivity, mode of imagination, affectivity, intelligence, judgment, will, of the author. But it is considered simply as expression. The task of the interpreter, his basic task, is empathy, *Einfühlung*. One feels one's way in to the author's mentality, to his mode of imagination, and so on. The interpreter's aim is to take upon himself the psychic, intellectual, rational, volitional modes of the author. He gradually arrives at this after years of intimate study of his chosen author, his specialized field.

In the third place, once one has taken upon oneself, inherited, the mantle of Elias and become able to think and write just the way the author did,

---

6 See above, p. 175, note 11.

7 An English translation of Schleiermacher's *Hermeneutik* by James Duke and Jack Forstman was published in 1977 by Scholars Press (Missoula, MT).

8 Now available as 'The Rise of Hermeneutics (1900),' chapter 3 in Wilhelm Dilthey, *Hermeneutics and the Study of History*, ed. Mudolf A Makkreel and Frithjof Rodi (Princeton: Princeton University Press, 1996) 235–60.

one is able to explain exactly why he wrote just what he wrote and why he wrote it in exactly that manner. One is able to interpret the author perfectly. In fact, one knows what the author means much better than the author himself did because the author is not able to explain why he wrote just these words in this connection and in this manner. A great part of the work of writing just pours forth. One has the main idea. As Cato said: *Rem tene, verba sequentur:* get ahold of your idea, of your matter, and the words will come. And that is the way most people write. They do not know all that the Romantic hermeneutics expects them to know or at least has the interpreter know about them.

Now Romantic hermeneutics has been under fire since the days of Husserl and Heidegger. They have brought out an entirely different approach to the problem of hermeneutics, the emphasis on the thing. It is not a matter of getting into somebody else's mind. It is knowing what he is talking about. And the first step there is to know the thing. 'Understand his words' is the second step. If those two don't suffice, well, you have to pay some attention to the author, but you don't get into the author. You don't become a mystic like St Paul to understand St Paul.

But there is a good deal of truth in this conception of hermeneutics. The element of truth in it I have attempted to express in saying that just as one has a commonsense understanding of other people's common sense who are one's companions, the people one lives with, so also there is a development of common sense that takes on a certain aspect of the common sense of another period, of other people. Insofar as the text is conceived as expression, *Ausdruck,* that conception of the text fits in very well with the way one understands a work of art, and it was about art that Winckelmann wrote. Insofar as one reaches the symbolic, intersubjective, artistic levels of meaning, or insofar as that type of meaning has its influence on the text, understanding the meaning of the text is of this type. That's a fairly good description, anyway, of the way one goes about understanding such texts. Insofar as one has similar experiences in intersubjectivity, in art, in symbols, one really gets to their meaning. If one has no conscious experience of a symbol emerging in one's imagination and of having a meaning for one, the thing is just a point on which one has a bit of a blind spot.

On the other hand, Romantic hermeneutics overlooks entirely the aspect of linguistic meaning by which it is true or false. Further, it dodges the issue of the transposition of a truth from one context to another context. It avoids that problem, which is a very obvious problem for the Catholic theologian. What is stated in the New Testament can be restated within a different context. The same meaning can be restated within a new context by the

Council of Nicea. Romantic hermeneutics eliminates the problem of that transposition by its somewhat mythical transposition of the interpreter inside the author's skin. It eliminates the difference of context. Finally, the criterion of reproduction is excessive. To understand what an author means, you do not have to understand things the author himself did not explicitly understand. He didn't understand or advert particularly to his mode of writing. The requirement, the criterion, set by Romantic hermeneutics is excessive.

2.1.5 Development of the Interpreter

We have considered understanding the thing, understanding the words, and understanding the author. There is a fourth element in understanding, and that is the development of the interpreter himself.

The major texts in letters, in religion, in philosophy, in theology are beyond the horizon of any average interpreter. They demand a development, a refinement, perhaps a conversion, a religious, a moral, or an intellectual conversion, a broadening of horizon, if the interpreter is to measure up to the level of those texts. The reader's initial knowledge is just inadequate, and he comes to know what the text is about just in the measure that he pushes the self-correcting process of learning to a revolution in his own outlook.

Consequently, there is to the work of interpretation an existential dimension, an existential aspect: what's wrong with me? The profounder, the richer, the truer a text is, the greater the need of the interpreter to discover what's radically wrong with himself.

Further, this existential dimension has another aspect. The classics in religion, literature, philosophy, theology are presented not only to individual interpreters. They ground a tradition. They are the formative tools of a culture. They create their own milieu. Insofar as one is born and brought up in that milieu, one is prepared in countless manners which one does not suspect for a capacity to interpret them, to understand what they are talking about. If the tradition is genuine, if it is authentic, a long accumulation of insights, adjustments, reinterpretations that repeats the original message for each age, then the preparation one receives unconsciously from one's milieu, one's background, one's schooling, one's teachers brings about the phenomenon exemplified by the disciples on the way to Emmaus in Luke 24.32. The disciples exclaimed: 'Did not our hearts burn within us when he spoke on the way and opened to us the scriptures?' Our Lord explained to the disciples the scriptures, and at his explanation their hearts burned within them. But their hearts burned within them because the interpretation that was given them was an interpretation for which they had been prepared although they did not find it out for themselves.

On the other hand, in the measure that the tradition is unauthentic, in the measure that it is a watering down of the original message, a recasting of it into terms and meanings that fit into the assumptions and convictions of those who have dodged the issue of radical conversion, in that measure a genuine interpretation, if presented to members of the culture, is met with sheer incredulity. In Acts 28, St Paul is in Rome. He preached to the Jews there, and some believed and some did not. St Paul quoted to them Isaiah: *aure audietis et non intelligetis.*[9] There in the one case one has people prepared by their tradition to understand the authentic meaning of the classical texts. And in the other case, one has people who are unprepared, who will listen with their ears and will not understand.

In that social or community dimension of the existential aspect of interpretation – inasmuch as I am involved, I am in need of radical change if I am to understand the text – one sees the importance of tradition. Gadamer, who is a Hegelian, writes in the left-wing encyclopedia *Religion in Geschichte und Gegenwart*, but in his *Wahrheit und Methode* he insists upon the importance of tradition in meeting hermeneutic issues. He attacks vigorously the Enlightenment precisely because it went about the work of reinterpreting the religious and humanistic classics of the past by laying down a premise that just destroys tradition, namely, a prejudgment against all prejudgments: *Vorurteil gegen die Vorurteile überhaupt.* And that judgment, that application of the Principle of the Empty Head, is a procedure that destroys any tradition and, consequently, destroys that prepared soil in which the more basic and finer products that are to be interpreted find their necessary preparation.[10]

2.2 *Judging the Correctness of One's Understanding*

On the act of judgment one has to note first of all that understanding the text is just a matter of a set of insights, and insights are a dime a dozen. Acts of understanding occur fairly freely, but that does not mean that they are right. I once addressed the psychotherapeutic members of the staff in a hospital, and one of the doctors said afterwards, 'Well, our patients get lots of insights, but they're not right.' That is something inherent in the insight. Human intelligence is infallible with respect to the image, with respect to what one is thinking of, but what one is thinking of need not be the totality

9 'You shall hear and not understand.'
10 A break took place at this point. What follows is found on Lauzon CD/MP3
   318 (31800A0E060).

of relevant data, and so it is not surprising that there are all sorts of interpretations of the same text. It would be surprising if there were not. Acts of understanding occur: one man sees this point, another man sees that, and so on. One goes along this line understanding the text; another goes along another. And they come up with different interpretations. They understand the same thing, words, author, and demands for development, but the results are different, and that is not surprising. Such is human understanding. It is infallible only *per se*, and the possibilities of the *per accidens* are rather large.

Consequently, there is always a need for judgment. The text makes sense if you take it in a certain way, but is that what de facto it means? Note the question, Is that what de facto it means? It is not a question of what it must mean. The meaning of a text is not something in the realm of absolute necessity. De facto, that is what was meant: you do not need a judgment that gives you more than that.

The criterion on the correctness of insight is always the same: does the insight hit the bull's-eye? Does it meet all the relevant questions? The trick to the question is: relevant to what? You have to have some term to which you refer your question – Does it meet all relevant questions? – if you are going to give a meaning to the word 'relevant.'

The simplest way of determining the meaning of that word 'relevant' is 'relevant to a determinate prospective judgment, a well-defined prospective judgment.' And from that it immediately follows that judgment on one's interpretation of the text, on the correctness of one's understanding of the text, is going to be a piecemeal affair. It will not take in globally all the acts of understanding one has on reading the text. It will tend to be of the type: 'At least the author means this; at least he does not mean that.'

Insofar as a man reflects on his understanding of the text and elicits acts of judgment, he does not sign a blank check – 'all my understanding is right.' He considers precise prospective judgments and pronounces this element to be certainly true, this to be highly probable ('I don't see how you could take it otherwise'), this to be probable, other points to be still obscure ('perhaps someone else will throw further light on them'), and so on. One gets in that judgment on the correctness of one's understanding a series of judgments with a series of qualifications.

The same point can be made in another manner. We have spoken about the hermeneutic circle: the whole is known through the parts, and the parts are known through the whole. We have said one evades that problem insofar as by a self-correcting process of learning one spirals into the meaning of the text, comes closer and closer, pins things down. However, we have to note the relativity of that word 'whole.' What does one mean by the whole?

The whole with respect to the words is the sentence; with respect to the sentence, the paragraph; with respect to the paragraph, the chapter; and so on to the book. But does one not go on to the *opera omnia* as the whole of which the book is a part, if one is going to understand what the author is driving at fully and exactly? Further, does one not have to take other authors into consideration: the people he was writing against, the opinions of those he was writing for, the antecedents, the state of the question before he began to write? And you can put a bigger whole around that whole. Where does this word 'whole' come to a stop?

So one is forced from a hermeneutic context, a context that has unity from a single mind, to a historical context in which there is an interplay of different minds; and it is significant not only to what they are thinking about but also to what they overlook. Once more, this relativity of the whole does not involve a total fluidity of meaning, a *panta rei* of meaning, but it does impose upon the interpreter a necessity for making restricted, qualified, limited judgments.

If one examines this dependence of the parts upon the whole, one quickly comes to the conclusion that, while the whole does determine the meaning of the parts, still it does so only from certain viewpoints. If you take the statement that Brutus killed Caesar, it can occur in a context in which Brutus is praised or it can occur equally well in a context in which Brutus is damned. The intention of the statement that Brutus killed Caesar will vary with the context, but at least it does not change the elementary nugget of fact that Brutus killed Caesar. It excludes the context in which the assertion is that Caesar killed Brutus or that Brutus did not kill Caesar. Any element in the text has a certain minimum of meaning which may not be fully determinate, that may be smaller or greater, but that is independent of the context. The whole determines the parts but it does not determine them totally. The parts fit organically into the whole of the meaning, but still the organs have their own character and function that to a certain extent can be determined from the organs themselves.

To take a contemporary example: in non-Catholic exegesis the Gospel of St John until a decade or so ago was read in a Hellenistic context. And that reading of St John in the Hellenistic context gave rise to a series of questions and problems and obscurities and doubts that was determined by that supposed context of this Gospel. The discovery of the scrolls at Qumrân has changed that context in the minds of a great number of interpreters. St John is read now much more in a Palestinian context. A large number of the ideas, the terms, employed by St John that were thought to be explicable only by a Hellenistic milieu are now found to have been common coin among the people at Qumrân. Consequently, the larger whole in which the Gospel is placed by the interpreter has changed, and the series of difficulties and questions that concern the interpreter has undergone a transformation. There is a new general perspective, at least for those interpreters who find Qumrân very significant for the interpretation of St John.

Still, this transformation of the larger whole, this change of the larger whole, does not involve much revision in a commentary on St John insofar as the commentary limited itself to an exact analysis of the text and was content to make cautious and restricted judgments on its meaning. I say this in illustration of the point that, while the part depends on the whole, it does not depend upon the whole in every respect. A solid commentary on St John that did not pay too much attention to the broader issues does not have to undergo too much revision, while another that was full of the Hellenistic milieu, if one accepts the view that Qumrân represents a type of Palestinian thought which is again occurring in St John, does undergo a considerable amount of revision.

The point I am trying to make is that, while the exegete tries to understand everything in the text that he can, nonetheless, when he comes to judge the correctness of his understanding, he makes a series of restricted and qualified judgments.

The point can be made in a third manner. When one approaches a text in an effort to understand it, one begins necessarily from oneself, with one's own questions, one's own interests. The further one advances in one's study of the text, the more one's questions and interests recede into a background, and one discovers what the questions were that the author was trying to answer, what the interests of the author were, what the interests of his readers were. And it is only insofar as one effects the shift from one's own preoccupations to the preoccupations of the author, from one's own *Fragestellung* to that of the author and his contemporaries, that one begins really to understand what the text is about.

However, there is always some indeterminacy with regard to the questions that the author was asking or attempting to meet, the interests he had. One can determine these things up to a point; but one has not exhaustive information upon the author's background, upon the things he read or knew. Insofar as the text provides a determination of what the author's concerns and interests were, one is on solid ground; but it is an incomplete ground. And once more one has a reason for saying that the interpreter's judgment on the correctness of his understanding is not a blank check in which he says, 'All my understanding is correct,' but a limited series of restricted and precise judgments.

So much for the first two tasks of the interpreter: understand the text, and judge the elements in one's interpretation that one can consider certain, probable, less probable, in need of further illumination, and so on.

2.3 Stating the Meaning of the Text

Now one might have the idea that stating the meaning one considers the correct meaning of the text is a fairly simple matter. On the contrary, it is the most complex of all.

Albert Descamps, in his article 'Réflexions sur la méthode en théologie biblique,' has certain particular views upon the nature of biblical theology, and they are worth considering.[11] His views are not the same as everyone else's. Biblical theologians are not uniform in their notions on what biblical theology is. But he is quite an intelligent man, and he has done a lot of work in the field, and his opinions are worth knowing.

The paragraphs that have been selected[12] regard the interpreter's account of the meaning of the text. He distinguishes biblical theology from exegesis by saying that exegesis is concerned with the total content of scriptures and biblical theology with the religious content of scriptures. He says that biblical theology will be as diverse, contain as many disparate elements, as there are biblical authors. In the limit there will be as many biblical theologies as there are biblical authors, and the interpreter, the biblical theologian, will above all respect the originality of each one of them.

Secondly, the investigator will appear to take a peculiar pleasure in slow procedures, in taking a long time to get anywhere. He will follow the route of the schoolboy, *des écoliers*. His descriptions will have the savor of ancient days. He will give the reader an impression of *dépaysement* – it's hard to translate: being out of one's own country, strangeness, archaism. His scrupulousness about authenticity will manifest itself in a choice of words that are as biblical as possible, in his care to avoid all hasty transpositions into a more recent terminology even when that terminology has the sanction of theological tradition. There is a whole problem of discretion, of prudence, in the choice of one's language in biblical theology. And when he talks about the choice of one's language in biblical theology, he is talking about the statement of the meaning of the text. Every general exposition, *tout exposé*

11 See above, p. 74, note 16.
12 Lonergan distributed one page from Descamps's article. He is partly translating and partly commenting as he presents the position there represented.

d'ensemble, will be constructed in the light of the conclusions of chronology and literary history. It will preferably be of the genetic type. For that reason, the question of authenticity in the inspired writers, while it may appear secondary in biblical theology, or while it is sometimes considered secondary in biblical theology, really has a decisive importance, because the presentation is genetic. Moreover, general expositions will be on the whole not very general. They will be rather particular. If they consider the totality of the biblical writings, they will be restricted to a single point of doctrine. If they have a complex object, not just a single topic, then they will be limited to a single book or to a limited group of books. With regard to the biblical theology that would embrace the totality or at least the greater part of inspired literature, it can do so only by remaining interiorly disparate after the fashion of a general history of Europe or a general history of the world, of man. There are those who dream – there is a certain point in that word 'dream' – there are those who dream, it is true, of a shortcut, a species of shortcut, of an exposition of the general plan of God throughout the history of the two testaments. And in that would consist, according to some authors, the principal task of biblical theology. But in fact, it seems to Descamps, a sketch of the design of divine providence belongs to biblical theology only in the measure in which a historian would find himself at home in that account of it. The believer arrives at the divine plan only through the many diverse intentions of the biblical authors.

Now that is one way of conceiving the communication of one's interpretation of a text. Note that Descamps wants to avoid the problem of a transition from the language employed in the Bible to a language used at a later time. He wants to eliminate that problem. And because he wants to eliminate that problem, his account of the meaning of the scriptures is going to appear strange; it is going to give people the impression of archaism; it is going to be a long, slow process as though one were a schoolboy doing the thing. Again, he does not want a general view. He wants the thing differentiated. He wants almost as many biblical theologies as there are biblical authors. And he does not believe in any shortcuts that give us a general view of the divine plan as revealed in the two Testaments. He wants to go about the thing the way historians would find making sense, namely, getting a little bit from this author and something else from another author, and seeing how they fit together. But then one may find it isn't too clear, if none of the authors tells us – in other words, the scrupulous historical approach.

2.3.1 Commonsense Communication

Now that is one view of the communication of the meaning of what one considers the correct understanding of a text. And, to give it a name, we may call it the commonsense communication of a commonsense understanding of the text. By 'common sense' here, I do not mean the kind of knowledge one finds in the man in the street. By common sense I mean a specialization of human intelligence concerned with the concrete, the particular, the factual. That is what common sense always is. But in the case of the interpreter it is a matter of acquiring the common sense of at least two and at times three millennia ago. The interpreter by understanding the text has acquired something like the common sense of another time. In the light of that common sense, he arrives at the meaning of the text, and the meaning he arrives at more or less is expressed in terms of that acquired common sense.

The problem of transposing from that apprehension to a contemporary mode of apprehension is avoided. The problem of synthesis, of putting together what is got in the separate books, is avoided. Descamps does not want any general history.

In that case the problem of communication is not a new problem. But, on the other hand, very little communication is likely to be achieved. If you talk like Isaiah, well, people are going to understand you just as well as they understand Isaiah. And if you talk again like Joel and all the other prophets and do not put them together, well, people will understand the relations between them from listening to you not an awful lot better than they would if they just went right ahead and read the Bible. That commonsense communication of that commonsense understanding of the text is best communicated in brief introductions to the sacred books and notes that explain all the points that the erudite person can clarify.

2.3.2 Scientific Communication

A second step, another mode of communicating a commonsense understanding of the text, would be a scientific communication of a commonsense understanding of the text.

Now such scientific communication rises spontaneously from the foregoing commonsense communication. The very effort at communication brings about the movement towards theory: the *Wendung zur Idee.*

One sees it very clearly in the composition of grammars. People read texts, and they find the same problems recurring, the same word endings recurring, the same prefixes. They make a systematic study of all this, and they write a grammar.

Again, in language, people proceed from understanding texts to the composition of dictionaries. They list all the different meanings in which each word is employed. Or they proceed from place names in texts to giving you at the present time a map of Palestine as it was about the year 1000 BC or 800 BC. Those are all specialized studies that proceed from the text, and they proceed to systematic statement. And they are just examples.

The exegete's task is to make use of this great number of specialized studies to bring them all to bear on the interpretation of each particular passage that he interprets. But insofar as he does so not only with respect to one passage but with respect to a long series of passages, he finds, too, that the same problems are recurring. Each act of interpretation is not something totally new. The same ideas keep cropping up again and again with slight differences in meaning. And so he begins to work out categories, to notice developments in categories, to classify different categories and relate them to one another. He begins the process of the movement towards theory. He is attempting to systematize the mode of thought and communication of the ancient authors. And so he heads into a scientific communication of the meaning of the text.

2.3.3   Foundations of Communication

In the third place, one can move a step further and ask about the foundations of a scientific communication of the commonsense understanding of the text. The commonsense understanding of the text remains fundamental, but one can remain simply with that and let other people learn one's meaning, one's way of talking, or one can move from a totality of texts to something more general that puts more compactly all that is to be learned. It puts it compactly perhaps with a little too much generality, without a sufficiency of differentiation and detail; but at least it does communicate in a more or less systematic fashion the totality of categories and relationships and modes of thought and developments that is to be found in the series of texts.

One may ask, however, about the foundations of this scientific communication of commonsense understanding of the text. And then one is confronted with a new type of problem, in fact with several things.

First of all, insofar as one is attempting a scientific communication of commonsense understanding of texts, one is moving beyond the explicit context of the single authors. Comparisons, classifications, the listing of categories, of their differentiations, the observation and explanation of genetic processes begin indeed from the context of each author, from the commonsense understanding of each author; but they go beyond it to ask and answer questions that the individual authors did not consider. One is moving from a hermeneutic level to a historical level as soon as one begins to classify and compare and list meanings and categories and genetic processes. So there is involved there a double step. One is moving away from the modes of thought of the authors to a synoptic view, the essence of their thought. And again, one is moving away from hermeneutics to history. The individual authors used the categories and meant the meanings of the terms and effected the developments, but they did not sit back and think about what they had done and tell someone about it. It is only the exegete that attempts that task.

There is another aspect to the same thing. The exegetes that do this work start each from his own native common sense. It is something that is too obvious to be discussed and too certain to be doubted, too clear to be explained. Everyone's common sense is that to him. He develops the common sense of another time. Still, his starting point is the point to which he spontaneously returns when he wants to tell you what the author really means. He can explain what he understands in the scriptures in contemporary language best of all to people who are nearest to him in mentality; and the further they get away, the greater the difficulty. Just as there is the possibility of moving from the particularity of each author to a consideration of what is common to all and the developments of that common element, and so of arriving at, moving towards, the concrete again, so one can do exactly the same thing with the interpreters as one does with the original authors. Just as there is a movement from the world of community to the world of theory with regard to the biblical authors, so there can be a movement from the world of community to the world of theory with regard to the exegetes. Just as one can understand developments in biblical thought, so one can understand developments in biblical criticism. There have been a lot of them, too.

So the problem of the scientific communication of a commonsense understanding of texts raises the problem of the movement from the world of community to the world of theory not only with regard to the authors but also with regard to the interpreters. If one is critical, one criticizes not only the Bible but also the critics. Otherwise, one's criticism is incomplete.

In the third place, there exist human sciences. They are concerned with complete generality, with the order of human living in family and society, morals and education, state and law, economics and technics. They are concerned with the meaning of human living as found in intersubjectivity and symbol, art and language, history and religion, literature, science, and philosophy. These human sciences exist. While they depend upon works of interpretation, still they reach a far greater generality than the process from community to theory that would occur within the limits of interpreting the authors in sacred scripture. These sciences have their results more or less assured. We know about the developments of language, the developments of phonetics, the developments of grammars, the general movement in the development of language from a great particularity in which one has several words for different kinds of two: a pair, a couple, a team, and so on, and only later does there develop a general word for two, any case of two, and similarly for absolutely everything else. Read the first volume of Cassirer's *Philosophy of Symbolic Forms*, on language.[13] He gives you a lot of comparative grammar there. The earlier the language is, the more concrete it is, and the poorer it is in abstract terms.

All these human sciences have a relevance to the problems that arise in the scientific communication of commonsense understanding of texts. Just as the interpreter will not hesitate to use grammars and lexicons, geographies and histories, in the interpretation of texts, so too he can come to use sociology, moral theory, theory of art, depth psychology. Depth psychology has been used an awful lot in comparative religion in recent years. The notable example is Mircea Eliade. There is a relevance of the human sciences towards a scientific communication of commonsense understanding of the texts.

2.3.4 Philosophy and Theology in Communication

There is a fourth point. There exist philosophies and theologies. We have already spoken of understanding the text as a development, a development in the interpreter himself. The radical problem of development in the interpreter is the problems of conversion, the radical change in his outlook.

Now those problems are thematized, made explicit, in the philosophies and the theologies. They objectify these radical fundamental problems and clarify them. They bring to light the importance of the basic orientations

13 See above, p. 58, note 4.

and attitudes of the individual. Those issues, though expressed in different forms in different texts, also exist there. They also are relevant to an understanding of the meaning of the texts. Bultmann's use of Heidegger's notions on authenticity and inauthenticity in his interpretation of the New Testament illustrates the general fact that those philosophic and theological issues not only arise later on: they arise in their own mode in the earlier period. And, consequently, there is something to be had from the philosophies and the theologies in a scientific communication of the meaning of the text.

We have been raising the question of the communication of a commonsense understanding of the text. Any understanding of the text is going to be of the commonsense type, a specialization of human intelligence with regard to the particular and the concrete. Each text is just the individual text that it is, and so interpretation in itself is always of the commonsense type. But when we come to the communication of that commonsense understanding of the text, when we ask the expert to tell us what he has found, we find, in the first instance, that he can attempt a commonsense communication of his commonsense understanding of the text, and then we get the tendency illustrated by Bishop Descamps. (He has been made a bishop since he wrote that paper.) In the second place, one can raise the question of a scientific communication of the commonsense understanding of the text, and the most obvious step in that is very readily taken. One compares the different authors; one finds the same sort of thing recurring with differences; and one moves to general statements that illustrate the viewpoint, the mode of thinking, the intentions, and so on, of the several authors, and one compares them with one another. One is stepping beyond the field of hermeneutics into the field of history, from the world of community towards the world of theory.

However, that process is performed differently by different experts. Each one of them is somebody with a mind of his own, which he uses. Everything he understands is *his* understanding, and all the judgments he makes are *his* judgments. And they start out from his habitual development. De facto for the last 100 or 130 years in which we have been having higher criticism of the scriptures, we have had all sorts of very different opinions. Just as there is room for classifying and relating with one another the original authors, so there is also room for doing the same thing with the exegetes. Further, there is a more general level of a source of categories, so to speak, supplied by the human sciences and perhaps to be supplied more adequately as these sciences develop.

To take a different type of instance entirely, it is possible for a man at the present time to understand the economics of the Roman Empire in a manner that far surpasses any understanding any Roman ever had of the economics of the Empire, simply because the human science of economics exists and has developed notably. And the same thing applies when one is moving towards a scientific communication of the commonsense interpretation of the text.

Fourthly, besides the relevance of human science towards this work of communication, there is also the more basic relevance, the source of radical differences that find their expression in philosophies and theologies.

2.3.5 Basic Context

If all these different considerations are to be put together, one comes to the question of a basic context. The basic context is roughly what I refer to in *Insight* in chapter 17 as the protean notion of being.

Context is a remainder concept. It denotes the rest that is relevant to the interpretation of the text. Material context is the rest of the documents and monuments that are relevant. Just how far that circle spreads is not too easily determined. We spoke about the relativity of the whole. Formal context is hermeneutic or historical. It is hermeneutic insofar as it is limited to the psyche, to the mentality, of an author. It is historical insofar as a sequence of authors is involved. Basic context is a heuristic notion. It is partly determined, very slightly determined, and partly to be determined, mainly to be determined. It is what becomes determined as the number of successful efforts at exegesis increases.

As a first approximation, basic context is the pure desire to know unfolding through experience, understanding, and judgment, and leading to the statements found on the one hand in authors and on the other hand in interpreters. Secondly, it is this concrete reality of the pure desire found in multiple instances that develops through time and that not only develops but also is subject to aberrations. The notion, then, of basic context is a notion of a reality that is one in its type, human intelligence in operation, and many in its instances, that is the ground of genetic relationships and the ground of dialectical relationships. It is the background of my description of theology as moving through the specialized fields.[14] Basic context

14 Lonergan refers here to the previous evening's discussion. See below, pp. 355–58.

is a context of contexts. It is not on the level of the author's understanding of what he means, or on the level of the interpreter's commonsense statement of a commonsense understanding, or on the level of the scientific statement of commonsense understanding. It is on the level that embraces all the lot. There is a peculiar logic to such a context. It includes terms used in different meanings. It includes contradictory statements made by different people.[15]

15 The seventh and final question-and-answer session was held later this day. See below, pp. 366–74.

1962-10

History[1]

I endeavored yesterday to outline a few ideas that seem to me basic in the problems connected with interpretation. Today there is offered a similar sketch with regard to history in its various meanings. History sets a recurrent task for the theologian, and certain clarifications may be helpful.

A fundamental distinction is between the history that is written about and the history that is written. The Germans have a distinction or sometimes make a distinction – it isn't anything rigid – between *Geschichte*, which means the history that is written about, the total course of human events, and, on the other hand, *Historie*, which is the history that is written. The history that is written about can be conceived vaguely as the total course of human events; or one can form a heuristic concept with regard to it, something to be known by the total set of true historical statements. In developing that heuristic notion, one forms one's general notion of history and of the methods of historical study. It is under that heading that what we shall have to say falls.

First of all, there is a fundamental clarification with regard to the notion of time. History is closely connected with the notion of time, and there is a certain clarification needed there of the relation of history and time. So

---

1 Friday, 20 July 1962, Lauzon CD/MP3 319 (31900A0E060) and 320 (32000A0E060). See www.bernardlonergan.com, 62200DTEL60, which, at least beginning with the second page, quite probably contains Lonergan's notes for this lecture. The notes are at some points fuller in content than the lecture itself, and the reader is encouraged to study them while reading this chapter.

that will be our next point. In the third place, we will discuss existential and narrative history, what the two terms mean; fourthly, critical history; and fifthly, *Historismus*. *Historismus* is a German term, and it has many meanings; but it is useful to consider it because of the interferences of philosophy and history. Sixthly, we shall attempt certain methodical classifications of historical studies. That will be subdivided under different headings: first, common historical research; second, historical essays; third, history and science; fourth, history and philosophy; fifth, history and tradition; sixth, history and religion; seventh, history and apologetics; and, eighth, the theological mediation of history. I can offer just rather incidental remarks on those rather enormous topics, but to have some idea with regard to each is at least helpful to me.

1 The Notion of Time

First of all, there is the notion of time. The Aristotelian definition of time is *numerus et mensura motus secundum prius et posterius*. The *prius et posterius* is spatial. On one's watch there are spatial differences, marked by numbers, and you can say the time by assigning a number: ten twenty-five. Or you can assign the time by a measure: ten hours and twenty-five minutes since midnight. That is precisely what Aristotle means by time. It gives rise to a problem: there are many motions, and so many times. That problem was solved by Aquinas in terms of the *primum mobile*, the first movement that provided a standard for all other movements, one standard time for the universe, the movement of the outer heavens; by Newton with his abstract time, the universal simultaneity; and, finally, by Einstein, with his transformation equations. That's enough for that topic at present.

2 History and Time

There is also a human time. It includes the material time that is numbered and measured, but it also includes something different. It is the *nunc entis mobilis*, and is contrasted with eternity which is the *nunc entis immobilis*. That basic notion of the *nunc* goes from the natural to the intentional order. In other words, *esse intentionale* is not contrasted with *esse reale* as though the one were real and the other were not real. *Esse reale* is divided into *esse naturale* and *esse intentionale*.

This *nunc entis mobilis*, then, has two components: the *esse naturale* of man and the *esse intentionale* of man. By his *esse naturale* man remains the same substance and changes with respect to his accidents. But by his *esse intentionale* he remains the identical subject throughout his life, and that identical subject by his psychological acts somehow transcends time. He recalls the past and anticipates the future as well as living in the present.

That extension over time introduces a new dimension into time, and it is that that is the possibility of history. One can change the subsequent actions of other objects by producing a change in them, but in man the recalling of the past may be a recalling of anything whatever, and any of those recollections will influence one's anticipations and exercise an influence upon one's actions, so that human action has an intrinsically cumulative aspect simply because, by his *esse intentionale*, which is an element in human time as experienced, there is not only the present moment, which is fixed by the *esse naturale* of his acts, but also the going beyond the present moment through memories and anticipations.

Now, this is an individual time, but it is interlocked with other individual times. Men live in a society. They cooperate, operate with one another, on the basis of a common understanding. That common understanding with the people you cooperate with over a given period or indefinitely is a determination that was reached in the past by some sort of explicit or implicit agreement and that through memory continues to exist into the present. In other words, the interlocking of individual times through social living gives a common time for the society and a social continuity. While any one individual may introduce a great deal of arbitrariness into his acts, the society cannot do so. Social action has to proceed on the basis of some common understanding. And while that common basis of common understanding can be changed at any time, still it is not changed without notice. People debate enormously about changes in the social setup. Even in a society that is said to be open to change, as contemporary democracies are – they boast of their openness, of the continuous changes in their social setup – people still have to preserve constantly this will to be open to change. It is very difficult to procure a constant will to be open to change.

3 Existential and Narrative History

These reflections on time lead into the distinction between existential and narrative history.

Existential history is the knowledge of the past that makes social continuity possible. If a man suffered amnesia, he would still be the same man, but he could not behave as the same man simply because he would not remember who he was, what his job was, what his place in society was, or what his obligations were. Similarly, if there were a national amnesia, the nation would vanish. We are all Canadians or Americans; but if we all forgot it, there would no more be Canada or the United States. That memory is an existential constituent of the society as continuous. If the society were simply discontinuous, if every day were a brand new beginning, there would be no social continuity. The possibility of that social continuity may be called existential history. The memory of the past is what makes social continuity possible. It is necessary in every society insofar as it functions as a society, insofar as its members are aware of their membership and of the common understanding under which they work together.

The whole of that existential history does not exist in one single locus. It is, as it were, parceled out among many minds. Each one remembers what regards himself and what regards the people who deal with him. He knows what is expected of him by others, and he knows what he can expect of others. It is in general in that form that existential history is parceled out among the many minds that make up the society. There is a rather vague general apprehension of these common rights and duties, but it is something very general. What actually functions as existential history is not some operative common element in memory in all its concrete details and variations. In other words, the many partial apprehensions that make up existential history are partial not only in the sense that they are incomplete but also in the sense that they are scattered among an indefinitely large number of minds.

Narrative history puts these partial views together. It tells who said what and who did what. In varying degrees it adds when it was said or done, where it was said or done, for what reasons, with what results, under what circumstances. And so narrative history effects the transition from the *vécu* of existential history to the *thématique*, from the vital, ordinary level of living to thematizing that living as a history.

That narrative history fulfills simultaneously many different functions. First of all, it is explanatory. Aristotle's efficient cause is the origin of movement, *hothen hē kinēsis*. Narrative history tells how things started. It may be mythical, but at least it tells how things started and what followed, and so it gives the members of the community some understanding, some explanation, of their setup. It draws attention to the broader aspects of the society as a whole in its main divisions, in its principal interdependences, in its origins and its developments, its setbacks, its perils, and its triumphs. One has some general view of the society from narrative history, which by the mere fact that it narrates how things started and what happened after that, communicates to the members of the society some understanding, some explanation, of the society. 'Why do we do things this way?' 'Well, so and so thought this, and someone else thought that, and they argued it out, and they came to this conclusion. And everybody is satisfied.' At least they know why things are done that way.

In the second place, narrative history is artistic. It is not an exhaustive catalogue but a selection, and the selection is in part determined by artistic exigences, by considerations of how much material can be worked into the narration without destroying its unity, rhythm, form, effectiveness. There is an artistic element that exerts a controlling influence in narrative history.

Again, it is ethical. It praises what the historian considers good, and it lays blame on the facts that the historian regrets and does not want to see recur.

It is apologetic. It defends the nation against its critics and particularly its foreign critics.

It is prophetic. It expresses a viewpoint on the present direction the society has taken, and it favors or does what it can to favor a given direction of social development.

Finally, it is existential because a social unit, as soon as it reaches a certain size, could not function merely by existential history. It needs this thematizing of existential history that is met by a narrative history that explains, that is artistic, ethical, apologetic, and prophetic as well as existential.

4 Critical History

Critical history revises narrative history, and it heads into the problem of a critique of historical reason. It proceeds from sources, from the totality of surviving monuments and documents. Its basis, accordingly, is not only existing narrative histories but also any other documents or monuments that may be available or may be discovered or searched for. It proceeds from the sources critically. It scrutinizes them for authenticity and trustworthiness. It locates their origin in place and time. It analyzes out exactly their precise meaning and bearing. It proceeds to an understanding of the sources, and it does not present itself simply as belief.

Collingwood in his *Idea of History*[2] illustrates the point by writing a short detective story in which all the witnesses are lying and all the clues are planted and the detective gets the criminal nonetheless. He is able to detect the

2 R.G. Collingwood, *The Idea of History* (Oxford: Clarendon, 1946) 266–74.

lies, then figure out why the lies are told and why the clues are planted; and through this process of reasoning he arrives at the criminal. The point is that the critical historian does not present his views as a believer. He is not believing either the people who are telling the truth or the people who are lying. He is like the detective, figuring out who is lying and who is telling the truth if anyone is lying. In other words, it is a matter of understanding the sources, and it has something of a pretense or claim to get beyond mere belief.

That understanding of the sources can be mediated by science. The historian can draw upon contemporary natural science, on contemporary psychology, economics, sociology, political theory, anthropology to reach a better understanding of the past. The obvious illustration, perhaps, of that use of a contemporary science to understand a past in a way that otherwise it could not be understood is Rostovtzeff's *Social and Economic History of the Roman Empire.*[3]

Further, that understanding of the sources, as it can be mediated by human or natural science, so also it can be mediated by a *Weltanschauung*, by a philosophy, by a theology, by a religion. An example of that is Butterfield's *The Whig Interpretation of History.*[4] Butterfield was able to write his *Whig Interpretation of History* because the Whigs were no longer the dominant force in academic circles.

This understanding of the sources that the historian reaches is communicated by a narration, by telling how it really happened, *wie es eigentlich gewesen*, in Ranke's famous phrase. In other words, the understanding of past events reached by the historian is understanding in the concrete. It is not an understanding that is formulated abstractly. It is the type of understanding that grasps the intelligible in the sensible, and it communicates that grasp of the intelligible in the sensible simply by narrating. The historian arrives at an understanding of a battle, and by narrating what happened in the battle he communicates, without mentioning, an understanding of the battle. In other words, you can communicate a point of view, an understanding of things human, simply by narrating; and that is the historian's mode. Insofar as he narrates what happened, simply because he is presenting data in a certain order, with a certain emphasis, in a certain direction, he communicates his understanding of the data.

The historian, then, does not operate professedly on any theoretical level. His type of intelligence is the commonsense type of intelligence,

3   See above, p. 53, note 25.
4   Herbert Butterfield, *The Whig Interpretation of History* (New York: Norton, 1965).

namely, the specialization of human intellect in the concrete and particular. By narrating about concrete, particular events and persons, he communicates his understanding of the history.

Now, in the nineteenth century there was an initial movement under the influence of Hegel that tried to do history in the light of Hegel's dialectical system and, consequently, a priori. And, secondly, there was a revulsion against Hegelianism by people known as the members of the Historical School: the brothers Grimm in linguistics and folklore; Niebuhr, Ranke, Droysen in the historians; von Savigny in the jurists. They all had the same idea: Nothing a priori. There is no need for any philosophy, any systematic viewpoint. All you have to do is sift the data, understand them, and communicate your concrete understanding by your narration. However, it was discovered later, notably by Dilthey, that, despite all their disclaimers with regard to any systematic or philosophical presuppositions whatever, de facto the members of the Historical School were living on the capital of the Enlightenment and Hegelianism. Just because they did not profess these things explicitly and draw conclusions from them did not mean that de facto that was not the way they were thinking. That led to Dilthey's attempt to do for historical studies what Kant had done for natural science. He never really got it done, but he did an awful lot of brilliant thinking with regard to it. You can conceive Kant as having eliminated metaphysics, but you can also conceive him as providing foundations for natural science. Those foundations were based upon a study of the achievement of the eighteenth century in natural science, particularly of Newton. Dilthey thought that we had come far enough in the art of history or science of history-writing for a person to reflect upon that achievement, particularly the achievement of Ranke, and work out the presuppositions of a possible history. That was his ideal.

5   *Historismus*

This brings us to the topic of *Historismus*. As I have said, the term *Historismus* is used in different meanings. Meinecke wrote a two-volume work on the development of *Historismus: Die Entstehung des Historismus*, published at Munich and Berlin in 1936.[5] Heussi in 1932 put out a very thin but care-

5   Friedrich Meinecke, *Die Entstehung des Historismus* (Munich: Leibniz, 1946). In *Method in Theology*, Lonergan refers to an essay by Meinecke in *The Varieties of History: From Voltaire to the Present*, ed. Fritz Stern (New York: Meridian Books, 1956) 267–88.

fully argued volume, *Die Krisis des Historismus*.[6] Karl Löwith vigorously attacked the relativism of *Historismus*. He emphasized that aspect of it. You get his viewpoint fairly briefly in an article in the *Eranos Jahrbuch*, 1952.[7] There is also his *Weltgeschichte und Heilgeschehen*, the third edition at Stuttgart in 1953.[8] Finally, there is Gadamer on truth and method: *Wahrheit und Methode*.[9] With regard to general bibliography on the subject, there is a paperback, *Philosophy of History in Our Time*, by Meyerhoff.[10] There also is a collection: Patrick Gardiner, *Theories of History*.[11] This is a large volume of selections from the chief people who have contributed to the method of history or the theory of history or the philosophy of history. Also, I think, it is pretty well fitted out with bibliographical references.

There are three different things to be distinguished to understand this discussion of *Historismus*: historical consciousness, historical relativism, and historical method.

5.1 Historical Consciousness

Historical consciousness is an idea of man. Among the existentialists there is a distinction between man's existence and his essence, and the Scholastic is surprised to learn that the essence is something you acquire after you exist. This is a use of the word 'essence' that does not make sense from a Scholastic viewpoint. As an example of how that meaning of essence arises, one can take Harnack's *Wesen des Christentums*.[12] It is a desire to know the essence of Christianity, but it is an attempt to know that essence through history. An understanding of the history of Christianity brings to light what the essence of Christianity is. Similarly, the understanding of a man, the way he lives, acts, and talks, brings to light the kind of man he is. You can say it is the person's intentional essence, what is essential to his mode of thought, judgment, will, affectivity, sensitivity, and so on. It is essence of the subject, essence as constituted by the intentional aspect of his acts.

6 Karl Heussi, *Die Krisis des Historismus* (Tübingen: Mohr, 1932).
7 Karl Löwith, 'Die Dynamik der Geschichte und der Historismus,' *Eranos Jahrbuch* 21 (1952) 217–54.
8 Karl Löwith, *Weltgeschichte und Heilsgeschehen: Die theologischen Voraussetzungen der Geschichtsphilosophie* (Stuttgart: W. Kohlhammer, 1953).
9 See above, p. 115, note 13.
10 *The Philosophy of History in Our Time: An Anthology*, ed. Hans Meyerhoff (Garden City, NY: Doubleday, 1959).
11 *Theories of History*, ed. Patrick Gardiner (New York: Free Press, and London: Collier Macmillan, 1959).
12 Adolf von Harnack, *Das Wesen des Christentums* (Leipzig: Hinrichs, 1908).

Now, historical consciousness is concerned with the intentional essence, if I may so speak, of men and human society. It is concerned with man not as nature, not as substance, but as spirit, subject, knower, chooser, agent. From this viewpoint the formal constituent of man, of his actions and institutions, his art, languages, literature, history, religion, science, philosophy, and theology is all in the intentional order. It is a matter of meaning. This intentional order develops, and the development of meanings is the development of man, of his institutions, of his actions, in all his fields of knowledge, in all the fields of action, in all cultural achievement, civilization, and religion. This development occurs in and through human meanings, purposes, actions. But it is historical precisely because it is not just what man intends, what man thinks of, that settles the results. It depends just as much on what the fellow is overlooking. The historical process moves not just in terms of human intentions but also in terms of their limitations, and the limitations reveal themselves in the blocks that the intentions meet precisely because they have been overlooking the point.

5.2 *Historical Relativism*

It is this element of history that involves something beyond what man may actually be thinking of that gives the Greek notion of *anankē* and *tychē*, necessity and fortune or chance, the Roman *fata volentem ducunt, nolentem trahunt,* the Christian divine providence, Hegel's *List der Vernunft,* the unseen hand of the laws of supply and demand, the Marxist dialectic resting on the forces and conditions of production, and so on. They are all referring to an element in history that arises precisely because, while the course of history is a matter of meanings and the development of meanings, of intentions and their execution, still, the results depend upon the interplay of these meanings, as the course of the battle does not depend simply on the plans of the generals but also upon the conflict between the plans and still further on what the plans overlook.

Now, that view of man can be carried through in all fields of inquiry without leading into philosophic difficulties or into some sort of philosophic relativism, precisely in the measure that it is supplied with an adequate philosophy for its purposes. Otherwise, what will happen? You will have the intentional essence of the historian settling what other intentional essences are and what their development has been; and the next historian comes along and places this historian within the historical process as a product not only of what was known but also of what was overlooked; and this man goes into the same things, and there develops the opposition of historical schools – and not only that opposition but a situation where there are no means of solving the problem, no ultimate criteria. Meinecke is mainly concerned with historical consciousness, but the approach through historical consciousness heads into a philosophic relativism insofar as an adequate philosophy for this new view of man is lacking. And insofar as prior to historical consciousness the philosophy had been classicist in its tendencies, concerned with the universal and the normative, and prescinding from the concrete details, it was not equipped to provide the directives, the type of norms that were needed by this historical movement.

Karl Löwith in his attack on Dilthey's relativism states that in Dilthey metaphysics yields place to the history of metaphysical systems. There is no human nature. There is the type 'man,' and that type is a Proteus; he changes as the meaning changes. Whatever happens to be thought or done is equally true, equally correct, equally right. There are no criteria. They are all human manifestations. Philosophy can make no claims to absolute truth. It is limited to getting the meaning, *Besinnung*, to understanding, to interpretation: *Besinnung, Verstehen, Deuten*. These change with every change in the historical process. Since *Historismus*, historical relativism, represents simply a stage in the process, it is due to go out too. But that is the contradiction in the position.

The difficulty with Dilthey arises because of his excessive reliance upon this intentional essence, his failure, as is necessarily the case in any idealism or criticism, to have not merely the intentional but also the natural order. Because the fundamental element in the intentional order belongs to a natural order that does not change, this exclusive attention to the intentional, taken by itself, separated from the natural, heads into a relativism that can hardly be escaped.

There is a certain amount of solution of the philosophic problems from the new confidence given in the light of the investigations of Husserl. And also, there is a chapter in Heidegger's *Sein und Zeit*, chapter 5 in the second part, that is thought to have made a fundamental contribution towards a solution.[13] But still, as Ebeling says, no one has the answers yet to all the problems about this. They are carrying on, but they know they have not got full answers to all the problems. They have some hope, and they believe in the historical-critical method, but the problems that are raised by historical

13 This would be the chapter 'Temporality and Historicality' in Martin Heidegger, *Being and Time*, trans. John Macquarrie and Edward Robinson (New York: Harper & Row, 1962) 424–55.

relativism have not been given any commonly accepted solution in the circles from which that problem arose.

5.3 Historical Method

Besides historical consciousness and historical relativism, there also is historical method. That is the main thing that concerns us, and it is with regard to that that Heussi wrote. By *Historismus* Heussi understands the way history was written about 1900. There are the fundamental handbooks on historical writing. Langlois and Seignobos's *Introduction aux études historiques* is still quoted.[14] It is still a fundamental manual in learning history, learning how to study history and how to write history. Similarly, Bernheim, *Lehrbuch der historischen Methode*.[15]

Heussi assigns four characteristics to the mode of writing history about the year 1900. The first is that the historian is concerned to determine the objectively already structured historical facts. To reach them he has no need of any set of systematic or philosophic principles. The structure is already there. All the historian has to do is to follow his method, and automatically he will arrive at a knowledge of what the true account of the facts and their interrelationships is. The crisis in *Historismus* is the rejection of that assumption.

The second characteristic is that historical objects are all related to one another. There is an intelligible interdependence of historical facts. The third is that there is a development. The idea of development, of historical progress or decline, is a key element in historical investigation. The crisis in *Historismus* does not affect the second and third characteristics. They remain just as they were around the year 1900. The fourth point was that historical studies are not concerned with profound issues, *die Tiefe der Dinge*, with the genuine content, the substance, the essence, the idea, the shape, the meaning of events. Such essays as Harnack's *Das Wesen des Christentums* were not historical; it was not something central to history but marginal. That type of study does not belong to history in the strong, full sense. On that fourth point, according to Heussi, the crisis in *Historismus*, this way of writing history about 1900, has affected it only slightly. History still does not claim to do any metaphysics of any sort. What Heussi was talking about was

14 C.-V. Langlois and C. Seignobos, *Introduction aux études historiques* (Paris: Hachette et Cie, 1898).
15 Ernst Bernhaim, *Lehrbush der historischen Methode* (Leipzig: Duncker & Humblot, 1894).

a crisis that arose among historians in Germany after the First World War. And his summary of what the situation was around 1932 is the significance of that work of Heussi.

However, one has in H.-I. Marrou, who is quite an eminent historian, in 1954, *De la connaissance historique*,[16] the claim, put forth on page 54, that if one really follows the standard method in historical investigation and in writing history as set forth by Langlois and Seignobos, according to their prescriptions, the more you set aside all preconceptions, the more you attend simply and solely to the critically established facts, the more the historian is driven simply to edit texts with footnotes. Such a history consists of a book of blank pages. That is the word of a man who has spent his life acquiring quite a reputation as a historian; that is his criticism of the fundamental handbook.

I asked the man that teaches method in the Church history faculty at the Gregorian what he thought of Langlois and Seignobos, and he said, 'Well, they have to start there, at least. There's no doubt about that. But whether you are going to grant that this method enables you to write history that says anything, well, that's a further point. After you have had your regular training along these lines, then it is up to you to decide whether you are going to stick with it.' It is a real issue. Descamps, in the article I quoted in *Sacra Pagina*, takes Marrou to task for his excessive skepticism, but I do not think that Descamps is understanding the real basis of the issues that Marrou is raising. Marrou is not a skeptic; he is disagreeing with a method. And inasmuch as Descamps holds that biblical theology is essentially a matter of applying literary and historical criteria, that biblical theology in its main lines is written just as well by an atheist as by a Catholic – both of them have to acknowledge that the people who wrote the scriptures were men of faith, but the fact that they themselves are men of faith does not affect the issue – there is in that position of Descamps a disregard, it seems to me, of the existential element in the historian. If the man is an atheist or a liberal or a modernist or a non-Catholic of any other type, there is some horizon there limiting him. And when he does history, he will be endeavoring to make the facts intelligible to himself, to people with his point of view. If a Catholic attempts to do biblical theology simply from the viewpoint of literary and historical criteria, there probably will be no difficulty because there is not this existential block, and that is the sense in which Descamps wants this; but he is overlooking the fact of this existential block, it seems to me.

16 Henri-Irenée Marrou, *De la connaissance historique* (Paris: Éditions du Seuil, 1954); in English, *The Meaning of History*, trans. Robert J. Olsen (Baltimore: Helicon, 1966).

However, I do not think there is any use going to either Heussi or to Marrou to find out just where the difficulties lie, because the way they put their points is philosophically unsatisfactory. In other words, while Marrou is somebody as a historian, while Heussi is someone as a historian, in their critique of the *Historismus*, in their critique of the methodology in the way history was done about 1900, they do not pin down the precise point. The precise point regards the question, Can history be written independently of any systematic, philosophic presuppositions or assumptions? That is the basic point. When Heussi says that you cannot draw any clear line between writing history and philosophic questions, I think he is expressing correctly his view. He says, for example, that history as the elaboration of the sources, as the critique of simple matters of fact, as the type of history-writing that is concerned simply with, or that mainly consists in, settling matters of fact, is not directly influenced by philosophic presuppositions. But the minute one gets beyond that – and it is almost impossible to write history without going beyond that – the fundamental questions arise, and you cannot say that the historian is independent of systematics. The way Heussi, however, expresses his difficulty is unsatisfactory. It heads right into a relativism, and it is very difficult for any of these people to get away from a relativism. Rothacker, whom I have referred to before, in his *Logik und Systematik der Geisteswissenschaften*, is ultimately a relativist.[17] For him all synthesis depends upon will, is led by will. On page 144 you have that statement, and again on page 149, and again on page 157. They are unable to provide ultimate answers to say how any synthesis can arise without invoking will or something similar.

The necessity of some philosophic assumptions becomes clear simply when one states that history is a set of propositions that purport to be true. Any propositions that are true have philosophic presuppositions. Whether the man who makes them knows it or not, they are there. Any methodical procedure has philosophic presuppositions whether the man who employs the method has a fully developed philosophy or no idea whatever of philosophy. The presuppositions are there; they can't be avoided. It is precisely because they can't be avoided that they are named philosophic. And so it was simply a naivete in the Historical School in the nineteenth century to presuppose that anything can be done without philosophic presuppositions. What you have to keep away from are false presuppositions; and you can get false presuppositions in, for example, the way that Heussi and Marrou express themselves.

17 Lonergan is referring to his mention of Rothacker in the second discussion period. See below, p. 284, note 3.

A point on which the issue arises concretely is what is called perspectivism. Subsequent events throw a light upon the past. The economic crisis of the 1930s forced an enormous development in economic theory, and that development of economic theory subsequent to the 1930s led to a reinterpretation of the economic history of the nineteenth and earlier centuries. The development of a contemporary science confers significance upon past events. There are several ways in which subsequent events throw light upon what went before. Consequently, there is to history what is called the perspective. In the perspective that arises at a certain moment, subsequent to the past that is being investigated, there is a whole new slice of that part of history that comes to light that before just was not perceptible.

In general, in history there is a relatively fixed object that depends on research, the analysis of texts, the determination of matters of fact, and, in general, what was known or could have been known by contemporary common sense. But what is known by contemporary common sense is not everything that enters into history. Churchill was magnificently placed to know everything that was going on in the Second World War. He had one of the positions of privilege. But his history of the Second World War is not the last word in the history of the business. History stands to what is known by contemporary common sense pretty much as self-knowledge stands to consciousness. All our waking moments are conscious, and everything we do during them is conscious. But that does not mean that we know ourselves. Similarly, the man who knows what is going on in his time is knowing what can be known by contemporary common sense, but history is concerned with more than that. And that 'more than that' is not relatively fixed but the relatively fluid element in history. It is what is brought to light subsequently. You can write the history of the battle after the battle is over and you know who won. But up to the decisive moment in the battle when things are settled, you would not know how to go about writing the history. You get the clue from the end of it. And similarly, when the war is over you can study the war. You have more light on it. And when a series of wars is over, the subsequent throws light on what went before; it increases the whole that is the object of your investigation; and similarly with the end of a people, of a state, of a type of government, of an art, a style, a culture.[18]

There are, then, new perspectives that arise in history by the passage of time, by subsequent events and subsequent understanding. Nietzsche

18 A break was taken at this point. The remainder of the lecture is recorded on Lauzon CD/MP3 320 (32000A0E060).

remarked that past events are pulled out of their shadows and placed in the sun of great men. A great figure in literature or in any human field of endeavor opens up new lines of thought, and the new lines of thought bring to light elements in the past, things that were significant in the past and that hitherto have been overlooked. Similarly, we say that *Novum Testamentum latet in Vetere et Vetus Testamentum patet in Novo.*[19] The New Testament throws a backward light upon the Old Testament. Something similar can be said with regard to Plato in himself and Plato in the light of Aristotle, or with regard to Aristotle in himself and Aristotle in the light of Aquinas; and so on. By subsequent developments in human science, in archeology, in knowledge of languages and various things of that type, there is in the course of time an opening up of new perspectives on the past.

Now one can acknowledge this fact of many perspectives on the past in two ways. One can be headed off into a relativism, and one is if one is not capable of solving the philosophic difficulties of relativism. On the other hand, one can speak of not a relativist but an absolutist perspectivism, namely, one that acknowledges the truth of the many perspectives, that conceives history as no more in possession of its ideal goal than is any other science, that affirms the possibility of the many perspectives being joined together into a single fuller view.

In that connection there would be room for a discussion of Bultmann's views on hermeneutics. For him, the way the question is put is the key issue. And by 'the way the question is put' he means something that develops historically, not just some individual way the question is put, but the way the question has to be put from the prior investigations that have gone on. That process brings one to putting the question; and once the question is put, the use of a method will determine what the significance of the past is from that particular viewpoint. He admits a multiplicity of viewpoints and a difference in perspective for every viewpoint. But, granted the determinate viewpoint, then the determinateness of the method will arrive at one correct interpretation of the text or the historical event. Where he is not clear is on the validity of the way in which the question is put. There is a lack there of foundations, and it is on that level of foundations that our main debate with these people lies.

And so, from that consideration of *Historismus,* namely, contemporary discussions of the problems of historical method and its unwilling involvement

---

19 The New Testament lies hidden in the Old, and the Old becomes clear in the New.

in philosophic issues – unwilling because, in general, exegetes and historians are not particularly interested or competent in philosophy – these questions bring to light fundamental aspects of history-writing and the way to deal with historians who are critics of Catholicism and of Catholic interpretations. That is how the issue of *Historismus* affects us, and also our own efforts at historical writing.

6 Methodical Classification of Historical Studies

We move, then, to an attempt at a methodical classification of historical studies. Just because history is a single word, one must not think that doing history is just one type of thing. One has to draw distinctions between different ways in which history is done and the different types of results that are arrived at.

6.1 Common Historical Research

First of all, let us take common historical research. Common historical research has at its disposal, first of all, contemporary instances of common sense, namely, the common sense of the historian; secondly, contemporary potential to develop a participation in the common sense of other times and places; and thirdly, a generally accepted set of methods and techniques (a) for the discovery, collection, classification, dating, editing, analyzing, evaluating, and criticizing of sources – what is to be done from each of those viewpoints is pretty well cut and dried; (b) for the determination of elementary facts: did Brutus kill Caesar? (c) for the determination of elementary interdependences: why did Brutus kill Caesar? what were the events that led up to it? and (d) for the determination of elementary developments of interdependences. By 'elementary' is meant what may unhesitatingly be left to common sense in its most common acceptation. Would you trust anyone to settle that, to investigate that issue, or would you not? If you would trust anyone of normal qualifications, then the question lies within the field of common historical research. It is the field on which universal agreement is easy.

For example, the history of France may be written by a Frenchman, but it could be written by a German, by an Italian, by an Englishman, by a Spaniard. And they are not all the same. There are elements in French history that you do not leave to everybody, but there are elements that you can leave to everyone without any difficulty. By common historical research is meant the field, the part of history, on which general agreement is easy. Whether it is a Catholic who does it or a Protestant, you can rely equally well on anyone. You do not feel any doubts about leaving it to anyone.

6.2   The Historical Essay

The second type of history to be considered I call the historical essay. The historical essay differs from common historical research by introducing a specially qualified common sense, a man who has very exceptional qualifications as a musician working at the history of music, or very exceptional qualifications as a psychologist working at psychological issues in history, and so on. The historical work is of the type of common sense, namely, the specialization of human intelligence that deals with the particular, the concrete, the factual. All history is of that type. But the common sense may be mediated by special qualifications, and people without the special qualifications will not see what another can see, will not find significant what he finds significant, will not come to conclusions that he easily arrives at, with the result that the history he writes, not merely in the light of common historical research, which is the highest common factor of all historical investigation, is something that can be appreciated only by people who take into account his special qualifications and are willing to rely on them.

The historical essay, then, confronts issues that cannot be left unhesitatingly to ordinary commonsense understanding, and it reaches an understanding of the past that will not be convincing to anybody and everybody. In other words, in natural science the arguments and the procedures are equally convincing to anyone. The issue is settled by an experiment. Anyone can see just where the needle is standing or whether the spark jumps the gap or anything that settles the issue. But that criterion of universal agreement which sooner or later is reached in the natural sciences cannot be applied to this type of history that I have called the historical essay. Its criterion is not going to be what is going to be accepted by anybody and everybody that investigates the field because, insofar as anybody and everybody re-performs that investigation, he will miss precisely the things that the special qualifications of this historian enabled him to see.

The function of historical essays – and by that I mean of flocks of them – is to raise deeper issues, to promote the education of historians, to effect in time a rising of the level of common historical research and, in the short term, to effect by their questioning the confinement of common historical research to the type of issues with which it is competent to deal.

6.3 History and Science

Thirdly, we consider history and human science, or history and science generally, but particularly human science.

There is a mutual dependence. There is the history of the science itself, and that can be done properly only by someone who knows the science. You cannot write a history of medicine if you do not know medicine, and you cannot write a history of mathematics unless you know mathematics, and so on. Again, this involves the mediation of a science beyond common sense. The historical work itself will be of the commonsense type of understanding, but that common sense is mediated not by other special qualifications but by knowledge of a contemporary science. If you know the science, you can pick out the key points in the development of the science.

When one compares history and science in the sense of human science, one gets the inverse phenomenon. Human science studies human data, data on human living. And most of the data are in the past. Human science is not based on human data of the moment. It can be, insofar as it is based, for example, in an experimental psychology, but in general, the data extend out into the past. Historical data are invoked. With this, one has a mutual dependence; the development of the human science depends upon historical knowledge, and inversely, the history of the science can be written only by a person who knows the science.

When a human science is employing historical data, one gets a conflict of competences. The human scientist has to be qualified historically. I don't mean he has to have done a course in history, but he has to understand what the historical techniques and procedures are, and he has to know how to use them and what you can get out of them, and he has to interpret his data as a historian would. On the other hand, he is not open to the criticisms of common historical research, in other words, of the people who do not know the science, who will miss the significance that this man grasps in the data. For example, consider the type of work that Eliade is doing. He is using depth psychology and his own studies of symbolic thinking to interpret the history of religions. Insofar as he is concerned with the history of religions, he is working in a historical field. Insofar as he is interpreting them from the viewpoint of symbolic meanings, to understand what he is doing a certain competence is required in depth psychology or the sort of thing that the depth psychologists have brought to light. Insofar as one is a historian of religion with no grasp of this business of symbolic meanings, however good one is at history, one is not competent to criticize Eliade. In other words, historical qualifications in specialized historical fields are not enough. You also have to have the scientific competence that is demanded. If one has the scientific competence and is fairly sure of one's historical ground, one need not bother about the criticisms of people who think that all history is common historical research.

6.4 History and Philosophy

After common historical research, historical essay, and history and science, we have history and philosophy. It is a matter of what I referred to yesterday as the basic context, or of what in *Insight* I call the protean notion of being.

We started from a world of interiority, of community, and of theory. But each one of the persons in the world of community is a case of interiority. He performs all the operations that the man who has come to self-appropriation knows about himself. Insofar as a man has arrived at self-appropriation, he knows the potentialities of any man, and he can reconstruct them. He knows that knowing is a matter of experience, understanding, and judgment, and that there is a further dimension added on by divine faith. He knows just what the effects of horizon and inauthenticity and the need of conversion are, and how the whole outlook is changed just by varying one of these factors in the subject. Consequently, he has a fundamental understanding of all the people in the world of community. He has an element that is highly indeterminate, that stands in need of further determinations, but his study of the historical data is a matter of reaching those further determinations.

Now that may seem to be something extremely abstract and irrelevant, but it is the sort of thing that makes history or any science possible. The positivist idea that the natural scientist is concerned only to ascertain with the greatest possible exactitude what the measurements are or what he sees, what the colors and all the rest of it are, is a total misconception of what the natural scientist does. The natural scientist works not only from below upwards, from data, classifications, measurements, comparing measurements, collecting measurements together, putting them onto graphs, and changing the graphs into a mathematical formula – the whole business of the determination of empirical laws. At the same time he is working from above downwards. He has got in physics a grasp of mathematical possibilities. He is able, from purely general considerations such as continuity or other equally general things, to write down mathematical equations of extreme generality, differential equations, or a postulate of invariance as in relativity, and from very incomplete knowledge of empirical laws and by these generalities pin right down what the results are going to be.

This downward movement from above is, of course, the thing that gives to physics its power and its sweep, that puts together these particular empirical laws into systems and gives the whole structure its forward drive. It's what's 'up there' that counts. It is not the people who are very good at measuring, but the Einsteins and Max Plancks who make physics into a highly successful science. And that is true all along the line. Insofar as you think of history simply as a collection of data, well, it remains just a collection of data, and you arrive at the criticism Marrou made of the method of Langlois and Seignobos. What does the historian do? Well, if he follows the prescriptions of Langlois and Seignobos faithfully, scrupulously, his history consists of blank pages. Marrou illustrates the point from Langlois's own work, which more and more tended towards what Marrou calls the blank page, the editing of texts and the writing of notes on the text. The methodological possibility of doing more than that is the fact that we possess a fundamental understanding of man; the historical data are determinations, further determinations, on something on which we already possess a good deal of knowledge. Anyone we write history about has to be a human being, and we have some knowledge of what that is. Insofar as one has arrived at self-appropriation, one has a set of fundamental determinate notions that receive their further determinations from the purely positive inquiry.

But the purely positive inquiry by itself does not take one beyond an enumeration. There has to be and there always is the intervention of insight when you get beyond that. And for anything on the large scale in history this other factor provides the upper blade of method: using one's self-knowledge to give knowledge of something that is common to all, that admits endless variation, that admits oppositions in development, that determines the various factors. That upper blade of method is the contribution of a critical philosophy to historical method. What one knows through self-appropriation is relevant to understanding the people who are written about by the historian. It is relevant to understanding the historians that do the writing. It is relevant to understanding the critics of the historians. It adds a normative element, the normative element that is implicit in such notions as horizon, authenticity, and conversion.

6.5 History and Tradition

The next topic is history and tradition. Earlier we distinguished existential and narrative history and said that the existential stands to the narrative as the *vécu* to the *thématique*. Narrative history, then, simply because it thematizes existential history, is a mediation of existential history, and it brings out in existential history its explanatory, artistic, ethical, apologetic, and prophetic aspects. Critical history broadens the basis on which historical investigation operates, by its systematic study of all the possible sources.

But we also saw that critical history heads into philosophic difficulties. Is the critical historian to have pre-philosophic presuppositions or is he not? The nineteenth-century Historical School in Germany was convinced that history is to be written without any systematic or philosophic presuppositions. That is a view that is very easily spread elsewhere with less awareness of what one is doing. That is just an illusion. You have philosophic presuppositions whether you want them or not, whether you know about them or not.

But there is a further aspect to that nineteenth-century movement, or to the general movement that has been going on from the sixteenth century. There is a recent book, put out at Göttingen in 1960. I have not read it, but the title is suggestive: *Die Säkularisierung der Universalhistorischen Auffassung.*[20] It deals mainly with the sixteenth and seventeenth centuries. The Christian world has its own general suppositions and understanding of the historical process. The birth, the rise, of secularism in the modern world implied a rejection of that view of the meaning of human life and human history and the discovery, the formulation, and the communication of another view of the meaning of human life.

Consequently, there is a relation between history-writing and tradition. Tradition is another name for what I have called existential history. Existential history is the possibility of social continuity, and tradition is handing on the achievements of the past from each generation to the next. Insofar as there has been that development of secularism that has been going on in recent centuries and insofar as the secularists had a great deal to do with the development of historical science, there is brought to light the relationship between a tradition and the writing of history.

What does the historian do? The critical historian no less than the narrative historian is engaged in knowing, in thematizing, the tradition that produced him, that produced his opportunities, that produced the problems of his time, that produced the difficulties of his time, that produced the situations in which he lives. He is thematizing that past tradition in which he lives, and by thematizing it he is communicating it, and he is communicating it from some determinate point of view, within the limits of some

20 Adalbert Klempt, *Die Säkularisierung der Universalhistorischen Auffassung: Zum Wandel des Geschichtsdenkens im 16. und 17. Jahrhundert* (Göttingen: Musterschmidt, 1960).

horizon. In other words, existentially the historian stands in a real relation to the tradition to which he belongs. Either he is carrying on that tradition and doing so creatively, or the opposite. In other words, conservation and creation, as Gilson remarked, are the same thing when God does them. Conservation and creation are not opposites. And the same is to some extent true of human affairs. To be a true conservative is keeping things alive, not killing everything. The opposite is sometimes taken as the meaning of conservatism.

The historian, then, may be a person who is mediating the tradition of the past, keeping it alive, passing it on; that is his existential function. Or his existential function may be just the opposite. His effort may be to destroy the tradition of the past and put a new one in its place, as was the effect of secularist history. It was eliminating the Christian view and the Christian meaning of human living and putting another meaning of history in its place, commonly the idea of progress.

Again, the historian may by his mediocrity be bringing about the inauthenticity of that tradition. He may be carrying it on professedly but not really understanding it and, consequently, unconsciously substituting for it something that is just not as good, a corruption of the tradition.

Finally, he may reduce the tradition to triviality by limiting himself to common historical research.

Now it is possible for historians to find all sorts of good, safe nooks and crannies in which these basic issues do not arise in their work. They are limiting themselves to just this point from just this viewpoint. They are carrying on the work of specialists, and they have no large ambitions. That is something that is possible for the historian to do. But that does not mean that the alternatives I have listed do not exist. One may evade what writing history really is by simply preparing the writing of history by highly specialized studies. Those preparations all head ultimately to a general presentation, and any such general presentation brings out the existential relation of the historian to his tradition. In that existential relation either he is reducing his tradition to triviality, or he is making it unauthentic, or he is conserving it in the creative sense, or, finally, he is endeavoring to be part of a movement that aims at destroying the tradition and giving rise to a new one.

If there is an existential decision involved in the historian's task when it is compared with the tradition – and existential decisions do not occur without acts of will, without decisions made by the will – does it not follow that all historical synthesis, as Rothacker claims, ultimately reduces to matters of will? According to Rothacker, it is only the problem of truth that is relative.

In other words, there is correctness. The historian or the human scientist can always be correct, perform all the operations demanded by his method, and be impeccable from a methodological viewpoint. As long as he does not raise any questions about truth, about rectitude, about ultimate morality, he remains on safe ground by remaining technical. However, as soon as you start talking about truth in the German sense of *die Wahrheit*, about rectitude, about proper orientations in human living, then your will is part of the picture, and, consequently, for Rothacker that part of the human sciences is something that is simply a matter of will; it is not a matter of science at all.

Now, if the historian's work involves existential decisions, an act of will comes in. But what is not true is that necessarily the act of will is something arbitrary. I would not have done the work I have done if I had not made decisions, personal decisions. But from that it does not follow that my attitudes are ultimately arbitrary. An act of will does not mean an arbitrary act. The act of will may be simply the consequence of intelligent and rational views, and insofar as it is, it is not the introduction of something arbitrary if the introduction is faithfulness to truth. The fact that you establish the existence of an act of will does not eliminate the possibility of a prior guidance by intellect. Consequently, that conclusion of relativism is unjustified. But it is a conclusion into which people almost inevitably fall whenever the nature of the act of judgment is systematically overlooked, when, in intellect, you have concepts and the combination of concepts, but the only instance of an absolute positing is by an act of will, an act of decision. In the idealist tradition, judgment in that sense is overlooked. In the Aristotelian tradition, judgment in that sense is not too clearly grasped.

6.6 History and Religion

My next topic is history and religion. The one point I want to remark on here is the experiment constituted by Toynbee's *Study of History*. He wrote the first six volumes on the assumption that history is concerned with the interdependence of historical events; in other words, the unit object of history is the civilization. You can write a history of Europe without bothering your head about China. There are and were in the history of Europe incidental contacts between Europe and China, but they were clearly incidental. The whole history of Europe marches forward, and it forms an intelligible unity, an intelligible unit-field of operations by simply selecting this geographical area and excluding others from the main concern because the relations are only incidental.

At the same time, he says you cannot write a history of Czechoslovakia or of France or of England taken as an intelligible unit of operations because you cannot understand the history of Czechoslovakia or of France or of England without continuous reference to what was going on in the other European countries. Consequently, the unit object of historical study is what Toynbee meant by a civilization. That was the assumption of his first six volumes.

With the next six, which came out twenty years later or so, that assumption had to be dropped. He shifted over to the view that the fundamental business in the writing of history is a religion, at least when religion reaches the level of the great world religions: Buddhism, Islam, Christianity, Confucianism. In the book edited by Gargan, *The Intent of Toynbee's History*, there is an article by Eric Voegelin which deals with this point. He brings out the contrast between the earlier and later volumes of Toynbee's history.[21] Toynbee, then, started out with one idea of history, and in his later volumes had to shift his basis to a consideration that the fundamental field is settled by religion. We can ask, Is the fundamental concern of history religion? Does religion provide the fundamental context in historical writing? One has one experiment in Toynbee. Is that a general truth? My main concern is to raise the point.

There is a further, general remark that can be made. Just as the world of community and the world of theory serve as a mediation of interiority, since it is through them that the subject really comes to appropriate himself, to know himself, so all three are a mediation of the sacred. All desire is ultimately desire of God. Similarly, all development that is the realization of desire is ultimately referred to God. There is an ultimate reference to God in all human affairs. That ultimate reference to God in all human affairs has been explicit in human consciousness in practically all cultures and civilizations until we reach our modern secularist society in which, as Nietzsche said, God is dead. There is the question of the fundamental importance of religion in the total field of history, and that question retains its full significance even though the civilization we are living in is professedly secularist.

6.7 History and Apologetics

This is just a note. The truth of Catholicism is not independent of singular and concrete historical facts located in the Near East during the first century AD. In other words, as St Paul says, 'If Christ did not rise, your faith is in vain.'

21 Eric Voegelin, 'Toynbee's *History* as a Search for Truth,' in *The Intent of Toynbee's History: A Cooperative Appraisal*, ed. Edward T. Gargan (Chicago: Loyola University Press, 1961) 181–98.

Our faith rests upon particular historical facts that occurred approximately 2000 years ago in a precise area. But that statement does not mean that the truth of Catholicism is to be settled by common historical research investigating the events of the Near East of the first century AD. Common historical research is just the highest common factor in historical knowledge. It is the part of history that anybody is willing to leave to anybody's common sense to settle, with certain restrictions. And because common historical research, at least in the sense we have given the term, has these limitations, it is not the implement to settle those facts.

Again, while the truth of Catholicism is not independent of precise and ancient historical facts, still these facts are not the one and only thing on which such truth is dependent. Truth presupposes the existence of a mind: *verum et falsum sunt in mente.* Supernatural truth presupposes the existence of a mind illumined by the grace of faith and not only given the grace, but also existentially responding to the grace. Truth about the past presupposes the mediation of a tradition: *fides ex auditu.* It is the massive, unparalleled tradition of the Catholic Church as existential history, as something prior to the mediation of historical research or historical essays, that always has been the fundamental mediation between the believer and the facts about Jesus of Nazareth. History is just the mediation of a tradition. It passes from the existential, from the *vécu,* to the *thématique.* But the Catholic faith ordinarily, in most individuals, is mediated simply by the tradition and not by historical investigation of the tradition. That is a fundamental difference between the Catholic position and any other Christian position. Any other Christian position – and I am speaking of the Western church – has to lay down as a premise that there has occurred some grave aberration in the course of history. The aberration may be placed in the Middle Ages or in the Greek Councils or in the transition from the primitive community to St Paul or in the transition from Jesus of Nazareth to the primitive community. But somewhere there has to be a break. Somewhere there has to be some separation. And it is only by historical investigation that that break can be claimed to exist. In other words, the Catholic position does not depend upon the mediation of history in the way that a non-Catholic, a Protestant, or a liberal position does. That is just a reformulation of Irenaeus's and Tertullian's insistence on tradition.

6.8 Theological Mediation of History

Finally, there is the theological mediation of history, the point I have already made when I spoke about the human good as corrupted by sin and restored by the redemption. That is the notion that I developed in *Insight* in chapter 20 – well, the corruption by sin in chapters 7 and 18 and the conception, the introduction, in chapter 20 of the supernatural as the one way in which the surd of sin can be eliminated from the human good. And I have developed that in the seventeenth thesis of my notes *De Verbo incarnato* on the meaning of the redemption. The meaning of the death of Christ is that death is at once the penalty of sin and the source of our salvation. There is a reversal of roles. What had been the penalty of sin becomes the source of our salvation. And that reversal of roles is the key Christian, Catholic point in history. The doctrine of loving your enemies and being good to those that hate you, that doctrine of the Sermon on the Mount, is what meets the problem of evil in human life, what breaks the venom of the virus of sin, stops it, as it were, in its tracks, transforms it into something entirely different. And that is the fundamental aspect, to my mind, of the intelligibility of history. I hope some time to add a further thesis to my *De Verbo Incarnato* that will bring that out somewhat more: the historical action of Christ.[22]

Now, I wish to thank you all very much, first of all for coming here and making this course a possibility; but also for your great patience in listening and being interested in what I have to say. I want you all to realize that I do not think I have got this whole subject under control. I realize that I shall have to put in many years yet before I will be able to write a book on the method of history. But also, in a quiet way, in listening to your questions I have learned where difficulties are and where things exist that I will still have to work out before I will be able to do the thing.

22 Volume 9 of the Collected Works of Bernard Lonergan, *The Redemption*, will contain the material that Lonergan is speaking of here.

1962

Discussion 1[1]

Question: What is theological methodology? Is it merely a critique, or is it more than a critique?[2]

Lonergan: We spoke this morning about the world of common sense, the visible universe, the world of community that everyone knows all about. It sooner or later brings about, or leads to, or heads into what Georg Simmel in his *Geschichtsphilosophie* calls *die Wendung zur Idee*, the turn to the idea, the movement towards system, towards conceptualization.[3] You not only have democracies but also people within democracies talking about what democracy is. This talk influences what in fact the democracy turns out to be. The ideas that are formed about democracy are usually quite inadequate, and the inadequate ideas please people who meet with a common consent and a certain amount of compromise that give you still greater inadequacy, and then what people choose to do differs notably from what they actually in practice perform. But there is still a transformation of the concrete social reality by the ideas that people have about that reality. There is an interaction between the world of theory and the more concrete world of common sense.

---

1 Tuesday, 10 July 1962, Lauzon CD/MP3 321 (32100A0E060) and 322 (32200A0E060).
2 This was one of three questions with which the discussion began. The other two had to do with inauthenticity and conversion. Lonergan preferred to begin with the question about methodology, but in responding to it he treated the other questions as well.
3 Georg Simmel, 'Die Wendung zur Idee,' in *Lebensanschauung: Vier metaphysische Kapitel* (Munich and Leipzig: Duncker & Humblot, 1918) 29–98.

But theories can be entirely about the concrete, the more immediate world of common sense. Then the theory can be worked out in pure form, and one will get different theories about what a democracy is or what a democracy should be and so on, and for everything else – what the church is and what the church should be. One can build up what the Marxists would call the ideological superstructure, the theoretical world, the doctrinal world. Its ultimates are in sets of definitions insofar as thinking is coherent. Insofar as the definitions fit together and don't lead to further contradictions, they cast a certain amount of intelligible light upon the whole subject; you have a coherent basic set of terms and postulates or something that heads towards the possibility of a formalization.

Now, when things reach that stage, everyone can read books about them; but not everyone will get the same ideas from the books; everyone understands them with a certain amount of his own ideas mixed in. Things like the point one misses, things that one doesn't think important, etc., one will skip over. One will go on to the part that appeals to one, and there you have an inadequate apprehension of what the theory is. That inadequacy of apprehension can arise from the existence of what we have termed horizon; that is, there are a certain number of things that one can do with facility, that one can apprehend with facility, that are within one's competence. That element of horizon arises when anyone reads any book. You get a certain amount out of it. In the introduction to *Insight*, I say that the fundamental problem is not to state all the true propositions – not that there is any harm in stating all the true propositions – but the fundamental problem is that stating all the true propositions doesn't do an awful lot of good. It does not do an awful lot of good because of what we have called horizon. Simply because one has a horizon of which one is aware or, more probably, not aware, and one wants to apprehend the object through this presentation, one understands as much as one can. One understands more on a second reading than on a first, and more on a third than on a second. But one doesn't read anything *n* times. There is an inadequacy of apprehension, and that inadequacy of apprehension of a theory is an instance of inauthenticity, *if* one thinks one knows all about it.

There is a further problem. A man can have an inadequate apprehension and know enough to note the inadequacy of his apprehension. But having doubts about the inadequacy of one's apprehension is not a universal phenomenon; it can be absent. Moreover, when a person starts arguing with someone else, there is a spontaneous tendency to say, 'This is what he said, it is simply that'; and people get into rather hot arguments about the subject, and so on. One can become convinced and reinforced in the conviction of the adequacy of one's apprehension. That is a fundamental element in the notion of inauthenticity as worked out by Jaspers in his *Psychologie der Weltanschauungen* (Psychology of Worldviews).[4] (Jaspers started off as a psychologist and gradually moved into philosophy. With his book, *Die geistige Situation der Zeit*,[5] he moves into an existential philosophy.)

That inadequacy of apprehension, that element of horizon, becomes something much more difficult to overcome. All our apprehensions are more or less inadequate, and we can always learn something more by adding on further insights, making something more adequate, more qualified, more accurate, and so on. But these further additions can be prevented by lack of attention, lack of education, lack of effort; and the element of inauthenticity can become rigidified by a lack of what I call conversion.

I described conversion as a reorganization of the subject. Newman was convinced of the truth of the Catholic Church as an abstract intellectual proposition somewhere around 1830 or 1835, when he was studying the Donatist controversy. Newman is an example of a man of great sincerity and honesty and care and objectivity in his judgments. It took him between ten and fifteen years more to take the step of becoming a Catholic. The fact that this time was taken by that man in becoming a Catholic reveals the difficulty there can be in a religious conversion. It involved a transformation of the whole development he had from childhood, boyhood, university career, his work for the Tractarian movement, and so on. It meant reorganizing his whole viewpoint, his whole set of reference terms. The terrific process that went on in those years of Newman's becoming a Catholic illustrates (one might possibly write a doctoral dissertation on it almost, studying his letters through that period) a transformation in his social relations, in his intellectual life, and so on. All that is involved in a religious conversion.

In moral conversion, fundamentally, the shift is from egotism, from myself as the center of the universe: what I desire and what I fear is what ultimately counts. One can, of course, build up a moral system on that basis in terms of the individual's last end. This idea of ends can be given an entirely different interpretation within a deontology in ethics. But that shift from a hedonism, hedonistic eudemonism to a deontology, not as an

4 See above, p.15, note 14.
5 Karl Jaspers, *Die geistige Situation der Zeit* (Berlin: W. de Gruyter, 1931; 2nd ed., 1933). In English, *Man in the Modern Age*, trans. Eden Paul and Cedar Paul (London: Routledge and Kegan Paul, 1951, 1953; Garden City, NY: Doubleday, 1957).

opposition between objective propositions – anyone can grasp that – but the changeover in me, that I no longer act as if I'm the center of the universe: that is conversion.

There is also an intellectual conversion. A lot of people are sure that *Insight* is idealist, Kantian, pragmatist, and I don't know what else; and there is no possibility of their seeing it as anything else. If you agree with Kant that the one and only way in which you can have immediate knowledge of an object is by *Anschauung*, intuition, taking a look, then either you hold that we know everything by taking a look at reality or else you are a Kantian. If you face the facts of human understanding, you must be a Kantian. M. Gilson is a celebrated, and justly celebrated, historian in philosophy. But for him, in his *Réalisme thomiste et critique de la connaissance*,[6] you have to get down to a look at reality or you are not a Thomist realist. If you hold that position, you are either going to assert, 'We see the real, we see the real, we see the real,' and pay no attention to psychologial facts at all, or else you will be driven into Kantianism. But what is not true is the fundamental Kantian assumption that the one way in which we have immediate relation to an object is by taking a look. *Verum est medium in quo ens cognoscitur*, and the *verum* in question is the logical truth of judgment, that is, *est* and *non est*. That is when we immediately know reality, and that isn't a matter of taking a look, it is a matter of making an affirmation. To grasp the difference as a theoretical point is not of itself a conversion. But to grasp the difference and make all its applications to one's thinking does involve a conversion. When I effected that conversion in myself, I felt for sometime, Well, isn't this idealism? And I was not brought up on any of this Gilson type of epistemology. I was brought up on the good old nineteenth-century business of the three fundamental truths: (a) the principle of contradiction, (b) the possibility of the mind to know truth, and (c) the existence of the ego. You couldn't say anything without implying those three truths; and therefore that's where one started from. At least, it was in the order of truth, in the order of true judgment; but that didn't mean anything to me then. Spontaneously, before we reach the age of reason, we form an awful lot of our ideas of reality; and they can remain with us for the rest of our lives, unless we change them. And we don't change them without knowing that we have changed them. Changing them is a revolution; you know something is going on; it doesn't happen unnoticed.

6 Étienne Gilson, *Réalisme thomiste et critique de la connaissance* (Paris: J. Vrin, 1939); in English, *Thomistic Realism and the Critique of Knowledge*, trans. Mark A. Wauck (San Francisco: Ignatius Press, 1986).

That failure of conversion – intellectual conversion, moral conversion, religious conversion – constitutes a wholesale block in all one's thinking. Take Fay's article on *Insight*, for example.[7] He just can't see what I'm saying. It is not a matter of getting something wrong here and there; it is a matter of being wrong all along the line! That is the point to an intellectual conversion. It is a revolution.

Insofar as the inadequacy is in our apprehension, that belongs simply to the fact that our intellects are potential. Angels know from the first moment of their existence all that they ever naturally will know. But the human race only through time and *distributive* in different individuals successively reaches the natural actuation of human intelligence. Human intellect is *in genere intelligibilium ut potentia*; consequently, there's always more we can learn about anything. It is this fact that constitutes the basic inadequacy in all our apprehensions, and it is inevitable.

That basic inadequacy can be complicated by the phenomenon of horizon. There's a beyond which to us is just a blind spot; we pay no attention to it. Each of us lives in his own little world: the world of the seminary, the world of the university, the world of the parish; and doctors and nurses live in the world of the clinic; etc, etc. To break out of one's little world is the broadening of one's horizon; and that horizon can exist in all sorts of ways, even in the ways of one's specialty. There are types of writers on one subject for whom one has no use; and one just doesn't bother reading them.

So the normal inadequacy of all human apprehension, the complication of horizon, and the further complication of a lack of conversion, lead to the phenomena of inauthenticity.

That is my analysis of the meaning of inauthenticity. It has been worked out descriptively by Jaspers, and I gave you a few indications of his presentation of the thing; and, again, it has been worked out in a different way by Heidegger. Heidegger is, in a sense, more fundamental, because Jaspers does not attempt to say what inauthenticity in itself is but rather inauthenticity as compared to such and such a doctrine. On the other hand, Heidegger treats inauthenticity as the renunciation of responsibility, the renunciation of being oneself. When Heidegger writes it out, or even when

---

7 C.R. Fay, 'Father Lonergan and the Participation School,' *The New Scholasticism* 34 (1960) 461–87. There are many pages in the Lonergan archives, some of them fragments, from an essay that Lonergan wrote in response to this article.

de Waelhens represents it in French,[8] it is a devastating and surprising presentation; and when one reads that you can see why that book went into all sorts of editions immediately.

These are particular presentations of the matter and I have referred to them.

Das Mann, in Heidegger, corresponds to the French *On le dit,* the inauthentic man. Who is *das Mann?* He is everyone and nobody, because everyone is saying just what other people say.

You have another aspect of this with Lord Keynes's illustration of the operations of the stock market. It is not a matter of knowing which is the good stock and so on, like short-term operations on the stock market; it is a matter of what he proceeded to illustrate in the following way: Let us suppose that a newspaper publishes a hundred photographs of a hundred beautiful girls and the competition is to pick out whom the majority will consider the six most beautiful girls – the majority of those who make choices. So it isn't a matter of picking out the most beautiful girl in one's own judgment or on any objective standard, or what one thinks other people will think are the most beautiful girls; but it is what one thinks other people will think other people will think. Similarly with the stock market, when it starts to go up and down; and what one thinks other people will think other people will think, that's what is going to happen. One can live human life on that level. It is living human life on that level that is the fundamental object of Heidegger's critique.

Method is an attempt to smash through those difficulties. The ultimate one can do in the world of theory is to set up a system; but one can't insure that people are going to understand it; one can't insure that they are not going to misunderstand it systematically.

I've done two detailed studies of Thomist thought: one on *gratia operans,* published in *Theological Studies* (1941, 1942)[9] and the other on *verbum* (1946–49).[10] In both cases, I became convinced that there was a systematic misinterpretation of Thomas in the tradition. It was an enormously complex thing, involving metaphysics and psychology and theology. Another example of the way a systematic mode of thinking holds is found in this business of the vital act. I have a series of snippets from all the works of St Thomas in which the sensation is produced by the object. There is no possibility of getting

---

8 See above, p. 18, note 20.
9 See above, p. 208, note 2.
10 See above, p. 12, note 11.

around it in any way, by any sort of distinction, the fact that sensation is produced by the object. In other words, it is a direct contradiction of the doctrine of vital act: the faculty producing its own act. But in the course of at
least fifteen years, that has made no impression on anyone except students;
and for it to make an impression would mean that one would have to reject
all one's views on endless topics.

Now, the idea of method is to move behind the world of theory to the
operating subject, just as one has the movement from the world of common sense, the visible world, the world of community, to the world of
theory when one writes a *Summa theologiae* or Euclid's *Elements*, or Newton's
mechanics, and so on. The subject as operating is the subject as nonob-
jectified. I can talk about the subject understanding, but when I do that the
subject is already objectified. What counts is the subject prior to that objectification, the subject as understanding, getting the idea, and being
aware of his getting the idea, and becoming aware of precisely what it is to
understand, having the experiences that eliminate the possibility of false
theories. Just as one can't talk about color to a blind man – in his own way
he might know that all of one's statements are perfectly logical but he
couldn't know what one meant if he was blind from birth – so the person
who doesn't attend to his own experiences in the effort to understand and
in understanding and to what he does with his acts of understanding will
not get what we mean. We must attend to the experiences themselves. We
must also attend to the experience of reflecting, weighing the evidence,
making judgments. It is not a matter of reading books on the subject; it is
a matter of using the books as a means towards attending to oneself.
Without that, movement towards method is inefficacious. And, of course,
you can't force anyone to do it. It is up to them to do it for themselves; the
subject has the ultimate responsibility. But if, at least, we pin the responsibility there, we are at the real source of the difficulties, and we can pin
down just what this aberration in the subject is, and what this blind spot in
the subject produces when he starts on his theories or on his practical activities in the world of community. It is a mediation: just as theory mediates
the world of community, so interiority mediates both theory and the world
of ordinary experience.

Question: I was wondering if that would imply that with each succeeding
generation it becomes more difficult for people to be authentic. Thus, a
man in any given field, let's say a logician, would be less able to be authentic, relatively authentic, because of the increase in the complexity of the

operations of other thinkers, and his inability to extend his horizon to areas that may be relevant to logic but come from another field.

Lonergan: The increasing complexity of the subject matter in a sense provides a greater opportunity for inauthenticity. But, on the other hand, it does not necessitate it in any way. With regard to your example of logic, if you apply the idea of method to it you will distinguish between logic as a manipulation of symbols in which what the logician does and what the computer does are not too different, and logic as a remove from that where logic deals with meanings. Then one has the intentional analysis of logic that is associated with John of St Thomas. (There is also Venn – or a name like that – he has presented in modern logic discussions in the United States this intentional-analysis viewpoint account of John of St Thomas.)[11] And you can take a step behind that to fundamental logic. What precisely are the bases of logical operations? Rational consciousness, the emergence of acts of understanding. And it is at this point that questions of authenticity and inauthenticity become relevant. Insofar as the logician holds that logic is merely a matter of manipulating the symbols, then all the logician knows is the formal implications of the type: not P without Q. There is this business of a material implication in their terminology – I think that is their terminology – that you have to have a nexus, an intelligible nexus between the antecedent and the consequent. Not P without Q: e.g., 'If Eisenhower is the President of the United States, then bananas grow on telephone poles' is a perfectly valid 'if then' proposition in symbolic logic, but there is no intelligible nexus between the antecedent and the consequent. Without that, they have in fact eliminated this 'if ... then.'

Now, there are the ultrapositivist tendencies among the symbolic logicians who take a step further. This material implication, this 'if then' meaning, is something purely subjective; it is of no more scientific importance than the conviction people used to have about the earth being flat. But at that point one is stepping into inauthenticity; one is eliminating the mind as having any relevance in logic. But to speak of authenticity in connection with logic is taking a rather hard example. The point about authenticity is never a question of the details; it is what is fundamental. Take Husserl's book, *The Crisis of European Sciences*, about 1954, published at The Hague.[12]

11 Lonergan is referring to Henry Babcock Veatch. See *Intentional Logic: A Logic Based on Philosophical Realism* (New Haven: Yale, 1952).

12 Edmund Husserl, *Die Krisis der europäischen Wissenschaften und die transzendentale Phänomenologie: Eine Einleitung in die phänomenologische Philosophie*, ed. Walter Biemel (The Hague: Martinus Nijhoff, 1954); in English, *The Crisis of*

The first third of it was written by Husserl, and the rest was put together from his notes. But that first third is a crackerjack; and his contention is that the more sciences subdivide and the more they become specialized, the more any notion of what science is in any strict sense disappears totally. And what do we get in its place? We get a clique with a set of conventions, where people pat one another on the back in their congresses; and the whole fundamental content of the Western ideal of science just vanishes. That is a fundamental criticism. As Husserl puts it, Is Western man just another anthropological type, or is there something in Western culture that represents an ideal of what humanity ought to be? Is science just another occupation like plumbing, or does it represent some sort of absolute? That was Husserl's question. Unauthentic science is dodging that question; they are doing what everyone calls science, and everyone knows what that means. Theology can be done in the same way. In the twelfth century, what was theology to a great extent? It was saying what St Augustine said. And it can be saying what St Thomas said; or saying what Pius XII said; and this is avoiding the issue of the subject as a science, avoiding all personal responsibility.

Question: Does method then become my method or the method of me as a theologian?
Lonergan: Yes. But it is transcendental. Your method is you operating as a theologian. In other words, that's its locus; but the same issues occur for everyone, perhaps not exactly in the same form, but they are recurrent: the idea of not setting up universal propositions which you apply to particular cases but drawing attention to concrete structures that recur in every instance. It is the latter which is the methodological approach.

I said it was transcendental because either you experience or you do not, either you understand or you do not, either you judge or you do not; and in either case the implications are there; in one case they rule you out of court, in another case you have to accept the consequences. It isn't a matter of absolute necessity.

Question: There is a greater stress, then, on subjectivity.
Lonergan: Yes. Interiority and subjectivity: they both mean the same thing, except that the people that talk most about subjectivity are also caught in philosophical difficulties and are immanentists; they don't grasp the significance of

European Sciences and Transcendental Phenomenology: An Introduction to Phenomenological Philosophy, trans. David Carr (Evanston, IL: Northwestern University Press, 1970).

the true judgment. For example, Bultmann's *Glauben und Verstehen*: there is understanding and there is believing.[13] Between understanding and believing there occur true or false judgments, and that element of the true or false judgment as not simply a comparison of concepts, a nexus between concepts, but an absolute positing, is something overlooked not only in the Hegelian tradition – read Hegel on judgment and the ideal judgment, where to say that man is rational is to say that there is an identity between the subject and the predicate and that the other judgments are dialectically imperfect forms of that perfect identity, that comparison between subject and object – it is not only in Hegelianism and the other idealists but also in Aristotle, taken over from Plato – the putting together of forms. For Aristotle it is putting together or separating, *compositio vel divisio*, and Thomas usually talks Aristotelian language. The key importance of the judgment is obscured in the Aristotelian tradition, as well as being excluded in the Hegelian; and in either case you tend to a form of immanence or of essentialism.

Question: To be a philosopher one must commit oneself – you mean this of any science?

Lonergan: Last summer I was in Seattle University, on my way back from St Mary's in California. It is a very lively place, and they got a group together; there was a doctor of engineering and a couple of doctors of physics, etc., and we went out to the villa house, had a swim and good dinner and a discussion. The doctor of engineering was saying that for a scientist science is an investigation that leads to a whole lot more investigations, and these in turn lead to more investigations. You're a big shot if you can do that, and that is all they have by way of a criterion. The development of science itself is run on a sort of pragmatic criterion; there isn't any reflection asking, What is science? And if anyone raised this question, as Husserl says, he would be given this field and told to specialize in it. However, nobody pays any attention to anyone else's specialty; that would be just a philosophical inquiry into the nature of science, or a phenomenological inquiry into the nature of science; and that is just another specialty. There is no readiness to accept the possibility of a field of inquiry that is architectonic, that rules the rest, that can say yes or no.

Question: In every pursuit of science that is authentic, is there this personal commitment?

13 See above, p. 97, note 13.

Lonergan: Yes. The big men like Einstein, Max Planck, etc., they are all that way. There are also the hewers of wood and the drawers of water; they fulfil a useful purpose.

Question: What is the difference between this commitment and the commitment of the theologian?

Lonergan: The commitment of the theologian is much more complicated. There is part of Einstein's autobiography in Schilpp's book *Albert Einstein: Philosopher-Scientist* where he says that intelligence is a frightfully delicate tree or plant that can grow only under the most favorable conditions. When he was a student, he says, there were so many courses and so many exams that it was almost impossible for intelligence to develop. At the present time the courses are much more numerous and the exams much more stiff and exigent and exacting, so it is absolutely impossible for intelligence to develop.[14]

Question: Should we tell Father General this?

Lonergan: Father General is occupied with many things; I'll talk to future Generals that may be around and are willing to listen.[15] Again, Einstein remarks that during his studies he had the good fortune to find a book that gave a popular presentation of the whole of physics, that attended to the fundamental ideas, and enabled him to understand the whole subject. This he looked upon as something precious in his life. He was obviously an extremely intelligent man, and he knew what it was to understand and, of course, that is what he was noted for. He would just add a little thing here and there, and a light would go over a whole field or more.

Again, Max Planck in his autobiography asks, What is it that puts a scientific theory across, that makes it accepted universally? Is it a matter of the accuracy of the observation, the keenness of the description? Is it a matter of the exactitude of the definitions and the postulates, the rigor of the deductions and all their implications? Is it a matter of complete verification of the hypothesis in all sorts of concrete data? No. It's a matter of the present generation of professors passing away or resigning their chairs.[16]

---

14 Albert Einstein, 'Autobiographical Notes,' in Paul Arthur Schilpp, ed., *Albert Einstein: Philosopher-Scientist* (New York: Macmillan, 1949) at 14–19.

15 This is obviously a Jesuit discussion, and the reference is to the Superior General of the Society of Jesus.

16 Max Planck, *Scientific Autobiography and Other Papers*, trans. F. Gaynor (New York: Philosophical Library, 1949) 33–34. This book was reprinted in 1968 and 1971 by Greenwood Press of Westport, CT.

That is the world of physics; so theologians must not be impatient if things are even a little slower than they are in the field of physics.

Question:[17] Can you explain the relation between the conversion effected in a good scientist or an authentic scientist and the conversion effected in one that receives faith? Is it a question of it being more intense or being more extensive?

Lonergan: The conversion in the scientist is a very partial affair, at least at the present time. Einstein had the conversion to intelligence away from the sensible. He wasn't the sort of man that wanted to put Piaget's work aside and try to do it all over again, in another way in which no use of intelligence is involved. He was a man for the ideas, etc. But while modern physics has pulled all the underpinnings out of the Galilean approach to the material universe, where the real was a matter of extension and motion and something that could be imagined and mathematicized or geometrized, Einstein's relativity and quantum theory have eliminated the possibility of imagining anything; and quantum theory has also eliminated the possibility of an imaginable process. But the only solution that the scientist can have, in my opinion, is, What do you know? We know what is. Still none of them are ready to make that statement; it has no meaning for them, as it had no meaning for Kant. It is something that is merely logical, to say that something is. We haven't got intellectual conversion in the scientific field yet, in the sense of moving to truth as an absolute, getting the significance of judgment; the correlation of the *verum* and *ens.* But there are all sorts of dedication and true intellectualism in the big scientists.

Now, the conversion to faith is a matter of going beyond what is the possible field of truth for a human mind; and you don't do that in virtue of the possible field of truth for a human mind; there is the whole business of the supernatural involved.

Question: Doesn't that depend on the object rather than on the subject?
Lonergan: Also on the subject; there is the light of faith, isn't there? The light of faith is the opposite to rationalism. Rationalism excludes the possibility of a revelation of truth beyond the comprehension of man. What's beyond the comprehension of man can't be true for a man. This is the rationalist thesis, and the light of faith is the opposite to that. But it isn't in

17 Part 2 of question-and-answer session of 10 July 1962, Lauzon CD/MP3 322 (32200AOE060).

virtue of human comprehension that you assert the validity of what is beyond human comprehension. That is where the light of faith comes in.

Question: My problem has been bothering me since the beginning of
Theology Digest.[18] I wonder if this sort of process is interfering with the true
good of theology or not. In digesting, popularizing, etc., is one distracting
and increasing to a certain extent the inauthenticity of many people who
think they know what they don't know?

Lonergan: There can be possible evils connected with things that are
counter-balanced by greater goods. For example, *Theology Digest* draws to
the attention of a lot of people things that otherwise they would have no
notion of whatever; one also has effective broadening of horizons there,
and that can be a good thing. I must confess that I'm not a steady student
of *Theology Digest*! But as far as I know, they draw upon articles from the
European field, current articles that are being published there all the time.
And without some sort of organ of that type there is a tendency for a country to become isolated. To give an example from my own experience, after
thirteen years teaching in Canada – six-and-a-half in Montreal, and six-and-
a-half in Toronto – and then teaching at the Gregorian, I discovered that
my students at the Greg *distributive* read everything that was written and
were ready to ask questions about it. They would ask me what I thought
about so-and-so's article in this and that, and I had to tell them that I didn't
know. There was no question of my reading all of it; but it made me aware
of what was being done, of the questions that were being raised, and so on.
So something like a digest can serve a very useful purpose.

All culture does involve this *haute vulgarisation*. Not everyone is intended
by divine providence to go beyond *la haute vulgarisation*. In fact, the vast
majority don't even reach it. There are different levels to be met. The
Communists have a way of presenting Communism for everyone. They can
talk to everyone, and they have a different story to tell everyone, and they
are effective on each level, to a certain percentage – about 30% in Rome.
And the Catholics too must do that. As a matter of fact, the weakness of our
apologetics is that unless someone has done three years philosophy and
four years theology people don't know what on earth you are talking about.
And the more we have a spread for the presentation of Catholic doctrine
the better. These are just some reflections on the subject.

18 The questioner was Fr Gerald Van Ackeren, s.j., editor of *Theology Digest* at
the time.

Question: You introduce quite a few new terms. What is the relationship and possibility of continuity in the usage of new terminologies vis-à-vis the traditional? For example, the full involvement of the human subject in the process of conversion and the traditional notion of the rational animal.

Lonergan: In relation to that problem, these notes were done by my students. Not all of them, but a sufficient number of them had followed my course on 'De Deo trino' and 'De Verbo incarnato.' My 'De Deo trino' takes the processions of the persons in terms of rational consciousness; they get a first break into rational consciousness there; that is in my *Divinarum personarum conceptio analogica*.[19] And in my *De Verbo incarnato*, Christ as subject is the final stage in the development of my theory of the hypostatic union.[20] We start off with the New Testament and go through the Greek councils, medieval thought on the person as substance, and then the question of Christ as subject, what is the subject in Christ? So there is that integration, de facto, in other writings.

But while the subject has not been a category in traditional theology, it is becoming a fundamental category at the present time. It is with that question of the consciousness of Christ that it is making its classical entry at the present time. Most of the theories on the subject are woefully inadequate. But still the question is there. And any question of method is impossible except in terms of the subject. The problems one has to deal with are in terms of the subject.

It is history that makes the difference. The conception of man as historical is not the conception of man who is potentially rational, where with the latter it makes no difference whether one is a St Thomas or a drunk, St John of the Cross or a lunatic; in both cases one satisfies totally the definition, *animal rationale*. Besides, there is the conception of man who at least is dreaming, preferably the dreams of the morning (Binswanger)[21] when the *Existenz* is projecting itself; there is the conscious living man who is using his

---

19 Bernard Lonergan, *Divinarum personarum conceptionem analogicam evolvit Bernardus Lonergan* (Rome: Gregorian University Press, 1957, 1959). The text was subsequently reissued in a modified form as *De Deo Trino: Pars systematica* (Rome: Gregorian University Press, 1964). The latter formed the basis of volume 12 in Collected Works of Bernard Lonergan, *The Triune God: Systematics* (see above, p. 153, note 12); appendix 4 contains passages from *Divinarum personarum* that were dropped from *De Deo Trino*.

20 Bernard Lonergan, *De Verbo Incarnato* (Rome: Gregorian University Press; Lonergan would be referring to the 1961 edition) 269–362. The text was revised in 1964.

21 Ludwig Binswanger, *Le rêve et l'existence* (Paris: Desclée, 1954).

intelligence, his will, his faith, etc. That is the object of historical study: the human good in which the formal element and the actual element lie in the level of the *esse intentionale.*

That is what the whole movement of Germany in the last century was concerned with. To the extent that the *esse naturale* was dropped from view you have an idealism or an immanentism of some sort; and that is what is behind this whole modern movement in Catholic theology which has come to the fore in the last century. The problems that came out were the idea of theology as science from the semi-rationalists like Hermes and Günther and Frohschammer, and so on. On the other hand, there was the tradition-alist movement in France; the Vatican Council met that. *Aeterni Patris* caps the thing by adding on St Thomas, the return to Thomas; and you have the movement towards a strictly scientific theology there. At the start of the century there was all sorts of talk about seminary reform, introducing more positive studies into the seminary, etc. Xiberta, in his *Introductio in Sacram Theologiam,*[22] gives a very full bibliography of that movement. It culminates in *Deus scientiarum Dominus,* in which ecclesiastical studies are reorganized, and *Divino afflante Spiritu* on scripture. To understand the problems we are dealing with we have to understand that German movement – the idealism, the *historische Schule,* Dilthey and his effort to organize the *Geisteswissen-schaften,* and the later movements that stem from Husserl and Heidegger, and what the German views are at the present time. This is forced upon us. The problem, at the present time, is not whether we are going to accept that or not; it is whether we are going to be able to master it and integrate it.

Question: Why is there so much Scholastic terminology in your work, in *De constitutione Christi ontologica et psychologica?*
Lonergan: That was written for students who I hoped knew something about the Scholastic tradition, and I wanted to get them into the other stuff; and it was a matter of effecting the transition. And it works. I have no diffi-culty in expressing myself in Thomist terms. On the other hand, in Thomism you have to be very careful; Thomas understood an awful lot more than he said regarding the business of consciousness, and so on.

Question: In your distinction between the interior and the exterior world, you mentioned that it took the rise of individualism with the decline of the

---

22 Bartholomaeus F.M. Xiberta, O.Carm. *Introductio in Sacram Theologiam* (Rome: Edizioni Carmelitane, 1949).

ancient great empires to bring this about. But isn't the child more aware of himself as an individual before he is aware of society?

Lonergan: Being aware of society: the child is, of course, a self-centered little animal. And there is Virgil's 'risu cognoscere patrem.'[23] I don't know if Piaget quotes Virgil, but the first time one of his babies smiled he says it was not a matter of any recognition of the father or mother or anything like that; it was the satisfaction of being able to do something it was trying to do.

To give a meaning to individualism, you have to have the social setup with reference to which one is speaking of the individual. The shaman in the primitive Asiatic tribe is an individualist. In Eliade's most fundamental technical work, *Le chamanisme et les techniques archaïques de l'extase*,[24] he presents the shaman as a type of mystic. Again, the Indian mystics were individualists, but they were not breaking away from a highly developed civilization – more in the case of the Indian mystics but not in the way it was occurring when the Greek Sophists arrived; the development of the Greek culture was on the margin of these ancient civilizations that had fallen down.

Again, one has the case of the individualism of the prophets, of men standing up against society. This is in a much more highly developed social milieu than the shaman in his central Asiatic tribe. The individual is mediated by the society; the individual develops within the society. As Newman says, the boy learns everything and believes everything that his teacher tells him, and then there comes the time when he starts thinking for himself. But it is what you learn before you start thinking for yourself that determines the quality of one's thinking for oneself. Heidegger's criticism is perhaps something inevitable and excusable; the faceless men, and so on, that Heidegger criticizes are incapable of thinking for themselves, and they welcome a return to a much more tribal type of existence.

Nisbet, in his *Quest for Community*,[25] describes the fundamental problem of modern society as the need for that mediation between the higher controls – for instance, something in Washington is frightfully far away – and

23 Lonergan said 'patrem,' perhaps purposely because of the Piaget reference that follows. Virgil wrote at the very end of his fourth Eclogue, 'Incipe, parve puer, risu cognoscere matrem' ('Begin, little boy, to acknowledge your mother with a smile').

24 Mircea Eliade, *Le chamanisme et les techniques archaïques de l'extase* (Paris: Librairie Payot, 1951); in English, *Shamanism: Archaic Techniques of Ecstasy*, trans. Willard R. Trask (Princeton: Princeton University Press, 1972).

25 Robert A. Nisbet, *The Quest for Community* (New York: Oxford University Press, 1953; reissued in 1962 under the title *Community and Power*, then again in 1969 under the original title).

individuals. To meet this problem one has all sorts of womens' clubs but no mens' clubs, because they know that there is not a damn thing one can do about it. If there were the intermediate levels of community and the use of symbols, a large number of social problems that exist at the present time would be solved. In other words, people aren't prepared to be the type of individual that they have to to be individuals in a modern society. The demands are much too great for them.

What I said about that individualism emerging at the point of the collapse of empires was from Jaspers' *The Origin and Goal of History*.[26] There was very markedly a necessity for an individualism to arise at that point. Everything before had been settled by the state, and now they were on their own, and they were going to be absolutely nothing. It occurred on the practical level and gradually moved to more theoretical levels with the prophets in Judea, the sophists and philosophers in Greece, and so on. That's Jaspers' thesis, and I tossed it out as an illustration. Also, Eliade's work on the Indian mystics can be taken as regarding another type, as can the modern individualist. Teresa of Avila was a terrific individualist, St Francis of Assisi, and so on.

Question: There is the accusation against you that this is such a thoroughgoing intellectualism. You have said about science that it is something to which the whole person commits himself. So there's the role of the will. And what about this notion that is around on faith as prior to understanding and more important than understanding?

Lonergan: I distinguish different patterns of consciousness and insist on the purity of each type and acknowledge the necessity of withdrawal and return, moving from one pattern of consciousness to another. In other words, I have no respect for the type of scientist that eliminates the scientific element from it, whether it's social science or biology or anything else, theology, philosophy. I'm opposed to the notion that there's nothing to science that you don't get in *haute vulgarisation*, that it has no exigencies beyond that. One would be better off and more honest not to pay attention to either. If one is going to do something, one should do it right. That is as far as the scientific side goes. But it's not my personal life.

In chapter 6 of *Insight*, I describe a series of patterns of experience; and they all exist, they all occur. But the thing is not to get them mixed up, not to live your whole life in the dramatic-practical pattern of experience and think that you're a crackerjack of a theologian or something else. That's inauthenticity, fake, phoney, and so on all along the line.

26 See above, p. 49, note 20.

Question: In the study of method does one have to or can one restrict one-self to one sphere, for example, the sphere of intellectual operations, or should one begin with a broader basis in the subject, or is there a broader base in the subject?

Lonergan: One has to have the preliminary education: One has to know languages and appreciate literatures, on the one hand. Otherwise one will not be able to do anything historical. And one has to have something in the way of a scientific formation, otherwise one will not have any real apprehension of what science is. That sort of thing will have to be presupposed. Again, in theology, if I am correct, positive theology and systematic theology are two phases of the same thing, and understanding the history of a doctrine is understanding the doctrine, and one can understand the history of the doctrine insofar as one understands the doctrine – they're mutually dependent. There are all the different levels of meaning involved in that. Take Hugo Rahner's articles in *Ascetik und Mystik* (the German one, not the French one) on the birth of the child Jesus from the heart of the Christian in Patristic letters.[27] That is the sort of thing one will find in the Fathers on sanctifying grace and the virtues. They don't talk in Aristotelian categories. And one has to be able to transpose from one pattern of experience to another. The whole development of theology is a transposition, an *Auslegung*, from the types of meaning of the Palestinian milieu and the Hellenistic milieu that went into the formation of the New Testament on different levels and in different ways. One has to be able to follow the continuity through. The job of the dogmatic theologian is not the job of a specialist. If you are a specialist, you are not doing dogmatic theology, because what the dogmatic theologian has to do is to put things together. He has to use the monographs, etc., but must go beyond them, because dogmatic theology is not on that level. You cannot disregard it or pretend that it doesn't exist or anything like that. This is the idea of dialectic. Anyone studying Tertullian won't be studying Origen at the same time; but you have to study both of them to see how they fit into a progression. Take Landgraf's work on the development of the theology of grace in the twelfth century.[28] That is the sort of thing that you have to read and understand, and see how it is true. This type of work throws a terrific amount of light on all that went before on grace and about the problems involved in getting to this notion of the supernatural habit that they reached about

27 Lonergan is probably referring to Hugo Rahner, 'Die Gottesgeburt: Die Lehre der Kirchenväter von der Geburt Christi im Herzen des Gläubigen,' *Zeitschrift für katholische Theologie* 59 (1935) 333–418.
28 See above, p. 158, note 4.

1230, and there is the absurdity of the Baius and Jansenius controversy in the sixteenth and seventeenth centuries. They just didn't know what went on in the twelfth century, and how these people were just steeped in Augustine, and just taught Augustine and nothing else. Yet they went beyond Augustine in this way, out of fidelity to Augustine, so to speak, on another level. The historical solution to a theological problem on that matter of grace in the twelfth and early thirteenth centuries, on the divinity of the Son in the Arian controversies in the fourth century, and so on – all the possibilities were envisaged by somebody or other. And it is knowing that history that constitutes the basis of a sound judgment on what is right, as distinct from the judgment of the church itself.

Question: You talked about passing from one pattern to another. Can you tell us something about the subject, what he is in the world, what meaning does he have? ·

Lonergan: Recall the distinction I drew this morning between the three meanings of the word 'presence.' The table is present in the room; the table is present to me; and for the table to be present to me, I must be present to myself. The third type of presence is not knowing an object. The only object I know when I know the table is the table; but I am aware of myself in some sense, and there is some meaning to that statement. Augustine describes this presence to oneself. When I am sound asleep, without a dream, I'm not a subject. I am a subject as soon as I start to operate psychologically. I am empirically conscious when I am lying on the beach gazing at the clouds going by and not asking myself the slightest question about anything. I become intellectually conscious when I start asking why, what, how often, that is, questions for intelligence, and getting insights and making formulations. I move to a third level of consciousness when I ask, Well, is that just a bright idea or is it true? when I weigh the evidence, and make a rational judgment. I become self-conscious when the judgment becomes a judgment of value, and I either accept or reject that value, because my acceptance or rejection of an objective value is also a judgment involving myself freely when I do so. Those different levels of consciousness are the steps in the fullness of the being of the subject.

The subject is always the one who is experiencing, not what is experienced; the one who is inquiring, understanding, conceiving, as distinct from what is inquired into, understood, conceived. He can be that too, but then it will be the subject as object. The one who is reflecting, weighing the evidence, judging; the one who is deliberating, choosing, making himself the kind of man he is to be by his choosing. A subject is a rather fleeting entity. You can never take it and put it between pincers and take a good look at it, because it is always what is doing the looking. But if you can get hold of the pattern of operations of the subject, you have also the pattern of the operations of any subject. And in answer to your question I give a very simple illustration. Did Matthew, Mark, Luke, and John know anything about *ens*? Well, if one means by *ens* the objective of the inquiring, reflecting subject, then either Matthew, Mark, Luke, and John had no brains at all, or else one says that they had the same notion of *ens* as I am talking about, which is quite a step and solves a lot of difficulties in the interpretation of scripture and the relationship between the scriptures and theology.

Again, it is the basis of a systematic methodical metaphysics. If all our knowing is a matter of experiencing, understanding, and judging, then the proper object of our knowing has to be a compound of potency, form, and act. You will find more details on that in chapter 15 of *Insight*.

Question: St Thomas spoke of man as a little spark of the divine flame? How would you define a person?

Lonergan: *Lumen intellectus nostri est similitudo quaedam creata luminis increati.* Intellect as *potens omnia facere et fieri* is an omnipotence in the intentional order. God is omnipotence not only in the intentional but also in the real order. So there's that similarity. Coreth in his *Metaphysik* raises the question of the pure perfections by which one proceeds to God; he says that the pure perfections are the perfections that admit infinity.[29] The intellect is a pure perfection: it is open to the infinite, it tends towards the infinite, towards the unlimited.

Question: In view of the study of interiority with a view to method, is it always necessary to begin from what is *prius quoad nos*? What is the starting point of theology?

Lonergan: Well, practically it is the *prius quoad nos*. My *De Deo trino* is divided into two parts. In one part I do the positive, and in the other part I do the speculative. The positive is presupposed by the speculative, because if you started off with the speculative – at least with contemporary students – they will say that one is making it all up out of his head, that's not science or theology in any possible meaning of the word; you will be working uphill with a terrific disadvantage. On the other hand, if you want your students to understand what the difficulties were in the apologists when they started talking about the *logos*, in Tertullian, in Origen, in the Arian controversies,

29 Coreth, *Metaphysik* (see above, p. 53, note 24) index, 'perfectio essendi ... pura et mixta.'

and so on, you will want to do the speculative stuff first. They get some sort of vague notion of what the problems are, but until they have done the speculative they really won't assimilate the other.

The speculative side answers the question, What on earth do you mean when you say God the Father had a Son? We all know what it means when we say that a human father has a son. But to answer that question to the last ditch, and not just tell people, 'That's a divine mystery, you fall down and adore,' or it is analogous but what's analogous about it? well, we don't quite get into that – if one excludes that type of answer, then the only answer is a speculative theology. And it is insofar as one understands the speculative theology that one can really understand the history.

De facto, in teaching the 'De Verbo incarnato' there's no question of starting with the redemption. One can do a Christology of St Paul and start with the redemption as Cerfaux did; but you can't do the 'De Verbo incarnato' that way, because you would seem to be contradicting everything the Catholic Church ever taught about Christ; it would seem you were saying that he wasn't God. But the redemption is the fundamental idea in the New Testament, and one gets into the *homoousion* in the fourth century. But students at the present time and probably students at most times start off with the positive stuff and gradually you bring them along. And this is the natural way: first of all the world of community and then its mediation by theory.

Question: Would you begin with a study of the revelation as it is in Scripture?
Lonergan: Yes.

Question: Would you begin with the *prius quoad nos* maybe considered also as the church presenting the doctrine to us today?
Lonergan: That depends upon the type of student you have. There is the problem of fundamental theology or apologetics. Fundamental theology is the field with the big methodological problems at present. Things like the Trinity, and so on, are treatises that are finished; and treatises like the mystical body haven't begun to be attempted yet. All the positive work has been done, but the categories in which one can think them have not yet evolved. Questions like the church, and so on, which have arisen and become prominent since the Middle Ages, these are things that haven't been categorized by medieval thought. It is there that the difficulties arise, and it is there that you have very complex questions. Does theology fall under the category of science or the sociology of knowledge? Do you want to put your question in those terms?

Question: You mention *quoad nos* and *quoad se*, but the analogy is between *causa cognoscendi* and *causa essendi*.

Lonergan: Also, yes. The New Testament talks the language of the community. The idea of God in the Old Testament is the one who did this. For example, in the Book of Samuel, Samuel tells the people all that God has done for them. And that was their concept of God, God known through narration. And the Messiah is the one who is to come. Those are the fundamental categories of the New Testament. When Paul talks to the Hebrews, to a Jewish audience, he talks about the God of his fathers, and tells the story of Israel in Acts, chapter 13. And later, one finds him talking to the Gentiles, and it is an entirely different mode of speech, as in the Areopagus. He's talking about the one who calls the rain and the sunshine, or whatever. Now that's the idea of God in the New Testament, the fundamental way in which God is conceived. And you have to give that to your students, otherwise they'll be in all sorts of difficulties about the way they're thinking about Christ in the New Testament.

It is *quoad nos*, insofar as it is historical: *quoad apostolos, quoad Urgemeinde, quoad* the first, second, third, fourth century, etc.

Question: But isn't there a way of looking at it *quoad nos* in this sense, that our community is a development of the original, and our community today is what is *nos?*

Lonergan: I think it is difficult to discuss the thing in the abstract. In *De Verbo incarnato,* I have ten theses on the hypostatic union. First, the terms are defined in such a way that one can verify them in the New Testament. The second concerns Apollinarism, Nestorianism, Monophysites, Monothelites, and that finishes off the movement from 380, say, to 680 A.D. Then we have the Scholastics on the person. The notion of the person in Augustine, Boethius, Richard of St Victor, St Thomas; and there are the metaphysical constituents of the person – I think it is post-Thomas really – in Scotus, Tiphanus, Suarez, Cajetan, Capreolus, and so on.[30]

---

30 The recording does not supply the end of Lonergan's response to the question.

1962

Discussion 2[1]

Question: Can you contrast your usage of the term 'method' with the term as it is commonly used? For example, kerygmatic method, Medieval method, Thomistic method, etc.

Lonergan: It would be easier to effect the contrast if I was told what was meant by kerygmatic method, Medieval method, and Thomistic method.

Question: What about kerygmatic method?

Lonergan: Kerygmatic theology, isn't it? Kerygmatic theology is the effort to give the type of theology that people can preach. The students say, Why do you give us all this stuff? Why not give us scripture and the Fathers and something that we can tell the people, a theology that is more immediately directed towards preaching? That is as much as I know about kerygmatic theology.

Question: It is a type of method?

Lonergan: I don't think so.

Question: You mentioned yourself yesterday Medieval 'method'; you went through the method of Abelard and Lombard.

Lonergan: Scholastic method.

---

1 Wednesday, 11 July 1962, Lauzon CD/MP3 323 (32300A0E060) and 324 (32400A0E060).

Question: The way you used the word 'method' there: Scholastic method; I think this is what we mean by the common ordinary use of the word. And we wanted to know if there was a contrast between this and the way you have been using 'method' in the title of this course?

Lonergan: There is perhaps insofar as I'm concerned primarily with the foundations. Regarding my notion of method: one has the world of community, the world in which we are born and educated, and live 99 percent of our lives; that world can be mediated by the world of theory. You can understand the world of community, and you can also mediate the world of industry and commerce and banking by an economic theory and understand how they work and know what to do to deal with crises. This was something that was lacking in the Depression of 1929 and 1930; it was the Depression that produced a radical change in economic theory, and it caused a number of topics to be accepted into economics that were taboo in the nineteenth century. That is the mediation of community by theory.

Now theory itself heads into difficulties. This appears in the multiplicity of philosophies, the multiplicity of views in the human sciences, but not so much the natural sciences because here the ultimate questions can be dodged up to a point. For example, Lindsay and Margenau in their book *Foundations of Physics*,[2] in the last chapter, start talking about the foundations. And they say that the ultimate criterion seems to be aesthetic. They are looking for the simplest equations to cover all the data. Those ultimate questions arise and appear in theology in the existence of different schools and the rejection of all schools. That problem of method is forced upon the philosopher, the theologian, the scientist by what may be called the systematic exigence, the move to systematic thinking in which the ultimate terms are precise. They are not defined by genus and species but by their mutual relations or, as Aristotle would say, by their proportion to one another: potency to act, matter to form, essence to existence, substance to accident; all those fundamental Aristotelian terms come out in pairs, and to understand them we have to understand their mutual dependence on one another. So the erection of systems gives rise to a critical exigence that is commonly expressed in terms of the principle or the demand that one show that what one is talking about is something that one knows or at least something that one can know. That throws one back on interiority. One needs a theory of

2 Robert Bruce Lindsay and Henry Margenau, *Foundations of Physics* (Woodbridge, CT: Ox Bow Press, 1981, reprint of 1936 [John Wiley and Sons] and 1957 [Dover Publications] editions).

knowledge, an exact account of what one's knowledge is and what its limits are, and so on, if one is to show that what one is attempting to know in one's theory is something that a man does know or at least can know.

When one meets this critical exigence by turning to interiority one has the foundations for method. Insofar as interiority mediates the world of theory and through theory mediates the world of community, or directly enters into the study of community, insofar as we are all made the same way, then one has method.

Method is the return from interiority to the world of theory and the world of community; and I think that is the fundamental notion of method. It is very general and holds for any type of inquiry whatever, because all inquiries are carried out by human minds. Insofar as the operations differ from one field to another, one gets special methods: the method that uses invariance and differential equations in physics, and the different methods one gets in all the different sciences. When you reach method based upon an interiority and you conceive it as a philosophy, it is a 'philosophy of,' and one can fill in the blank by adding on the determinations of the different subjects: philosophy of science, philosophy of nature, philosophy of religion, philosophy of society, and so on, adding the further determinations that arise from a particular field.

Erich Rothacker, who is more or less in Dilthey's line of thought, put out at Bonn in 1947 – I think it was part of a series of handbooks – what he called 'The Logic and Systematics of the Human Sciences.'[3] He conceives all the human sciences as involving three elements: the history of, the foundations of, the doctrines of. The history enlarges the foundations. If one studies the history one arrives at what the basic presuppositions of the subject are. There are histories of religions and foundations of religions, and the two are interdependent. From understanding the history and the dialectic one will get the normative element as history heads into doctrine, and one will arrive at a doctrine. For example, in the study of law there is the philosophy of law and the history of law and legal doctrine or jurisprudence.

I said, with regard to Scholastic method, that it was implicit. It wasn't St Thomas or Scotus that wrote *Die Geschichte der Scholastischen Methode*, it was Martin Grabmann around 1909.[4] And it wasn't St Thomas or Scotus that

---

3 Erich Rothacker, *Logik und Systematik der Geisteswissenschaften (Handbuch der Philosophie)* (Munich: R. Oldenbourg, 1965). The book was first published in 1927 and reissued in 1947.
4 Martin Grabmann, *Die Geschichte der Scholastischen Methode*, 2 vols. The book was originally published in 1909, and an unaltered edition was issued in 1956 (Munich: Akademie-Verlag).

reflected on the history of Scholastic method, it was Congar in his article on 'Théologie' in the DTC.[5] Thomas and Scotus *did* theology. And until theology is done, until one has a first-class creation such as St Thomas's work, one hasn't got the objectification of theology that can base the reflective work of method.

If one thinks that theological method can be found by studying the *Summa theologiae* of St Thomas, well I think one is off to a bad start. Any *Summa* is just a part in the medieval movement. The medieval movement starts off – an exception is Anselm, he antedates the Scholastic method in a certain sense; he was a purely speculative type; he dealt with all the hard questions and mysteries he could find: predestination, grace and liberty, the Trinity, etc. He picked out all the hard things in theology and discussed them. But the weakness in Anselm is that he hasn't got the positive basis that is needed for a theology. The positive basis came in with people like Abelard and the books of *Sentences*; they just went to work systematically in the fashion of their time, collecting all the passages from the Fathers and the Scriptures that bore on particular points. That work of the twelfth century provided the positive basis for commentaries on the *Sentences*. One can read St Thomas's commentary on the *Sentences*, where he is commenting on Peter Lombard; it is evident from the question that there is a hundred years between the two. Thomas is discussing things that bear no relation to what the Lombard was saying. It represents a hundred years of progress since then, and the thing runs on. But the fact that they got so far beyond the state of the question when these collections were made is evidence that there were terrific advances in systematic thinking, and these had to break away from the *Sentences*.

Take the first book of the *Sentences*. St Thomas is all over the place. There is one question on *De Deo Uno*, and another on *De Deo Trino*, and so on, shooting back and forth. There is no order in the presentation, at least by later standards of the *Summa theologiae*. The *Summae* represent attempts at systematization: picking out one's fundamental concepts and expressing everything in terms of those fundamental concepts. So the *Summa* is just part of a total method that was being carried on by a medieval community. When we think of medieval theology in that way, we think of a method that was implicit there and can't be made explicit at the present time and followed very successfully.

What is going on at the present time in a certain sense is that biblical scholars are presenting problems for systematization by the more speculative

5 See above, p. 3, note 2.

theologians who work it into their system for the presentation of doctrine. The same sort of thing is going on. The function of method is to understand what is happening at the present time.

Question: Does that mean you have to go back to theology? What is the relationship between philosophy and theology?
Lonergan: The problem of the relationship between philosophy and theology is a terrific problem, if all that one has are concepts and propositions. They are two different fields, so what's the use of bothering with philosophy when one is doing theology? However, if one realizes that one is performing certain operations in each field, using the brains God gave one, then one can escape the division of fields and see that there is something common to both.

There is a mistaken notion of theology: philosophy is carried on by the natural light of reason, and faith is beyond the natural light of reason; we can conceive theology as faith helped along by reason, which adds on certain conclusions. If one conceives theology that way, one has something totally distinct from philosophy. But you can conceive theology also as the Vatican Council seems to have done, as *ratio per fidem illustrata* not *fides per rationem adiuta*; you have the native light of intelligence given a further light from faith and the two operating as a unit. Insofar as the light of faith is involved, it isn't natural; but the light of faith illuminates only the answers to the question, *An sit?* It doesn't answer the question, *Quid sit?* The light of faith is the light needed to make an assent, a judgment, and the theologian's judgments will have supernatural objects, and they will presuppose his faith and include his faith insofar as they are properly theological. His faith will be operative, and because his faith is supernatural those operations will have a supernatural element in them somewhere.

But insofar as the theologian is answering the question, *Quid sit?* – what do you mean by the supernatural? what do you mean when you talk about God having a son? – he is trying to understand and, as is known, he gets no new species of the supernatural order. He begins from *ex analogia eorum quae naturaliter cognoscit*, as the Vatican Council says. From those analogies, and from putting together the different analogies, he arrives at some understanding of the mysteries. Understanding is not beyond the range of human intelligence, because it is just analogous. It is not *quoad substantiam* supernatural, though it is *quoad modum*, that is, in view of the problem, in view of the truth he is dealing with.

While the truths of faith are beyond the range of natural human knowledge, the truths of faith are not beyond the capacity of human intellect, because human intellect is supernaturally elevated and human intellect assents to them. The human intellect has the job of assimilating them and making them fructify thirty or sixty or a hundred fold in human living. Insofar as the truths of faith are properly assimilated, insofar as one knows what they mean, then one can live them. Otherwise they're a precious something or other wrapped up in a napkin and buried in the ground.

Question: What is the meaning and function of interiority?

Lonergan: Another name for interiority is subjectivity. However, subjectivity is usually associated with some immanentist philosophy; one gets into subjectivity, and one can't get out of it. Interiority is illustrated by the spiritual life. The more a man progresses in prayer the less he uses his theology. The prayer of simplicity eliminates the imagination and reduces discourse to occasional aspirations. One is moving into a sphere that is quite different from the world of community and the world of theory. Again, Thomas à Kempis states that it is better to feel compunction than to define it. When you feel compunction, you're in the world of interiority. When you define compunction, you make an object of what goes on in you. This making an object of it is something quite different; it is a reflection on, an objectification of, something that is prior to the reflection and the objectification. That prior something is what counts. Having the prior something doesn't exclude the defining and the objectification. As a matter of fact, the objectification mediates the experience and enables you to say that it is better to feel compunction than to define it. If you had no objectification at all you wouldn't be able to discuss or compare feelings and the definition of feeling. As soon as you use the word 'compunction,' the objectification has occurred. Of course, you can feel compunction and not know what's going on. Knowing what's going on is a conceptualization, an understanding, of one's experience. The fundamental element to interiority is that it is interior; it is always there, immediate, given. No matter what you objectify, no matter what your object is on the level of sense, on the level of understanding, on the level of conception, on the level of reflection and judgment, on the level of deliberation and choice, there is always the one who chooses, the one who deliberates. It's quite distinct from what he's deliberating about, what he's choosing, usually. And so on for the other operations. You have to have the soul present to itself, in Augustine's language, for anything to be present to it; and it is insofar as one understands the structure of the operator that one can understand the structure of the *operata*. The structure of the operator is something that you can't fool with, something you can't eliminate. *Naturam expellas furca, tamen usque recurret.*[6] You can't get around nature. For example, the argument in the eleventh chapter of *Insight*: there is no revising of the reviser. There is the relativist position: science is never more than probable; science is the highest form of human knowledge; therefore the highest form of human knowledge doesn't admit certitude. To be able to say that, to make a universal statement about science, you have to understand the structure of our knowing. And if you understand the structure of human knowing, are you certain of it? If you are not certain of the statement that science is always subject to revision, it won't hold.

Again, we can take this problem another way. We can say that any attempt to revise this analysis of knowledge will involve the discovery of new data that haven't been taken into account in this theory, and it will involve an understanding of these data and all the other data, and it will lead to the judgment that this view is better than the previous one. You have there experience, understanding, and judgment, and that is all the original theory stated. The very possibility of a revision presupposes this same structure.

But that structure can be refined. This is just a simple instance of it, and it can be worked out in full. For instance, there is my reference to horizon, lack of conversion and the presence of conversion, authenticity and inauthenticity; on this basis you are able to locate a writer, say, the various Patristic writers. And you are able to locate the people who wrote monographs about them. You have a principle of criticism not only of the original authors but also of the people who write about the original authors. From that you can proceed methodically, systematically, to deal with the historical process of a literature and a doctrine.

Question: Can you relate interiority to St Thomas's two kinds of wisdom? The emphasis that you are putting on the subject, who remains the same and does not become the object, at least approaches theological wisdom and in a way this connatural wisdom, the wisdom through charity.
Lonergan: St Thomas has two wisdoms: (1) the wisdom expressed in Aristotle's *Metaphysics*, and (2) that which comes as a gift from the Holy Ghost. What is wisdom? *Sapientis est ordinare,* and the wise man *simpliciter* orders everything. To order everything, you can think simply in terms of the object, and that is the way Aristotle went about it. Insofar as you add on the

---

6 'You can drive nature out with a pitchfork, but it will always return.' Horace, *Epistolae,* I, 10, 24.

structure of the subject you have a further principle of pinning down just what this order is and how the order develops in different individuals. There is not a sufficient grasp of it in the child for him to be said to have reached the age of reason. There is not a sufficient grasp of it in the minor for him to be held responsible before the law, and one can compare the degree of wisdom reached in successive individuals. That type of extension of the notion of wisdom is necessary if we are going to go systematically into history and into notions of development in history.

The gift of the Holy Ghost is that by which the soul is *facile mobilis per instinctus superioris motoris*. In the *Nicomachean Ethics* there is a passage in which Aristotle describes or discusses the pilot who gets the ship into port because he knows the art of navigation, and the pilot who gets the ship into port without the art of navigation is said to have fortune. The explanation of the man of fortune is that he is moved by some superior instinct. St Thomas from the universal necessity of the *initium consiliandi* generalizes this, and it is on that level that he puts the gift of the Holy Ghost in his general systematic presentation, insofar as I understand it. The virtues are what make a man perfect. The just man naturally does just acts, as fire moves upwards; the charitable man spontaneously does charitable acts, and one can expect him to do such acts because he has the virtue. But no finite perfection results in perfect action. Consequently, there is need for a further direction from the Holy Ghost. The gifts of the Holy Ghost are the adaptation of the subject, his subordination to a superior principle of direction. And that would be along the lines of the gift of wisdom.

Now, charity is something that is isomorphic with the fundamental structure of intelligence and rationality. Charity is to love God above all and your neighbor as oneself. That charity destroys the spontaneous egoism of the human animal. Man insofar as he is an animal has a set of instincts to preserve himself and those that belong to him. The universe is centered around him; he doesn't apprehend the whole universe, he apprehends as much of it as concerns him and his spontaneous activity. That orientation is something that has to be overcome, surpassed, gone beyond, if he is to perform intellectual operations properly, because intellectual operations are detached, disinterested, concerned with the truth and only with the truth. Intellectual operations must be freed from wishful thinking and from fears which lead to hesitancy or doubt. The subject's light of intellect is, in a sense, at war with the spontaneous animal center; it is detached. This is the same sort of orientation as you have with charity. Insofar as the subject has charity, he will by his will be given the orientation and have the orientation, and that will have a backward influence on his intellectual operations. The man of charity will be free from the party spirit, from personal ambitions that can destroy his intellectual life just as much as his moral life. This is the participation in wisdom through connaturality, through charity, something one gets as a gift from the Holy Ghost. Wisdom is something connected with and resulting from charity.

Question: St Thomas got as far as distinguishing acts by objects.
Lonergan: St Thomas said as much as he possibly could to the people of his time. One has to have some sort of an audience and, as a matter of fact, Thomas spoke beyond his time and was condemned. St Thomas was hardly noticed by Scotus, who paid more attention to Henry of Ghent and other people. Generally, they would discuss Thomas without quoting him. We must remember that Thomas was not then the great St Thomas that he is now, but rather a condemned author. There are a lot of things in St Thomas, at least from my study of him, that show that he knew about many things that he did not mention. Take the matter of consciousness. There is the account of consciousness in Augustine, which is more explicit than in St Thomas. But Thomas can quote these passages in Augustine and interpret them correctly and then not pay any attention to them a few pages later. He is saying what can be said in his milieu. So when I say this about Thomas, I am talking about Thomas generally, what is obvious from the viewpoint of common historical research, insofar as historical work attempts to state what nobody can fail to see.

Question: Are you adding the subject? That can be in two ways, through the will and charity, the infused way. The other is intellectual.
Lonergan: Insofar as we are working on the method of a science, it is intellectual. These other influences will be there: overcoming horizons, overcoming inauthenticity, etc. But the structure of the subject is important with regard to fundamental questions of meaning. What do you mean by matter and form? Matter stands to form as phantasm stands to insight. You can have the experience of insight with the help of imagination and know exactly what you mean, and because any act of human intelligence is going to involve sensibility and intelligence, any proportionate object, any proper object of human knowing, is going to involve matter and form. So hylomorphism is, as it were, self-evident once one gets hold of oneself and knows what one is doing when one is knowing. Besides, one can answer any question that may arise with regard to matter and form simply because one

has at the basis of one's thinking not just concepts that seem to be pulled out of nowhere, but terms that stand in a relation that resides in one's own inner experience.

This is one aspect of interiority. Then, another aspect is this business of horizon, authenticity, conversion, and so on, and that has to do with the critique of subjects. Insofar as one is studying development – development is not just a straight line – there are always the people who are on the wrong side, and the struggle between them. There was not only Athanasius, there were also the Arians; not only Cyril of Alexandria but also the Nestorians; not merely Chalcedon but also the Monophysites; not only Augustine but also the Pelagians. Everything comes out through a fight.

Why do we pick one rather than the other? How does one know that these fellows are wrong? Well, we know it through the teaching of the church, yes, but the theologian's job is not simply to say that the church is right. The church tells him that his noblest task is to show how the results of what has been decided by the church correspond to the scriptural data. It's only insofar as one has some method of judging the process that one is able to do that. And one has some method of judging the process insofar as one can set up what interiority is and what its aberrations can be.

Question:[7] How do you recognize method?

Lonergan: Everyone has it, but to attend to it is the trick. To make consciousness thematic, the transition from the *vécu* to the *thématique*, from the implicit to the explicit, from what you understand in commonsense fashion to what you can systematize, define exactly – that is where the difficulty arises. Anyone can find out what it is to see by opening and closing his eyes. He not only sees the picture and doesn't see it when he closes his eyes, he also causes an experience that occurs within his consciousness. In one case he is not seeing and now he is seeing. You can pick that out in your consciousness very simply; it's a matter of sensation; one knows the difference between being hit and not being hit, etc. On the sensitive level it is perfectly simple, but we begin to find it difficult as soon as we get to the level of intelligence, because one intellectual act is just one experience, and as soon as the thing becomes habitual, well, one doesn't notice it anymore. One has to make another discovery; one has to have a series of experiences of insights to become familiar with just what the insight is, the thing that made Archimedes shout *Eureka*, the thing that brightens up the students' faces

7 The recording moves at this point to Lauzon CD/MP3 324 (32400A0E060).

and that, when it's missing, causes you to get the blank stare, and you know it. A teacher can just work on that; he'll know right away if they are getting what he is saying or not.

There is a further level of judgment, which is still more difficult. Because there is an element of personal commitment in it, we are more easily conscious of our judgments than not. When you have to make a judgment, you have a period in which you say, 'Well, I don't know what to think about that.' But you think it over, and say, 'Well, that seems to be right.' Again, your acts of will: did you consent? Well, what is that element of consent? It's hard to pin down. One has to engage in introspection; but people have a false notion of what introspection is; they think it is taking a look. However, it is something on the side of the subject, the third type of presence. The stock objection to the proof of freedom is that one can be conscious that one has performed this act but one can't be conscious that one could have performed the opposite; what could be isn't given in consciousness. One doesn't have consciousness of possibles, one has consciousness of facts, what de facto is there. But the free subject is the dynamic principle of performing either act. That free subject is conscious of his potentiality; that is where the consciousness of freedom resides. It resides on the side of the subject, on the side of the active principle and not on the side of the act that's posited as a result. It is on the side of the principle that consciousness of freedom resides. But to hear the formulation of it doesn't give you the experience.

Question: Could you repeat that?
Lonergan: The subject is the principle of the act. He is not merely the empirically conscious principle of the act. By empirically conscious, I mean the feeling of coldness when I touch the metal part of a chair. As Merleau-Ponty says, the subject is extended in space. The statue represents the conscious hunk of space that is my body – that is not Merleau-Ponty, it is Susanne Langer. Empirical consciousness: consciousness of the fact that I'm seeing and not seeing. Intellectual consciousness: I'm inquiring, understanding, I'm intelligent as opposed to the intelligible. Rational consciousness: when one is making a judgment one is rationally conscious; one is demanding the unconditioned and judging whether or not one is getting it. If one gets it one must judge, and if one doesn't one can't. Rational self-consciousness: if the judgment is a judgment of value, either one accepts that value or rejects it. Then one is the rationally self-conscious principle of the act of choice; and it is the rationally self-conscious principle of the choice that is conscious

of the potentiality of accepting or rejecting. It is not the consciousness of the act posited that is the consciousness of liberty; that's just consciousness of a fact. One gets consciousness of possibility insofar as one is consciously the principle, the cause, that could do either.

Question: Is method of theology part of theology?
Lonergan: Yes and no. Yes, insofar as the principle of theology is not *fides per rationem adiuta* but *ratio per fidem illustrata*; the first element there is *ratio*. And that is the substantive subjective element in theology. How do you do theology? By using your mind. But it isn't using a mind that isn't illuminated by faith, it is using a mind that is illuminated by faith. Consequently, method in theology is method that goes beyond philosophy; its fundamental principle is more than the fundamental principle of philosophy. It is a transformed mind, but it is a mind, and it isn't faith. In *Denzingertheologie*, what does theology consist of? It consists of saying what the church has said. In other words, it is a rejection of what the church has said, because the church has said that we are to follow St Thomas and that there is some fruitful understanding of the mysteries that we can attain. And the church doesn't attempt to offer theological explanations. It settles disputed questions.

Question: What about this rational self-consciousness?
Lonergan: Rational consciousness and rational self-consciousness. The will is rational self-consciousness, that is, when one is on the level of deliberation. Because the act of will not only determines what's going to happen to the microphone if I kick it or don't kick it, it also determines the sort of person I am, the contributions to my habits. We make ourselves what we are by acquiring habits. So the will is a two-edged sword, so to speak. Its fundamental importance is what it makes of me, not the objects. And that is the element of self-consciousness in rational self-consciousness – these deliberations.

Now, for the intellect to function it is enough if I don't interfere. The act of will that is required is noninterference by wishes or fears in the intellectual process.

Question: Is this the place of the intellect?
Lonergan: There is an ascendancy of intellect in me that is demanded of me by my rationality. My will cannot be good if my intellect is not right, not objectively good. In that rationality, one may ask oneself, How is it that the proofs for divine revelation are solid? So many people don't see anything

here at all. But we may not think these things out to the end; the process can be cut off at any stage. Intellectual probity is a matter of maintaining the rational.

Question: Does a person mature into an intellectually good person without having wanted to?

Lonergan: No. But in a sense it is *per accidens* because there is a sense in which intellect is prior. There has to be some sort of probity in a specialized sense that is an intellectual probity, an element that is brought out by de la Rochefoucauld's statement that everyone complains about their memory but nobody about their judgment.

Question: Where does sin fit in?

Lonergan: It can be due to a bad act of will; but really the will is always heading towards the good. It is by omission, a non-acting of the will, that one gets sin; either one doesn't inhibit an incipient evil process or one fails to consent to an incipient good process. In other words, there isn't a positive entity that constitutes the sin; ultimately the sin resolves to a privation.

Now, to separate our intellect and will is going to be a simply theoretical task at any time. In the concrete, a man decides the kind of mentality he is going to have to a great extent, by deciding to go to this university rather than that one, by deciding to read these books rather than those, by all sorts of things like that, acts of will, and so on, often made without any awareness of their implications.

Question: This probity of the intellect is in the very nature of the intellect itself. What about intellectual conversion?

Lonergan: Insofar as the subject is unconverted, insofar as he is the center for himself of the universe, there will be the impediment there. And to overcome that impediment will involve intellectual conversion. Intellectual conversion is very well illustrated by the Stoics. The Stoics had a very high morality, and Stoic morality had a considerable influence on St Thomas. But the Stoics were materialists. For the Stoics the real is something material. So they had the moral conversion but they didn't have the intellectual conversion.

Question: Their presuppositions aren't intellectual conversion.

Lonergan: There is the struggle between the two. One has something of the same in Kant, who has a very elevated morality but at the same time his doctrine in the 'Transcendental Aesthetic' is that there is no immediate knowledge of an object except by *Anschauung*, and that is the basis of all materialisms.

Question: How does the commonsense world mediate theology?
Lonergan: It builds theologates! It supplies the cash to send people to institutes on method in theology! Divine revelation was in the terms of the commonsense world. Does that answer your question?

Question: I was thinking of applying theology to common sense.
Lonergan: On that level: I was teaching theology at the Gregorian to people from sixty-four nations and all sorts of cultural backgrounds. I can't tell them how to preach because I don't have the sixty-four different backgrounds; one has to be intimate with a given milieu, with the people one is going to talk to, before one is able to say something that will mean something to them. What the dogmatic theologian does is to provide the unconscious principles that will enable the Catholic preacher to talk to his people and, at the same time, talk as a Catholic. I think I illustrated this before in the difference between the Catholic priest and the Protestant minister. The Protestant minister spends all his week preparing his sermon: he reads all the latest books and all the latest periodicals and writes his sermon out. The Catholic priest is busy in the hospitals, schools, teaching catechism, visiting the sick, preparing the bazaar and the bingo, and hearing confessions, and perhaps late Saturday night he prepares his sermon and he preaches his sermon on Sunday. One finds with Catholic priests all over, they say the same thing. But the Protestants have as many doctrines as they have ministers. And what makes the difference? It is Scholastic theology and learning theses. The Catholics are, at least, trained with a party line. They have it, and it influences everything they say and think in the religious field, whether they think about it or not. Theology has to offer, on the level of those determinants that make preachers in different continents, in different countries, in different cultural milieus, at different times, that which makes the same their different repetitions of the biblical message in the Catholic sense. It is because theology is on that higher level that it can do this work.

We have a responsibility to the initial deposit of faith; and the movement from the world of community to the world of theory is an effort to maintain that continuity; it is an explicit effort to maintain that continuity and to ensure that continuity. The Vatican Council states that there is a deposit of faith, the doctrines of faith, given to the church, not as though it was some human discovery that was to be developed by human talent over time, but as a deposit that was to be retained without change down the centuries. However, in a certain milieu it has to be expressed so that it will be understood by all sorts of people; it has to make possible that vital intercourse and, at the same time, preserve that identity, to have a freedom from the modes of expression, so that all Catholics are united and don't have to become Jews of the first century. To eliminate this as a precondition of being a Catholic, one has to have this dogmatic theology.

Question: I'm thinking about Rahner writing about work and communications and other applications. What about that?
Lonergan: That sort of application, I imagine, would start out as a phenomenology that takes an instance of work and understands it, brings out its meaning. Insofar as the meaning that is got at is Catholic, one has a theology of work.

Question: And that would be universal?
Lonergan: That's the technique for doing it, eh? Insofar as one is using one's theology to make the meaning one draws out of work a Catholic meaning, one is using theology.

Question: Is that what you are saying about these worlds needing integration?
Lonergan: Yes. It is an instance of mediation in the sense that a man who is an economist can write a history of a country and will understand things that a man who isn't an economist won't understand, and so on for any type of theoretical knowledge. Theology is mediating the operations in the commonsense world, the world of community.

Question: Can one turn that around and have the *sensus fidelium* mediating theology, and thereby contributing to the development of dogma, as in the case of the Immaculate Conception and Assumption; is there a mediation from common sense to theology?
Lonergan: That is more the perpetuity of the deposit of faith, isn't it? It is leading to a dogmatic definition: that this is so. And it isn't the theologian in the Catholic Church that fulfills the role of the apostles and the prophets, as Karl Barth does for his Protestant communion; the church says what is so. There is a difference between the function of the magisterium and the function of the theologian. The *sensus fidelium* is for the theologian a criterion of what is so, but it isn't up to the theologian to say this is what the *sensus fidelium* is.

Question: That's what will get the theologian started. Isn't that something like mediation?

Lonergan: That's faith. Faith is fundamentally in the world of community, though, *fides ex auditu*. The development is an *Auslegung*, an interpretation, of what is there implicitly, a making thematic what is there on the level of experience. But it has to be there before it can be explicitated.

Question: Can you discuss the assertion that the human good is formally constituted by meaning?

Lonergan: There are the levels of the human good, there are the elements of the human good, that are natural in the cruder sense of the term 'natural.' In other words, meaning is something that is higher up, the form as opposed to the matter. You can take the view of man that prescinds from all meaning, that prescinds entirely from the *esse intentionale*, and say man is a rational animal, and by rational I mean a potency so that a lunatic, or an infant, or a moron, or St Thomas Aquinas, or Einstein are all equally men. And that is a view of humanity that gives no significance to history, no significance to development; if you don't want to pay any attention to those things you're off to a good start.

But human living is not that; human society is not that; the *esse intentionale*, the element of meaning, enters into everything in human life. And that is the element, meaning, that develops and makes history. What is a law court apart from meaning? It is a lot of noise. Or a parliament apart from meaning? It is a lot of noise. Cut out the meaning from human life, and it is something like what the existentialists call nausea. It is meaning that makes human living human. We don't think of human living in terms of idiots and infants. The element of meaning is the element that is constitutive of all human institutions. If you eliminate meaning, the family ceases to be a family. If you eliminate meaning, one's state or one's society ceases to be a state or a society. Without meaning you have no language, no art, no symbols, no literature, no history, no science, no religion – religion is meaning; there are the motions of the liturgy, but the motions have a meaning. What is called historical consciousness is reference to that particular constitutive function of meaning in human action, in human living. The nihilist is a person for whom life has lost all meaning. Nietzsche can say God is dead; that is to say that, in the nineteenth century, culture reached the point in which the existence of God was not something that anyone could rationally affirm. God meant nothing to men in that cultural milieu; God was dead, and Nietzsche was keenly aware of the fact. He was aware that practically all the meaning in the genesis of the culture that he belonged to, and all its surviving institutions, had a religious basis. And saying that God was dead meant a complete revolution of everything; one had to remake the whole thing.

We shall all be judged, each man shall be judged, according to his works, and his works are his rational, deliberate works, they are works informed by meaning. Christianity is a doctrine and an order; in both cases it is a matter of meaning. The word of God is a meaning; the body of Christ is an order, and an order is the realization of something intentional. The possibility of Catholicism being a transformation of human living, of the world, is the fact that the world already is formally constituted by meaning. That is the significance of statements such as Cassirer's, that man is a symbolic animal; he is an animal all right, but he is an animal who makes signs and uses symbols. What are wars fought about? They are fought over meanings. All the great movements are great movements because they are full of meaning. As meanings develop, institutions change. Change the meaning of marriage and you change the reality of marriage; change the meaning of the state and you get a different state. There will be some abstract definition that all states can satisfy, but they are not the concrete realities that constitute the good of order within which men live. Education is the transmission of meaning.

Question: What is your notion of the surd? Is that the opposite?
Lonergan: To develop this would take considerable space and time. I developed it in the seventh chapter of *Insight* and also in chapter 18, where I discuss the idea of effective freedom. The surd, sin, is irrational; it is not *secundum rectam rationem*, it is against reason. Why did Adam sin? Why did the angels sin? If there was a reason it wouldn't have been a sin. Adam may have been able to think up excuses, but if he had a reason it wouldn't have been a sin. So when one asks why, one is asking a mistaken question. And if the question why is a mistake the object must be lacking an intelligibility that you would expect an object to have. That is what a surd is. It is something that lacks the intelligibility one would expect an object to have. You would expect that the diagonal is commensurable with the side of the square, but it is not. There is no common measure, no matter how small, that will go an even number of times into the side and into the diagonal. One would expect that if one were allowed to take something as small as you please one would find something that would fit, but one can demonstrate that this is impossible. So the ratio between the two is a surd. There is not the intelligibility there that you would expect.

Sin is the case of the ultimate surd; it's a case where your expectations aren't justified. One expects the rational appetite to will rationally, but it doesn't. There is not only this irrationality in the act of the will but there is also this lack of rationality, of intelligibility, in the action and in the situation that the action brings about. You make the situation, and when the surd and the situation lack intelligibility, then you have objective evidence for false conclusions. One steps into *Realpolitik*: 'One has to live, I'm not a tough.' It's all right to be an honest man if you are living among honest men, and it is all right not to be a murderer when no one around one is a murderer; but change the social situation and people will cry, 'I've got to live.' There is the dialectic of sin on two levels: on the practical level of the people who say, 'I've got to live,' and then on the theoretical level, the people that say human intelligence is not an instrument for setting up norms that can't be lived by; what we have to do is think out a new philosophy, a new ethics, a new religion, and so on, that will be in conformity with the objective facts. As the objective facts get worse and worse, the new ethics, the new religion, the new philosophy, keep getting worse and worse. That is the social surd expanding in the world of community and in the world of theory. It is a succession of ever lower syntheses.

[(1)] One supernatural religion in the Middle Ages gave rise to several supernatural religions at the Reformation. The result was that there were the religious wars. This was the first lower synthesis. (2) Religious wars don't make any sense, so let's go by the light of reason and put aside all supernatural religions, right religion. This was the second lower synthesis. (3) But as for the appeal to reason, it was discovered afterwards that the light of reason seemed to differ considerably from one man to the next. So the next lower synthesis was liberalism: respect everybody's opinion. (4) But when one respects everyone's opinion and everyone follows his own opinions you can't deal with social evils, and so on. So you have to give society the power to handle the whole business, and so one arrives at the next lower synthesis, that is, the totalitarian state. If you want to move into this gradually, you will have creeping socialism, but you get there in the long run. And in the totalitarian state what does theory become? It becomes ideology, the instrument on the intellectual level for controlling the situation. The surd, in its expansion, ends up with an elimination of any normativeness on the part of human intelligence and reason. You are left with the balance of forces, the balance of power, economic determinism, and the myth: Rosenberg's myth in the twentieth century or the Marxist myth of the classless society. The only way to overcome this downward sweep of history is that we must rely on

redemption and grace. We must transform evil into good. There is the old
dictum: according to Aristotle *actio* and *passio* are one and the same *motus*.
But the action of crucifying our Lord was as wicked as possible, and the action of our Lord in suffering the crucifixion was as good as possible. The
actio and the *passio* are the same concrete reality, still they differ by the wills,
to cause the one and undergo the other. You have there the transformation
of evil into good. Death, which was the penalty of sin, became the means of
redemption. That is the fundamental Christian symbol. Faith, hope, and
charity, besides their role as theological virtues in bringing us to God, are
also the means of transforming the evil in the world. That is all in chapter
20 of *Insight*.

In theology there are treatises of different degrees of maturity. To them
there is nothing left to be added. For example, St Thomas's treatment of the
Trinity is the most mature of all the theological treatises. But there are other
theological treatises that have barely put their nose above water. And they
are the ones that have to do with reflection on the sciences, the social sciences, and so on. There is so much emphasis on the legal aspect, for example, in the treatise on the church simply because the one human science
that is of considerable ancient lineage is the science of law. Insofar as we take
over and assimilate and make our own the other human sciences we will be
able to develop an adequate treatise on the church and its role in history.

Question: What is the connection of the schema of the human good to the
previous discussion of object, subject, and operations?
Lonergan: The human good is a matter of operations that are cooperations. And the human good insofar as it is cooperations raises the question, How do they cooperate, what do they cooperate for? The operations:
on the second level of the scheme we have the habits, and we spoke of
habits, operations, objects. The object of a singular operation or cooperation is a particular good. But the habits are concerned with the sequence,
a recurrence of goods. Insofar as the operations are cooperations, insofar
as the human good is socially mediated, you have institutions. The basis,
the common understanding that underlies cooperation, is what gives one
the good of order. That isn't an ultimate account of the human good; you
have to add on liberty and orientation, personal relations and terminal
values. When you do all that you have an initial scheme for discussing the
world of community, and the world of community is one of our ultimate
fields, it is one of the fields in which development occurs. It stands in antithesis to the world of interiority, to the world of theory, and to the ultimate which is God. The discussion of the human good is a transition point

which makes concrete the discussion of the world of community, the world of theory, and the world of interiority.

Question: There seemed to be an abrupt transition for us from the intellect to the will. Did the transition seem as abrupt to you?

Lonergan: It's abrupt to me because I have two packs of notes! One corresponds to the typewritten stuff and the other, equally big, which I hope to work in some time in the course of these two weeks. The stuff on the human good was pulled out of the second stack; and the reason I pulled it out was that I didn't want to start talking about the world of community, of common sense, and so on, without giving some sort of scheme that would enable one to tie things together. In that scheme, I think, one does succeed in putting together a lot of things that otherwise would be unrelated. Why isn't he saying anything about personal relations? Why isn't he saying anything about freedom and how does it fit in with institutions? Development, in its conspicuous form, is the development of institutions; but what do institutions mean? They have their meaning from the rest of the setup. It's like Aristotle's definition of the soul. Aristotle has two definitions of the soul, and neither was simply in terms of the soul. What is the soul? It is the *actus primus corporis organici*, and in that case the soul is related to the body. Or the soul is *primum quo vivimus, sentimus, intelligimus*, and then the soul is related to operations. The soul in itself is just an abstraction. It is similar for all the things that I've put down in that scheme of the concrete human good. Another point to it, of course, is to get away from the bias of classicism that doesn't consider the concrete: you get the good when you get the laws all made; and there you have it. The human good *est in rebus; bonum et malum sunt in rebus*. The intelligibility, the fundamental intelligibility, of each of those things in that scheme lies in its relations to the others. The relation of the levels: the particular good, the good of order, terminal values. Cooperations, institutions, personal relations, orientations, habits, operations. It also illustrates the mediation of society and the individual. Again, I didn't mean just intellectual operations when I mentioned operations; it is any operation at all. It is the baby sticking out his hand and putting something in his mouth. There are combinations of three types of development: development of the eye, development of the hand, and development of oral muscles.

Question: Discuss the meaning of freedom in the schema on the human good.

Lonergan: It is the ordinary meaning of the word 'freedom.' Man can do this or that; he can do this or not do it. He can do good or evil; and man is not only a center of capacities and needs, a center of perfectibility, he is a free center. Because he is free he can be orientated one way or another: to the dialectic of decline, the dialectic of sin, or the dialectic of redemption. That is the ultimate choice. And as the individual is orientated, so are his personal relations, and then you have all the implications of these personal relations, like Hegel's celebrated dialectic of the master and slave, Fessard's imitation of that in the Jew who is the child of God in the Old Testament but becomes rejected, while the pagan becomes the Christian. In other words, there are the two potentialities, the potentiality of the good to become sinners and of the sinners to be converted.

1962

Discussion 3[1]

Question: What is the distinction between moral conversion and religious conversion?

Lonergan: There needn't always be a distinction, but there can be. If one ceased to be an Epicurean and became a Stoic, one would undergo a moral conversion. The Stoics had a very elevated morality in terms of the order of the universe. It was taken over by St Thomas and the Catholic tradition. Their moral doctrine was quite distinct from their philosophic doctrine, which was materialist. A religious conversion: it depends on what religion you're talking about. If you're talking about the Catholic religion, you're moving from the natural order to the supernatural order. You're performing supernatural acts; particularly, the supernatural order makes demands that in a way conflict with humanistic ideals. One could be following purely human ideals and be a rationalist, and exclude the very possibility of the supernatural. I don't know if rationalism can be defended, but there could be a case in which one has an intellectual conversion, not be a materialist, and a moral conversion, accept a Stoic morality, and yet not be a Christian or a Catholic.

Question: Why did you add religion as a third category in conversion?

Lonergan: You can have religious conversion without moral conversion. *Fides* need not be *formata*. It can be *fides informis*: 'I'm a good Catholic, but

---

1 Friday 13 July 1962, Lauzon CD/MP3 325 (32500A0E060) and 326 (32600A0E060).

I'm not a fanatic about it; I don't go to Mass on Sunday or eat fish on Friday. I'm not living with my wife. But I'm a good Catholic. I'm not trying to kid myself.' Such a person is a Catholic, but there's a lack of a moral conversion there. And you can have the religious conversion and the moral conversion without the intellectual conversion. You can be holding a doctrine in your philosophy that is equivalent to a naive realism, that when pushed becomes a materialism.

Question: In what sense is God the object of theology?

Lonergan: According to St Thomas God is the *subject* of theology. That difference of subject and object: the subject stands to the habit as the object does to the act. It's rather a subtlety. God is the object of theology, in that God is what theology deals with, principally. St Thomas discusses the question of a Christ-centered theology, and he doesn't accept it. His reason is ultimately that what is significant about Christ is that he's God, and it is divinity that is the mystery: the ultimate object of human intellectual desire and the object in terms of which everything else that theology treats is illuminated.

Question: Where is that in St Thomas?

Lonergan: The first question of the *prima pars*. Just where, I don't know. But he's talking about the object of theology. He discusses the different views of theology at his time. I'm speaking approximately.

Question: The issue for us was how can you study God as an object? That seems to remove the personal element.

Lonergan: That is something that we're coming to. It was at the tail end of this morning's lecture.[2] Max Scheler distinguished different specialized types of knowing: for knowing values, for knowing persons, for knowing realities, for knowing science. They're all separate departments. It is fundamentally from Max Scheler that there is derived this business that God is not an object. If your fundamental intellectual category is not *ens* – it's only by *ens* that you can unify the whole of human knowledge, and Scheler hasn't got that notion of being – the result is that knowledge falls apart into several separate watertight compartments. You know a person by performing with that other person a certain type of operation, working in common with him to a common end. That's how you know a person. And Scheler can use that to develop terrifically personal knowledge.

2 See above, p. 127, note 26.

The special type of activity that brings to light knowledge of values is intentional feeling. Fundamentally, the apprehension of values is a matter of loving or hating. Scheler builds up all apprehension of values in terms of that. Insofar as loving is loving some object, it is the vivid and effective form in which there is an apprehension of a value. And he develops that no end with his phenomenological method. But the fundamental weakness of that approach is illustrated by Scheler himself. When he wrote *Vom Ewigen im Menschen*[3] he wrote as if he were a Catholic, and at the time he was more or less acting and thinking as a Catholic, although he denied later that he ever accepted all these things that the Roman theologians want people to believe. But he dropped his Catholicism entirely in the later years of his life and became fundamentally a dualist. And in his philosophic position there's no reason why he shouldn't.

Now, we have to take advantage of all these new techniques and elements that are added on by phenomenology. Scheler runs parallel to Heidegger in the development of phenomenology, and he's had a terrific influence in Germany, but it has spread out all over, and people who draw this distinction between persons and objects depend ultimately on Scheler in one way or another. They may not accept completely his formulation of it, and then you get a further remove, and they are not even aware of any dependence on Scheler. But it is that type of thinking that leads to those distinctions. If you're knowing an object, you're not knowing a person; and if God is a person, you can't know him as an object.

Now you have to bring in the personal element, of course, but you bring it in objectively: it's by saying what is true that you really know it. If that type of knowing has no meaning for someone, then the intellectual approach has no meaning for him. It becomes a psychological problem. But I'll admit it's a hard case. In other words, if your theology and dogma are in the world of theory, that means there is a real problem of transposition, of communication, of putting it within the range of people who have no tendency in that way at all and for whom it means nothing. That's a real problem, but it isn't solved by making the type of distinction that Scheler made, which just leaves you bankrupt. This doesn't mean someone, to be a Catholic, has to spend three years doing Scholastic philosophy and four doing Scholastic theology. The person who has that training is not going to preach that, because he's not teaching a class when he's preaching. The influence it will have on his dealing with people may be unconscious. I've used twice in the

3 See above, p. 134, note 5.

discussions the difference between the Catholic priest and the Protestant minister. The minister spends all week preparing his sermon. He reads all the latest books. He knows his scriptures very well. He may know the Fathers very well. And he puts everything he has into his sermon. The Catholic priest is teaching catechism in the schools and going to the hospitals and bringing communion to the sick in their homes and taking care of the bingo and bazaars and hearing confessions. On Saturday night at 10 o'clock he's lucky if he has time to look up the Gospel and sketch a few ideas for his sermon the next day. But the Catholic priests all over the world preach the same thing, and the doctrine of the ministers varies from one pulpit to the next, with the latest book they happened to read and the review they happen to be interested in. And what causes the difference? It's the party line drilled into the priests during four years of theology. And they may think they have forgotten all about it and that it means nothing to them, but it gives them an outlook, a fundamental interpretation of the meaning of scripture; and it gives that community the doctrine that makes the unity of the church.

Now, there is that real influence of the theological formation upon priests throughout the world. If you ask most priests what theology means in their practical pastoral life, they'll say, 'Well, we had to go through it, but it's not what counts now at all.' It does count in a way they're quite unaware of. And it counts in a very fundamental and significant fashion. One can turn that over. How does one deal with a person who gets 100 in religion and yet it doesn't mean anything to him? Well, it may be the case of Mortimer Adler, who says, 'Well, according to your own doctrine, according to St Thomas, you have to have a supernatural gift of grace, and knowing all the rational part of this doesn't mean a thing.' But usually it is not that. God's grace is given to everyone. The problem is a little more complicated than that. And there is the problem of communication. But the problem is to be tackled by a person who knows the milieu, knows the mentality of that person, and can pick out the weak spot and make his contribution toward his conversion. But St Paul himself couldn't convert everybody. In the later chapters of Acts, when Paul arrives in Rome, he preaches to them, and St Luke says that some believed and some did not believe, and Paul quoted Isaiah, 'With their eyes they shall see and shall not see and with their ears they shall hear and shall not hear' (see Acts 28.26–27). Many are called and few are chosen. There is a mystery of divine faith there too. But there is the concrete problem. Just as there has been in the past that adaptation, that movement back, spontaneously, almost unconsciously, from theological training to dealing with one's parish, with one's people, with one's pupils, so that can be pushed further and has to be adapted as one meets with new situations. The function of dogmatic theology is to provide the background from which that can be well done. The theologian cannot, unless he's teaching a homogeneous group as in a diocesan seminary, add on the practical applications and the practical ways of going about things. That's as far as I've got with that problem. But it's a real problem, and it's not solved by something like Scheler's specialized types of knowledge. There is a truth there, but it's not a matter of pushing these specialized types of knowledge to the point where you get separate departments. Knowledge of God as a person is also knowledge of God as an object. God is. That's how you know God: knowing the truth of that proposition.

Question: When we look at this problem from the point of view of the various worlds you've illustrated, does that mean that when we study God in theology in the theoretical world this necessarily includes the religious world? Or is it something more profane?

Lonergan: Well, a person can study theology as though it were a profane subject, and a person can study theology and constantly be distracted off to prayer. Insofar as he's being distracted off into prayer, he's moving into the world of the sacred. Insofar as theology is mediating his religion, it's in the world of the sacred. But in itself it's just a matter of learning, an intellectual discipline. Just as a man can be doing all sorts of good works in the community, spending his nights and days, and it's not a mediation of his religion, it's just getting the job done, *effusio ad exteriora*, as it's sometimes called, and on the other hand it can be a mediation towards God, something in the world of the sacred. But the world of the sacred is a further dimension added on to something. And the sacred, the divine, is always mediated. We haven't got immediate knowledge of God in this life.

Question: In the example you gave of the Catholic priest and the Protestant minister, you noted how the Catholic priest has behind him all this theological context. Is this the dogmatic-theological context that you are talking about?

Lonergan: Yes, it is. A Catholic priest has no doubt that Jesus Christ is God. That isn't a problem for him. Insofar as it becomes a problem for him, he's exceptional. For the Protestant minister, the question is agonizing, if he hasn't ruled it out of his consideration. What on earth could it mean? When the ecumenical movement sent to Bultmann their fundamental requirements for anyone to belong to the meeting, they had down there that Jesus

Christ was God, and Bultmann said, 'What on earth do you mean?' It's only a few odd places in the New Testament where it is said that he is God, and you can make objection to those. He's always called 'Lord,' and so you can put down 'Lord,' but that can mean absolutely anything. We know what we mean by faith, but in non-Catholic circles, what is faith? It may be a sentiment – fiduciary faith, and so on; as long as it's irrational, it will be faith.

Question: Is this dogmatic-theological context the *sapientia* about which you were talking?

Lonergan: The context also is a *sapientia*, because a *sapientia* is an ordering of everything, and that context orders things. It is an instance of the *sapientia*. It's what you take for granted when you talk, what you would say if someone asked you what you meant, even though you don't think about it explicitly.

Question: Would the content of revelation be in the world of community?

Lonergan: Yes, fundamentally that is what it was. It was the history of the Jewish people and the promise of the Messiah; and Christ fundamentally is represented in the New Testament as the fulfilment of this hope. There is Vincent Taylor's work and Cullmann's work on the titles of Jesus,[4] and there is development in the whole series of titles up to the point where they speak of Christ as God and try to express his divinity in all sorts of ways. The transition to theory occurs at Nicea, where they are forced to use a language that is not in the New Testament. That language of Nicea is simply a formula that refers back to the New Testament. The real meaning of the *homoousion* is what we have in the Preface, 'Quod enim de tua gloria, revelante te, credimus, hoc de Filio tuo, hoc de Spiritu sancto, sine differentia discretionis sentimus.'[5] The predicates that are given to the Father are also predicates of the Son and also predicates of the Holy Ghost. And where are those predicates? They are what God has revealed about God's glory, the *kabôd Yahweh*. There is nothing that is more scriptural than the glory of God. What we know by faith from revelation about the *kabôd Yahweh* is just as true of the Son as it is of the Father: that's the meaning of the consubstantial. It is a summing up of whatever is said about the Father in scripture, just as the fundamental formulation of the doctrine of Ephesus occurs in the fourth canon of Cyril's chapters against Nestorius; the apostolic and evangelical

---

4 Vincent Taylor, *The Names of Jesus* (New York: St Martin's Press, 1953); Oscar Cullmann, *The Christology of the New Testament*, trans. Shirley C. Guthrie and Charles A.M. Hall (London: SCM Press, 1959).
5 For a translation, see above, p. 26, note 35.

predicates about Christ are to be attributed not to two persons or two subsistents but to one. They're not divided up among two. It's moving to the world of theory by simply talking about the expressions that occur within scripture, within revelation. But by the mere fact that you have moved on and are reflecting back on and using compendious statements with respect to these expressions, you have moved into a world of theory. Or at least you have put the premises from which you are forced into a world of theory. This is the continuous process in every department of human life. It occurs not only in religion, in the Catholic Church; it occurs also in the state, in industry, and all the rest. Men do something, and they ask themselves, What are we up to?

Question: Cardinal Bea has made a statement that the word of God is a living revelation of himself, and that it is difficult to distinguish whether it is something like an eighth sacrament or something in the sacramental area. This causes a special problem for scriptural theologians when you say that scripture studies fall into the realm of objective study and that they're not always an interpersonal relation between the speaking God and the person. Is that an inadequate analogy, or what?

Lonergan: Well, I haven't got a too pure idea of what Cardinal Bea said.

Questioner: The main idea is that God is actually speaking here, just as much as you are speaking to me. This can hardly be anything but a personal relation between God and the individual or the group. How do the scriptural theologians get beyond the actual interpersonal relation so that they are studying scripture objectively?

Lonergan: Scripture can be taken in several ways. Any text can be taken in several ways. You can use the New Testament as a basis for working out a grammar of *koinē* Greek. You can use it as a basis for working out the geographical place names in the first century AD. There are all sorts of viewpoints from which you can study it. The existence of all those possibilities reveals the possibility of an objective studying of scripture. The question of exegesis is a matter of using all these specialized studies regarding the scriptures and their environment, the contemporary literatures and parallel literatures, to throw light upon the meaning of the text. I hope to give attention next week to this business of interpreting a text.[6] It's a rather long affair, and it's being discussed a great deal at the present time, especially in

6   See above, chapter 1962-9.

Germany. But when the meaning of the text is placed in a religious context, when it mediates between the subject and the ultimate, then it's properly religious. But the professor of exegesis doesn't get up and repeat his meditation in front of his class. There's obviously a difference between the two.

Question: At the beginning of the second class, after the summary of the first class, why was the question of the human good introduced? What was its connection with what preceded and what followed?

Lonergan: Well, at the beginning of the second class, we also skipped the division between a first problematic and a second.[7] Moreover, I have two packs of notes equal in size, and one is reproduced on the mimeographed sheets you have in Latin, and the other is something that is not reproduced, that belongs to that second problematic. And I'm throwing in things from the second pile as I give out the first.[8] The reason I threw this in was, first of all, that if I speak about the world of community it might not convey something very precise, very concrete, very meaningful. By putting in the social mediation of the human good, one sees how all these aspects of the life of community are interrelated. It is in terms of such interrelations that each one of the terms has its meaning. Just as the soul was defined by Aristotle, in a definition that has survived two thousand years, by relating the soul to the body and to its operations, so any definition, any intelligent account of anything, is a matter of relating it to other things. That set of relations involved on those three levels ties together or provides a basis for tying together all the fundamental aspects of community. It is a means of expressing what the world of community is. The world of community develops, but it doesn't develop within a closed compartment. It has the movement toward theory, *die Wendung zur Idee*. The community comes to a point where it wants to understand itself and has to understand itself to go on, and you not only have law, but you have the history of law, the philosophy of law, the jurisprudence that lays down the doctrine regarding the law at the present time. And similarly for all other human institutions.

As for its connection with what preceded, we spoke in general of subject, habit, operations, objects. The social mediation of the human good is a matter of operations and cooperation building together into the concrete good of

7 This refers to the structure of Lonergan's course the preceding spring, 'De methodo theologiae.' The relevant material will appear in cwl 23.
8 The two problematics structure the course 'De methodo theologiae' that will occur in volume 23. Lonergan's notes, he is here telling us, have to do with what there he calls the first problematic.

order. So it transposes general talk about operations, which I had illustrated from Piaget's study about children, into the context of ordinary human living towards which the education of children tends, in the context of community.

As for its connection with what followed, the fundamental problem about studying developments is to find some way of classifying them. Now, the development of institutions is one means: the state developed from this to this to this, the law developed from this to this to this, the economy developed from this to this to this, and so on. I offered a general classification of developments through mediation, where 'X is mediated by Y' gives a classification of developments in terms of their interdependences with one another. But one wants a notion of the field within which development occurs, and that's added by the social mediation of the human good.

Question: In the discussion of worlds, what would be the definitions of 'sacred' and of 'profane'? Should these two worlds be separated on principle?

Lonergan: The sacred is what is ultimate. We have no immediate knowledge of God. Therefore, our knowledge of God is all mediate. All desire ultimately is for God, according to St Thomas. Again, God is ultimate. And God is not an object that we can master. The Trobriand Islanders whom Malinowski described in his *Magic, Science and Religion*[9] knew perfectly well what they had to do to get crops sown, reap the harvest, and so on. They were just as commonsense and practical and intelligent and rational about it as anyone else. But the whole thing was penetrated with myth and magic as well. What we would call the profane order was not something distinct from it. That indistinction of the profane and the sacred is something that we cannot get hold of in our modern Western consciousness. Wordsworth would recall it from his childhood. The profane was open to the sacred. There was no distinction between them, and there is no distinction between them in the primitive mind. A spade is never just a spade. Nothing is ever *just* something. You have in Augustine the distinction between *ratio superior* and *inferior*, as it were a reflex formulation of something like that attitude. It's the difference between Bonaventure and Thomas. For Bonaventure, there is no knowledge of the world by itself. It's only analogously that the world is said to be. God is what is, and the function of the world is simply to be a theophany, a manifestation of God. If you don't look at things that way, you're lacking in wisdom. There is no room for philosophy as an *ancilla theologiae*, in the sense

9   Bronislaw Malinowski, *Magic, Science and Religion* (New York: The Free Press, 1948; repr. Westport, CT: Greenwood Press, 1984).

that philosophy teaches you something that is simply true. Philosophy teaches you something true only insofar as philosophy teaches you something that leads you further on to God and makes you know God better. That complete openness of everything to the divine, to the beyond – primitives don't consider it adequately, but they have that openness there.

Similarly, in Jung's study of the collective unconscious, symbols that are fundamental or elementary manifestations are products of undifferentiated consciousness. Symbols are open to the divine in the same way as the experience of the world of the primitive is open to the divine. All symbols are polyvalent. They have many meanings, on many different levels. We have to distinguish between Jung and Eliade's interpretation of Jung's data. I'm giving you Eliade's interpretation; I'll give you Jung later. But Eliade's interpretation of Jung's data is that the unconscious or preconscious processes that are going on without the consent and against the will of the subject when the subject is moving to what Jung calls individuation, that is, individual perfection, are homologous, isomorphic to, parallel to, analogous to the processes that are conceptualized in alchemy. Alchemy was not merely a matter of transmuting base metals into gold. It was also aiming at a transformation of the subject and a domination of the world. Chemistry only represents a very minor portion of alchemy. The higher part of alchemy is represented by the nineteenth-century idea of progress, man's increasing domination over nature. And there's a further dimension of alchemy in the transformation of the subject. You have the same type of parallel to all this in the Hermetic literature. And the alchemists, of course, are not merely fifteenth- and sixteenth-century Europeans; they're found in first- and second-century Egyptian thought, and in China in an earlier period; and Eliade traces it back to primitive blacksmiths and miners. All this is parallel. And the Christian revelation in terms of death and resurrection is the same thing; *anima humana naturaliter christiana.*

That is Eliade's presentation. The field of death and resurrection is found in all sorts of nature religions and in initiation rites, and so on. In Eliade's presentation of it, these things are parallel. For Jung, the real thing is the preconscious process, and the rest is just projection. And what is projection? Projection is imagining you see what's out there when you're merely projecting. 'Projection' is a term that proceeds from naive realism, and if the real is what you know when you know the true, you shift from Jung to Eliade's presentation, in which these several forms are homologous, and, as the Christian tradition has it, the *anima humana* is *naturaliter christiana.*

Now the definitions of sacred and profane: the profane is this, the immediate world, that we can dominate and manage, that one can go ahead and do what one wants to do with – I am my own master, and I am free. The whole modern world is created by that attitude. The individualist who does not depend on tradition and revelation – that's the past, but I'm a rational being, I know I'm a rational being, I know what a man can do, the past history of mankind has been determined by men using their own intelligence and their own will, and that's what we're doing. We're creating the modern world. That is in large part what the modern world is. That's the profane world: independence of God to the extent where God is not acknowledged at all; in Nietzsche's words, 'God is dead.' That's the secularization of the world, the elimination of the sacred.

The definition is in terms of what is attained in human operations adequately, the proper object of human intellect and activity, and on the other hand, what is always beyond, what man never properly grasps, and that is the divine. It's a definition that is based on the capacities of the subject, upon a division in consciousness between the two.

Should the two be distinguished in principle? Well, the two are distinguished as a matter of fact, and we have to accept the facts. Whether it would be good for things to be otherwise is a utopian question because we can't change the facts. But all progress, all development is a matter of differentiation and integration. One may say it must have been very fine to be a primitive when everything was open to the divine, but it not only meant the sacralization of everything profane but also the secularization of everything sacred. Christopher Dawson made the remark that the characteristic point of Christianity was that it took sex out of religion. Sex is not an intrinsic or prominent part of Christianity, but it is in other religions. That's a case where you're preventing the secularization of the sacred. Development is by differentiation and integration. The development has occurred. We can't change it. Our task is not to attempt to revert to the original indifferentiation but to integrate the two that have been differentiated, neither to eliminate the profane nor to profanate the sacred, nor on the other hand to eliminate the sacred and to secularize it. It's a matter of alternation between one and the other. The two don't mix easily. St Teresa was able to be in a high mystical state and carry on all sorts of practical activities at the same time, but she felt herself cut in two, a sort of mystical schizophrenia.

Question:[10] Why have you decided on these four worlds as describing the whole situation? What is the basis of your choosing these?

---

10   The discussion continues on Lauzon CD/MP3 326 (32600A0E060).

Lonergan: The distinction between the world of theory and the world of common sense is the different structure of consciousness that is had in ordinary living and in the intellectual pattern of experience. In the intellectual pattern of experience, a man is like Thales; he's the absentminded professor, and the absentmindedness is just an external characteristic, it's nonsense unless he's really doing something. But a man in the intellectual pattern of experience is dominated by purely intellectual concerns and criteria. He's out of this world, in the ordinary sense of the expression. When Newton was working out his theory of gravitation, he had a terrific state of concentration that went on over a long period, and he'd barely bother eating his meals. Or when Thales was looking at the stars and didn't see the well at his feet and tumbled into it: that is either a myth or a fact, but it expresses that differentiation of consciousness.

Secondly, the difference between the inner and the outer is founded on the opposition between subject and object. There's no consciousness without an object and an operation with respect to the object. But the object isn't present to anyone, there's nobody home, unless the subject is also present to himself at the same time and in a different sense of the word 'presence.' That opposition is ineluctable. It is just as ultimate as the difference between the two patterns of consciousness, between science and common sense.

Finally, there is the opposition between what everyone can master by his operations and what is always beyond his reach, and that's the basis of the sacred and profane.

Piaget thought of development as operations becoming differentiated, combinations of differentiated operations, grouping of the totality of combinations of differentiated operations, and then grouping of groups. But that doesn't go on smoothly. It runs into ultimate radical antitheses between subject and object, theory and common sense, sacred and profane. And when any type of analysis runs into a brick wall, you can capitalize on that and use it as a basis of setting up a new way of analyzing or describing this process of development. I've attempted to do that through the mediation of the subject.

Question: Do you regard that list as exhaustive?
Lonergan: No, I don't say they're exhaustive. They're three that are clear to me at the present time.

Question: You were talking about the separation of the profane and the sacred and of integrating through the back-and-forth between the two.

This seems to exclude what we're told to do, to bring Christ into the world, to bring the sacred into the practical level following the principle of the Incarnation.

Lonergan: I'm not saying that one cannot do an awful lot of interpenetrating. But at least going by ordinary experience, there's quite a difference between one's state of consciousness, one's operations, when one's saying Mass, or reciting one's breviary, or making one's meditation, or saying one's beads, and, on the other hand, when one's eating one's meals, chatting with one's friends, however much one wants to bring Christ into the world. De facto, that difference is there. Now one can have the one pouring over into the other more and more and more, and the greater the sanctity the more that occurs. But at least there is the fundamental problem, and the simplest form of integration is oscillation: at least one can do that. What I propose is that at least we start from the ordinary facts, and if we can we move on further. I don't want to discourage anyone!

Question: Is this the problem of integration you're talking about later, with regard to the old Greek idea of science and the modern? Or is that an integration of objects?

Lonergan: Integration is as diverse as the things to be integrated, put together. Just as development involves endless types of differentiation, so the problem of integration is just as manifold and diverse as are the different forms of differentiation. But this is a fundamental problem of integration. In other words, Greek science and modern science both are in the intellectual pattern of experience. The reason why I insist on this is because there has been in recent years, since the Second World War, a continuous clamor demanding from theologians that they do what no scientific doctrine can possibly do. They want a theology that integrates the world of interiority, the world of community, and the dogmas of the church and the doctrine of St Thomas Aquinas. My answer is that it's not going to be done. They are asking something that is not done by fixing some unification either in the world of theory or in the world of community or in the world of interiority. There are ultimate limitations to the human spirit, and we have to face them and take them into account and build up on the basis of those limitations. Once the limitations are recognized, one can endeavor to bring Christ into the whole of one's life as much as one can and live in the perpetual presence of God. But that's something to be achieved. It's not something that you expect a schoolmaster to hand out to all his pupils and have them pass an examination on.

Question: Is this problem of integration the problem that Teilhard de Chardin was working on in *The Divine Milieu?* In particular, the integration of religion and science, bringing religion into the scientific world in a meaningful way.

Lonergan: I'd say that what is legitimate in the work of Teilhard de Chardin, insofar as it's legitimate, is the legitimacy of limited objectives. The fundamental problem at the present time is that there are all sorts of people who are at the peak of human culture in scientific fields and at the same time their ideas on religion are most elementary. Teilhard's achievement was that he was able to talk religion to people who felt the need of it, or maybe didn't feel the need of it but at least were helped enormously by him, even if they didn't come the whole way to the church. I think such limited objectives are legitimate, and a good work at the present time. But if one tries to say that what's essential to Catholic truth is contained within these limited objectives, then one is wrong.

Question: There is a difficulty of integrating everything objectively in theological science.

Lonergan: What I do say is that when you do perform such an integration, you're integrating everything insofar as it's an object of a theoretical subject.

Question: So it is the subject who is not integrated. The science is integrated.

Lonergan: Yes.

Question: What is the relation of the discussion of worlds to theology and to theological method?

Lonergan: Theology as a science is within the world of theory. Its relation to theological method is that theory has to be mediated by the subject, if you're going to get your fundamental concepts and your fundamental operations clear, if you're going to eliminate from them in something like a methodical order or in a regular fashion the influence of horizon – it means nothing to me, therefore let's forget about it – and the influence of a lack of conversion. As I say in the introduction to *Insight*, the problem is not to enunciate the true propositions. The problem is to prevent the true propositions all being misinterpreted. It's a problem fundamentally of a lack of conversion, and when the problem of a lack of conversion combines with horizon and is pushed a little further, you get problems of authenticity.

They're the fundamental problems. They're the sort of thing that make people say, 'Well, look at theology. It's just a mass of disputed questions. If we just learn what's down in Denzinger and what's *de fide definita* and listen to the Holy Office when they tell us something more that's connected with it, we have all the theology that counts. What's the use of the rest? Why spend four years at that?' It's a problem for a lot of people. At the same time, unless theology clears up this attitude, it cannot deal effectively with the continuous mass of material that's constantly being poured upon the dogmatic theologian. A specialist in St Paul can't read all the contemporary literature on St Paul. The dogmatic theologian can't read all the contemporary literature not only on St Paul but on St John, on the Synoptics, on the Old Testament, on the apostolic Fathers and the apologists and the Greek Fathers and the Latin Fathers and the councils and the heretics and the Scholastics, and so forth. One department in which you know just where they stand is Patristic studies. You have Altaner.[11] There isn't a comparable book either for scripture studies or for medieval studies. But the first thirty-seven pages of Altaner give you indications of the different fields that are being studied and the fundamental works in those fields. And with every Father he mentions he gives you a few pages of bibliography from different viewpoints. What is the dogmatic theologian to do about all that? If we are to handle that mass of material in any fashion, we have to know precisely what we're doing. And we have to eliminate the disputed questions, or if different people have different views on where the disputed questions are going to be eliminated, at least we have to make some sort of a stab at that. It's nearly two centuries since Kant wrote on the possibility of philosophy as a science, and we have to face the fact of the possibility of theology as a science if we're not going to be pushed against the wall and have the magisterium simply take over.

Question: When you speak of the possibility of theology as a science, do you mean this great mass of material?
Lonergan: Yes, and the fact that it's very hard to know what you can do about it. Take the Gregorian, where we have a limited number of people teaching dogma and ever so many more teaching this and that and that and that and that – all things under the sun, and they're all good. History of religions: an expert spends his life studying Chinese religion and Chinese

11 Berthold Altaner, *Patrologie: Leben, Schriften und Lehre der Kirchenväter* (Freiburg: Verlag Herder, 1958); in English, *Patrology*, trans. Hilda C. Graef (Freiburg: Herder, and Edinburgh, London: Nelson, 1960).

history. He comes in and does his course. Another man knows about 200 dialects of tribes in Central Africa, and he comes in and does his course. And so on. Another on India, another on the Gnostics and the relation of that to the early Greek Fathers of the first three centuries. All sorts of things – liturgy, missiology, all sorts of scripture. The students are reading all sorts of periodicals and books. They don't read them all, but when you have 1700 students in your theological faculty, they cover an awful lot of ground, more ground than 50 professors can. Well, how do you put all of this together? It's all very well to dump this out on them, but how do they put it together if the professors can't put it together? That's the second stage of the problem. The third stage of the problem is, Well, what do we agree on apart from the things that are *de fide definita*? Very little. The closer things are to *de fide definita*, the more the agreement, and the further away, the less. That is not carried on the way the scientists do. A new scientific theory comes out. It may be necessary to wait until the present generation of professors resigns before you're going to get unanimity among scientists, but when they do resign you get it. Theological problems keep on going for centuries. It makes no difference how many generations die off. It would be more like science if you got agreement when the older professors died off. But is there any reason why we should hope for that at the present time in light of our past experience? There isn't unless we get down to the study of the method of theology. What are the roots of the thing? Existentialism has a brutal way of approaching things. This idea of authenticity is just about as crude and blunt an instrument as you can want. But if they do it, if the philosophers do it, it may be what we need too.

Question: If you had a group studying theology with a method of theology and with this type of commitment to the intellectual process that you describe, do you feel that these problems would be solved?
Lonergan: I think an awful lot of them can be cleared up.

Question: And your blunt instrument?
Lonergan: Ultimately, it's that. At least a lot of the questions could be eliminated. For example, when the theologian asks himself about the question of the *constitutio* of the hypostatic union, that question has different meanings for different groups, and there's no awareness of that as far as one can see. To have a method that would lead to settling on one meaning of that question would clarify the question and put an end to the perpetual repetition of all the existing theories – and if anyone makes a new contribution to

the subject, it's just another theory. One isn't advancing by doing that. And we've reached the point where people are disgusted. That isn't science, and it doesn't help, and they have an awful lot to say.

Question: In the treatment of the integration of worlds, do you criticize some of the modes of integration as an ideal? Are these modes listed in an ascending order of importance?

Lonergan: Integration by elimination is not an ideal. It's dodging the issue – the journalistic world, the combination of the visible universe, the world of common sense, and the profane. Then the simplification, a schematic notion of Brahmanism, on the one hand, integration of the intelligible world, the world of the subject, and the world of the sacred, and on the other hand, as Atman, the absolute subject, and again the integration of the profane, the objective, and the world of common sense, which is the world of appearance. Those are not integrations. Just as in the primitive all worlds are undifferentiated, just as primitive consciousness is undifferentiated consciousness, so when the differentiation arises, you have to bring together the different elements. To eliminate any one of them is not to integrate. The integration is the most analogous of all possible terms, because differentiations are endless. But insofar as there are the radical antitheses, the initial fundamental solution is oscillation. There's a time for everything. You don't make an 8-day retreat for 365 days of the year. You take some time for a retreat, 8 days. For 357 you're doing something else. You don't meditate all day. You meditate for so much time in the morning. And so on and so forth. That's the normal solution.

Question: When you mentioned transposition and sublimation you moved into Christian charity. I don't understand how you did this.

Lonergan: In the other three, fear is significant. The object of fear is overcome: St George and the Dragon. The object of fear is euphemized: Jonah goes down into the whale's belly and is no worse for it. It may be unpleasant for the three days he's there, but afterwards he's just as good as ever. And alternation from one to the other, as in any synthetic symbol, of which the best known is the Tao. In all cases, the fear remains. It's either mastered or euphemized, or you switch from one to the other. But *caritas foras expellit timorem*. The only evil is the evil of sin. Still, there is that, and one can ask oneself whether one is in charity. The problem arises in another dimension, in the dimension of one's personal relations with God and one's neighbor.

Question: It's a new problem of integration.

Lonergan: Yes, you eliminate the old problem of fear, but you have a new problem on a different level, the problem of charity. Do I really love God? Do I really love my neighbor as myself? It's not what I'm going to do about what I'm afraid of. The problem is changed; it's raised to a higher level; but there's still a problem. That's transposition.

Question: In the phrase 'accedit quae dicitur conscientia historica,' what is the meaning of 'conscientia historica'?[12]

Lonergan: It's a crackerjack. It's the transition from substance to subject, from man conceived as what is common to St Thomas Aquinas and a lunatic, what is common to Einstein and a drunk, to man conceived as an empirically, intelligently, rationally, morally conscious subject, man as he is when he's at least dreaming, and particularly man as he is at his best moments. Secondly, once you've made the step from substance to subject, the *esse intentionale* assumes an enormous importance. It presupposes the *esse naturale* of man. Still, as soon as you ask what kind of a man he is, you enter into the order of what he thinks, what he understands, what he considers true, what he chooses, what he proposes, what his intentions are, what his goals in life are. That's all within the psychological-intentional order. And it is that psychological-intentional order that settles our eternal destiny when we appear before the tribunal of Christ to be judged each according to his works – it's not the metabolism of our cells that we'll be judged on, or anything else that pertains solely to the *esse naturale*, it's the *esse intentionale* of our acts of knowing and willing. Not only that, though. Further, Cassirer says that man from the viewpoint of a phenomenology of culture may be defined as a symbolic animal.[13] Georges Morel, in his *Le sens de l'existence*, goes further and says man is a symbol.[14] And to get the point of that, the ultimate meaning of a man's life is often summed

12 'To this is added what is called historical consciousness.' The Latin sentence appeared in the notes that Lonergan distributed, and will be found in the material on the course 'De methodo theologiae' in CWL 23, with a translation by Michael G. Shields.

13 Elsewhere Lonergan refers in this context to Ernst Cassirer, *An Essay on Man: An Introduction to a Philosophy of Human Culture* (see above, p. 58, note 5). See Bernard Lonergan, *Topics in Education* (see above, p. 5, note 6) 78 note 82.

14 Georges Morel, *Le Sens de l'existence selon s. Jean de la Croix* (Paris: Aubier, 1960–61), vol. 3: 39. See a fuller quotation in Bernard Lonergan, *Philosophical and Theological Papers 1958–1964* (see above, p. 55, note 26) 101, note 11.

up in a gesture. Christ dying on the cross is a tremendous act of meaning, and it's the meaning of his life, Christ dying and rising. It's the meaning he has with this world, the world in which we have to turn from sin to God. Not only is meaning something that's formally constitutive of human living, but meaning develops. History is history of the development of meanings and orders that are constituted by meanings. The human family is a Christian family or a Roman family or whatever kind of family it is in virtue of meanings. Meaning constitutes human order. Law, the state, society, the economy all are what they are in virtue of meaning, and these meanings develop. As the meanings develop, the human orders develop. Historical consciousness is understanding man, human reality, in terms of the historical development of meanings. When one apprehends man through historical consciousness, one suddenly becomes aware of the significance of divine revelation, which is a meaning transforming all other meanings, and it grounds an order, the mystical body of Christ, to transform all other orders. Historical consciousness is something that has developed out of German romanticism and German idealism and various types of historical study. It has been batted around in various ways, and it is something new, it's the novelty of modernity. It is the source of all our fundamental problems in theology. We spoke of the mass of material by which the theologian is assailed. Its fundamental source is that development of historical consciousness.

Question: One of the things that keeps coming up along these lines – for instance, in the United States we have had a large group of intellectuals join Islam. For them the development of historical consciousness has led to the fact that Islam itself is the great saving order of man. Why is it necessarily so that historical consciousness will naturally lead to the mystical body of Christ?
Lonergan: I don't say it will naturally lead there. I say that when you grasp what is meant by historical consciousness, you see that revelation is not just more talk, that it is something that enters into the constitution of human living, if meaning enters into the constitution of human living, because revelation is a meaning. If human living occurs within orders and the mystical body is a transformation of all other orders, again you see the significance of the Catholic religion. The advantage of Islam is that it doesn't involve you in the supernatural, which is hard for human pride.

Question: Is theology a sacred or profane science? In this context, what is the implication of the sentence on p. 19 of the notes, 'Theologus e contra ita est subiectum theoreticum, ita mundo intelligibili inhaeret, ita normas scientificas in omnibus observat ut mundanam quandam sapientiam quaerere videatur?'[15]

Lonergan: 'Ut videatur,' 'he seems to be.' In other words we're dealing with an objection. 'Let's get over all disputing, all this proving theses, and get a theology that gets down on its knees and prays. That's a real theology.' Well, it isn't. The Catholic religion not only transformed the world of community and the world of interiority. It has assumed the mission of transforming the world of theory as well. And if it's attempting to do that, you mustn't be a phony and try to pass something else off in place of it. You have to meet theoretical exigences. Just as taking care of the sick can be directed to God, so also can science, and particularly the science that regards God. But in itself, it's performing operations that are *quoad modum* supernatural in that they presuppose the truths of faith. But there's a conception of theology as proceeding from the principle 'Faith which is aided by reason,' where reason comes along and adds further conclusions to the faith. I do not believe that on that basis one can have any adequate conception of theology. According to the Vatican Council, *ratio per fidem illustrata*, a transformed reason, is what reaches the understanding of the mysteries. In other words, the knowledge of faith is above natural human knowledge, but both the knowledge of faith and natural human knowledge occur within the human intellect, and they have to be integrated by and in human intellect. That integration is the work, not of faith alone, not of reason alone, but of a transformed human reason, a *ratio per fidem illustrata*.

Question: Must one have faith to study theology?
Lonergan: I don't know much about these 'must' questions. They belong to the world of a deductivism, where you settle what must be. Any judgments I can make are true as a matter of fact. I'm not able to demonstrate a priori or a simultaneo the existence of God, and similarly with all my other judgments. They depend on matters of fact. There is an element of experiential objectivity in them. I think it is true that if one hasn't got faith, one won't bother one's head about studying theology. One won't take it very seriously. One can be interested in it as a curiosity, just as one can be interested in Brahmanism from a detached viewpoint. And one can do it historically.

15 'The theologian, on the other hand, as a theoretic subject is so deeply immersed in the intelligible world and so observant of scientific norms in everything that he seems to be seeking a worldly wisdom.' Translation by Michael G. Shields, to appear in CWL 23.

There's nothing to prevent a non-Catholic from going to work and writing an intelligent book on the evolution of Catholic dogma or the evolution of Catholic theology. A priori and per se there's no difficulty to it. But the work he does will differ radically from the work of a Catholic theologian, simply because he's not existentially involved. And insofar as he's existentially involved, he's against it. The fact that he is against it existentially will show up in his work. In general, as soon as one moves from the level of natural science to human science, philosophy, or theology, existential involvement starts. It means something to me. It demands me being different from what I am. It's a thorn in the flesh. You haven't got the same detachment about it that you have about the electrons.

Question: Could one come by reason alone, without faith, to the conclusion that Christ is God?
Lonergan: I don't think so. It isn't a conclusion. It is an act specified by a supernatural object. And an act with respect to a supernatural object is a supernatural act. And a supernatural act isn't performed by reason alone. However, Fr Dhanis at the Gregorianum also wants to prove the divinity of Christ in fundamental theology. You can't persuade everyone about everything!

Question: But, going over what you said this morning, by natural theology you come to the conclusion that God can neither deceive nor be deceived. Then historically, this man did things that are beyond the powers of nature. He raised the dead to life. This man said that he was God. Could one possibly draw the conclusion that he must be, without grace?
Lonergan: The conclusion he can draw is: I can and ought to believe that he is God. He's accurate. And if he draws that conclusion, what follows from what 'I can and ought to believe'? I will to do what I can and ought to do. When he makes that act of will, there's the *imperium* for the assent of intellect, and then he believes that Christ is God. And from the moment at which, in the reflective act of understanding, he has grasped the sufficient evidence for affirming that he can and ought to believe a mystery, he foresees necessarily what it heads to. Supernatural grace, the light of faith, enters into the occurrence of that reflective act of understanding. That's the point where the supernatural enters in necessarily; de facto it will enter in before that to eliminate other objections and difficulties, blocks that occur along the way. But that's the point where the supernatural specification of acts begins, in my opinion.

Question: If you're familiar with Billy Graham's method of asking for a decision, would you comment on that? Is that an act of faith, or what is it?
Lonergan: It depends on the object he presents and the way it's understood by the individual.

Question: He asks them to make a decision for Christ, and all they have to do is march forward.
Lonergan: Well, it's the type of concrete fact that's extremely difficult to analyze and can vary from one individual to the next. It can be anything from an intense psychological experience to a genuine supernatural act. I don't think the theologian can do more than give general principles.

Question: Speaking about positing the act of judgment as being a responsibility or a commitment, does this necessarily mean that an act of the will follows it?
Lonergan: Only when the judgment is a judgment of value. Then the act of the will doesn't necessarily follow. It follows freely.

Question: And that's why a man like Mortimer Adler can come up to an act of judgment with regard to the Catholic faith and not take the next step.
Lonergan: Yes, if what's lacking is good will. But ususaly what is lacking is not the naked act of good will. One sees things coming from a long way off. Defense mechanisms don't have to thought out. The key thing is to see through them.

Question: Suppose you have a person studying, and he makes the judgment, 'Christ is God,' if he is an integrated or converted person in the sense of authentic, this for him would be faith, wouldn't it?
Lonergan: Yes. And the analysis is something different from what people are conscious of.

Question: If the ancient concept of science is that it was of the universal and abstract and necessary, and if there was no science of the singular, the concrete, and the *per accidens*, and if on the other hand the modern concept of science is that it can be of the singular and concrete and *per accidens*, how can the modern affirmation be integrated in the face of the ancient denial?
Lonergan: You have to select what is true in the ancient affirmation insofar as it is true, and show how the further affirmations also are true. One truth doesn't contradict another. The intelligibility that is discovered in

the singular is not understanding the singular as a material singular but on the other hand it is not an understanding that says, 'Let's forget about anything singular and stay with universal concepts.' Besides the universal concept there is the scheme that combines with the universal concept an act of understanding and an image, or an image of a series. When you get these images of a series mediated by acts of understanding and terminating in concepts – for example, supposing there is an evolution of every living thing in this world, and one understood in all its details just how that evolution took place, one would have an act of understanding in which de facto was verified an intelligibility that could be other than de facto it is. That would be science in the modern sense of the word 'science' and it would be understanding particulars. One can say it is possible to have another world in which exactly the same course of evolution took place through the same *per accidens*, and it could be, but to know whether there is or not, you'd have to do a tour of exploration of the material universe. By considering that possibility, one saves the truth of the statement that by understanding one doesn't understand the singularity of the singular. But that is acknowledging an intelligibility in the particular that is not acknowledged at all or taken into account by people who insist that science is of the universal and we must attend to universal concepts and pay no attention to imaginative schemes. In other words, when I set forth this ancient ideal of science, I said I was talking about what stuck out like a thumb in reading Aristotle and what everyone is ready to grant Aristotle holds. There are all sorts of qualifying remarks you can make by reading Aristotle more thoroughly, and there are some points on which you have to argue strenuously to show what Aristotle really meant. There's an awful lot of stuff in Aristotle that doesn't fit in with the average acceptance of the word 'Aristotelian.' I believe that modern science can be integrated with Aristotle, but it can't be integrated with popular or semipopular or commonly accepted views of what Aristotle held.

1962

Discussion 4[1]

Question: What is the relationship between freedom and the act of faith? Where does freedom come in the act of faith? Where do you place the freedom of the act of faith? Given the perception of the motives of credibility and credendity, how is it possible *not* to make the act of faith?

Lonergan: With regard to the freedom of the act of faith, one can distinguish between a freedom *in causa* and an essential freedom. The freedom *in causa*: a man chooses to go to a Catholic university instead of to a secular university, or vice versa; and implicit in that choice are the influences he will undergo during his whole university course. Each element is not singled out explicitly, the object of a free act; still, by making that decision with regard to his education, he opens himself to one type, series, set of influences, and by choosing the other to another set. There is a freedom *in causa* there. It is something distinct from the freedom exercised in each particular act.

With regard to the act of faith, what makes the main difference between believers, Catholics, and non-Catholics is largely that freedom *in causa*. Newman, at the end of something like ten or fifteen years, progressed from the position in which he had some sort of intellectual conviction that the Catholic Church was true, when he had his suspicions with regard to the Donatist movement, to a final acceptance of the Catholic faith. He required that long period to recreate his own mentality, to break the assumptions, the associations, and so on, that had come to him with his education, with the

1 Monday, 18 July 1962, Lauzon CD/MP3 327 (32700A0E060).

tradition in which he had been brought up and make a complete turnover. The ultimate decision was free, but the process also was free. He kept concerning himself with these religious questions; he kept his mind on the job.

In *The Screwtape Letters* Screwtape is advising the young and inexperienced devil how to handle these people who start to become interested in religion. He told them that one of his subjects was once in the British Museum reading a book and getting the idea that there might be something to this business of religion, and he didn't disturb him. He let him read on. Finally, when the time came, the man took out his watch and looked at it. It was time for lunch, and the man went out of the Museum and into the bright sunlit air, and he saw a glorious red double-decker bus going by, and the newspaper boy came up to him and said, 'Paper sir'; and he got back his sense of reality. He forgot all about this religion. In the mere fact that one keeps interested in a question on religion until one comes to the point where one is to make the act of faith, one is exercising one's freedom all along the line. One is maintaining one's interest, one is reading the further books, one is asking the further questions and gradually finding answers to them. It is that freedom *in causa* that by and large makes the conspicuous difference between converts and non-converts, and again between Catholics who have doubts and overcome them and Catholics who have doubts and don't overcome them.

On the other hand, there is an essential freedom in the act of faith itself. We said that there is a preamble: the reflective act of understanding that grasps an unconditioned, a virtually unconditioned; I can and I ought to will to believe that the mysteries are true, or that what the Catholic Church asserts is true. From the reflective act of understanding, there follows the judgment of possibility and value. Now that is not the infinite good, good from absolutely every respect; it does not necessitate the will. A man can see that the one rational thing he can do is to become a Catholic; but he isn't necessarily rational; men can sin. You can't prove an act of will. Suppose you have all the antecedents of the act of will and the act of will itself. This does not mean Q follows from P. Q follows from P if the will is rational – one can say that. But the human will is not necessarily rational; man is not impeccable. At least, there is that element of freedom.

There is a further element of freedom insofar as that judgment of value does not present the infinite good to the will. Does that meet the question?

Question: Does the act of faith follow upon the act of will?
Lonergan: Yes. I will to believe the mysteries. That is the *imperium* of the assent of faith. The assent of faith is not essentially free, it is denominatively

free, it is an act in the intellect. The act that is essentially free is the act in the will.

Question: Where does supernatural grace necessarily come in?
Lonergan: The reflective act of understanding, because its object includes the mysteries. The preambles de facto head towards the mysteries in this order. But one could have the same preambles when the revelation merely made natural truths accessible to all.

Question: What about accepting something that is not a mystery, a natural truth revealed by God?
Lonergan: You're dealing either with a man who knows the truth or with a man who doesn't know the truth. If you follow Suarez, you'll say it could be both *scitum et creditum*, and if you follow St Thomas, you'll say it couldn't.

Question: Do the credibility and credendity judgments and the supernatural feature in such an act?
Lonergan: Not if the object is natural. It is because the formal object, the object of the act, is supernatural, a truth beyond the human realm, that we appeal to the authority of God, the science of God, *as we don't know it.* Insofar as we appeal to God's knowledge insofar as we know it, we are within the field of naturally known truth and naturally knowable truth. But the mysteries are what cannot be known without revelation. It is an extension of the field of truth, and the ultimate basis of that extension cannot be something within the field. The mysteries by their very nature exceed the created intellect.

Question: Don't you admit the *obiectum formale quo* is supernatural?
Lonergan: By the *formale quo* you mean the motive. The motive is supernatural, but you know it is supernatural because the *formale quod* is supernatural.

Question: I'm thinking of a case where the *formale quod* is not supernatural. Can you not have a supernatural *formale quo*?
Lonergan: You can. It's a one-package deal. For example, by one act of faith we believe all that God has revealed, which includes both the mysteries we can't know naturally and certain truths that are not universally accessible, though they could be known naturally. If there is nothing supernatural in the *formale quod*, why should you say that the *formale quo* is supernatural? It's an abstract possibility, but the abstract possibility of things being that way is not a reason for saying that it must be that way.

Question: Did you not say God does give the light of faith to those who can't easily understand natural truths?

Lonergan: No, I was speaking of the object of faith, saying that revelation is necessary that the truths of salvation be known. There are in the actual object of revelation both natural truths and supernatural truths. The *obiectum formale quod* is the *verum formale*, and the particular propositions, particular truths, are the *obiectum materiale*. That *formale obiectum* is *formale quod*, the *verum*, and why is it true? Because God knows. And it's God knowing something that is beyond what we know of God by analogy.

Question: What is the *formale quod* again?

Lonergan: The *formale quod* is *verum*. The *formale quo* is the motive, God knowing and revealing.

Question: Is that the same whether the material object is natural truth or supernatural truth?

Lonergan: Well, if the material object includes supernatural propositions, the whole thing necessarily is involved in the supernatural order. There is an *illuminatio intellectus*, and that is something distinct, supernatural, in the intentional order. And there is the *inspiratio voluntatis* with regard to the act of will.

Question: Where do *gratia sanans* and *elevans* fit in?

Lonergan: There is *gratia elevans* in the end, and there is *gratia elevans* with regard to the *praeambula*, the process to this final act, because man cannot long observe the natural law *quoad substantiam* without grace; and in particular because this process is heading towards a supernatural end, you need a superior direction there coming in. The man is directing himself to an unknown objective. Now those graces could theoretically be non-supernatural. However, there is a theological opinion to the effect that de facto in this order all graces are supernatural, *elevans*. There is never a grace that is merely *sanans* and not also *elevans*. That's an opinion.

Question: And that would hold even if the material object were natural truth?

Lonergan: No, not if it were purely natural truth. It's because of the mixture.

Question: Can the *formale quo* be mediated by the world of theory? The precise motive is the personal knowledge of God, which would be in the world of community and interiority. I don't see how theory can mediate that.

Lonergan: Theory doesn't mediate it, except in a person who is theoretical and has theoretical difficulties. Even on the level of *praeambula*. If you're going to convert Rudolf Bultmann, you have to go into the world of theory.

Question: I can see how this motive *quo* is supernatural, which is the authority of God revealing. Now can the authority of God revealing be found in the *praeambula* as an object of natural reason investigating and judging?

Lonergan: The question doesn't arise in the *praeambula* except insofar as you're anticipating the end of the journey. This motive is the motive of the principal act; it's believed along with the object. We believe it is true because God is the first truth. For example, in sight you have the object color, the *obiectum formale quod,* and the motive *formale quo,* light. You see the color because of the light; you don't see any colors in the dark. This 'becauseness' is not part of the object of sight. However, the judgment is an intrinsically rational act, it is *to* the object because of the motive. Now, the whole thing is anticipated when you make the reflective act of understanding. However, a person who is just inquiring is just inquiring. For example, is the New Testament a first-century document or is it a second-century document? You settle that not on whether God can reveal truths that you can understand or not. You may have to appeal to the transcendent authority of God insofar as there are elements in the revelation that you have to say to yourself: well, if God revealed it it's got to be right. But you have to stick to the point if you are to settle whether it is a first- or second-century document. This is faith from the viewpoint of knowledge. Faith is not just that. We're not considering all the aspects of faith.

Question: In what sense is the act of faith its own ground?

Lonergan: In the sense that the motive is believed along with the object; that is a way of expressing it. The assent of faith is to an object because of a motive. It is not like sight which doesn't know that it sees the color because of the light. But the judgment is an act with respect to an object because of the motive.

Question: Doesn't that have overtones of *credimus quia credimus*?

Lonergan: It may seem to, but there are two questions. Faith as such is not my knowing, it's my taking over what someone else knows. I don't know that the mathematical tables are true; I believe they are true. The person that knows is somebody else who made them and checked every step. My believing that the tables are true may be reasonable, but it isn't the same as holding them as true because of my knowledge. Holding them as true because of belief can be rational; its rationality consists in the fact that holding that to be true is a good for my intellect. I know it to be a good for my intellect when I arrive at the judgment of credibility and credendity, which is a judgment of possibility and value. And the rationality of the act of faith lies in the preambles, the reflective act of understanding, the judgment. The rationality of the act of faith, however, is not knowing truth, holding something to be true because I know it is true; that wouldn't be faith at all, or belief. It is holding something to be true because it is reasonable for me to believe that it is true.

Question: By motive you mean ...
Lonergan: Cur? The ultimate reason why it's true, God beyond what we know of God. 'Inter creatorem et creaturam non potest tanta similitudo notari, quin inter eos maior sit dissimilitudo notanda.'[2] God as the ground of the truth of the mysteries is God qua in the *dissimilitudo*, because we can't naturally know the mysteries.

Question: If one makes an act of faith because one judges it is a good thing to hold that these things are true, why is it that some people don't make the act of faith?
Lonergan: It's because they don't see that it's good for them. The rationalists hold that nothing is good for a human intellect except what the human intellect can know. *I* may not be able to know that Einstein's relativity is superior to Newton's mechanics, but some human intellect can. Einstein can. The rationalists will say that it is all right for me to believe that relativity is superior to mechanics, even though I don't see why it should be. I can say that it seems to be a little crazy, but still I can accept it because the truth they are knowing lies within the possibility of a human mind. When you start talking about a truth that lies beyond the possibility of a human mind, what mind are you using when you talk about it? Has truth any meaning in that context? Do you mean anything when you start talking about truths that lie beyond the capacity of the human mind? The rationalists will say, 'Well, it may have a meaning for God or somebody else but it has no meaning for us.' To meet that objection you have to appeal to the fact that just as there is an analogy of *ens* so there is an analogy of truth. There is what is true to us, and what is true for us stands to us just as what is true to God

2 'Any similarity, however great, that is discovered between Creator and creature will always leave a still greater dissimilarity to be discovered' (DB 432, DS 806, ND 320).

stands to God. And God can reveal to us. The rationalists will have some difficulties about that too. Then there is the whole question of the fact that God did reveal; and that happened two thousand years ago. Well, how is one going to know that? They ask an awful lot of questions. They say of these Catholics, 'Well, they are pious people and they do a lot of good, and the Catholic Church is a venerable institution, and so on. But don't try to tell me that there is anything rational about it, that it's a good for human intellect to go in for that sort of thing.'

Question: If a person can convince himself, does the act of faith follow?
Lonergan: Not necessarily. The act of faith is free. He isn't necessarily rational. According to St Thomas, there are many ways to a goal, I know there are many ways to a goal, and my will determines itself with regard to selecting a particular one. There is the contingency of a course of action, the intrinsic contingency, the fact that this is not the infinite good that is presented to the will; that is the positive basis of freedom.

Question: How would this analysis obtain with regard to a seven-year-old?
Lonergan: With regard to a seven-year-old person making an act of faith, perhaps I can say one thing on it. Gadamer, who is a Hegelian, did a fair amount of work writing in *RGG* (a German periodical); in 1960 he put out a book, *Wahrheit und Methode*, about five hundred pages of fine print.[3] He is dealing with the problem of hermeneutics, and he comes out flatly on the inevitability of a tradition. He says that the Enlightenment has its fundamental principle in its prejudgments against all prejudgments. Insofar as the Enlightenment aimed to liquidate the Christian faith and the Catholic Church, it was using a highly efficacious technique, but to generalize that principle or to accept that principle is simply the destruction of any civilization. There is the tradition, and it is through the tradition that one becomes capable of one's culture, one's capacity for philosophy, for understanding the works of the past, for participating in the achievements of the past, and so on. To block out all prejudgment is simply an attempt to liquidate a tradition; it is an irresponsible act.

The seven-year-old in making his act of faith has some apprehension of God. We will come to some more points on the transmission in later lectures. Prior to any written history there is an existential history that is the possibility of the society; for example, if I suffered amnesia I wouldn't know

3 See above, p. 115, note 13, and p. 221.

that I was a priest, or a professor of theology, or that my address in Toronto is 3425 Bayview; I wouldn't know if I was married or not, had any property or not, and so on. I couldn't continue to be myself. Similarly, a society has to have awareness of itself as a society. That is its existential history, and it is transmitted without being noticed. The fundamental transmission of the truths revealed by Jesus Christ is the existential history of the Catholic Church. That's the *signum levatum in gentibus*. It is a tradition two thousand years old. We stand in an entirely different position from the Liberal or the Protestant. The Protestant needs a critical history to show that corruption started at some point: in the Middle Ages, in the Greek Councils, in the step from the *Urgemeinde* to St Paul, or from Jesus to the *Urgemeinde*. They have to find a break somewhere, in order to be themselves; they can't have simply existential history. But in divine providence that's the way the church lives.

I don't know if that says anything towards solving the problem of the seven-year-old child and his act of faith; it is essentially this sort of thing: existential history. His mother is the product of what was founded on the prophets and apostles. The child may apprehend the whole of tradition in his mother and father. They are members of the mystical body. To study the psychology of the seven-year-old child and know how this applies is a highly specialized question.

Question: How can the child make this act?
Lonergan: If he makes the act of faith, it is dependent upon an act of will, and that act of will has a supernatural object, and consequently there is the inspiration of the Holy Ghost acting upon the will. The will has some intellectual presentation of a value, and that presentation of a value includes believing the mysteries, of which the object de facto is supernatural. Consequently, that act is supernatural. Insofar as it is rational it is preceded by some sort of grasp of the sufficiency of the evidence. But the problem becomes specifically a question about the seven-year-old insofar as one asks, 'What precisely has the seven-year-old in mind when he has some apprehension of the sufficiency of the evidence?' The child does not have a horizon that spans two thousand years, and so on. At least we find it hard to think that, no matter what the child may be capable of doing. But the tradition is the continuity of the initial deposit of faith in an existential history. That continuity is something that the historian can study, inadequately, and knows about inadequately. But Catholic faith does not depend upon a knowledge of history in the same way that a Protestant or a Liberal position will have to. They have to claim that at some point there is a corruption in

the tradition. One could turn the thing around and say we have to prove that there isn't. In trying to tackle this problem of the child's act of faith, I would say, 'Collect all the facts one can about the case and understand the case in the light of the facts.' You're working in a vacuum when you want to go from a completely general analysis of the process and apply it to a hypothetical seven-year-old of whom you know nothing except that he is seven years old and his mother told him. His mother probably had a lot to do with it. The sound procedure is to begin from the other end, the empirical end.

Question: You said that with someone who believes supernatural truths, the object of which is supernatural, if he believes because his parents told him to believe, the motive would not be supernatural.

Lonergan: Well, if it's merely that. But if his parents told him to believe it because God said so, it's something different. There is a division between truths that are naturally knowable and truths that are not naturally knowable. If you have a principle that is competent to ground all naturally known truths and is not competent to ground truths that are not naturally knowable, then you have to have a transition to a new order. You have to have a principle that is sufficient to ground that new order somewhere. That principle is not the natural light of human reason; ultimately, that principle is God himself. And that principle comes to us insofar as we have the illumination of intellect and the inspiration of the will by the Holy Ghost. We become attached to that principle.

Question: The intentionality, the type of cognitional act here, is not different from the normal type of act.

Lonergan: There's no difference on the level of understanding. Anything you understand about the supernatural order you understand by analogy with the natural order. But the judgments are with respect to objects that cannot be naturally known. Those judgments are intentional; the judgments of credibility are intentional; the reflective act of understanding is intentional.

Question: Discuss the object of faith as conciliar pronouncements. One has the *fides divina*, what's in scripture, and *fides catholica*, what is taught by the church. There is the distinction between the *fides catholica* and the *doctrina catholica*, what is taught by the church but not taught as a matter of faith. Then there is the speculative theology of St Thomas. Are they all the same?

Lonergan: There are, at least, beginnings of theory that are objects *de fide catholica, de fide definita*. The consubstantiality of the Son: this involves a theoretical element; such a notion has a theoretical element. There is the distinction between person and two natures, two properties, two operations, and two wills in Christ. The supernatural insofar as it is explicit in certain elements in the [First] Vatican Council is a pure theorem arrived at in the course of about a hundred years, between 1130 and 1230 AD. Theologians were stumbling around trying to deal with Augustine, and finally about 1230 AD they caught the point; as grace is above nature, as faith is above reason, as charity is above friendliness, as merit before God is above the esteem of men, so there are two entitative orders which are disproportionate. One is supernatural and the other natural. That was the theorem, and there was an explosion; it was a terrific discovery, and it simply transformed theology and solved countless problems that they had simply been baffled by. This whole thing is described by Landgraf, in the first volume of his *Dogmengeschichte der Frühscholastik*.[4] Now there are those theoretical elements that have entered into what is believed explicitly by the sufficiently informed Catholic. In other words, there is no impossibility of theoretical elements becoming objects of faith, insofar as the church guarantees them. Those theoretical elements are not different truths from those revealed in scripture; they are the same. The same truth admits expression in different contexts. What is expressed in the context of community, of common sense, can also be expressed in the context of theory. There is not just one possible expression of a truth, and so we have continuity.

Insofar as Scholasticism represents a certain type of approach, it represents the transition from the world of community to the world of theory. The authority of St Thomas is something that the church recommends. It has never been thought that all the statements of St Thomas are binding on a Catholic. One simply couldn't say this because St Thomas himself changed; he doesn't say the same thing all the time, all his life long.

Question: How strong is the church's commitment to St Thomas, for example, in *Aeterni Patris*?
Lonergan: That is a difficult question. There is a minimum sense of infallibility that is infallibly defined. The pope speaking *ex cathedra* on matters of faith and morals has the infallibility that Christ wished his church to have. That is defined by the [First] Vatican Council. Most, but not all, theologians say that papal infallibility is not just limited to that, but the further extension is not infallibly defined.

4 See above, p.158, note 4.

Secondly, there seems to be a great reluctance on the part of the central government of the church, to put it vaguely, to state just what is settled for all time and what is settled for these particular issues at this particular time. I think there is no doubt that the pope speaks both ways. If he is addressing a congress of the Italian obstetricians, he is not necessarily announcing truths that hold for everyone at all times, but he wants to tell them something that is important at the time. But if you get into a debate with anyone and state that the pope was just talking in this way, well, the other fellow will want to chop off your head: 'You want to reject what the pope says.' There is a lack of clarity on those issues, and it is very difficult for the theologian to inform the teaching church that a greater clarity is desirable. It is up to the teaching church to give the greater clarity when it sees fit. There certainly are documents that everyone will regard today as superannuated; all you have to do is go back far enough. For example, the letters of Gregory and Alexander condemning Aristotle at the University of Paris: that is not the sort of thing you can quote effectively against someone who is following St Thomas; he will be able to show endless documents in favor of the authority of St Thomas. But those other documents were written by a pope just as much as the later ones. So you have to acknowledge, especially if you go back far enough, that the popes are talking for the good of their own time; they are saying the best thing to be done at this time; though a fuller view of a topic may be possible later on. I think that the Biblical Commission was appointed at the early part of this century simply because they didn't want to involve the Holy Office; they didn't want to give the authority to the Holy Office. They felt that some direction to biblical studies was necessary; but they didn't want to involve the authority of the Holy Office in those directions because they weren't too sure just where things stood. I think there are a lot of elements like that. It is very difficult for a theologian, until a number of centuries have passed, to attempt to clarify the issue; and really, it isn't his business; he isn't the teaching church.

Question: What is the difference between dogmatic theology and biblical theology?

Lonergan: With regard to the comparison between dogmatic theology and biblical theology, it is a topic about which we will have something to say later on. But in general, there are several views on what the biblical theologian should do, held by biblical theologians; that is the first point. Secondly, the one that seems best to me is that the biblical theologian's job is to understand the scriptures from the viewpoint of the mentality of the times; it is fundamentally a type of literary-historical study. However, it is not merely that because faith, I think, comes in a little more than Bishop Descamps recognizes. In an article he wrote for a biblical convention at Louvain about 1957, I think he presses that aspect a little too far.[5] The task of the biblical theologian is to tell us all he can about what is the meaning of each part of the whole of the scriptures, and that is a task that progresses indefinitely. The dogmatic theologian is not concerned to start where the biblical theologian leaves off; the basis of dogmatic theology is not the totality of conclusions of the biblical theologians. The conclusions of the biblical theologian are some less probable, some more probable, some certain, and so on. And the more he presents a synthesis, a rounded view, that is entrancing and effective, and so on, the more likely it is that he tends towards the probable and the certain.

The dogmatic theologian uses scripture the way a doctor uses the report of a patient on his illness. He doesn't attempt to enter into the patient's feelings, and he wants to pick out things that are clear and certain and definitive, and on them he bases his judgment. The dogmatic theologian is content with a minimum that is certain; he won't base his case on one text; he will want to have as many different texts as possible, so that if the exegesis of this text changes, then the biblical theologian won't be tied down to that, he'll be free to let his science develop.

There are two parts: dogmatic theology as something that has already been achieved in the church; and as something to be achieved. There is the past *augmentum intelligentiae, scientiae, sapientiae*, and the main business of the teacher of theology is to communicate that. But as there was development in the past so there is development in the future. And the biblical theologian as getting all he can out of scriptures is the fundamental source of that further development of dogmatic theology. We will attempt to say more about that later on.

Question: Do biblical theologians pertain to the world of theory?
Lonergan: That is a complex question. The fundamental interpretation is commonsense understanding of commonsense understanding. The people who are written about or the people doing the writing in the scriptures are in the world of community, the world of common sense. Common sense is a specialization of human intelligence that deals with the concrete and particular. To know what this concrete and particular common sense of these

5 See above, p. 74, note 16.

people of the past was is a commonsense operation. So the fundamental task of exegesis is in the field of common sense.

However, it too has its *Wendung zur Idee*, and every text isn't something entirely new; the same meanings recur, or slightly different meanings recur. One gets a movement towards distinguishing categories, the genesis of categories, and oppositions, and so on. There starts a reflective process on the job of interpreting. And so you move from a commonsense interpretation of commonsense facts to a scientific presentation of the totality of these commonsense interpretations. When you take that step, you become involved in all sorts of theoretical complexities. Descamps attempts to avoid that further step. But we will have a full session on this problem later on.

1962

Discussion 5[1]

Question: Not all thematization is dogmatic evolution, but all dogmatic evolution is thematization. What would you say to this proposition?

Lonergan: Yes. In other words, there are all sorts of thematizations; every sermon is in fact a thematization of the gospel text that is preached on. It is only insofar as there are a whole series of thematizations involving similar topics that you start getting further questions: How do you reconcile this? The Middle Ages started off with a *glossa* of the scriptures and collections of passages from the Fathers; and when they started to compare them they didn't seem to fit, at first sight. There arose a problem of reconciliation, and their tendency was to find simply a logical reconciliation by drawing distinctions. That is a necessary type of solution. But the idea of introducing the dimension of time into theology is to explain an awful lot of these oppositions; it is not simply a logical reconciliation of concepts and distinctions; it is a matter of explaining the evolution of thought, the development of thought. The genetic process also accounts for a great deal of the apparent oppositions, apart from logical distinctions. Does that meet the question?

Question: With regard to all dogmatic evolution being thematization, what about the Assumption? I don't quite see that it works there.

Lonergan: Well, in the Assumption there is very little in the way of the introduction of new concepts. If one holds that Christ rose from the dead and one

1   17 July 1962, Lauzon CD 328 (32800A0E060).

adds on Mary too, then one is not going beyond the categories of original Christianity; it is finding another application for them.

Question: Is that thematization?
Lonergan: Well, you're stating the thing explicitly, and saying, 'That belongs to the deposit of faith.' You are placing it within the dogmatic-theological context. Insofar as they ask further questions about it, insofar as the definition involves a little more precision than is found in the Gospel narratives about the resurrection of Christ – still, it's not typical of dogmatic evolution.

Question: Is it a move from the world of common sense to the world of theory?
Lonergan: No, not in any notable way. Perhaps insofar as the Resurrection goes beyond the world of common sense too; but it doesn't go beyond the Catholic world of common sense, so to speak.

Question: But in general, dogmas are thematization?
Lonergan: Yes. In other words, the statement covers the general line of dogmatic evolution, and in general dogmatic evolution doesn't reach the level of pure theory. The consubstantiality of the Son is defined, but what you mean by consubstantiality is not defined, except implicitly from the context. 'One person with two natures' is defined, but there are Catholics who have opposed theories about what constitutes the person metaphysically. What is the nature of the hypostatic union? The Church doesn't push right into the systematic theological field, usually, de facto. The church can always pass judgment and say this theory is right and this theory is wrong. The church is not limited; at least no theologian would undertake to limit the church. On the other hand, de facto the tradition has not been to do that. However, if one wants to understand in a general way what the process of dogmatic evolution is and the problem regards the introduction of new concepts and new modes of speech, and so on, then I would say that the dogmatic evolution, in that respect, consists in a thematization, in a process of clarification, a movement towards theory.

Question: Are there degrees of thematization?
Lonergan: The degree of thematization differs in different cases. The fundamental developments are (1) the trinitarian doctrine, in which the key element is the consubstantial; (2) Christological doctrine: one person and two natures; (3) the idea of the supernatural, habit and act. There is then the field in which the categories are not as yet fully developed. For example,

categories as to the instrumental causality of the sacraments; that has to be broadened out. There is also everything regarding history and the mystical body, and the church; all these need further development.

Insofar as there is a movement towards the speculative order, to something distinct from the modes of speech and thought of the New Testament, there is a very clear thematization. To take the instance of the Assumption, in which one states of Our Lady something similar to what was stated of Our Lord with regard to his resurrection, well, there isn't the same newness to the statement that there is to the affirmation that the Son is consubstantial with the Father.

Question: How does the dogma of the Immaculate Conception fit in? Did Scotus make a contribution here?

Lonergan: I think it was a contribution. It set up a common doctrine of a theological school. It exerted historical influence on the matter. But it is very difficult to give a quick evaluation of a process that went on over some 550 years, especially since it is a long time since I taught any thesis on that subject. In the movement towards any dogma, there are the positions, the statements that head on towards the development and add up to it, and the contrary statements; and by the elimination of their weaknesses they shift opinion over to the other side. Scotus's argument was the sort of thing that solved logical difficulties with connection to the Immaculate Conception. The Immaculate Conception is a quite different type of dogma from the Assumption. It presupposes an evolved doctrine on grace and on original sin. It presupposes a prior evolution, although it regards a particular truth with regard to a particular person.

Question: Is what you are presenting a philosophy of theology?

Lonergan: The difficulty with that statement is that in the tradition of the Catholic Church philosophy is conceived as something known by the natural light of reason. It is not thought of existentially. Our methodical account of the nature of theology includes the act of faith, a supernatural act, among its foundations. In other words, our method of theology has as its foundations not only experience, understanding, and judgment in the light of human reason, but also in the light of faith, as made by a member of the body of Christ, a member of the church, under the direction of the church. All those elements enter into our foundations. If you want to call it foundations of theology, fine. If you want to call it philosophy of theology, then you will have to add on a qualification if you don't want to be misunderstood.

The fundamental thing about the analysis is, of course, interiority. Interiority is the field from which you get your foundations, your basic terms, your basic relations. In the cognitional order they are experience, understanding, judgment, not only in the light of personal knowledge but also in the light of belief, and not only belief but also divine faith. Those are the fundamental operations. That provides the ground for your theory; and since all the members of the community are also subjects with an interiority of their own, it provides also foundations for understanding the community.

As for the historical process, one analysis of the human sciences from the German viewpoint of *Geisteswissenschaften* involves the three elements of (1) foundations in any human science, whether it be law, linguistics, art, and so on, (2) history, and (3) doctrine. Studying the history will bring to light the foundations, especially the history of the study of art. And the history as containing immanent norms can be the grounds of a doctrine. We have an interdependence of the three. You will have the foundations or philosophy of law, the history of law, and jurisprudence. Similarly, there's one's aesthetic theory, history of art in different civilizations and cultures, and so on, and perhaps a doctrine on art or a theory of art, etc., etc. And this can be applied to our study. You can study the history of dogma, the development of dogma, in such a way that you bring to light the foundations as the thing develops. This is the way de facto historically they arose.

But you have to avoid the difficulties that Duméry is in. Duméry, an extremely brilliant person, within a few years published first of all *Le problême de Dieu en philosophie de la religion*[2] – a small, thin book, but the notions are right out clear; *Critique et religion*,[3] a rather large book on the relations between criticism and religion; and *Philosophie de la religion*, two volumes, at least that I have seen.[4] And the lot went on the Index promptly, and the Holy Office wondered how on earth he ever got an *imprimatur*. His idea, fundamentally, was that dogmatic theology was just a cookbook for getting people into heaven; it is a practical science. The dogmatic theologians don't attempt any criticism of the Catholic religion or any critical evaluation of the symbols, the

---

2 Henry Duméry, *Le problême de Dieu en philosophie de la religion: Examen critique de la catégorie d'absolu et du schème de transcendance* (Bruges: Desclée, 1957); in English, *The Problem of God in Philosophy of Religion: A Critical Examination of the Category of the Absolute and the Scheme of Transcendence*, trans. Charles Courtney (Evanston, IL: Northwestern University Press, 1964).

3 Henry Duméry, *Critique et religion: Problèmes de méthode en philosophie de la religion* (Paris: Societé de l'édition d'enseignement supérieur, 1957).

4 Henry Duméry, *Philosophie de la religion: Essai sur la signification du christianisme*, 2 vols. (Paris: Presses Universitaires de France, 1957).

rites, and so on, on which the Catholic religion lives. There is a need for a philosophic criticism of the religions to evaluate them: you presuppose the end that the religions are aiming at, but you evaluate the means they employ and consider whether they are conducive to the end or not. This criticism is conducted on a purely philosophic basis. The philosophic basis is Husserl; he added on a fourth reduction to Husserl's three. There is the eidetic reduction, going to the essence as conceived by Husserl: not an essence in the sense of what you know by insight but more or less knowing the meaning of the universal. Husserl is concerned to find for science foundations that are absolutely necessary. And the idea of the reduction is to clear away the chaff so that finally you will be left with what is absolutely necessary. The eidetic reduction goes from the particular, the contingent, to the essence. There is, secondly, the phenomenological reduction; you get rid of the natural attitude in which you think that everything about you is real; you just drop all that. At the same time, you drop all questions of existence, because existence is contingent. The third reduction is the transcendental reduction; you reduce all objects to the subject. You explain all objects as products of the subject. Duméry added on what he called a fourth reduction, the henological reduction, a reduction that is connected with the *hen*. It is under the influence of Plotinus, ultimately. The One is first; and what you know about the One is that it is beyond any categories. God is the absolute One, and you don't introduce any of this multiplicity of God knowing the possibles or any of that stuff which contradicts the absolute unity of God. In that, he is following a man who is in quite good standing. Jean Trouillard, the author of *La purification plotinienne*[5] and *La procession plotinienne*,[6] is the thinker behind Duméry. He did his studies in Plotinus. Connected with them is Joseph Moreau, who teaches at Bordeaux. He had a book out recently on phenomenology, *La conscience et l'être*.[7]

Duméry was working on the research foundation of the French government; and after his books were placed on the Index, he was more or less finished with the church. He asked to be defrocked; so he is not functioning as a Catholic priest.

We have there that difficulty of saying that the foundations are philosophic – very dramatically presented.

5 Jean Trouillard, *La purification plotinienne* (Paris: Presses Universitaires de France, 1955).
6 Ibid.
7 Joseph Moreau, *La conscience et l'être* (Paris: Aubier, 1958).

Question: Is the development of speculative theology more philosophical or more a matter of a better understanding of the sources of revelation?
Lonergan: It is both. The earlier development, fundamentally, is a development in philosophy, simply because there is a certain logical priority to it; and also there is a certain greater fundamentality to it. But it heads right into the other.

Let me try to substantiate this. To my mind, what was the first thematization, the practical thematization, of the sources of revelation and of the New Testament was contained implicitly in the preaching of the Gospel and in the passing on of the teaching of the Apostles. It occurs continuously in the New Testament in connection, principally, with the the word *logos*: *ton logon didaskein* and *akouein*: preaching the word, teaching the word, and listening to the word. You can get the references to *logos* in any Greek concordance. There is the act of teaching and hearing. For example, at the transfiguration we have the words, 'This is my beloved Son in whom I am well pleased; *hear ye him.*' Hearing in the New Testament is not simply oral attention; it includes the act of will, the openness to listen to the Gospel, to obey it. All that is implicit in the *akouein.* God the Father doesn't simply want you to listen to Jesus Christ and then go on your way. It is a listening that is an openness, an obedience, a following. All follows upon the *logos*, and the *logos* is the message; there is the work of preaching and the duty of listening to the Word. As the Law for the Jews implicitly contains the idea that the Law is to be obeyed, so the Word in the New Testament is something to be believed. You're not really apprehending the meaning of the New Testament message unless you're believing it. And there follows from that simply as a practical procedure the exclusion from the church of the people who don't believe, the mutual control of the bishops over one another, which was the primary type of more general control, the determination of the canon, all these earlier phenomena in which the dogmatic element in Christianity is coming to the fore. And a council like Nicea, the first ecumenical council, is just pushing to a logical conclusion an issue that was disputed all over the East. That fundamental characteristic of Christianity, that it is a dogmatic religion that has something to teach and considers that what it teaches is true, is basic.

We arrive at that implicitly because there is nothing in the Council of Nicea or in the anathemas about being true. But 'if one says so-and-so, then *anathema sit.*' It is a practical consequence; if you do not acknowledge what the Church teaches, then you are excluded. There is an implicit emphasis on truth and an implicit thematization of this aspect of truth. And the first problem is, Well, what do you mean by being true?

There is the elimination of the symbolic attitudes of the Jewish Christians and of the Gnostics in the first stage. In the second stage, there is the elimination of naive realism. Naive realism is clear in Tertullian but spread among his contemporaries and predecessors. In Irenaeus, are souls purely immaterial, without shape or figure? Well, you can prove the contrary. The parable of Dives and Lararus: if Lazarus had no shape or form, he wouldn't have any finger to dip in the water and put it on Dives' tongue. There are passages in Clement of Alexandria that show a similar tendency. They didn't have any notion of the immateriality of spirit; this was something that came in with the Middle Platonism of Alexandria, where the notion of the spiritual order is very clearly and firmly formulated. But what is spiritual reality? What is reality is conceived in Platonist terms. Arius put the issue in biblical categories, so to speak – creature and creator. Is the Son a creature or is he not? And, of course, creature and creator are not biblical categories in that form. If you want to prove that God is creator from the scriptures, well, you talk about him dominating everything, and it is insofar as you use the word 'everything,' *omnia*, that you can deduce our later philosophic notion of creation. But the issue was put, and fundamentally it is settling philosophic categories: creatures and creator. Is the Son creature or is he not? But at the same time it's raising the theological question, What do you mean by 'Son'? Is divine sonship something different from being created? How does something originate without being created?

The Fathers of the Church were not in the least concerned with philosophy; they were doing philosophy, but they were doing it implicitly. What Athanasius thought he was doing was defending the honor of Jesus Christ; and that is the level on which the debate was carried on. Similarly, Cyril against Nestorius. They were raising philosophic issues but they were concerned with religious truths and safeguarding them. All the trinitarian and Christological questions followed on. They were clarifying philosophic issues while dealing with religious and theological truths; the two are not separate. The distinction comes in the Middle Ages when they distinguish between the natural and the supernatural. The separation of philosophy from theology comes with Descartes when he was doing just philosophy; he wasn't doubting anything about faith, but he was doubting absolutely everything else. And so you get the separation of philosophy from theology.

Christian philosophy is fundamentally a theological creation and a theological tool. There is no separation between philosophy and theology in St Thomas. There is the distinction between the natural and the supernatural order, but to set up a distinction is not to separate two domains or two subjects. Theology heads into some imperfect understanding of the mysteries: the Trinity, the Incarnation, and so on. The understanding is very imperfect. This involves theology as a science, as a technical domain; but it is just a complete misunderstanding of theology to say, 'Well, all this is philosophy.' Theology is a science, and even when it is using philosophic concepts it is using what it itself originated for its own purposes and what it uses for its own purposes.

A more recent example is Vagaggini's article on St Thomas as a rationalist published in 1959. Its contention is that while St Thomas constantly claimed that he wasn't demonstrating the mystery of the Trinity, still in the back of his mind in a vague sort of way there is this Anselmian idea of the *rationes necessariae*, and while he says he isn't demonstrating, still he is doing exactly the same thing that Anselm did. Anselm thought he was demonstrating, and Aquinas did a much better job of it than Anselm did.[8] For Vagannini, everything is philosophic unless you're quoting scripture, the councils, or the Fathers; anything apart from that is philosophy. Well, that isn't true. There is a domain of knowledge with its proper concepts that is worked out by *ratio per fidem illustrata*. There is a certain field that is common to all the sciences apart from theology, and the foundations of it are philosophy. But there is the transformation of those foundations by the introduction of the act of faith. There is the transformation of the basic operations; there is the transformation of all the categories employed.

Theology is just as much a subject with its own proper concepts and its own proper criteria as is physics, chemistry, biology, sensitive psychology, rational psychology, philosophy of man, science of man. Theology has its own proper concepts, and when they become theoretical it is just obtuse to say that they are philosophic, as if everything theoretical is philosophic.

If you conceive theology as *fides per rationem adiuta*, then you will arrive at a position similar to Vagaggini's. You have philosophy and all the human sciences, and you have faith and what you know by faith, and you have an occasional little help from one to the other. You can tag on theological conclusions to the truths of faith, but that has no relation to the theology that has developed over the past centuries. That theology is the work of human intelligence and rationality as illuminated by faith and seeking an understanding of the truths of faith. It is a work that has a hypothetical parallel to what philosophy would be if we were in a state of pure nature.

8 C. Vagaggini, 'La hantise des *rationes necessariae* de saint Anselme dans la théologie des processions trinitaires de Saint Thomas,' *Spicilegium Beccense I*, 103–39.

Question: What do you mean by the Catholic understanding of philosophy 'prescinding from the existential situation?'

Lonergan: Take, for example, an existential philosophy or an empirical science of man. An existential philosopher doesn't suppose himself to be in a state of pure nature; for example, here I am and this is the sort of life I'm faced with; such is human living and this is the world as it actually is. Similarly, the human sciences don't study the ideal family or the ideal state or the ideal type of education. They study the states, the families, the types of education, the forms of law that exist and function. Now, with regard to man as he actually exists, he is born in the state of original sin; he is born in a world in which he needs God's grace to observe the merely natural law *quoad substantiam* for any notable period of time; he has a need for grace, and grace is given to him; God gives everyone grace in some measure, and he either accepts that grace or refuses it. The existential situation is penetrated by theological facts. A merely rational attempt to understand it is inadequate. But traditionally, Catholic philosophy, because it was in a classicist milieu, dealt with man as if he were man insofar as he is naturally known.

Question: Is a real philosopher-Christian then impossible?

Lonergan: Well, no. It is not impossible, but it only goes so far. And insofar as it faces these further issues, then it is preparing the way for theology; it is raising questions which it cannot answer. You can explain the moral impotence of the human will without any theology, as I do in chapter 18 of *Insight*. But to find an answer for the moral impotence of the human will you need a theology and a religion, first the religion and then the theology.

Question: How does the theologian know what is the *verum* in the text without the thematization of the data?

Lonergan: The determination of what is *verum* in the text in general is the proper field of the exegete; the theologian depends on the work done by the exegetes, and he doesn't attempt to duplicate their work. However, because exegesis is an empirical human science, it isn't simply a matter of eternal and necessary truths; it is a science that develops, in which opinions are probable, and so on; and there is no objection whatever to that fact. By all means, let the exegetes develop their field as much as they can. The development of a human science, of any empirical science, in general is through making mistakes; if you want to exclude the possibility of their making mistakes you will almost certainly exclude the possibility of their making any advance; you will confine advance to non-Catholics. The exegete to do his job has to have a certain scientific free play.

You will find in *Sacra Pagina* an article by Cardinal Alfrink, as well as the article by Descamps that I have already cited, alluding to this point, namely, that the modern biblical scholar is going to make developments, and there are going to be mistakes, and so on, and so a distinction has to be made between strictly scientific work and Catholic teaching – let them make their mistakes in private, as it were; and that is a way of dealing with the problem. Again, the pronouncement of the Holy Office a year ago to let the Catholic exegete be as prudent as possible in publishing his results was along the lines of these articles. However, the dogmatic theologian is out to show that some truth that is *de fide definita* is contained in the sources. He wants to find it certainly in the sources, and no matter how much future development there is going to be in scripture studies he wants to be certain of it here and now and not wait till kingdom come before he meets the *nobilissimum theologicum munus* of showing how the doctrines that are defined, in the sense in which they are defined, are contained in the sources. Consequently, he develops a set of special techniques that are not the techniques of the exegetes. I started saying something about them this morning when I spoke, for example, of heuristic definition as illustrated by the *logos*.[9] What is meant by the *logos* in St John? You can give a certain answer if you are content with an answer that isn't telling you everything there is to be known about the *logos*. In other words, this element of probability and uncertainty enters in just in the measure that you attempt to explain everything. If you limit what you are out to do, the possibilities of certitude increase.

Question: What would be the difference between a heuristic approach and fundamentalism?
Lonergan: Fundamentalism is, as far as I know, an anachronism. It is reading the scriptures with a present-day mentality and attributing that mentality to the original authors.

The dogmatic theologian will presuppose that the scriptures are a set of canonical books, that they are inspired by the Holy Ghost, and that they are without error. Insofar as the definition of the *logos* is heuristic, it says that the *logos* was *in principio*, it is not settling what St John meant by *principio;* that is an open question. But it means, at least, something more definite than *logos* necessarily will mean. *Per quem omnia facta sunt* doesn't mean *per quem nihil factum*

9 See above, p. 181.

est; at least that much is clear from the meaning of the text. The exegete will illuminate the text from all sorts of angles, but the more light he throws on it the less certitude becomes. A second exegete with regards to *in principio* may add on something else. I said that the *logos* is God in the sense that *theos* is not *ho theos*. I don't suppose that heuristic definition burkes any questions, but it provides a basis that no matter what answers the critical scholar is going to give, and whatever further light is going to be shed, it is going to be light thrown on this. And this as it stands has a certain determinacy.

In other words, if one thinks the Prologue is to be understood in terms of its sources then let's gather all the sources. But how do you understand the sources? In the light of their sources? And those sources in the light of their sources? There is a fundamental understanding communicated by the text itself on which a lot of questions can be asked; but not absolutely everything is questionable. Just how much is questionable and how much is not is a difficult point to decide; you can't settle it a priori. But at least you have the datum; and insofar as you approach the scriptures as true you are approaching them as inspired documents, without error, whatever other explanation is given.

The dogmatic theologian, I believe, bases truths of faith not upon the most lucid and brilliant account of the whole idea in John's Gospel, because you will have Dodd writing in 1954 and somebody else writing in 1955, and somebody else writing in 1956, and so on. There is an awful lot to be said for all of them, but they are not all exactly the same. And you'd expect the same thing happening in 1964 and 1965 and 1966 too. It's been going on for over a hundred years, so we know what happens. Dogmatic theology isn't a corollary that changes every year with the developments of biblical scholarship.

Question: I got the impression this morning that the theologian bypasses the data more than you seem to be saying now. Now you seem to be saying that he does consult the exegete, and he gets all that the exegete has to say, and then he takes what is perhaps the substance of this message.

Lonergan: If you consider any empirical science you will find that its results are probable insofar as revision is possible. But not everything can be revised. You can't revise the data. Because there is a canon of scripture, that canon, insofar as it is settled by the Council of Trent and the [First] Vatican Council, stands apart from other contemporary documents. The meaning of scripture will be changed by the discoveries at Qumrân in a manner far greater for the person who doesn't believe in the inspiration of scripture than by a person that does. Because the person that does believe doesn't believe that what is new in Qumrân has been inspired. But for the person who doesn't have any satisfactory view on inspiration, it is just another religious document, and so is Qumrân, and we understand the first century in the light of both. Insofar as scripture is something inspired, it is a particular field.

Now, to size up just what can be revised and what can't be revised depends on two factors: (1) one's knowledge of what a science is and how it develops; that is the theoretical component, the upper blade of the scissors; (2) the lower blade of the scissors comes from the type of thing that escapes revision. My second point was that the dogmatic theologian collects similar passages. If you have one text of scripture that really proves a thesis, why bother about any others? The point is that it is much easier to effect a revision on the current interpretation of one text than it is to do so on twenty texts that are more or less similar and scattered through the New Testament. You would have to have developments in interpretation over a wide field. In other words, the possibility of revision is cut down.

I don't say that all arguments from scripture are exactly the same type. For example, in proving the divinity of Christ, you would have to do a very long and complex investigation of what is said about Christ in the New Testament. But the dogmatic theologian doesn't do it in the same way as the exegete does it. The dogmatic theologian does it in the light of his purpose, and his purpose is not to rediscover as completely as possible the Palestinian mentality or Hellenistic-Christian mentality in the first century. It is to take what can be settled as true in those passages, what cannot be avoided.

Question: But would a better understanding of the Palestinian mentality help one to discover the passages that are true?
Lonergan: It is one thing to understand the text in the light of the people who wrote it, and I have no objection against that whatever. But it is another thing to make it one's life work to find out what precisely that Palestinian mentality was. And I don't think that it is the job of the dogmatic theologian to spend his life finding out what that Palestinian mentality in the first century was. He makes as much use of that as is possible, as is available; but it isn't the whole story by a long shot.

To handle that more fully, one has to go into what precisely is hermeneutics, what goes on in the mind of the interpreter. Such a problem doesn't lie on the level of data. There has been in Catholic theology a problem of introducing a historical mentality, and that is the break. But once that is introduced the main problem is passed. In other words, the sheer anachronism of reading back into the New Testament later categories, or starting out from present-day common sense and interpreting scripture in that way – I have no desire whatever to defend that. But that isn't where the problem is by a long shot. There are fundamental differences in the interpretation of the New Testament, and those fundamental differences don't arise because one man is a better scholar than another or one man knows more about it than another. They arise from the a priori that people have and don't know they are using. The dogmatic theologian's job is mainly to deal with those a prioris.

Question: If one is going back to a commonsense mind, what mind is one going back from?
Lonergan: The exegete starts off from his own common sense, and he gradually develops the common sense of the earlier period, just as you can come to understand the mentality of your parishioners. And understanding the mentality is understanding what they would say and do under certain typical situations that commonly arise. Similarly, one can understand a Jew or a Greek of the first century and what he would say or do under certain typical circumstances and common situations. That is acquiring the common sense of another time. All that process is the self-correcting process of learning; and that is the fundamental entry into the New Testament mentality.

Question: Are their findings certain or probable?
Lonergan: There are things that are probable, and there are things that are certain; and which is which is not settled by any general discussion or a priori.

Question: Is he just reading categories into the scripture?
Lonergan: 'Reading categories into' is a particular application of the great principle that you know by taking a look at what's out there. Either it is out there or it is not; and the man who sees what is out there is right and the other fellow reads his own mind into what is out there. That is a fundamental error on what the exegete or interpreter does. What's out there are black marks on white paper in a certain order. And if the exegete or interpreter gives you anything distinct, in any way different from those same black marks on white paper in the same order, then it is due to his personal experience, his personal intelligence, and his personal judgment, or it is due to his belief in what someone else told him. And that someone else telling him is variations in sound, and anything over the variations in sound is due to his use of his experience, intelligence, and judgment. And if you arrive at something

that is true, that is absolutely so, if you make a judgment, 'It is,' then you are not a relativist.

Question: But there is the possibility of being wrong?
Lonergan: If you have faith there is a certain complexity there. But there is no historical problem whatever that Brutus killed Caesar, and, in general, among people who have investigated even in a general way the events of the first century AD, there is no historical problem about the fact that Jesus suffered under Pontius Pilate. And to have more than that is quite possible. However, the question of hermeneutics will occupy us later.

Question: What is the relation of the concern of the exegete to the biblical theologian and the dogmatic theologian? Where do they meet *quoad verum*?
Lonergan: The exegete, according to Descamps, is concerned with the total content of the scriptures. The biblical theologian is concerned with the religious content of the scriptures. Descamps's idea of biblical theology is that biblical theology is conducted fundamentally under the criteria of literary and historical study. It is done just as well by the pagan as by the Catholic. Both have to acknowledge that the authors in these scriptures were believers, but conducting the operations is done equally well by the two, by either one or the other. He also holds that the method is not a hybrid method that is half theological and half historical but is fundamentally a straightforward literary-historical method. After you have settled in that fashion what the religious content of the scriptures are, you add on the truths you know from faith – this is the word of God – and draw conclusions from that. You can add on the truths you know from the church: that these scriptures are free from error. And what is free from error? This you know from your literary-historical method. I don't think this account of biblical theology is adequate, but it is the most satisfactory I've seen.

What is the relation between the biblical theologian and the dogmatic theologian? First of all, the biblical theologian investigates to the full what the religious content of the scriptures are. In part, he prepares the work of the dogmatic theologian, just as the patristic scholar prepares the work of the dogmatic theologian, or the student of the councils prepares the work of the dogmatic theologian. The dogmatic theologian is engaged in making use of a long series of preparatory studies, prior and preparatory from his point of view. From the viewpoint of the biblical theologian, he has his defined field, and he studies and develops it as an empirical human science or an empirical religious science: in other words, according to his ideas of what his investigation is. The dogmatic theologian has two parts to his task: to carry on the tradition – that is his main part, and the biblical theologian aids him in that by his prior investigation of scripture – and the further task of future development, making some contribution to that. He finds his fundamental stimulus in the findings of biblical theologians going beyond the present achievement of theology. In similar, though lesser, fashion the patristic scholars do the same sort of thing as do historians of theology who study the heresies.

1962

Discussion 6[1]

Question: A question was asked about breaking theology up and having different professors teaching different divisions of each thesis in dogmatic theology, and another question had to do with the unity of everything that goes on in theology. Lonergan chose to begin by considering these questions together.

Lonergan: One can think of positive empirical science applied to the series of books in the Old Testament and to the series of authors in the New Testament, and to the Apostolic writers, the Apologists, the Greek Fathers, the Latin Fathers, the medieval theologians. This will suffice for our present question. Insofar as one is conducting an empirical human science one is seeking to understand texts, to grasp the meaning of texts – the detailed discussion of which we will leave till tomorrow when we discuss hermeneutics, which is the problem of stating what the meaning of a text is.[2] However, to anticipate slightly, not every text needs an exegesis; not every statement needs an exegesis; otherwise, the exegesis would need an exegesis, and the second exegesis would need a third, and so on to infinity. In other words, there are cases, and there have to be cases, in which the meaning of the text is plain right at the start. If you don't admit that, then you are in an infinite regress. However, there are blocks to understanding texts. A person you know very well understands your meaning without too much trouble. The more two people have the same background, read the same books, go to

---

1 Wednesday, 18 July 1962, Lauzon CD/MP3 329 (32900A0E060).
2 See above, chapter 1962-9.

the same school, college, and university, and think alike in all things, the less difficulty they have explaining just what they think on any given point. Get people from different countries, as they are brought together in Rome, and they all find one another to be a little strange and odd. But after a while they come to understand their point of view a little better, and they end up saying, when they are heading for home, 'Thank God we don't have to bother with that any more.' In other words, the other peoples' common sense is good enough for other people, but we have our own. There is always a problem of communication the moment the common sense of any two persons begins to diverge. And the greater the divergence, the greater the difficulty of communication, and the greater the elaboration required to explain to another what one means.

If you try to read Karl Rahner, or any German theologian or Catholic German philosopher, you are struck at once by a difference of vocabulary, and you really catch on to it in the measure that you understand the movement of thought in nineteenth-century Germany. There are a whole host of terms they use that automatically are meaningful to them, but we have to feel our way into them, even though they are talking our position in philosophy and theology. When you move from Catholics to Protestants, and different groups of Protestants, well, your statements are much more easily misunderstood. And when you move to different cultures – Russian, American, etc. – the problems of mutual understanding mount still further. We have this differentiation of developments of common sense at the same time in the same world. For example, when I was teaching theology in Toronto earlier, there was a Hungarian student who had done his teaching period as a scholastic in Japan, and he told me of a missionary who was working in a small village in Japan, and he spent six years arguing with the local bonze on the principle of contradiction. For the bonze there was the Great Mountain Fujiyama, and there were several ways up the mountain; there were several religions, and they all take one to God; and he saw no reason for becoming a Catholic. To put the point that there was one religion that is true and that other religions are false ultimately turned on the issue of the principle of contradiction; and it took him a great deal of time to put that across. For our Western culture, stemming from the Greeks, the Hellenistic civilization in the Mediterranean basin, the Scholasticism of the Middle Ages, the formation of the universities, and so on, the principle of contradiction is just too obvious to be discussed; but that is because our culture includes the world of theory to a notable extent. In the high civilizations of the East, in China and Japan, there is not the same combination of theory with the world of common sense, of community, of intersubjectivity. I believe Chinese is a language structured for intersubjectivity; there are all kinds of flourishes to it regarding 'my humble personal situation,' 'your exalted personal situation,' and so on. Anyway, this man spent six years trying to convince the bonze of the principle of contradiction, and when he convinced him he became a Catholic, and the whole village became Catholics too.

The problem of communication is something entirely different. Just as there are those differences in space in the world of the present time – for example, preaching the faith in Central Africa is quite a different problem, as it is also in New Guinea – so there are also problems in going back in time; and unless one has performed, at least once in one's lifetime, serious historical work in which one gets away from all the presuppositions of one's own mentality at the present time, one doesn't really understand what the task of the historical thinker is. If one does it once, then one knows the sort of thing it is, one knows practically, concretely; one has a real apprehension, to use Newman's phrase, of what the task is, and one can size up what it is going to be in parallel cases.

Once the necessity of developing a historical sense is clear, one can begin to extrapolate, and one finds that in each of these fields what people are doing is working towards the meaning understood by the writers in the texts that have survived. One does that by the self-correcting process of learning. One reads one thing, and one gets a little bit of light, one reads other passages and reads this one over again, and so on and so forth, and insights pile up, and after one year or two or three or four or five, one gets to the point where one is familiar with the way of thinking and talking of the author. The amount of material that one has collected becomes enormous, and without doing that work one really doesn't follow it. One doesn't realize what has been done, and one doesn't move into the mentality of another age without doing that.

The specialist of any field that I have enumerated is building up something like the common sense of that period. It is a highly specialized thing, a very specialized acquisition. He can communicate it in a rough sort of fashion by telling you about it, by writing a book about it, and so on. But a full and adequate communication of it would be like trying to teach someone common sense; and you can't teach common sense. Either they get it for themselves or they don't get it at all.

Moreover, it happens that there are several experts in all these fields, and they don't all think exactly the same thing. They disagree with one another slightly or greatly and all sorts of points in between. Moreover, the experts of one generation succeed the next, and there are differences along the line there. For example, to devote oneself only to the study of the major epistles of St Paul, to know them inside out, and to know all that has been written about them, is a little more than a man can do in his lifetime. And similarly for everything else.

Moreover, because there are many opinions on many points, there is such a thing as specialized studies in all the fields, and it consists of studies that are developing; and what one learns strictly is history: what was said, what was done, by such and such a people at such and such a time.

Now, history is neither positive nor speculative theology. It isn't positive theology, according to the assertion of *Humani generis*, and it isn't speculative theology, as is evident to everyone. But positive theology uses all this work; it doesn't undertake to compete with the specialists in any field; it uses their results from a viewpoint that does not belong to the specialist in that field. If one wants to know Tertullian's position in the development of the trinitarian doctrine, one can select two types of passages mainly in one work, his *Adversus Praxean* – there are corroborative passages in other works as well – and in one case he is talking about God in one way, the way that predominated at Nicea, and in other texts he is talking about God in another way. The mere presence of those two elements, as it were, assigns or fixes Tertullian's position in the development. Tertullian's position in the development isn't part of the business of the specialist's work on Tertullian. The specialist is not concerned with Tertullian in his relations to Origen, to Arius, to Athanasius, to the Council of Nicea. But that is precisely the viewpoint of the positive theologian.

Similarly, the positive theologian has his primary source in scripture; but he is concerned not from the viewpoint of getting down to where one is understanding absolutely everything in every verse, every allusion, every reason why every text is just what it is. He is concerned with scripture as the document that represents the starting point of the Catholic tradition; and that is his main work: communicating and justifying the contemporary dogmatic-theological context. He is concerned to pick out from that the things that are certain, that no exegete can possibly get around, no matter how well he understands the thing, no matter how much further light is thrown upon it. Similarly, he is concerned to use all the material that goes along the line.

The specialist's study is study that aims – just as any science aims – at the complete explanation of all phenomena; it wants to know everything about a given writer, to understand everything. As long as there are passages that are not clear or are not clear to everyone, the task still remains; it is unfinished

business. It is an aim at complete understanding of a given text. The aim of
the theologian, whether positive or systematic, is not that. His aim is to communicate, and perhaps to develop, the existing dogmatic-theological context. He is concerned to distinguish sharply between what is certain and what
is probable, between what is more probable and less probable; he is concerned with truth. But any empirical science aims at some understanding,
even though it is only probable; it hopes to get to what is certain, an understanding of everything; but it proceeds to that goal by putting forward probable views and correcting them by more probable views.

I think the fundamental point is to grasp that difference of viewpoints. To
really understand it, one has to do historical work and realize just what is
demanded in the historical interpretation of a text and what it means. But
insofar as one does that work, one is aiming at explaining everything, and
one doesn't insist on certain explanations; one wants some explanation,
and if there is any weakness to it then someone else will come along and
point that out, and give a better explanation of it, or it will be left an open
question; science develops in the scientific group.

The purpose of the theologian is not complete understanding of scripture, nor complete understanding of each of the patristic writers, nor complete understanding of everything that happens at a Council, and so on.

At the Council of Chaldedon there was clearly an opposition between the
Egyptian group and the group centered around Byzantium, around
Constantinople; and that opposition became much more obvious at the
time of the Monothelite controversy, and at the time of the Persian invasion, and then the Arabic invasion. The people of Syria and Egypt were
delighted by the Persian invasion; they felt themselves much better off than
under the people in Constantinople. And they more or less opened their
doors to the Arab invasion. In other words, there are all sorts of sociological
and other secular historical tensions involved in these controversies, say,
between Monophysites and followers of Chalcedon, and so on. The dogmatic theologian isn't concerned to communicate to his class the whole
historical picture regarding Ephesus, the whole historical picture regarding
Chalcedon, the whole historical picture regarding the monothelite controversy of the seventh century, and so on. If he did, he would never finish,
never get to the point.

Moreover, understanding everything is not the sole means by which one
can understand anything about a text. That's true if you presuppose that
the right type of hermeneutics is Romantic hermeneutics, that the method
and nature of hermeneutics is to get into the other fellow's mind and think

the way he thinks, and so understand absolutely everything he says better then he does himself. If that is your only idea of interpretation, then the only way in which a dogmatic theologian can make use of scripture is by waiting until the scripture scholars finish all their tasks – which is to wait till kingdom come. Empirical sciences develop indefinitely. The dogmatic theologian has to find the key points and get certain answers from the texts. His use of the texts is technically different, his purpose is technically different, his viewpoint is technically different. His job is to communicate the essentials of the Catholic faith and to understand not St Paul, not St John, not Justin Martyr or Tertullian or Athanasius or Cyril of Alexandria; it is to understand the Christian faith. More accurately, the object of his concern always is God.

So, with regard to this proposal of having different people teach each of the subjects, if they are dogmatic theologians then they will teach dogmatic theology; but if they're biblical scholars, patristic scholars, conciliar scholars, aiming at a complete understanding of each of those documents and specialized in that field, they won't teach theology at all, they will teach history.

Question: Would you say that positive theology can be identified with historical theology?
Lonergan: By historical theology, do you mean history, the complete understanding of a text, or the complete understanding of a series of texts?

Questioner: Not the complete understanding, no, but the development of the dogma, for example, the movement toward Nicea.
Lonergan: Yes, well, that is positive theology. If you distinguish between hermeneutics and history, in hermeneutics you are concerned with the expression of one mind. In history, the fundamental example is the battle. You have the battle plans of both generals, and neither the battle plan of one general nor the battle plan of the other determines the course of events. History is concerned with the course of events. Hermeneutics is concerned with the intentions of a human agent. The battle plans don't settle what happened. What happened is the resultant, partly of the victorious general's plans, partly of the defeated general's plans, and partly of what either of them overlooked. History results largely from what has been overlooked by everybody, what is going forward despite the intentions of men. 'Man proposes, but God disposes.' Or there is Hegel's *List der Vernunft* or the economists' unseen hand of the laws of supply and demand; it is what the agents overlook.

Now, when you start considering a series of authors you have moved from hermeneutics proper to history. You take into account, not only what they considered but also what they overlooked; you are using comparative method to move towards an application of genetic and dialectical method – the dialectical method will take care of the part they overlooked. In a sense you are placing them in a context of what they didn't think about. Hermeneutics is not concerned to say what a man overlooked and didn't think about; it aims to arrive at what he did think about and what he didn't overlook. That is a broader context, and it is historical in the large sense.

Now, history is not concerned to understand everything about that historical process; there are all sorts of determinants coming into that historical process. You don't understand Origen unless you know Middle Platonism and its representatives. You don't understand Tertullian without knowing a good deal about Stoicism, even though Tertullian's use of Stoic formulae doesn't seem to be accurate. A recent work by Spanneut treats the Stoicism of the Fathers from Clement of Alexandria to Cyril of Alexandria.[3] It complements Arnou in the DTC on the Platonism of the Fathers.[4] Just the amount of Stoicism in Tertullian and his milieu – to determine those questions lies beyond the proper interests of the positive theologian; he has to be able to pick out the elements that make for the development. And he picks out those elements fundamentally by an understanding of horizon, authenticity, the need of conversion: intellectual, moral, and religious. They are the fundamental points of change.

More generally, there comes in here the use of human science in historical studies. We will say something more about that some other time.

Question: Can you say something about the unity of theology?
Lonergan: Theology is concerned with God. God is the subject of theology, according to St Thomas. And God may be known in three ways. Each of them involves the principle and the medium, the means. The principle may be the divine essence, and the means may be the divine essence, and then you have the beatific vision: God is known immediately in himself. The principle may be the natural light of human reason and the means the created universe as known by the natural light of reason; and then you have natural theology. The principle may be reason illumined by faith, and then

3 Michel Spanneut, *Le stoïcisme des Pères de l'Église, de Clément de Rome à Clément d'Alexandrie* (Paris: Éditions du Seuil, 1957).
4 R. Arnou, 'Platonisme des Pères,' *Dictionnaire de théologie catholique* 12 (24) 2258–2392.

the means is the word of God transmitted in the body of Christ. It's in the order of meaning. The mediation of theology is a science in which the principle is reason illumined by faith, and the means is not the divine essence itself, nor the essences of created things, but a meaning – something in the realm of meaning, in the sense of *esse intentionale*, the word of God. That word of God is transmitted in the body of Christ: a social order and a social message, a message socially transmitted.

Because of the medium, the word of God transmitted by the church, by the body of Christ, there is relevant to theology the historical development of doctrine; there is the process of transmission. That process of transmission is also the process of the development of dogma and the development of theology. Because the means of transmission, the medium of the science, is a revelation transmitted through a church, the history of the science of theology itself is an integral part of teaching theology. To teach physics you don't have to teach the history of physics; to teach mathematics you don't have to teach the history of mathematics. A good teacher will select points out of the history to put his teaching of the mathematics across. He will explain so-and-so's problem and how he solved it. This is a pedagogical technique. But the development of dogma, the starting point and the subsequent development of dogma and the subsequent development of theology, since they are part of the medium of the science, pertain in an internal way to the science. They pertain in a more intimate fashion than the created universe pertains to natural theology.

However, the word of God and the church as the means of transmitting to us the word of God, communicating to us the word of God and giving us the rules according to which we interpret the word of God – that is not end but means. In natural theology you have to know something about creatures to be able to conclude to the existence of God and proceed analogously to the attributes of God, to have some analogous knowledge of the attributes of God. But still, knowing creatures is not the point to natural theology. Similarly, the word of God and its transmission is, in theology, a means. What theology is concerned with is God and all things in their relations to God. You don't get the knowledge of God of dogmatic theology by dropping out the means; the means is part of the way in which you know. But the means is not the end. Positive theology is concerned with the element of foundation, the element of certitude, in your knowledge of God. But when I speak of a systematic theology that more closely approaches the end of theology, when I say it more closely approaches the end, I mean its concern is with the end, some understanding of the mysteries.

Now, one may say that speculative theology doesn't communicate much in the way of understanding the mysteries. If that is the case, then it is the theologian's job to make it something more. One may say that it is going to be pedagogically efficient only for a few, at most for seminary students, and not for all of them; and that, again, raises a practical problem. And one always has to do the best one can in one's situation. But the unity of theology is that theology is concerned with God and other things insofar as they bring us to God. It is when we are concerned with the end of theology, the end of the development of dogma, the end of the development of theology, that we are concerned with that subject that is the subject of theology.

Question: Would you say that theologians who are advocating a more practical approach are revolting against a false systematic theology?
Lonergan: Theology can head off to a blind alley very easily. The sermons of the Fathers thematized the scriptures; the Scholastics thematized the Fathers. What was twelfth-century theology? One can say very briefly, with a slight injustice, theology in the twelfth century was a matter of saying what Augustine had said. And theology since the thirteenth century is very often a matter of saying what St Thomas said or what St Bonaventure said, and so on. And when you start thematizing not scripture, not the Fathers, not the Scholastics thematizing the Fathers, but when you start thematizing on the Scholastics, you can lose contact with everything else and be dancing around in a circle. In other words, there have been defects in theology, and there is at the present time a fundamental enrichment of theology going forward from positive studies. That fundamental enrichment has a greater range of teachability. I'm quite ready to grant everything along that line. But it remains that theology is concerned with God; and there is room in the Catholic Church for an occupation not merely of the world of interiority and the world of community, but also of the world of theory.

Moreover, while everyone finds meaningful and effective the more concrete presentations of religious truths that are possible through scriptural study, study of the liturgy, study of the Fathers, and so on, there also is not absent from the minds of even the simplest men the profounder questions. They want to know whether you hold that Jesus Christ is God really and truly, or not. There was a book put out by a pair of Anglican authors called *Convictions*; they were discussing convictions in Protestant circles, and they remarked that the layman, in the last resort, wants to know whether or not there is any fire behind all the smoke that comes forth from the altar.[5] The ultimate questions about whether it is so or not so and precisely what is so and what is not so are the real questions, the fundamental questions; there isn't much to be said about them, the average man isn't able to discourse upon them, but he wants a clear yes or no, he wants the possibility of clear answers; and it is systematic theology that deals with that; it is dealing with the faith on a very real and extremely serious level.

Now, to say something on the unity of practical theology. Insofar as one reaches truths, one goes on to judgments of value; and when judgments of truth move over to judgments of value one is in the practical order. The revelation to the Jews was a revelation of a law; it was truth as practical. It was 'Do this and don't do that.' There was a speculative motive that we can discern behind the prohibition of images in the Jewish cult; but it wasn't an explained prohibition; it was just 'You don't do this, and you don't do that.' There is a fair amount of ridicule of the pagans adoring images. But fundamentally in the Old Testament the revelation is the law; and there are the great psalms that we say on Sunday from the breviary praising the justice and the justifications of God.

The law is a true judgment that regards actions, the *verbum spirans amorem*. The judgment of value is the source of acts of will. The transition from the order of truth to the order of values is very simple. With regard to what we hold to be true, we either live it or else we suffer an inner contradiction; and if we can't bear the contradiction, either we are converted back to the light that is in accord with our lights or else we dim the lights, we become rational or we rationalize. Practical theology stands to speculative theology as rational self-consciousness stands to rational consciousness. Is that enough on that point?

There is also the truth in scripture. The truth in scripture sets the problem for old-time Protestants who followed scripture and nothing else, according to its plain meaning. The sixteenth century was full of movements that wanted to get back to the simplicity of scripture, the plain and obvious meaning of scripture. They wanted to liberate themselves from all this medieval theology, particularly the decadent theology they knew. But while it is true that according to the possibility of hermeneutics there

5 It is quite likely that Lonergan is referring to a book called, not *Convictions*, but *Foundations*. More fully: *Foundations: A Statement of Christian Belief in Terms of Modern Thought*, by Seven Oxford Men, B.H. Streeter, R. Brook, W.H. Moberly, R.G. Parsons, A.E.J. Rawlinson, N.S. Talbot, W. Temple (London: MacMillan, 1912). See Lonergan's reference to this book in *Philosophical and Theological Papers 1958–1964* (see above, p. 55, note 26) 262. The editors are grateful to Charles Hefling for his advice on the question.

must, at least, be some texts that don't need an exegesis, otherwise the attempt at exegesis is futile, still there do exist problems of exegesis, and some of them are solved with certainty and some with probability and some are not solved yet, and there are further questions. And answering any set of questions usually gives rise to a further set of questions on a further level. Knowing the meaning of a text is not something that is done simply and easily. It is almost the definition of a classic that it is never perfectly understood, but that the educated man and the man who educates himself are always finding more in it. And if that is true of the human classic it is also true of the word of God. We have *Humani generis* to tell us that the sources of revelation are never exhausted.[6]

While the dogmatic theologian has no objections to the use of the technique of empirical science that advances through less probable to ever more probable interpretations, still his concern is to find the truths that the church says are certainly contained in the sources of revelation and to show to the best of his ability that further developments aren't going to eliminate them.

The question had to do with *verum et falsum sunt in mente, bonum et malum sunt in rebus.*[7] What do you mean by scripture? Do you mean the book? Do you mean the book as being read? Do you mean the book as being read and understood? And is the understanding probable or certain? Or do you mean the truth in the mind of the hagiographer? Or do you mean the truth that God intended to communicate? There are all these different meanings of truth.

Question: Which is your meaning?
Lonergan: One can use them all. The theologian is concerned with the scriptures as true. He is concerned with the point that scripture is not just the expression of a mentality, as is a work of art, the expression of a subject, of a purely experiential pattern of experience that one objectifies. Romantic hermeneutics is concerned with interpreting texts from that viewpoint. It's not meeting. One can think of the scriptures as a meeting point with God; while there are other ways of meeting God besides dogmatic theology, the dogmatic theologian meets God through the scriptures on the level of truth. There is a good deal more to religion and religious experience than that, and the other parts are easily thought to be more vital and more important. Some of them are, and some of them aren't. Intellectual virtues are

---

6 DB 2314, DS 3886, ND 859.
7 Lonergan is referring to the way the question arose in the group, which had to do with the relation of this principle to the notion of the *verum* in scripture.

virtues *secundum quid,* and virtues in the will are virtues *simpliciter,* according to St Thomas. But dogmatic theology is a special field, a special study for a special end, and its approach is through truth. It thematizes the aspect of truth. You can consider in the scriptures not only expression or meeting; you can also consider them as a witness, an example of first-century *koinē* Greek or a type of language, and place it in the general study of languages, the development of languages, or a tool for knowing geography. The scriptures can be studied from all sorts of viewpoints. The dogmatic theologian studies them to determine the truth that he believes God to have revealed.

1962

Discussion 7[1]

Question: What is meant by horizon? Is horizon proper to the world of common sense, or more proper to it, or can it be found in all worlds?

Lonergan: Horizon is the limit of the field of light or the limit of the penumbra beyond which there is just complete darkness – one can take it as either one. What lies within one's horizon is what one can apprehend, choose, what one is willing to do, and what one has the necessary skills to do, whether it is in the world of common sense or the world of theory or the world of interiority. The world of theory can easily be beyond an individual's horizon; to a great extent the world of interiority is beyond one's horizon if one is an extrinsicist; but horizon is not limited to any particular world. It is most easily illustrated within the world of common sense because that is the world we are most familiar with. There are the horizons of the different professions: theology professor, clergy, medical profession, lawyers, judges, politicians, trade union leaders, etc. They all have their apprehension of the world, and they know that there is an awful lot of other stuff around it, but it increasingly has no interest for them, they have no familiarity with it. It is a de facto limitation that occurs in everyone.

To be a specialist and nothing but a specialist is to have a very restricted horizon. The horizon is determined by one's de facto acquired habits and skills. Something is not beyond one's horizon if one does not have to learn to understand it, if one does not have to be persuaded to do it, if one does not have to practice to do it. Playing the piano is beyond my horizon.

---

1 Thursday, 19 July 1962, Lauzon CD/MP3 330 (33000A0E060).

Question: What exactly do you mean by 'understanding the thing' in your discussion of hermeneutics?

Lonergan: One can read and understand an author in order to know the thing. One reads books to learn about things; that is perfectly true. We distinguished four elements that are understood in understanding a text; and the first and simplest to talk about is the thing. If you understand the thing in general but do not understand the particular aspect the author is talking about, you have a good background for learning about the thing from him. But to be sure you really understood him, it is well to invoke either experiments one imagines or experiments one performs. If you are doing mathematics, you also do examples; and if you study literature, you also write essays, and so on. In other words, a text can be a tool for learning about the thing.

But in general the more you know about the thing itself the better prepared you will be to understand and to provide an accurate interpretation of what the author has to say about it. Understanding the thing is not going to be understanding the author; but in the measure that you understand the thing, you are prepared to learn more about it from the author, and insofar as you learn more about it, your examining the thing and going back to the author will enable you to see just how much about the thing the author says that you think is correct. That criticism of the author makes your interpretation all the more precise. There can be all kinds of mutual influences, one way and the other. But if you know nothing at all about the thing, if you are reading about something you know nothing about, then every time the word occurs it is just an x in the text, and the more concrete and simple the examples you take, then the more obvious it will be. There are problems in interpreting ancient languages. We know most of the verbs, but we cannot figure out what some of the nouns are about, and the reason is that today we haven't got the tools that these people were talking about. If one comes to a highly mechanized civilization, there are simply some things that one can't express in a primitive language, they have never seen it. When the tribes in which totemism still exists first saw an airplane they first set out to know what relation they were to the airplane, because everything is relative to them, everything is categorized by relations. There are relatives in the sense of some sort of blood relations; but all their categorization is through relationships in the obvious human sense.

Question: The theology of Schmaus is very helpful in teaching college theology, and yet it uses very little philosophy. What do you have to say about that kind of theology?

Lonergan: With regard to philosophy and theology, the theology I'm talking about is theology in the full sense. One teaches as much of it as one can to any given group. It depends upon the group and also upon the measure you're willing to force the pace. Insofar as there is a demand for exactitude, for stating precisely what you mean, all you mean, and nothing but that, you are going to start using techniques, and among them metaphysical techniques. The fundamental use of metaphysics in theology is, Do you mean something or do you not? and if you have two propositions, Do they mean the same thing or do they not? The principle of metaphysical equivalence is worked out in chapter 16 of *Insight*. Most so-called metaphysical questions in theology simply reduce to that: put down your true propositions on one side; and, on the other side, the metaphysical conditions of the propositions being true.

There are a series of statements about what from the thirteenth century has been named sanctifying grace, about its properties. What is the metaphysical condition of them being true? That there be a certain entity received in the soul of the just. If one has it, then all these propositions are true of him. They are formal effects of having sanctifying grace. If one can have some and not others, then the ones that are not necessary are secondary effects that are said to be capable of being impeded. Most of metaphysics can be reduced to that. Do the two propositions mean different things or do they mean the same; do they mean something or do they mean nothing? If they mean nothing, you don't need something *a parte rei* – you're just talking through your hat. But if you are not just talking through your hat, then you mean something, and there is some corresponding reality implied. What is that reality? You have further propositions; does the same reality account for their truth, or do you require a further reality? Are you saying the same thing when you make the second statement as when you make the first, as far as real difference goes, or are you not?

Practically all the metaphysical questions in theology reduce to that, as far as I know. And the three fundamental metaphysical realities are in the order of potency, form, and act. Relation, I believe, is not a distinct one. You divide these three up into substantial and accidental, natural and supernatural. That's about the whole equipment, and their function is to determine whether one is saying something or nothing, whether one is saying the same thing or something different.

Now, there undoubtedly are hordes of college students that couldn't possibly grasp that; and in that case it is better to leave out the metaphysics. They may not be interested in whether you're saying something or nothing or whether you are saying the same thing or something different. But you do what you can with the audience you have.

Question: Is it possible to talk about the relations in the Trinity without using philosophical terms?

Lonergan: What do you mean by philosophical terms? Do you think the Trinity is a philosophical object? If you are only using philosophical terms, you won't be able to say anything about the Trinity. Are 'three persons in one nature' philosophical terms? Is the divine nature as treated in the Trinity philosophically known? The analogy goes one step further, does it not? You have to use the technique of analogy, but if you read Basil of Caesarea or Gregory of Nyssa or even Gregory Nazianzen, the five theological orations which he preached in the church of Constantinople to the ordinary Constantinopolitan audience, you will not find anything there that is not in the Preface on the Trinity: *in personis proprietas, in essentia unitas, in maiestate adoretur aequalitas*; there are a few things more but not much more.

Question: Is there not a need to give philosophical definitions of nature and person?

Lonergan: Not at that level. Everyone knows what they mean when they ask, What is it? They have some idea of it. Otherwise they wouldn't ask the question. About the divine essence, what we know is what we express when we ask what it is; and we know that we don't know what it is, except analogically. If you start from the thing historically and consider Eunomius's objections against the existence of the Trinity, you will find Gregory Nazianzen's answers the necessary thing, and nothing seems very difficult about them. You can complicate the thing endlessly by philosophic questions, and you can complicate the issue endlessly by historical questions, but I think the fundamental difficulty is that people get into a state of paralysis. Just as, when you offer a mathematical illustration, people say, 'Well, I never understood mathematics, don't tell me that.' A lot of the difficulties are fictitious, and a lot of the difficulties come from mistaken attempts at metaphysics. There's been an awful lot of muck written in the field, too, and the function of the critical problem is to clear it away. If a person doesn't know metaphysics, then it would be much better for him to keep away from it entirely when teaching theology, because he will only communicate his mistaken and confused notions.

Question: Can a person get this entirely in the field of common sense?

Lonergan: I wouldn't say that. What I would say is that people don't want to remain entirely in the field of common sense. People who remain entirely in the field of common sense don't belong to our civilization. They have fundamental problems which they handle only symbolically, and moreover, their symbolic thinking easily degenerates into myth. We have millennia of human experience to establish that fact. The reason why contemporary commonsense thinking doesn't degenerate into myth is because of the presence in the culture of theory. If people are getting a college education they are generally willing to move beyond the level of common sense. They want to know exactly what you mean and whether you mean anything or whether you mean the same thing by the two propositions.

Question: In interpretation there are a series of wholes, and how do you determine the whole that is relevant to any prospective judgment?

Lonergan: I don't think it is possible to determine what *the* whole is. I think that is what creates the problem of judgment in the interpretation. You understand the parts in the light of the whole and the whole through the parts, and that is the hermeneutic circle, which is complicated by a further point: the relativity of the whole – where do you stop? The line of thought that I suggested on the matter was the fact that the broader the whole, while it does have an influence, still it has only a limited influence. It can't change everything about the meaning of the text. The reason I brought up the example of St John in the Hellenistic context and within a Palestinian context, as it has more recently been tended to be taken, is the fact that that difference doesn't disqualify everything in commentaries on St John on the supposition that he was writing in a Hellenistic context. The more the writer who was contemporary with the earlier view restricted his statements to an analysis of what the text is saying, the more he was content to put things together in the light of the text itself. The less he thought that you could understand St John by assigning his origins, and understand the origins by assigning their origins, and so on to infinity without ever understanding anything in itself – the more he found the meaning within St John himself – the less this shift in the broader context would tend to invalidate his judgments. So my suggestion was modesty in these judgments.

You do not attempt to settle from every aspect or point of view just what the author means. Insofar as your judgment does that, it is open to further revision, and it can't be more than a probable judgment. But there are things that you can get out of the text by considering the words themselves, the way in which the author handles things, and so on. And by knowing the difference between the two you can concentrate on the one and know enough to be discrete in speaking about the other.

Another example I gave was that you can have in a text that Brutus killed Caesar. The contexts can differ enormously, but you have something in that statement that the context cannot change. It can't mean that Brutus didn't kill Caesar; the context is never going to imply that. There is an element of meaning that is given by the text that can have its meaning more fully determinate from the context. That plus that comes out of the context has to be determined by the context. There is something to the text itself that determines the context, and there is the mutual influence; but the mutual influence is on different levels, in different ways. This is the *esprit de finesse*. There is no set of rules to tell one how far one can go. An exegete is good or poor just in the measure that he can exercise that *esprit de finesse*. The more he is carried off by abstract theories the more likely he is to be wrong. And the more he has had a humanistic training and developed a sensibility in the use of words, in the way words are used, and in the type of meaning that an author attempts to communicate, the more delicate and precise and limited will be his statements, and they will be pretty solid. This is one aspect of the matter.

Question: There are difficulties, though, in relating to the modes of expression.

Lonergan: One has to be aware of the genetic series of modes of expression and of ideas, and the further you go back the less there is any automatic differentiation between them. If a person writes a book today, a small book with a beautiful cover on it, with nice pictures in it, and the book starts off, 'Once upon a time ...,' you know that it is a fairy tale. And, of course, the interpreter has to be aware not only of those differences in modes of writing at the present time, but also of the fact that the further you go back the less these things are differentiated from one another, and the more they tend to merge in a single piece.

Newton's mechanics was purely scientific but he called it 'The Mathematical Principles of Natural Philosophy'; he thought he was doing philosophy, or if he didn't think so, which is quite probable I think, still he was yielding to the mode of expression of his time. The early Greek philosophers wrote in verse. Empedocles wrote in verse; Plato wrote a literary dialogue; the Aristotelian corpus approaches to the treatise. So there is the development of the genre proper to philosophy. But the further you go back the less these things are distinguished. All these things have to be kept in mind. But if we are talking about the first century BC in Rome and the year that Brutus killed Caesar, there isn't any reason for supposing that the author is mythical. In other words, you can have the idea that practically the whole of Latin literature was written by medieval monks. While it's a difficult thing to dispose of in a way, on the other hand it's simply ridiculous.

It's an abstract question, because we have not taken a text and built up the understanding of the thing, the understanding of the words, the understanding of the author, and the development in the self. The judgment is something that supervenes. But the point I want to make is that there are qualified judgments that can be made, and when the proper qualifications are made, then the judgments are not open to revision. Your understanding is not given a blank check of approval; but with regard to precise issues you may say that this author means this, and one can judge pretty securely. But what is behind that judgment is, of course, the *esprit de finesse* or Newman's illative sense. You can't get a machine to do that job for you.

Question: If you know your insight is invulnerable, you judge. You had some remarks about not being able to teach common sense. But how do people grow in common sense, and especially grow to the stature of the inspired author?

Lonergan: I worked out in the sixth chapter of *Insight* a detailed description of the process of developing in common sense, as well as I could express the thing – the first ten pages of chapter 6 on common sense and its subject. The thing is taken up again from the viewpoint of judgment in the tenth chapter under commonsense judgments. It's a matter of catching on to one thing and catching on to something else, and so on, and either you hit your head against a wall by making mistakes or you learn not to make the same mistake twice. You either use your head to keep out of difficulties or you end up in hot water; and you find it easier to keep out of hot water if you use your head. Your insights accumulate, you come to understand the situation in which you are, and that understanding moves towards a limit in which you can understand, usually by the addition of one or two further insights, just what to say, just what to do, in that milieu. That is the ordinary type of development in common sense. It is the same sort of thing as learning a language; you learn it by writing prose compositions, and your first prose compositions are packed full of mistakes. Teaching Latin, you start the boys off with the rudiments, and they translate simple sentences with a noun, a verb, and an object; and they learn the noun, the subject, in the nominative case, and the verb in the right tense and person, and the object in the accusative case, and then you add on the dative case, and so on. And by making lots of mistakes they gradually learn to do it right. And things keep getting more complicated all through the course. The advantage, for example, in Latin is that it gives you the bare bones, the bare structure. Greek will add on all sorts of finesse in the ordinary, elementary, human sphere. If you learn to write a modern language, a correct literary style in a modern language, the things you have to deal with are on an entirely different level. You start doing descriptions, translating descriptions or characterizations from English, say, into French. It gives you an enormous attention to detail, to every aspect of the words you are using. You become aware of the resources and potentialities of different languages, of just what can be said and what cannot be said in them. When I write in Latin I say what can be said in Latin, and I don't attempt to say in Latin what I would say in English because the language has not the resources for expression that a modern language has. And that literary formation, that linguistic formation, is a basic stage in the formation of anyone who is going to interpret ancient texts. It is the sort of thing that comes to one gradually over the years. People like that are not made over night; it is a matter of adding insight onto insight and getting to know how to handle this and how to handle that.

When I was studying philosophy at Heythrop, there was an American who went up to Cambridge in the summer to study Greek prose composition under a tutor. What the tutor would do every morning was to open the *London Times* and translate the first leader. He translated it into Platonic Greek, turning all the English metaphors into metaphors that would have been familiar to Plato, the sort of metaphor that Plato would have used. He could give you a version right off, like that, of first-hand Platonic Greek, handling the leader in the first editorial of that morning's *London Times*. After he had finished he would say, now Plato might have been completely coherent with himself and could have expressed it this way; and he would give another example using all the metaphoric expressions that were in the leader. And in that sort of work there is a complete transposition of all the thinking. He would be able to give you the exact way in which one would find in Plato the idea presented. If you want an approach to the sort of thing he was doing, get Donovan's *Greek Prose Composition*, 3 volumes. It was composed for sixth-form boys in our school, St Aloysius, in Edinburgh; it was the work they did in Greek prose composition before going to the university.

Now, that is a matter of knowing what it is to know a language, what humanistic training is. The ability to do that is something that is built up over years of gaining familiarity with the language, exploring the potentialities of the language. You just can't communicate that to anyone; one has to learn it for oneself; one has to do the apprenticeship.

You can't teach common sense; in general that is true. A person has to have a certain amount of *nous* before he can profit from teaching and reading. The maths tutor I had at Heythrop, Charles O'Hara, would insist on one's mistake. He would say, a wise man makes mistakes but he never makes them twice; and he would make it very plain to one why one shouldn't do it twice. By learning not to do things twice, you pick up an awful lot. This is the acquisition of common sense, and it occurs in this field of interpretation. But it is just as complex an acquisition as a child learning a language. How does a child learn a language? He learns it by insights. He gradually becomes more correct in his expressions.

Now, I wasn't talking about measuring up to the level of the inspired author; the inspired author is inspired by the Holy Ghost, and one doesn't measure up to the level of the Holy Ghost. I was speaking quite generally of the classics; and people can read and reread the classics, and find something new in them every time. There is the story about Victor Hugo when he was seeking entrance into the French Academy; he had to do the circuit of all the existing members and solicit their vote. At that time, Victor Hugo was the most celebrated poet in France. But when he introduced himself to one Academician, the man had never heard of Victor Hugo, and he asked 'Don't you read?' and the man said, 'At my age people don't read, they re-read.' That's the thing about the classics. There is always more to be learned from the classics, and one gradually moves up to them.

PART TWO

Avery Cardinal Dulles's Notes for Lonergan's 'A Five-Day Institute: The Method of Theology,' 13–17 July 1964, Georgetown University

Titles of the lectures as given in the program:
13 July: The Contemporary Problem
          A.M. Factors External to Theology
          P.M. The Internal Situation
14 July: Reason Illumined by Faith
          A.M. Human Knowing as Operational Structure
          P.M. Transformation of the Structure by Faith
15 July: Differentiation of Methods, I
          A.M. Foundations
          P.M. Positive Theology
16 July: Differentiation of Methods, II
          A.M. Dogmatic Theology
          P.M. Systematic Theology
17 July: Special Questions
          A.M. The Development of Dogma
          P.M. The Argument from Scripture

1964-1

The Contemporary Problem[1]

Medieval crisis led by appearance of Aristotle – led to 13th century.
Today: 1. Shift in ideal of science
    2. Empirical human science – study of man as he concretely is in family, mores, education, economy, law, etc. Foundation of all such studies = enlargement of concept of meaning.
    3. Historical consciousness
    4. Emergence of philosophies that can handle preceding – that can deal with historical, etc.

1 Shift in Model of Science

In Middle Ages, theology as queen of sciences. But science taken in Aristotelian sense. Modern science has (a) enlarged field of science and (b) changed notion of science itself.

    Theology is analogously a science – but analogous to what?

---

1 Notes for lectures on Monday, 13 July 1964.
2 Notes directly connected to this section may be found in a searchable 17-page pdf file on the Lonergan Archive website, www.bernardlonergan. com, at 85400DTE060. Of these pages, 14 are typed, consecutively, while 3 are handwritten additions. The reader is advised to study this file along with the present section.

(i) Greek science concerned with the necessary. Modern science concerned with de facto empirical intelligibility – e.g., law of falling bodies – rate of acceleration (g) is intelligible but not necessary. Modern science is hypothesis + verification. Necessity becomes peripheral. Some things still regarded as necessary. But science doesn't center on necessity.

(ii) Greek science concerned with eternal, immobile. Becoming is characterized *ex termino.* Continuum is not intelligible, but only goal. Modern science concerned with the temporal. Intelligibility attained in process, in dialectic. Intelligent.

(iii) Greek science concerned with universal. Insisted upon abstraction. Necessity and intelligibility found in universals. Modern science concerned with concrete – things as they are. Modern method uses universals to get as close as possible to the concrete. Process of evolution.

(iv) Greek science concerned with *per se.* No connection between redheaded and trombone player. Modern science concerned with *per accidens.* Study statistics.

(v) Greek science concerned with formal object – *ratio sub qua.* Element of abstraction in notion of formal object. Modern science defines a 'field' – region to be mastered. Means of mastery: a method.

(vi) Greek science ruled by logic. Logical deduction from definitions and principles to conclusions. Modern science starts with insights, gets hypotheses. Draws conclusions. Tests these by confrontation with the data – correction: new hypotheses, etc.

(vii) Greek science concerned with essence – intrinsic ground of necessity, etc. Modern science (a) pluralism – reality too rich to be compressed into a single definition. Ellipse is attacked [?] as cone-section etc. – different ways of getting to reality of ellipse using different techniques. Some only through use of computers. Several approaches needed. (b) perspectivism: mitigation of historical relativism. In history different things become significant. Was Apollinaris denying human soul or human subject [in Christ]? Subsequent event throws earlier event into new perspective.

(viii) Greek science concerned with four causes. Modern science aims at complete explanation of all aspects.

(ix) Greek science is *certain,* otherwise is not science. Modern science is not certain. Positive doctrine = best available opinion at present time.

(x) Greek science is individualist + permanent. Habit is individual. Modern: collectivist + in process. Scientific achievement = collective good of the scientific community. Science can't be mastered by a single mind. E.g., in physics, men who do experiments are not able to do theory – and vice versa. Handed on not by 'great books' [but] by floating library.

The theologian does not have to make a choice. Choice has been made for him. *Deus scientiarum Dominus* introduced more positive theology + invasion of positive studies into theology. They are under direction of modern idea of science.

2 Notion of Meaning[3]

Only part gets into definition:

Finality may be conscious or unconscious. Conscious finality = intention. Fundamental intention is comprehensive, global, determinable. Meaning is a determined intention.

Unformulated meanings: intersubjective, symbol, artistic, ...

(i) Intersubjective meaning occurs in encounter. What acting adds to text of play. Encounter itself already has a meaning – my coming to see her sets into motion dynamism developed by past encounters. Human communication is not work of soul hidden in recesses of body emitting Morse code signals. Bodily presence is that of the incarnate spirit – reveals itself by every shift of eyes, etc. Immediate revelation of the other as a person that operates and changes me and the way that I apprehend. Automatic adaptation of subject to the other as manifest, smile has a meaning – highly perceptible – difficult to suppress. Noises of street can't be repeated because they have no meaning. We don't learn to smile. Smiles have all sorts of meanings – friendliness, delight, etc. Meaning depends on interpersonal situation.

[Not] conceptual meaning – doesn't distinguish. It is a revelation of subject. You can bring out by phenomenology (a) the unformulated meaning – but smile can't be replaced by a formula. Give meaning of joke! There is a level of communication prior to distinction between I and Thou. A shriek frightens us; the fear becomes *our* fear. Max Scheler, *Die Formen der Sympathie*[4] – also, Buytendijk, *Phénoménologie de la rencontre*:[5] Desclée.

(ii) Symbolic meaning: affect laden in the percept, evokes image and they mutually reinforce each other. Freudian investigation modeled on family relationships – e.g., House of Thebes (Oedipus etc.)

Jung: Symbols of transformation, conversion, death.

3 The fifth page (third typed page) of the archival item mentioned in note 2 locates this discussion in the context of historical consciousness as distinct from the classicism treated in section 1.
4 See above, p. 198, note 11.
5 F.J.J. Buytendijk, *Phénoménologie de la rencontre*, trans. into French by Jean Knapp (Bruges: Desclée de Brouwer, 1952).

Eliade: Preface to *Myths, Dreams + Mysteries*, orig. French edition – has good critique of Jung.[6]

Durand, *Les structures anthropologiques de l'imaginaire.*[7] Grenoble. Doctoral thesis.

Dominant reflexes: e.g.

(α) Keeping balance. Mothers spend [time] by child learning upright position. All overtones of falling – Fall of man, etc. Synthesis = image of St George and dragon. Dragon synthesizes all objects of horror. Overthrown by man.

(β) Swallowing – sweet, warm, comfortable. Not just 'falling down.' Euphemization of previous object of terror. Composite image of Jonah and whale. Jonah is swallowed, none the worse.

In ways like this one deepens the unformulated meanings.

(iii) Incarnate meaning – that of a man, or character in his life or outstanding achievement. E.g., Benedict Arnold, George Washington. Passion + Resurrection of Christ is incarnate meaning. Combines intersubjective + symbolic into one.

G. Morel: *The Meaning of Existence in St John of the Cross.*[8]

(iv) Artistic meaning: Suzanne Langer, *Feeling and Form*, Scribner, 1953.[9] Huyghe: *L'art et l'âme*, Paris, 1961?[10]

Unformulated meaning becomes dessicated when formulated.

(v) Linguistic meaning – (a) everyday language.

(b) Technical meaning – multiplied as civilizations develop.

E. Cassirer: *Philosophy of Symbolic Forms*[11]

K. Jaspers: *Origin and Goal of History*[12]

H. Frankfort et al.: *Before Philosophy*[13]

E. Voegelin, *Order and History*[14]

Redfield: *Primitive World*[15]

---

6 Mircea Eliade, *Myths, Dreams, and Mysteries: The Encounter between Contemporary Faiths and Archaic Realities*, trans. Philip Mairet (New York: Harper, 1960).

7 See above, p. 65, note 12.

8 See above, p. 320, note 14.

9 See above, p. 201, note 12.

10 René Huyghe, *L'art et l'âme* (Paris: Flammarion, 1960).

11 See above, p. 58, note 4.

12 See above, p. 49, note 20.

13 See above, p. 58, note 3.

14 At the time of these lectures, the first three volumes of Eric Voegelin's *Order and History* would have been published: vol. 1: *Israel and Revelation*, vol. 2: *The World of the Polis*, and vol. 3: *Plato and Aristotle* (Baton Rouge: Louisiana State University Press, 1956, 1957). The fourth volume, *The Ecumenic Age*, was published in 1974, and an incomplete fifth volume, *In Search of Order*, was published posthumously in 1987.

15 Robert Redfield, *The Primitive World and Its Transformations* (Ithaca, NY: Cornell University Press, 1953).

B. Malinowski – *Magic, Science and Religion*[16]

Omits all feeling, intersubjectivity, dry as dust. Precise point stated precisely and clearly. Moves to second power when concerned with control of meaning itself as in grammar, logic, epistemology, metaphysics.

Plato's early dialogues represent transition from everyday logic to technical meanings. From common sense to technical language. Phenomenology attempts to formulate unformulated meanings.

Fries: *Die Kath. Religionsphilosophie der Gegenwart.*[17] Points out that 2 phenomenologists can take same phenomena and get different insights. You still need development and judgment.

(c) Literary meaning floats between unformulated and technical. Euclid made all sorts of fallacies because [he was] not perfectly logical – Literary meaning: one intends to communicate with others not present.

Floats between technical and laws of imagination and feeling.

Langer, p. 243. Move from class to individual, from negation to overcoming, from excluded middle to ambivalence, from single theme to condensation of several.

Negation: Nothing is happening. 'Only the sleep eternal in an eternal night' (Swinburne). Positive description of the negative.

Condensation: Incompatible themes combined in mixed metaphors etc. studied by Freud.

Meaning evolves. Different languages can handle different meanings. Evolution of meanings involves differentiation of consciousness.

Classical culture was that of standard man. His reason was Reason. Modern man regards classicist as a particular anthropological species.

Finds himself to his liberation responsible to construct his own world.

Meaning is constitutive of human reality. Same human nature is different in Thomas Aquinas and a lunatic. In world of intended objects man develops his cultures and civilization.

Questions

Question: Until recently law was about the only human science on which theology drew for its development. Now we draw on sciences that are not yet mature.

Lonergan: We lack theoretical conceptions from psychology and sociology needed for development of treatise on the mystical body.

16 See above, p. 59, note 7.
17 See above, p. 86, note 7.

Question: Are the two ideals of science incompatible?

Lonergan: We must retain both. God is field of absolute necessity. The First Vatican Council applied Greek ideal to God. In the contingent human field modern notion of science is more fruitful. Intelligibility of creation, redemption, etc., is not Aristotelian. Scotus attempted to find that type of intelligibility and ended up a voluntarist. Modern ideal uses necessity whenever it shows up.

Objection: Aristotle is more nuanced than this. Holds every subject matter has its own methodology. Conversely, contemporary methodology calls for some sort of necessity for de facto intelligibility.

Lonergan: Nature: grace is not a necessary relationship, though you can find necessities in it. Theology can't be reduced to contemporary ideal of science – cf. later.

Question: Brunner on non-objective knowledge of persons.

Theory

(defines its terms) —————————— Interiority (data of consciousness)

Indian culture

Community

(arises on intersubjectivity)

Lonergan: Brunner operates in community. Differentiation of consciousness is involved here. See *Insight*, ch. 6. Insight works in a different way in interpersonal relationships. Classicist world is conceived as normative. Dropping it creates a crisis of values. Positive theology is undermining all the proofs they have from scripture, from the Fathers, etc. You can't rewrite the first 21 councils of the church. We must find how transpositions can be made.

de Lubac, *Surnaturel*[18] – Epilogue produced an explosion. Held gratuitous has to do with personal relations. Nature in Hegelian philosophy is opposed to spirit. Lonergan influenced by Newman's *Grammar*. Also Plato, Augustine; picked up Maréchal. Doctoral work on Thomas – The man much better than his followers.

De Deo Trino is example of finished treatise. Not much more to add. Redemption needs use of human and historical sciences. Experience: Insight: Judgment.

Husserl's *Einklammerung* is OK unless you make it universal and take rudder off the ship. Phenomenology focuses on aspects not attended to, and this makes experience richer.

18 Henri de Lubac, *Surnatural: Études historiques* (Paris: Aubier, 1946).

AFTERNOON LECTURE, PART 1: FACTORS EXTERNAL
TO THEOLOGY (CONTINUED)[19]

2 Notion of Meaning *(continued)*

Differentiated consciousness gives rise to subject of Thales and the milk-maid. Two forms of consciousness. Newton working out gravitation totally absorbed in theory. Absent-minded professor is absorbed in world of theory. Others think in imaginative and common-sense terms. Eddington spoke of two tables in front of him, one of which was mostly empty space. For boy, giraffe is mostly neck. Each science has its own technical language. Different method of inquiry and investigation. Scientists' is systematic. They relate things to one another; common sense relates them to us.

Other patterns of experience: The mystical.

Meaning as constitutive of human reality. – When a man starts to dream. When he awakes meaning is much more so. When he asks, reflects, deliberates, etc., he becomes more and more himself. So meaning is constitutive of our symbols, of our living with others, loyalty, faith, our projects, plans, goals, etc.

Meaning is constitutive also of human communication and hence of community and rises out of common meanings. Community of understanding. Strangers are strange because they do not share this. Community of knowledge rests on agreement. Community of commitment – love, loyalty, faith, etc. Limited commitments of contract, friendship, etc.

People can become mutually incomprehensible when this breaks down. Way open for quarrels and war. Newman's *Idea* says university must create community of knowledge. Cf. C.P. Snow's *The Two Cultures.*[20]

Three meanings of word 'world' – i.e., totality of objects.

1 Immediate sensitive apprehension – for infant.

2 Mediated by meaning – acquisition of language enlarges world. Liberal or general education enables one to control world mediated by meaning. World of common sense, history, etc.

3 Mediated and constituted by meaning. Human institutions are ultimately determined through meaning. Family is constituted by meaning – Accepted notions of state determine what state is – democracy in US does

---

19 The same archival item as was mentioned above in note 2 contains notes relevant to this section.
20 C.P. Snow, *The Two Cultures and the Scientific Revolution* (New York: Cambridge University Press, 1959).

not equal democracy in England. Johann:[21] when one moves from nature to history the world becomes unstuck. Human institutions. World becomes different for convert or apostle.

3 Historical Consciousness[22]

Man's world has always varied in time – more rapidly today. Man is acutely aware of massive fact of human existence. Modern man has made the world. He has done it and knows he is responsible. Ever-decreasing importance of ancient models. Modern man has investigated other worlds – voyages into lands of past and distant places. Whole of history stands in evolutionary perspective. Freedom is a factor in constitution of world in which man lives. Tradition in sense of what used to be done – we find we need to reassess. Classicist tradition looked on 'up to date' as a matter of fancy or fad. But to modern man to be out of date is to try to live in a world that no longer exists. *The – 'isms'*

Some discovered by historian – e.g., feudalism

But others mean a new approach to human living coming to consciousness: (a) Political, (b) Econ (c) Literary (d) Religious (e) Philosophic etc.

Every 'ism' tries to organize the whole universe. It is really the historical consciousness become constitutive. The ontological aspect of *historismus* – The reality of man is historical.

Modern philosophy has developed with modern human sciences. Cf. tomorrow morning for this.[23]

AFTERNOON LECTURE, PART 2: THE INTERNAL SITUATION[24]

1 Description of theology
2 Method = is concerned with operations not object.
3 Contemporary problem

21 It is not clear to whom Lonergan is referring.
22 The same archival item (85400DTE060) contains notes relevant to this section, at the typed page numbered '9.'
23 Notes on modern philosophy relevant to Lonergan's preparation for the 1964 institute may be found in the same archival item, on the typed pages numbered '10' through '14.' These notes are far more extensive than what it seems Lonergan presented on the following morning.
24 Lonergan's lecture notes for this section may be found in a 5-page searchable pdf file on the Lonergan Archive website, www.bernardlonergan.com, at 85500DTE060. See also 472A0DTE060.

Modern notion of science carried into theology by 'positive theology' – i.e., *oratio obliqua*: What did X hold?

B. Xiberta, *Introductio in S. Theol*[25] gives bibliography of protest. literature.

Deus Scientiarum Dominus introduced positive teaching into seminaries. Cf. bibliographies in *Biblica*, Altaner, *Patrologie* – sigla for collections, etc. Medieval: *Bull. de Théol. ancienne et médiévale*. Theol. in general: *Eph. theol. lov.*

Effort a generation ago was to get positive studies into theology –

Newman's theorem [in *Idea of University*]: To omit part of knowledge is to distort the whole. Cf. Fergal McGrath, *The Consecration of Learning*.[26]

Conversely to add a new field is to change the whole. New sciences are flourishing but transformation of the whole is as yet only a disquieting confusion.

The 'person' – Augustine asked, 'quid tres?' Replied: The name we use is person. Boethius, Richard of St Victor, St Thomas give definitions – Third stage: You are forced into metaphysics to decide what definition to adopt – Scotus, Capreolus, Cajetan, Suarez, etc. Then a shift to psychological study of consciousness – Descartes, semi-Rationalists – confusion of consciousness with person. Phenomenology then distinguishes 'I-Thou' from 'I-It.'

Another instance: Bossuet held what is new is heretical because not *ubique, semper* and *ab omnibus*.[27] Later the development of doctrine sets up periods. St Thomas when he speaks of love means primarily *habitus*. Modern writer begins with experienced affects.

Today appeal to Augustine and Thomas leads to a historical inquiry into what the man really meant – and you have taken 2 months off from your course. You can't teach dogmatic theology and history at once.

Formerly theology was a solid block of doctrine. Today theology is getting impacts from all sorts of movements due to positive studies.

Theology finds itself in great problem. Differences in language in classical and contemporary consciousness. Philosophy that fits in with the one doesn't fit in with the other. In unified theology one may use one or another or no notion of science. Affective modes of consciousness can't be both classical and modern. You must use some philosophical *ancilla* – but what will it be? The massive entry of modern science, historical consciousness, and positive studies into Catholic theology is demanded by historical

25 See above, p. 274, note 22.
26 Fergal McGrath, *The Consecration of Learning: Lectures on Newman's* Idea of a University (Dublin: Gill, 1962; and New York: Fordham University Press, 1962).
27 Vincent of Lérins, *Commonitorium pro catholicae fidei antiquitate et universitate adversus profanas omnium haereticorum novitiates*, ed. Adolf Jülicher (Frankfurt: Minerva, 1968), para. 2.3.

quality of Catholicism. You can't simply pour new wine into old bottles. Tension between departments, generations, etc.

Problem of method in theology comes partly because exigence for change tends to be hidden. Theologian is not a specialist in the sciences where the change is taking place. Theologian tends to regard question of nature of science, etc., as 'speculative' – i.e., *insoluble* and irrelevant.

Boyer, Garrigou-Lagrange, were not concerned with these issues. So too contemporary students of positive theology are not concerned. Contemporary biblical student is not a modernist – wants to prescind from these theoretical issues. Wants to master techniques.

E. Husserl, *Die Krisis der europäischen Wissenschaften und die transzendentale Phänomenologie.* Hague, 1954.[28] The more specialized a science becomes the less it is influenced by theoretical notion of science. Theorist of science is regarded as another specialist, so no one pays any attention.

Men in positive field are there because they never liked philosophy and theory. In Protestant theology the situation is different because you have men like Bultmann who will think out the consequences theoretically; and that gives them the initiative.

Positive studies and dogmatic theology of a sort are undermining each other. Dogmatic theology was supposed to put down clearly what everybody agrees on. This leaves only formulae to be recited and believed. Biblical studies embarrasses this dogmatics by endless difficulties, and they capture minds of students by offering an account that gives some understanding – even if only first century.

Conversely, epistemology is undermining positive studies. Scientific history was von Ranke's method. A. Richardson, *History: Sacred and Profane.*[29] Gadamer, *Wahrheit und Methode* Tübingen 1960[30] gives good account of Dilthey. Dilthey wanted to do a critique of historical reason. But he discovered that Ranke etc. was full of ideas from the Enlightenment. Carl Becker in US, Karl Heussi, *Die Krisis des Historismus*[31] – history as done by competent historians as of about 1900. Marrou's critique of Langlois and Seignobos.

Hermeneutics also is facing epistemological questions. Fundamental thinking must be faced for exegesis.

---

28 See above, p. 62, note 10.
29 Alan Richardson, *History Sacred and Profane* (Philadelphia: Westminster, 1964).
30 See above, p. 115, note 13.
31 See above, p. 240, note 5.

Questions

Question: Does meaning or free action constitute the reality?
Response: Freedom pertains to the order of meaning and intention. Meaning is conscious finality. Human meaning is determination of transcendental determination towards being. There is a creative, effective order of meaning.

Levels:

(a) Potential
(b) Formal intelligence – cognitional – *dat formam*
(c) Judgmental – *dat esse*
(d) Effective – appetitive

Husserl does not admit grasp of the real but is left with transcendental ego. Caught in idealist trap. Tries to get community of egos.

Because Protestant theology is centered on Bible, there is no place else for speculative theologian today.

Objection: Modern Catholic biblical commentaries try to apply meaning to church today.
Lonergan: *Sacra Pagina* – Descamps' 'Réflexions [sur la méthode en théologie biblique]' and Spanish article for authentic biblical theology are contradictory.[32] Descamps works way into mind of Isaiah till he and pupils talk Isaiah's language. Job of going to ... 'Biblical Movement.'

There is a conception of biblical theology that proceeds from understanding of scripture to pulpit prescinding from Councils, etc.

Objection: In theology you can't prescind from relevance, i.e., in terms of salvation.
Lonergan: Other views make no clear distinction between dogmatic and positive theology – Lonergan holds precepts of different methods call for different disciplines.

32 See above, p. 74, note 16.

1964-2

Reason Illumined by Faith[1]

MORNING LECTURE: HUMAN KNOWING AS OPERATIONAL
STRUCTURE

Vatican I: Two orders distinct both in principle and object

Ratio fide illustrata is mating of the two. Today our concern is not with
objects but with method – i.e., operations which theologian performs in
dealing with object.

Operation: 2d act.

Dynamic structure: Cf. *In Boethei de Trinitate*, q. 5 on abstraction. Thomas
points out you can't abstract foot from animal because its intelligibililty
depends on its function – i.e., animal.

Structure: an element which with others forms an intelligible entity.
Form, matter, *esse* are not things but structural components.

So this morning we shall speak of human knowing. Knowledge, objectivity, consciousness.

1 Knowing

'Know' in wide sense includes any cognitional activity – even stupid gaping
or imaginative insight (into unreality) or reckless judgment. But experience
is really a component in human knowing. To know, you must experience,

---

1 Notes for lectures on Tuesday, 14 July 1964.

understand, doubt, and judge reasonably. Judgment is the ultimate in which process reaches completeness.

Admiratio (*thaumezein*) lifts to level of insight. Doubt raises to level of search for evidence. Third elevation: process of deliberation leading to practical judgment and decision of will. Leads to a responsibly ordered life.

Practical judgments and decisions
Judgment of truth
Understanding   concepts, theories, hypotheses
Experience ⟶

Only by adverting to one's own 'experience' of understanding, etc., does one grasp what it is.

Understanding is prior to concepts and differs from sensory seeing. [At this point Lonergan used the familiar example of the first problem in Euclid's *Elements*, to construct an equilateral triangle on a given base in a given plane.]²

So too, definition of circle in terms of constant radius depends on understanding.

Euclid's system logically incomplete because he has theorems that can't be proved from his own postulates – based on commonsense insight into sensible data. Nobody noted the defect in first proposition of Bk 1 for 2000 years.

To illustrate act of judgment is more complex. Cf. *Insight* ch. 10. It is an act of understanding of the rationally conscious subject.

Human living is a structure of operations – experience, understanding, and judgments.

2 Objectivity

(a) *Experiential objectivity.* Contained in presentation of data/evidence. Is my hand white? If seen vs. paper, response is no. But other elements also needed to have objectivity in full sense.

(b) *Normative objectivity.* B. Russell uses postulate that there is no postulate that applies to all classes. This is said to be not objective – i.e., lacks intelligible coherence. It is self-refuting. If normative objectivity is lacking people complain that you are talking nonsense – incoherently. (Synthesis of concepts)

2 See above, pp. 85–86, and note 4.

(c) *Absolute objectivity*. A matter of fact – is it a dog or a wolf that I am seeing? Either statement would be coherent. Call is for certitude. (Weighing
evidence in process of judging)

3 elements are all required for objectivity.

Empiricists, Essentialists, and Rationalists emphasize one component.

Materialism, Idealism, Realism

3 Consciousness

You are conscious when you understand and when you don't. You are conscious of inquiry, imagination, doubt, reflection, deliberations and choices.

On basis of consciousness you can inquire into consciousness.

Modern type of philosophy, as opposed to Greek or medieval.

Prenote. Modern philosophy may hark back to earlier modes.

Greek: Sharp discontinuity between theory and practice, wisdom and prudence, necessity and contingency. Prudence takes care of contingencies.

Modern: Discontinuity tends to disappear. Philos. concerned not so much
with wisdom as with realm of prudence, etc.

1. characterized by shrinking of realm of necessity. Euclid regarded as
one of many geometries.

J. Ladrière of Louvain on Gödel.[3] Roure on principles of identity and
non-contradiction.[4]

S. Breton on crisis of reason in contemporary thought.[5] These men
question possibility of a perfect logical statement. Pure reason dominated 17th-century philosophies.

Hegel's new logic of necessity is considered indefensible by most
commentators.

---

3 Jean Ladrière, *Les limitations internes des formalismes: Étude sur la signification
du théorèmes apparentés dans la théorie des fondements des mathématiques* (Louvain:
Nauwelaerts, and Paris: Gauthier-Villars, 1957). See Lonergan's references
in *Phenomenology and Logic* (see above, p. 77, note 17). 49–62.

4 The reference may be to Marie Louise Roure, *Logique et métalogique: Essai sur
la structure et les frontières de la pensée logique* (Paris: Vitte, 1957).

5 Edmond Barbotin, Jean Trouillard, Roger Verneaux, Dominique Dubarle,
and Stanislas Breton, *La crise de la raison dans la pensée contemporaine* (Bruges:
Desclée de Brouwer, 1960). See Lonergan's review in *Shorter Papers*, vol. 20
in Collected Works of Bernard Lonergan, ed. Robert C. Croken, Robert M.
Doran, and H. Daniel Monsour (Toronto: University of Toronto Press,
2007) 234–36.

For Christian, world is contingent, man's choices add more contingency. Christ's redemption is gratuitous.

2. Penetration of theory into practice. Discontinuity tends to vanish. Modern math and science are wedded to practice. Theory [in] human science – e.g., sociology – aims to understand and hence control concrete reality.

3. Breakdown of naive realism. You need a whole series of insights to grasp any subject as a whole. So understanding is *not* like just seeing! Relativity and quantum theory eliminated imaginable space-time manifold and continuous trajectories. Modern physicist knows only that his equations are verified. Modern historical method.

Psychology: Piaget on development of subject-object distinction, not based on seeing.

4. *Logic* deals with objects in general. *Method* shifts from logic to operations – scil. all cognitional activities. The *subject* is revealed by the way he performs the operations.

5. Transition from *per se de iure* subject ('any reasonable man') to *de facto* self-constituted subject. Modern philosophy proceeds from philosophers that exist. World of man is both constituted and mediated by meaning. Critical problem is root of all the disputed questions – and are the ones that strangle theology. It must be faced.

AFTERNOON LECTURE: TRANSFORMATION OF REASON BY FAITH

1 This Transformation Affects the Levels of Data, Understanding, and Judgment

1. In natural science the datum is simply the given – e.g., place of needle on the dial. In human science, the data include a meaning – a commonsense, everyday meaning. In a human science, the fact that this is a law court pertains to the data.

Dilthey worked out distinction between *Naturwissenschaften* and *Geisteswissenschaften*.

Human sciences don't attempt to follow so closely method of human science.

In theological science the fundamental datum is word of God. This word is authoritative, not to be contradicted. For the believer that word is 'true.'

Loca theologica distinguished by M. Cano. Reducible to Scripture and Tradition.

In theology as distinct from human sciences you are committed to accept the meaning of the data as true.

2. On level of understanding –

Human understanding is not measure of intelligibility of God's word. Vatican I said that one couldn't know strict mysteries without revelation and even after revelation they are not demonstrable from created things. But reason illumined by faith can attain a very fruitful understanding from connections with one another, with creation, and with end of man.

3. On level of judgment –

A divine sociology of knowledge is needed. Revelation has been entrusted not to theologians or individual believers but to the church.

Theology is a science in an analogous sense because its data, mode of understanding and of judgment differ markedly from other sciences. But in all the sciences including theology the fundamental intention is good and true. Theology is not an entry into the absolutely other. Modally it differs from natural and human sciences but the operations are basically the same.

Positive theology mainly considers data, systematic deals with understanding, dogmatic theology is concerned with judgment (assent of faith). Foundations is concerned with relation of these to one another and to other sciences.

2 Mediation[6]

Popularized in philosophy by Hegel. Cf. Niel's *De la médiation dans la phil. de Hegel.*[7] Aristotle had already spoken of middle term.

1 Tim 2.5 Christ the one Mediator. Hegel influenced by the theological notion of mediation.

(a) Mediation in general. Any factor that has a source and derivatives may be said to be immediate in source and mediated in derivations and expressions.

Cases: A watch = a constant movement – movement from mainspring, constancy from balance wheel. Mutual mediation and causality – since each affects the other. So supply of oxygen and flow of blood and nutrition. Operations that pertain to whole body are immediate in one place or another.

On the psychic level what is immediate in intelligence is mediated in rest of psyche, etc. On level of evidence: first principles (immediate) and conclusions.

---

6 See www.bernardlonergan.com, items 87200DTE060 and especially 87300DTE060 for material pertinent to this section, which draws comments from both of these items. See also the paper 'The Mediation of Christ in Prayer' (see above, p. 55, note 26).

7 See above, p. 55, note 27.

In theology, the four parts exhibit mutual mediation.

(b) Self-mediation. Organism is functional whole, it mediates itself in growth. The organism generates its own organs in such a way that at each moment it remains a viable organism. H. Driesch's experiments on sea urchins showed that growth is determined by teleology.

Processes of specialization and differentiation of parts.

There is a phylogenesis of species which mediates itself by reproduction – to mediate sustenance of further species.

Animal organism – introduces element of intentionality.

(c) Self-mediation through self-consciousness. Development is one of increasing autonomy. Individual learns about himself through his activities and then wants to decide for himself what he is to do. Existential commitment: man sets own goal for himself, disposes of himself in love, in loyalty, in faith (in family, state, Church).

Human community formally is an intentional reality constituted by meaning.

(d) Mutual self-mediation. Man arrives at existential commitments not in isolation but in togetherness.

Act of *faith* – an existential commitment. Individual is depending on the mediation of history. By his witness he is a point of mediation for others to be helped or hindered regarding Christianity.

Theology: Thematized knowledge of God mediated by the body of Christ. 'Vécu' – contained in living. You don't attempt to reflect on it. 'Thematized' stepping out of mainstream and trying to say what is going on. Diary is thematizing one's living. Everybody is conscious of all his human activities. Thematized – not just *exercite* but *signate*. All Christians have knowledge of God – but theology articulates, evaluates, grounds, etc.

Knowledge of God is immediate in beatific vision. Mediated either by reason or by faith. Fundamental passing on of the Christian witness is entirely distinct from historical study of the Christian tradition. Mediation by body of Christ is by illumination and inspiration of Holy Spirit (subjective aspect). Objective aspect – content of the tradition. In positive theology we concentrate more on data.

Responses to Questions

Reason illumined by faith – reason is owl that sees only by night. Illumination is in darkness of faith. Reason and faith as an operational structure. Reason is transformed by faith. The metaphor of light has to be transcended.

Theologian needs illumination of Holy Spirit. Process of development of dogma is not strictly deductive.

In sciences, belief is essential. No mathematician bothers to check the logarithm table. Scientists are a believing community. No one of us can be a news service. But theory of general relativity, etc., are human achievements. Cf. analysis of belief in last chapter of *Insight*.

Mediation between sciences. Various branches of theology influenced by one another.

End of natural desire for Thomas is 'quidditative' knowledge of God. But a person has not got an essence, he has a secret which he reveals when he chooses – a Who.

This is in another sense a what too.

Faith is on level of truth. Rousselot held *les yeux de la foi* – didn't sufficiently distinguish between insight and reflective judgment. Believer understands only with images. But there is an extension of affirmation and an enlargement of domain of truth. *Lumen fidei* is for affirmation not for understanding.

1964-3

Differentiation of Methods I[1]

MORNING LECTURE: FOUNDATIONS

Differentiation of methods is necessary because one cannot pursue different ends simultaneously. Different ends require different methods.

Reflection on whole process of experience, understanding, and judgment = foundations.

Foundations for theology is not fundamental theology in sense of foundation for reason.

Horizon: 'Founding circle' – limit of field of visibility. Husserl generalized this notion. We shall use as variation on Aristotelian-Thomist notion of *formal object*. Defined by correlatives of pole and field. Pole is subject, field is totality of objects. Potency is defined by its formal object. Scholastic concept concentrates on object and commonly conceives this abstractly: *ratio sub qua objectum attingitur*. Pole is *concrete* subject. Field is a *totality* of objects. Horizon embraces *both* pole and field.

Horizon originates with regard to vision. For different standpoints there are different horizons and different totalities of objects. There is a central region which is luminous, then penumbra and finally outer darkness. What is beyond horizon is what subject knows nothing about. He couldn't care less. In penumbra: vague knowledge, of minor interest, what one talks about only casually. What is fully within horizon fully engages attention. Each lives in his own world – of law, politics, religion, industry, commerce, home, etc.

---

1 Notes for lectures on Wednesday, 15 July 1964. Relevant to these notes is www.bernardlonergan.com, 86400DTE060.

Analysis of horizon:

Absolute horizon. Everyone draws the line somewhere. What cannot be known and is regarded as worthless. Everyone draws the line somewhere no matter how liberal or openminded he may claim to be. (Cf. 'discredited statements.' [AD addition])

Relative horizon. Doctors and lawyers know about one another's worlds. They do business with one another. We acknowledge relative differences and admit their necessity. It is a matter of a person's *development*.

Absolute horizon is a matter of *conversion*. Makes the world a different place for him. Conversion is intellectual, moral, or religious. Changes basic orientation of one's living.

Relative horizons differ socially according to measure of one's competence.

Historical differences, environments, differences in individuals.

This type of foundation regards the operative subject who is doing theology. But he is understanding others who are also doing it.

Psychological differences (individuals)

J. Piaget – genetic epistemologist

Flavell

J. McV. Hunt – work on IQs [*Experience and Intelligence*[2]]

Piaget's analysis complements that of Aristotle. Studies operations, developments, and provides unity which is lacking to Thomas's catalogue of virtues and vices. Starts from 'natural' habits present in infant, developments occurring from rudimentary operations which are inefficient. Specialization of these habits with regard to particular objects. These different operations combine. Playing a piano combines many operations.

Flavell, *Developmental Psychology of J. Piaget.*[3]

Piaget holds any new operation has assimilation and accommodation. Thomas in *Summa contra Gentiles* has topics (chapters) with some 20 arguments on each. Same operations repeated with regard to different questions. Differentiation with regard to these. He goes through a group of operations with adaptations to special questions. Picks out the operations relevant to the matter.

2 Joseph McVicker Hunt, *Intelligence and Experience* (New York: Ronald Press, 1961).

3 John H. Flavell, *The Developmental Psychology of Jean Piaget* (Princeton: Van Nostrand, 1963).

Different levels of development. (a) Immediate (infant). (b) Mediated by imagination, thought, language. (c) Operations with respect to control of imagination, use of language, etc. Reflective disciplines in process of education (grammar, etc.).

Social aspect with regard to relative horizon:

Individual	Social	Final
1. capacity, need　operation	cooperation	partic. good
2. plasticity, perfectibility, habit		
= group of operations (Piaget)	institution	good of order
3. liberty, orientation, conversion	relations	terminal value

Good of order is a series of particular goods – breakfast every morning. The relevant group of operators. In economics – when there is a slump the interconnections change, but the individuals retain their ability to work.

Formal element in good of order is the order itself – one that de facto exists and functions.

Institutions – family, mores, state, economy, etc. They are to society as habits to the individual. Children fight about particular goods but men fight about good of order. Terminal values are the values incorporated in a good of order. The justification of monogamous marriage, democracy, etc. *Personal relations* rest upon institutions – channel them. But more intimately depend on *orientation and conversion* of the individual – his moral conversion, etc.

The field of social horizon is the good apprehended as practically possible. We needn't bother our heads about things beyond that realm.

Social horizon considers what limits field to actualities but it grasps the significance of the ideals in virtue of which men operate. Ergo it doesn't accept empiricist blindspot. Conversion is change of ideals which has impact on what actual situation will be. Being practical doesn't mean being shortsighted. Marx was longsighted, has influence today.

Historical differences:
Consciousness differentiated by Greeks according to theoretical and practical life.[4]

Theoria of Greek Fathers is not *theoria* of Greek philosophers but is much more like Indian interiority.

4　At this point some schematic diagrams appear in Cardinal Dulles's notes, which are here omitted due to lack of clarity as to their meaning.

Different types of theologizing. Relative horizon helps determine what a man will say.

Absolute horizon –

1. *Normative subject.* People don't make statements that deny the dynamics of all human operation – having experience of intelligence, judgment, moral judgment. The normative subject is rationally conscious. Truth, goodness, and value cannot be ignored.

2. *Deviations.* The normative subject is always present but not always attended to. Insofar as a man actually controls operations he may fall into deviations such as *extrinsicism* of truth. Theory of *fides scientifica* rests on fallacy that truths are out there. What God reveals is true in God's mind and in mind of believer, but not elsewhere – out in the air. The Trinity etc. are not true 'out there.' Truth is misconceived in this theory. Tendencies to extrinsicism. The foundation lies in the subject judging. People want criteria that are more public and more easily accessible than intelligence and judgment. They want experiment, necessary demonstration, common consent, etc.

Work on mathematical foundations in this century. Desire to escape from responsibility of subject and set up some extrinsic, 'inspectable' criterion.

3. *Neglected subject, truncated subject.* Leap from understanding to decision is required. Act of will required for decision. Element of judgment is often eclipsed, as though one moved directly from understanding to decision.

Essentialism is temptation because Platonism conceives judgment as composition or division of concepts. Hoenen holds that judging is positing synthesis already made rather than synthesizing.[5] For Aristotle man is a soul in a body. You can't be an Aristotelian and accept [Council of] Ephesus – because Word didn't assume a man.

The perennial philosophies – The various ways in which subject can be neglected and truncated.

4. *Actual subject.* Period of development: One decides more and more for oneself. Finds out more and more for oneself. I am always making myself. Habits acquired spontaneously are extremely hard to break. Question: What kind of man am I to make of myself? *Drifter* fails to face the critical moment. Such people want a Führer.

Existential subject deliberately sets about choosing what to do with himself. Decision repeatedly has to be made in fidelity. *Existenz* giving himself an essence.

5 Peter Hoenen, *La théorie du jugement d'après St Thomas d'Aquin* (Rome: Gregorian University Press, 1946). See Lonergan's very positive assessment of this work, in *Verbum* 106–107 note 2.

Existential subject is the man himself in his interiority. Ignatian *Exercises* is technique for existential decision. Decision may be authentic or inauthentic (differing from normative subject). Contradiction in operations arises from inauthenticity and gives basis for counterpositions.

Foundation is concrete theologian who founds himself existentially. Theologians whom we examine either are or are not 'authentic.' Counterpositions and their reversal brings about progress.

Responses to Questions

The normative subject is all of us in our *transcendental structure*. Capacity and exigence for human development. For theology normative subject includes reason transformed by faith – religiously converted.

Contradiction between *performance* and *content* reveals departure from normative subject in actual subject. Cf. Lonergan, 'Metaphysics as Horizon' (review of Coreth).[6] You can set up contradiction between what Kant says and his saying so. Counterposition. Cf. *Insight*, chapter on method of metaphysics.

Application in theology – if person doesn't accept what Church teaches. Theologian is an organ of mystical body for thematization of knowledge of God.

Normative subject: The invariants present in (a) any rational subject and (b) any believer. You can experience in yourself your own drive to understand, to be reasonable. No one complains about his own judgment but we complain about our memory, which is not in our control. Normative subject is what one finds in himself.

The normative subject is not known when we are thinking about objects. Being present to myself is not presence of object but is condition of presence of any object. One has to identify the object thought of in one's own inmost being and find himself, not some abstraction. Everyone has experience of some insight ... In 'horizon' we do objectify, but *the object mediates the subject. Insight* is self-appropriation, finding of oneself – and that is the foundation. This finding is essentially incommunicable but spark can jump. Finding it as normative is basis of criticism of what one has done and what one finds in others.

Normative subject in theology is not just experiencing data, nor is it experiencing data to which a meaning is assigned, but there is truth element involved. *Divine* truth on second level of operation. Theologian is a member of mystical body, judges within the church – and hence the natural intelligence must be transformed.

6 See above, p. 119, note 22.

For examination of theologian's writings in light of his authenticity. Rosmini's understanding is one of gazing. Religiously he was pious, etc., but intellectual conversion is not the same thing. This analysis provides clues to where things can go wrong.

Normative subject – concrete universal. Husserl's project to get transcendental ego – *eidos* of *ego* seems to be similar. You must objectify – but objectification is mirror in which subject finds himself.

Objection: Thomas, *De veritate*, q. 10, a. 8, would seem to say subject is present to itself as first act.
Lonergan: Thomas used psychological introspection to arrive at results. But he didn't say he was doing so. With regard to consciousness he is not as consistent as Augustine. His expression is sometimes less accurate. Soul in first act may mean simply soul. *Mens* in Augustine is subject. When Thomas uses this term it may be clue to finding what Thomas thinks about subject.

Question: What do you mean by obnubilation? How does it compare with rationalization?
Lonergan: A type of inauthenticity contrasting actual subject with what he thinks he is. A person can think he is a Christian, or Thomist, without being so. Doesn't advert to differences. Has no other means of expression. Obnubilation runs through all he says. A school often becomes inauthentic because disciples are not of founder's status. So too in a religious order. The normative subject is objectified as great leader but not understood.

Rationalization. One knows what one knows but knows it imperfectly. The rationalizer is perfectly clear-headed. Makes universe square with all the conclusions.
Differences between intellectual, moral, and religious conversion.

(a) *Intellectual* – capacity to use own mind develops. Children have to discover difference between imagined and real world. Childish notions of objectivity, etc., must be exchanged for others which are constitutive fully developed capacities.

(b) *Moral* – man a center in environment. As a psyche, each man is a similar center. Considers self as just one in the community.

(c) *Religious*

Triple conversion. Three do not occur simultaneously. Nicea represents emergence of intellectual conversion in Catholic dogma.

Authentic subject: normative subject as actual

Intelligible emanation (Crowe)

1. Understanding
2. Judgment (expression of reflective understanding)
3. Love (complacency) (delight, consent to being)
4. Conscience (what ought to be done). Deals with being as possible.
Level of concern.

AFTERNOON LECTURE: POSITIVE THEOLOGY[7]

Christianity is historical religion. Origins in a given historical milieu. Tradition – handing on the good news down through the ages. Four factors shaped post-medieval positive theology:

(a) Printing made publication of texts and monographs possible.

(b) Decadence of Scholasticism in 14th and 15th centuries. Positive theology presented as an alternative. Theology in comparison deprecated.

(c) Pursuit of antiquarianism. Cf. A. Richardson on the *érudits*.

Jansenism, etc., aim to restore true Augustinianism.

O. Chadwick on development of doctrine presents Bossuet's theology as Gallican.[8]

Theology in French more historical than in Spanish.

(d) Dogmatic theology aimed at presenting doctrine common to all.

Positive theology presented as supplement to Scholastic (Cano, etc.).

Positive theology used as a weapon for polemics.

19th century – Romanticism, *Historismus*, Positivism, and Existentialism – appeal to texts to correct.

We mean [by positive theology a] specific technique: Theology in *oratio obliqua*. Just what was thought about God by Isaiah, Paul, Athanasius, Aquinas, etc.? Narrates theology of particular writers. Not my theology. It aims not at settling what Church teaches but to provide information needed if one is to have a theology based on original revelation and its transmission. Criteria: experiential objectivity.

Philip Donnelly on *finis* of creation.[9] Why didn't Vatican 1 quote Thomas? Their defense vs. attack that was missing point fails to make clear that they too

---

7 For lecture notes relevant to this section see www.bernardlonergan.com, item 85600DTE060, first (unnumbered) page.

8 The reference is probably to Owen Chadwick, *From Bossuet to Newman* (Cambridge: Cambridge University Press, 1957).

9 Philip Donnelly, 'Saint Thomas and the Ultimate Purpose of Creation,' *Theological Studies* 2 (1941) 53–83.

were not missing the point. This sort of thing happens when the tradition is not well known. Blindness of saying there is *consensus Patrum* when there is not.

Positive theology aims only to be a *functional part* of theology.

It doesn't analyze foundations, nor does it explain what Church imposes or how truths are to be understood. But its specific function has a certain *relative autonomy.*

Commonsense matters of fact resist certain philosophies, as Gilson points out. Law of falling bodies depends on notions of distance and time: The law possesses a certain independence in accuracy of its correspondence with data. Einstein's theory of relativity penetrated into formulation of many laws but didn't require doing the experiments over again. Laws of Newton remained in substance, put into a new framework.

So text submitted to theology has meaning which must be fitted into one or another theory. An inadequate relative horizon or a mistaken absolute horizon will somewhat distort. But there is a basic core that remains regardless of changes in theoretical superstructure. Having the facts makes error much more difficult. Interlocking set of texts in one author will make his mind fairly clear.

The names of Christ can be divided into four classes: (1) Christ = expected Messiah. (2) Son of Man as present to apostles in lifetime. Prediction of Passion and Resurrection. (3) Lord – Christ as present to early community. Made Lord and Christ on Resurrection. (4) To correct notion of divinized man – the name Son, opposed to Father (*Deus Pater*).

Knitting together and accounting for differences puts you onto something determined by text, minimally influenced by horizon of the interpreter. Tends to become *l'acquis*. Interpretation based firmly on solid and complete knowledge of text.

Note differences of positive theology and empirical scientific laws: Natural science explains (*Erklärung*), aims to state relations of things to one another, though this must be qualified for quantum mechanics. Commonsense type of understanding is not a matter of arriving at universal laws but getting insights which suffice to understand this instance. Doesn't proceed by scientific hypotheses. In common sense there is no strict definition, nor would it help much. 'A stitch in time saves nine.'

Dogmatic theology aims to say what Catholics must believe. Restricts itself to what is clear and certain and common to everyone. Moves toward Vincent of Lérins's norm. *Positive* theology aims to study John and Paul in their individualities. Its results are not always certain. Works in terms of lesser and greater probabilities.

To confuse dogmatic with positive theology means to ask wrong questions. Dogmatic theology has different concerns and perspectives. Johannine distinction between *verbum* and *verbum caro factum* is not same as our distinction between divinity and word incarnate. Leads to anachronism. St John insists on the knowledge of Christ: he knew the mysteries he was revealing. But John didn't distinguish between his divine and human knowledge.

If dogmatic and positive theology are not distinguished you will be asking your questions rather than his. What St Thomas would have thought about boy scouts if I had been St Thomas.

Positive theology includes: (1) Getting the text – critical editions, who wrote it, when, why, what sources, etc.? Theology uses the best handbooks with relevant articles in current periodical literature.

(2) Interpretation. Questions of hermeneutics – principles of right interpretation. *Per se* the meaning of texts is clear or you would be involved in infinite regress. But there are blocks in interpretation of some texts. Hermeneutics deals with some typical blocks. (a) In ages when there are different theories of knowledge, as today, the discipline is lively. (b) Also because of emergence of historical consciousness. (c) Modern man busy creating a modern world. Brought about an exigence for reinterpretation. Trying to eliminate the Christian view of everything. Scriptures restored to predogmatic context of history of religions, etc. Marxism represents such a principle of universal reinterpretation.

The operations of interpretation itself:[10]

1 Understanding the text

2 Judging how correct interpretation of text is

3 Expression of judgment based on understanding.

1 (a) Understanding *things or objects* spoken of in text. A text can be used as means of learning about things. But we usually presuppose understanding of things author is talking about. Blind man will not understand detailed discussion of colors. We must connect text with something in our experience.

Epistemological problem. If interpreter first has his own understanding he will not be presuppositionless, lest he settle in a priori fashion what text must mean. Principle of empty head. If you know by taking a look you need only look. But in that case you will see only a set of signs. Man with fullest understanding with respect to thing is the one who has best understanding of text. Previous development of interpreter's intellect is all to the good.

Doctrine of Enlightenment was perfect where you were out to destroy and wipe out past and make people start again. Cf. Gadamer, *Wahrheit und Methode*, for critique.

---

10 The material on interpretation presented in this section and at the beginning of the next is not included explicitly in archive item 85600DTE060, but can be found in the 1962 document that forms the appendix to this volume. See also archive item 85900DTE060.

(b) Understanding the *words*. The term x may refer to x_1 or x_2. Writer may mean x_1 and interpreter thinks it means x_2. He should discover what is x_1 which would make sense of the text. Controversialist will say the author is talking nonsense. Cf. *Insight* ch. 6.

Hermeneutic circle. Meaning of word depends on paragraph ... chapter ... book ... *opera omnia* ... environment in which author writes, etc. Meaning of text is an intention unfolding itself through many parts. Parts determined by whole. Understanding grasps both parts and whole. Self-correcting process of learning. You may have to reread after you have finished whole book.

Rules of exegesis – who, when, for whom, *quibus auxiliis*, etc. A man can observe all rules and be just a pedant. Rules don't guarantee that interpreter will be intelligent man.

(c) Understanding the *author*. Need for long and arduous use of self-correcting process. When rereading the book fails to clarify we have to study man and his times.

(d) Changing oneself.

Questions and Responses[11]

When interpretation bears upon interpretation of Scripture it is closely related to what is a matter of faith. Vatican I says it is office of Church to decide what is correct interpretation of Scripture. Positive theologian insofar as he proceeds along lines of scientific method doesn't pretend to solve difficulties.

Also, text of Vatican I is normative, and at same time positive, theology. Anyone who reads theology will have more detailed knowledge than the church requires from every Hrr [?]

A synthesis – made in faith.

Romantic hermeneutics.

There is history which is constitutive of the community – tradition in a wide sense. Existential history. Historical Catholicism gives this to the cradle Catholic. Existential history goes by belief. For Collingwood the 'scientific' historian is not a believer. Scientific history belongs to thematization as opposed to the *vécu* of Christianity.

Catholic has a commitment to unbroken truth of existential history.

Question: Special problem in theology is that we don't get to the revealed object except through the discourse we are studying.

11 In this section it is not clear at times where the questions stop and the responses begin. The editors interpret a couple of the paragraphs as exchanges.

Lonergan: From a particular text we have the whole faith. *Positive theology* –. The absolute horizon is determined by the faith of the subject. He will not exclude evidence that points to Jesus being the Son of God.

Question: The texts investigated are for the interpreter authoritative – and they will be used for dogmatic and speculative theology.
Lonergan: From a methodical viewpoint, a sound method for interpretation of [the Letter of] Barnabas would be about same as for interpretation of a late New Testament text. The interpreter has no special technique for use on an inspired text.

Positive theology is engaged in problems; systematic theologian is concerned with things that are already certain and defined – and seeks to find them in the texts.

Meanings of Scripture are normally 'literary' rather than technical – hence openness [is] to be turned various ways.

Faith is constitutive of the horizon for positive theology. Controls questions which can and cannot arise.

1964-4

Differentiation of Methods II[1]

(c) *Understanding the author.* To understand the words often requires one to understand the author. We can understand other people even when they think differently than we do. We say, 'That's just like you!' Acquisition of the field – gradual accumulation of data with commonsense grasp of mentality of another way of life. Not a matter of defining terms, constructing hypotheses, etc.

Romantic hermeneutics speaks of *Einfühlung.* Herder, Winckelmann, Schleiermacher, Dilthey. Conceives the text as the *Ausdruck* of the writer. Feeling oneself into the writer's soul. You become able to write and speak in same way. Romantic hermeneutics gets right down to particulars. Conceives text rightly from point of view of unformulated intersubjective symbolic meanings. Weakness is oversight of element of truth or falsehood in linguistic expression. A smile is neither true nor false. This element of truth under transposition to another milieu possible. It implies you don't know what Paul is talking about till you get into his mind but [that] doesn't enable you to get out and speak to another time. Truth will de facto be expressed under some limitations but what is truly stated within any prior context can only be stated within another context. Element of transposition is essential to theol. Catholicism = universality.

---

1 Notes for lectures on Thursday, 16 July 1964.

(d) *Development of interpreter.* An intellectual, moral, or religious conversion may be necessary. Only after he has changed himself can he get on author's wave-length. Perennial divisions of mankind in interpretation of the great texts are rooted in the necessity of breakthrough by conversion. After conversion, much mopping up is necessary.

Classics create a milieu and produce the mentality needed to understand them. Gadamer: *Wirkungsgeschichte.* That is what classics are. Create their own tradition. Tradition if authentic will open up the sources. If inauthentic it will obscure the true meaning because of those who are not ready to submit to total conversion. Enlightenment presupposition of no presuppositions destroyed tradition, and understanding of the original sources was destroyed.

Newman: Better to start by universal belief than universal [doubt].

2 Judgment of one's correctness in interpreting the text –

Does it answer all relevant questions? 'Relevant' entails reference to a prospective judgment.

The interpreter is forced to resort to limited judgments on meaning of text by hermeneutic circle. Expanding element in the object forces interpreter to limit himself to closely confined judgments: At least the author did not mean that. Meaning of parts is *affected* by meaning of whole. There remains a hard nugget. Statement that Brutus killed Caesar favorable to either Brutus or Caesar, but can't be put in context that Caesar killed Brutus. Gospel of John may be read as background of Hellenism or Dead Sea Scrolls, but still a careful study of John himself will not be thrown out by either. Dodd's study written independently of the Scrolls.

3 Statement of meaning of the text –

(a) A. Descamps *Sacra Pagina* 1, Théol biblique.[2] Holds biblical theology attends to religious element in the scriptures. Commonsense expression; the writer's commonsense views. Can be communicated in seminar. Will stick to author's mode of expression, evading problems of transposition. Will avoid exposé that ranges over the various books of scripture, etc. P. 142f.

But there is a real problem of properly expressing at present time what scholar finds in text.

(i) There is an area of human expression free from hermeneutic problems. Once one is within the circle. No hermeneutic literature on what Euclid meant. All who think they understand agree as to what he meant. But there are endless commentaries on Plato.

2 See above, p. 74, note 16.

The dogmas of the church in general do not raise such great problems – '*homoousion.*'

(ii) There are divisions that exclude communication. Absolute horizons may so differ that communication will not carry. Incommensurable views. One may dismiss it as obsolete.

Without some absolute horizon every demonstration is meaningless.

(iii) Area where hermeneutics are minimal – e.g., statements about external human action, artifacts, time-series of artifacts. These easily find equivalents in any sufficiently [advanced society].

(iv) Literary statements about transcendent objects raise maximum problems. With regard to objects beyond experience one must use either a technical or metaphysical language. In religion statements about transcendent objects are at their maximum. Religion as lived must be expressed in literary language.

(v) There is a non-exegetic solution of this hermeneutic problem. The sources give rise to a tradition. There will be divisions in the tradition due to ambiguities in the sources. These divisions work themselves out in history. The questions about the meaning become explicit and conscious on a technical level.

MORNING LECTURE, PART 2: DOGMATIC METHOD[3]

This brings us to question of *dogmatic method.*

(a) Concerned with point in *Humani generis* on *munus* of dogmatic theologian. Relation between defined dogma and the sources.

(i) The dogma is not in the sources interpreted anachronistically. This would be a vicious circle. No evidence of any consciousness in NT authors of 3 Persons + one [God].

The connection is not any simple-minded deduction.

(ii) The sources are not the sources as interpreted by Romantic hermeneutics – if you want to solve dogmatic problems.

(iii) Nor is it in sources interpreted by naive historical realism. The Fifth Gospel with the *ipsissima verba*! Dogmas take source from the canonical books. Works from meaning of text to dogmas. Whether sources can be reduced to something earlier is another question.

---

3 See the second and third (unnumbered) pages of archival item 85600DTE060.

(iv) Nor is it in sources as investigated by positive method. Positive method aims at complete understanding of data – attends to what is obscure, doubtful. Aims at probabilities lesser and greater. Dogmatic theology aims at results that at present are attainable.

Dogmatic theology aims at finding how this doctrine of Church has its foundation or is contained in sources. Question comes from outside the sources, unlike positive theology.

Attends chiefly to what is clear and certain in many NT writers. Concerned with minimum certainties of the text.

(b) Other side of issue is: *What are the dogmas?* Dogmatic method may be applied either to past or future development of dogma. We attend first to past development. Doesn't take the isolated dogmas at random. Subsequent definitions depend both on sources and on earlier dogmas. Was Cyril or Nestorius in accord with Nicea? Dogmatic theology takes advantage of actual process of development to line up the dogmas in the most satisfactory order. Good order.

(c) What is link between sources and dogmas? Understanding the sources and understanding the dogmas are interconnected. You can't write history of math unless you are a mathematician. Inversely, to understand subjects of human or religious order you must understand the history. (Richardson lacks understanding of systematic method and hence reduces to understanding the history.)

Understanding the history is not same as endless information. Greek councils did not apply Greek philosophy to faith. Discovering key moments in genesis of doctrine – key points at which blocks arose and were overcome. This is quite different from what is meant by history. Butterfield's work on *Origins of Modern Science 1300–1800*.[4] Asks where there began the modern scientific mind. Shows that before about 1700 contributors to science couldn't defend their discoveries because they lacked systematic ground to stand on vs. Aristotelian assumptions. In other words, there are questions in history which arise on the higher level. Same type of history is relevant to understanding of dogma. Cf. Lonergan on how Christian thought moved from NT to Nicea (*De Deo Trino*).[5]

Is the transposition a really valid one?

(a) There is thematization of the *vécu*. But the absoluteness of the word of God gives element of affirmation which gives rise to dogmatic development. If affirmation has a meaning it implies an ontology.

4 Herbert Butterfield, *The Origins of Modern Science: 1300–1800* (New York: Macmillan, 1951; rev. ed., New York: The Free Press, 1966).
5 Lonergan, *The Triune God: Doctrines* (see above, p. 25, note 30) 28–255.

(b) Transposition from one pattern of experience to another. A second type of identity.

(c) Transposition of implicit to explicit by way of deduction.

[Questions?]

Important for all 64 nations to have a means of apprehending, however jejunely, what the whole Church must believe – to avoid falsifying the message. The Protestant minister spends a lot of time preparing sermon. But Catholic priests say pretty much the same thing because they have absorbed the party line – a fundamental identity of meaning secured by arid set of dogmatic theses. Dogma concentrates on strategic issues which channel all the other statements one will make. Assures priest there is fire behind all the smoke coming from the altar. Without it you may have intense spirituality. The ultimate questions do arise. Since 4th century you can't be a Christian without putting the question of divinity of Christ, etc.

The idea of *Wirkungsgeschichte* seems to apply outside the Christian tradition. People in Western [world] in UNESCO can discuss education and know what each other means – but when we discuss with Orientals there is a problem. In Greg[orian], no one is too anxious to direct thesis by Indian.

Traditional manuals on church settle power issues: Who is boss? Effort is now very much to get away from juridicism, which was only method possible so long as only human science was law. To exploit notion of people of God we will have to exploit sociologists.

Nicea is the beginning of all dogmas. But there was no awareness that a whole chain was being started. Nor did Chalcedon distinguish between nature and person in any technical sense. Real distinction would be thought out later.

Office of dogmatic theology – (1) apologetic function. (2) Understanding the whole tradition can consequently be done by backward method (retrogressive). (3) Provides model for future development. Dogmatic function is 'highest' because it deals directly with truth value.

Dogmas are to be believed by divine and Catholic faith – so you can't have dogmatic pluralism. But there are different dogmatic theologies in sense of reduction to data of sources. The dogmatic truth will be differently expressed in different cultures.

AFTERNOON LECTURE: SYSTEMATIC THEOLOGY

If one pursues two goals at once one attains neither.

Vatican I gave charter for systematic theology. Reason illumined by faith ... attains a very fruitful understanding: from (a) analogy of things naturally known and (b) connection of truths with one another and with man's last end.

Prayer that understanding may increase in whole church (DB 1800).

Positive theology – oratio obliqua.

Dogmatic theology – transition to rarified Catholic statements on a hermeneutic level that escapes existential problems. But the declaration of obviously mysterious dogmatic definitions makes this clear. Hence we have *fides quaerens intellectum.* The systematic theologian must bring out full riches derived from dogmatic and positive.

Systematic theology aims at systematic understanding. Doesn't ask what is so but how and why. A correct understanding, of course. Of course all the operations are involved to some extent in all three branches of theology. Questions can easily arise in systematic theology that pull one away. The three levels mediate one another. Drive of inquiry transforms sensible data into images, illuminates these by intellectual drive (*intellectus agens*). Yields definition, hypothesis, theory. The outside object as being is agent cause and as *finis* it is goal.

In theology the object is God as revealed. Any theological act of understanding will of course be finite and imperfect and analogous. This knowledge will also be obscure – because you don't know what the non-understood 'more' is. Further, the theological understanding develops in time. Cf. DB 1800.

The knowledge moreover is synthetic – it attempts to put together the different elements with one another and with man's last end.

'Most fruitful' for *melior est conditio intelligentis.* The more developed is the understanding, the fuller the apprehension of God's revelation will be.

When human inquiry proceeds to an end, it anticipates the end by putting questions and problems.

Development of medieval theology. Launched by Anselm, who however did not command the positive data. Abelard's *Sic et non.* 158 propositions, with reasons for affirmation and negation. Work was scandalous at the time because he gave no answers. He was doing what Gratian had done in Canon Law: *Concordantia discordantium canonum.* Cf. ML 178: 1339–1610. Peter Lombard – four books each of about fifty distinctions. Remained the fundamental text in theology from 1150 to 1608 (Estius). Put the question and left lots of open questions for the *prudens lector.* Successive commentaries differ radically, for the commentators took account of development of theology in intervening centuries. Real issues had changed.

The systematic problem: to find which of a set of questions to take first.

1 *Sapientis est ordinare.* Key question should be able to be asked without presupposing solutions to others. And answer should illuminate at least one other question. St Thomas in Preface to *Summa* complains that order of Lombard is not economical. If you have solved key problems you have virtually solved the rest. *Scientia est de conclusionibus* – in sense of development of understanding.

(*Problematik* = theory of a problem) In some cases the initial solution is met by a fuller understanding of key problems which enable you to solve another set of problems. Theology must moreover develop in relation to philosophy, literature, culture, science – enrichment by expansion into other fields.

If a critic finds the solution not satisfactory he will find all the other solutions unsatisfactory. An inadequate understanding of the correct solution generates a mass of pseudo-problems. This mishap can occur in many ways because of many possibilities of misunderstanding. Decadence: New problems are not put in right order. Result is morass of confusion.

The people who come after are disgusted by the multiplicity of theologies. Some fail to understand the aim of systematic theology. They don't advert to act of understanding and see that it can be expressed in various conceptual frameworks – e.g., Aristotelian. Thus insights of scripture or Augustine can be expressed in Aristotelian terms. John Peckham begged Holy See to condemn paganization of theology by the Aristotelians. He failed to see that Aristotelian concepts were being applied to understanding the mysteries.

Third stage after total misapprehension will be that the data are denied – which throws problem back to positive, dogmatic, and fundamental theology.

Systematic theology is based on analogies from the natural order. Common principles in theology regard the transcendentals – principles that recur in *any* scientific undertaking. Proper principles differ for each branch of science. Lonergan thinks that many current theories of consciousness of Christ are based on lack of effort to think what consciousness is. The theologian can't take position that he is not a psychologist. Knowledge of natural finite object on which you base your analogies is presupposed. So you must study society to be able to apply this to the church. If you want to do theology of symbols you must learn about symbols first. Otherwise you operate under analogy of your own imagination.

Rapid development of sciences make it possible to develop theology rapidly. For continuity of theology it is important that the new analogies be in continuity with the older. Men who want to move too fast usually end by setting things back. Lonergan in *De Deo Trino* integrates modern notions of consciousness – God a self-constituting existential subject. So too you can find that Monothelites were talking in terms of experience of consciousness. (?? [– in AD's notes])

Understanding of itself is neither true nor false. On further level of reflection one asks, Is it so? Understanding of mysteries must be a true understanding.

Dogmatic definition gives some points of departure and limits. But there are many doctrines on which we have little or no dogmatic definition. Systematic theologian will work from interpretation of the common and clear teaching of scripture. But then it will be asked, Is the understanding true? The understanding of itself has value of hypothesis. Its validity is judged by whether it provides *some* understanding of this mystery. If it fails to satisfy, you use it till you can get something better. In certain cases we have no hope of attaining any other analogy. Lonergan holds this for psychological analogy on divine Persons.

Questions

In fundamental theology ('Foundations'), one treats once and for all the difficulties that go to the root of all theology – e.g., critique of Bultmann.

Foundations imply dogmatic or critical realism, which can then be applied in other treatises. Tertullian used a naive realism – the Son is divine because he is made of the right stuff – in Stoic line of thought. Origen in Platonist camp gives subordinationist explanation of Trinity. Idealisms on pattern of Platonism will recur in different centuries.

K. Rahner – Parallels between *Verbum* articles and *Geist in Welt*.[6] Philosophy – cognitional theory and epistemology and metaphysics of proportionate being. You integrate in terms of transcendent concept of God, etc. Philosophy automatically becomes 'philosophy of' – certain cognitional activities – e.g., of natural or human sciences or of art and literature or of education. Use of philosophy in theology involves an *Aufhebung* of philosophy as K. Rahner says in *Hörer*.[7] Theology takes over primacy that philosophy had; it retains philosophy in its entirety; transformation of philosophy.

6 Karl Rahner, *Spirit in the World*, trans. William Dych (New York: Continuum 1994).
7 Karl Rahner, *Hörer des Wortes: Zur Grundlegung einer Religionsphilosophie* (München: Kösel-Verlag, 1963).

All mysteries deal with *quid sit Deus* – i.e., understanding of God in himself. Aristotle held God is *intelligentia intelligentiae* (or rather a separate substance is). Thomas broke up into Unlimited and angels. Beatific vision is communication of divine self-understanding which is lacking to theology in this life. *Ipsum intelligere = ipsum esse.* Supernatural grace is such by intrinsic relationship to the divine essence. Our experience of grace gives us only conjectural knowledge of it. Theological understanding is about a blind spot – a negative – a focal spot which is not luminous. That is our analogous understanding of mysteries. This setting up is a purely technical task.

There are sets of theories which systematically eliminate certain possibilities: Contingent predications about God imply a term ad extra. This can be used to eliminate a whole series of pseudo-problems. Fundamental part plays its role here. Systematic is positive analogous understanding, using ...

Foundational method differs from philosophy because its foundation is reason illuminated by faith. If speculative theologian says, 'I will tell you what is true regardless of differences between philosophical schools,' that is ruinous and gives rise to just complaints. If one is seeking certitude one doesn't get far in developing of understanding, and vice versa. The speculator is apt to overlook detailed facts and vice versa. Three tasks. General survey to establish differences and relations between the three levels.

1964-5

Special Questions[1]

MORNING LECTURE: DEVELOPMENT OF DOGMA[2]

No one today disputes that it occurs. Not all dogmas evolve in just the same way. Some general features may, however, be singled out –

Evolution of dogma may be conceived on analogy of universalization. Universal: *Unum multis commune* {*in re*
{*in mente*
{*reflexum*

What was singular in mind of Christ became common by its diffusion to Apostles and to the believing Church. The process of teaching involves *universale in mente*. There are obvious differences between the way different minds assimilated. Each had his own *modus recipientis* which is brought to light by positive theology. Daniélou, *Théologie du judéo-christianisme* (Tournai-Paris, Desclée, 1958),[3] shows tendency among them to conceive Son and Holy Spirit as angels on a larger scale. Analogy of angels in Isaiah's vision was used. Angels above all other angels chanting, 'Holy, Holy, Holy.' Gnosticism, while it had some roots in Samaria, was more Hellenistic in its *modus recipientis* – led to heresy.

When people learn, they make some adaptations of what they already have. Christian doctrine did not lie in these differences of apprehension. Catholic faith is what is common – *quod ubique, ab omnibus.*

---

1 Notes for lectures on Friday, 17 July 1964.
2 See the fourth (unnumbered) page of archive item 85600DTE060.
3 See above, p. 25, note 32.

Third step is *universale reflexum* – stage of definition. According to Ignatius of Antioch the Christians are to follow the bishop. And there was communion of bishops. There was an element of prescinding from individual differences arising in particular cultural milieu. When a dogma is defined you have a *universale reflexum* emerging. Hippolytus on Noetus. He was excluded because they never heard his doctrine before, not handed down. Excommunicated by local presbyter. When heresies arose such as Sabellianism there were determinations which moved toward formulation of common object. E.g., Apostles' Creed in Rome second century fundamentally anti-Marcionite. Dogma of Nicea is a clear effort to define by introducing a technical term because scriptural terminology not adequate.

Another aspect in evolution of dogma is transition from hermeneutic problems and movement to form of expression that lies outside hermeneutic problems. Literary expression involves considerable use of metaphor. 'Splendor gloriae et figura substantiae eius' (Hebrews 1.3) may depend on Philo but ultimately on OT language. Gives high notion of who Son is. Doesn't put question whether Son is truly God, which would be anachronistic till 4th century.

Hermeneutic problems [are] at minimum in technical scientific thought.

Further aspects to evolution of dogma: on side of object, subject, evaluation of process, and interpretation of process.

On objective side: Dogma is not simply a repetition of statements in scripture. There is an element of unification – movement from many scriptural statements to one that implicitly contains these many. This is notably true with regard to divinity of Son.

On subjective side: Differentiation of consciousness. Gospels are addressed to the whole man. When man works for a concrete end he is inspired by images, his intelligence works out means to the end, will tend toward it. Differentiated consciousness – in an intellectual pattern of experience the imagination cools down. Imagination is merely for sake of judgment. Affects in abeyance. Will pursues only the good of intellect. The man becomes a specialist. The dogmas are engaged almost exclusively in instruction of intellect. Question precisely what the truth of the matter is.

Much criticism of dogmas can be met on this level. It is asked, Why substitute arid formulas for the vital expression of the word of God? The meaning of dogma is relatively clear. Further, we are not choosing between Gospels and dogmas. Utility of dogmas for the *rudes* is more debatable – perhaps their value as orientations for future development of individual should not be ignored in catechetics.

Question of judgments on value of dogmas. Fundamental question is whether they are true. For undifferentiated consciousness they are not religious. As man becomes more cultured, the religion has to become differentiated with differentiation of the consciousness. To exclude this intellectual side becomes equivalent to secularism – for what is not intellectually respectable is rejected or kept only as a matter of form.

Hermeneutics of the process. Element of context is present in all our judgments. When people deny our statement we exegete our own judgments – make clarifying statements. Context is clarifying statements that *would* be made.

Evolution of dogma is across a plurality of contexts.

$$\longrightarrow$$

Along each vertical the consistency must be logical. 'Universe of discourse' includes coherence, possibility of deductions, etc. But the universe of discourse is limited. Other statements can be made outside that universe of discourse.

Evolution of dogma includes processes that are not simply logical. The dogmas do not follow in objective, logical fashion. You can make it look consistent by introducing what are called implicit propositions. But these 'implicits' were not in minds of the original writers so far as we can determine by textual evidence. Apostles did not think about these matters, nor does it follow from their mode of expression.

In theological treatise there is no need to work into minds of biblical and patristic writers what positive exegetes deny is there. We must admit development into new universes of discourse.

In math we shift frame of reference. Same point in space may be $x + x_1$, from different points of reference. There are rules for moving from one frame of reference to another. In development of dogma these relationships are more complex than in math.

Higher-level history is necessary to understand development of dogma. In a Council you must figure out what the issues were. Mere fact that process ended this way in church guided by Holy Spirit tells us there must be some connection there. '*Objektiver Geist*' – inevitability can be discerned in the concrete events themselves. This may be inauthentic except in decisive decisions taken in church.

If one appeals to foundations we have set up, we can see source of most of difficulties which have been raised. Typical types of aberrations. Stoics were ethically very fine but they were materialists – their universal *logos* was real because material fire. Spanneut wrote on Stoicism of the Fathers from Clement of Rome to Clement of Alexandria.[4] Accepted materiality of the

4 See above, p. 360, note 3.

spiritual world – departed souls. Subordinationism of Tertullian is a naive way of conceiving the Son's divinity. Block was philosophic, preventing early Fathers from speaking in accordance with Nicea. Origen falls into subordinationism as in order of intelligence, of idea, Platonically. In Nicea we get a dogmatic realism which is not yet critical. Picking out key points in the process. Counterpositions in Tertullian and Origen can be understood in terms of philosophical development. There you can see a dialectic in process from Gospels to Nicea. The dogma of Nicea doesn't come from nowhere. One can see unity across this span of development.

In building up a treatise, the strictly dogmatic part should be presented in order in which councils follow one another. Each decision raises new problems, later resolved by new decisions. In Christology go from Nicea to Ephesus (Nestorius vs. Cyril) (after some consideration of Apollinaris). Distinguish between key process of major dogmas and mopping up process to fill in gaps, analogous questions, etc. Perhaps this is relevant for question of *impeccantia Christi*, Assumption BVM.

Is there some new increment in process of development??? Lonergan says Apostles had all the knowledge but not the new mode of apprehension – to conceive and express it adequately. No new truth is arrived at in the dogma. Apostles were in a state of tension groping for symbols and concepts to express their insights. Infused *species* mean precisely a capacity for understanding. Apostles were talking to people and hence limited themselves to what they felt they could communicate. The more you communicate the more you can communicate.

AFTERNOON LECTURE: THE ARGUMENT FROM SCRIPTURE

There is truth 'in' scripture – a process 'from' scriptures – and an argument 'according to' scripture {correspond to positive theology, dogmatic theology, systematic theology}.

(A) 'In' scripture. Principle can be starting point in scripture for a dogmatic development. We can ask what is explicitly in scripture. Question comes from the later dogmatic development. Positive theologian wants to find what is the question of the text of the original writer. In dogmatic study the question comes from outside. You are not aiming at complete understanding of text. You will concentrate on common elements because he wants to arrive at common affirmation of faith.

Common difficulties: (1) Anachronism reads later questions into earlier discussions. Older style of dogmatic theology abounded in these. (2) Archaism is the complementary error. If not in the earlier, it must be an aberration. Protestant *sola scriptura* didn't admit progress across new modes of expression. Example of *Filius Dei* in Synoptics, Acts, Romans 1, and even Hebrews, which cannot be understood as divine generation.

Different 'schemata' of different theologies – e.g., Alexandrian *logos=sarx*, Antiochene (*Deus-homo?*). There are schemata in NT which help us in our present problem. [a] Texts where our Lord is conceived as the expected one: Christ = Messiah. Scheme is a concrete mode of apprehension – sensible or imaginative or a set of words, plus a certain understanding (in historical terms of a people's expectation). (b) Son of Man – Christ present to his apostles or passages about second coming. Neither (a) nor (b) deals with question whether Christ is God and man. (c) Christ after Resurrection: *Kyrios.* In many passages he seems to be conceived as a deified man. *Dominus* doesn't yet mean Yahweh in Acts 1. (d) A fourth scheme is retrospective. Before Abraham was I am. Deal with pre-existent Christ.

This analysis by schemata provides clues to difficulties which can be raised. Collect a large number of texts which obviously establish that Christ is more than man. *Multipliciter divina participat.* Then texts which bring us closer to divinity: (a) utilization of OT titles and predication of attributes proper to God. E.g., title 'Son' (*simpliciter*). Names 'Father' and 'Son' are used more frequently, name θεός almost disappears. (b) Expression in Hellenistic context. 1 Corinthians 8.6 – one Lord *per quem omnia.* Colossians, Ephesians, etc.

(B) Argument *from* scripture. Movement from scripture to the dogmatic statements. Show how contexts determine movement of the objective spirit to give connection with later teaching of Church. *Wirkungsgeschichte.* The classic creates the tradition. Where there is obscurity there will be conflicts in the tradition but a normative line will establish itself (cf. Foundations), Argument (B).

But take as example Christ's knowledge as man. This could not be directly discussed in scriptures because question could arise only in context of distinction of two natures. Then the question of divine and human operations becomes pertinent. Here you must use:

(C) Argument 'according' to scriptures. Helpful analogy is in physics: satisfying the boundary conditions. If Christ has a human intellect he must have some human knowledge – but what is it like? We can't show directly that John asserted Jesus had beatific vision. But we can say if I put my question, what would be in accordance with the testimony of John? John says, The one speaking knows the Father and is revealer.

If I hold that Christ as man had the beatific vision, I can read John without difficulty. If I hold he didn't I must constantly make distinctions when reading John, which run counter to intention of his Gospel. See how Lonergan develops this in his *De Verbo Incarnato.* Scripture is boundary condition which selects as boundary conditions which of two theological answers is to be preferred. Lonergan argues from function of Christ as revealer. Scripture doesn't indicate that Christ had faith. Nor was he ignorant of the mysteries. We are not asking what John would have said if I had asked him my question. Words of Christ are the doctrine of the Father. Continuity must come through Christ's human mind. If you say Christ as God knew Father this doesn't satisfy John's intention.

Trent on Romans 5.12 probably did not intend to do more than assert that the text has this dogmatic significance; there is continuity. It doesn't affirm what is in Paul's mind. If what I find in scripture is not in conformity with Trent, I study scripture some more.

Compare questions of interpretation of constitution. Similar to interpretation of scripture. Analogies could be found.

Christ developed through stages corresponding to Piaget's description of child learning.

Intuitive knowledge of God contains no intrinsic ordering to any human expression. It is *ineffabilis.* It is not *intelligibile in sensibilibus.* In human intellectual drive you have pure desire to know which unfolds on three levels of experience, insight, and judgment. Christ's beatific vision expressed itself in his living. He made himself a man of a certain character under given cultural conditions. Living of Christ as expression of beatific vision makes effable the ineffable. Learning required human development of *effabilis* from zero. He works not toward an end but from an end. *Superabundantia amoris* is expression and manifestation of the end already attained – *agapē* rather than *eros.* Christ's love is pure donation. In making effable you have constant influence of beatific vision. Child in Temple asked questions because he wanted to know. Development runs along with normal spontaneity. The act of judging is a commitment of the person – the point of impact of the beatific vision.

'Transcendental Philosophy and the Study of Religion,' 3–12 July 1968, Boston College

1968-1

Method[1]

I think I'd best begin by giving the chapter headings of the book I'm projecting. It will help you in the question periods to have some idea of the things that are better to leave until later and the things that can be handled right away in the question period each day. The first part of the book consists of six chapters, and the titles are, first, Method; second, Functional Specialties; third, Horizons and Categories; fourth, The Human Good, Values, Beliefs; fifth, Meaning; and sixth, Religion. It will mainly be with those six chapters that we will be concerned. Perhaps I will go on to a later section, but what the later section has to do with will appear in the second chapter, Functional Specialties.

In general the first six chapters are a hermeneutic circle: you understand the whole by understanding the parts, and the parts by understanding the whole; however, we start from the part that is the presupposition of what follows, and that is method.

In regard to method, first of all a brief observation. There are in general three possible approaches to the topic of method. The first is to say that method is not a science but an art, not something learnt by lectures or books but in the laboratory or in the seminar, that what counts is concrete example, imitating the master, listening to his criticisms, and so forth. In

---

1 Wednesday, 3 July 1968, Lauzon CD/MP3 481 (48100A0E060). Lonergan had been introduced by David Tracy. The basic topic of the first lecture is 'Method.' The lecture is based on a manuscript that became chapter 1 of *Method in Theology*. The second lecture (below, p. 441) begins by completing this introductory topic.

other words, it is a prolonged process of getting hints here, there, and everywhere, watching someone doing a job who is good at it and listening to his criticisms of the way you do it. I think that this is true for initial thought on method and also true for the finer points in any specialized area. The whole business cannot be thematized and objectified. There are things that we do learn only in the laboratory or seminar.

However, there also is a second approach to the topic of method. It was employed by Aristotle, and it has been employed in modern times. That is to pick out the conspicuously successful science, to analyze and study its procedures, and on that basis to define what science really and truly is. The other sciences that are less successful, insofar as they are similar to it, also get the name of science. Insofar as they are dissimilar, well, they have a lower status in the pecking order. For Aristotle, the conspicuously successful science was arithmetic and geometry, and, as Sir David Ross says in his introduction to the *Prior and Posterior Analytics*, throughout his writings Aristotle always seems to assume that anything short of mathematics is only by courtesy given the name of science.[2]

In modern times it is the natural sciences that have that position. They are something quite different from mathematics. And the human sciences, insofar as they conform to the procedures of the natural sciences, are allowed some share of the glory of the name of science; insofar as they differ, well, that is just too bad; they are doing the best they can and as well as they can.

However, this second procedure, while it is all very well for the successful science, is not too good for the others, because, while they get some direction insofar as they resemble the successful sciences, still, where they differ they have no help at all, no direction. And that is the status at the present time of the human sciences and very particularly of our discipline, theology.

Accordingly, what I am proposing to do in this first chapter is to work out a third way. My procedure will be first of all to derive a preliminary notion of method from the successful science; secondly, to go behind that to cognitional theory; thirdly, to find in that cognitional theory the properties of a method, method in the sense derived from an analysis of the natural sciences; and finally, to determine the functions of this very general method in relation to other methods.

2 W.D. Ross, *Aristotle's Prior and Posterior Analytics* (Oxford: Oxford University Press, 1949) 14.

1 A Preliminary Notion

First, then, a preliminary notion. Method is a normative pattern of related and recurrent operations yielding cumulative and progressive results. We're going to consider that definition term by term.

There are operations, the operations are distinct, each is related to the others, the relations form a pattern, and the pattern is described as the right way of doing the job. There is an indefinite repetition of related operations within the pattern, and the results of the repetition are not the same thing over and over again as on the assembly line, but cumulative and progressive.

There are, then, the operations. Methodologists of science praise the spirit of inquiry, and inquiries recur. They praise exact observation and description, and observations and descriptions recur. They demand that problems be accurately defined, and problems recur. They praise above all discovery, and discoveries recur, hypotheses, the working out of the suppositions and the implications of the hypotheses, devising experiments to check the hypotheses.

These operations, then, are distinct, they recur, they are related. It is inquiry that transforms mere experiencing into observation. If you have a precise question that you are asking, you begin to attend to the data in a more specific fashion simply because you are inquiring. Similarly, your observations will move into your descriptive categories. The descriptions give rise to conflicts or apparent conflicts, and then you get problems. The problems sooner or later lead on to discoveries. The discoveries are formulated in hypotheses, the hypotheses have to be formulated with great accuracy, all their presuppositions clarified and all their implications worked out. Doing that suggests possible experiments that would test the hypothesis. All these operations, then, are related to one another; one leads into the other.

Finally, the results are progressive: the operations include new discoveries. And they are cumulative: the new discoveries have to be integrated with previous discoveries, the new insights added on to all previous insights. So you get a cumulative result. It is not a series of unrelated discoveries: the new discoveries have to be integrated with the prior discoveries.

Such, very briefly, is a notion of method: *a normative pattern of related and recurrent operations yielding cumulative and progressive results.* If you think of method, as Gadamer seems to do in his *Wahrheit und Methode,*[3] as simply a set of rules that can be followed blindly by anyone, then method in that

3 See above, p. 115, note 13.

sense is, of course, the method of the assembly line, the method of the New Method Laundry. It does not yield any new or any progressive results. It gives the same thing over and over again. A scientific method has to be a source of discoveries, and, of course, discoveries as well as syntheses – being cumulative, the addition of a new insight integrated with the old – are things that cannot be predicted. They can be made more probable by the whole scientific setup and the encouragement given to scientists of various kinds, but they cannot be predicted; they are new emergences.

Again, I am not conceiving method as a set of rules, but rather as a normative pattern of relations between operations. From that normative pattern of relations between operations, rules can be devised. But I am conceiving the method not in terms of rules but in terms of that normative pattern.

Again, note that the operations are not merely logical operations. It is not simply a matter of operating on propositions, on terms, classes, relations. Non-logical operations are included, such as inquiry, observation, discovery, experiment, synthesis, verification. Moreover, it is this conjunction of logical and non-logical operations within a single recurrent pattern that constitutes the vitality, the ongoing character, of a modern science. The logical operations alone tend to what is eternal and immutable; you get perfectly defined terms, adequately formulated principles, rigorously drawn conclusions. That logical ideal is something that one can always aim at in one's expressions, but de facto there is the ongoing process of science from the fact that you have other, quite different operations added in, such as inquiry, discovery, synthesis, and so on. The logical operations tend to consolidate whatever has been achieved, the non-logical to move the process a step further.

Again, method is not putting movement within logic, as Hegel did. Hegel invented a logic within which there is a movement, his dialectic. Still, that movement occurs within a closed system. The method in science is open; it is moving on from any position to further discoveries, and what future discoveries are to be is not something that is contained within any system.

So much for our preliminary notion of what we mean by method: a normative pattern of recurrent and related operations yielding cumulative and progressive results.

2 The Basic Pattern of Operations

We now have to take a second step and discover in ourselves a basic pattern of operations. Later we will go on to say that that basic pattern satisfies the definition of a method, but at the present time what we are aiming at is the self-appropriation of our own operations.

The operations in question are seeing, hearing, touching, smelling, tasting, kinesthetic experiencing, imagining, inquiring, understanding, conceiving, formulating, reflecting, marshaling and weighing the evidence, judging, deliberating, evaluating, deciding, speaking, doing, writing.

I assume some familiarity with these terms, and I ask about their pattern. And to arrive at the pattern is to arrive at what I would name an explanatory apprehension of the operations. To arrive at the pattern is to know the operations in their interrelations, so that the operations themselves become one's basic terms, and the basic relations are the relations between them.

Fundamental clarity in any science is achieved through defining. But defining presupposes other terms, if it is explicit definition. Mathematicians at the present time go beyond explicit definition to implicit definition, in which no terms are presupposed. They set up a basic vicious circle in which the terms are clarified by their relations to one another and the relations are clarified by the terms that they relate. That is the fundamental set, and it is such a fundamental set that we are aiming at when we are endeavoring, each for himself, to heighten consciousness of our own operations in their own spontaneous relationships.

The book *Insight* is a five-finger exercise on that process of self-appropriation. And even there, no more could be issued than an invitation to the reader to do it in himself and for himself. No one else can do it for you. So I am not attempting to prove anything or demonstrate anything to anyone or persuade them of anything, but merely to suggest that if you try this and keep at it long enough, you may get satisfactory results. Method is a matter of how *you* do things. And what one will get out of these exercises is not going to be Lonergan's view, but what you find in yourself; you'll be genuinely yourself, just that. Mainly in this part, which is the sticky part of course, I am trying to recall my book *Insight*, and I will mainly be clarifying the terms. Perhaps my terminology is a little clearer, more precise, better worked out than it was in *Insight*.

I begin with general reflections on the operations that I listed, in which we will clarify the words 'intending,' 'intentional,' and on the other hand 'conscious,' 'presence,' 'awareness,' 'experiencing,' 'introspection,' 'levels of consciousness,' and so on.

First, then, the operations are transitive. They have objects in the grammatical sense. One sees colors and shapes, one hears sounds. The verb 'see' has the object 'colors,' the verb 'hear' has the object 'sound.' They are transitive not only in the grammatical sense; they have objects not only in the grammatical sense, but also in a psychological sense. The objects become present to me through the operations. If I close my eyes, the operation of seeing does not occur. I open them, and I do see colors and shapes before my eyes. Seeing is a very good operation to work with, because you can turn it off and on at will by opening and closing your eyes.

So the operations are transitive. They have objects. They have objects not only in the grammatical sense, but also in the psychological sense. By the operation one becomes aware of the object, and in the operation the object becomes present to me. That psychological sense is what is meant by 'intend,' 'intention,' 'intentionality': my awareness of objects and the object's presence to me.

Second, the operations in the list are operations of an operator. The operator is named the subject. The subject is subject not only in the grammatical sense: I see, I hear, I inquire, I understand, I define; but also in a psychological sense, namely, in the operation I am present to myself, and my operation is present to me. Myself as seeing occurs when I open my eyes and ends when I close them. I can get a first experience, or a precise direction to experience of consciousness, simply by opening and closing my eyes. In the operation 'seeing,' there is not only the object seen, there is also given the operation seeing and my seeing; and it is this psychological sense of 'I see,' of being subject, not merely the grammatical subject of the verb 'see' but the psychological subject of the operation seeing, that is meant by 'conscious,' 'consciousness.'

Whenever any of the operations in the list occurs the subject is conscious, and the operation is conscious in a different sense. While the sense is different, the subject and his operation are co-conscious. Moreover, none of the operations in the list occurs in dreamless sleep or in a coma. So the operations in the list have a twofold psychological dimension. By the operations, objects become present to the subject, and the subject and the operations become present to the subject. The presence of the object is called intention, intending, intentional, intentionality. The presence of the subject is called conscious, consciousness.

I have used the words 'presence' and 'aware' with regard to both, but the presence, the awareness, in the two cases is different. Insofar as an object becomes present, it is what is attended to, what is intended, what is seen; it is on the side of the object. But my being present is not something attended to, something seen, something heard, or anything like that. It is on the side of the seeing. I am present not as attended to but as attending, not as intended but as intending. It is a different type of presence; it is presence on the side of the one who attends, intends, and for that reason one can give one's whole attention to the object without in any way losing one's consciousness. Attending to the object is in one dimension, and the attending of the subject is not another object. The spectator does not have to become part of the spectacle to be conscious.

This can be a tricky thing insofar as one is apt to think of all knowing, all awareness, as a matter of taking a good look. Set that a priori down, and demand that everything conform to it, and you get into all sorts of difficulties with regard to consciousness. For example, the word 'introspection' literally suggests an inward looking. If you try to look inwardly you do not get anywhere. What you have to do is let your span of interest, your span of attention, expand. Normally, our consciousness of ourselves is peripheral. We are attending to the object. But one has to let interest and attention widen. You don't drop your looking at the object; you add on to that yourself experiencing yourself as seeing. You do not have to be told that you are seeing when your eyes are open; you simply experience it.

Again, when I say that you experience yourself operating, that experience is not another operation; it is the operation itself. The operation has two dimensions: a dimension of intentionality and a dimension of consciousness.

Now, it is quite simple to advert to one's consciousness of things like seeing and hearing, and so on, because those operations are very easily produced. It is fundamentally the same type of problem, but the conditions are not as easily fulfilled, when you talk about experiencing an insight, because the insight has to be occurring for you to experience it, and you don't produce insights at will. You can take things that you already understand and set up the conditions for the occurrence of the act of understanding in their regard. Or you can take something new and come to understand. To come to understand something new, and to become familiar with the occurrence in yourself of the insight, frequently enough is quite a long haul.

Now, all I am doing is giving a general indication of what it is to appropriate oneself in one's conscious intentionality or intentional consciousness. Just as I suggested you do for seeing, so you can do for the whole list of the operations. But the task is considerably longer than anything that can be attempted in this course of lectures. I once gave forty hours on *Insight* to a group, and it was not too much to give people all the help that can be given in this matter.

Next, I want to distinguish different levels of conscious intentionality. I gave a list of about sixteen or so operations, but they differ in their intentionality and in the type of consciousness. By distinguishing different levels we can see that just as there are two kinds of presence, the presence of the object and the presence of the subject, so there are different kinds of intentionality and different kinds of consciousness. All the different kinds satisfy the statements that have been made so far, but now we have to attend to further differences.

First of all, there is the dream state and the waking state. Our conscious intentionality in the dream state commonly is fragmentary and obscure. One needs the therapist to clarify this.

In the waking state, four distinct levels of conscious intentionality can be distinguished: (1) the empirical, (2) the intellectual, (3) the rational, and (4) the responsible.

At the empirical level, there are the data of sense and the data of consciousness. At the intellectual level, there are inquiry, insight, and formulation. Fr Richardson, an authority on Heidegger, mentions *Verstehen, Auslegen, Aussagen*.[4] The insight is the *Verstehen*, and the formulation is the *Auslegen*. This correspond to St Thomas's *intelligere* and *verbum*. At the rational level, there are reflection (Is that so?), reflective understanding, and judgment. At the responsible level, there are deliberation (Is it worthwhile?), evaluation, and decision.

With respect to those four levels of consciousness, we want to distinguish two movements. Start from the data of sense. One moves on to understanding what one experiences sensitively, and to judging one's understanding, passing judgment on one's understanding. By passing judgment on one's understanding, one comes to what are called facts; and when you know the facts, there arises the question, What am I going to about it? One moves on to deliberation, evaluation, decision. This is the movement up from the data of sense.

However, there is also a movement across. All of these operations are conscious, and being conscious of each one of them is the task I was speaking of. Insofar as one is conscious one has the data of consciousness, and you can repeat the process: inquiry, insight, formulation, etc., with regard to the data of consciousness; reflection, reflective understanding, and judgment with regard to your understanding of the data of consciousness; deliberation, evaluation, decision, with respect to the facts regarding oneself. That is the second movement.

In other words, the process, the intellectual, reflective, and deliberative levels of consciousness can reflect on all the data of consciousness, and that

4 Lonergan is referring to lectures given earlier in this three-week program by Fr William Richardson, s.j., then of Fordham University.

reflection on the data of consciousness is self-appropriation, heightening of one's consciousness.

Now, with regard to the second movement I want to make certain observations. The first has to do with qualitative differences of the levels of consciousness. Sensations, the empirical level in which the data of sense become present, are not conspicuously different in us from the experience we attribute to the higher animals. But in us they are the materials for a second level; and the second level is something quite different from the first. On the first, something is given, something that is intelligible, something that we can understand. But the second level is not merely intelligible; it is intelligent. It is intelligence inquiring, intelligence moving towards understanding, intelligence coming to understand, intelligence formulating in the light of what it has understood. And that act of intelligence as distinct from the mere passive intelligibility of the data of sense gives us a first qualitative difference in the levels of consciousness.

This experience of intelligence that you can have by suitably setting yourself problems and coming to their solutions surrenders to a third level of consciousness which I called the rational. I remember once I addressed a group of psychiatrists on the general topic of insight; and one of the therapists said to me afterwards, 'Our patients get a very large number of insights, but they are wrong.' Insights are a dime a dozen, and it is only insofar as they accumulate, insofar as they complement one another and correct one another that one moves to anything approaching an adequate understanding. Consequently, the insight always has to be submitted to critical consciousness, to the rational level of consciousness. There one is not trying to understand as intelligence does or glory in the fact that one has understood as Archimedes did when he shouted, 'Eureka!' On this level, the rational level, one is standing back, demanding evidence, bowing only to evidence, refusing to go beyond evidence, concerned with an absolute that is so exigent that the positive results of all the modern sciences are just probable, all subject to revision. This is the rational level, the level of critical consciousness.

Finally, there is the fourth level of consciousness, as responsible, as conscientious. On the third level, one arrives at what is so, or what can be so. On the fourth level, there arises the further question, What is to be done about it, What am I to do? This level is evaluative. I ask, Is this worth while in an absolute sense, and not merely, Is this going to please me? There is the possibility here of the emergence of benevolence and beneficence and genuine loving and a fuller self-transcendence than the self-transcendence of knowledge.

Consciousness, then, as you move from level to level, becomes different qualitatively. It moves from merely experiencing to intelligent experiencing, and then critically exigent intelligent experiencing, and, finally, responsible deciding. It is always the same subject, but it is a fuller self that is emerging as you move up the different levels of consciousness.

Moreover, as there are differences in the quality of consciousness, so too there are qualitative differences in the objects intended. The intending of sense is receptive and formative. We do not simply respond to every impression that comes to us from every angle. We select the *Gestalt*, and that is what one apprehends. You can walk along a noisy street talking with a friend, and your ear picks out the sounds that have a meaning and disregards all the rest. If sense becomes strictly creative, one is involved in hallucination, and that is abnormal, but imagination is not only representative but also creative.

With understanding you move on to an entirely different type of object. By understanding you don't come to apprehend something that is given; what you apprehend in understanding is a unity or relationship that possibly is relevant to the data. Consequently, of itself, it is something that is hypothetical. It is only going to be something more than hypothetical when you move on to the level of judgment, the rational level.

In the judgment, one moves beyond the subject; there is a cognitive self-transcendence in the judgment. When I say something is so – 'I am sitting here, talking my head off' – that is so. I am not saying what appears, what seems to me, what I'm inclined to think, what I'd like to say. All these relate the proposition to something about me. When one says, 'That is so, that is all that there is about it, that is a fact,' one has reached a point of self-transcendence. Sense experience and understanding achieve a measure of self-transcendence; sense experience moves you out of yourself; understanding constructs your world; but it is in judgment that you get to something independent of yourself. Finally, in deliberation, evaluation, decision, there can be a fuller self-transcendence. One can become a principle of benevolence and beneficence, capable of genuine loving.

Besides the distinction of the levels of consciousness and the qualitative differences of the consciousness itself and the objects intended, we have to draw a distinction between the categorial and the transcendental. Categories are determinations. They have a limited denotation. They vary with cultural variations. They can be illustrated by Levi-Strauss's totemic operators (something like our names for professional hockey and football teams: Bruins, Colts, and Bears). They can be explicitly named categories, as Aristotle's substance, quantity, quality, relation, action, passion, time, place, posture, habit. They need not be so named, as is the case with Aristotle's four causes, or his genus, difference, species, property, accident. They can be the products of scientific achievements, the concepts of physics, the periodic table of the chemists, the evolutionary field of the biologists, or Heidegger's existentials, drawn from existential phenomenology. Categories, then, are determinations; they have a limited denotation, they vary with cultural variation, and they are illustrated in various ways. The transcendentals are comprehensive in connotation, unrestricted in denotation, invariant through cultural change. One needs the categories for determinate questions and determinate answers. But the transcendentals emerge in questions as of a kind. In the question on the second level of consciousness, the intellectual level, the question for intelligence, asking what and why, what for and how, you are trying to understand, and that effort as such heads for the intelligible. Insofar as you talk about the intelligible as what the second level is aiming at, you have objectified the transcendental notion, which is the question itself. The objectifications will be subject to cultural variation, and they can be mistaken, but the question is something native to the human mind, and you get a new edition of man, a new variant, if you start to change the questions themselves.

Similarly, the question on the third level of consciousness, Is that so? asks about the truth of one's understanding and the reality of what you take to be a fact. It heads not merely to the intelligible but to the true and the real.

On the fourth level of consciousness we get the questions, Is that worth while, Is it merely an apparent good or is it truly good? That issue arises on the fourth level, and you have the transcendental notion insofar as the question arises, itself, in the spontaneity of the human spirit. You have the transcendental concept insofar as you objectify that question.

Now, I said that the transcendentals are comprehensive in connotation, unrestricted in denotation, invariant through cultural change. They are in questions as of a kind: questions for intelligence, for reflection, for deliberation. There is a radical intending that moves us from ignorance to knowledge. The human mind not merely comes to know, it intends what it is trying to know. The question goes beyond the data. When I ask, Why is that so? I am not asking for a further datum; I am asking for an intelligible unification and relationship that is never a datum, though it may be verified in the data. It is simply distinct, something that is possibly relevant to the data.

So not only do we know something, but we know that there is an awful lot of other things that we don't know. There is a known unknown. We can have not only ignorance, but also *docta ignorantia*, which knows things we don't know. And that is because we are able to ask more questions than we are able to answer, and also because we intelligently, reasonably, responsibly move beyond what we don't know to come to know the unknown.

So there is a radical intending. It is not the intending of any cognitional content, but the awareness of ignorance moving on to something beyond. It is a priori in the Kantian sense. It is not a datum. It is simply going beyond the data. So much is presented, and I ask for something distinct, beyond it. It is unrestricted, because our answers only supply us with the materials for further questions. We have enormous libraries, and we need even bigger ones, because our present libraries just enable us to ask more questions more intelligently and more accurately.

The transcendental notions are comprehensive, as opposed to any meaning of the word 'abstract.' We know what we mean by the concrete insofar as we advert to those questions. The questions, the transcendental notions, intend the unknown whole. They manifest this intending by the fact that questions keep recurring. Any answer gives rise to further questions. You cannot cut the questions off, or say to the questioner, 'This far and no further.' That is obscurantism. You can say of any given question that that is a mistaken question, or a misleading question; but you cannot cut out questioning itself; that is a radical refusal of the human spirit.

The transcendental notions are comprehensive because they go beyond any amount of knowledge that we have. They want, they head us towards, a complete understanding of everything about everything; as the scientist says, the complete explanation of all phenomena. That is not something that we know, it is something that we intend by the fact of inquiry.

Finally, we have to distinguish elementary and compounded operations and objects. The elementary operation and object are such things as seeing and seen, hearing and heard, understanding and understood, judging and judgment. Each of these operations is a knowing in an elementary sense of the word 'know.' 'I know it.' 'In what sense?' 'I see it, or I hear it.' But human knowing, in general, is something distinct from that elementary sense. When you say that you know a man, or that you know mathematics, or that you know physics, that knowing is not any single operation; it is a compound of operations on the four levels of consciousness. What we mean when we refer to persons and things or the world or anything like that is the compound object. Thus, compounding is the work of the transcendental notions.

The objects are linked to one another. What is experienced is what is to be understood by the fact that one asks what or why or how with respect to one's experience. Again, the understood is what is to be affirmed or denied;

one is aware of the fact that one's understanding can always be completely wrong, and one wants to check if it is really so, if in fact one has got it. What is affirmed or denied is what is to be pronounced or denied to be something worthwhile. The movement is up from elementary objects or partial objects to an object compounded of elements from experience, elements from understanding and formulation, and, finally, the element added on in judgment. That compounded object is reached through the interconnection between the transcendental notions. Fundamentally, there is just one single thrust of the human spirit that unfolds. As it unfolds, it reveals these successive levels. We aim at what is good. To know the good we have to know the real; to know the real we have to know the true; to know the true we have to understand; to understand we have to attend to the data. These transcendental notions are intimately connected; they seem to be just simple variations on a fundamental theme.

Finally, this basic pattern of operations that I have been talking about is a dynamic pattern, in two senses of the word 'dynamic.' It is dynamic materially insofar as its elements are operations, just as in music or in a dance; the elements in the pattern are themselves movements. Secondly, the basic pattern is dynamic formally. It puts itself together, it assembles its own parts. We wake up and start experiencing. Shortly, we are not just having impressions; intelligence supervenes along with reflection and judgment and deliberation, evaluation, decision. This formally dynamic pattern that assembles itself is not blind but open-eyed; it is attentive, intelligent, reflective, reasonable, responsible; it is the self.[5]

3 Transcendental Method

This basic pattern of operations satisfies the definition of a method. It is a set of distinct operations, the operations are related to one another, they keep recurring, the pattern in which they recur is normative, that is, it is the pattern that is dictated by human intelligence, rationality, responsibility, and it yields cumulative and progressive results – the human race has progressed. It is that basic progress of the human race that makes things like science and methodology possible. The unthematic takes precedence over the thematized. The thematized will give you a better knowledge of yourself, a more exact apprehension of yourself, a heightened consciousness. But what counts is not any concept of intelligence, but the fact that you are

5 A break was taken at this point. The recording continues on the same CD/MP3.

intelligent, not any account of reasonableness but the fact, the human spiritual reality, of your reasonablenss and similarly of your responsibility. They are what do the work; and while they do the work by setting questions and criteria, they themselves are unquestioned. If you question intelligence, you want to do it intelligently; you have already acknowledged the exigences of intelligence.

So that basic pattern satisfies the definition I gave of a method. Moreover, it is a transcendental method. It is not confined categorially to any generic or specific type of result, to any limited field of investigation. Other methods aim at meeting the exigences and exploiting the opportunities of particular fields. But this general pattern aims at meeting the exigences and exploiting the opportunities of the human mind itself, which operates in all fields.

That concern, then, for this total pattern is both foundational and universally relevant. It is foundational, because it is knowing the basic elements in any pattern of operations and any method. It is knowing the basic building blocks you are going to be working with. It is universally relevant, because it is always worth while to know precisely what one is doing.

Now, in a sense everyone knows and everyone observes transcendental method. Everyone does so insofar as he is attentive, intelligent, reasonable, and responsible; and these are the conditions of the possibility of being an authentic human being. Inasmuch as one is inattentive, unintelligent, unreasonable, irresponsible, one moves away from the normal human concern to some form of madness. On the other hand, in another sense it is quite difficult to be at home in transcendental method, because it is not something achieved by reading books or listening to lectures or analyzing language. It is a matter of heightening one's consciousness, and one heightens one's consciousness to objectify it. This is something each one has to do in himself and for himself. It is only in the measure that one does so for oneself and in oneself that one will know precisely what one is doing when one is doing x. Without that heightening of consciousness, without that self-appropriation that I have tried to indicate (inadequately in the limited time), this lecture and all subsequent lectures will be like a disquisition on color read to the blind. You have to get these experiences clearly to know what the words mean. There is an entry into oneself, a heightening of one's consciousness, that is the meaning of the words.

Now, in what does this process consist? It is a process of objectifying oneself from the evidence supplied by oneself. There are a larger number of operations. We will pick one out from each of the four levels. We will talk about experiencing, understanding, judging, deciding, and let these represent all the operations on each of the four levels, respectively.

This process of objectification is a matter of applying the operations as intentional to the operations as conscious. The operations become conscious insofar as you start from the data of sense, inquire, understand, formulate, reflect, weigh the evidence, judge, deliberate, evaluate, decide. In the occurrence of the operations is to be found consciousness of the operations; it is a dimension of the operations themselves. Insofar as this consciousness has been elicited, there are available the data of consciousness to which you can again apply the operations, this time as intentional, to the operations as conscious. You can inquire about the data of consciousness and come to understand them and formulate what you have understood, reflect on your formulations, weigh the evidence for the accuracy of your formulations, make your judgments, and decide on your methods.

Consequently, objectifying means that one first has to experience one's experiencing, understanding, judging, deciding. The experience there is just conscious. The operations are intrinsically conscious as well as intentional. One cannot perform them without some consciousness of them. That consciousness may be peripheral. One has to expand attention, broaden interest, so that the operation itself, and not merely the content, the object, is brought to light – one lets it appear, as Heidegger would put it. The first step, then, is experience: heightening one's consciousness of one's experiencing, understanding, judging, deciding.

Secondly, one has to understand one's experienced experiencing, understanding, judging, deciding. The operations are experienced not in isolation but in their concomitance. When you experience, inquiry arises and leads to insight; insight may lead, depending on the level of culture, to a formulation, and so on. It is not merely that the operations are conscious but that the process is conscious. In other words, we are dealing with a field that differs from the field of external data. Hume remarked that we don't see causality, all we perceive is succession. But in consciousness, where you have the subject operating, you have not only succession but the emergence of intelligence upon the givenness. You, as intelligent, put inquiries about the given because it is not understood, with the purpose of understanding. You are working from the inside. Not only the operation, but also the process itself, is conscious.

Sensitive process is spontaneous, vital, psychic, but intellectual process is something more. The connections are much more palpable, precisely because one is intelligent. The connections of intelligibility such as one can find in one's sensitivity are like the connections one can find in external data. But in intelligence the connection between inquiry leading up to insight and the insight, the act of understanding making one intelligently operate in a given situation, this process itself, is within consciousness. Similarly, in the rational process there is a critical demand for evidence, the refusal to assent with insufficient evidence, and the necessity of assenting because the evidence really is sufficient. The process itself is conscious, not merely the single operations; and similarly for the deliberative process.

In other words, the higher one goes in the levels as one understands the relations which unite the different operations, the more the understanding is an understanding of the unity of consciousness itself: its unity by its intelligence, its unity by its rationality, its unity by its responsibility. One does not have to assemble an unrelated multiplicity. One is conscious of a unity, and it is only by an analysis that one can distinguish the different elements in it.

Thirdly, one has to affirm the understood relations of experienced experiencing, understanding, judging, and affirming. Do these conscious and intentional operations occur? It is very rare that anyone who is not blind or deaf or something like that will say that never in his life did he have the experience of seeing or hearing or tasting or smelling or touching or imagining or perceiving or feeling or moving, and if he did appear to have such experience, then it was merely appearance, since all his life long he has gone around like a somnambulist. In other words, anyone who wants to say, 'These operations don't occur in me or if they occur they are not conscious,' is uttering an enormous paradox.

Further, no one prefaces his lectures with the statement that he personally never had the most fleeting experience of intellectual curiosity, of inquiry, of striving and coming to understand, of expressing what he had grasped by understanding. Insofar as we are unintelligent, we don't tend to let it out!

How rare is the man that prefaces his articles with the reminder that never in his life did he experience anything that might be named critical reflection, that he never paused about the truth or falsity of any statement, that if he ever seemed to exercise his rationality by attending to the evidence and weighing it, still, that was mere appearance; he was not doing that at all.

How uncommon are those that preface their books with the warning that never in their lives have they acted responsibly, and least of all were they concerned with achieving something worth while in writing and publishing the present volume.

In brief, conscious and intentional operations exist, and anyone who wants to be counted out has only to disqualify himself by claiming that he is a non-responsible, non-reasonable, non-intelligent somnambulist.

The operations exist. Do they exist in the alleged pattern? Isn't that pattern merely hypothetical? We have got some understanding, but someone else will come along and understand it ever so much better, and this process will keep going on indefinitely. We have got a hypothesis that human understanding provides, but there will be further hypotheses that will radically change the picture.

Well, first of all, we have to distinguish two senses of the pattern. There is the pattern itself constituted by one's own intelligence, reasonableness, and responsibility: the unthematic that we are thematizing. On the other hand, there is the objectification of the pattern in concepts and judgments and words and sentences. To revise what is objectified is quite possible. But to revise the pattern itself is a matter of putting out a new edition of man as something radically different from what we have known him to be. Revision does not regard the pattern itself, but the objectification of the pattern.

Further, there is no doubt that any account of the pattern can be improved on; there are always further things to be learnt, further complexities that can be discovered, fuller and more adequate accounts that can be given. However, there is a restriction on the changes that can be introduced, and they are contained in the very notion of the possibility of a revision. For there to be a revision, one has to advert to data that hitherto have been overlooked. The understanding of these data has to involve a revision of the understanding that previously had been held. Because we now understand more data better, we have a more probable judgment now to make. And one takes the trouble of doing all this discovering further data and understanding things better and arriving at a more probable judgment on the matter, because one is interested, one considers it worthwhile to get things straight and know them accurately. Accordingly, the possibility of a revision includes the pattern that we have been expounding all along.

There is, then, at the root of transcendental method, a rock, the fact that the possibility of revision also limits the possibility of revision. Your revisions cannot arrive at something which excludes the possibility of revision, because then you would be excluding revision itself. Just as you have to have some invariant pattern in order to say that revisions are always possible, similarly that invariance of the pattern that grounds the possibility of a revision also limits the possibility of revision.

So much for the notion of transcendental method. It is the spontaneous pattern of intelligent, rational, responsible consciousness as it is in the subject, unthematic. And we talk about transcendental method not to have a basis in some objective set of statements, but to be aware of ourselves.

Insofar as we are attentive, intelligent, reasonable, and responsible, we are the first principle, where 'principle' means, not a logical proposition but a reality whence other things proceed. We ourselves are the first principle qua authentic beings, qua attentive, intelligent, reasonable, responsible, for the construction of methods.

There remains in this chapter a final section on the functions of transcendental method, but I think we'd best leave that until the next lecture.[6]

---

6 The first question-and-answer session was held later this day. See below, pp. 569–79.

1968-2

Method (continued), Functional Specialties, and an Introduction to Horizons and Categories[1]

The day before yesterday, I did most of the first chapter on method, and first of all I noted that there are three approaches to the notion of method: first, a purely empirical approach, where method is more an art than a science; secondly, a selective approach, where one picks the successful science and analyzes it and wishes all other sciences to be science insofar as they conform to it; that's quite unsatisfactory for the less successful sciences that need more help really than anyone else; and consequently we were trying to work out a third approach through an analysis of human cognitional structure, from which one could proceed to the proper method of any academic discipline or science or whatever you want to call it.

Accordingly, I worked out a preliminary notion of method from natural science, namely, a normative pattern of related and recurrent operations yielding cumulative and progressive results. I then went on to study the basic pattern of operations, the pattern in which we experience, understand, judge, and decide. Finally, I argued that that pattern satisfied the definition of a method, and since the method so determined was not limited to any particular category of objects, but simply was based on the transcendental notions, the basic questions that are the dynamism of the human spirit, that method was transcendental.

1   Friday, 5 July 1968, Lauzon CD/MP3 483 (48300A0E060) and 484 (48400A0E060). The lecture begins by completing the material of lecture 1 on method. Lonergan then moves to the topic of functional specialties, then planned as chapter 2, and he concludes the lecture by introducing what was then his third chapter, 'Horizons and Categories.'

There still remains a final section of that first chapter, namely, the functions of transcendental method. What does transcendental method do for the special methods, for the method of physics or chemistry or theology or history or anything else?

1 The Functions of Transcendental Method

Transcendental method is the core of all methods. All methods are a matter of attending, coming to understand, judging correctly, deciding on the right procedures. Transcendental method points out that is what one does, and the special methods particularize what one attends to and how one goes about understanding in a particular field.

Fitst, then, transcendental method sets the basic norms for all methods. Methods are not just a matter of authority: 'So-and-so said so.' They are not just a matter of pragmatism, success: 'It works!' They have to work, of course, but it is not just pragmatic. There are the transcendental precepts: Be attentive, Be intelligent, Be reasonable, Be responsible. They are the fundamental normative element in any method.

Second, transcendental method provides the science, or theology or any subject, with a critical basis. There has been, as Kant complained, the scandal that the scientists engaged in natural science agree, but the human scientists, the philosophers, the theologians endlessly disagree. Transcendental method indicates a solution to that problem; namely, it brings to light, it heightens our consciousness of, the operations we actually perform. The big source of the irreducible oppositions in the human sciences, philosophy, and theology is a conflict between the way one actually operates and the way one thinks of one's operations. Transcendental method brings to light, What am I doing when I am knowing? Why is doing that knowing? and What do I know when I do it? These are the three fundamental questions. Differences over the third can be reduced to differences over the first and second; differences over the second, epistemology, can be reduced to differences in the first, cognitional theory. Where cognitional theory is at variance with what a person actually is doing, then a contradiction comes to light, and you can say that at least this is wrong, you will have to find some other way of going about it. The outstanding example is, of course, Hume. He conceived human knowledge as a matter of relating impressions by custom, by habit. If that is what the human mind is, then no mind is original. But Hume's mind was extraordinarily original. This sort of criticism can be worked out against any cognitional theory in which what one is doing is one thing and what one is saying is another.

Third,[2] transcendental method provides a basis for dialectic. This critical approach can be applied to every cognitional theory, whether explicit or merely implicit as in a method of hermeneutics, a method of history, and so on. One can line up systematically the positions and the counterpositions, all the places where cognitional theories run into conflict with the operations that are performed in presenting the cognitional theory.

Fourth, transcendental method provides a basis for systematic thought. Ordinary definitions in terms of genus and difference always presuppose a set of as yet undefined terms, and the fundamental problem in any science (or any academic discipline, if you don't like the word 'science') is to fix those fundamental terms. The definitions have to be, in that case, implicit. The terms are fixed by their relations to one another, and the relations are fixed by the terms they relate. Now, transcendental method is becoming aware of a set of operations and processes, which when objectified are terms and relations. The cognitional theory provides a first circle of terms and relations. Epistemology takes you on further. The correlatives to those operations are objects, and so you can move on to a metaphysics, where metaphysics is not understood as something speculative – what being is made of: all water, according to Thales; all spirit, according to Hegel – but simply the correlatives to the cognitional operations: what corresponds to judging, what corresponds to understanding, what corresponds to experiencing.

Fifth, transcendental method provides other methods with continuity but not at the price of rigidity. It provides a principle of continuity. It eliminates an ultimate relativism because it is immune from revision at a certain point. It can improve, but it is not subject to the revolutionary revisions that would eliminate the meaning of the word 'revision' itself. On the other hand, cognitional theory can always be further refined, and so even one's basic terms and relations can vary over time, can become richer. And that, of course, is precisely what is needed. We have to find a middle way between a mere relativism, on the one hand, and simply eternal truths that cannot develop, if we are going to deal with a developing religion, developing dogma, developing theology in human history.

---

2 In the lecture Lonergan said 'Thirdly,' and then changed to 'Fourthly,' apparently assuming that the material on the three basic questions had been his third point. But the text of *Method in Theology* indicates that the third function begins here, and that the material on the three basic questions belongs with the second function. Accordingly, the enumerations given in the lecture have been altered to conform to those in the book.

Sixth, transcendental method has a heuristic function. 'Heuristic' comes from the Greek word *heurisko*, to find, and something is heuristic insofar as it leads to finding things out. The fundamental technique is to name the unknown, to state all you already know about it, and to use that to arrive at what you still have to learn. In algebra, if you are asked to find a number, you say, 'Let x be the required number,' and you fiddle around with the diagrams and find some equation regarding the x, and you solve the equation, and you get your result. In physics, you say, 'Let the unknown law be some indeterminate function.' And you find out by experiment or by general considerations the sort of thing that will tighten down the type of function that has to be. You are talking explicitly about the unknown and using all you can to find out about it, to pin it down more and more closely. All method is a process of exploiting that intending of what is already unknown, naming it an x, or naming it an indeterminate function, $f(x,y,z,t) = 0$. All method is an objectification of the transcendental notions. The question, What is it, or why is it so, or how is it so, or what is it for? is the primary instance of this heuristic function. When in ordinary language one talks about the 'nature of' light, the 'nature of' life, what do we mean? Especially if you don't know what light is, what life is, what do you mean when you talk about the 'nature of' it? You mean what you will know when you understand it, if you do understand it. But already you can intend what you do not know, and that is the dynamism of the human mind; it is this heuristic business. Since in transcendental method one lines up these transcendentals and says just what they do, one has the basis for all heuristic activity, which is all methodical activity.

Seventh, transcendental method is foundational. All special methods in general are derived from accumulated experience of investigators in their respective fields. But besides special norms, there are common norms, and besides problems peculiar to special fields, there are interdisciplinary problems. Inasmuch as special methods are grounded in transcendental method, sciences can be mobilized within the higher unity of vocabulary, thought, orientation, criticism; they can attack interdisciplinary problems coherently, complement one another effectively, attack more fundamental problems that now are neglected. The methods of the particular sciences are not expressed simply in terms of the interests of that science, but reduced back to their roots in transcendental method. All the sciences will have one common root. They can develop a certain measure of common norms, common vocabulary, common modes of criticism. On that basis they can work together in team-like fashion on interdisciplinary problems.

Eighth, transcendental method is relevant to theology. Theology has its methods derived from experience in the past. But its methods are, however peculiar to theology, nonetheless the work of human minds performing the same basic operations in the same basic patterns of relations as common sense, the natural sciences, and the human sciences. It is true that one attends, inquires, reflects, decides differently in the natural sciences, in the human sciences, and in theology. But at no point is there a transition from attention to inattention, from inquiry to indifference, from being critical to being uncritical, from being responsible to being irresponsible.

Ninth, the objects of theology are not beyond the reach of transcendental method. Theology is not something entirely different, totally other. The transcendental notions are unrestricted, they regard all intelligibility. They are not measured by what we can attain, but by what we can ask about, want to understand, want to know. That is why we can know that there is much we don't know: by the questions we ask and cannot answer. They regard everything about everything, and what is outside everything about everything is simply nothing at all, and theology is not about nothing at all.

Tenth, transcendental method is not a new resource in theology. Theologians always had minds and always used them. Transcendental method does not give them minds or cause them to use their minds, or make them more intelligent or more reasonable or more responsible. It helps them make better use of a resource they have always had.

Eleventh, theology has a problem of relating itself especially to the human sciences and to philosophy; and its conception of unified science, in the past, has been derived from Aristotle. The Aristotelian conception of science is in terms of subject specialization, in terms of the results achieved. A science for Aristotle is 'certain knowledge of things through their causes.' The things are picked out, the different sciences are distinguished by their formal objects, and each science is supposed to be a logically coherent whole. That conception of the sciences, the hierarchy of the formal objects, is the way in which an Aristotelian or a Thomist conceives the unification of the sciences. That is all very well as long as the sciences are simply a set of fixed results, but as soon as all the sciences are ongoing processes guided by methods, then what is fixed about them, what is set about them, is precisely the method, not their present situation. The unification has to come through the methods because a modern science defines itself, is itself, through its method. The Aristotelian ideal of necessary causes and immutable effects conceives science as logically ordered results, distinguished by formal objects and related by relations between formal objects. Modern sciences are on the move; they are fixed not by a formal object, but by a method. The only unification is through the unification of methods, and while methods change, still they change only slowly, and method in no way is incompatible with developing science, developing religion, developing dogma, developing theology. The other conception is always tending towards fixity, eternal truths, *philosophia perennis*, and so on. On the other hand, method is the pattern of change.

Finally, a word on philosophy and theology.[3] First of all, we can get away from the old metaphor about that relationship, namely, that philosophy is the handmaid of theology. This does not illuminate or guide us very much. Secondly, we won't speak about philosophy in general, but of three precise questions: (1) cognitional theory: What am I doing when I am knowing? What are the operations? (2) epistemology: Why is doing that knowing? Why are those operations constitutive of knowledge? (3) metaphysics: What do I know when I do it? in the sense of a general semantics: how do I distinguish metaphor from reality in the literal sense? The theologian is interested in these questions, not because philosophers in the past and to some extent in the present are interested in them. He is interested in them whether the philosophers are interested in them or not. He is interested in them because they regard method, and because they regard the method of theology itself, in its most fundamental aspects. The theologian is concerned with those questions because theologians have minds and use them, and it is worthwhile for them to know precisely what they are doing when they are using their minds. In that fashion, one eliminates the tendency to brush aside questions – 'Oh, that's just philosophy, we need not bother our heads about that, I'm a specialist, I'm a theologian.' If you are a specialist and a theologian, you are using your mind, and it is worthwhile to know precisely what you doing when you do use it. That is the point to considering method. So much for chapter 1.

2 Functional Specialties

2.1 Three Types of Specialization

Now we have to move from a pattern of related and recurrent operations yielding cumulative and progressive results to a pattern of such patterns. Theology has become specialized, highly specialized. It has not one method, but a set of methods, and so it has to be conceived not simply as *a* normative

---

3 In *Method in Theology*, this point begins with the words 'In the twelfth place.'

pattern of related and recurrent operations but as a normative pattern of normative patterns. The second patterns there are the functional specialties.

Specializations can be conceived in three different ways, all of which are legitimate. First, there is what I will call field specialization. It divides up the data. Not everyone can examine all the data of all subjects. Field specialization divides up the data. You can divide up the objects to be studied in theology: the scripture, patristic, medieval, Renaissance and Reformation, Enlightenment, modern theological studies. And you can start subdividing right away. You can divide scripture into the Old Testament and the New Testament, and the Old Testament into the Law and the Prophets and the Writings, and you can cut them down further, and you will discover that there are far too many books written for you to keep up with it. Field specialization, then, makes it possible for certain parts of the library and the periodicals to be neglected by some people.

Next, there is subject specialization. Subject specialization divides up not the data but the results. There are not only data, there are also results that are being produced. That's what fills up the library. Subject specialization divides up the results to be taught. We have in a university departments, subjects, courses. You investigate the Old Testament according to different parts, but you teach Semitic languages, Hebrew history, religions of the ancient Near East, Christian biblical theology: different subjects. They are results that have been put together.

Thirdly, there is functional specialization, and it divides the process from the data to the results. It distinguishes different stages in the process. At each stage there is a different pattern of recurrent and related operations. And those recurrent and related operations are applied to the results of the previous stage.

For example, the textual critic studies the families of the manuscripts and so on, and arrives at what he considers the critical text, the most likely original writing that constituted this book. When he's finished, the exegete comes along and works out what this writing meant. The first question is, What was written? and the second, What does it mean? The second is the exegete's task. He performs a different set of operations. He doesn't get a new set of data. He operates on the data provided by the textual critic. But he performs a different set of operations. He isn't doing over what the textual critic has already done. He's doing something different. When you divide up the Old Testament into the Law, the Prophets, and the Writings, the specialists in the field specializations are doing pretty much the same thing, each with respect to his proper field of data. But here the thing is cumulative. We are dividing up the process from data to results. The textual critic does one thing. The exegete works out the meaning. The historian comes along, and he takes the commentaries and the monographs of the exegetes, and he tells us what was happening, what was going forward, from these sources: he writes a history; it's a third level. And then the critic comes along, and he finds there are different exegetes and you get different interpretations from them, and you have materialists writing history, and idealists, and Catholics and Protestants, and Germans and Frenchmen and Englishmen and Americans, and they're all writing different histories, and you have criticism of all these differences and you have a sort of dialectic.

Again, to go into a different field, there are experimental physicists and theoretical physicists. The theoretical physicist has a wonderful knowledge of mathematics, but he can't handle the cyclotron. He has to get the experimental physicist to do that work for him. And the experimental physicist can't figure out what experiments are worth trying. He has to ask the theoretical physicist, What is worth doing? And when he gets his results, he has to ask the theoretical physicist, What does this mean? It is not a new set of data there, as when you go from the Law to the Prophets. It's the same data, but different operations are performed at successive levels. That is the notion of functional specialization.

Functional specialization is a very interesting thing, simply because the successive stages are related to one another. They are tied together of their very nature. They are successive stages in a single process. Consequently, while field specialization separates and divides up the field indefinitely, so that, as the classic statement has it, you know more and more about less and less, still this notion of functional specialization shows how things come together towards results, how they can pile up. So the notion of functional specialization divides and clarifies the process from data to results. It prevents the confusion of methods. If you haven't got a clear distinction between textual criticism and exegesis and history, you'll be applying the principles or precepts of one department or stage to operations elsewhere. 'Why aren't they doing this? Well, so and so did it. And so and so is a textual critic, not an exegete.' But you have to have the distinction of those different tasks, the different tasks to be performed, and the different ways of doing it.

Secondly, it links field specialization with subject specialization. And finally, it helps overcome the endless diversity and disconnectedness of field specialization.

2.2 An Eightfold Division

Now, I am going to conceive theology in terms of eight functional special-izations. First, I'll give some rough outline of what is meant in each case. That will be merely descriptive, a mere indication of what I'm talking about. Later I'll go into the grounds for picking out exactly those eight and not any others, and further, the principles by which one will clarify just what pertains to each one of the eight.

These eight will be chapters 7 to 14. The first chapters are more or less setting up the field, and then the discussion of each one of these eight will be the more practical side of method in theology.[4]

My eight are: research, interpretation, history, dialectic, foundations, doctrines, systematics, communications.[5] I'll say first in a general sketch something about each of the eight.

First, research. It makes available the data relevant to theological investiga-tion. Research, then, is concerned to make available the data for theology. It is either general or special. Special research is concerned with assembling the data relevant to some particular question or problem: the doctrine of X on the question Y. Such special research operates all the more rapidly and effect-ively the more familiar it is with the tools made available by general research. General research locates, excavates, and maps ancient cities. It fill museums and reproduces or copies inscriptions, symbols, pictures, statues. It deciphers unknown scripts and languages. It collects and catalogues manuscripts, pre-pares critical editions of texts, composes indices, tables, repertories, bibliog-raphies, abstracts, bulletins, handbooks, dictionaries, encyclopedias. Perhaps someday it will give us a complete information retrieval system.

Secondly, while research settles what was written, what signs were made, what traces were left, interpretation asks what was meant. It grasps that meaning in its proper historical context, in accord with its proper mode and level of thought and expression, in the light of the circumstances and intention of the writer. Its product is the commentary or monograph. It is an enterprise replete with pitfalls, and today it is further complicated by the importation of the problems of cognitional theory, epistemology, and meta-physics. Bultmann's use of Heidegger in writing a theology of the New

---

4 In *Method in Theology*, there were five 'background' chapters, and the individual functional specialties occuped chapters 6 to 14, with two chapters being devoted to history.
5 This seems to be the first public statement on Lonergan's part of the eight functional specialties.

Testament is also the importation into theology of metaphysical and epistemological questions. So it is necessary for the theologian today to be able to meet those issues not only on the abstract philosophical level but also on the concrete level of a hermeneutics, of a method of interpretation.

Thirdly, history may be described as basic, special, and general.

Basic history tells where (places, territories) and when (dates, periods) who (persons, peoples) did what (public life, external acts) to enjoy what success, suffer what reverses, exert what influence. I'm conceiving basic history as the sort of history you can trust anyone to write. It makes as specific and precise as possible the more easily recognized and acknowledged features of human activities in their geographical distribution and temporal succession.

Special histories tell of movements, whether cultural (language, art, literature, religion), institutional (family, mores, society, education, state, law, church, sect, economy, technology), or doctrinal (mathematics, natural science, human science, philosophy, history, theology).

General history is, perhaps, just an ideal. It would be basic history illuminated and completed by the special histories. It would offer the total view or some approximation to it. It would express the historian's information, understanding, judgment, and evaluation with regard to the sum of cultural, institutional, and doctrinal movements in their concrete setting. It's what was going on, what was going forward or coming apart.

History, as a functional specialty within theology, is concerned in different degrees and manners with basic, special, and general history. In the main it has to presuppose basic history. Its substantial concern is the doctrinal history of Christian theology with its antecedents and consequents in the cultural and institutional histories of the Christian religion and the Christian churches and sects. Finally, it cannot remain aloof from general history, for it is only within the full view that can be grasped the differences between the Christian churches and sects, the relations between different religions, and the role of Christianity in world history.

Our fourth functional specialty is dialectic. While that name has been employed in many ways, the sense we intend is simple enough. Dialectic has to do with the concrete, the dynamic, and the contradictory, and it finds abundant materials in the history of Christian movements. For all movements are at once concrete and dynamic, and Christian movements have been marked with external and internal conflicts, whether one considers Christianity as a whole or even this or that larger church or communion.

The materials of dialectic, then, are primarily the conflicts centering in Christian movements. But to these must be added the secondary conflicts in historical accounts and theological interpretations of the movements. The conflicts occur on the theological level and on the level of historiography.

Besides the materials of dialectic, there is its aim. That aim is high and distant. As empirical science aims at a complete explanation of all phenomena, so dialectic aims at a comprehensive viewpoint. It seeks some single base or some single set of related bases – they may be related contradictorily – from which it can proceed to an understanding of the character, the oppositions, and the relations of the many viewpoints exhibited in conflicting Christian movements, their conflicting histories, and their conflicting interpretations.

Besides the conflicts of Christians and the distant goal of a comprehensive viewpoint, there is also the past and present fact of the many diverging viewpoints that result in the conflicts. Such viewpoints are manifested in confessions of faith and learned works of apologetics. But they also are manifested, often in a more vital manner, in the unnoticed assumptions and oversights, the predilections and aversions, the quiet but determined decisions of scholars, writers, preachers, and the men and women in the pews.

The study of these viewpoints takes one beyond the fact to the reasons for conflict. Comparing them will bring to light just where differences are irreducible, where they are complementary and could be brought together within a larger whole, where finally they can be regarded as successive stages in a single process of development. Comparison is to human studies what experiment is in the natural sciences; you can't experiment on men; it's setting up oppositions. Just as experiment reveals opposition between your hypothesis and the data, the comparative method compares different types of data with one another, and is confronted with differences there.

Besides comparison there is criticism. Not every viewpoint is coherent, and those that are not can be invited to advance to a consistent position. Not every reason is a sound reason, and Christianity has nothing to lose from a purge of unsound reasons, of ad hoc explanations, of the stereotypes that body forth suspicions, resentments, hatreds, malice. Not every irreducible difference is a serious difference, and those that are not can be put in second or third or fourth place, so that attention, study, analysis can be devoted to differences that are serious and profound.

By dialectic, then, is understood a generalized apologetic conducted in an ecumenical spirit, aiming ultimately at a comprehensive viewpoint, and proceeding towards that goal by acknowledging differences, seeking their grounds real and apparent, and eliminating superfluous oppositions.

So much for the first four.

The fifth is foundations. As conversion is basic to Christian living, so an objectification of conversion provides theology with its foundations. By conversion is understood a transformation of the subject and his world. Normally it is a prolonged process, though its explicit acknowledgement may be concentrated in a few momentous judgments and decisions. Still, it is not just a development or even a series of developments. Rather, it is a resultant change of course and direction. It is as if one's eyes were opened and one's former world faded and fell away. There emerges something new that fructifies in interlocking cumulative sequences of developments on all levels and in all departments of human living.

Conversion is existential, intensely personal, utterly intimate. But it is not so private as to be solitary. It can happen to many, and they can form a community to sustain one another in their self-transformation and to help one another in working out the implications and fulfilling the promise of their new life. Finally, what can become communal can become historical. It can pass from generation to generation. It can spread from one cultural milieu to another. It can adapt to changing circumstances, confront new situations, survive into a different age, flourish in another period or epoch.

Conversion, as lived, affects all of a man's conscious and intentional operations. It directs his gaze, pervades his imagination, releases the symbols that penetrate to the depths of his psyche. It enriches his understanding, guides his judgments, reinforces his decisions. But as communal and historical, as a movement with its own cultural, institutional, and doctrinal dimensions, conversion calls forth a reflection that makes the movement thematic, that explicitly explores its origins, developments, purposes, achievements, and failures.

Inasmuch as conversion itself is made thematic and explicitly objectified, there emerges the fifth functional specialty, foundations. Such foundations differ from the old fundamental theology in two respects. First, fundamental theology was a theological first; it did not follow on four other specialties named research, interpretation, history, and dialectic. Secondly, fundamental theology was a set of doctrines on the true religion, on the divine legate, on the church, on the inspiration of scripture, on the theological loci. In contrast, foundations present, not doctrines, but the horizon within which the meaning of doctrines can be apprehended. St Paul said (1 Corinthians 2.14) that 'a man who is unspiritual refuses what belongs to the Spirit of God; it is folly to him; he cannot grasp it.' Theological foundations set forth the horizon within which the spiritual doctrine has its meaning. And a distinction between the horizons within which religious doctrines have their meaning [and the horizons in which they cannot be apprehended]⁶ is foundational to theology.

Sixth, doctrines express judgments of fact and judgments of value. They are concerned, then, with the affirmations and negations not only of dogmatic theology but also of moral, ascetical, mystical, pastoral, and any similar branch.

Such doctrines stand within the horizon of foundations. They have their precise definition from dialectic. The foundations exercise a selective principle with regard to the dialectic. The dialectic does not take sides. It reveals opposition. Foundations do take sides, and when you've taken sides, then from the dialectic, the history, and the interpretation, you can get your doctrines.

Seventhly, systematics. The facts and values affirmed in doctrines give rise to further questions. Doctrinal expression may be figurative or symbolic. It may be descriptive and based ultimately on the meaning of words rather than on the understanding of realities. It may quickly become vague and indefinite. It may seem, when examined, to be involved in inconsistency or fallacy. The functional specialty 'systematics' attempts to meet these issues. It is concerned to work out appropriate systems of conceptualization, to remove apparent inconsistencies, to move towards some grasp of spiritual matters both from their own inner coherence and from the analogies offered by more familiar human experience.

Finally, there are communications. In systematics theologians talk to one another. In communications they learn to talk to the rest of the world. Theology has to explain how one is to communicate to all peoples, all cultures, all classes. And further, it has to be able to effect the transpositions necessary to do this and to use creatively the diverse media of communication that exist today.

2.3   Grounds of the Division

So much for a rough description of what is meant by these eight specialties. Now we want to know, Where does this list of eight come from, and what are the principles to be invoked in working out these different things, in delimiting further and clarifying the relations between them?

First of all, we can say we have a posteriori de facto at the present time distinctions between textual criticism, exegesis, history, apologetics, fundamental

---

6 The words in brackets are an editorial addition. See *Method in Theology* 131.

theology, dogmatic theology, systematic theology, pastoral theology, and that these distinctions approximate fairly well to what I am talking about in talking about those eight. However, those eight that I have just listed are more or less eight different things. When you get the notion of functional specialty, you have the eight related intrinsically, organically, to one another, and so we have to move to what it is that sets up these eight.

Fr Richardson quoted Ebeling dividing theology into *Wort* and *Antwort*.[7] This has been a very traditional distinction. We listen to the word, but we also bear witness to it. In the Middle Ages there was the *lectio divina* but also the *quaestio*. You read and then you wondered what it meant; you asked questions: Does it imply this and that? We assimilate the tradition, but we also hand it on. We encounter the past, but we take our stand towards the future. We study theology *in oratione obliqua*. What did Isaiah and Jeremiah, Paul and John, Augustine and Aquinas, Luther and Calvin have to say about God? We want to know what they said and what they meant. That's theology *in oratione obliqua*, quoting somebody else. But there is also theology *in oratione recta*. What am *I* saying? What do *I* get out of it? How do *I* apply it to human living at the present time?

So there are two phases to theology: the phase of listening, of reading, of assimilating the past, of encountering the past, of being challenged by the past, of studying what other theologians or writers have said, and on the other hand bearing witness to the word to which one has listened, raising and solving questions that arise, handing on the tradition, taking one's stand to the future, speaking one's own mind. That gives us a basic division of theology in two phases, and that is the difference between the first four and the second four.

In ordinary living, we operate on all four levels of consciousness at once. But as soon as things start getting tight, we start concentrating all four levels on the end of one level. And since there are four levels, you can get four functional specialties. If you use experience, understanding, judgment, and decision to settle just what the data are, you're doing research. But if you use all four to understand what the data mean, you're doing interpretation. If you're using all four to make your judgments of fact – what happened? – you're doing history. When you find that different people write different histories and make different interpretations, you're confronted with a conflict, and with the conflict you're on the level of decision yourself, whether

7 Again, Lonergan is referring to lectures delivered earlier in the Institute by Fr William Richardson, s.j., on Heidegger and hermeneutics.

it's a decision about methods or about content. In other words, the functional specialties arise inasmuch as the four levels of intentional consciousness each have their proper end, and one can devote all one's efforts to the end of one level.

That's for the first phase. Similarly in the second phase, our foundations are fundamentally a *Weltanschauung*, a conversion. The conversion is presupposed, but the conversion fundamentally is an act of decision, adopting a *Weltanschauung*, and its objectification is a horizon. It's on the level of decision. On the level of judgment, of what is so, we have doctrines. On the level of understanding, interpretation understands the text, but systematics understands the thing. And finally, after one has been through all these seven, one has something to say, and one produces new data, and that's communications.

I think that's fairly clear. We have experience, understanding, judgment, and decision. In the first phase, the phase of listening, there are research, interpretation, history, and dialectic; and in the second phase, there are foundations, doctrines, systematics, and communications.

There is a further point with regard to the first phase. As one moves up in the specialties, the objects that one is dealing with become enriched. In research it's just data. In interpretation it's data with a meaning. In history you're beginning to meet people, and they're doing things. And in dialectic you have encounter with other persons, and some people bearing this witness to Christ and others bearing another witness, and so on. You're on the fully personal level when you reach the fourth level. And so, theology as encounter – where does it start? It's when you get up to dialectic.

Further, these functional specialties are not in watertight compartments. They're organically interdependent.

2.4   The Need for the Division

Next, what is the need for this division? I've said that it already exists in some form, but the trouble is that the form in which it exists leaves those several things in apparent independence. The point to setting up eight functional specialties as a way of dealing with the whole mass of theological data is that one has one theology in which all the parts are related to one another. You're going to have all the divisions coming from field specializations, all the divisions coming from subject specializations. Still, you'll have a central core in which everything comes together.

The need, then, for functional specialization is not just a matter of convenience. You can attribute a good deal of field specialization and subject specialization simply to the fact that the load is too big for one man. To keep up with all the literature on St Paul and the Pauline letters at the present time is too much for one man, and so one man will take the great epistles and someone else will take the Pauline school, and someone else the Pastorals. And to read all that is put out on that and to keep up with it will keep them quite busy. Similarly, it's too much for one man to teach the whole of theology, and so you chop it up into different treatises and have different people teaching different treatises. But the need for the functional specialization is not just that. It's because there are different tasks to be performed, and the different tasks are performed in different manners. Textual criticism is a quite different set of operations from exegesis, and so on right along the line. Different ends are pursued by different means, different means are employed in accord with different rules, and method is concerned with setting up the basis for those different rules.

Further, the different tasks exist at the present time. Once theology reaches a certain stage of development, the two phases separate. From the seventeenth century on, there is the distinction between positive and Scholastic theology, later between positive and dogmatic theology. That was pretty much separating the two phases. With further specialization you get the phases breaking up into their four functions.

Further, there is the need to curb totalitarian ambitions. One person is working in one functional specialty, and if it's not conceived simply as a functional specialty it tends to want to be the whole show. What is theology? Well, the only thing that counts is systematic theology or biblical theology or dogmatic – that's where you're really certain, and so on; and you want to brush aside the rest. These totalitarian ambitions are cut down to size when it's clear that there are eight functional specializations and that, while none of them can get along without the others, still each has its own task and each needs the others to do its task properly.

Further, there's the need to curb excessive demands. If the eight aren't separate and acknowledged to be separate, people will say, 'This piece of work isn't any good because he isn't doing everything that a person could possibly do.' But if a person works at one functional specialty and does a good job, he's making a very serious contribution to theology; and if he's able to say, 'This is what I'm doing,' and other people know what he means, then he'll be able to do his job properly.

This notion of functional specialty: I stumbled upon it. You'll find the traces of this stumbling in the second volume of my *De Deo trino*, where I'm separating dogmatic and systematic theology, doctrines and systematics as

I call them now, and in the introductory part of the first volume of my *De Deo trino*, where I'm separating dogmatic and positive theology, and I'm pushing that in this present stage to its full logical conclusion.[8]

Without the distinctions, then, persons doing systematic theology will be asked, Is it certain? Well, systematic theology is not certain. It's like scientific theories; they're probable. But to understand something about things is better than to understand nothing, even though it's not yet certain, as all the sciences demonstrate. But if the systematic theologian is constantly being dogged by the question, 'Just how certain is that?' he'll never get anything done. Similarly, the dogmatic theologian, if he's asked, 'Well, how do you explain this? How do you expect me to believe that? What sense does it possibly make?' he's being asked questions that lie outside his specialty. He's out to determine what is the doctrine of the church and where on earth it comes from. That's a task in itself, and similarly for all the other tasks we've been lining up.

2.5   A Dynamic Unity[9]

Finally, we have to speak of the unity of theology. First of all, there is theology as becoming distinct from religion, and secondly, there are the different phases of theology becoming distinct and the different specialties within each of the phases. But they still remain connected, and we have to see how they are connected.

Now, the unity of a subject in process of development is not static but dynamic. If you try to impose a static unity upon it, you will eliminate its development, and you put anyone who tries to develop anything in an extremely awkward position. The logical ideal tends to the static. It wants terms to be absolutely clear, fixed, sharply defined. It wants principles to be as exactly laid down as possible, and deductions to be as rigorous as possible. But in a dynamic unity, we have the unity of a process. The development is from the undifferentiated through differentiation and specialization to an integration of the specializations.

---

8 See Lonergan, *The Triune God: Systematics* (what here he is calling the second volume of *De Deo trino*; see above, p. 153, note 12), chapter 1, and Lonergan, *The Triune God: Doctrines* (the first volume; see above, p. 25, note 30), Prolegomena. While Lonergan uses the word 'traces,' 'anticipations' would be more accurate.

9 The recording continues on Lauzon CD/MP3 484 (48400A0E060).

Initially there was just the Christian religion. There was no distinction drawn between religion and theology. The distinction that does arise is something that arises not merely in the case of religion and theology. It's a universal phenomenon, in all departments of human living. To understand the reason why that distinction arises is of fundamental importance for someone who wants to know what theology is about, what it's trying to do.

First, then, the principal part of human living is meaning. A man's life is not what goes on when he is in a dreamless sleep or a coma. If he dreams, there is something that is specifically human that is coming out, something concerned with meaning. And in his waking time he is busy intending, speaking, doing, and his intending, speaking, doing is all concerned with meaning. Meaning is involved in it. It's never just purely, only meaning, but meaning is a part of it, and a directive part of it.

Now in any human movement, its principal part is a common meaning. You have several people forming a community for a given end insofar as they share some common meaning or set of meanings. The more the movement spreads, the longer it lasts, the more it is forced to reflect upon that common meaning, to bring that common meaning out of an unthematic state where everyone understands it and knows what's meant and you don't have to mention it, to the thematic, when it's stated just what the movement is about; to distinguish this meaning from other meanings, to guard it against aberrations. As rivals come and go, as circumstances and problems change, as issues are driven back to their presuppositions and decisions to their ultimate consequences, there emerges what Georg Simmel has called *die Wendung zur Idee*, the shift towards system.[10] And this is true not only of religious movements but also of political, social, artistic, literary, scientific, philosophic movements. They have to know where they are going, and they have to say so, in order to give the movement its coherence, its differentiation from other movements, to prevent it from being captured by other movements. The occurrence of this process is the history of Catholic, Christian doctrines, and in a later stage the history of its theology. The writing of the several elements in the New Testament resulted in objectifications, putting down in writing parts of the Christian message. Forming the canon was a bigger step in that direction. The Apostolic Fathers, the apologists, the teachers in the schools at Alexandria and then at Antioch, and then the great Councils of Nicea and Chalcedon were all elements in this objectification, this statement, this clarification of what the Christian message is. Nicea went

10 See above, p. 260, note 3.

beyond scripture. It used a word and a formula that didn't occur in scripture, and that caused fifty years of incessant tumult in the church. Chalcedon took a step forward and used the word *physis* in a sense that didn't occur not only in scripture but even in any of the earlier Fathers. And the result of trying to clarify that was Byzantine Scholasticism. Medieval Scholasticism went much further. It reviewed the whole of Christian reality, asking questions about it and building up toward systems and *Summas*.

Now, there naturally arises the question, Is not this academic theology such as began in the Middle Ages just a cultural superstructure that is totally alien to religion? It *is* something that is distinct from religion. There is no doubt about that. And theology can be good or bad, and insofar as it's bad it certainly is alien to religion. But the good is distinct from it and related to it, in symbiosis of mutual influence, religion grounding theology, theology grounded in religion and clarifying it, broadening it out, opening it. What is good for religion and what is good for theology are distinct things, but each helps and reinforces the other. Again, theology is not something for everyone. Just as the differentiation of religion and theology is a differentiation, so to apprehend both and give them their due calls for a differentiation of consciousness. There are people of common sense who have no use for theory, and they never grasp any theory, and they live their lives, and they are quite excellent lives. But there is a differentiation of consciousness that enables a man to confront what Whitehead called the bifurcation of nature.[11] A man looks around and finds a nice wooden desk in front of him and sees the chair, and they're nice solid objects, and so on, and as a modern physicist he realizes that there's much more empty space here than there is matter, that there are only electrons and neutrons and protons, and really you can't localize them or imagine their movements. He's living in two different worlds, the world of common sense and the world of theory. To be able to think of the two and relate one to the other without confusing them calls for a development of consciousness. To try to hand theology to a person without that differentiation of consciousness is to try to impose on him something that he cannot absorb, cannot assimilate. On the other hand, when a person has a differentiated consciousness – he's a good physicist or a good historian of religion – and his theology, his knowledge of religion, is what he learned from his mother's knee so to speak, his religion is going to suffer from that. Either it is going to be brushed aside as something merely childish, or else

11 Alfred North Whitehead, *The Concept of Nature* (Ann Arbor: University of Michigan Press, 1957), chapter 2, 'Theories of the Bifurcation of Nature.'

he'll have to learn theology and develop religiously as he has developed in other fields. In other words, the function of theology is for the cultured consciousness, not for everybody; and there it is necessary.

Finally, the aim of the distinction of theology from religion is not simply differentiation. I used the word 'development' for the distinction between theology and religion, for the relations between them, and for the way to conceive them in their relations.

Next, though, there is a differentiation within theology itself. We already mentioned the *lectio divina*, the *quaestio*, the *Sentences*. Peter Lombard collected the opinions of scripture and the Fathers on a series of points, and then there were the commentaries on the *Sentences*. I think the last commentary on the *Sentences* was written about 1608 by Estius. So Peter Lombard remained the positive basis for all this speculative systematic theology that went on for about 350 years on the basis of his work. Scholastic and positive, dogmatic and positive: that distinction of the two phases is of long standing.

What is the root of the crisis of the so-called opposition at the present time between biblical and dogmatic theology? Its root is that the older type of theology that comes from the Middle Ages and was modified in various slight ways up until the year 1900, say, or even later, has been under Aristotelian influence, the Aristotelian notion of science. Not that theology ever accepted and applied that rigorously, but its thinking about itself was on the background of Aristotle's *Posterior Analytics*. But the positive theology that developed during the nineteenth century and in Catholic circles principally during the twentieth has its origins in German *Philologie*. Friedrich Wolf, who wrote on Homer and divided Homer up into several parts and speculated on the origins of the Homeric poems, conceived *Philologie* as the total reconstruction of a culture in the light of a perfect knowledge of its language, its grammar, its literature, and all its archeological remains. That ideal of *Philologie* was of course first applied to classical antiquity, but it spread out, it included all cultures, and in particular its application to the biblical field, the Old and New Testament, has been the background of the development of modern scriptural studies, modern patristic studies, and modern medieval studies as well. That concept of what these studies are was something quite different from what came out of the development of the *quaestio* in the medieval period.

Now, the conception of theology as eight functional specialties in two phases bridges over that split. It's able to retain everything in the way of foundations, doctrines, systematics, and communications, on the one hand,

and on the other hand everything in the way of research, interpretation, history, and dialectic, the oppositions that emerge when those things are done. And it conceives it as eight parts of a single whole, not as two theologies – biblical, patristic, medieval, on the positive side, and then dogmatic, systematic, pastoral, on the other, six theologies if you wish – but as one theology with eight functionally interrelated parts.

Now we have to consider the unity that emerged in that eightfold division. There is the unity of the first phase, and that unity is not a logical unity. One part does not stand to the other as premise to conclusions or as universal to particular, or any similar logical relationship. What we have is four partial objects that cumulatively are assembed into a total object. They are four, and the four constitute an ever fuller response to the moving object, the total moving object, which is the body of Christ. The structure is essentially an open structure. Experience is ever open to further data, understanding to greater penetration, judgment to more detailed information, more nuanced pronouncements, more adequate perspectives, dialectic to the elimination of mistaken issues, the clarification of real conflicts, and so on. Moreover, the four are in reciprocal dependence. It is obvious that interpretation depends upon the research, for example, the editing of critical texts. You get very clear interpretations from the fellow who explains how a mistaken reading of the text is a very intelligent statement about some thing. You can hear the textual critics talk about the exegetes on that one. But also, the research depends on the interpretation. There is interpretative work involved in the research itself. Again, history obviously depends upon the research and the interpretation. But the opposite is also true. You can do your textual criticism insofar as you can work out the history of the manuscripts, their affiliation, their family relationships; and that is a matter of history. Again, the interpretation has to set this document within its historical context. Finally, dialectic comes out of the previous three. But there is a reciprocal dependence. A few years ago, I was in Los Angeles in a discussion with philosophers and scientists, and the question arose about the unending development of the sciences, and the chairman of the chemistry department said, 'In the last five years, the theoretical developments in the field of chemistry have enormously increased our field of data.' And similarly, the theoretical work involved in the dialectic brings to light elements in the data, elements in interpretation, elements in the history, that before were in their shadows. Nietzsche says that the historian pulls a man of genius out of the shadows in which he was confined during his lifetime. It is the later thinking that asks the questions that bring out the new light.

Now this reciprocal dependence of the four specialties of the first phase is most easily achieved when one man does all four specialties. And note, it's a distinction not of specialists but of specialties. It's different tasks. If one man can perform all the tasks, fine. What has to be kept separate are the tasks because they are performed differently. The distinctions are wanted so that the different tasks are performed each in its proper manner. However, the more the specialties develop, the more refined their techniques, the more numerous and delicate the operations they perform, the less possible it becomes for one man to do all four well, and then recourse has to be to teamwork. And you can have teamwork insofar, first of all, as the fact of reciprocal dependence is understood and appreciated. Not only is that understanding required; one has to be familiar also with what is called the *acquis*, what has been settled, what no one has any doubt about at the present time. You're doing a big thing when you can upset that, but you have to know where things stand at the present time, what has already been achieved, to be able to see what is new in its novelty as a consequence. There is a necessity of easy and rapid communication. The point to the university, the research school, the publications, the periodicals, the books, the congresses, is the easy and rapid communication of people working in specialized fields which are reciprocally dependent.

The movement of the first phase is from the almost endless multiplicity of data through many interpretative unities to more comprehensive narrative unities – the monograph will be on a single aspect of some author's work, the history will pull together several manuscripts – to dialectical oppositions running through the interpretations and the histories and what is interpreted and reported in the histories. That is the movement of the first phase.

The second phase is from the unity of a grounding horizon, the foundations, through doctrines and systematic clarifications to communications with the almost endlessly varied sensibilities, mentalities, interests, and tastes of mankind. Again, in the second phase the process is not deductive, from premises to conclusions. It is a movement through successive and more fully developed contexts: from the foundations, which is just the horizon, to the doctrines, which give a shape within that horizon, to the systematics, which clarify, make the shape meaningful, and finally to the communications, which transpose the message to all the different wavelengths.

Foundations provides a basic orientation. Applied to the conflicts of dialectic, it takes sides, throws light on the ambiguities of history and interpretation, and becomes a principle of selection that leads to doctrines. Doctrines tend to be regarded as mere verbal formulae until their ultimate meaning is worked out and their coherence is assured by systematics. Systematics reveals what there is to communicate, but there remains the problem of the creative use of the available media, the task of finding the appropriate approach and procedure to convey the message of the gospel to peoples of all cultures, classes, and times.

Now the dependence as I have spoken of it is from foundations to doctrines, from doctrines to systematics, and from systematics to communications. But the dependence is also reciprocal. It is not only doctrines that give rise to problems in systematics, problems for understanding, but also communications. Again, it is not merely systematics that clarifies doctrines, but doctrines can draw upon systematic formulations to acquire accuracy and clarity. Finally, while conversion is formulated as horizon, still it has not only personal but also social, historical, and doctrinal dimensions.

There is, then, a reciprocal interdependence of the four specialties in each of the two phases. It is further clear that the second phase depends on the first. The first is mediating theology, the body of Christ as it has existed and still exists, manifesting itself to us more and more as one moves up from mere research, making the data available, through interpretation and history, to the personal confrontation where it is presented by the opposed interpretations and histories. The second phase is mediated theology, theology as of God and of all things in their relations to God. There is an opposition reflected in the question, Is theology reflection on the mystical body, or is theology about God and all things in relation to God? It is both, but as mediating theology, it is the first, and as mediated theology in the second phase, it is the second.

The first phase, again, is field specialization rising up through the four levels of experience, understanding, judgment, and decision. And the second is theology as subject specialization, descending from horizon or conversion through doctrines and systematics to communications. The second manifestly depends on the first. That has been the whole presentation. But one can ask, Does the first also depend on the second? Here the greatest care has to be exercised. There is a dependence of the first phase on the second. But undue influence absolutely has to be avoided. If there were undue influence, the second phase would become independent of the first. It would be dictating to the first what it should be. And it becomes isolated and sterile if it does that. Its life is out of the data, out of the first phase. And if it starts acting too strongly back again, it's corrupting the first phase, corrupting the challenge that comes to it from the first phase.

464   Part Three: Boston College Lectures, 1968

What, then, is undue influence? The questions that arise in the first phase have to be met not by an appeal to the second phase as an a priori but out of the resources of the first phase itself. It's easy enough to spot in somebody else's work a bias from positivism or existentialism or any other 'ism,' but the effective answer is not that. The effective answer is to go over the work in scholarly fashion and pin down just what's wrong. Stephen Neill speaks of Lightfoot, the man who edited the Apostolic Fathers,[12] and he speaks of him with delight, as a man who could just cut short the mistaken view. If Neill had anything to say about it, every first-year student would have to read 500 pages of Lightfoot. Baur put forward his view on the late appearance of the New Testament writings. Lightfoot went ahead and cleared up the question of which of Ignatius of Antioch's epistles were authentic. Then he dated them. And when he had the authentic epistles separated from the unauthentic, and the authentic ones dated, he had the means of settling what were the latest dates at which a great part of the New Testament could have been written. And no one ever heard of Baur's opinion after that. It just stopped it. It's that kind of work that is the proper work of the first phase; that is the work of the first phase meeting its problems out of its own resources. It's much shorter and simpler to say where this fellow is theoretically wrong, but you don't stop his position that way. There are a lot of other people who aren't going to argue on that basis. But if you put your answer down out of the resources of that phase, you make a real contribution to that field, and you can end the matter, because there are in the first phase the resources to deal with its own problems. It can't deal with them all, because some of them are things that don't really belong to the first phase. But that answer from the first phase is an important thing, and not to do that, or to be negligent about or slovenly about it or lazy about it is, of course, to let the second phase really suffer because it is not having the challenge and not being given the problems that are needed for its vitality here and now, at the present time.

But once this has been said, it remains that there is mutual interaction between the first and second phases that is quite legitimate. This interaction is between history and doctrines and between foundations and dialectic.

First, it is between history and doctrines. Everyone knows today that if you want to understand the doctrine, you do the history of it. It is through understanding how the doctrine developed that you understand just what

12 Stephen Neill, *The Interpretation of the New Testament, 1861–1961* (London: Oxford University Press, 1964) 36–59.

The Robert Mollot Collection

it means. But the inverse is also true. If you want to do the history properly, you have to understand the doctrine. If a man doesn't know mathematics or chemistry or medicine and he wants to write a history of those subjects, his history will be a mess. He will be all the time overlooking things of real significance and playing up minor matters. His language would be inaccurate or out of date, his emphases mistaken, his perspectives distorted, his omissions intolerable. One really has to understand mathematics or chemistry or medicine to write the history of it, to see what was significant, to pick out the key points and the breakthroughs. What is true of those subjects is also true of religion and theology.

Again, there is an interdependence of dialectic and foundations. Foundations objectify conversion, and while there may well be more than one account of authentic conversion, still they may tend to a certain similarity. In virtue of that similarity, they should tend to reduce the multiplicity laid bare by dialectic and to weaken its merely polemical tendencies. I spoke this morning of this matter in St Paul, 'The unspiritual man does not apprehend it.' Friedrich Heiler, in an essay in a volume on the history of religions (a 1959 volume, University of Chicago), on methodology, states that there are seven common features to all the high religions, and by the 'high religions' he means some seven religions besides Christianity. This point that foundations is the objectification of conversion is not something that's going to be in Christianity with nothing like it elsewhere, but on the contrary there is something very similar, at least if one can trust that list set down by Friedrich Heiler there.[13]

From the two interdependences, therefore, on the level of foundations and dialectic and on the level of history and doctrines, there results at least indirectly an interdependence of both the phases – with the limitation, however, that the second phase must not exert undue influence on the first.

I conceive dynamic unity, then, as the interdependence of the four functional specialties in each of the two phases, as the interaction of the two phases, and as the interaction of theology and religion. There remains the interaction of religion and the world, which is a further point.

Note, then, finally, that functional specialization involves a distinctive notion of theology. Field specialization, if it's taken as the guide, gives us series

13 Friedrich Heiler, 'The History of Religions as a Preparation for the Cooperation of Religions,' in *The History of Religions*, ed. Mircea Eliade and Joseph Kitagawa (Chicago: University of Chicago Press, 1959) 142–53. Note the development in Lonergan's notion of conversion from the position of 1962 expressed above. See p. 32, note 3.

of different theologies: theology of the Old Testament, theology of the prophets, theology of John, theology of Paul, of the different Fathers, and so on. Subject specialization gives us theology as science of God and of all things in their relation to God, as known under the light of revelation and faith. Functional specialization, taking functional specialization as one's key, brings these two together and allows each its full significance and role, without thereby tending to neglect the other. Moreover, it conceives theology not as a deduction from the truths of faith, but as, primarily in its first phase, a reflection on the religious fact. It gives theology the same fundamental shape as any human science, especially any human science like the history of religions that reflects on man's past and exercises an influence on his future.

Finally, while all these things that I've been distinguishing are interconnected, still, as in any similar case, one first of all has to draw the distinctions before one can posit the relations. The development in the understanding of theology itself is a matter of a movement from the undifferentiated through differentiation and specialization to their integration.

So much for chapter 2.

3 Horizons and Categories, Introduction[14]

Chapter 3 is entitled 'Horizons and Categories.' The first section is 'Meaning as Horizon,' and the second 'Method as Horizon.' I think I can run through these fairly quickly, and then we can have a question period. That will do it for today.

Literally, horizon is the line where earth and sky apparently meet; it comes from the Greek for 'bounding circle.' It recedes as we advance and closes in behind us. It divides objects into visible now, and not now visible, according to one's standpoint. As one moves about, one's standpoint changes, and the objects that are within one's horizon change. What is within one's horizon is now accessible to vision. What is beyond one's horizon one cannot now possibly see. So much for the literal sense.

But besides the literal sense, there is also a metaphorical or analogous sense. As the range of our vision, so our interests and our knowledge are limited. Within our horizon, within the world of our interests and knowledge, there is all we care for, know about to some extent, great or small. What is beyond our horizon is what we know nothing about and care less.

---

14 See www.bernardlonergan.com, item 18490DTE060.

Horizons may be compared in three ways. They may complement one another; they may be related genetically; they may be opposed dialectically.

First, there are complementary horizons. There are different interests, skills, knowledge in workmen, foremen, supervisors, technicians, engineers, managers, doctors, lawyers, professors, and so on. But each knows about the others, and each has some general idea of what the other does. Each recognizes the need for the others, and no one is willing to take up the other fellow's work and do it for him. Together, they constitute a common world. Each complements the other. Each knows something about the others. They work together within a common world. Yet the focus or what is fully a matter of interest varies from one man to the next. Their horizons are complementary.

Genetic horizons are related to one another as successive stages in some process of development. The later includes the earlier but diverges from it, dropping some elements, changing others, adding still others. They are not complementary, because they are not simultaneous. They are parts of the same biography or the same history.

Horizons may be dialectically opposed. Then each has some awareness of the others, but this inclusion is also a rejection and a condemnation. The other's position is ascribed to wishful thinking, the acceptance of myth, ignorance or fallacy, blindness or illusion, backwardness or immaturity, infidelity, bad will, a refusal of God's grace. The rejection may be passionate, and then the suggestion that one should cultivate openness makes one furious. But rejection may also have the firmness of ice without any trace of passion except perhaps a wan smile. Both genocide and astrology may be beyond the pale, but the former is execrated, the latter is ignored or merely amuses.

So we've compared horizons in three different ways: as complementary parts of a single world, as genetically related, and as dialectically opposed.

Horizons also differ in their structures. In the first place, horizons are structured. Learning is not just an addition to an already acquired store but rather an organic growth out of what already is known, and so there is always context. Our intentions, our statements, our deeds all occur within contexts, and it is to contexts that we appeal when we explain our deeds – 'What are you doing? What are you up to?' – or when we clarify, amplify, qualify our statements – 'What I really meant was this' – and appeal to the context within which we made our judgment. When you explain your goals, you give a context.

Husserl, who did terrifically delicate analyses of practically everything, said that to describe even a single perception without any mention of the comprehensive horizon of a world as its encompassing frame of reference was to give a mutilated account of the perception. Perceptions and all our acts of intentional consciousness are within the context of their past and in a movement towards their future.

Further, regulative of our learning is our interest. We take the trouble to attend and learn in accord with the values we respect and the satisfactions we prize. But the values that are respected and the satisfactions that are prized can vary from age to age, group to group, man to man, and within the lifetime of each one of us, so that the variation of horizons from the context from which they are built up in learning and the influence of values and satisfactions give rise to different structures in horizons. Values and satisfactions are great determinants of horizons, and you can have different scales of values, different values highly prized and others ignored. That gives rise to enormous differences in horizon.

Now we have mentioned this matter of horizon because our conception of method and of method in theology in terms of functional specialization determines a horizon in doing theology. We have conceived theology methodically, that is, our very conception of what theology is has been the conception of functionally interdependent sets of normative patterns of related and recurrent operations. This method fixes a horizon. It conceives theology as an ongoing process of a certain type of complexity. It will serve to clarify the point if we indicate the divergence between this position and that of Aristotle's *Posterior Analytics*, which from the thirteenth century provided the background from which the nature of Catholic theology, at least, has been discussed; and secondly between this position and the series of more specifically theological positions that have characterized Catholic theology since the thirteenth century.

The *Posterior Analytics* really has never had any great direct positive influence on theology, but theology has been conceived relative to it, on some sort of analogy to it, and without any real breakaway from it. Today I'll only take this difference from Aristotle. I think it's important not because of any great familiarity that people have with Aristotle, but because of the unconscious influence that is contained in the tradition, that isn't really recognized as such, and that spontaneously is appealed to as something definite and determinate and undisputed.

The crucial difference of modern science from the *Posterior Analytics* is that in the *Posterior Analytics* science is conceived as knowledge of the causal, the necessary, the immutable, while, on the other hand, modern science is knowledge, not of the intelligibility that must be but of the intelligibility of what can be. The law of falling bodies was worked out by Galileo some four centuries ago and has been verified directly and indirectly countless times in the last four centuries. But it is not a statement of the way bodies must fall. It is not a necessary law. Bodies could fall in some other fashion, according to some other law. The falling would still be intelligible in that manner. It does not have to be a constant acceleration over narrow ranges; that is not necessary, and no one ever thought that that was necessary (although I'll have to bring in some qualifications presently). But physical laws are hypothetical. They have to be verified; they are true because they are verified, in the measure that they are verified; and when their verification becomes questionable, out they go. They are not what must be.

Now it is true that in the nineteenth and early twentieth centuries the Aristotelian notion of necessary law was accepted. People spoke of the necessary laws of nature and even of the iron laws of economics, the impossibility of miracles, and so on. But that position has broken down. The breakdown began with the discovery of the possibility of non-Euclidean geometry. It went further when Einstein used the non-Euclidean geometry in physics with his relativity theory. It went still further when quantum theory predicts alternative probabilities. It goes even further with the limitations on deductive systems formulated by theorems of the Gödelian type. Finally, in mathematics at the present time, no one holds that mathematics is deduced from self-evident necessary principles. The vast majority of mathematicians are content if they can find some way of showing that their axioms are not contradictory. There is a school that wants more than that; they want some positive intelligibility; they are called the intuitionists; but that is the mathematical position. That notion of necessity is not a notion that is central to modern science; it is a notion that at most is marginal.

Now the Aristotelian notion of science has always been nothing but an embarrassment in theology. God is necessary in himself, if you please, but he need not have created the world; he need not have destined us to a supernatural end; and he need not have redeemed sinners. To drop Aristotle on this point is to drop a series of pseudo-problems. There are the problems of showing that the mysteries can't be demonstrated, all the business about rationalism and semirationalism. Well, nothing is demonstrated in the Aristotelian sense.

Again, to drop Aristotle is to reveal the real worth of systematic theology. When you have this idea that science is of the necessary, theological explanation is described as *convenientia*, and if you think of intelligibility in terms of demonstrations, then *convenientia* is an argument that does not prove. What is the good of that? What is the good of systematic theology, if all it does is give you arguments that do not prove? Well, what you get in systematic theology is the same type of intelligibility, the hypothetical intelligibility that has to be verified, and only insofar as it is verified is it true. That is the type of intelligibility that you have in physics, chemistry, biology, and there it is very highly respected, and it can be just as highly respected in theology.

There are a series of corollaries. Aristotle distinguished between science and opinion. Science is of the necessary; opinion is of the contingent. Modern science aims at scientific opinion, the best opinion available at the present time. It is a science of the contingent, of this contingent world in which we live.

For Aristotle, theory regards the necessary, and practice regards the contingent. Theory is necessarily non-practical because it deals with what cannot be other than it is, and you cannot do anything about what cannot be other than it is; it cannot be practical. Modern theory and practice are two stages in consideration of exactly the same objects, and theory is eminently practical. The ivory tower of necessity just vanishes in the modern context.

Again, there are implications for wisdom and prudence. For Aristotle, wisdom is the first, concerned with the ultimate causes. Prudence concerns the contingent affairs of men. But man in his historicity, the historical destiny of peoples and nations, our lives and our cities, is not simply a matter of prudence. We need an awful lot of wisdom. We have to get wisdom and prudence together.

Again, the vehicle of Aristotelian science was the syllogism, and there was a sequence of syllogisms concluding the necessary properties of things from their essences. This presupposes self-evident principles from which the deductions can be made, and a purely logical concept of science. The whole of science is contained within the conceptual and the verbal. But de facto such principles do not exist in modern science. Aristotle, in the *Posterior Analytics*, book 2, chapter 19, gives an account of the way scientific discoveries are made, and his account is accurate. But discoveries made in that fashion are hypotheses; they are not necessary truths.

To accept method in theology is to drop this deductivist ideal, with its necessary first principles known to be necessary by God and revealed to us, from which, while we don't see them as necessary, still, we can deduce all the conclusions. That deductivist setup in theology goes out when you conceive theology methodically, when you conceive it as an ongoing process with continuity and without rigidity.

Again, truth is contextual. The meaning of any statement depends upon the context. But it makes a vast difference whether that context is conceived as a unique and fixed set of necessary and immutable truths or as an ongoing process that develops historically, that contains in a living unity knowledge and belief, certainties and probabilities. Aristotle himself was not taken in by his logic. Though he was the discoverer of logic and formulated it in the *Prior* and *Posterior Analytics*, he consistently preached the doctrine that one should distinguish different subjects, different degrees of accuracy, rigor, coherence possible in different subjects, and so on; he is constantly harping on that theme. But it is one thing to preach this doctrine and another to enable people to form some idea of what the actual context of statements is.

Controversialists might be defined as people who suppose that the context of statements is some logically formalized deductive system that enables them to demonstrate what one must have meant whether or not any such meaning ever entered one's head. It presupposes that the context is something that has been worked out with all the rigor of a formalized logical statement. One of the advantages of the transition from logic to method is that it facilitates an apprehension of the nature of contexts. Within the framework of method the function of logic is limited, first, to the fact that it consolidates what has been settled; it reveals defects still to be overcome; it presents an ideal towards which expression always strives, but this ideal is never supposed to be an accomplished fact. The demand is not for clarity but for increasing clarity. Total clarity simply means that conceptual development has come to a dead end. Understanding is always expected to increase, and as it increases, concepts will become fuller, more precise, richer in implications. There is a demand for coherence, but it is a limited demand. It does not lead to the rejection of contrary statements, each of which is backed by some evidence, and both of which may some day prove to be complementary aspects of a single truth, though now you can't show that they are complementary; you don't know what the single truth is.

Full respect is paid to logical rigor; but full respect is also given to subtler and richer procedures such as the moving viewpoint. The context of methodical work contains a degree of indeterminacy and of openness and a need for further advance that is not present when you conceive context on a logical model of first principles and conclusions. That type of context is the context in which methodical thought has to be conceived.

Next, there is the ivory tower versus the existential subject. If science were the deduction of necessary conclusions from self-evident principles, then it can hardly be conceived that anyone could fail to apprehend what is self-evident or to deduce its necessary implications. The scientist, then, can be prescinded from; he cannot help but be employing right reason. It is a terrific effort to miss what is self-evident, to blind himself to that; or to fail to draw necessary conclusions from it. So you can deal with the per se subject, an ideal subject, a *de iure* subject. You don't have to think of concrete existing human beings with all their failings. And so in the eighteenth century, from the Enlightenment on, and still a good deal today, people appeal to right reason.

When method replaces the necessitarian notion, values and choices play a fundamental role. Method regards operations. Operations have motives and occur because of choices. Method is within the context of action and consequently of motives and values and choices. To say that is to say that a science cannot be value-free. There is always, at least, the value of the science itself there. Followers of Max Weber have been pointing that out by explaining the way in which this *Wertfreiheit* has to be understood.

Moreover, the more the several methods of the sciences are based on their root principles, namely, Be attentive, intelligent, reasonable, responsible, the more the science is seen to depend on the authenticity of the existential subject, and, inversely, the clearer it is that science has the value of being one of the ways in which the existential subject can realize his authentic being.

Finally, there is the contrast between habit in the mind and science as possession distributed in the community. Deductivist science suggests the view that science can be tucked in the mind of an individual as a habit. But method results in sciences so vast that no mathematician knows all mathematics, no physicist knows all physics, no chemist knows all chemistry, no biologist knows all biology; and there are no omnicompetent theologians today. The modern discipline is not in a single mind; it is distributed among a scientific community. Not all of it is to be learnt by everyone because not all of it can be learnt by everyone. But the ideal becomes the ideal of the scientific community; one must have in one's community someone such that between all the members of the group taken together there is always someone who is able to handle any particular issue that arises and, on the other hand, to slap down anyone who is merely freewheeling, talking without any basis.

Again, teaching theology is not a matter of teaching the whole of theology; it's a matter of initiation into method exercised in its various forms and a selection of topics in accord with the future work of the student.

I think we can stop there and go on Monday to the contrast between the horizon of method and the various stages in the history of theology especially from the thirteenth century until the present day. Now we'll have any questions that may have occurred to anyone.[15]

15 There do not seem to have been any questions; at least none were recorded.

1968-3

Horizons and Categories[1]

1 Horizons (continued)

We continue with 'Horizons and Categories.' Last time I spoke of the meaning of horizon, comparison of horizons, distinguishing them as complementary, genetic, and dialectical, and the differences of structure in horizons. I went on to method as horizon, and in particular to the difference between the traditional Aristotelian approach, however qualified, and the implications of horizon. Particularly the notion of necessity was fundamental in Aristotelian science, and it is marginal in modern science. We dealt with the many implications of that, especially with regard to the way the context of the statement of a truth is conceived, whether it is conceived in accord with some logical ideal or more in terms of the ongoing process of method. Again, I spoke of the abstract subject as opposed to the existential subject, and of science or a scientific discipline, not as a habit in some individual's mind, but as a possession distributed in the scientific community.

There is a second contrast, namely, the methodical approach in theology in comparison with what especially Catholic theology has been in its history. Catholic theology in its history has never been anything purely speculative. The seminal work, the great speculative person was, of course, St Anselm, who handled all the more difficult questions in theology, the speculative issues. His influence has been very small simply because his thinking was

---

1 Monday, 8 July 1968, Lauzon CD/MP3 486 (48600A0E060). The lecture is devoted to completing the chapter entitled 'Horizons and Categories.'

not informed with the terrific range of information that we will find 150 years later in St Thomas Aquinas. This terrific range of information that you find in St Thomas and his contemporaries starts from Peter Abelard's seminal work *Sic et non*. It consisted of 158 propositions, and he produced texts from scripture, quotes from the Fathers, arguments from reason, to establish both sides of the contradiction with regard to each one of the 158 propositions. It provided, and was an initial exploration of, the Catholic tradition in scripture and the Fathers, and it set up the medieval mentality, the arguments from reason. It was fundamentally a positive work and fundamentally a challenge from the past: Which side are you taking and why, in each of these 158 propositions?

Out of that developed the technique of the *quaestio*. The *quaestio* starts off with arguments or quotes on one side: *Videtur quod non*, and arguments and quotes on the other side: *Sed contra est.* Then there are laid down the principles of solution: *Respondeo dicendum quod.* And finally, specific solutions are offered to each of the apparently opposed texts.

The technique of the *quaestio* in Aquinas's *Summa* has become highly formalized. If one wants to see the *quaestio* as a real business dealing with real issues, then go to *De veritate*, q. 24, a. 12. There the question is whether the sinner without grace can long avoid further mortal sin. In the Commentary on the *Sentences*, 2, d. 28, St Thomas had held that he could, and now he holds the contradictory opinion; he is changing his mind. He has twenty-two texts on the *Videtur quod non* and eleven on the *Sed contra est*, and the principles of solution run over columns in the Vivès edition. But it is the technique of the question as a live procedure, and it was a live procedure as long as new texts were coming in and real problems were being met.

The *quaestio* expanded into the set of *quaestiones*, and the set would be on particular topics: *De veritate, De potentia, De spiritualibus creaturis*, and so on; or a commentary on the *Sentences* of Peter Lombard. Peter Lombard's *Sentences* were the medieval combination of Rouët de Journel and Denzinger, texts from the Fathers and the Councils. They wrote commentaries on them and raised questions; and by the time you get to St Thomas's commentary on the *Sentences* of Peter Lombard, the questions Thomas is asking and answering have hardly any relation to the texts of Peter Lombard. The discussion of over a hundred years has been going on, new matters have been added, and the discussion includes all the development of the previous hundred years.

There were several collections of *Sentences*, but Peter Lombard's was the one that survived best because he did not try to settle issues but just gave the texts and said the prudent reader will now, perhaps, be able to figure things out. He was a bit of a positivist. Two things are to be noted. First of all, this procedure of writing a commentary on the *Sentences* that is going over the whole field of theology as it was then conceived or of writing a *Summa* as did St Thomas – either the *Contra Gentiles* or the *Summa theologiae* – sets up a new problem of coherence. In other words, they were dealing fundamentally with the coherence of the texts brought in from scripture and the Fathers, and the coherence of that thinking with the medieval mind, and consequently the arguments from reason. But they found themselves in a new problem of coherence when they asked, How are all these responses to these questions coherent? You need some common basic vocabulary, mode, set of concepts, *Begrifflichkeit* as the Germans say, to be able to answer coherently all these questions. And it was that that gave Aristotle the entry into medieval theology. Aristotle did provide a fundamentally coherent apprehension of man and of nature, and the theologians, by analogy, extended this to God, grace, the economy of salvation, and so on. So Aristotle enters intrinsically into medieval theology as the one who provided the language, the technical language, the systematic thinking that enabled theology coherently to answer a whole series of questions and not merely to create a new problem of coherence in place of the old one.

This imposing edifice of medieval theology had one basic defect. It dealt with its sources fundamentally in a logical fashion. What it was seeking was logical coherence. It did not entertain the notion of development and reconciling opposed texts on the principle that this is a later development of the earlier position. The historical component, the problem of development, was not part of their system of solution, and consequently there was a fundamental defect in the medieval development of theology of being non-historical, where I mean by 'historical' a process of development of religion, development of dogma, development of theology. They were developing theology at a terrific rate themselves, but they were not adverting to the fact that the Fathers had developed, gone beyond the New Testament, and to the fact that they were going beyond scripture and the Fathers. The fundamental problem in method in theology, at the present time, is precisely integrating that historical element into theology.

The Renaissance with its classicism attacked Scholasticism. But it was enamored with eternal truths, unchanging laws, fixed ideals of perfection, and it had little sense of history. The Reformation, initially, was anti-Scholastic but it soon developed a Scholasticism of its own. Those who are called the 'Old Protestants' had very much the same mentality as their Catholic opponents, from the viewpoint of a Scholasticism.

Petavius, perhaps the founder of Catholic positive theology, knew that Justin Martyr did not talk the language of Chalcedon, and instead of thinking in terms of development, he thought of him as probably a heretic. Melchior Cano worked out a new approach to theology. From the Middle Ages on to about the sixteenth century, they wrote commentaries on the *Sentences*. The same doctrine was being argued around; there wasn't new material coming in, or only to a very slight extent. Melchior Cano did work out a new approach in which there was room for study of scripture and study of the Fathers, but there was no provision made for any fruits to be derived from this further study of scripture or the Fathers; the same Scholastic theses were still being expounded; and all he was getting was a new type of proof for the old theses. Again, the notion of history was not operative.

Finally, the dogmatic theology that took shape in the manuals was marked by the great presupposition of *semper idem*: if the faith is always the same, then a man with the faith today will have no difficulty understanding the Old Testament or the New Testament or the Fathers, medieval writers or Reformation writers, and so on. There is that absence of historical perspective. The difficulty with the manual is not anything connected with the thesis technique; that is just a pedagogical device and a rather fine pedagogical device. The difficulty is the supposition that one man can compose the thesis and give arguments from all over. He can do so only by using secondary sources in a non-expert way. The difficulty is that while the manual is a very good pedagogical technique as an end product, still, it has to be an end product of teamwork if it is going to be a first-class thing – and anyway the manuals are going out. The fundamental difficulty with it is the assumption that one man can master all and really be at home in the whole business.

Now, this long-standing resistance to the historical approach has gradually broken down. The nineteenth century learnt about the development of dogma and the history of theology in the Patristic and medieval periods. The twentieth century has greatly developed that, gone far beyond it, and the resistance to the historical approach in scripture studies came pretty well to an end with *Divino afflante spiritu*. There are still some pockets fighting, but the historical approach is in right across the board. Moreover, despite the nineteenth-century attempt to resurrect Thomism, at the present time Catholic theologians are drawing on such fresh sources as personalism, phenomenology, existentialism, and historicism as necessary means for formulating the theology that is being born. Karl Rahner put it as follows: traditional neo-Scholasticism is just not in the contemporary discussion;

and if the theologian is to think in contemporary terms, well, he has to do his own philosophizing.

The interest, then, of the question of method in theology stems from the fact that we have this terrific breakthrough. We have as big a challenge as was faced in the Middle Ages, or a bigger one. What we are going to do about it is a fundamental question. And that is the question of method.

I started out speaking of horizon, the horizon as fixed by method in contrast to an Aristotelian position or in contrast to the non-historical elements in traditional Catholic theology that have been overcome. The problem of the historical approach no longer exists, seriously, in Catholic theology.

2 Categories

I move on now to the question of categories. I mentioned the fact that medieval theology found its coherent conceptuality, its *Begrifflichkeit*, by the two steps of, first, taking over Aristotle's apprehension of man and of nature, and secondly, proceeding analogously from this conception to some conception of God, grace, the economy of salvation, and so on.

Categories for a contemporary theology open to history have to be somehow transcultural. They have to be such that one can use them in moving through the 2,000 years of the church's history, in going still further back into Old Testament times, in speaking to all cultures and classes in the modern world. There has to be at least a transcultural root to them, and the possibility of transcultural categories lies in connecting them somehow with transcendental method. Transcendental method, precisely because it escapes categorial limitations, has transcultural possibilities.

Three observations are in order. First, there is a sense in which transcendental method is transcultural, and there is a sense in which it is not. It is inasmuch as it is non-thematic, *in actu exercito*, inasmuch as it is a matter of the transcendental notions, the thrust of the spirit in inquiry, reflection, deliberation; of the operations that follow upon that thrust; of the structure of the operations; of the objects specified as correlatives to the operations. For example, what do you mean by form? What you know insofar as you understand. What do you mean by act? What you know insofar as you judge. What do you mean by potency? Something connected with the empirical residue of what's given, whether given to sense or given to consciousness, something of the purely given. There you have your objective terms defined as correlatives to cognitional operations. In that sense, there is a transcultural element to transcendental method.

On the other hand, inasmuch as transcendental method is thematized, objectified, it obviously presupposes a notable cultural development and is open to still further development, though not to radical revision.

Secondly, the derivation of transcultural categories from transcendental method may be done in two ways. Firstly, one may simply sketch procedures, and that's the methodologist's task. Or one may work the transcultural categories out in detail, and that is the task of the theologian dealing with specific problems in specific areas. So all you are going to get from me is a sketch of how it can be done, some idea on how it can be done.

Thirdly, I distinguish a general derivation and a special derivation; and I understand this in a parallel fashion to the medieval distinction which used Aristotle when thinking of man and of nature but proceeded from Aristotle by analogy to think of God and of grace.

3 General Categories

First, then, general derivation, general categories. How does one get from transcendental method to general categories? I indicate five ways of going about it. One starts from what I call the basic structure: the transcendental notions, the operations, the structure of the operations, and the correlative objects. One can: (1) complicate that structure, (2) turn to concrete instances of it, (3) fill it out, (4) differentiate it, (5) set it in motion. I will illustrate each of these.

(1) Complicate the structure. First of all, there is the basic structure: experiencing, understanding, judging, deciding. It can be complicated in various ways. One way is the commonsense development of intelligence studied in chapters 6 and 7 of *Insight*. A second way is the classical, statistical, genetic, dialectical heuristic structures worked out in *Insight*: classical, in classical science; statistical, when you start taking concrete events into account; genetic, in biology; dialectical, dealing with the concrete, the dynamic, and the contradictory.

Again, metaphysics is an integral heuristic structure. It complicates the fundamental business of experiencing, understanding, judging, and deciding by having several instances of this in certain relations.

Similarly, the second chapter, on functional specialties, was a complication of the basic structure. We have the four levels (experiencing, understanding, judging, deciding) occurring in two phases; and the effort concentrates on the end of the first level, the second level, the third level, and the fourth level. This happens twice and so you get eight. It's a complication of the basic structure. As presented, it was a complication of the basic structure. As a derivation of special categories, it was for theology. But something similar will be required whenever you have an academic discipline that deals with man's past with a relevance to his future.

First, then, complicate the basic structure.

(2) Turn to concrete instances of it. From the individual subject of conscious and intentional operations, turn to many such subjects, to their grouping in society, and to the historical succession of such groups. The basic structure becomes an a priori for the individual in the group, for the group, for the history of the group.

(3) Fill it out. Experiencing, understanding, judging, deciding. Experiencing what? Understanding what? Judging what? Deciding what? Fill it out with details. Now you have a good deal of this in *Insight*; and we will have two chapters, the fourth and the fifth, concerned largely with that business of filling out, on the human good, values, beliefs, meaning. So there is a move to the concrete.

(4) Differentiate. In *Insight* the distinctions are drawn between the biological, aesthetic, intellectual, dramatic, and practical patterns of experience. Peoples' experience goes into different patterns, into different modes. The person having an aesthetic experience is not the same person playing a game of baseball. Experience is flowing in a different mode; those distinctions are drawn in *Insight*.

Again, there is the authentic and the unauthentic subject. The subject is authentic insofar as he is attentive, intelligent, reasonable, and responsible, and unauthentic insofar as he is failing in any one of these. Again, the authentic subject is the basis of what may be called positions, and the unauthentic of what may be called counterpositions. Again, we have a topic treated in *Insight*.

One can distinguish different worlds and differentiate the worlds of common sense, theory, interiority, and religion. There is Whitehead's bifurcation of nature: the everyday view of things (trees, animals, and so on) and the further theoretical view. The biologist goes with his son to the zoo and both look at the giraffe. The boy notices the long neck and the short tail, and so on. But what does his father see? He sees an interlocking set of systems: the skeletal system, the muscular system, the digestive system, the vascular system, the nervous system, interlocking and giving you this living thing. This giraffe is one way of having all these systems interlocking and functioning. Is this the same animal? Yes. But there are two entirely different apprehensions of the same animal. One of these is the theoretic apprehension, the other the commonsense apprehension. Common sense studies the giraffe in relation to me: what he looks like, and so on. The biological apprehension understands the relations between all the different parts of the giraffe and their unity. There is a systematic exigence that leads to the separation of the world of common sense and the world of theory. People want to get things accurately, work out all the implications, and so they pull right out of things as related to us in order to get them related to one another. This not merely gives one two different worlds; one gets two different languages. The biologist's and the physicist's language is highly technical. You also have two societies. The scientist talks with other scientists in a technical language, and he goes home and talks with his wife in the language of common sense. You get a completely different setup.

How does one relate these two worlds? You're driven back to the subject, something like transcendental method, if you're going to relate them. That brings out the world of interiority.

Finally, there is the world of religion. God is never immediate in any way, and this gives a fifth world. I did not mention the world of immediacy, the world of the infant before he starts using language. Language gives a terrific increase in the size of one's world. The world of immediate experience is always a very small affair. What is within reach is a narrow strip of space-time through which I am moved.

That is another way in which the basic structure is differentiated. Differentiated consciousness is a way of being at home in successive worlds: the world of common sense, the world of theory, the world of interiority, the world of religion, the world of immediacy, what is immediately given. And what is meant by differentiated consciousness? Precisely the ability to be at home in any one of those worlds, to shift easily from one to the other. And, of course, it is the refusal of that shift when people say: 'Oh, it's abstract; it's no use; it's not practical; it's no good.' What do they mean? All they mean is that they have an undifferentiated consciousness, that the world of theory is alien to them, something into which they are not yet prepared to move. Or the world of interiority is something into which they are not yet prepared to move.

(5) Set the structure in motion. The basic structure is dynamic, both materially and formally. It already is essentially in motion. It is materially dynamic, in that it consists of operations. It is formally dynamic, in that it assembles the operations in the appropriate pattern. We have the simple notion of the heuristic structure. Heuristic structure in the simple case is: what is X, say, fire? Fire, for Aristotle, was one of the four elements. Fire for

chemists previous to Lavoisier was something attributed to phlogiston. Fire for subsequent and contemporary chemists is a process of oxidization. Well, how do you use the same word for three entirely different things? How can you be talking about the same thing? There is nothing in common between the process of oxidization and one of the four elements. The point is that prior to any of the answers: A_1, A_2, A_3, there is the inquiry with respect to phenomena of this kind. That is the fundamental meaning of the question. Experience: the sight of fire. Question: what is it, what is going on, what's up? The question: that's the heuristic structure; and the same heuristic structure can successively give rise to different answers whenever you have a development. The unity of the different answers lies not in something in common to the answers, but in the common question that all the answers tried to deal with and successively did so.

Again, what is a person? This is a standard question in theology, and there are all sorts of answers down the ages. For Augustine, there are three persons in the Trinity. What is meant by person? Well, Father, Son, and Holy Spirit. There are three, but three what? There are not three Gods, three Fathers, three Sons, three Holy Spirits. What are there three of? Well, by person or subject, Augustine said, I mean what there are three of in the Trinity. This is person conceived heuristically. I don't know what a person is but by person I mean what I will know when I know what there are three of in the Trinity. This is the question purely, the heuristic structure. Boethius, Richard of St Victor, and Aquinas gave three successive definitions of the person; and that was all very well, but the definitions gave rise to metaphysical questions, and the later discussion is in terms of the metaphysical basis of these definitions, and you have Scotus, Capreolus, Typhanus, Suarez, de la Taille, and maybe some others. They conceived person metaphysically, in a metaphysics of the person. With Descartes, you move on to the person as conscious subject, and subsequent philosophy turned to that. Today the person is described phenomenologically: how do I relate to you, or I to Thou? There is the phenomenology of the person. This is a series of answers to the same fundamental question, and when you are historically minded, as a contemporary theologian has to be, you have to be able to move over the lot. You are getting a transcultural concept insofar as you have a transcultural question that is answered differently in successive contexts.

Again, there is the issue of development. There are several answers, but how does one move from one answer to the other? That is the question of development. Development in general is from the undifferentiated through differentiation and specialization to a new integration in which the specializations are united. The prior way of doing a thing was of very low efficiency. By differentiating elements in the operation and having different people specialize on different elements, you get far greater efficiency and perfection in your operations; but you have to pull them all together into a new whole. There are the different types or cases of development, like the succession of higher viewpoints in *Insight*. A universe that involves both classical and statistical laws is a universe in which an emergent probability can be discerned – another topic discussed in *Insight*. Again, there is authenticity grounding progress; unauthenticity grounding or giving rise to the social surd; and religion as redemption saving us from unauthenticity and from decline.

Moreover, there is chapter 17 of *Insight*, on interpretation aiming at a universal viewpoint that moves over different levels and sequences of expression; it is development of this sort of heuristic structure along with development in between the elements.

So much for the general idea of generating transcultural categories or something close to transcultural categories from the basis in transcendental method.

4 Special Categories

We now turn to special derivation, the derivation of categories that are specifically theological.

Here there are two steps: (1) What is the basis? How we are going to get in the specifically theological element? (2) Once we get it in, how do we use it to get specifically theological categories?

What is the basis of the specifically theological? We start from the notion of self-transcendence. Man achieves his authenticity in self-transcendence. He has a horizon and lives in a world in the measure that he is not locked up in himself. The first step is his sensitivity. It is something he shares with the higher animals but, while they live in a habitat, he lives in a universe because he asks questions and his questioning is unrestricted.

There are questions for intelligence. They ask what and why and how and what for. The answers unify and relate, construct and serialize, classify and generalize. Man moves out into a world through his intelligence.

There are further questions for reflection: Is that so? Now he has moved beyond imagination and guesswork, idea and hypothesis, theory and system, to ask about reality. Here there is a new type of self-transcendence. He is moving to what is independent of himself. He wants, not what appears, not what he imagines, not what he thinks, not what he would be inclined to say, not what seems to him to be so, but what *is* so. This is self-transcendence, but still it is only a cognitive self-transcendence.

With questions for deliberation, self-transcendence becomes real.[2] It is in the order, not merely of knowing, but also of doing. To ask whether or not this is worth while, whether it is not apparently but truly good, is to ask not about pleasure and pain, not about comfort or ill ease, not about sensitive spontaneity, not about individual or group advantage, but about objective value.

Because we can ask such questions and live by the answers, we can effect in our living a real self-transcendence, the possibility of genuine benevolence and beneficence, of real collaboration and of true love, of swinging completely out of the habitat of an animal and of becoming a genuine person in human society.

Now, real self-transcendence becomes a habitual reality when one falls in love. Then, one's being is a being-in-love. Such being-in-love has its antecedents, its causes, its occasions. But once it has blossomed forth, it is not an effect. It becomes a first principle. It takes over. From it flow one's desires and fears, one's discernment of values, one's decisions and determined actions. As Augustine put it, *Amor meus, pondus meum.*[3]

Being in love is of different kinds. There is the love of intimacy, of husband and wife, with its fruit in the family. There is love of one's fellow men, with its fruit in the achievement of welfare. There is the love of God with one's whole heart and one's whole soul, with all one's mind and all one's strength. It is the love of God poured forth in our hearts by the Holy Spirit that is given to us (Romans 5.5). It is a love that grounded St Paul's conviction that there is nothing in death or life, in the realm of spirits or superhuman powers, in the world as it is or the world as it shall be, in the forces of the universe, in heights or depths, nothing in all creation that can separate us from the love of God in Christ Jesus our Lord (Romans 8.38–39).

The question of God is implicit in all our questioning. That is a point that I will return to in chapter 6 when we start treating religion specifically.

2 See Bernard Lonergan, 'Faith and Beliefs,' in *Philosophical and Theological Papers 1965–1980*, vol. 17 in Collected Works of Bernard Lonergan, ed. Robert C. Croken and Robert M. Doran (Toronto: University of Toronto Press, 2004) 35 note 9, for a brief history of the transition from the expression 'real self-transcendence' through 'performative self-transcendence' to 'moral self-transcendence.'

3 Augustine, 'Pondus meum amor meus,' *Confessions*, book 13, chapter 9. See *The Confessions of St Augustine*, trans. John K. Ryan (New York: Doubleday Image, 1960) 341: 'My love is my weight.'

There is a problem of exposition: we want to get categories, theological categories, but to talk about religion adequately, we will first of all have to treat of things like the human good, values, beliefs, meaning. So this is really an anticipation of chapter 6. And I think I can argue that as the question of God is implicit in all our questioning (a point to be developed in chapter 6), so being in love with God is the basic fulfilment of our conscious intentionality. It fulfils conscious intentionality qua transcendental, qua unrestricted. Because it fulfils conscious intentionality in its transcendental aspect of being unrestricted, it brings a deep-set joy that can remain despite failure, humiliation, privation, pain. The same fulfilment brings peace, a radical peace, a peace that the world cannot give. It is a fulfilment that bears fruit in the love of one's neighbor, the love that brings about the kingdom of God on earth.

On the other hand, when people trivialize human living, or when they are fanatical in their pursuit of finite goals, one can suspect, perhaps, a deviation of their capacity for loving God. Conscious intentionality implicitly contains the question of God. I am not saying 'knowledge of God' but 'the question of God.' And its actuation by being in love with God, by infused charity, provides the basis for specifically theological categories. But just as one has to labor – and in this many fail through no great fault of their own – to bring out into the open one's experience of one's conscious and intentional operations in general, so one has to labor to identify in one's inner life and its more outward fruits what is meant by the words 'being in love with God.' One does not take an insight and put one's finger on it and find it. So there is the same problem occurring in a more fundamental fashion when we start looking for infused charity in our lives.[4] Just as one is not to conclude that one is non-intelligent because one has little or no success in identifying one's experience of insight, so a fortiori with respect to the exploration of one's spiritual life, one is not to conclude that one's spiritual life does not exist or that one is not in the state of grace simply

---

4 Note that, while 'being in love with God' is here identified with 'infused charity,' in *Method in Theology* it is identified with sanctifying grace. See Lonergan, *Method in Theology* 289. In his explicit treatments of grace in more metaphysical terms, Lonergan consistently followed Aquinas in distinguishing sanctifying grace and charity. See, for example, *The Triune God: Systematics* 470–73. A major question of interpretation is whether his later work identifies them. In the last of the question-and-answer sessions in the 1974 Lonergan Workshop at Boston College, Lonergan admitted he had amalgamated the two into one. The recording of this session appears as 81500A0E070 on the website www.bernardlonergan.com, with a corresponding transcription at 81500DTE070.

because one does not find the evidence for it in consciousness. The analysis of consciousness is an extremely difficult thing. In fact, spiritual directors might deplore people trying to look for that in their experience, on the ground that it was so discouraging. But saying that it is not there is not the only solution to the question. One may not have found it. In fact, the difficulty of the techniques, the difficulty of knowing exactly what you are looking for, are other explanations that are more likely to be true.

Now, just as there is an intellectual and moral self-appropriation that grounds transcendental method, so too there is a religious and Christian self-appropriation that grounds the extension of transcendental method into theology. What I am saying is something similar to what was suggested by Fr Richardson during his lectures: a *Daseinsanalyse* for theology.[5]

Finally, as our Christianity commonly is more an aspiration than an achievement, we have to have recourse to the Christian community, to its store of experience, its traditional wisdom, to awaken in us what is latent in us, to stir our feelings even though our minds are only partly open, even though our wills are not yet ready.

So much, then, for an indication of the basis of a specifically theological extension of transcendental method. Transcendental method is based on the self-transcending, conscious, intentional operations of man. As the question of God is implicit in that structure, an ultimate fulfilment of that structure lies in infused charity. Infused charity as an ultimate actuation of conscious intentionality gives the basis for a specifically theological method, just as a general analysis of that structure gives the general basis for doing any science.

We have been setting up the basis for the derivation of specifically theological categories. Now we turn to the derivation itself and, as before, we complicate, turn to concrete instances, fill out, differentiate, and set in motion.[6]

(1) Complicate. The matter of complicating has already been done in chapter 2 when we set up the eight functional specialties of theology.

(2) Turn to concrete instances. From the subject in love with God to subjects, their togetherness in community, the history of the salvation that is being in love with God, the function of this history in promoting the kingdom of God among men. It is turning to concrete instances, the group, the history of the group, the role of the group in human history.

---

5 See above, p. 430, note 4.
6 Compare the account of the special categories in *Method in Theology* 290–91.

(3) Fill it out. Being in love with God is exceedingly simple, but it is also exceedingly rich. To fill out the basic structure is to work out a theology of Christian subjectivity that pays special attention to psychology, phenomenology, history, fieldwork, that involves blending into the theology not merely dogmatic but also ascetical and mystical and pastoral theology. So much for the filling out.

(4) Differentiate. Just as one's humanity, so too one's Christianity may be authentic or unauthentic. And when it is unauthentic there is a watering down of the Christian religion. The unauthentic subject thinks of himself in Christian categories without living them. There results an abuse of the language, a watering down of the Christian meaning or, again, the meaning of religious life. There can develop from that a pathology of Christianity: the different ways of being unauthentic and the way in which they give rise to divisions, oppositions, controversies, denunciations, hatred, bitterness.

(5) Set in motion. Human authenticity provokes progress. Christian authenticity is a fuller and more effective self-transcendence. It promotes progress more fully and more effectively. Besides, it is a self-sacrificing love. It overcomes evil not with more evil but with good, and that is the real way to combat corruption and decline.

I have been indicating, then, first, a general derivation of categories from transcendental method. Then, after setting up a basis for a specifically theological position, namely, the infused love of God, the gift of the Holy Spirit to us, in similar fashion I have shown how specifically theological categories could be derived. And, of course, the methodologist merely sketches. It is up to the theologian dealing with specific problems in particular areas to develop the thing in detail.

5 Use of the Categories

I have been talking about how we derive the categories; now I will say something on their use. I have been indicating the way in which we can obtain something that contains transcultural validity of some sort. Insofar as you start using the sciences, you get down to the thought of a particular place and time. But if it is pinned on to something transcendental, when it becomes revised, the whole thing won't vanish; there will always remain the transcendental basis on which the thing is pinned.

The base of the general derivation of the categories was the authentic or unauthentic man: attentive or inattentive, intelligent or unintelligent, critical or uncritical, responsible or irresponsible.

The special base is the authentic or unauthentic Christian, genuinely in love with God or failing in that love, and the consequent Christian or un-Christian outlook and style of living.

Derivation of the categories is a matter of the human and Christian subject effecting a self-appropriation and employing this heightened consciousness both as a basis for methodical control and as an a priori, a set of categories for understanding other men, their social relations, their history, their religion, their rituals, their destiny.

The use of the categories occurs within the functional specialties, and so in research, interpretation, history, dialectic, foundations, dogmatics, systematics, communications. Again, the use and the development of the categories occurs in interaction with data. The categories receive further specification from data. At the same time, the data set up exigences not merely for further clarification; they can lead to the development and correction of the categories. There is, then, a scissors movement, an upper blade and a lower blade. It is not just one knife you are working with. Physics is not just observation and experiment; it is not just mathematics; it is the interaction of the two: the selection of physical theories out of the vast range of mathematical possibilities in the light of data and experimental results. In similar fashion, theology is neither purely a priori nor purely a posteriori; it is the interaction between the categories, the special and the general categories, and the data. With the categories you can ask precise questions. From the data you can learn, not merely what the answers are or move towards the answers, but also correct your questions.

Karl Rahner has spoken of a *Fundamentaltheologie*.[7] I don't know if I have entirely grasped his meaning, but insofar as it seems to be the kernel of theology, something that should be communicated at least to every theological student, I say it would be, perhaps, an account of the origins, genesis, development, present state, and possible future adaptations and improvements of the categories in which Christians understand themselves, communicate with one another, and announce the Gospel to the world.

6 Theologians and Scientists

The determination of the categories will be drawing on the sciences, especially the human sciences, and very specifically the science of religion.

7 See Karl Rahner, 'Reflections on the New Task for Fundamental Theology,' in *Theological Investigations* 16 (London: Darton, Longman & Todd, 1979) 156–66.

Consequently, something has to be said about relations in general between theologians and scientists.

Medieval theology, by its baptism of Aristotle, not merely secured for itself the basis for a coherent conceptual structure, but also set itself in relation to the extensive group of scientific investigations contained in the Aristotelian corpus. Theology was at one with both philosophy and science because the one Aristotle represented both philosophy and science. While the Aristotelian scientific investigations contained a mighty effort towards clarity, precision, coherence, and as well the fruits of far-ranging inquiry and observation, they tended to be regarded, not as a modest beginning to be completed and supplemented and extended, but rather as a treasure to be preserved intact for all time. So the relations of theology and science tended to be conceived by theologians as relations between well-ordered collections of static results, relations fixed by formal objects that assign each discipline its own territory, relations controlled by logic that demanded of each discipline its external as well as its internal coherence.

This notion of the relations between theology and science has to be transformed in the contemporary context. Theology and science are not collections of well-ordered results, but ongoing processes. They are ruled not by logic alone, but by method. And since method ultimately rests on transcendental method, on the authenticity of the existential subject, the relations are concretely relations not of theology and science, of two abstractions, but of theologians and scientists.

A basic task the theologian has to deal with is to help overcome the birth trauma of modern science. Modern science comes out of the thrust of intelligence and questioning that was the medieval world. Perhaps no one has paid better tribute to it than Whitehead in his *Science in the Modern World.*[8] Here is the recognition of the logical work or thrust of the Middle Ages and its influence in setting up the Western scientific tradition. But modern science developed in opposition to Aristotle, to Aristotelians, to theologians, to ecclesiastical power. There is a certain amount of myth mixed in with that, but that is the birth trauma, and there results from it a fierce resentment against any suggestion of any interference with scientists by theologians. Hence it is important that theologians be clear about possible differences between theology and science.

8 Alfred North Whitehead, *Science and the Modern World* (New York: Macmillan, 1926).

There are six possibilities of conflict. (1 and 2) Either the theology or the science is insufficiently developed at some specific point. Conflict would end if there were fuller, more accurate knowledge. (3 and 4) Either the theologian or the scientist fails in human authenticity. (5 and 6) Either the theologian or the scientist fails in Christian authenticity.

In the first pair, there is lack of development in theology or in science. Then the remedy is to encourage the needed development. The remedy is not deducing scientific conclusions from theological premises, or theological conclusions from scientific premises. The remedy, again, is not deduction and denunciation but dialogue and encouragement.

Secondly, if the difficulty is a lack of Christian authenticity either in the theologian or in the scientist, recourse has to be had to prayer. Infused charity is God's gift, and God gives his grace to those who ask. 'If you being evil know how to give good gifts to your children, how much more will your heavenly Father give the Holy Spirit to those that ask him.'

If the difficulty is the second pair, namely, a failure in human authenticity, the remedy is transcendental method. This follows from what I have been saying. However, it easily appears hopelessly idealistic, mere fantasy. Transcendental method not only is difficult, but also it cures a malady most people do not know that they suffer from. There is a lack of motivation. However, there are grounds for some hope. First, theologians are afflicted with the problem of method. Some are ready to implement even a difficult solution. In the measure they succeed, others can be expected to join them in time. Nothing succeeds like success, so if we get a bit of success we can hope for more. Second, scientists are not wholly complacent. The horror of nuclear weaponry has made scientists reflect on their vocation, and it has made possible future scientists doubt any vocation to scientific work. Further, human scientists especially – not all of them, but for example what is called the third force in psychology – would welcome a line of solution. Indeed, the human sciences suffer from the same fundamental methodological problem as theology. The successful sciences are the natural sciences. One tells the theologians and the human scientists to do like the natural sciences, and that to the extent that this cannot be done there is a second-rate type of science or no science at all. The human scientists are in that position, and they are aware of the fact. People like the people in the third force, or people working in the history of religion at the present time (such as the people in the history of religions in the books put out in Chicago)[9] are confronted

9 See above, p. 465, note 13.

with the fundamental dilemma. Insofar as they follow strictly the methods of the natural sciences they empty their investigations of everything specifically human. If they do not, then they become involved in the chaotic disarray of the philosophies. And neither alternative is acceptable to anyone who is genuinely human and genuinely scientific. The scientist does not want to surrender his autonomy to a whole series of philosophies that can't get along and don't know what they are doing or at least can't come to terms with one another. On the other hand, if the human sciences imitate the natural sciences accurately, well, the human element just goes out. You get a man like Skinner who says that one arrives at a psychological explanation when one has a robot that will do it. He is not joking; he wants to base social reform on that scientific basis.

The dilemma, however, is not quite rigorous. Transcendental method is not just another philosophy. Essentially, it is an attempt to rise above the many philosophies. Further, it is conceived on the analogy of science. Just as natural science proceeds from the data of sense, through inquiry and understanding, to conception and judgment, so too transcendental method proceeds from the data of consciousness, through inquiry and understanding, to conception and judgment. It differs inasmuch as it deals with a privileged area of data: data on the operations that produce common sense, science, philosophy, and theology, and revise the lot of them. Moreover, what transcendental method brings to light is not simply extrinsic to science. It is not alien to the scientist to know what he is doing when he is doing science, why doing that is science, and what is to be known by doing it. It is not alien to the scientist to free his mind from the cognitional myths that generate the chaotic disarray of the philosophies. It is not alien to the scientist to acknowledge the plain fact that he is deliberately pursuing the value 'knowledge,' that science, so far from being value-free, is grounded in the pursuit of a value. Nor need this fact disturb him. Truth is a case of value, and there is no conflict between truth and value, for both are fruits of the movement of human authenticity, the movement of self-transcendence.

So far from being alien, transcendental method is especially relevant to the human sciences. For it is the existential subject treating the existential subject, his coming to self-appropriation. It supplies the a priori not only on every human scientist but also on every object of human science. The human scientist is a structure of conscious and intentional operations, and any human object is similarly such a structure.

Once the human scientist does proceed on that basis, namely, using transcendental method both for controlling his own operations and for providing himself with an a priori on his object, he is able to liberate himself from imitating natural science and set up shop for himself.

I have been discussing the relations of theology and science in terms of possible areas of conflict. I have stressed the concrete, dynamic personal aspects of these relations. Where the old logical context could lead to the conclusions of the Inquisition, the contemporary context of method recalls rather the parable of the cockle (Matthew 13.24–30).

Besides possible conflicts, there are also possible uses, and I'll say something very brief on this topic.

There is the use of theology to the scientist, and it seems to be threefold. First of all, the use of theology is to keep his religion on the level of his other cultural activity, to prevent his religion from appearing childish, outworn, antiquated, irrelevant. If his apprehension of religion is not on the level of his knowledge of other things, then it will take on the appearance of something childish, outworn, antiquated, irrelevant.

Second, to curb tendencies of science to claim omnicompetence – the only way to go about anything is the scientific way. This results when clearheaded and carefully controlled knowledge in the field of science is not balanced by equally clearheaded and carefully controlled knowledge in other fields. In that case, the non-scientific appears just to be idle opinion, and the only competent way of doing things is the scientific way. There has to be made available to him a highly competent technical type of theology that he can respect.

Third, the more the scientist is acquainted with a first-rate theology, the more he becomes capable of joining theologians in teamwork on interdisciplinary problems; and that is a concern at the present time.

What is the use of science to the theologian? First of all, it is necessary if the theologian is to speak to contemporary man. Science and history are the distinguishing marks of modern culture. Just as the Fathers of the church justified their assimilation of Hellenistic culture by appealing to the way the Israelites despoiled the Egyptians when they fled from the country, so too contemporary theology must be the assimilation of religion by a culture, by a contemporary culture. Thus, medieval theology was not just constructing a science. It was making the Greek and Arabic cultural traditions that were invading and flooding the West something that could become compatible [with] and leave fundamentally unchanged the Christian religion. We have the same problem at the present time, and it is to a great extent by its dealings with science, the assimilating of theology to the culture, the assimilating of religion to the culture and the culture to religion, that that fundamental task of theology is to be performed.

The use of science is manifold. It will vary with the phase of theology and the functional specialty. This is something to be treated in the later chapters when I am treating each of the functional specialties separately. But in general, sciences, the human sciences, and above all, the science of religion offer theology information, models of procedure, accounts of structures, analyses of processes, and analogies that throw light on specifically theological topics. The theologian has to borrow from reputable sources. He has to be critical of what he borrows, both from the viewpoint of human authenticity and religious authenticity. But he has to do this to extend his data, to make more determinate his general and his special categories. And in chapters 4 and 5 on the human good, values, beliefs, meaning, we will be doing that sort of thing.

7 Pluralism

The final topic in 'Horizons and Categories' is pluralism. It is something characteristic of our times, and by it I do not mean a relativism but simply a manifoldedness. Knowledge of man is knowledge of many races, peoples, states, cultures, religions, histories. It is pluralist both in its subject and in its object. In its subject it is not known by the individual but by very large scientific communities with a great diversity of horizons. Its objects are many and in motion: sets of ongoing processes, developing, declining, recovering in different ways at different rates in greater or lesser degrees of interdependence.

Such knowledge is under the sign of method. It uses logic to consolidate gains, to point out ambiguities and inconsistencies. It does not use logic to construct an ideal context so clear, consistent, rigorous as to be motionless. Still, it is not mere multiplicity and diversity. There is a common source in the attentive, intelligent, reasonable, responsible subject, and method ensures progressive and cumulative results. There is a common source; the methodical procedure, the cumulation of results, and progress from further discoveries tend to bring things together.

Still, there is a pluralism to the modern world that did not exist before, that was not apprehended in classicist culture. Classicism had a normative apprehension of culture. Its ideals were eternal verities. Its classics were immortal works of art. Its philosophy was a *philosophia perennis*. Because its apprehension of culture was normative, it was thought of as universally valid. It distinguished between the educated, the cultured classes, and, on the other hand, the people or the natives or the barbarians; and anyone was entitled to move over if he got the education. But there was this normative idea of culture, and, consequently, there was only one culture because the conception of it was normative. And, similarly, there was the distinction between the theologians and the *simplices fideles*.

Pluralism is broader in its interest and has an empirical notion of culture. Culture is the meaning of a way of life, the meaning and evaluation put upon a way of life. The social is the way of life in family and mores, education and society, state and law, economy and technology, church and sect. That is the way of life. But the meaning and evaluation put on that way of life is the culture. And with the modern empirical notion of culture it is obvious that there are many cultures, and this pluralism is broader in its interests, richer in its sympathies, more zealous in its efforts to understand. It recognizes the real basis of pluralism as it recognizes that horizons are determined largely by values and choices. That pluralism appears in the contemporary church in its ecumenism and its interest in non-Christian religions.[10]

10 The second question-and-answer session was held later this day. See below, pp. 580–93.

1968-4

The Human Good and Values[1]

The title of the chapter[2] is 'The Human Good, Values, Beliefs.' There are seven parts: first, the human good; second, development as operational; third, the development of feelings; fourth, progress and decline; fifth, the notion of value; sixth, judgments of value; and seventh, beliefs.[3]

The point to this is that we will wish to speak about the good of religion, religious values, religious beliefs; and one can do that only insofar as one has said something about each of these in more general terms. In other words, unless you want your theology to be locked away in an ivory tower, separate from anything else, then you have to consider things in their generality. You have to relate the good of religion to the human good, religious values to other values, religious beliefs to other beliefs.

1 The Human Good

First, then, the human good. The good is always concrete. The good is never an abstraction, just as reality is never an abstraction. However, to apprehend the human good, one needs something in the way of a scheme, something that will suggest to one the great variety of questions connected

1 Tuesday, 9 July 1968, Lauzon CD/MP3 487 (48700A0E060) and 488 (48800A0E060).
2 Lonergan is referring to what at this point was chapter 4 in the draft of what was to become *Method in Theology*. This material, somewhat revised and reordered, became chapter 2 in the final edition, 'The Human Good.'
3 The first six parts are covered in the present lecture, while the material on beliefs was presented at the very beginning of the next.

with thinking about the human good. If all one knows about the good is *id quod omnia appetunt*, and the human good as *id quod omnes homines appetunt*, you are finishing the question off a little too briefly. And so I will proceed to inflict something in the way of a scheme.

Individual		Social	Ends
Potentiality	*Actuation*		
capacity, need	operation	cooperation	particular good
plasticity, perfectibility	development, skills	institution, role, task	good of order
liberty	orientation, conversion	personal relations	terminal value

That provides topics for exploring different aspects of the human good. In general we will proceed by implicit definition; namely, terms are clarified by their relations, and relations are clarified by the terms they relate. Derived terms can be defined by previous terms, but basic terms are only clarified by their relations to one another and the relations by the terms. If one follows this principle rigorously one can get terms of excessive generality. Mathematicians use implicit definition rigorously, and their terms have a generality beyond anything they anticipated when they started out defining them that way. We are going to use all these terms in their ordinary meaning, but they acquire clarification through their interconnections and their relations to one another and the further questions that they raise.

First, then, we will relate four terms from the top row: capacity, operation, particular good, and need. Individuals have capacities for operating. People do things. Operating procures instances of the particular good. By an instance of the particular good I mean any entity, any object or action, that meets a need of a particular individual at a given place and time. The needs are to be taken in the broadest sense. They are not restricted to necessities. They are wants of every kind.

Next, relate four terms from the third column: cooperation, institution, role, task. Individuals live in groups. Largely, operating is cooperating. There results a pattern. The operations of one individual are connected with, related to, the operations of another. The pattern is fixed by roles to be fulfilled or tasks to be performed. These roles and tasks are found within an institutional framework. Such institutional frameworks are the family and manners, mores, the way people do things, the accepted way of doing things;

society and education; the state and the law; the economy and technology; the church or sect.

I have distinguished ten types of institutions, very general things. And each of them gives rise to roles and tasks. Individuals, by operating, by performing these tasks, fulfilling the roles within institutions, are operating on a generally agreed, accepted basis. The institution is the commonly understood and already accepted basis and mode of cooperation. Institutions tend to change only slowly. Change, unlike breakdown, involves a new common understanding and a new common consent. The fact that I alone am talking here and you are not trying to stop me or arguing what should be done, and so on, presupposes an institutional framework, an already accepted common understanding and common consent to what is going forward. If we had to figure that all out, well, we would not be having a lecture. If you examine any other part of your day you find that. The institution is a framework of roles and tasks which consists in a commonly understood and accepted basis and mode of cooperating.

Third, there is the set of relations of the remaining terms in the second row: perfectibility, development, skills, the good of order. The capacities of individuals are plastic and so perfectible. The infant has to learn to move all his members and develop skills. Because he does that he has a terrific capacity for performing. The skills of acrobats, musicians, typists, and all different types of skills that the human being can acquire are based on the terrific plasticity of the human infant. The fact that we are able to have our members controlled in connection with meanings, that the body becomes a vehicle for meaning, is another instance of the terrific plasticity of the human being. That plasticity and perfectibility admit the development of skills of all kinds, and the skills that are developed are the skills that are demanded by the institutional roles and tasks.

But besides the institutional basis of cooperation, there is the concrete manner in which cooperation is working out here and now. The same economic setup, the same economic institution, is compatible with both prosperity and recession, with both boom and slump. There is the wide difference in political life and in the administration of justice under the same constitutional and legal arrangements. The same rules for marriage in the family generate now bliss, now misery. There is the concrete way in which things are working out, and that is the good of order.

The first is the particular good: what meets the need of an individual at a given place and time. The good of order is the way in which the cooperating within the institutional framework is working out. This concrete manner named the good of order is distinct from instances of the particular good but not separate from them. The particular good regards them singly, in their relation to the individual whose needs they meet. But the good of order regards all the instances of the particular good as recurrent: my dinner today for me is a particular good; dinner for everyone that earns it everyday is part of the good of order. An individual's education is a particular good, but education for everyone that effectively desires it is part of the good of order. The actual way in which the system works out in the concrete is what is meant by the good of order. It is not merely a sustained succession of instances of types of the particular good like meals or classes; it is not merely the recurrent manifold; it is the order that sustains this recurrence. It is the ordering of operations so that they are cooperations and ensure recurrence of all effectively desired instances of the particular good. It is the interdependence of effective desires or decisions with appropriate performance by cooperating individuals.

There are two elements to that good of order: the ordering of operations so that they will really be cooperations, and a connection between one's performance and the meeting of one's own demands for the particular good.

This good of order, then, is not some design for utopia, some theoretic ideal, some set of ethical precepts, some code of laws, some super-institution. It is quite concrete. It is the actually functioning or malfunctioning set of if-then relationships guiding operators and coordinating cooperators. It is the ground whence recur or fail to recur whatever instances are recurring or fail to recur. It has its basis in institutions but it is also the product of much more, of all the skill and knowhow, all the industriousness and resourcefulness, all the ambition and fellow feeling of a whole people adapting to each change of circumstance, meeting its new emergencies, struggling against every tendency to disorder.

So much for the terms in the first two rows. There are the terms in the third row: liberty, orientation, conversion, personal relations, and terminal values. Liberty means not indeterminism but self-determination. Any course of action is only a finite good; it is open to criticism; it presents alternatives, limitations, risks, drawbacks. The process of deliberation and evaluation is not itself decisive. We experience our liberty as the active thrust terminating the process of deliberation by settling on one possible course of action and proceeding to execute it. Insofar as the thrust of the self regularly opts for the true good, not the merely apparent good, for the value, the self achieves real self-transcendence, he exists authentically, constitutes himself an originating value, and brings about terminal values, namely, a good of order that is truly good and instances of the particular good that are truly good. Insofar as our decisions have their principal motives, not in the values at stake, but in the calculus of the pleasures and pains involved, one fails in authentic human existence, in being an originating value in oneself and in society.

Liberty is exercised within a matrix of personal relations. In the cooperating community persons are bound together by their needs, by the common good of order that meets their needs. They are related to one another by commitments freely undertaken, by expectations aroused in others by the commitments, by the roles they have assumed, by the tasks they meet to perform. These personal relations are alive with feeling. There are common feelings and opposed feelings about qualitative values and scales of preference. There are mutual feelings: one responds to another as an ontic value or as just a source of satisfactions. Beyond feelings there is the substance of community; people are joined insofar as they share experiences in common, insofar as their insights are similar or complementary, insofar as their judgments of fact and of value are alike, insofar as there are parallel orientations in their lives. On the other hand, they are separated, estranged, rendered hostile when they get out of touch, when they misunderstand one another, when they judge in opposed fashions, when they opt for contrary social goals.

So personal relations vary from intimacy to ignorance, from love to exploitation, from respect to contempt, from friendliness to enmity. Personal relations, then, bind the community together, or divide it into factions, or tear it apart. More specifically on personal relations, there have been a number of noted studies. There is the dialectic of master and slave in Hegel's *Phänomenologie des Geistes*. Fessard's *L'actualité historique* discusses a dialectic of Jew and Greek.[4] Hegel's master and slave: simply by the fact that the slave is always doing everything for the master, always doing the work, the slave becomes the really genuine human person, and the master degenerates – an inverse dialectic. And there is something similar in Fessard. Very concretely, there is Rosemary Haughton, *The Transformation of Man: A Study of Conversion and Community*.[5] It is an extremely concrete study of conversion, of development; while it has a somewhat narrow outlook, the outlook of the home and very intimate personal relations, it is very penetrating.

4 See above, p. 40, note 8.
5 Rosemary Haughton, *The Transformation of Man: A Study of Conversion and Community* (London: G. Chapman, and Springfield, IL: Templegate, 1967).

Then again, on describing feelings, techniques, and some theory, there is Carl Rogers's *On Becoming a Person*.[6]

So much for liberty and something on personal relations.

Terminal values are the values that are chosen. They are true instances of the particular good, a true good of order, a true scale of preferences regarding values and satisfactions. The terminal values are correlative to the originating values that do the choosing, the authentic persons achieving self-transcendence by their good choices. Originating and terminal values can coincide, since man can know and choose authenticity and self-transcendence. Then, when each member of the community wills authenticity in himself and promotes it in others insofar as in him lies, then the originating values that choose and the terminal values that are chosen overlap and interlace.

Finally, orientation and conversion. Presently, we shall have to speak of the orientation of the community as a whole, of progress and decline. But for the moment our concern is the orientation of the individual in the orientated community. The root of the orientation lies in the transcendental notions that enable and require us to advance in attention, understanding, true judgment, and response to values. This possibility and exigence become effective only through development. One must acquire skills and learning to become a competent human being in some walk of life. One has to grow in sensitivity and responsiveness to values if one's humanity is to be authentic. And development is not inevitable, results vary, there are human failures, mediocrities, and there are the continually developing people with achievement varying according to their initial backgrounds, their opportunities, their luck in avoiding pitfalls, and with the pace of their advance.

Orientation is, so to speak, the direction of development. Conversion is a change of direction and, in general, a change for the better. One frees oneself from what is unauthentic in one; one grows in authenticity; harmful, dangerous, misleading satisfactions are dropped. Fears of discomfort, pain, privation have less power to deflect one's course. Scales of preference shift. Errors, rationalizations, ideologies fall and leave man open to be what he should be. On various aspects of growth see Abraham Maslow's *Toward a Psychology of Being*.[7] It is about the psychology of growth, peak experiences, and that sort of thing.

6 Carl Rogers, *On Becoming a Person* (Boston: Houghton Mifflin, 1961).
7 Abraham Maslow, *Toward a Psychology of Being* (Princeton, NJ: Van Nostrand, 1962).

The human good, then, is at once individual and social. Individuals do not just operate to meet their needs, they cooperate to meet one another's needs. As the community develops its institutions to facilitate cooperations, so the individuals develop skills to fulfil roles and perform tasks set by the institutional framework. Though the roles are fulfilled and the tasks are performed that the needs be met, still all is done, not blindly but knowingly, not necessarily but freely. The process is not merely the service of man, it is above all the making of man, his advance in authenticity, the fulfilment of his affectivity, the direction of his work to the particular goods and the good of order that are worthwhile.

So much for a sketch of the human good. As for the concrete way in which the human good is achieved, the concrete meanings of doing good, fitting within that framework, advancing it, correcting its errors, its aberrations – these are topics on which I wish to say something presently.

2 Development as Operational

What we have been saying about the human good is something that is a general invariant structure that can be specified more particularly in any given society at any given time; all these questions arise. But development is over time. We had something to say about development under the actuation of the individual, but we are going to consider now in more detail two types of development: development of operations, and development of feelings.

This development as operational will be discussed by drawing on three notions borrowed from Jean Piaget, who has written some twenty-five books on educational psychology, and a number of books on other things: genetic epistemology, symbolic logic, and that type of thing. The three notions are adaptation, group, and mediation. Piaget conceives learning, development, as an adaptation; and in the adaptation he distinguishes two elements: assimilation and adjustment. Assimilation: one operates on a new object in a new situation, basically by recalling the appropriate operation in a somewhat similar situation on a somewhat similar object; that's the first element to it. The second element is a correction, a process of trial and error, that moves away from the operation that first you would want to try by changing it, modifying it, to suit the object or the new situation. So there are those two elements: the element, then, of assimilation, using already learnt operations or spontaneously occurring operations that you don't have to learn, and the second element, changing that operation so that it fits the object, fits the situation better.

As adaptations occur to ever more objects, a twofold process goes forward. First, there is an increasing differentiation of operations; there are more and more different operations that can be performed. Piaget has two volumes on the first two years of life of his three children, in which he studies day by day what they learnt to do that they could not do before, from every viewpoint: learning to use their mouths, their hands, their eyes, coordinating hands and eyes, and so on, choosing objects, learning to walk, learning to master the space in which they moved about – endlessly detailed descriptions of just what went forward.[8]

As operations occur to ever more objects there is a twofold process going forward. There is an increasing differentiation of operations; there are more and more different operations that can be performed, and there is a greater multiplication of different combinations of differentiated operations. The baby develops oral, visual, manual, bodily skills and masters an ever greater variety of combinations of these different skills.

What is meant by mastering? Because Piaget gave a very precise meaning to this mastering, he was able to lay down series of stages in child development: the type of problem a boy of eight should be able to do, and a boy of nine, and so on, on the average. People who did not want to be bothered with his theory tested everything he did in his experiments, using it here in America and in England, before his theory, his analysis, was accepted. The book on that that best presents his theory, the theoretical side of Piaget, is John H. Flavell, *The Developmental Psychology of Jean Piaget*.[9]

Piaget introduces the mathematical notion of group, and while there are other very tightly defined elements in the definition of group for the mathematician, one element will suffice for our purposes, namely, any operation is matched by an opposite operation; any combination of operations is matched by an opposite combination. The little toddler, at first, toddles over from his mother to his father; and then his mother will smile at him, and he will toddle back and won't know that he is going back. It is when he knows that he is going back that he has grouped his set of spatial operations, his moving about, and has acquired a mastery of this business of going around. There is a period when he hasn't got this, when he is always disorientated and needs someone to tell him where to go or bring him.

With regard to that notion of group, when operations and combinations of operations are performed unhesitatingly and the reverse can

8 See above, p. 7, note 9.
9 See above, p. 396, note 3.

occur unhesitatingly, then there is mastery on a certain level. And the fact that Piaget was able to define, pick out, just what the groups of operations were meant that he was able to have an experimental verification of his theory.

The third element is the notion of mediation. Operations are immediate if the objects are present. Seeing, hearing, touching are immediate to what is seen, heard, touched. But by imagination, language, symbols, our operations become compound. They are immediate with respect to the image, the word, the symbol, and mediate with respect to what is imagined, meant, symbolized.

By learning to speak, and in general because of mediate operations, one can learn to deal not only with what is present and here and now, but with the absent, the past, the future, the merely possible, the ideal, the normative, the fantastic. By learning to speak, the child moves out of the world of immediate surroundings to a larger world revealed by the memories of other men, by the common sense of the community, by the pages of literature, the labors of scholars, the investigations of scientists, the experience of saints, the meditations of philosophers and theologians. That is the world mediated by meaning. What we mean by the real world is not the world of immediacy: what you can see, touch, and so on; that is just a narrow strip of space-time, of each individual's experience. But by language one moves out of that world into a world mediated by meaning.

This distinction between immediate and mediate operations has a very broad relevance. It sets the world of immediacy apart from the larger world mediated by meaning. It provides a basis for distinguishing between lower and higher cultures. In a lower culture there is a world mediated by meaning but the meanings are not subject to effective control. Myth and magic cannot be fought, simply because there is no technique; there has not yet been developed a way of controlling meanings. Myth is a meaning, but mistaken, and it is in the indicative mood; magic is in the imperative mood, and, again, it is a mistaken meaning. In a higher culture there are developed reflex techniques that operate on the mediate operations. In other words, what you are meaning now is the operation by which you refer to something which is not present. The mediate operations are further mediated by a process of reflection: alphabets replace vocal with visual signs, dictionaries fix meanings, grammars control the inflections and combinations of words, logics promote clarity, coherence, rigorous discourse, hermeneutics works out the different relationships between meaning and meant, and philosophies discuss the basic differences between worlds mediated by meaning.

Finally, among the higher cultures, there are at least two types of control. There is the classical type of control which set up ideals, norms, that it considered absolute and permanent and unchanging. And there is the modern type in which the controls themselves are within an ongoing process. Part of the main problem in method in theology, at the present time, is precisely that shift from the classical type of control to the modern.

There are differences in the differentiation of consciousness. With this development of meaning, this world mediated by meaning, there is the emergence of different worlds. Children play: 'Let's play house.' They know it's not for real, but for fun. They are able to live in a world of meaning that is constructed just for their pleasure and for their development also. Piaget has a lot on the play of children and on their imitation.

Similarly, their elders shift to worlds mediated by the reflexive techniques. They not merely have a world mediated by meaning, but they have a higher set of operations by which they control their meanings. This world of theory, this higher set of operations, may be felt to be abstract, but they know that it is very relevant to their dealings with the real world.

Again, aesthetic experience is moving into another type of world. One is stopped by beauty; one is slipping out of the routines of ordinary living. One's sensitivity can become simply a matter of ready-made living in a ready-made world: with the red light you go on the brake, with the green light you go on the accelerator, and so on. You're not seeing red or green; you're simply responding, moving along with the traffic. The aesthetic experience pulls one out of that ready-made world, that set of ready-made actions, and moves one into deeper and fresher rhythms of apprehension and feeling.

Again, the mystic is dropping this world mediated by meaning, and the transcendental notions in their reaching for God, their intention of God, are not mediated by images of any kind.

So the relevance of Piaget goes beyond the field of educational psychology. It enables us to distinguish stages in cultural development, and also man's breaking away from this in play and in aesthetic experience, and in contemplative prayer. Moreover, any technical proficiency can be analyzed as a group of combinations of differentiated operations. What do you find when you read successive chapters of St Thomas's *Contra Gentiles*? In the first chapter, twenty-eight arguments on this point; in the second, thirty-six on that point; in the third, about thirty. It seems to be pretty much the same stuff coming out in each chapter, but there are differences. What we are getting are different combinations. There is a series of differentiated operations and combinations of them; and Thomas has one combination dealing with a question in this chapter, and another combination of perhaps somewhat differentiated operations in the next; and a third combination, and a fourth, and so on. Or take the concert pianist: a terrific range of groups of groups of combinations of differentiated operations. It is not only good for the analysis of individual operations but also group operations. The technical proficiency of a team, a team of football players or hockey players, and so on, the skilled workers being grouped by the entrepreneur, the coach, the impressario: new combinations grouped in new ways for new ends. That type of analysis runs very broadly.

3 The Development of Feelings

Here I'll draw mainly on Dietrich von Hildebrand's *Christian Ethics*[10] and Manfred Frings's *Max Scheler*.[11]

Dietrich von Hildebrand distinguishes nonintentional states and trends, and, on the other hand, intentional responses. Nonintentional states: I'm feeling tired, irritable, in bad humor, anxious. They are states, very, very real, and so on, states of feeling, but they are not directed to objects. There are also nonintentional trends or urges: hunger, thirst, sexual discomfort. They are not responses to an object; you are feeling hungry, and you discover what's wrong, I need something to eat. States have causes, trends have goals. But the relations of the state to the cause or of the trend to the goal is simply a causal relationship. It is not an intentional relationship to a present object.

The intentional responses, on the other hand, are relations to objects that are somehow presented. The feeling arises from the object; it is an answer to what is intended, represented, and so on. It relates the subject to the object. Feelings give intentional consciousness its mass, drive, momentum, power. And without feeling, all this business of experiencing, understanding, judging, deciding is paper thin. What carries people around, gets things done, and so on, and what is being alive, is feeling. Through our feelings we are massively and dynamically orientated not merely in a world of immediacy but in the world mediated by meaning. Feelings respond not merely to concrete objects, but to objects that are meant. So our feelings are for persons, for our respective situations: past, present, and future;

10 Dietrich von Hildebrand, *Christian Ethics* (New York: David McKay, 1953).
11 Manfred Frings, *Max Scheler* (Pittsburgh: Duquesne University Press, 1965).

about evils to be lamented and remedied, about the good that can, must, might be accomplished.

I distinguished nonintentional states and trends, and, on the other hand, intentional responses. Intentional responses regard two main classes of objects. On the one hand, the agreeable and disagreeable, what satisfies and dissatisfies, what is pleasant and unpleasant, and, on the other hand, values, the ontic value of the person or qualitative values such as beauty, understanding, truth, virtuous acts, noble deeds, great achievements. The response to the value is an incipient self-transcendence. The feelings that respond to values are what carry us to self-transcendence. The response to the agreeable or disagreeable, the pleasant or unpleasant, is ambiguous. The pleasant can be what is truly good but it may also be only apparently good, and similarly the unpleasant may be truly bad, but it may also only be apparently bad. Consequently, there is that distinction added to Scheler by von Hildebrand.

Feelings don't simply respond to values without discrimination, they do so in accord with some scale of preference; and so one may distinguish vital, social, cultural, personal, and religious values in an ascending order.

Vital values: health, strength, grace, vigor. Spontaneously we prefer them to the trouble, unpleasantness, work, and so on, that may be needed to maintain them. Spontaneously we are moved to despise anyone who sacrifices vital values simply for the sake of pleasure or the avoidance of pain.

Again, there are social values. It is the good of order conditioning the vital values of the community; and the social values, the good of the community, are esteemed by the individual more highly than the vital values.

Cultural values presuppose the vital and the social, but they rank higher. Not on bread alone does man live, but on every word that proceeds from the mouth of God. In general, the cultural value is the value, the meaning, the significance that attaches to a way of life, to the whole setup of the human good.

There is the personal value, which consists in the individual's self-transcendence, in his loving and his being loved, in his being an originator of values, an inspiration and an invitation to others.

Finally, there are the religious values, of which we said something yesterday. We will have more to say on these when we come to the chapter on religion.

As skills develop, so also there is a development of feelings. Fundamentally, our feelings are spontaneous; they are not like the motions of our hands that we have at our bidding. But once feelings arise they can be reinforced or curtailed. We can advert to them, approve of them or disapprove of them. And if we approve of them, we can reinforce them; if we disapprove of them, we can curtail them, turn to something else, and by that advertence, approval or disapproval, one can change a merely spontaneous scale of preferences; one can enrich and refine one's feelings. A great part of education is setting up a climate of discernment that will lead to the approval or appreciation of true values and true preferences.

Feelings as intentional responses are not merely transient; they are not limited to the time of apprehending values. Some, of course, are transient, some can be repressed; but there also are feelings, notably love, which, when reinforced, accepted with full deliberation, are so deep and strong that they channel attention, shape horizons, direct life. A man and a woman in love are loving at all times; their particular acts flow from a prior state, their state of being in love.

There are also aberrations of feelings. Scheler developed the theory of *ressentiment.* He took the idea from Nietszche and corrected it. Fundamentally, his notion is that *ressentiment* arises when a person who is inferior is confronted by a value in another person and his reaction is not the attempt, the desire to acquire that value, but a refusal of it, a refusal to acknowledge it as a value and a consequent throwing out of gear of his whole scale of values in all his thinking.

Finally, always it is better to be aware of one's feelings rather than to try and disregard them, not acknowledge their existence, when they are not the sort of thing one approves of. There is the whole question of neurosis, as conceived by people like Karen Horney and especially Carl Rogers. Just as in transcendental method the idea was to experience one's experiencing, understanding, judging, and deciding, and being able to name and identify those acts, so Rogers's program for the people who need help is to help them let their feelings come out into the open, and name them, know what they are. It is transcendental method applied to feelings.

4 Progress and Decline

The notions of progress and decline provide another aspect of the human good. Newton conceived his planetary theory in three steps. The first approximation was his law of inertia: bodies keep moving in a straight line, unless there is some force pulling them away from it. Secondly, the law of gravity: bodies attract one another according to this law of gravity, the law of inverse squares; and mathematically one can conclude from that that any such body will move in a conic section: a hyperbola, parabola, or an ellipse, or even a circle under very ideal circumstances. So we have the planets moving around the sun in ellipses. But the planets also gravitate towards one another, and so they move in perturbed ellipses; there are three steps in working out that movement.

Similarly, you can take three steps in an approximation to the course of human history. And the first is like the law of inertia: what happens under a very ideal supposition is that a body on which no forces at all are acting moves in a straight line, at the same velocity, for ever and ever. The first is, then, what happens if everyone is always attentive, intelligent, reasonable, and responsible. What happens is progress. They advert to the human situation, they attend to it. They are intelligent: they see how things could be done better. They agree to do what is better. They have the project, counsel, decision. They put it into effect, and they see what the results are, and what the defects of it are. They correct those defects and get more bright ideas. The thing rolls on and on and on. Things keep getting better and better. This progress proceeds from the assumption that everyone always is an originating value, humanly authentic. There follows a continuous flow of improvements.

However, we move on now to the second stage in our analysis. What happens insofar as people are inattentive, unintelligent, unreasonable, or irresponsible? What happens then is various forms of aberration, of decline. They may take the three main types as in chapter 7 of *Insight*: individual bias, group bias, and general bias.

Individual bias: the individual is taking care of himself and not worrying about anyone else. He is looking for all the loopholes in the institutional framework that enable him to get more out of it than he is putting in. Insofar as such individuals are relatively few, and you can take care of them with prisons, and so on, all is well. But when they become very numerous, you can't put them all in prison. The law starts winking at certain types of ill-doing, and you start getting a legal system, a system of justice, that favors certain groups and classes over others. From that you get the Marxist criticism of the law favoring the class.

Again, individual bias is, of course, something that is always disapproved of by all the groups. But when you have group bias, well, everyone in the group is all for it. Insofar as the group with the bias is in a controlling position, it promotes progress and development everywhere in the society but especially for itself, and it provides a market for doctrines and theories that will justify its way of proceeding and attribute the misfortunes of others to their indolence and stupidity, their lack of energy and good will. Society divides into the haves and the have-nots, and the dominant group has its own ideology justifying itself and is very surprised when the other group works out an opposite ideology to bring about the revolutionary situation.

Then there is general bias. Insofar as we are all people of common sense, and common sense is specialized in the concrete, the particular, the immediate, it is very, very weak at paying any attention to long-term results and consequences, and it doesn't want to envisage them, it doesn't take them into account. One gets a general bias there simply by the fact that any specialty tends to have a narrow view. Common sense is a specialized form of intelligence, but it doesn't know that it is just a specialized form of intelligence. You have to move on to something else to realize that common sense is just a specialization in the particular and concrete.

In general, the unauthenticity that brings about decline by individual, group, and general bias has a further effect, a deeper effect; namely, it produces objectively absurd situations. It is non-attentive, non-intelligent, non-reasonable, non-responsible, and the situation produced by that type of action differs radically from the situation produced by progress. The progress type is increasing the intelligibility of the situation because the situation is the result of intelligent action. Insofar as the situation is intelligible, it is the sort of thing that intelligence can deal with. But the situation created by sin, by inauthenticity, is the realization of the absurd in the situation, and the absurd is not something that intelligence can manage. The situation becomes unmanageable: it becomes, simply, a balance of forces, or a balance of determinisms; people are unhappy and discontented and repudiated and rejected.

The third element in our approximation to history is, What can be done to overcome the absurd situation and the souring of human lives that results from the absurd situation? The answer worked out in chapter 20 of *Insight* is self-sacrificing love. Trying to introduce violence of any kind simply adds to the evils already existing. But it is self-sacrificing love, overcoming evil with good, that is the possibility of human redemption. It is insofar as one does for others not in terms of what they have done for you, but by giving where they have failed to give, that the human situation can be righted.[12]

5 The Notion of Value

I have been using the word 'value' rather freely. The question arises, What is meant by value? A fundamental element in that meaning is the question,

---

12 A break was taken at this point. The remainder of the lecture and the discussion session are found on Lauzon CD/MP3 488 (48800A0E060).

Is that worth while? Is that truly good? This is the question for deliberation, the question not as formulated, but as the subject in his dynamism, in the dynamism of self-transcendence, in the deliberative moment that he expresses through such a question as, Is that worth while? Just as the questions, What? How? or Why? and so on are verbal expressions of the question for intelligence, the subject as trying to understand, so the question for deliberation is the question of the subject moving to real self-transcendence. Just as there is an intention to trying to understand that is moving one from ignorance, from non-understanding, to understanding, and just as the question for reflection, Is that so? is moving one from ignorance to knowledge, so the question for deliberation is the beginning of real self-transcendence, and it is intending what we call value.

Such transcendental notions are the dynamism of conscious intentionality. They promote the subject from lower to higher levels of consciousness. They mediate between ignorance and knowledge, or between cognitive and real self-transcendence. They refer to objects immediately, while answers refer to objects because they are answers to questions. The transcendental notions promote the subject to full consciousness, they direct him to his goals, and they provide the criteria [for] whether or not he is reaching his goals. There is not only the question for intelligence, but there is the satisfaction provided by the act of understanding. When the understanding is incomplete there is the dissatisfaction that gives rise to the further question. Again, with the question, Is that so? there is a demand for evidence that is sufficient, the impossibility of rationally assenting without that evidence, and a necessity for a rational assent when that evidence is forthcoming. Finally, the transcendental notion of value is not only reaching for real self-transcendence, but it also offers the criterion of the happy or unhappy conscience, according as one's judgments of value and one's acting correspond to that effort that leads us towards real self-transcendence.

Further, the transcendental notions are concrete. Questions for intelligence keep on until one has understood everything about everything. Similarly, the notion of reality, of being, is completely concrete. It is everything about everything. There is a similar element of the unlimited connected with the transcendental notion of the good, the value, the true good aimed at, insofar as any finite good is a possible object of criticism. There is an element not merely of wanting the good, but also of disenchantment with the finite good, the disenchantment that brings to light the limitations of every finite achievement. Real self-transcendence plunges us into love, but it also makes us aware of how much our loving falls short of its aim. In brief, the transcendental notion of the good so invites, presses, harries us, that we could rest only in an encounter with a goodness completely beyond its powers of criticism.

So much for value as a transcendental notion.

6 Judgments of Value

Next, judgments of value. Judgments of value are simple or comparative. They are simple: *x* is truly good or only apparently good. Or they are comparative: *x* is better than *y*, or more important, or more urgent. Judgments of value are objective or subjective inasmuch as they proceed from the self-transcending subject or do not proceed from the self-transcending subject. In other words, the criterion of the judgment of value is the authenticity of the judge. Is he moving towards real self-transcendence? Just as the objectivity of the judgment of fact is a cognitive self-transcendence, so the objectivity of the judgment of value has its criterion in a real self-transcendence of the subject.

Judgments of fact and judgments of value differ in content but not in structure. They differ in content: one is about what exists, the other is about what ought to be; one is what is so, the other is what one approves or disapproves. But they do not differ in structure, for in both there is the distinction between the meaning and the criterion, the definition and the criterion. The definition of truth is correspondence with reality, but the criterion is the fact of sufficient evidence for making the judgment, or what I have analyzed as the virtually unconditioned. Similarly, in the judgment of value, what the judgment means is that this really is good or better. But the criterion is whether the subject is really transcending himself or not.

Judgments of value go beyond merely intentional, merely cognitive self-transcendence, without reaching the fullness of real self-transcendence. The fullness of real self-transcendence is not merely knowing what is good; it is also doing it. If one knows without doing, then, unless one is humble, one goes in for rationalizations, trying to make out to oneself that it is not really good, and so destroying the basis of one's moral being.

Still, the judgment of value is beyond the sphere of facts. There is a moral element even in the judgment of value; it is the first step towards benevolence and beneficence and true collaboration and love.

Intermediate between the judgments of fact and the judgments of value lie the apprehensions of value; and these apprehensions are given in our feelings: vital values, social values, cultural values, personal values, religious values. We ask questions and recognize correct answers; but also we respond with the stirring of our very being as we glimpse the possibility or the actuality of real self-transcendence. There is a thrust of feeling that carries us towards self-transcendence, and that is an apprehension of value distinct from the merely transcendental notion and something prior to the judgment of value.

In the judgment of value one has to distinguish three components. First, there has to be a knowledge of human life, of human possibilities proximate and remote, of the probable consequences of actions. Without this knowledge of human reality and human living, of things as they are and as they occur, one can have very fine feelings and moral idealism, but probably one will do more harm than good. The judgments of value have to have a basis in concrete human reality. Again, moral feelings are not enough. They have to be criticized, and that criticism will vary with the community: there is honor among thieves, but that does not mean that stealing is fine. One's finer feelings are things that can become totally irrelevant to the situation in which one is. It is all very well to be kind and gentle and considerate, and so on, if one is living with people who are kind and gentle and considerate. But if you are living with a group of thugs, you find that you are not going to survive on that basis. There is a conditioning of one's possible moral attainment by the society in which one lives. So there is also a critique of feelings and a development, an advance in one's feelings, and this development of knowledge and of moral feelings heads one to existential discovery of the self as a moral being, of the significance of personal value, of the person as an originator of values, and of the judgment of value as the door to fulfilment of oneself or to loss of oneself. The experience of one's frailty or of one's wickedness raises the question of salvation.

So these judgments of value occur in contexts: in the context of the community in which one lives and in the context of one's own development and growth. There is the context of the person who is growing and developing; and that can go on all one's life long: growing in knowledge, in skills, in responses to values, in openness to further achievement, insofar as one's life comes under the gift of grace, of infused charity. As St Augustine said: *ama et fac quod vis*, love and do as you please.[13] Insofar as one's living is being in love with God, then that love will be the discernment of one's values, and one's doing in accordance with that love will be acting perfectly.

13 The exact quotation is 'Dilige, et quod vis fac.' Augustine, *Epistulam Ioannis ad Parthos*, VIII, 8. The editors thank Roland Teske for providing this reference.

On the other hand, there is another context, a context of deviations, of neurotic needs – this is a phrase from Maslow – and of things people have to do because of neurotic need, things that do not contribute anything to their growth; or there is a refusal to risk, a distortion of a scale of preference, a context of soured feelings, of bias, rationalization, ideology, even hatred of the good as in Scheler's account of *ressentiment*; and this *ressentiment* may be either confined to the individual or spreading out into the community.

Finally, there is the ultimate basis of the judgment of value. Joseph de Finance in *Essai sur l'agir humain*[14] distinguishes between horizontal and vertical liberty. Horizontal liberty is the exercise of liberty within a settled horizon, within a determinate horizon and a corresponding existential stance. Vertical liberty is the exercise of liberty that selects an existential stance and a corresponding horizon. That exercise of vertical liberty may be implicit, the liberty of the person who is growing and moving into a fuller and more accurate horizon.

Now, the ultimate foundations of judgments of value are to be found in the exercise of vertical liberty. Insofar as you are already within a horizon and assuming it, your judgments will depend upon it. But the really foundational judgments of value are those that select the horizon. Here you may discern a vicious circle in my account of the judgments of value. In a sense there is one, but it is the vicious circle that you find in Aristotle's *Nicomachean Ethics*. Namely, what is the meaning of virtue, or where is the meaning of virtue? It is where the virtuous man puts it. The basis, the empirical basis, of an ethics is the concrete existence of virtuous men. Insofar as you have virtuous men, you can find out what the virtuous acts are, and without that presupposition you have not de facto got an existential basis for your ethics.

In other words, the transcendental notion of value, the feelings by which we apprehend values, the judgments we make about values, the happy or unhappy conscience that we have as a result of our judgments and decisions and acts, all tend towards our moral development. But if you want the really true judgment of value, you go, not to the person who is still developing, but to the person who has developed. And that is the point of the Aristotelian business: virtue lies where the virtuous man places the value.[15]

14 Joseph de Finance, *Essai sur l'agir humain* (Rome: Gregorian University Press, 1962).

15 Lonergan indicated that he would take up the section on beliefs on the following day. The third question-and-answer session was held later this day. See below, pp. 594–604.

1968-5

Beliefs and Carriers of Meaning[1]

1 Beliefs

Chapter 4 was on the human good, values, and beliefs, and we treated everything except beliefs. We are treating belief in general, not yet religious belief.

The appropriation of one's social, cultural, religious heritage is largely a matter of belief. What we find out for ourselves is a very small fraction of what we know. We rely upon the experiences, the insights, the judgments of others; and this reliance is not merely on the experience, understanding, and judgment of our contemporaries, but also of our ancestors. The reason why man has progressed in the last 200,000 years (if that is the age of man) is because of the cumulative tradition down the ages, the handing on. The extent to which even things that we to some extent find out for ourselves rest in a context of beliefs, and the extent to which things that we find out for ourselves are dependent on beliefs, may be illustrated very simply by our knowledge of the positions, the relative positions, of the major cities in the United States. We all know about them; we have seen maps. But are the maps right? Well, who would want to deceive us? Still, we don't know.

---

1 Wednesday, 10 July 1968, Lauzon CD/MP3 489 (48900A0E060) and 490 (49000A0E060). The treatment of beliefs concludes the presentation of what at this time was chapter 4, 'The Human Good, Values, and Beliefs.' The remainder of this lecture treats what *Method in Theology* calls the carriers of meaning, which are presented at the beginning of the chapter on meaning, at this time chapter 5 in the evolving manuscript.

Moreover, the map-maker doesn't know; he relies upon a large number of surveys made by different parties. There is no one who knows all the relative positions out of his own knowledge, or it is a very rare person. We are sure that the maps are right, because roads are built and property is bought and sold, and the airlines travel, and so on, in accord with the maps; they all work on the maps. Still, we don't do all that traveling or buying and selling; we believe that too. A certain amount of our knowledge depends upon personal experience that we have checked, and we are sure that there is an awful lot more that other people are checking. But we are sure that they know. We don't know. Our knowledge is within a terrific web of believing.

Science is often contrasted with belief. But the scientists do as much believing as anyone else. The scientist finds out certain things for himself; he makes his own personal discoveries. That is his knowledge; he knows that. He can check another man's work, go back to the principles on which his hypothesis is based, work out all its implications, repeat his experiments, and he will know it on his own personally generated knowledge just as the original discoverer did. But scientists don't waste their time doing that. There will be a bit of checking when a new idea comes out, but people will prefer to proceed by indirect verification. Indirect verification presupposes the other result is correct until you have reason to suspect it is wrong. Galileo about four centuries ago formulated the law of falling bodies. That law was verified directly by Galileo, and it has been verified directly by other people too. But most of the verification has been indirect. That law has been presupposed every time a house has been built, any time any mechanism of any complexity was constructed and fault was never found with it. There have been four hundred years of indirect verification, which is much more momentous than the verification performed by this or that man in his laboratory. Still, we believe that that indirect verification exists; we have not done it; it has been done by different people for four hundred years. A scientist's knowing is within a web of believing.

Believing is a matter of making the division of labor possible in the field of knowing; and that division of labor in the matter of knowing is just as important for knowing as the division of labor is important in the industrial commercial sphere. The division of labor, as I have suggested, extends down the centuries. It is not merely people at the present time dividing the labor, but they are going by what was learnt before. In other words, human knowledge is a common fund. One draws upon it by believing, and one contributes to it by the things one can add to what is already known. So there result common sense, common knowledge, common science, common values, common climates of opinion.

Not all of what is believed is true. There are also oversights, biases, errors; but one does not get rid of them by eliminating all belief. All you achieve by eliminating all belief is a primitive mentality. You wipe out ninety-eight percent of all you know when you eliminate all your beliefs. The issue is to be critical in one's believing, and being critical is not a matter of simply refusing to believe or of being stubborn about believing, or anything like that. When you find in yourself that you have a mistaken belief, you start out from that mistaken belief and go into other beliefs that are associated with it, that are connected with it. Maybe they are mistaken too. Further, you go on to the mistaken believer to get to the root of the trouble. Why did you accept them? Moreover, this critical side has to be accompanied, and is better when it is preceded, by a positive acquisition of what is true. Newman says he would sooner believe everything than doubt everything according to Descartes's precept of doubting everything; because if you doubt everything you have no basis from which to work; if you believe everything, what you have that is true will develop and gradually cast aside what is mistaken.

Such, in general, about belief. Now, what exactly is the process, the act of belief? The first step is the possibility of belief. The process of believing is possible because what is true is not something private but something that essentially is public. It rests upon reaching an unconditioned. What is unconditioned does not depend upon the subject that makes the judgment. It is something that is independent of the subject, and in that sense it is fundamentally public. It is independent of the mind that grasps it; it is the fruit of a cognitive self-transcendence. I cannot give another my eyes, but I can report accurately what I see. I cannot give another my understanding, but I can report accurately what I understand. I cannot give another my judgments of facts and values, but I can report accurately what those judgments are.

A second step, with regard to the analysis of belief, is a general judgment of value. It approves the division of labor by which human knowledge develops, the fact that we depend upon one another for what we know. It approves that division of labor, not just today, but down the centuries. It is willing to correct this or that belief, and it wants to do this whenever it finds belief to be mistaken. But it is not going to reject belief generally, in principle, because that means simply a return to the little that any individual can learn in a lifetime; and that is very small indeed. Even a genius contributes very, very little to the sum of human knowledge.

The third step is a particular judgment of value. This witness is trustworthy, this expert is competent, this leader or statesman or authority can be trusted. The point at issue is whether this person whom you are believing is himself critical of his sources, whether he attained self-transcendence in his judgments of fact, whether he attained real self-transcendence in his judgments of value. These things, in general, cannot be directly investigated. But they can be tested indirectly. If there is only one expert, well, you really don't know whether he is an expert or not, whether he is competent or not. But if you find that there is a series of experts, and that they independently say the same thing, or if distinct witnesses who give every sign of reliability independently give the same report, one indirectly checks upon the possibility of believing this particular statement or claim.

Besides the general judgment – we should believe what is credible, and this is credible – one comes to the decision to believe. There is a decision involved in believing. Believing is attaining truth through the mediation of what is good. The division of labor in coming to know is part of the human good. My taking part in the human good of knowing, a common fund of knowing, is a thing I do not by knowing what is true, but by knowing what is good for my mind. I test the testimony in various ways. I come to the conclusion that it is the sort of thing that pertains to the common fund of human knowledge, and I participate in it through a decision.

Finally, on the decision to believe there follows the act of belief, which is an assent of the mind to this as good for my mind. And what is good for my mind is true.

Now any analysis of belief makes one a bit skeptical about it, and so let's take a concrete example of someone who believes. The engineer has a little problem, and he whips out his slide rule and moves it along, back and forth, and gets the answer in about a quarter of a minute. He knows how the slide rule works and why it works. However, the slide rule depends upon logarithmic and trigonometric tables that he has never worked out. He does not know whether or not they are accurate; he believes them to be accurate. He has every reason for believing them to be accurate. Moreover, he never took his slide rule and tested it against the tables. Do the distances between the markings correspond to the numbers on the tables? He never did that; he believes that it is right; at least he never had any reason to doubt the accuracy of his slide rule, and of course it would take him a couple of years to get down and work out for himself all these tables and do all this testing. He believes his slide rule to be accurate, both to be well founded in tables that he has never worked out and to correspond to those tables. Are you going to say that the engineers are behaving improperly in believing their slide rules? Are you going to think they should take the time necessary to find out for themselves that their slide rules are correct or not?

Finally, if my account of belief appears to you novel, then perhaps your previous views on belief were mistaken and were mistaken beliefs about belief. If that is so, the critique of beliefs implies that if you happen to reject your previous views on belief, then my account implies that you should find out whether there are any other beliefs from a similar source or of a similar nature associated with your previous views on belief and find out why you accepted them. In other words, introduce a critique of mistaken beliefs and the mistaken believer.

So much for belief and chapter 4 on the human good, values, beliefs.

2 Carriers of Meaning

Chapter 5 is on meaning. The first four sections are on carriers of meaning, the embodiment of meaning in intersubjectivity, in art, in symbols, and in language. These are four different ways in which meaning is embodied. Then there is a section on the analysis of meaning, on meaning and interiority, on functions of meaning, and finally on meaning in history. The last two sections have not been written yet; they will be a bit sketchy.

2.1 Intersubjectivity

I will treat first of all intersubjectivity itself, intersubjectivity of action and of feeling; and then, intersubjectivity of meaning.

Intersubjectivity of action: there is a 'we' that results from friendship, associations, comrades, collaboration, being in love. But there is a prior 'we' that is prior to the distinction between 'I' and 'thou,' and that prior 'we' is something vital. It is the basis of intersubjectivity. If someone is going to hit me, I spontaneously raise my arm. If I am standing by someone and he starts to fall, I spontaneously hold him, to prevent his falling. I don't first think of preventing his falling and then do it. Perception is involved and action, but I perceive my own action when it is going on. It's as though we were all members of one another before we started distinguishing each from the other.

This intersubjectivity appears not only in mutual aid, as in the examples I gave, but also in the different types of common feeling. Max Scheler distinguishes four aspects of common feeling. Two of them are intentional responses, in the sense used yesterday. There is the perception of an object, and on it follows the response, the feeling. Two are independent to some extent of perception. The first of the first pair is community of feeling, where two people are responding together to the same object. For example, the parents of a dead child are responding to the fact that their child is dead; both feel deep intense sorrow; they are not acting on one another; they are responding to the same object; but they respond together, and that is community of feeling.

On the other hand, there is fellow feeling. If someone else came into the room, observed the sorrow of the parents, and began responding to their sorrow, began to feel sympathy, to share their sorrow, that would be fellow feeling.

Psychic contagion has a vital rather than an intentional basis. It is sharing another's emotion without adverting to the object of the emotion. One enters a room and everyone is laughing, and one starts to grin, and one does not know what they are laughing at. Others are weeping, and one begins to feel sorrowful. You don't know the cause of their grief, but you do begin to feel sad. An onlooker, without undergoing another's ills, is caught up in the feeling of extreme pain expressed on the face of the sufferer. Scheler calls that psychic contagion. One shares another's emotion without having oneself the grounds of that emotion, and this psychic contagion, according to Scheler, seems to be the mechanism of mass excitement in panics, revolutions, demonstrations, strikes, where personal responsibility tends to disappear, intelligence decreases, and a domination of drives over thinking emerges along with readiness to submit to a leader. Such contagion can be deliberately provoked, contrived, built up, exploited, by political activists, by the entertainment industry, by religious and especially pseudo-religious leaders.

Distinct from psychic contagion is emotional identification; and it occurs in two main ways. First, when the differentiation between the parties is not developed or insufficiently developed; and in the second case, when there is a retreat from the differentiation. The undeveloped differentiation has its basic illustration in the emotional identification of mother and infant; it also appears in the identifications of primitive mentality, the members of the tribe; or in the earnestness with which a little girl plays with her doll. She identifies herself with the mother and also projects herself on the doll.

Or perhaps differentiation has occurred, and there is a retreat from that differentiation. Scheler uses this in his explanation of hypnosis. It occurs in sexual intercourse, or in the group mind: members identify with their leader, spectators with their team. In both cases, the group coalesces into a single stream of instinct and feeling. In the ancient mysteries the mystic became divine in a state of ecstasy, identified with the god. This process of emotional identification is most commonly experienced in spectators watching their team.

Now, I have spoken of intersubjectivity manifested in action and in feeling. There is also intersubjective meaning, and we will illustrate it in a single instance by the phenomenology of a smile. I am drawing largely on Susanne Langer's *Feeling and Form*.[2]

First, then, a smile has a meaning. It is not just a certain combination of movements of lips, facial muscles, and eyes. It is a combination with a meaning. Because that meaning is different from the meaning of a frown, a scowl, a stare, a glare, a snicker, a laugh, it has a name of its own, a smile. Because we all know that that meaning exists, we do not walk around the streets smiling at everyone we meet. We would be misunderstood.

A smile is highly perceptible. Our perceiving is not just a function of the impressions made on us, but it is a matter of organizing perceptions. What is already organized in some fashion is therefore all the more perceptible. One can converse with a friend on a noisy street and pick out the rather low sounds made by the friend's voice and disregard all the other sounds. Why? Because what he is saying has a meaning. Again, even an incipient smile is easily perceived; it is a *Gestalt*, as they say.

Smiling is natural and spontaneous. We do not learn to smile as we learn to walk, to talk, to swim, to skate. We do not think of smiling and then do it. We just do it, usually. Nor do we learn the meaning of smiling as we learn the meaning of words. We make the discovery for ourselves, and again the meaning of smiling doesn't seem to vary from culture to culture the way the meaning of gestures will vary.

A smile has something irreducible about it. It cannot be explained by causes outside meaning. And it cannot be elucidated by other types of meaning. It has its own meaning. This can be brought out by comparing the meaning of the smile with linguistic meaning.

Linguistic meaning tends to be univocal, but smiles have a wide variety of different meanings. There are smiles of recognition, welcome, friendliness, friendship, love, joy, delight, contentment, satisfaction, amusement, refusal, contempt. They may be ironic, sardonic, enigmatic, glad or sad, fresh or weary, eager or resigned. Smiles have not the univocity of words and no tendency towards the univocity of words.

2 The correct source of this is the work of F.J.J. Buytendijk. See above, p. 379, note 5.

Linguistic meaning may be true in two different ways: as opposed to mendacious and as opposed to false. A smile can be mendacious; you can smile and smile and be a villain. But it can't be false as opposed to true.

Linguistic meaning contains distinctions between what we feel, desire, fear, think, know, wish, command, intend. The meaning of a smile is global; it expresses more what one person means to another; it has the meaning of a fact and not the meaning of a proposition.

Linguistic meaning is objective. It expresses what has been objectified: there is *Verstehen, Auslegen, Aussagen;* the *Auslegen* objectifies. The meaning of the smile is intersubjective. It supposes the interpersonal situation with its antecedents – why has he come to see me? – and all the memories of past meeting, and so on. It is a recognition of the present situation, and moreover it is a determinant within the situation, an element in the situation as process, a meaning with its significance in the context of antecedent and subsequent meanings. The meaning of the smile is not about some object. It is rather an immediate revelation of the subject. It is not the basis of some inference, but rather in the smile one incarnate subject is transparent or, again, hidden to another, in a way that antedates all subsequent analysis of body and soul, sign and signified. The subject is not hidden away in a body, in some recess of the body, sending out signals in some form of Morse code. The subject, the intersubjective subject, is revealed in all the manifestations of his intersubjectivity. What I said about smiles can be extended; one can go on to all other facial expressions and all gestures, and so on, the whole gamut of the actor's art, mode of communication, carrying of meaning; and that carrying of meaning is meaning of a personal, interpersonal nature. It is not meaning that has been objectified yet.

2.2 Art

Meaning in art is like intersubjective meaning in some respect, insofar as we haven't got a distinction yet between meaning and meant. But you have an objectification of the meaning.

According to Langer, art is the objectification of a purely experiential pattern. Pattern may be abstract or concrete. There is an abstract pattern in the indentations in the grooves of a phonograph record or the musical score. The concrete pattern is the pattern realized in these movements, these tones, these colors, these shapes. The pattern is a pattern of internal relations. The elements that are patterned are related to one another; they can't be unrelated, and their relations as representative of something else are not part of the pattern. Art does not have to be representative.

Besides the pattern of the perceived, there is the pattern of the perceiving. And, as the sensible in act is the sense in act, we have the same pattern recurring there. When sounds, or anything else, are patterned they are easily perceived, easily repeated. One can repeat a tune or a melody but not a succession of street noises. Verse makes information memorable: 'Thirty days hath September, April, June, and November.' The verse helps one. Decoration makes surfaces visible; you can perceive simply because it is already patterned, and perceiving is a matter of taking the impressions that can fit into a pattern; so what is already patterned is perceptible. Patterns can be built up on the organic analogy: the roots, the trunk, the branches, the shoots, the leaves, the flowers, and the fruit. The complexity can mount indefinitely.

The pattern in question is a pure pattern. It is pure inasmuch as it excludes alien patterns that instrumentalize experience, where one's senses can become merely an apparatus for receiving and transmitting signals, the ready-made subject in the ready-made world. I have already spoken of that. Or sense can function simply as the instrument of scientific intelligence; it sees what fits into technical categories, it observes them all. An entomologist can see so much more in a bug than you or I, because he has the categories to differentiate all the different aspects of the bug. Or sense may have imposed upon it some theory from physics, or physiology, or psychology, or epistemology that is not simply the nature of sense itself at all. Sense, then, can be subjected to alien patterns. When you talk about a purely experiential pattern, you mean that the experience is not under the control of some alien pattern, some other interest.

Again, in art the pattern is purely experiential: it is of colors that are visible and not the stereotypes that are anticipated; of shapes that are visible and so in perspective, not of shapes as really constructed, as known perhaps to touch but not to sight; what you can see is what comes out in an awkward photograph; things are in perspective but we don't see them that way. We see them as they are constructed; we are imposing the shape upon what are visual materials.

Not only is anything alien or any stereotype excluded by the purely experiential, but the experiential pattern is allowed its own retinue of associations, affects, emotions, incipient tendencies. There may arise out of the pattern a lesson, but there isn't a lesson to be imposed upon it in the manner of didacticism or moralism or social realism.

There also accrues to the experiential pattern the experiencing subject with his capacity for wonder, for awe and fascination, with his openness to adventure, daring, greatness, goodness, majesty. There is sought the purely experiential pattern, for purposes not of impoverishment but of enrichment. It curtails what is alien to let experiencing find its full complement of feeling, its own proper pattern, to let it take its own line of expansion, development, organization, fulfilment.

So experiencing becomes rhythmic; one movement necessitates another, and the other in turn necessitates the first. Tensions may be built up to be resolved; variations multiply and grow in complexity yet remain within an organic unity that eventually rounds itself off.

The aesthetic experience takes us into a different world. One may say that the world of the artist is unreal, illusory, or one can say that it is revealing a deeper reality. But in any case, we are transported from the space in which we move to the space within the picture, from the time of sleeping and waking, working and resting, to the time of the music, from the pressures and determinisms of home and office, of economics and politics, to the powers depicted in the dance, and from conversational and media use of language to the vocal tools that focus, mold, grow with consciousness. We will say something more on that vocal-tool business when we speak later on meaning and language.

As the world is transformed, so too the subject is transformed. He has been liberated from being a replaceable part adjusted to a ready-made world and integrated within it. He has ceased to be a responsible inquirer investigating some aspect of the universe or seeking a view of the whole; he has become just himself, emergent, ecstatic, originating freedom.

This is the purely experiential pattern. Now the work of art is an objectification of a purely experiential pattern. It could be expressed in the way that the art critic talks about the work of art; but that would not be the proper expression of that purely experiential pattern. The proper expression of the elemental meaning of the purely experiential pattern is the work of art itself. That meaning lies within the consciousness of the artist, but, at first, it is implicit, veiled, unrevealed, unobjectified. The artist is aware of it, but he has to get it out. He has to get hold of it. He is driven to behold, inspect, dissect, enjoy, repeat it; and this means objectifying, making it explicit, unveiling, revealing.

This process of objectifying involves what is called psychic distance. For elemental meaning is just experiencing. Its expression involves detachment, distinction, separation. The smile or frown expresses intersubjectivity; the feeling is felt. Artistic composition recollects emotion in tranquillity, in Wordsworth's phrase. It involves insight into the elemental meaning, a grasp of a commanding form, that has to be expanded, worked out, developed; and the subsequent process of working out, adjusting, correcting, completing the initial insight.

The result, the work of art, is an idealization of the original experiential pattern. Art is not just autobiography. It is not telling one's tale to the psychiatrist. It is grasping what is or seems significant, of moment, concern, import to man. Or it is the denial of any significance. It is truer than experience, leaner, more effective, more to the point. It is the central moment with its proper implications that unfold without the distortions, the interference, of the original pattern.

The proper apprehension and appreciation of the work of art is not any conceptual clarification or judicial weighing of evidence. The work of art is an invitation to participate, to try it, to see for oneself. As the mathematician withdraws from the sciences that verify to explore possibilities of organizing data, so works of art invite us to withdraw from practical living to explore possibilities of living in a richer world.

Now, to take that general scheme of Langer's and apply it to the different art forms, to drawing and painting, statuary and architecture, music and dance, epic, lyric, and dramatic poetry, this you can see in Langer's *Feeling and Form* for yourselves. But the fundamental element is that there is a meaning to a purely experiential pattern, to this form. Consider a band's tune giving us a march; you get a lift from it whether you want to or not. There is an elemental meaning to the purely experiential pattern, and the work of art objectifies it. In the liturgy there is an objectification of the sacred, of the hierophany.

2.3 Symbols

A third carrier of meaning is the symbol. I will mean by a symbol an image of a real or imaginary object that evokes a feeling or is evoked by a feeling. We shall speak of feelings, objects, and images, symbols as evocation, and some attempts at explaining symbols.

Feelings are related to objects, to one another, and to their subject. They are related to objects: one desires food, fears pain, enjoys a meal, regrets a friend's illness.

Feelings are related to one another in many ways. Through changes in the object, one desires the good that is absent, hopes for the good that is sought, desires the good that is present, fears absent evil, becomes disheartened at its approach, sad in its presence. When you get changes in the object, you get changes in the feeling.

Feelings are related to one another through personal relations: love, gentleness, tenderness, intimacy, union go together. Similarly, alienation, hatred, harshness, violence, cruelty form a group. So such sequences as offense, contumacy – I offended you, I'm glad I did it – judgment, punishment, or again, offense, repentance, satisfaction, forgiveness. Feelings may conflict yet come together. One may desire despite fear, hope against hope, mix joy with sadness, love with hate, gentleness with harshness, tenderness with violence, intimacy with cruelty, union with alienation.

Feelings are related to their subject. They are the mass and momentum and power of conscious living, the actuation of his affective capacities, dispositions, habits. They relate him to a world mediated by meaning, not the world of immediate apprehension. Because our feelings are intentional responses to things that we intend and mean and think about, we live in a world mediated by meaning.

Now, with regard to objects and images, the same objects or images need not evoke the same feelings in different subjects. And inversely, the same feelings need not evoke the same symbolic images. There are two points: differences in affective response, and how this affect effects the symbols as images of real or imaginary objects. The difference in affective response may be due to differences in age, sex, education, state in life, temperament, existential concern. More generally, the difference in affective response depends upon the individual's history. One has had a certain affective development, and that development may or may not have included aberrations, and consequently you get different affective responses to different objects. Because of this, one can talk about undifferentiated and transformed symbols. Symbols are undifferentiated inasmuch as different symbols awaken the same response. Consequently, such symbols as are affectively undifferentiated and awaken the same feeling response can be interchanged and can be combined to obtain a more powerful response. And it is in that organization of affectively undifferentiated symbols that you get the difference between the symbolic and the artistic. The monsters of mythology are just bizarre; they are not artistic. But they do combine – the dragon, for instance, does combine all the different objects that awaken fear and horror and disgust and terror, and so on. It's an amalgam of all the ways of exciting a single set of responses.

Again, compound affects call for compound symbols, and each member of the compound may be a conglomeration of undifferentiated or only slightly differentiated symbols. St George and the Dragon combines St George on his horse, lifted up, able to manipulate his hands, in the light, seated with power, the spear in his hands; all ascensional symbols are there, the whole of ascensional symbolism is there. And the meaning of that ascensional symbolism has been connected with the dominant reflex by which you maintain your balance, and all the affectivity that was involved in learning to walk, standing upright, and keeping your balance. At the same time, there are not only all the values of ascensional symbolism but all the disvalues of its opposite; you have them in the dragon: the danger of falling and being bitten, devoured, blinded at birth by the fire from his mouth, and blinded by the smoke, and so on.

Now there can be a transvaluation of the symbol. The conquest of terror replaces the dragon as insignificant fancy by the whale that swallowed Jonah. He was drowning, he went down into the jaws of the mouth, and three days later without suffering in the least bit he was landed on the shore. There is transvaluation in that you have in the whale and the drowning all the same type of disastrous things presented as in the dragon, but this time it's not so bad after all, there's nothing to worry about; the feelings are transformed. There has to be this transvaluation. A lack of this transvaluation of symbols seems to point to a block in development. It's one thing for a child and another for a man to be afraid in the dark.

As for symbolic evocation, symbols obey the laws of image and feeling, not of logic. Insofar as communication is on the ordinary human level, or to the degree that it becomes affective, the logical elements tend to be replaced by symbolic devices. One moves from the logical class to the representative figure, from the univocal to the word with multiple meanings, from rigorous proof to overwhelming with a manifold of images that converge in meaning, from the principle of excluded middle to the *coincidentia oppositorum*, the coincidence of opposites, from negation to a rejection by overstatement, and from linear meaning – one thing at a time in proper order – to the condensation that presents all one's concerns just all together in a moment. In other words, insofar as image and affect take over in one's writing or thinking, there is a movement away from the logical to the laws of image and feeling. The power of the symbol is to recognize and express what logical discourse abhors: the existence of internal tensions, incompatibilities, conflicts, struggles, destruction. You can get that expressed rather elaborately, however, in a dialectic or methodological viewpoint that can embrace what is concrete, contradictory, and dynamic. But the symbol did this before dialectic was thought of, and it does it for those who are unfamiliar with dialectic. Finally, even those who are familiar with dialectic need the symbol in a certain dimension of their own being. The symbol meets needs that the refinements of method and dialectic cannot, for example, the need for internal communication.

The phrase 'internal communication' is Carl Rogers's, but I'm not sure that my meaning is identical with his. What do I mean by this internal communication? Organic and psychic vitality must reveal themselves to intentional consciousness. Inversely, intentional consciousness has to secure collaboration of organism and psyche. Again, the apprehension of values occurs in intentional responses, in feelings; and there is a need for feelings to reveal objects, to evoke objects, and for objects to awaken feelings. It is through symbols that mind and body, mind and heart, heart and body, communicate. That communication of body, mind, and heart is the internal communication that is effected by the symbol.

Moreover, the proper meaning of the symbol is this internal communication. It is an elemental meaning, in which meaning and meant have not yet been distinguished, as the smile is prior to the phenomenology of the smile, and the purely experiential pattern prior to the work of art. It is a meaning that fulfils a function in the imagining and perceiving subject, as his conscious intentionality develops and/or goes astray, as he takes his stance to nature, his fellow men, and before God. In other words, you don't have to have, besides the symbolic meaning, a conceptual meaning as well. The symbolic meaning does its own work in the field of internal communication, whether you have it analyzed and explained or not. It effects that communication of mind and body, mind and heart, heart and body. The proper context of the meaning of the symbol lies in the process of internal communication in which it occurs; and to this context, with its associations, memories, and tendencies, the interpreter has to appeal if he is to explain the symbol.

The interpretation of the symbol is going outside the field of the symbol. It is a transition from an elemental meaning in an image or percept to a linguistic meaning. The linguistic meaning will have its own context; it will be some theory of interpreting symbols, and that theory may be right or wrong.

De facto there are many such interpretive contexts to which the linguistic meaning appeals. First of all, there are the therapeutic interpretative systems: the psychoanalysis of Freud, the individual psychology of Adler, the analytic psychology of Jung. The initial oppositions are diminishing. There is Charles Baudouin, professor of psychology in Switzerland, who uses simultaneously or alternatively Freud and Jung.[3] He uses Freud for

3 In *Method in Theology*, Lonergan gives a reference to Charles Baudouin, *L'oeuvre de Jung* (Paris: Payot, 1963). Subsequent references for this section are taken as well from *Method in Theology*.

the archaeology, going back to the causes, and it is connected with objects. He uses Jung for the teleology, the dynamism exhibited, the forward constructive elements in the psyche. And he will shift from one to the other in the same case.

Ricoeur in his book on interpretation, *Essai sur Freud*,[4] complements that position of Baudouin. His interpretation of Freud is, of course, that Freud is doing an archaeology in his interpretation in terms of infancy and childhood, and so on. But he holds that Freud's position presupposes the existence of a process of development; otherwise, you could not have the regression. You would be beyond anything to regress to unless there also was a teleological process. So again, without introducing Jung, Ricoeur's long volume has the same tendency as Baudouin's. Erich Fromm speaks of the interpretation of dreams as an art; and one develops one's own art.[5] Carl Rogers aims to provide the patient with an interpersonal situation in which the patient will be able to come to grasp, to have some acknowledgement, awareness of his own feelings. The mythology is there but he does not bother about it. He just is asking the person all the time, more or less repeating what the person is saying in other words, helping him to objectify what he is experiencing.[6] At the opposite pole there is Frank Lake, who has an enormous volume entitled *Clinical Theology*.[7] His theory is from Pavlov, and his technique is LSD 25. His patients relive birth traumata, feel the forceps on their foreheads, the umbilical cord wrapped around their necks choking them. Pavlov's experiments were in terms of taking pain beyond the threshold of endurance, with the result that the subject just flips over and gives no reaction at all or ceases to give proportionate reaction, gives no reaction at all, gives the opposite reaction. I think that there are four different steps in the experimental results of Pavlov taking people beyond the threshold of pain and, according to Frank Lake, the cases he treats are precisely that type of case; they are the really extreme cases: birth traumata relived, the holocaust of suffering the infant or the child has been through. It's fascinating, though; he says that the mythology is there, but it is really secondary; it is not the important thing.

4 Paul Ricoeur, *De l'interprétation, Essai sur Freud* (Paris: Payot, 1963); in English, *Freud and Philosophy: An Essay on Interpretation*, trans. Denis Savage (New Haven: Yale, 1970).
5 Erich Fromm, *The Forgotten Language*, chapter 6: 'The Art of Dream Interpretation' (New York: Grove Press, 1957).
6 Carl Rogers, *On Becoming a Person* (Boston: Houghton Mifflin, 1961).
7 Frank Lake, *Clinical Theology* (London: Darton, Longman & Todd, 1966).

Now, besides these therapeutic interpretative systems, there are the non-therapeutic. Gilbert Durand, a pupil of Bachelard, has quite a large book in which he organizes vast ranges of symbols around three dominant reflexes.[8] A reflex is dominant if, when it is called in, you neglect absolutely everything else. If you're going to lose your balance, you stop talking and do everything you need to recover your balance. Maintaining one's balance, one's equilibrium, is a dominant reflex. Swallowing is a dominant reflex. When anything goes wrong with swallowing one loses interest in all else. The same with mating; it is a dominant reflex. Around those three St George and the Dragon is the one for equilibrium. The opposite one is for swallowing, going down into the dark: there is nothing wrong with that, it is quite pleasant as a matter of fact, but it is just the opposite of the ascensional symbolism you have for maintaining one's equilibrium. There is alternating from one to the other, in any form of rhythmic shift from both sides: the tree surrounded by the green sward in the sunlight sending up its branches while its foot penetrates down into the earth where it draws all its nourishment. You have in Durand a perfectly simple explanation of vast ranges of symbols that is totally independent of any therapeutic context.

Then Eliade has collected, compared, and integrated vast ranges of primitive religious symbolism.[9] Northrop Frye has reduced literary myths, the literary stories, to three different cycles: cycles of day and night, of the four seasons of the year, and the course of the organism's growth and decline. From these three, he has constructed a matrix from which symbolic narratives of literature can be built up, all the variations: tragic, comic, epic, and so on.[10]

Moreover, there is what is called the third force in psychology: people like Abraham Maslow with his book *Toward a Psychology of Being*,[11] and a large number of books of that type in which the psychologists are turning from the sick to the well, to the people who develop, who keep on growing. They are called the unmotivated because, apparently, among previous types of psychology a motive is, What's in it for me? If you have that you have a motive. So these people who are not simply thinking of what's in it for me are called unmotivated. It's a queer terminology.

8 See above, p. 65, note 12.
9 Mircea Eliade, 'Methodological Remarks on the Study of Religious Symbolism,' in Eliade and Kitagawa, eds, *The History of Religions* (see above, p. 465, note 13) 86–107.
10 Northrop Frye, *Fables of Identity: Studies in Poetic Mythology* (New York: Harcourt, Bruce & World, 1963).
11 See above, p. 499, note 7.

Finally, there is a man who is not looked upon favorably by people in the field, at least for this business, Mowrer. He has a book, *The Crisis in Psychiatry and Religion.*[12] I'll tell you what his thesis is, and you can investigate it further for yourselves if you wish. He says that most people in asylums have not the problem of mistaken guilt but of real guilt. And it is the clergymen who know about the real guilt, not the psychiatrists. This does not fit into the categories of mental illness; it is something entirely different. He says the only people who believe in Freud at the present time are clergymen who are counsellors; and he has other juicy statements. He is a bit off the beaten track; but just how good he is I don't know.

Finally, there are the existentialist interpretations of dreams. Ludwig Binswanger uses the existentialist movement, and in America Rollo May. There is also the logotherapy of Victor Frankl in Germany. For them, the dream is not just the twilight of human living; the dream can also be the dawn of the transition from nonpersonal existence to a person living in his world.[13]

So much for the meaning of symbols. It's a meaning that occurs in internal communication; but it also influences linguistic meaning, insofar as the analysts show that it is very rare that one has literal statements that are simply accurate. Not all language is of the type, 'This is a cat.' When it moves away from that, you are moving into the rules of affect and image, and so on.[14]

2.4 Linguistic Meaning

Besides intersubjective, artistic, and symbolic carriers of meaning, there is also linguistic meaning. By its embodiment in language, in a set of conventional signs, meaning finds its greatest liberation. Conventional signs can

12 O.H. Mowrer, *The Crisis in Psychiatry and Religion* (Princeton, NJ: Van Nostrand, 1961).

13 Ludwig Binswanger, *Le rêve et l'existence*, Desclée, 1954, introduction (128 pp.) and notes by Michel Foucault. Rollo May, Ernest Angel, Henri F. Ellenberger, eds, *Existence: A New Dimension in Psychiatry and Psychology* (New York: Basic Books, 1958). Rollo May, ed., *Existential Psychology* (New York: Random House, 1961). Rollo May, 'The Significance of Symbols,' in *Symbolism in Religion and Literature* (New York: Braziller, 1961). V.E. Frankl, *The Doctor and the Soul* (New York: Knopf, 1955); *Man's Search for Meaning* (New York: Washington Square Press, 1959, 1963); *The Will to Meaning* (Cleveland: World, 1969). V.E. Frankl et al., *Psychotherapy and Existentialism* (New York: Washington Square Press, 1967).

14 A break was taken at this point. The remainder of the lecture, along with the discussion following, are found on Lauzon CD/MP3 490 (49000A0E060).

be multiplied indefinitely. They can be used reflexively in analysis and control of linguistic meaning itself, and in a description of intersubjective, artistic, and symbolic meaning.

In contrast to the freedom and flexibility of linguistic meaning, intersubjective and symbolic meaning seem restricted to the spontaneities of human living together; and whatever conventions the arts may develop – there is an element of convention in the arts – still, they are limited by the materials in which colors and shapes, solid forms and structures, sounds and movements are embodied. The first point, then, is the freedom, liberty, flexibility of linguistic meaning.

Now the moment of language in human development is illustrated first of all by the story of Helen Keller's discovery of what this writing on her hand, this touching on her hand, really meant. It meant a name. It was a terrific emotional experience when she got that insight. She was obviously emotionally carried away and immediately started asking the names of about twenty other objects on the way into the house. This happened when out pumping water from the well. Her enormous interest in learning other names exhibits the significance of naming, simply naming, for human consciousness. In the ancient civilizations, there is a terrific amount of prizing of names; the name is something very extraordinary. Sometimes it is said that for the ancient civilizations the name stood for the essence of the thing, but essence is a later Socratic question of finding definitions. The real significance of the name is that it is the human achievement that brings conscious intentionality into sharp focus. When you can name it, your effort at apprehension comes to a sharp focus, it fixes on something definite. That is the key step in human consciousness setting about the double task of ordering one's world and orientating oneself within it. Insofar as one has names, one can do that with a precision and a clarity that otherwise is not attainable.

Moreover, conscious intentionality develops in and is molded by its mother tongue. We not only learn the names of what we can see and feel, but we can attend to and talk about the things insofar as we can name them. The names or the verbs pick out the aspects of things that are pushed into the foreground, the relations between things that are stressed, the movements that demand attention.

So different languages develop in different manners, and the best of translations can express, not the exact meaning of the original, but the closest approximation possible in another tongue. There is not any exact correspondence, word for word, between languages; it just does not exist. The point to knowing the original is to know the meanings of any given term as it is employed in the original. A good translation will use five or six different words for any one word in the original, according to the differences between the two languages. But if you are just stuck with the translation and don't know the way the original is using the same word, you are blocked in grasping the meaning to a great extent. That is the importance of knowing the original language, the original text.

Besides molding the development of consciousness, language structures the world about the subject. Spatial adverbs and adjectives relate places to the place of the speaker; tenses of verbs relate times to his present; moods correspond to his intention to wish or exhort or command or declare; voices make verbs active or passive and shift subjects to objects and objects to subjects. Grammar, on the one hand, almost gives us Aristotle's categories of substance, quantity, quality, relation, action, passion, place, time, and so on. On the other hand, Aristotle's logic and theory of science are deeply rooted in the grammatical function of predication.

Symbolic logic proceeds in an entirely different fashion. First of all, there is the proposition, then the combination of propositions, simply their being together: there are not any if/then relationships in the classical propositional calculus; it's a mathematics of combinations. The fact that Aristotle does depend so much on grammar is partly an advantage, but it is not purely an advantage; there is a verbalism inherent in Aristotelianism that one has to escape; and one is escaping it in my emphasis on method.

Moreover, as language develops there emerges a distinction between ordinary, technical, and literary language. Ordinary language is the vehicle in which the human community conducts its collaboration in the day-to-day pursuit of the human good. It is the language of the home and school, of industry and commerce, of enjoyment and misfortune, of the mass media and casual conversation. It is transient. It expresses the thought of the moment, at the moment, for the moment. That transient character is, of course, being overcome by the tape recorder.

It is elliptical. It knows that a wink is as good as a nod; that full statement is superfluous and would only irritate. It is based on common sense; and what is common sense? It is a nucleus of habitual insights such that with the addition of one or two further insights one will arrive at a proper understanding of any of the series of situations that are liable to arise in ordinary living. You have that basic nucleus of insights; and to deal with any concrete situation you have to take a look around and see what's up, what's going forward. But you have a general nucleus so that one or two more insights will enable you to know just what to say and what not to say, what to do and what not to do.

Now, the whole orientation of common sense is centered in the subject and regards the world as related to him, as the field of his behavior, influence, action, as colored by his desires, hopes, fears, joys, sorrows. As shared by a group, this nucleus of insights is common sense, the common sense of the group. There are many common senses because there are many groups. The common sense of a Russian is one thing, and the common sense of an American is another, and the common sense of a Frenchman is a third, and so on. And you can get subdivisions in the different classes.

Common sense is common sense if it is the common sense of your group. Insofar as you have your own views, well, you're a bit odd. Insofar as it is the common sense of another group, well, that's being strange; and when you travel about the world and live in foreign countries, you find them all strange. Their common sense is not yours.

Next, there is technical language. The commonsense development of human intelligence yields, not only common, but also complementary results. There starts, after the primitive fruit gatherers, the specialization of hunters, gardeners, fishers. New groups, new ends, new tasks are calling for new words. The division of labor continues and fosters the specialization of language. A distinction emerges between words in common use that refer to what is generally known about particular tasks, and, on the other hand, the technical words or the jargon employed by craftsmen or experts or specialists when they speak among themselves. Eventually human intelligence shifts from commonsense development to theoretical development, when it is seeking knowledge for its own sake, when logics and methods are formulated, when a tradition of learning is established, different branches of learning are distinguished, and specialties multiply; then technical language becomes enormous. You have dictionaries for chemists, and so on.

Finally, there is literary language. Literary language is the language of a work, a *poiēma*. It is not something transient. It is not transient expression of the moment, and it is not something restricted to a technically specialized group. But it is a work, something written or something to be learnt by heart. While ordinary language is content to supplement the common understanding and feeling already guiding common living – it adds on the further little hint or suggestion or movement that is needed to complete mutual understanding – literary language aims not only at fuller statement – it is not so elliptical – but it also attempts to make up for the lack of mutual presence, the lack of intersubjective meaning. It would have the listener or reader not only understand but also feel; and it aims at evoking, provoking the feeling. So where the technical treatise aims at conforming to the laws of logic and the precepts of method, literary language tends to float somewhere between logic and symbol. The symbol is guided by the laws of image and affect, and the treatise is guided by the laws of logic and method, but somewhere in between you will find literary language, and consequently, the shift from the class to the representative individual and all those things that I have already enumerated.

We now say something about the so-called figures of speech. What are figures of speech? They are the result of literary language being analyzed by the theoretical mind and judged by logical standards. Literary language does not follow simply the laws of logic. It does not aim at literal statement; it aims at communicating. Consequently, it is floating in between the logic of the treatise and, on the other hand, the laws of the symbol. The distinctions of simile and metaphor, and metonomy, and so on, drawn by Aristotle, for example, in his *Rhetoric*, are not something such that the literary person first of all has a literal meaning and then dresses it up with figures of speech to affect the reader. The literary expression is the spontaneous expression, and the strictly logical expression is an ideal to which theoretical minds are trying to make ordinary and literary language conform; they express this in terms of the figures of speech.[15]

15 The fourth question-and-answer session was held later this day. See below, pp. 605–16.

1968-6

Analysis of Meaning
and Introduction to Religion[1]

1 Elements of Meaning

We spoke yesterday on the carriers of meaning, the ways in which meaning is embodied in intersubjective expression, in art, in symbols, and in language. Finally, we turn to the analysis of meaning, and first of all, to elements of meaning.

Distinguish sources, acts, and terms. Sources of meaning are all conscious acts and all intended contents, from the dream state right through the four levels of waking consciousness. The fundamental division is between transcendental and categorial meaning.

'Categorial' means the determinations reached through experiencing, through understanding and conceiving, through reflecting, weighing the evidence, judging, through deliberating, evaluating, deciding. One reaches determinate contents. But prior to what the Germans call *Begriff*, all determinate contents, there is the *Vorgriff*, the effort to arrive, the effort of attending, the effort of inquiring, the effort of reflecting – is it so? – the effort of deliberating; and there you have the transcendental active part of meaning, the intending that gradually becomes more and more determinate as we advance in experiencing, understanding, judging, and deciding.

So much for the sources of meaning, then: all conscious acts and all intended contents. Their fundamental division is into categorial (determinate)

---

1 Thursday, 11 July 1968, Lauzon CD/MP3 491 (49100A0E060) and 492 (49200A0E060).

and transcendental, which are comprehensive (not abstract), invariant, and universal, in the sense of carrying one right through to the concrete; what is intended is always everything about everything.

Secondly, acts of meaning. We distinguish acts of meaning into potential, formal, full, active or performative, and instrumental.

Potential meaning is the elemental meaning we spoke of in intersubjectivity, in the purely experiential pattern, in the symbol. In the elemental meaning, the potential meaning, the distinction has not yet been made between meaning and meant. It may be illustrated by the smile as simply intersubjective determinant of the interpersonal situation; the work of art prior to interpretation; the symbol as internal communication prior to the analysis of it by the therapist.

Again, according to the Aristotelian theorem, acts of sensing and acts of understanding are potential meaning. The intelligible in act is intelligence in act; the sensible in act is the sense in act. You can have sounding without ears, longitudinal waves in the air. But you can't have hearing without ears. You have sounding in the sense of longitudinal waves, but not in the sense of something that is heard or hearable. The sound in act is hearing in act; again, the color in act is seeing in act; color in potency, sight in potency, are distinct.

Next, formal acts of meaning. A formal act of meaning is an act variously named conceiving, thinking, considering, defining, supposing, formulating. Here the distinction between meaning and meant has emerged, the difference between the definition and the defined. But just what the difference is has not yet been determined, and the function of judgment on the next level of consciousness is precisely to determine the status of what is conceived, defined, considered, whether it is something that really is or whether it is merely a mathematical entity or hypothetical or logical or transcendent. That distinction arises in the full act of meaning, which is the act of judgment: this is so; there is a logarithm of the square root of minus one.

Fourthly, there is the active or performative meaning. I really mean it! This emerges on the fourth level, the level of deliberating, evaluating, deciding. There will be more to be said about that later, when we speak of the functions of meaning.

Finally, there is the instrumental act of meaning, the expression that externalizes, exhibits for interpretation by others, the potential, formal, full, or performative acts of meaning of the subject. As both expression and interpretation may be inadequate or faulty, instrumental acts of meaning provide the materials for our eighth chapter on hermeneutics, on interpretation.

Besides sources of meaning and acts of meaning, and five kinds of acts of meaning, there are terms of meaning: what is meant.

First of all, terms of meaning have various stages. In the potential act of meaning there is no distinction yet between the term and the act. In formal acts the distinction emerges, but its precise nature is indeterminate. In full acts the distinction is carried out to the end; one settles whether or not A is; whether it is a real thing or just an object of thought. In performative acts, one is on the level of real self-transcendence; one is settling one's attitude to A; what one will do for B; whether one will attempt to bring about C.

In the terms of meaning there arises the distinction between spheres of being. We have already had occasion to mention this in the discussion periods.[2] We say that the moon exists and that there exists the logarithm of the square root of minus one. 'Is' is used in quite different senses, and those different senses give different spheres of being. There is being in each case, because in each case the judgment rests on a grasp of a virtually unconditioned. But you have different spheres of being because in the different cases different conditions are making the conditioned virtually unconditioned; there is a different fulfilment of conditions. To say there exists the logarithm of the square root of minus one means that you can arrive at the conclusion of what that logarithm is by proceeding from appropriate mathematical premises. But you don't mean that these mathematical entities are entities such as is Boston College, or you, or myself. In the other case, when you talk about real being, the fulfilling conditions have to be the data of sense or the data of consciousness. Beyond the restricted spheres of being, the world of human experience, and, then, the still more restricted spheres – the merely logical, the merely mathematical, the merely hypothetical, the merely figurative, the mythical, and so on – at the opposite pole from these, there is the transcendent sphere of being. Our affirmations of things in this world rest upon grasping a virtually unconditioned, something that de facto has its conditions fulfilled, something that is contingent. But the fundamental criterion of judgment is simply the unconditioned. The virtually unconditioned is what we can get in the world of our experience, but the intention of our judgment is for the unconditioned *simpliciter*. So there is a transcendent sphere of being.

Now what I have been giving you is a realist account of the different spheres of being. You can get as many different accounts as you can have philosophies. If you ask the empiricist about the full term of meaning, he

2 See below, p. 585.

does not talk about grasping the virtually unconditioned; he appeals simply to experience: What is a man? Look around, see them; they are all around here. The idealist points out to the empiricist, yes, it's all very well to take a look but we do an awful lot more than that. We inquire and understand and conceive, and do an awful lot of constructing and relating; and that is necessary for our knowledge to be human, not just to be mere gaping, unintelligent gaping. So while he rejects the empiricist's account of knowledge, still he accepts his account of reality, and rejects that as something we know. Consequently, he is in an idealist world, and you can keep on differentiating the different types of idealism and different types of empiricism.

So much, then, for the elements of meaning. We distinguished sources, acts, and terms. Sources: all conscious acts, all intended contents divided into transcendental or categorial. Acts: potential, formal, full, performative, and instrumental. Terms vary with the acts, and then to this we added spheres of being and pointed out that our account of spheres of being was a realist account.

2 Exigences

The next topic concerns the different exigences that arise within meaning. There is the differentiation of consciousness that results from meeting these exigences. Finally, we discuss the unity of such a differentiated consciousness.

Originally, consciousness is undifferentiated, homogeneous. Meeting the exigences of meaning results in a differentiation of consciousness. Consciousness begins to operate in different worlds, and, at first, it is very troubled by this, because it wants to get synthesis by returning to undifferentiation, homogeneity. You have to get beyond that and accept the differentiation of consciousness and find a dynamic unity in the fact that you are able to relate these different worlds and move easily from one to the other.

The first exigence that appears is the systematic exigence. The classical illustration of it is in Plato's early dialogues. Socrates stood in the market place in Athens and asked people, 'What do you mean by courage? What do you mean by temperance? What do you mean by justice?' No one was going to say – least of all any Athenian – that he had no notion at all. They all knew perfectly well what they meant by courage; they knew a coward when they saw one; and similarly for temperance and justice. No one was going to say that he had no notion of what justice was. But on the other hand, they were not able to answer Socrates' questions. He pointed out that all he wanted was a definition that applied to every instance of justice, for example, and to nothing that was not justice; and what was this that they were talking about when they were talking about justice? They would bat the thing around, and Socrates would say, 'Well, I don't know; I'm just trying to find out. I know enough to know that I don't know.' That was his advantage over the other people. In Aristotle's *Ethics* there is a definition of virtue in general; and there are definitions of all the virtues; there is a whole Greek vocabulary with regard to virtue. And each virtue is flanked by two vices: a vice that sins by excess and a vice that sins by defect. But now, if you take up the *Nicomachean Ethics* you will find that you are no longer in the context of people coming along in the market place and listening to Socrates' questions and trying to answer them. Aristotle has gone to work and built up a whole context in which these answers can be given. He has a doctrine of habits and a doctrine of the mean, and so on. There is a whole theoretical context that has to be constructed in order to make it possible to discuss the questions and work out answers to the questions raised by Socrates. Within the commonsense context you can raise the questions, and you can start working out answers to them, but by the time you have got answers rounded out you are in a theoretical world, and you have given technical meanings to words that already existed or found new words, as the case may be. Again, you have moved from the world of common sense into the world of theory; and that is just one example of it. That moving from the world of common sense to the world of theory occurs in every science. Every science, in the measure that it turns the corner, becomes explanatory, operates with fundamental concepts that do not refer to the data of sense. Mass is not weight; temperature is not the feeling of hot or cold. Things may be of the same temperature, but if one is metal it will feel colder, and if it's wood it will feel warmer. There is the shift to what Aristotle would call the *quoad se*, or as we would put it in term of modern science, to things in their relations to one another. The periodic table relates the elements to one another, according to the relations constitutive of this table.

So that is the systematic exigence. Common sense builds up its world by a self-correcting process of learning, adding one insight on to the other. It does not aim at universal principles, universally valid. Instead of principles it has proverbs, and the meaning of the proverb is: it is worthwhile paying attention to this. I don't say that it will hold in every case. 'A stitch in time saves nine.' If it holds in a number of cases that it's better to do something right away than to wait until tomorrow when you'll have to do three times as much work, still it is not giving you a universal principle in the scientific sense. It is using a metaphor, the stitch. The stitch refers to anything that you might do. 'Look before you leap.' It may not mean merely looking before you do, and it may not mean leaping either. That is the way common sense thinks. It has its proverbs, and they are true in a large number of cases. What the cases are, well, you advert to the fact when the case arises. It's an entirely different mode of thinking from the systematic mode that sets up theories and builds up a world of theory.

The result, of course, of meeting the systematic exigence, is that one has two worlds: a world of theory and a world of common sense, the world of tables and chairs and the world of electrons and neutrons. And there arises, as a result, the critical exigence. There are communications between the world of common sense and the world of theory. The questions that theory answers first arise in a commonsense context. The corrections of the theory can arise in a commonsense context, but the corrections are in the technical language of the theory. You have the two worlds – not only two different apprehensions of one and the same world, but two languages. People have to learn the technical language if they are going to move into that sphere. And you have different societies. People who know the language and have grasped the theory can talk to one another; but if someone else comes along there have to be very, very long explanations before he catches up.

About theoretical language, last summer at the theology congress held in Toronto, there were on the panels one gentleman in each case that supplied the money, the financers of the congress, and the questions they usually raised went along the lines, as one man put it, of the following: 'It would be much easier to understand if you used four-letter words more frequently.' Langdon Gilkey fielded this one very nicely; he went on with this and that, but he finally made the point and said: 'People who are interested in a subject, in chemistry, in physics or mathematics, and so on, are willing to take the trouble to learn the theoretical language.' It is a fundamental point.

We go on to the critical exigence. How does one relate these two apprehensions of one world, these two languages, these two modes of coming to know? The mode of coming to know of common sense is something quite distinct from the coming to know in science, and that throws us back into a world of interiority. The world of common sense and the world of theory have to be related, and the critical exigence drives one back into the world of interiority. Because one has two apprehensions of one world, one is confronted with questions about knowing and objectivity and reality. What am I doing when I am knowing? Why is doing that knowing? What do I know when I do it? These are the questions of the different schools of philosophy.

With these questions one turns from the outer worlds of common sense and theory to the appropriation of one's own interiority, one's subjectivity, one's operations, their structure, their norms, their potentialities.

In its technical expression such appropriation resembles theory but in itself it is a heightening of intentional consciousness, an attending not merely to objects but also to the intending subject and his acts. As this heightened consciousness constitutes the evidence for one's account of knowledge, such an account by the proximity of the evidence differs from all other expression. It is self-expression in a theoretical mode.

Thirdly, from the world of interiority there is met the methodical exigence. Because one knows what one's acts are, and their norms and potentialities and structures, one is able to construct a transcendental method that deals just with the potentialities of the human mind, and then one can enlarge this transcendental method according to the different exigences of different fields of inquiry: the natural sciences, the human sciences, theology.

Finally, there is the transcendent exigence. There is to human inquiry an unrestricted desire for intelligibility. There is to human judgment a demand for the unconditioned. There is to human deliberation a criterion that criticizes every finite good. There is to man some thrust towards the infinite which Augustine expressed in the words: 'Thou has made us for thyself, O Lord, and our hearts are restless until they rest in Thee.' So, one moves to a fourth world: the world of religion. There is, then, a world of common sense, a world of theory, a world of interiority, of heightened self-consciousness, and finally a world of religion. At the start, interiority and theory don't exist, and religion is not differentiated from the world of common sense. As one develops, consciousness itself differentiates in four ways. The life of prayer becomes something of its own, just as distinct from the life of common sense dealing with persons and things, or theoretic life dealing with theory, or philosophic inquiry into subjectivity. These four become four different things. One moves from one to the other, and one relates them to one another in terms of the different exigences I spoke of: the systematic, the critical, the methodical, the transcendental.

One does not seek homogeneity. For example, there is a lot of objection against theology, that it is not religion. Well, there is a stage in religion in which there is no differentiation between it and theology; it's all of a piece. But as theology develops, it differentiates from religion and enters into relations with religion and is of use to religion as religion is related to it and founds a theology: and you have two things that are distinct. But you must not attempt to give that distinction to people whose consciousness is not yet differentiated. In other words, it is not a matter of distinguishing merely two worlds, but also two apprehensions, and a person who has not yet got the second apprehension is not going to know what this theology is about. It won't be theology unless it is identified for his consciousness with religion.

3 Functions of Meaning

The last two sections of this chapter on meaning have not yet been written. However, roughly they are, first, on the functions of meaning, and secondly, on meaning in history. I'll say something on both.

Functions of meaning: we have the formative, communicative, cognitive, effective, constitutive. Meaning does different things. So besides elements of meaning and different structures of consciousness and different carriers of meaning, there are different jobs that meaning does.

Meaning is formative. It is a component that completes man's being. That is clear insofar as the sources of meaning are his conscious acts and all intended contents. But, in particular, what am I thinking of when I say meaning is formative is what I said yesterday about linguistic meaning, the meaning of the word, the discovery of the word in Helen Keller's terrific experience when she first caught on to the use of language. The meaning completes the effort of intentional consciousness to pick out things and relations. There is a function of the word as a completion of consciousness, a focusing of consciousness, that otherwise remains somehow inchoate and frustrated. There is the function of the symbol in internal communication and, in general, the completion of man by meaning. This formative function of meaning and the constitutive function are hard to distinguish; but they have different spheres of influence, so to speak.

Meaning is communicative. This is the most obvious aspect of meaning: one person talking to another, communication; and common meaning as constitutive of community. There is community insofar as people have common experience, understand things in similar or complementary fashion, share common judgments of fact, and have common commitments, whether they are the common commitments of the family, or of the state, or of a faith.

Meaning is cognitive. Most of our talk in these eight lectures has been about meaning as cognitive. But we also spoke of meaning as deciding, meaning in the acts of decision. We know things by meaning them. Knowing is a matter of meaning as opposed to looking; this is a fundamental epistemological discovery. The object is what lies ahead, what we mean, what we intend; not something we look back at.

Meaning is effective. The people that came out on the Mayflower did not find any of the cities, or roads, or industries, and so on, that are in this country at the present time. There is a world of human artifacts between us and the virgin forests and plains. In that producing there has intervened meaning. You mean a road before you build one; you mean a factory before you build one. Acts of meaning guide all man's transformation and exploitation of nature: meaning is effective.

Finally, meaning not only plays a role in transforming nature, it also plays a role in the constitution of human community. All human institutions come into being through decisions, and decisions involve acts of meaning. The family, mores, the state and the law, society and education, economy and technology, church and sect, all have an element of meaning that is part of their being, that makes them be what they are. You change the state and the law by changing the meaning. If you start reinterpreting the law you get a change in it, because constitutive of the law is its meaning. It's not the whole thing to it; but it's a constituent part.

4 Meaning in History

Now those different functions of meaning may be more or less developed. The cognitive function in Western society at the present time is developed to an incredible extent, but it just does not exist at all in illiterate peoples. As the different functions develop differently, you get a different total pattern, and there we have, I think, the possibility of working out the relations between different stages in a culture. According as the formative, communicative, cognitive, effective, constitutive functions are achieved differently, forming different structures, you get differences in the culture.

I've already made certain very broad comparisons. There is the meaning without any control over it, as when myth and magic run rampant. You have the victory of *logos* over *mythos* in the Greek period. Myth and magic come under control, and the control is classical, in terms of universal norms and ideals and laws. The shift from classical to modern culture is a shift in the controls; the controls become invariants in an ongoing process.

That is a very, very broad distinction, but I think that a more detailed study of these different functions of meaning and the comparison of the degrees of development provide some sort of an indication of what might be done towards a general theory of cultures.

So much for meaning, which is chapter 5.

5 The Question of God

We now go on to chapter 6 on religion. We have five sections: the question of God; religious values; religious expression; faith; and conversions and breakdowns.

First, the question of God. The question of God is a question of ultimates. It takes very many forms. There is living polytheism: there are 800,000 divinities in Shintoism, I believe. But in its purest form the question of God arises out of the very structure of conscious intentionality: from inquiry into inquiry, reflection on reflection, deliberation about deliberation.

Inquiry is unrestricted, and so we can inquire into inquiry itself. We recognize the fact that we come to understand our world insofar as we have acts of understanding that satisfy us, that give rise to no further questions on that point. But we can wonder why on earth it is that the satisfaction of our understanding should be knowledge of a real world. What connection is there between the two? Why should the world be something that conforms to the way we understand, so that when we do understand we are knowing the world? There arises the question, Must there not be an intelligent ground, if the world is intelligible? That is one way of putting the question about God. It is the question of God in the form of the question of the reality of intelligibility.

The same question can arise when we reflect on reflection. We ask, Is that really so, have I understood correctly? And figuratively we say that we come towards the answer to that question by marshaling and weighing the evidence. I've attempted a more technical, exact analysis of what happens in the tenth chapter of *Insight*. The formula there was, We reach an act of reflective understanding in which we grasp a virtually unconditioned, a conditioned whose conditions have been fulfilled. The world of our experience is known to be a world of contingent beings, precisely because anything we know about it or in it is just a conditioned whose conditions happen to be fulfilled. The data are there: the conditions are fulfilled. But there is something unsatisfying to our rationality about a world that merely happens: everything in it merely happens, as a matter of fact, to be so. And we note that while we are content with grasping a virtually unconditioned when we say that something is, still our real demand is for the unconditioned. There is a presupposed thrust to the unconditioned that is prior to the merely virtually unconditioned, as the virtually unconditioned is prior to the merely hypothetical, the merely logical, the merely mathematical – the spheres of being. In the way in which we seek evidence, we are seeking really an unconditioned. There is the intention of the unconditioned prior to the intention of the conditioned whose conditions are fulfilled. And so, in a second way, there arises the question of God: the question of the transcendent, something that is beyond being as we know it, but is being in the sense that it is an unconditioned.

Thirdly, we can deliberate about our deliberation. We stop ourselves short and ask, Am I doing something that is truly good, or am I just kidding myself? Is it really worth while? We can go further and ask whether it is worth while bothering about whether things are worth while. Is this whole process from the nebulae, cosmogenesis, the evolution of life in all its forms, human history, is that something that is worth while, something that is truly good? The only way it could be would be if it were the product of a moral agent running the show because he considers it worth while. And so the question of God arises on the moral level, the question of the goodness of the universe, where goodness is a question of the value of the universe, in the sense in which we have been using the word 'value.'

So note the nature of the question of God, as I have been raising it. I said that it can be raised in all sorts of ways; the whole history of religions illustrates the enormous variety of ways in which that question can be raised. But what I'm saying is that it is contained, it is implicit, in the very nature of our intentional consciousness in its capacity to ask about itself: inquiry into inquiry, reflection on reflection, deliberation about deliberation.

Put in that form, the question of God is not any matter of image, feeling, a father image, for example; any question of feeling, of concept, of judgment. All that will pertain to answers to the question. What I am positing is simply the question, and the question about God is questioning turning back on itself, asking how the world that will be known by answers can be intelligible, asking about the sphere of transcendent being, of the formally unconditioned that underpins the reality of a world that is only virtually unconditioned; asking whether asking whether things are worth while is itself worth while. Are we in a universe of value or just the *Geworfhenheit*, something thrown out, meaningless?

Because the question of God is located in the originating powers of conscious intentionality, it is a question that can be manifested in very many ways, in the many varieties of human culture, and in the many stages of man's historical development. But such differences are secondary. They easily introduce elements that overlay, obscure, distort the pure question that questions about questioning. The obscurity and the distortion presuppose what they obscure and distort, and so it follows that however much religious and irreligious answers differ, however much the questions that actually are raised explicitly differ, still, at the root there is the single transcendental tendency of the human spirit that questions, that questions without restriction, that asks about the possibility of an intelligible world, about the ground reality behind contingent being, about the worthwhileness of deliberating, and so about what we mean by the word 'God.'

The question of God, then, lies within man's horizon. Unless man is reaching for the intelligible, the unconditioned, the worthwhile, his transcendental self-transcending subjectivity is mutilated. But the reach of his intending, not of his achieving, is unrestricted. There lies within man's horizon a region for the divine, a shrine for ultimate holiness. It cannot be ignored. The atheist may pronounce it empty, the agnostic may urge he sees nothing there. But their negations suppose the spark in our clod, our native orientation towards the divine.

That is the question of God, then, in its transcendental form. Putting it more concretely in terms of a number of philosophical complexities, one can ask some certain questions like, What is an object? Can a person be an object? Can God be an object? What about God and verification? What about the God of the philosophers and the God of religion? I'll say a few words on each one of those topics.

The word 'object,' etymologically, regularly means what stands opposite, what is set opposite, what lies opposite. The Greek is *antikeimenon*, lies opposite; the Latin *obiectum*, our 'object'; the French *objet*; the Italian *oggetto*, again, what lies, is thrown opposite; the German *Gegenstand*, what stands opposite. Object, then, in its etymological sense is something lying or standing opposite, presumably, a spectator. The theory of object in that sense was worked out with perfect rigor by Kant. In the first sentence of the 'Transcendental Aesthetic' he says that no matter how many ways we may know objects mediately, still, there is only one way in which our cognitional operations are related immediately to objects, and that is by *Anschauung*, intuition. And in us he acknowledges only sensitive intuition. From that it follows that the categories of the understanding have no immediate relationship to objects; they can become related to objects only insofar as they are filled out with an *Anschauung*. Similarly, the ideas of reason have no immediate relationship to objects; they attain a relationship to objects insofar as by guiding the use of the categories, when the categories are applied to sensible objects, they indirectly become relevant to objects. Consequently, the Kantian world has to be a world of phenomena, of what is given by sense. The objective element is the sensible content.

One gets a similar position by a different route in logical atomism, positivism, empiricism. The logical element is acknowledged. How does it refer to reality? You go back to your sensible data, and there you get the same position Kant had, in a much simpler fashion.

Now, throughout the nineteenth century there was a series of efforts to break away from the Kantian position, and they consisted in laying an emphasis on the subject. In Kierkegaard, it is faith, the leap of faith. In Schopenhauer and Nietzsche, it is the will. There is, even in absolute idealism, an attempt to break away from Kant too: in Fichte, Schelling, and Hegel, but still more so in people like Kierkegaard, Schopenhauer, and Nietzsche; and in our century in phenomenology, existentialism, and personalism. In these there is an attempt to save human values by emphasizing the subject. It is in that movement, that attempt to get away from Kant or logical positivism, by an emphasis on the subject, the person, personal existence, the will, faith, that these questions about God as object arise.

But none of these attempts, at least for me, are satisfactory. My position is to go to the root of this matter, this Kantian notion of the object, the etymological meaning of the object and the Kantian deduction of the implications of that notion of the object, and say, How are our cognitional operations related directly, immediately, to objects? My answer is, in the question. The immediate relation to the object is the intending of the question; and the mediate relation is in the answer, the experience of the answer, because experiencing and conceiving and judging are the way in which to get the answers to the question. The answer is related to the object because it is the answer to the question. You are already intending what you want to know when you are striving, when you are questioning. That is an entirely different meaning of the word 'object' from Kant and from the people trying to break away from the Kantian position in the nineteenth century and early twentieth century in existentialism and positivism. It is also a meaning of the word 'object' that breaks from naive realism. The object, then, is what we intend when we ask questions; and we come to know something about it insofar as we answer the questions. It is an object of human knowledge where human knowing has to be distinguished from the knowledge of the animals.

Objectivity, then, in that conception of the object is self-transcending subjectivity. We transcend ourselves cognitively when we are saying what is so, not what seems to me, what appears to me, what I imagine, what I would like to think, what I feel like saying, and so on, but what is so: there is no doubt about it. You have got beyond things related to yourself by appearing and being thought, and you are saying something that is; it is a cognitive self-transcendence. And you have a real self-transcendence in benevolence, beneficence, true collaboration, really loving.

The operations of intending and performing the further operations of working out answers to questions for understanding, for reflection, and for deliberation is a process of self-transcending, and it is in that process of the subject as transcending himself that one reaches the objective.

Now, can a person be an object? In Max Scheler, in his position in his phenomenology, the answer is very emphatically no. One person knows another as a person only through what he calls a *Mitvollzug*, mutual intersubjectivity in act. One comes to know another person in cooperating, co-performing. But on the notion of object as I have expressed it, obviously a person can be an object. We transcend to them. One transcends one's own subjectivity insofar as one comes to know and affirm the reality of another. And just as there is a self-transcendence in loving another, so there is a lesser self-transcendence in knowing another. In that sense of the word 'object,' there is no question whatever that a person can be an object.

Similarly, one knows another through intersubjectivity; there is no doubt about that. But in intersubjectivity of itself we are not yet at the stage where there is a distinction between meaning and meant. And, just as in self-affirmation the subject becomes the object – as affirming the subject is subject as subject, but as affirmed the subject is subject as object – so similarly for the 'we.' The 'we' of intersubjectivity is the 'we' as acting. But we can affirm the 'we,' say that we are acting; and then the subjects becomes objects.

Again, can God be an object? God can't be an object in the Kantian sense, in the sense of logical atomism, or empiricism. Solutions by way of Kierkegaardian faith or will or existence or any kind of subjective, personalist attempt at a solution may express peoples' religious convictions. But there is the question of God, and there are answers to that question, within the context of the principles one can lay down and the conclusions one can draw. And just as one affirms persons, so one can affirm God's existence; and in that case God is an object, in the sense in which I have defined the word 'object.'

However, with regard to that business of God as object, note this. The life of prayer, as it develops, tends to drop more and more all intermediary images and concepts. The thrust of the transcendental notions comes to operate more and more on its own, and that is the basis of mysticism. But there are several stages on the way; and as prayer to one's Father in secret moves towards its purity, it tends to drop images; and in that sense God is the objective of our striving rather than an object.

Again, there is the question of God and verification. There is an essential difference between the approach to God in the Aristotelian context, the Scholastic context, and in the context of modern science. The eighth book of Aristotle's *Physics* moves from this world to God beyond this world, the immovable movers. The Aristotelian notion of causality is a notion that can extend beyond the universe of sense, by analogy and development. On the other hand, modern science essentially is knowledge of this world. It adds nothing to the data except intelligible unities and relationships; and its addition is a possibly relevant hypothesis that has to be verified. There are no data on the divine, and consequently, there cannot be an empirical science about the divine itself. Moreover, there is no possibility of a verifiable principle relating this world to God. To have a verifiable principle you have to have both terms in the data. And so modern science is something that systematically is concerned with this world, and only with this world. We have, consequently, a different type of question when we ask about God in the present situation from what there was when the Aristotelian world view was accepted.

Now, is it true that every principle has to be a verifiable principle in the scientific sense? What do you mean by 'principle'? Do you mean by principle a logically first premise, or do you mean by principle first in an ordered set, so that the mind itself is a principle? It is an originating power; it is the source of all propositions. If you take principle in that general sense, then the mind itself is not something that has to be validated by any type of verification. You have to use your minds to verify, and, consequently, you presuppose the validity of your mind every time you appeal to the principle of verification. It is in the unrestricted thrust of the transcendental notions that one finds the premises for concluding to the existence of God, for moving beyond this world to God.

Finally, there is the question of the God of the philosophers and the God of religion. The word 'philosopher' is extremely ambiguous. There are all sorts of philosophies, and while all may be wrong, not more than one can be right. So when you talk about the God of the philosophers, you are setting up a dummy that you can tear down by refuting all the philosophies you know to be wrong. Usually, what is meant by the God of the philosophers is the God in a deductivist, conceptualist, rationalist viewpoint; and his existence is demonstrated, not by any existing person, but by right reason, by the *per se, de iure* subject. As that type of philosophy is very definitely out at the present time, so the God of those philosophers is out.

However, when one speaks about the God of the philosophers, one need not be subscribing to a rationalist, deductivist approach to philosophy. The question of God, as I put it, is God as the intelligent ground of the universe, as the formally unconditioned, and as the ground of value, God as good. If you mean by God all three: intelligent, unconditioned, and good – and that is what we do mean by God – then the third element arises, can be reached, only in the response of an existential subject, in the exercise of vertical liberty, the liberty that is setting up a horizon, founding a horizon. Fr de Finance distinguishes between the exercise of liberty within a horizon and the exercise of liberty that changes the meaning of one's life, changes one's horizon.[3] And it is in an exercise of vertical liberty, when one accepts the evils of this world as not destroying the goodness of God, when one is taking that stand, that the full acknowledgment of God, as we understand God, occurs. It is the act of an existential subject. That God is intelligent, God is unconditioned, I think, are things that can be concluded from the nature of our knowledge. Regarding God as good, you can set up a metaphysics of the good in terms of the intelligible and conclude to it that way. But the personal acceptance of that view, and not saying, 'Well, that can't be so,' involves the acceptance of a world view that involves a decision and God's grace.[4]

6 Religious Values

Already we have had something to say on vital, social, cultural, and personal values. Now we treat religious values. The response to the question of God is not only a statement about his existence and nature, but also a response to his goodness, the adoption of a *Weltanschauung*. It is a response to the originating value that is God and the terminating value that is the created universe. Elsewhere I have spoken about God's nature and existence, in *Insight* chapter 20: God as apprehended in cognitive self-transcendence.[5] In religious values we have a real self-transcendence.

The original feature of this real self-transcendence is that the existential subject thereby is constituting himself, not just to the human good, to his fellow men, to their needs, to their development, but to God as originating value, and to the world as terminal value. So the human good is taken up within an all-encompassing good. Before, the only originating values were men. Now, God is understood as originating value. Before, terminal values

3 See above, p. 512, note 14.
4 A break was taken at this point. The remainder of the lecture is found on Lauzon CD/MP3 492 (49200A0E060).
5 It is likely that Lonergan meant *Insight* chapter 19, or perhaps chapters 19 and 20.

were just human achievements. Now, we understand the whole universe as terminating value. Before, an account of the human good related men to fellow men and to nature. Now, human concern reaches beyond man's world to God and God's world. Men now meet, not only to be together and to settle human affairs but also to worship. Men develop not only in skills and virtues but also in holiness; and the limit of human expectation ceases to be the grave.

I was saying that the response to God generates religious values by setting the human good within the whole universe and conceiving God as the originating value. To conceive God as originating value and the universe as terminal value implies that God too is self-transcending and that the world is the fruit of his self-transcendence, a work of his love, the expression of his benevolence, the realization of his beneficence. We say God created all things for his glory, the manifestation of his excellence: there is a striking phrase in St Thomas, 2-2, q. 132, a. 1, ad 1m, in which he says that God seeks his glory not for his sake but for ours. Just as the Father seeks the well-being of his Son – and his Son is his glory – for the sake of the Son, not for the sake of the Father. That second addition there, that's my own; but he has just this short phrase, *Deus quaerit gloriam suam non propter se sed propter nos.* It is a far simpler answer than the very complicated explanations that you will find in the *Acta* connected with Vatican I on God creating the world for the manifestation of his glory. God has made us in his image, for our authenticity consists in being like him, in self-transcendence, in being origins of true values, in true love.

Already we have had occasion to distinguish acts of love and being-in-love. Being-in-love, once it has been brought about, becomes a first principle. As love of neighbor, it unites one with him or her in a common achievement of the human good. Being-in-love is the *mit* of the *Mitsein*. As love of God, it is not love of someone with whom one is working at one's side, so to speak; it refers back and around and forward. It refers back to the first lover: *Deus est Caritas*, God is love – in the first epistle of St John. It refers around to all men, for all men are made in the image of God. And it is in men and through them and with them that God's glory is achieved. And it refers forward to promote progress and offset decline. It does so not just for the sake of achievement, not just for the good of men, but at the deepest level for the good of men because that is the glory of God. Man's excellence is the glory of God. It is sought by God for man's sake.

Religious values are the values that arise in and from real self-transcendence in response to God. But self-transcendence in response to God is an ultimate in self-transcendence. All loving is self-surrender; but love of God is love of a Being beyond criticism. There is nothing, on his part, that could ground our introducing qualifications or conditions or reserves of any sort whatever into our love for him. And so love of God is a unique, total loving. Of its very nature it is otherworldly, pointing beyond anything finite. It is a love that actuates the unrestricted character of human conscious intentionality. And because it actuates that unrestricted character, it is fulfilment in a singular manner. The love of God is also joy. St Paul, listing the fruits of the Spirit, begins with charity, joy, peace. Being-in-love with God is a fount of joy that remains despite failure and humiliation and privation and pain. It is peace, the peace the world cannot give, the peace into which one may enter, almost palpably, when one prays to the heavenly Father in secret. Such love, joy, peace transform a man or woman; they banish the emptiness, the unrest, the alienation, the flight from one's depths that haunt lives lived without God. Full love, joy, peace enhance all one's virtues, press against all one's defects; they make a man a power for good, zealous in achieving. Relating man to God, they also relate him to all mankind and to the whole cosmic and historical process. On all persons and things, on all events and deeds, they shed a new dimension of meaning, significance, value.

Religion, then, and progress are bound together. They have a common root in man's cognitive and real self-transcendence. To promote either is to promote the other indirectly. Again, religion places human efforts in a friendly universe, reveals an ultimate significance in human achievement, strengthens new undertakings with confidence; and, above all, religion can undertake the supreme task of undoing decline. Decline disrupts a culture with conflicting ideologies; it inflicts on individuals and groups the social, economic, psychological pressures that for human frailty amount to determinisms. Decline multiplies and heaps up the abuses and absurdities that breed resentment, hatred, anger, violence. It is not propaganda or argument but religious faith that will liberate human reasonableness from its ideological prisons. It is not the promises of men but religious hope that enables men to resist the vast pressures of social decay. If passions are to quieten down, if wrongs are to be not ignored, not just palliated, but removed, human possessiveness and human pride have to be replaced by self-sacrificing love. Men have to come to acknowledge their individual and group sinfulness, to accept their real guilt, to amend their ways, to learn with humility that the task of repentance and conversion is life-long.

I have been speaking of religious values in their two aspects: the aspect of the relationship to God as fulfilment within the human person; and as a source of proper human action in this world. I have to go on, next, to religious expression. I have been speaking of religion in an extremely interior sense, namely, being in love with God. But there also is religious expression; and there there arise very complex questions which we shall attempt to say something about tomorrow.

1968-7

Religious Expression,
Faith, Conversion[1]

1 Religious Expression

The sixth chapter, on religion, treats the question of God and religious values. We did that part yesterday. There remain three more sections: religious expression, faith, and conversions and breakdowns. First, then, religious expression.

Religious values may be briefly referred to as values connected with, arising from, ultimate concern. Our conception of religion in that section on values had to do primarily with religion conceived in its roots, as simply ultimate concern, as authentic human existence with regard to God and God's world. The primary and ordinary manifestation or expression of ultimate concern is not any technically formulated question about God, not any transcendental analysis of ultimate concern, not any ontology of the good or philosophic proof of God's existence, but the endless variety of the religions of mankind. These religions are more than ultimate concern. In the measure they are authentic they express, reveal, communicate ultimate concern. But by going beyond ultimate concern to its expression they risk inauthenticity.

The more primitive the religion, the less its expression is differentiated from the rest of its ambient culture, and so the less it is capable of functioning independently and so of resisting sociocultural decline. On the other hand, when religion develops into a separate entity within a culture it can function with some independence and initiative of its own. But this will

1 Friday, 12 July 1968, Lauzon CD/MP3 493 (49300A0E060).

not guarantee authenticity, and it brings added risks of resisting cultural advance on the pretext of maintaining its authenticity or, on the other hand, of seeking integration with a culture and mistakenly joining with the forces of decline. There is, then, when one moves beyond the pure kernel of religion that we were talking about yesterday, the risk of corruption of one kind or another. Either it differentiates from the culture or it does not. If it does not, it can hardly function independently; and if it does, it is open to more complex difficulties.

Religious expression develops from an initial global or undifferentiated expression, where ultimate and proximate concern, the sacred and the profane, are not distinguished, separated, specialized. Each penetrates the other. What we would term profane is sacralized; and what we would term sacred is in the profane. All activity expresses some concern, but here the concern that is expressed is at once ultimate and proximate. The religious expression is not specifically and exclusively religious, but included globally with other types of expression. Even after differentiation has gradually been established, individuals and groups can slip back into forms of expression and patterns of expression in which religion as lived, felt, revealed, once more is global.

The differentiation or separating out of religious from other elements in human life sets the objects of ultimate concern apart from other objects. The one concern of human authenticity, the concern to attend, to understand, to judge truly, to choose responsibly, remains one and the same. But it expresses itself differently with respect to different objects. Specialized activities with a religious significance are developed. A division of labor in the performance of the activities emerges, and religious expression becomes a distinct part of the cultural statement on the meaning and value of human life, while the propagation and development of that expression are entrusted to a social institution.

The root of this differentiation is the difference between questioning experience and questioning questioning itself. We found yesterday that the question of God is implicit in questioning questioning. When one questions experience, one is concerned with this world, with the set of objects of possible immediate human experience. But when you question questioning, the reference is otherworldly. The object of ultimate concern is to be known, not by questioning experience, but by questioning questioning itself. This does not imply that the object of ultimate concern is totally other, that there is a complete break, that it transcends all human categories absolutely, even the transcendental intending. It is the ground of intelligibility, truth, being, value, in the whole universe, and these are related to both ultimate and proximate concern. It is the ground to whom alone man surrenders himself totally, and thereby achieves the love, joy, and peace of authentic fulfillment. It has the character of a response, man's self-transcendence answering divine self-transcendence, a finite being-in-love answering divine love.

However profound and powerful, however intimate and personal, that response to God must be expressed, or else it will be incomplete, unfinished, broken off. But in the specific religious expression we must distinguish whole and part, to avoid certain confusions and pitfalls connected with secularization theology. On that topic there is Bob Richard's book, *Secularization Theology*, Herder and Herder, New York, 1967.[2] Also very helpful, I found, is Colin Williams, *Faith in a Secular Age*, 1966, in a paperback.[3] I don't agree with a lot of the things he says. But he puts his points very well, and some things he says are quite true.

There is the distinction between total specific religious expression and partial religious expression. Total expression is an imitation of divine love. The total expression of one's response to God imitates divine love. Just as that love expresses itself by creating the universe and by loving and providing for rational creatures, so too, one's loving response to God finds its expression and outlet in loving God's creation. Effectively, it is a love that extends to all that God has done, is doing, or will do. Effectively, it turns to the persons that here and now can be comforted and helped, and to the present tasks of promoting the human good and offsetting decline. It is concern with the kingdom of God, not just the church but the kingdom of God. It is religious in its source because it is a total love of God. But there is a sense in which it is secular in its term. The total expression is religious in its source, for this is loving God with one's whole soul and all one's mind and all one's strength. Its term is the whole of creation. It is not confined to what is specifically religious, ecclesiastical, theological. It reaches out to the whole of this world, and in that sense it may be called secular. Yet it is not to be confined to this life, for its measure is all that God brings about.

If total religious expression is in a sense secular, still, it is not secularist. It does not exclude religion as church or as theology. It includes them as parts within a larger whole, and it limits them to their functions within that whole. When I was a student of theology, the kingdom of God was identified

2 Robert L. Richard, *Secularization Theology* (New York: Herder & Herder, 1967).
3 Colin Williams, *Faith in a Secular Age* (New York: Harper & Row, 1966).

with the church.[4] That has been eliminated by Vatican II. The church is God's instrument, one of God's instruments in this world, for promoting the kingdom of God, but the kingdom of God regards the whole world.

The reason why there should be not merely this pursuit of the kingdom of God, but also what is called the ecclesial dimension, is that man just does not simply act. He pauses and reflects on the meaning and value of his acting. He criticizes it and seeks to improve it. Nor is this reflective pause an unworthy deviation from the primary business of acting. It is the source of all development, which proceeds from initial global undifferentiated operations, through differentiation and specialization to new and more effective integration. This reflective process happens in all other components of human living, and it also happens in the most basic of them all. Man reflects on his love of God. Whom is he loving? Is it really love? How can it be strengthened and refined? In what ways can it be communicated and shared? He realizes this love is a gift, yet it is a gift to be cultivated by human effort. He holds that his neighbor is to be loved in every way, and he also sees that communicating, or doing something to share with the neighbor, this love of God is the greatest benefit he could give him. And so he comes to such conclusions as the cultivation of the inner life by prayer and self-denial, mutual support in communal worship, the specialized functions fulfilled by various members in the social institution named the church. In other words, those specialized functions, that specifically religious activity, is something that pertains to the expression of religion, not as the whole of it, but as a functional part, the reflective part that helps its development.

Both the total and the partial religious expressions are variables. The total expression as effective is always love of one's neighbor. But the human good progresses and declines, and so the good to be done and the decline to be undone vary with place and time. Similarly, specifically religious expression is fixed in some aspects and variable in others. The higher achievements of the inner life tend to transcend image and symbol, concept and system, and so have a dimension of independence of historical change and cultural content. On the other hand, manners of speech, modes of emotional communication, cultural and social forms are historical variables. As they change, specifically religious expression has to keep step, neither resisting progress nor siding with decline.

---

4 This identification can still be found in the sixth chapter of Lonergan's trinitarian systematics. See *The Triune God: Systematics* 495.

In this specific religious expression, there is the possibility of inauthenticity. Specific religious experience and expression can promote development of ultimate concern or be a carrier of decline. To admit specific expression is to admit cultural activities and social functions in which inattention, incomprehension, unreasonableness, and irresponsibility can find their way. As these distort other forms of progress, so also they distort religious development. The salt loses its savor. The religious man neglects the beam in his own eye to fumble with the mote in his brother's.

I'm saying, then, that there is something true about secularization theology insofar as the church is distinct from the kingdom of God and charity extends even to the Samaritan. On the other hand, I cannot accept the idea that religious expression and specific religious expression is superfluous, that it can be dropped entirely, that we can have a religionless Christianity, because I think that any sort of movement involves an element of reflection on itself, and the specifically religious is that element of reflecting on religion. And, moreover, the religionless theologians keep right on with very highly specific religious tasks: they write theology.

Another point is Christian atheism: this is another facet of the complexities of our day. It can be Christian inasmuch as it experiences ultimate concern and gives it, at least, its primary and essential expression in love of all mankind. It is atheist because, on practically all up-to-date philosophies, there is no way of coming to know about God. And it is Christian and atheist because it deems it absurd to surrender ultimate concern merely because its philosophic abilities or interests are not equal to the task of coming to know about God or believe in him. That is the analysis of a possibility; it is not a historical study of any of the figures at the present time who speak in that manner.

Now, that theoretical entity which I set up, in the sense that it is Christian, has religious experience, sincere religious experience. It is atheist because, at the present time, not only are the philosophies incompetent to arrive at knowledge of God or even exclude it, but also, something like Karl Barth's fideism is a thing that can collapse. It is faith with no props; and while it can carry on with people that are carried by Barth and carried by their religious experience, it is the sort of thing that just collapses like that.

Now, while this position is a possibility, is it likely to be stable? I think its stability is doubtful, not merely because the philosophic issues can be resolved, because philosophy has never been a redeemer, but also, when God is not acknowledged, ultimate concern ceases to be otherworldly. It ceases to be ultimate. Then either there is no total self-transcendence, life is trivialized, and man is alienated from himself. Or there is total dedication to some worldly cause; and religious otherworldly dedication to a this-worldly cause easily falls into fanaticism and spreads havoc.

So much, then, for the general topic of religious expression. There is the fact that there is a stage in human development when it is not specifically differentiated, when the two, the proximate and the ultimate, merge. The nature of the differentiation means, on the one hand, that it should not lead to a narrow religious mind serving religion simply for its own sake, instead of serving God's creation, and, on the other hand, that one should avoid the extreme of these people who speak of a religionless Christianity. Insofar as they mean that religion can be corrupted, that is perfectly true. It can be a carrier of decline; it can promote irreligion. But what has to be done about that is to undo the decline in religion, as you undo the decline in anything else.

2 Faith

My second topic this morning is faith. I conceive faith as the knowledge born of religious love, of being in love with God. Pascal spoke of the reasons of the heart which reason does not know. 'Le coeur a ses raisons que la raison ne connaît pas.' In terms of my analysis, reason would be man as experiencing, understanding, and judging. The heart's reasons would be the feelings that are intentional responses to values, where intentional responses to values have the two aspects: an absolute aspect, in which you recognize the value as objectively good; and the relative value, in which feelings express a scale of preferences. And the heart that knows the heart's reasons is the subject of the fourth, existential level of intentional consciousness, in the dynamic state of being-in-love. So the distinction between the mind and heart, the heart and reason, would be the distinction between the subject on the fourth level, as distinct from the subject just on the other three levels. And the heart's reasons would be the apprehensions of value.

I have spoken on this already, probably in answering questions, but also in my statement on religious values, but I'll briefly go over the nature of religious love, to go on to the knowledge born of religious love.

It is an otherworldly love without conditions, reserves, qualifications. It is otherworldly, for only idolatry would directly bestow it on anyone or anything in this world. I don't mean by that that human love is not a total self-surrender, but there are limitations to it that would have to be dropped when it is a question of the love of God.

This total love is a dynamic state. Reaching it is an exercise of vertical liberty: one is entering a new horizon. Once reached, it is distinct from, prior to, and principle of subsequent judgments of value and acts. It is the fulfillment of man's capacity for self-transcendence, and as fulfillment it brings joy and peace. It radiates through the whole of one's living and acting, opening one's horizon to the full, purifying one's intentional responses to values, rectifying one's scale of preferences, underpinning one's judgments of value, simplifying issues by moving them to a deeper level, strengthening one to achieve good in the face of evil.

As religious, this total love is the love of God poured forth in our hearts by the Spirit who is given to us (Romans 5.5). And this can be experienced in many ways. There are many ways in which people talk about religious experiencing, and I think that each one should reflect on his own life, and become aware of how the grace of God has been acting in it; in that way one will arrive at an account of religious experience that means something to him. There is no reason why the manifestations of grace should be the same in everyone. It can be experienced in many ways. There are the expressions that ring a bell, at least, with a number of people with whom I have spoken. It is the quiet undertow of one's living that reveals itself only in a deep and obscure conviction that one cannot get out of trying to be holy. It is what is nurtured by a life devoted to prayer and self-denial, and becomes intensified in that way, and can transitorily redirect consciousness away from the world mediated by meaning. In St Ignatius's rules for the discernment of spirits, there is one rule that speaks of consolation that has no cause. And Karl Rahner says that 'no cause' means when it is not directed to an object; it is moving away from the world mediated by meaning; and it can be just a very slight movement.

However personal and intimate, it is not solitary. It can be given to many. The many can recognize in one another a common orientation in their living and feeling, in their criteria and goals. From a common communion with God, there springs a religious community.

This community of faith invites varying expressions. The expressions may be imperative: love the Lord thy God with thy whole heart; narrative: the story of the community's origins and development; ascetic and mystical: the way towards total otherworldly love taught practically; or theoretical: teaching the wisdom, goodness, and love of God, his intentions and purposes in the universe.

Any given community may have a compound of two or three or four. The compound may synthesize them, or take one as basic and use it to interpret and manifest the others. The particular compound of a particular community may remain unchanged for ages, or periodically develop and adapt to new social and cultural situations.

This community of faith can be historical and doctrinal. It is historical in that communities endure, new members replace old, and expression becomes traditional. Thus religion becomes historical. In the general sense, it exists over time, but it can be historical in the deeper sense that total loving, ultimate concern, has the character of a response, an answer to a divine initiative that may not only be the act of creation, but also a divine entry into human history and a communication of God to his people. Such has been the religion of Israel and Christianity.

This has implications for our understanding of revelation. Man's life is informed by meaning. We are living humanly when we are awake, when there is an element of meaning in our lives, not when we are asleep. Revealed religion means that there is a divine entry into the meaning that informs human living.

As response, faith takes on a new dimension. It remains the power of total loving to reveal and uphold all that is good. It remains the bond that unites the religious community in mutual recognition, that directs common judgments of value, that purifies beliefs. But it becomes recognition of God's own love, a hearkening to the word of Emmanuel, of God with us. The history of its origins and developments becomes doctrine as well as narrative; faith takes on the dimensions of belief. As the subject grasped by ultimate concern can discern others similarly grasped, so too he can discern God's expression of his total love not only in nature but also in history.

Faith, then, I have been describing as the eye of otherworldly love and the recognition of God's own love. Such recognition is on the level of personal encounter. Newman's device is *cor ad cor loquitur*, heart speaks to heart. The first four of the functional specialties – research, interpretation, history, dialectic – gradually elevate the object with which one is dealing. Insofar as you are dealing with research, you are dealing simply with data; insofar as you are doing interpretation, the data have a meaning that you are trying to determine. Insofar as you move on to history, you are dealing with human beings bearing witness. And in the fourth, dialectic, you are confronted; you have personal encounter of the oppositions of the dialectic. Religious conversion is a response to that encounter; it is on the level of encounter. The community as fellowship of love at the service of mankind is the sign raised up among the nations; and its members speaking from the heart speak effectively to those whose hearts the Spirit fills.

Faith subsists and is propagated on a level quite beyond philosophy or history or human science. The latter are the work of Pascal's reason: of experience, understanding, and judgment. But faith is the eye of an other-worldly love, and that love itself is God's own gift. It is on the level of feelings, values, beliefs, actions, personal encounters, of community existence, community action, community tradition.

However, to say that faith subsists and is propagated on a level beyond experience, understanding, and judgment, on the existential level, in no way implies that faith is without experience, understanding, and judgment. There is a unity to human consciousness; and the higher levels do not suppress but presuppose and complement the lower. Without experience, there is nothing to be understood; without understanding, there is nothing to be judged; without judgment, there is nothing to be loved, valued, achieved. On the positive side, the many operations come together and cumulatively regard a single, identical object, so that what is experienced is what is to be understood, what is understood is what is to be affirmed, what is affirmed is what is to be evaluated. The partial objects cumulate into a single object, and faith cannot be separated from the others, although its distinctive characteristics are found on the existential level.

On God as object, I said something yesterday,[5] and I want to say something perhaps a little more refined today. God is not an object among the objects acknowledged by positivists, empiricists, Kantians. He is not an object of natural or human science. He is not an object in the naive realist sense in which an object is 'out there' and a subject is 'in here.' He is an object for intentional and real self-transcendence, inasmuch as people think of him, affirm his existence and attributes, fear, worship, and love him, speak of him and praise him: in other words, in the sense of what is intended, not in the sense of what is looked at. For an object in the sense of what is intended is simply the content of self-transcending intentionality, or what the content refers to. The above acts are acts of such intentionality, and they refer to God. The possibility of God being an object within a horizon rests on the unrestricted character of intending.

However, God is also subject in a unique relationship, insofar as the love of God is given to us. It is a unique relationship; it is not the same sort of relationship as you have in mutual love between human beings. They are, as it were, collaborators in a common task, in a common way of life. They are a 'we' in which one is beside the other. But the love of God that tends

5 See above, p. 547.

to get away from images and concepts and systems and cultural media is a relationship to God as the one who is loved; and the 'I-Thou' is prior to any conceptual or any other type of objectification. It is a subject-to-subject relationship, not of the lateral type that we have in human love, but of a reference back to God and forward to the whole of God's creation, and laterally, love of one's neighbor because of love of God.

Now that love of God, relationship to God as subject, can be objectified, or I would not be able to talk about it. When I start talking about it I'm objectifying it, and then God as subject becomes subject as object; just as when I speak, I speaking am subject, but I speaking of myself am speaking of subject as object. I have objectified myself when I speak of myself.

Consequently, the movement from a purely philosophic approach to God to a religious approach is the difference between conceiving God as object, operating on the first three levels mainly, and objectifying the relation to God as subject, subject as object. There is a difference between a religious discourse based upon religious experience and, on the other hand, philosophic discourse which does not take that into account.

Now, there are people that try to say that the God of Abraham, Isaac, and Jacob is not the God of the philosophers. To me that is breaking down the unity of human consciousness, the capacities of human consciousness to develop. There is a greater fullness and richness to God as apprehended as the subject that is objectified as compared with God just as object. But it is all in the one process of self-transcendence. The intellectual, the moral, and the religious are three stages in human self-transcendence, and they are intimately related to one another. To try to separate them, to say it is a different God that you have an intellectual apprehension of, may be a very sound response to feelings, but if you want a real distinction you have to have contradictory predicates, and there are no contradictory predicates there. To say that *A* is not *B*, you have to have something about *A* that you can't predicate of *B*, and you do not have that in this case; it is a continuous development.

3 Conversions and Breakdowns

Conversions may be intellectual, moral, or religious. I will have something to say on each one, although I have probably said a lot on them already.

Intellectual conversion is a radical clarification, and consequently the elimination of an exceedingly stubborn and misleading set of myths about reality, objectivity, and human knowledge. It distinguishes the world of immediacy and the world mediated by meaning. The distinction noted is made in the world mediated by meaning. Distinctions occur only there, not in the world of immediacy. It acknowledges the reality and priority of the world of immediacy, but the acknowledgment is effected by meaning. It grants that without the world of immediacy, we would never arrive at a world mediated by meaning. But granting this is an act of meaning. It goes on to point out that any questions one asks about the world of immediacy or any answers one gives only serve to make the world of immediacy one of the objects meant within the world mediated by meaning. Finally, it adds that any account of human knowing, of its criteria of objectivity, of the universe thereby known, must be an account, not simply of the world of immediacy but of that world and of the intricate process from it to the world mediated by meaning. In other words, an account of objectivity is not just an account of experiencing. It has to be an account of the normativeness of intelligence and rationality, of trying to understand and demanding sufficient evidence, and of the absoluteness contained when by grasping an unconditioned one assents unconditionally.

The cognitional myth, at least for visual Western man, is that the real is 'out there now,' and that objectivity is a matter of taking a good look. That is not merely in philosophy. It penetrates hermeneutics, it penetrates the writing of history. There has been a *Krisis des Historismus* in this century, and it is largely getting over mistakes about objectivity. Carl Becker is the main person on this problem in the States; but there are others in Germany and France, and so on.

When that has been said, it follows that when the criteria of the process of setting up the world mediated by meaning are ignored as merely subjective, so that experiencing is what counts and understanding and judgment are purely subjective elements, the result is an empiricism. When it is discovered that human knowing is anything but just taking a good look, that it is all sorts of other things, that it proceeds on at least three levels, and the empiricist notion of reality is retained, you get a negation of empiricist reality without any other reality coming in its place, and so you get an idealism. It is only when one uncovers intentional self-transcendence in judgment, in the process of coming to know, that a critical realism becomes possible. This is not merely a technical point in philosophy. Empiricisms, idealisms, and realisms name three totally different horizons with no identical objects. When an empiricist is saying what he means, he is intending something that no idealist can know about, talk about, or think about, and no realist either. The same holds for the other two.

You get this in the sciences. The empiricist interpretation of quantum theory is that it cannot be about physical reality because it does not deal with objects, but only with relations between phenomena, and not very determinate relations at that. The idealist agrees – of course, it deals with relations between phenomena – and adds that of course the same is true of all theories and of the whole of human knowing. The critical realist will disagree with both because any verified hypothesis probably is true, and what probably is true refers to what in reality probably is so. The emphasis is on the judgment.

Again, what are historical facts? For the empiricist they are what was 'out there' and capable of being looked at. For the idealist they are mental constructions carefully based on data recorded in documents. For the critical realist, they are events in the world truly mediated by acts of meaning. They are known through acts of meaning.

We have had a lot in this century on demythologization and myth. There are psychological, anthropological, and philosophical answers to the question about myth. But besides these, there are also reductionist answers. Myth is narrative about entities not to be found within an empiricist, an historicist, an existentialist horizon. That notion of myth takes one's horizon as the measure of all things, and in that way that type of criticism is just the introduction of a reductionism.

I have given illustrations from science and history and in talk of demythologization, but illustrations can be multiplied indefinitely, for philosophic issues are universal in scope, and some form of naive realism seems to appear utterly unquestionable to visual Western man until he has an intellectual conversion. As soon as he begins to speak of knowing, of objectivity, of reality, there crops up the assumption that knowing is a sort of looking. To be liberated from that view, to discover intentional self-transcendence in the process of coming to know, is to break often long-ingrained habits of thought and speech, and to acquire the mastery in one's own house that comes of knowing what one is doing when one is knowing. It is a conversion, a new beginning, a fresh start.

Second, moral conversion changes the criterion of one's decisions and choices from satisfactions to values. As children or minors, we are persuaded, cajoled, ordered, compelled to do what is right. As our knowledge of human reality increases, as our responses to human values are strengthened and refined, more and more our mentors leave us to ourselves so that our liberty may exercise its ever-advancing thrust toward authenticity. We move to the existential moment when we discover that our choosing affects ourselves more than the chosen objects, and it is up to each of us to decide for himself what he is to make of himself. It is the time for the exercise of vertical liberty, and then moral conversion consists in opting for the truly good, for value against satisfaction, when value and satisfaction conflict.

But it is not just that initial moment. It has to spread out in the whole of one's living. One has to keep developing one's knowledge of human reality and potentiality as it is concretely in the developing situation. One has to keep distinct its elements of progress and decline, to continue scrutinizing one's intentional responses to values and their implicit scale of preferences, to listen to criticism and protest, to remain ready to learn from others. For moral knowledge is the proper possession only of morally good men, and until one has merited that title one has still to advance and to learn.

Thirdly, there is religious conversion. It is being grasped by ultimate concern. It is otherworldly falling in love. It is total and permanent self-surrender without conditions, qualifications, reserves. But it is such a surrender, not as an act, but as a dynamic state distinct from, prior to, and principle of subsequent acts. It is revealed in retrospect as an undertow of existential consciousness, as a fated acceptance of a vocation to holiness, as an increasing passivity in prayer. It is interpreted differently in the context of different religions. The Christian tradition distinguishes, from Augustine on, between operative and cooperative grace. Operative grace is, to use a passage from Ezekiel, plucking out the heart of stone and putting in the heart of flesh. That is God's action. God operates on us. Cooperative grace is using the heart of flesh to transform all one's living.

There are the relations between the three conversions. The three are modalities of self-transcendence, and their relationships can be best described, when all three are in the same person, in terms of sublation. I'm using sublation in Karl Rahner's sense[6] rather than in Hegel's sense; namely, if one takes moral conversion as higher than intellectual, and religious conversion as higher than moral, then the higher goes beyond the lower, introduces something new and distinct, puts everything on a new basis, yet so far from interfering with the lower or destroying it, needs it, includes it, preserves all its proper features and properties and carries them forward to a fuller realization within a richer context.

Hence, moral conversion goes beyond the value 'truth' to values generally. It promotes the subject to a new, existential level of consciousness and establishes him as an originating value. But this in no way interferes with or weakens his devotion to truth; he still needs truth, for he must apprehend reality and real potentiality before he can respond to its value. The truth he

6 Karl Rahner, *Hörer des Wortes* (Munich: Kösel, 1963) 40.

needs is still the truth attained in accord with the exigencies of rational consciousness. But now his pursuit of it is all the more meaningful and significant because it occurs within and plays an essential role in the far richer context of the pursuit of all values.

Similarly, religious conversion goes beyond moral. Questions for intelligence, for reflection, for deliberation reveal the eros of the human spirit, its capacity and its desire for self-transcendence. But that capacity meets fulfilment, that desire turns to joy, when religious conversion transforms the existential subject into a subject-in-love, a subject held, grasped, possessed, owned through a total and so otherworldly love. There is then a new basis for all valuing and doing good. In no way are the fruits of intellectual or moral conversion negated or diminished. On the contrary, all human pursuit of the true and the good is included within and furthered by a cosmic context and purpose. And as well, there now accrues to man the power of love to enable him to accept the suffering involved in undoing the effects of decline.

It is not to be thought, however, that religious conversion means no more than a new and more efficacious ground for the pursuit of intellectual and moral ends. Religious loving is without qualifications. This lack of limitation, though it corresponds to the unrestricted character of human questioning, does not pertain to this world. Holiness abounds in moral goodness, but it has a distinct dimension of its own. It is otherworldly fulfillment, joy, peace, bliss. In Christian experience, these are the epiphenomena of a being-in-love that is the gift of a loving, if mysterious and uncomprehended, God.

Sinfulness, similarly, is distinct from moral evil. It is the privation of total loving, a radical lovelessness. It can be hidden by sustained superficiality, by evading ultimate questions, by absorption in all that the world offers to challenge our resourcefulness, to relax our bodies, to distract our minds. But escape may not be permanent, and then instead of fulfillment there is unrest, instead of joy there is fun, instead of peace there is disgust: a depressive disgust with oneself or a manic, hostile, even violent disgust with mankind.

Religious conversion is from sinfulness to holiness, from radical lovelessness to otherworldly being in love, from captivity to the powers of darkness to redemption and liberation in the kingdom of God. Sin is not just moral fault but an offense against the goodness of God. The fact that I have sinned calls forth both regret and sorrow for the past and the firmest purpose not to sin in the future. Can such detestation, such sorrow, such purpose change anything? The Christian answer is the mediating death and resurrection of Christ. For in Christ, God was reconciling the world to himself.

Besides conversions there are breakdowns. What has been built up so slowly and so laboriously by the individual, the society, the culture, can collapse. Intentional self-transcendence is neither an easy notion to grasp nor a readily accessible datum of consciousness to be verified. That the real is what you feel may be crude, but for most it is convincing. Values have a certain esoteric imperiousness, but can they outweigh carnal pleasure, wealth, power? Religion, undoubtedly, had its day, but is not that day over? Is it not an illusory comfort for weaker souls, an opium distributed by the rich to quieten the poor, a mythical projection of man's own excellence into the sky?

Initially, not all but some religion is pronounced illusory, not all but some moral precepts are rejected as ineffective and useless, not all truth but some kind of metaphysics is condemned as mere talk. The negations may be true, an effort to offset decline. But they may be false, the beginning of decline. In the latter case, some part of past cultural achievement is being destroyed. It will cease being a familiar component in cultural experience, it will recede into a forgotten past for historians, perhaps, to rediscover and reconstruct. Moreover, this elimination of a genuine part means that a previous whole has been mutilated, that some balance has been upset, that the remainder will become distorted in an effort to fill the vacuum, to take over the functions once performed by the part that has been dropped. Finally, such elimination, mutilation, distortion will have to be ardently admired as the forward march of progress, and while they may give rise to objective grounds for further criticism, that can be met by still more progress, by way of still more elimination, mutilation, distortion.

Once a process of dissolution has begun, it tends to perpetuate itself. Nor is it confined to some single uniform course. Different nations, different classes of society, different age groups can select different parts of past achievement for elimination, different mutilations to be effected, different distortions to be provoked. Increasing dissolution will then be matched by increasing divisions, incomprehension, suspicion, distrust, hostility, hatred, violence. The body social is torn apart in many ways, and its cultural soul has been rendered incapable of reasonable convictions and responsible commitments. For convictions and commitments rest on judgments of fact and judgments of value. Such judgments, in turn, rest largely on beliefs. Few indeed are the people that pressed on almost any point must not shortly have recourse to what they have believed. Such recourse can be efficacious only when believers present a solid front, only when intellectual, moral, and religious skeptics are a small, and as yet, uninfluential minority.

But their numbers can increase, their influence can mount, their voice can take over the book market, the educational system, the mass media. Then believing begins to work not for but against intellectual, moral, and religious self-transcendence. What had been an uphill but universally respected course collapses into the peculiarity of an outdated minority.

So much for the process of decline, on which you can get a lot more in Toynbee's *Study of History*. And that does it for the three topics that I had in this morning's account of religion, namely, religious expression, faith, and conversions and breakdowns. And we now have a break followed by a question period.[7]

7 See Discussion 1968-6 below, pp. 626–33.

1968

Discussion 1[1]

Question: Do you exclude the possibility of another animal developing that won't work in this irrevisable structure?

Lonergan: I don't know anything about that. In other words, I'm going on 'what do you mean by revision now?' If we have some evidence for considering some other possibility, we will take that into account and proceed in accord with the evidence. I'm not given to speculation.

Question: How does memory fit into these operations or into this scheme that you have given us here?

Lonergan: Well, enormously. In other words, I've been giving you a cross-section, but experience accumulates: you remember the past, and in the light of it you anticipate the future – sensitive memory. Insights accumulate – intellectual memory. Your judgments accumulate. We say that a child reaches the age of reason at the age of seven. That is, by that time, after seven years, he has learnt enough to be able to make a few good judgments. But he is a minor until he is twenty-one. He can't make too many good judgments; he isn't responsible before the law in civil matters. The development of judgment is a terrific accumulation.

Question: With regard to the heightening of one's consciousness as opposed to intention, is it possible to be stunted in that development so that one is not conscious of one's operations and only operates as a response to phenomena?

---

1 Wednesday, 3 July 1968, Lauzon CD/MP3 482 (48200A0E060).

Lonergan: No. People are always conscious, as far as I know; there is no evidence that people aren't conscious, except if they are in a coma or a deep sleep, a dreamless sleep. Even when one dreams, one is conscious.

Question: Heightening one's consciousness is something one has to do personally?

Lonergan: People can give you help and tips, and tell you what to attend to and so on. I didn't attempt, for example, to give any heightening of understanding as an experience this morning, simply because there are so many different varieties of it; and to go through the lot is rather long. The first eight chapters of *Insight* illustrate insights.

Question: Why does consciousness always have to be on the periphery?

Lonergan: There is the span of attention, you can attend to more or less. And that is heightened. Piaget says that until a child is able to deal with an object it may be embarrassed by its presence but it can't do anything about it; it requires the process of assimilation and adjustment, what he calls an adaptation. And gradually the child is able to deal with that object. I remember once in a group of philosophers and scientists, the question was put, Is science going to continue developing indefinitely? And the professor of chemistry said. 'Well, in the last five years the theoretical developments in chemistry have increased enormously the range of data with which we deal.' In other words, you don't apprehend the data without the conceptual apparatus.

Similarly, you can think of an approach to therapy, such as that of Carl Rogers, where he wants people to be able to admit into some sort of explicit consciousness the feelings they feel and are conscious of, in the sense in which I'm using the word 'conscious.' A person can have feelings but they may not be objectified.

Question: Is it not introspective and intentional work?

Lonergan: It is not introspective in the sense of taking a look in. You can work in two ways. You can advert to that element in consciousness, emphasize it, for example, by opening and closing your eyes, and similarly for the other acts. There is that emphasis on that side. On the other hand, insofar as you have the conceptual apparatus at your disposal, you have the materials for naming different elements in your consciousness and identifying them. It is an investigation like any other investigation, and there is a constant intercourse, a dialogue, between the data and the insights and formulations.

Question: But I don't see how consciousness itself is made different.

Lonergan: It is heightened. If I put an equation on the board you will apprehend it much better if you know what it means. Consciousness, without the conceptual development, the intellectual side, is there, it is given, but you haven't got hold of it properly. A number of therapists have come out with explicit statements to the effect that the so-called unconscious is not unconscious at all. Stekel is rather brutal about it. He says that we are not dealing with things that people don't know anything about; they know all about it but they won't admit it. Karen Horney says they don't know it, but it registers. Hostie, who writes about Jung, says that for Jung, an object is not conscious unless it is objectified. And I think the German origins of a lot of this come from the word *Bewusstsein*, because *Bewusstsein* means being an object, being known, and what is conscious is not yet an object.

Question: Are you planning to have more certitude in transcendental method than in scientific method?

Lonergan: The scientists are more certain of their methods than they are of their results. Their methods change much more slowly than their theories and systems. What I say about transcendental method is that it is not open to radical revision, simply because by revision you mean a certain process, and the transcendental method is identical with that process that you mean by revision. In other words, the thing bends back on itself at a point. You don't have that in any scientific method. It doesn't mean that any objectified account of the cognitional process or the cognitional and volitional process is guaranteed to be immutable – not at all. One can say that there is no unimpeachable account of the principle of contradiction, and while people could work one out that met all the objections that anyone has thought of up to now, still, this doesn't guarantee that in the next ten years somebody else won't find some more difficulties so that you would have to shift things around to get an adequate formulation of it. There is always that problem in the formulation. But, on the other hand, insofar as you define precisely what you mean by revision, you have a limitation on the possibilities of revision, a limitation of the radical transforming revision. The revision that adds to accuracy and clarity and precision and that enriches is always possible.

Question: Is transcendental method trying to write something like a *Prior Analytics?*

Lonergan: In Aristotle, that was syllogism, and it had to do with terms, and propositions to a lesser extent.

Question continued: You talked about looking at method materially and formally, and isn't that like prior and posterior?

Lonergan: No, that 'materially and formally' had to do with dynamic materially – it consists of operations, movements – and dynamic formally – it assembles itself.

Question: A scientist wouldn't use the term 'transcendental method,' so why do you use it?

Lonergan: Well, it is transcendental simply because it is not categorially determined to some particular field. But it is the starting-off point for any method. I gave a sketch in my second section this morning, a preliminary notion of method. And I gave a sketch of method in the natural sciences, just a sketch. All the elements there are also in our preliminary notion.

Question: But the scientist's method might change?

Lonergan: Yes. But where it changes is not in a shift from attention to inattention, from intelligence to stupidity, from reasonableness to silliness, and from responsibility to irresponsibility. It is a more detailed intelligence, a more precise attention, a more precise kind of reasonableness, and so on. This is how scientific method changes and develops.

Question continued: There is a real, very close relation between the unthematic and the thematic. The thematic is really limited by the unthematic, I think. As you mentioned, the unrevisability is not absolute but limited.

Lonergan: Yes.

Question: Is it correct to say that the analysis and exercise of transcendental method has been the concern of philosophers right down the ages?

Lonergan: Insofar as they've been good. You find that element recurring. It is in Heidegger's *Daseinsanalyse* and Jaspers's *Existenzerhellung*, and so on.

Question: You would hold this to be the core of philosophy?

Lonergan: What is not this, the theologian need not bother about in philosophy.

Question: Why are there so many different accounts of method by philosophers? (The questioner gave the brief example of Husserl.)

Lonergan: There is what has been called the liberty of making mistakes, and in philosophy this is rather large. For example, Husserl is very definitely marked by his beginnings. He began as a theorist of mathematics; he discovered the difference between objective meaning and psychological event; that was the big thing he did. Saying that two and two is four is something more than a certain psychological event that goes on in me. Then he had the Aristotelian ideal of science in terms of necessity, and that pretty well stayed with him all his life: moving to the necessary, eliminating all the contingent. His successive reductions are a matter of eliminating the contingent and getting hold of the necessary. That concern for the necessary, to my mind, is Aristotelian and just the opposite of modern science, which aims at an intelligibility that is hypothetical, the intelligibility of what can be, not of what must be. The law of falling bodies has been verified for four hundred years directly and indirectly, but it is not a statement of what must be but of what de facto is so. You have all these variations because if one man gets off on the wrong foot, the next man is dealing with him, and so on.

Question: It seems that transcendental method is necessary, and yet you approach it looking for the hypothetical. The process has to be what it is because it is exhaustive and there are no alternatives.
Lonergan: Well, it is not necessary absolutely but hypothetically. Socrates, while he is sitting down, necessarily is sitting down as long as he is sitting down. If I'm intelligent, then there is an instance of intelligence, if intelligence means 'If this, then this,' and so on. But it is the de facto empirically existing subject that is the basis of everything I'm saying. And I'm asking each subject to be his own basis and to find in himself what his own basis is. He exists contingently, de facto. He needn't exist, and he needn't be exactly this sort of person. So I don't say that for all time all are going to have this structure. But if you have it, then that's the basis on which you proceed.

Question: Is there any essential difference between my affirmation of reality and your affirmation of reality?
Lonergan: Oh, yes. My own affirmation is based on my own immediate experience, and so on. I have plenty of evidence that the next man is just as intelligent, reasonable, responsible as I am, but it isn't the same kind of evidence. In other words, he has his own immediate evidence.

Question: Did you say that insight may lead to a formulation, depending on the level of culture?
Lonergan: Yes. In other words, the possibility of formulation is the possibility of having a language in which one can speak about these things and

having an audience to whom one can speak about them. You can't go into elementary school and start talking about insights, because the children would say, 'Oh, a dog understands; if you call him he comes,' and so on.

Question: So you meant something technical by formulation, not just another word for insight.
Lonergan: I mean something technical, to some extent.

Question: In your levels of consciousness, you distinguished a vertical movement and a horizontal movement, and the distinction was not clear to me.
Lonergan: You need the vertical movement for all your operations to occur consciously. You start out from the data of sense. When you are conscious, distinctly conscious, of all the operations, you can start naming them, relating them to one another, experiencing the relations as the spontaneous movement of your consciousness from one to the next; and that spontaneous movement now is intelligent, now is reasonable, now is responsible. You can make the judgment that no one is going to claim to be a non-responsible, non-reasonable, non-intelligent somnambulist – or very few, and we needn't worry about them. This view can't be revised as long as you have some precise notion of what you mean by revision, some precise and plausible notion of what you mean by revision. The horizontal movement is from the data of consciousness to the objectification of the subject and his operations. The vertical movement is from the data of sense to physics, chemistry, biology, and the human sciences, history, and so on. So you really have the two in conjunction in the human sciences, to some extent.

Question: When you talk about a horizontal movement or a vertical movement and relating on each of the levels: inquiry, insight, formulation, from reflection to judgment, and from deliberation to evaluation to decision ...
Lonergan: Well, that also is true but it is a different viewpoint from the one I was using just now. In other words, you can use horizontal and vertical in terms of that diagram. But you can use it again in terms of proceeding from data of sense to the full actuation of consciousness, and then from consciousness to its objectification. This is a scheme, and actual process bounces up and down and across every way. And there is the cross-section, the cumulative process; memory is very essential.

Question: Don't we often go from sensation to affirmation, and is this not essential for survival?

Lonergan: You are running along in such a case on your acquired insights. Is this a house? Well, you don't have to figure out what a house is.

Question: [The precise words of the question are not clear, but the same questioner was relating the previous question to Hume.]
Lonergan: Causality is a case of intelligibility, something grasped by insight. It is part of constructing the object. If you conceive knowing as taking a look, you can just empty this all out and get down to sense data, phenomena, and so on.

Question: [The same questioner pursues the issue, referring to the survival mechanism as a short system.]
Lonergan: These elements are all operative in what you call the short system, except that you have your judicial context already made, the actual development acquired, and you see that no further insights are needed to say that this is a house or this is my wife, etc.

Question: [The same questioner pursues the issue further.]
Lonergan: In other words, we are healthy animals long before we develop intelligently and rationally.

Question: [The same questioner pursues the issue yet further.]
Lonergan: Is it to affirmation? You can have the healthy animal, and you can have what I am calling human knowledge. And you can have human knowledge reinterpreted on the animal basis, and you get a sort of naive realism out of it. You can have a rejection of the animal basis as what human knowledge really isn't without denying that that's the right notion of the real, and then you get an idealism. There is a whole set of possibilities, and these are the fundamental philosophic options. And the individual himself can develop differently.

Question (same questioner): What about phenomenology? Does it not miss the point on this?
Lonergan: In general, phenomenology is in the idealist tradition, and it hasn't got hold of the key step from what seems to me to what is so, the grasp of an unconditioned, an absolute, that grounds that. But I wouldn't subscribe to any blanket condemnation of phenomenology. What the phenomenologists are doing is having insights without calling them insights. They are seeking insights. Their weakness is on the level of judgment.

There is a lack of a criteriology that can be had only by understanding the way insights develop. There are weaknesses to phenomenology, but, on the other hand, it has done an awful lot of good.

Question: [The same questioner asks whether the one who starts from sensible data does not go back to sensible data for confirmation.]
Lonergan: They're in a new context now. There is the sensitive flow, the flow of insights and formulations; the insights are structuring the sensitive flow. Insofar as this process of insight structuring the flow, and meeting every further question as it arises, is done intelligently, you have a link, a normative link between the data as given and the formulation in your conception. In other words, insofar as intelligence has been developing in accordance with the demands of intelligence, you have this link. You have an 'if, then': if these data, then a house; if these data, then my wife, or whatever you please. Consequently, on the level of judgment you put together the link, the 'if, then,' and the givenness of the data, and you get whatever your formulated object is. That is a general sketch of the way in which judgment proceeds. Now, to apply it to all the different kinds of judgments, see chapter 10 of *Insight*. And note, this is not a formulated syllogism. If it were a formulated syllogism, then you would have to have the prosyllogisms that set up your premises. This is just an analysis of the way in which consciousness builds up its objects and judges whether they are.

Question: [The question asks whether Lonergan's theory of meaning holds that the meaning of a term referring to a private mental act is had by reference to the mental act rather than to the term being publicly meaningful and then being used in referential ways. If one accepted the latter theory of meaning, it would seem that the meaning of terms could not come from reference to the private mental acts.]
Lonergan: First of all, this reference to private mental acts is not a universal theory of meaning, it is simply meaning with regard to private mental acts; it is not meaning in general. I say that each person has to find the acts in himself and do his own objectifying, and if he can't, then anything I have to say won't be helpful to him. And the real ground of publicity is not the fact of a consensus; things become public when they move from the level of what appears to me, what seems to me, to what is so, to the unconditioned; I grasp the unconditional grounding judgment; that is the ground of publicity. It may be a probable publicity or a certain publicity, as the case may be. You can approach the matter from the viewpoint of pragmatism and positivism, and say, 'Well, at least it will be public for us because this is the sort of thing we are

going to agree on.' And that is all they mean by it. If you want a theory of meaning based on that, well, then, I'm not going along with it.

Question: According to Wittgenstein, the meaningfulness of language has to be essentially public and is only derivatively private or else it couldn't function as a language.
Lonergan: *In facto esse,* yes; *in fieri,* how do you show it? I don't believe it holds *in fieri,* because I don't see how language could develop, at least the language about personal acts or internal acts.

Question: I think it could be shown how it could be developed, but in a different way. In your terminology a concept is an inner word, which means that it is understood by analogy with an external word. So the primary meaning comes from the external. This shows how it develops.
Lonergan: That's the history of language. Can there develop a language about internal acts at all? The meaning of the term 'insight' as I am using it, and as people who agree with me understand it, comes from the fact that they've had an experience of insights. Now, the experience of insights that they've had has become known as an experience of insights by using more or less standard examples that have become public to communicate them. You can take theorems in geometry, and so on. There is a certain amount of using the public, there is also using the internal experience. And anyone who doesn't have the internal experience would be for me like a blind man hearing about colors.

Question: Doesn't the meaning come from the way in which the term was used in the language?
Lonergan: That is true also, but that isn't the only meaning of the term. In other words, the meaning of words is not just other words.

Question: But it is meaningful only within a system of language. There are presuppositions on how these terms are used referentially.
Lonergan: If you get into presuppositions, you can have a whole metaphysics presupposed. But that isn't to my mind a useful approach. As for my presuppositions on meaning, I have an account of meaning in *Insight* and there will be a further account in the fifth chapter of this course.

Question: Do you have to have a theory of meaning presupposed at the start of *Insight?*

Lonergan: You don't have to have a theory of meaning presupposed; that is just a logical ideal presupposition. I don't do my thinking within a deductivist system.

Question: Are you speaking of isolated acts? Isn't there a structure?
Lonergan: What I'm talking about here is not a set of isolated acts but a pattern of acts, internally related, and you experience the relations, as well as the acts.

Question: So when you speak of deciding as an operation or an act in itself, it has this complexity?
Lonergan: Yes. Perhaps with regard to Fr MacKinnon's question, to go back to it, my tying up terms with experiences occurs at a very specific level in the process. You have a development of chemistry, say, up to the periodic table, and then the definition of all chemical elements in terms of the periodic table and blanks in it for new things that are to be discovered. That is arriving at a basic conceptuality or *Begrifflichkeit*. And in my thought, no matter how this process of arriving at a precise experience of these different kinds of acts in their relations goes on in any particular individual, my basic definitions in cognitional theory are terms and relations set up in correspondence with experienced acts and processes. From that I will get my terms in epistemology and my terms in a general semantics or metaphysics. My metaphysical terms are the correlatives to the terms referring to the terms and relations in the cognitional theory. It is the switch-over from what I call the descriptive to the explanatory stage in a science. There are other terminologies. The positivists usually refer to the explanatory as the descriptive and think of the explanatory in terms of something you can imagine – like the lines of force in Faraday's conception of electromagnetism. But that is a terminological difference. I think you know the difference in a science when you move from one type of thinking to another. And it is with regard to that shift that I'm correlating experiences and basic terms.

Question: On what level do you want to place the meaningfulness of language?
Lonergan: It depends on your aim. Aristotle worked out his psychology, and Thomas worked out his psychology, with metaphysical presuppositions. However, in that way one is never able to clear up metaphysical ambiguities, at least from the psychological viewpoint. You will have the ambiguities imported into your psychology. Insofar as you can arrive at a pattern that isn't

revised, you can set up a basis and see how the different philosophies emerge from that one basis with different presuppositions. In other words, it is a critical problem.

Question: What do you do prior to coming to the critical problem?
Lonergan: You deal with the people that exist and their interests.

1968

Discussion 2[1]

Question: I have a problem about the conversions and their meanings. How do I ever know that, when I accept something on the authority of God, this is an act of supernatural faith as distinct from a natural acceptance of something on the authority of God. If we're going to reflect on our being Christian, how can I ever know that I'm authentically a Christian? I can accept the fact that I can be aware of my act of faith qua assent, but qua supernatural, qua activated by grace, how can I be sure? Can I experience an act of faith qua supernatural?

Lonergan: Aquinas, when he discussed this question, said that you can't have scientific knowledge of the fact that you are in the state of grace, and I imagine that it is the same thing with regard to the supernaturality of your faith, because supernaturality means an intrinsic ordination of the act to the divine essence or the beatific vision. And until you have the beatific vision you can't know whether that relationship is there or not. Consequently, you can't have scientific knowledge. The scientific essence of the supernatural is the relation to the divine essence, and until you know God by his essence you won't know whether that relationship is there or not – scientifically. However, as conjectural – 'By their fruits you shall know them' – you can have good grounds for believing that you are in the state of grace in which your faith is supernatural, from its fruits.

---

1 Monday, 8 July 1968, Lauzon CD/MP3 485 (48500A0E060).

Question: So you can experience the effects of grace?

Lonergan: Yes. And it is manifested in your living, in your convictions.

Question: You extrapolate from this that your experience of believing here and now is a supernatural act of belief, and hence you can reflect upon this as a further self-transcendence?

Lonergan: Well, the thing I'm taking is not belief and not even faith but charity. And, as I said, because our Christianity is usually more in aspiration than in effect, we have to fill it out in various ways. [Reading from his text]: 'Finally, as our Christianity commonly is more an aspiration than an achievement, we have to have recourse to the Christian community, to its store of experience, its traditional wisdom, to awaken in us what is latent in us, to stir our feelings even though our minds are only partly open and our wills are not yet quite ready.'

Question: Is there a scientific element to the supernatural?

Lonergan: There is the intrinsic relation of charity or faith or hope to the divine essence, to God as he is in himself. Scientific knowledge of that includes knowledge of God as he is in himself.

Question: You say, then, that if I accept through my acts out of love merely because it seems to me to suit my cultural environment, I should be able to recognize this by way of your transcendental method?

Lonergan: I don't know that I was setting up something sharply differentiated. I was giving the characteristics of that love, and it is something that develops with the development of the spiritual life. It becomes more conscious over time. But what is your vocation? Is it something that you can't get out of? That reflecting on your own life, over time especially, seeing the things that moved you one way and another and why you acted as you did: in that way you discover grace acting in your life.

Question: But I'm never present to grace as I am to experience, understanding, judging, deciding?

Lonergan: No. It is not the same way. It is something much more fundamental in you – 'You have not chosen me, I have chosen you.'

Question: In other words, there is some deduction in there?

Lonergan: No – some analysis, some finding out that you are not alone. It is the sort of thing that has been neglected, first of all, because Scholasticism has been terrifically objectivist; and secondly, because this technique of heightening consciousness of what is going on in oneself is extremely difficult.

Question: Can you think of it as the new *esse?*
Lonergan: Do not think of it that way. In other words, think of it as on the subjective side, think of it in terms of contrasts: the trivialization of human life, where the religious part of man is ignored; or the fanatical pursuit of finite ends, where religion is taking a wrong manifestation. We will go back to this in the sixth chapter; I am really anticipating now.

Question: What is the relationship between human authenticity and Christian authenticity? Human authenticity is achieved through transcendental method, while apparently Christian authenticity is superior to that, at least in the orientation it has and the profundity that it achieves. How does this relate to pluralism, especially when Christianity is one religion among many? Would one have to be authentically Christian in order to be humanly authentic so that Christianity would be the norm for all other religions?
Lonergan: We can go about it a posteriori. Friedrich Heiler, 'The History of Religions as a Preparation for the Cooperation of Religions,' *The History of Religions*, edited by M. Eliade and J. Kitagawa, Chicago: University of Chicago Press, 1959,[2] takes seven points that are common to all the higher religions, and he lists them and develops them. And they all come from something similar to this love of God that I was talking about, this being in love. And that fits in with the Catholic position quite easily, because God gives sufficient grace to everyone.

Question: So Christian authenticity would just be necessary for those who are Christians, and the authenticity that Christianity brings could be brought to them by any of the higher religions?
Lonergan: The comparison of the different religions and what they achieve and so on is something for a posteriori study. When I was talking about this this morning I was using Christian authenticity in contrast to human authenticity in the sense of being attentive, intelligent, reasonable, responsible. When I was speaking about this further authenticity I was speaking of an actuation of the element of the unrestricted that is in human conscious intentionality. That thrust to self-transcendence that is constitutive of the whole actuation of the human spirit has in it a place for

2   See above, p. 465, note 13.

something that moves to otherworldliness, to something that is not of this world – the relationship to that. In that sense, the question of God is implicit in human conscious intentionality. And I conceived infused charity as an actuation of that, in that precise respect of the unrestricted, the otherworldly. I am speaking about it as a fact, quoting St Paul; I am speaking about it as a fact, quoting Friedrich Heiler for the high religions. And, I think, going backwards to the earlier stages of the high religions, the more primitive stages, its main difference is cultural, modes of expression, and so on.

Question: So it is the experience that is normative, not Christianity?
Lonergan: As I was talking this morning, yes. I haven't unfolded Christianity; I am unfolding the extension of transcendental method into theology. But it's true of Christianity: there is this charity in Christianity. But I'm not doing traditional apologetics or traditional fundamental theology, or anything like that.

Question: I am wondering if it is authentic because it is Christian or Christian because it is authentic?
Lonergan: Well, it is what it is. Draw on any adjective that you please. But it isn't the same as 'attentive, intelligent, reasonable, responsible.'

Question: If you say authentically human and authentically Christian.
Lonergan: Take it as authentically religious.

Question: So you are talking Christian as religious?
Lonergan: If you want to quarrel about the word 'Christian,' I'll throw it out and say 'religious.' But I am not identifying Christianity with religion or religion with Christianity, or anything like that.

Question: Are you talking about authentically human and authentically religious?
Lonergan: Yes. But, of course, I don't mean that you are inhuman when you are religious; please save me that!

Question: What does being authentically religious add to being authentically human?
Lonergan: That love of God above all things, with your whole heart, your whole soul, all your mind, and all your strength.

Question: The word 'God' is important there?

Lonergan: Yes, but can we drop this till chapter 6? Our hearts are restless until they rest in Thee. Does that mean something to you? That's Augustine, and it means something to Bultmann. The question of God is implicit in this human dynamism.

Question: You were throwing out a challenge to the theologian. What was that?

Lonergan: I'm afraid that isn't big enough a clue. Could you tell me a little more about what I said?

Question: You said this was a challenge for theologians.

Lonergan: Does anyone have the context?

Question (another person attempting to clarify): Working out the categories as the theologian's job, as opposed to the methodologist, who presents the procedures for doing that.

Lonergan: Yes, but I don't know that I used the word 'challenge.' [Reading from his notes:] 'The kernel of theology, if that's what Rahner means by *Fundamentaltheologie*, then it is perhaps an account of the origins, genesis, development, present state, possible further adaptations and improvements, in the categories in which Christians understand themselves, communicate with one another, and announce the Gospel to the world.' Is that it?

Question: I think it was with regard to the data of faith that you get to apply your transcendental method, the act of conversion – you talked of some sort of *Daseinsanalysis* of the act of faith.

Lonergan: What I am doing in introducing a further authenticity besides human authenticity is the sort of thing or question that was raised by Fr Richardson: would there be a *Daseinsanalyse* of the Christian?

Question: Does your methodology leave open the determination of the relationship between the natural and the supernatural? Perhaps there are several different ways of conceiving the relation between the two. Is it specified in your methodology? Does your methodology lay a structure for a particular relationship, or for any relationship?

Lonergan: Well, I add a general derivation and a special derivation of the categories parallel to the Scholastic use of Aristotle for an apprehension of man and of nature and an analogous set of concepts based upon Aristotle for their conception of grace; they conceive grace as habit and act, and so on. The analogous concepts apply to the supernatural order, the economy of grace. But we have to expand terrifically what the Scholastics did. For centuries, the one human science, practically, was law. That is why we have so many juridical analogies of things conceived simply in juridical terms. We have to draw our analogies from all the fields of all the modern human sciences and study those aspects, and even study things like the sociology of religion, which studies the social aspects of a religion, and the psychology of religion, and so on. Fundamentally, the meaning of natural and supernatural is in the patristic statement: *Christus nostra sumpsit ut sua nobis daret.*[3] The *nostra* are the natural and the *sua* are the supernatural.

Question: Going back to your quest for God, the innate quest for God in man, I believe you are stating now that this is an extension of the original question of the human spirit to the level of faith?

Lonergan: Yes. This is really the sixth chapter, but I better say something about it! We have our questions for intelligence. But why should the universe be intelligible? Why should the understanding have anything to do with knowing the universe? Is there an intelligent being behind the universe making it intelligible? It is a question about God. Again, the different spheres of being. There is the logarithm of the square root of minus one. There is a moon. There is Boston College. Quantum theory is an acceptable hypothesis or theory, and so on. To talk about genera and species is to speak about logical entities. How do you distinguish between the different spheres of being? There isn't a logarithm of the square root of minus one in the same sense as there is a Boston College or this institute. Where do these differences arise? Well, they arise in the criteria of the judgment. Every one of our judgments rests upon a grasp of a virtually unconditioned: if A then B, but A, therefore B. But the conditions to be fulfilled vary. The conditions for a mathematical statement are that it can be derived from acceptable mathematical axioms. The axioms are simply postulated; it is true that there exists the logarithm of the square root of minus one, if you can derive it from a suitable set of postulates. It can be done, therefore it exists. But if you say Boston College exists, well, you have to have an idea of a college and verify it in a whole institution. It is a matter of concrete data. The mathematical can be merely mathematical only in virtue of the real. You have to have the real presupposed to say this is merely mathematical or merely logical or merely

3 Christ assumed what is ours in order to give us what is his.

hypothetical. It has to presuppose the real, otherwise it wouldn't be merely mathematical – if mathematics was all that there was.

We now come to the further step, the transcendent. While we know God by grasping a virtually unconditioned, still, God is not just a conditioned whose conditions happen to be fulfilled. That is not what anybody means by God – a contingent being. He is formally unconditioned. He has no conditions. So the total negation of conditions that you have in God is something that is presupposed even by the real world.

Question: How does that differ from St Anselm's proof for the existence of God?

Lonergan: Well, it differs because I'm talking about a real mind; I am not comparing concepts. Then, the third level. The whole process from the nebulae, the cosmogenesis, the evolutionary process, the historical development of man: in that whole process is the first occurrence of morality, of moral goodness, of real self-transcendence, found in man? Or is this process itself something that is fundamentally morally good? Is there a moral author of the universe? Here the question of God arises again. And those questions come right out of the very structure of conscious intentionality in man. The question of God is implicit in the structure. It comes out of the structure. The question of God is not something totally outside the human horizon, something to which people will say, 'Theism and atheism are both totally irrelevant.' In that case, God would be something outside, beyond the human horizon. When you say that the question of God is implicit in man's conscious intentionality, you are saying that the question of God is part of the human horizon, that there is a place for that question. Your horizon either will be theist, or there will be a blank somewhere, you will be an agnostic, or if you deny God you will be an atheist, or you will be trivializing religion or putting religious power or force upon a finite object. That's a proposal.

Question: With regard to the giraffe, and the father and the son: You said that the difference between common sense and theory rests on a difference in the subject. Is it that so much as it is the function of the knowledge, that is, the common sense as opposed to the scientific? I'm not sure what you meant by differing in the subject.

Lonergan: It is a difference in the object and the function and in the context. The subject too has to be able to move outside his commonsense world, what Whitehead called the bifurcation of nature. The theoretical apprehension of things is in terms of the relations of things to one another. You measure and then correlate the measurements: you are relating things to one another. The relationship to human senses vanishes. It has slipped out simply by the process of relating measurements to one another and setting up functions that give you this relationship between the measurements in general form, and then working out theories that relate different empirical laws, bringing them into a system. That whole structure is an apprehension of the world. But it is a quite different apprehension, a systematically different apprehension, from the commonsense way of going about things, in which the thing is always related to the subject and to his modes of apprehension and his needs.

Question: So 'theoretical' would mean that distance between the sense data, etc.
Lonergan: Yes. You have it in every science that becomes properly scientific, insofar as there emerge terms that have no direct sensible correlate, like mass, temperature, electromagnetic field, periodic table, evolution.

Question: In your various patterns of experience, where would you find a place for aesthetic experience?
Lonergan: It is neither common sense nor scientific. We will have something to say about that in chapter 5 on Meaning. We will be studying different carriers of meaning. Meaning is realized in language, it is realized in symbols, it is realized in art, it is realized in intersubjectivity.

Question: In the study of religions, when you get to the comparison of structures, is that bringing comparative religion into its own as an explanatory science?
Lonergan: Insofar as you move that way, it moves into explanatory science. The more theological it becomes the more it moves towards an explanatory science. In other words, Eliade as a historian, as a morphologist, as a phenomenologist of religion, will take the question so far but he won't talk about the reality of God or the reality of what these hierophanies refer to. The theologian has to face those further questions, and he tries to teach them.

Question: If you were to rework your Trinity courses and make these eight functional specialties very clear and state the transitions between them, how would you go about re-editing them? Or would you re-edit them?

Lonergan: My work on the Trinity is the start of this thing. The second volume, the *pars systematica*, separates systematics from the dogmatic side, the question of intelligibility – understanding the thing from the question of certainty, which is the dogmatic side. In the introduction to the *pars dogmatica* we separate dogmatic theology, the genesis of the dogmas, the historical genesis of the dogmas, from positive theology, which hasn't got the specific concern.[4] When we say that Lebreton was rather too apologetic in his approach to his treatment of the Trinity, for example, we mean we are taking a more positive approach: what really happened, what was going on in the second century or the third century? Now that positive stuff breaks down into the four: research, interpretation, history, and dialectic.

Question: Would the *verbum* articles fit in as interpretation or as foundations?
Lonergan: More as interpretation. Foundations is a horizon. You take a realist and an idealist, and have them both speak. There is no statement made by the idealist that refers to a realist world, and there is no statement made by the realist that refers to an idealist world, providing they are both presenting their own views. In other words, the interpretation of every statement differs. So the statements are not ultimately what determine the meaning; they are already within a world, within a horizon, an idealist one or a realist one. Similarly, St Paul says that the unspiritual man is not going to grasp a spiritual doctrine; it is meaningless to him; he cannot grasp it. This is a question of the religious horizon, within which religious statements have meaning and are significant. That is the foundational question; it is the objectification of conversion.

Question: Would something like *Insight* therefore be a foundational document?
Lonergan: Insofar as it is self-appropriation, insofar as self-appropriation generates a horizon that people didn't have before, insofar as it is an invitation to a conversion.

Question: How would your search for transcultural categories compare with Bultmann's attempt to demythologize the New Testament?
Lonergan: In his *Theology of the New Testament*,[5] Bultmann deals with the theology of the New Testament and he interprets Pauline and Johannine

---

4 These two volumes are now available as *The Triune God: Doctrines* (see above, p. 25, note 30) and *The Triune God: Systematics* (see above, p. 153, note 12).
5 Rudolf Bultmann, *Theology of the New Testament*, trans. Kendrick Grobel (London: SCM Press, 1955).

terms in terms of *Daseinsanalyse*. That is demythologization in the sense, first, that St Thomas was demythologizing when he was using Aristotle and analogies from Aristotle in his scripture commentaries and in his theology; that is one aspect of it. It is demythologizing in another sense insofar as, for Bultmann, the only objective statements are scientific statements; the objectification of religious experience is necessarily mythical, with the exception of the kerygma. That is the point Buri pulled him up on. Why not go the whole way and call the kerygma a myth too? In other words, just as you will move from things you can directly experience to concepts like mass, temperature, periodic table, and so on, and just as the classifications of plants and animals become explanatory when they are put within an evolutionary context, so in theology there is a movement towards a systematics, in which you really grasp what you are talking about and say it out clearly. As Enrico Castelli remarked, there is no hermeneutic literature on scientific treatises. Euclid's *Elements* was written 2300 years ago. You have to work to understand them, but there is no dispute about what he meant. There can be different interpretations insofar as there are different mathematical theories, and so on, and that can't be helped; but what Euclid was talking about is undisputed. People find Euclid difficult, abstract, and technical, and they find the four gospels very clear and helpful, in that they talk to the heart of man, are sacramental. And yet the hermeneutic literature on the gospels is endless. An element in the theological process is precisely that movement towards clarity. Just where does metaphor begin and end? As for demythologization, well, perhaps the first instance of it is Clement of Alexandria.

Question: Can all theological categories be transcultural, can this goal be attained?

Lonergan: I don't think you want to attain that, because you want to talk to your culture too. But you don't want to be so lost in it that you are conceiving every other culture in the same way and think that we all have to be little Ciceros talking Latin and thinking in Latin categories, and that the criteria for the seminary set down at the Council of Trent have to be applied to the conversion of Africa, that they can't have a native clergy until they get that type of culture. The meaning of the transcultural is that you get enough determinations from transcendental method that your interpretation and apprehension of different cultures is linked by the transcendental element, which can be extended by complicating it and proving it in concrete instances and filling it out, differentiating it, and setting it in motion. But doing those things moves you into the categorial, and the more that occurs, you are introducing determinations that are subject to revision. In other words, theology is being written in each generation for the needs of that generation and for the needs of its apprehension of other generations and other cultures. The point to the transcultural is that it is not an abstract something that fits all but rather the series that enables you to move from any one to any other. That way you can be concrete. Abstraction, where the whole is one thing and you cut off a part, is one thing. But serialization, where you have single and double relations, and so on, that is where you are dealing with the concrete. You are dealing with the concrete, even though you are dealing with and thinking of these various relations or that series of relations. Structures like that are essentially concrete, just as the intention of being, of the intelligible, is intending the concrete, not any abstraction. There is a false emphasis in the Aristotelian and Scholastic (more in the Scholastic than the Aristotelian) notion of abstraction. They wanted a science of the universal and necessary. Why? Because you got the necessary only when you abstracted; as long as you remained in the concrete you were dealing with things that could move and be changed. There is a mistaken emphasis on the abstract there. Modern science is not concerned with any abstractions. It wants to know the concrete reality in its fullness, the complete explanation of all phenomena. Similarly, theology moves towards that: not to a set of truths that will take you through life and provide you with sermon material for every Sunday throughout the year.

Question: Are your transcultural terms anything more than a common language? I'm not sure why you put 'transcendental' in there. For instance, when two scientists from different cultures are talking, is it not just the language of the science?
Lonergan: It is the common language of theologians.

Question: Why the transcendental method, then? I don't see what that adds to it?
Lonergan: It's a rather fundamental difficulty. You're going back to the whole notion of transcendental method, what it means. Any human being can attend or not attend, be intelligent or not intelligent, reasonable or unreasonable, responsible or irresponsible: let's say 'adult.' And that is a fundamental thing.

Question: That seems very obvious to me.
Lonergan: Of course, it is obvious.

Question: I am wondering about the relationship between methodology and theology, which functional specialty does methodology fit into?
Lonergan: The eight functional specialties are the unfolding. I said method is a pattern, a normative pattern of related and recurrent operations yielding cumulative and progressive results. Now theology is a specialized subject: there are field specializations, there are functional specializations, and there are subject specializations. What are these functional specializations? I gave you a list of eight, so theology is not just some one method, it is a set of eight methods, a set of eight normative patterns. Now as to that set of eight normative patterns, you can study them singly, and those will be chapters seven to fourteen: research, interpretation, history, and so on. Or you can be developing certain fundamental notions that will be relevant to the lot, and in the third chapter we are talking about 'Horizons and Categories.' In chapters 4 and 5 we will be working in general at the 'Human Good, Values, Beliefs' and 'Meaning,' so in chapter 6 we will have a start for talking about the good of religion, religious values, religious beliefs, religious meanings, and that will give us the generalities from which we shall proceed to deal singly with each of the eight functional specializations.

Our first day, on Method, was taking the first step in the business. Our second, on functional specialization, was extending the notion of method into theology. 'Horizons and Categories' is setting up theology as something beyond a merely methodical business; this is something specifically theological: what one's horizon is and how his categories can be set up, and how theology can be related to non-theological disciplines.

Question: What about horizontal and vertical movements?
Lonergan: That talk of horizontal and vertical has to do with very general notions on method: experiencing, understanding, judging, deciding. The experience: is it data of sense or data of consciousness? Insofar as it is data of sense it is the vertical movement. But that makes all your operations, brings into play all the different types of conscious operations. You will start from data of consciousness then: advert to the experience, understand what is experience, judge your understanding, and decide to obey the norms set up by it.

Question: With regard to the question of functional specialization and its importance in theology, would you say that as in the Socratic maieutic man tries to mediate his experience, understanding, and judgment no longer

592   Part Three: Boston College Lectures, 1968

through ordinary language but through a technical language and a shift towards theory, so now what you're trying to do is a whole new step or leap in mediation, so that the mediation is no longer simply through a technical language but this technical language is able to thematize certain operations of the human subject, so that you could speak of it as a basic mediation, because a technical language can always be referred back to the operations of a subject, and therefore you're opening up a possibility of a basic dialectic of technical languages that may be originating from an inauthentic subject. So functional specialization could have almost unlimited potentialities; for instance, in Jaspers' notion of the axial period, when the thematizing through technical language gave an axial period, and this heightening of consciousness that you're talking about would be actually a higher control, a basic control of meaning.

Lonergan: Yes. That's the point to it. It is to have a set of basic terms and relations that can be complicated in several different ways, all of them verifiable, and to use that as your starting point. In other words, instead of doing what the Scholastics did in taking their fundamental terms and notions from Aristotle, you take them from the operating subject, his own experience of himself, his self-appropriation, and the Christian or religious subject's self-appropriation.

The differentiation of common sense and theory finds its basis in interiority, what I've been calling transcendental method: going into the subject, studying his operations. Interiority provides the possibility of universal method, of transcendental method.

Question: How does the use of transcendental method liberate the human scientist from the model of the natural sciences?

Lonergan: The fundamental liberation is to get hold of the fundamental significance of the notion of meaning. The natural sciences appeal to the data as given, just as given; you need names to be able to point them out, to talk about them, and so on, but it is what's given that counts. Between the given and the human sciences there is always a layer of commonsense meanings. You can send into a law court all the physicists, chemists, biologists, with all the equipment they want, and they can count and weigh and measure and compare, dissect to their hearts' content, but they'll never discover the law court. Ask the porter, on the way in. That layer of meaning that makes the data for human science data for a human science is the difference, one aspect of the difference, between the natural and the human sciences. Once you admit that significance of the level of meaning, you are liberating your science from a terrific emphasis on charts and measurements. You don't measure meaning, and meaning is what is significant. Again, hermeneutics becomes a fundamental tool, and history becomes a fundamental tool, because meanings change over time, the contexts change over time.

1968

Discussion 3[1]

Question: Were you dealing with ethics or metaethics?

Lonergan: I was not dealing with any precise ethical question. You might call it general ethics or the elements that touch upon general ethics. What I was talking about was the human good. I wasn't talking much about obligations. I was concerned to talk about various aspects of the human good: about human development, individual and social, about the notion of value and judgments of value, and about the complexity of the judgment of value: just what is the criterion in the judgment of value? What are the general criteria such as apprehensions of value, the transcendental notion of value, individual self-transcendence, the good conscience? You have to have these functioning in a fully developed person. We are getting judgments of value all along the line. We say that a child of seven can distinguish between right and wrong, but we call him a minor till he is twenty-one. And we don't give him a chair of moral philosophy till considerably later.

Question: Does this schema on the good follow from the transcendental method or does it follow from the objective pole?

Lonergan: It is something worked out from the objective pole but it also includes the subjective pole too: capacity for developing, capacity for operating, needs, and so on. They are aspects of the human good. Really, the key business is the final part: the particular good, the good of order, and the terminal values. Children fight about the particular good; men fight about the good of

---

1 Tuesday, 9 July 1968, Lauzon CD/MP3 488 (48800A0E060).

order: democracy, totalitarianism, and so on. And they do fight about it because of the values that are being realized in the different orders. Projecting
that back on the individual and on the society, you pick out the things that are
relevant to those three. Those three are the basis of the scheme.

But the point to it is to be able to talk about the good, first of all, concretely; and secondly, the complexity of the human good – there are all
sorts of components to it – and to think, at the same time, of the individual
and the social aspects, and the way in which they interlock.

Question: Does it follow from some things you've been saying that authentic man will emerge with high frequency only out of a rich and developed
culture?

Lonergan: I think if you talk about human authenticity resulting from God's
grace – there is a thesis in theology to the effect that the sinner without grace
cannot long avoid further sin: moral impotence, the necessity of prayer.

Question: But what if we want to prescind from theological solutions to human problems?

Lonergan: Well, if you prescind from theological solutions you are talking
about a world that doesn't exist. I don't think I would be answering the
question if I prescinded from real factors in the situation.

Question: So fully differentiated consciousness goes with authenticity?

Lonergan: You have to have a good deal of authenticity to move in that direction, to be interested in it. On the other hand, you can be authentically
human without being highly cultured.

Question: Is there not a higher probability, in a developed culture, for the
emergence of authentic people?

Lonergan: I don't think so. They can say *corruptio optimi pessima*, right away.
All progress is, de facto, accompanied by decline in one way or another. I
am not laying down any laws about it or anything like that. I don't say that
decline is necessary but I don't say that it is going to be necessarily avoided
either. As far as the Gospel goes, the need for taking up your cross daily and
following Christ is not something restricted to a certain period in human
history. It was laid down rather generally. Similarly for the necessity of prayer: lead us not into temptation. These precepts are general precepts. They
also speak of a new heaven and a new earth, but that is in a different stage
of the process.

Question: What is the relationship between moral conversion and intellectual conversion, and between moral and religious conversion? You seemed yesterday to see more relation between moral conversion and intellectual conversion. You were talking about religious conversion, particularly about the structures in Heiler's analysis of the higher religions, and I began to wonder about the differentiation between moral and religious conversion. In Buddhism, for example, religious conversion would seem to me to be very much like moral conversion, where you would be centering your life about the good and the true. Also *Insight* seems to involve intellectual conversion, and theology religious conversion, but related to both is moral conversion.

Lonergan: Religion is concerned with the holy, with God; and the holy is not the same as the good; it is a particular type of the good. The Buddhist has great concern for morality, but he also has great concern for holiness, for prayer. Religious conversion, or religion as I have been thinking of it, is concerned with the unrestricted element in the transcendental notions: the good beyond criticism, being that is not just contingent being, a new order of being, transcendent being, the possibility of a universe being intelligible, and so on. The moral is concerned with the rationality and the responsibility of one's decisions, the values they realize. Religious values are values that are realized, but they are a specific type of value. They have a great influence on the moral: love of your neighbor follows from the love of God and has its concrete meaning and concrete manifestations in the love of your neighbor, in your love of God. Still, the love of God is something distinct, and you love your neighbor as an overflow from that love of God. Moral conversion is implicit in that love, but you can have types of moral conversion that are not specifically religious. This may be difficult or rare, but there is no contradiction between a person being morally upright and non-religious.

All three conversions are related; all three are stages in the process of self-transcendence. And to reach any one is a powerful factor in moving on to the others. Intellectual conversion came into the church in the Arian controversy, it seems to me. Up till then they had been preaching the word and insisting on the word and serving the word – all the expressions you have in the New Testament and in the teaching of the doctrine and Christian life. There is a terrific insistence on the word. But the word as something true, as the measure of reality, only comes with Nicea. You have in Tertullian a materialism: the Son is divine because he is made of the right stuff. And in Origen you have a Platonism: the Son has to be a different essence from the Father; otherwise, he is not distinct from him. The Father is goodness itself and divinity itself, but the Son is neither of those. He is the *logos* itself, the truth itself, and so on. There are different essences in the Father and the Son; otherwise, they are not distinct for Origen. You arrive at a position regarding your thought about God being in terms of true propositions, with Nicea. This is swinging over to a dogmatic realism which is equivalent to a critical realism de facto, although not in its intellectual structure. This more or less came to the Christian Church through the implications of preaching the word.

   An intellectual conversion therefore occurs three centuries after the start of Christianity roughly. It is implicit in prior preaching of the word. Moral conversion is immediately preached along with the gift of charity, and it is implicit in it. Does that satisfy the question?

Question: Just a little more on moral conversion being implicit in religious conversion.
Lonergan: Love of neighbor in your love of God. If you love your neighbor, you're satisfying all the law and the prophets.

Question: To say that the church had an intellectual conversion at Nicea – do you mean a critical sort of conversion? As you have said yourself so often, the early Christians were not blind, stupid, silly. Intellectual conversion is part of their religious conversion from the very beginning. It seems a little far-fetched to me to say they weren't intellectually converted.
Lonergan: Well, what about Tertullian? If it is real it is a body! The Son is divine, why? Not because he is equal to the Father, not because of any attributes he has, not because he is not subordinate to the Father. He is divine because he is made of the right stuff. Is that an intellectually satisfying position?

Question: Well, he was satisfied with it.
Lonergan: I'm not saying that he was dissatisfied with it, I'm saying he wasn't dissatisfied with it, and that was the trouble. You have that in the West. When Nicea came out, the West was just stunned. The bishops of Rimini all agreed with what the emperor told them to sign, and Jerome remarked that the world woke up astounded to discover it was Arian. It took fifty years before they reached some sort of a settlement on the business, after Nicea. The period from about 325 to about 365 was a complete mess, with endless councils. Origen's doctrine on the Son, again, is good Platonism, but it isn't the doctrine we have in the Preface of the Trinity: 'Quod enim de tua gloria, revelante te, credimus, hoc de Filio, hoc de Spiritu sancto, sine differentia

discretionis sentimus.'[2] We give exactly the same attributes to the Father, the Son, and the Holy Spirit. Or we give to the Son and the Holy Spirit what we know of the glory of the Father from revelation.

Question: These were poorly formulated, but isn't there a matter here of faith?

Lonergan: I'm not talking about an intellectual conversion in the sense of accepting the faith. I'm talking about an intellectual conversion in the sense of converting your intellect, changing over your notions of what you mean by real and what you mean by true. Every big scientific advance is escaping from a myth, and intellectual conversion is escaping from a myth about knowledge. It is implicit in the preaching of the word because the emphasis is on the word and on its truth, but it becomes explicit in a much more pronounced fashion with the councils. The big objection to the dogmas is precisely the objection of the intellectually non-converted. It means nothing to them, it is just words, formulae.

Question: Can we go one step further and say that when we convert from a classicist world view to a modern world view the Church will go through another intellectual conversion?

Lonergan: Well, it won't be the same sort of thing. It is a cultural shift, just as with the Middle Ages there was a cultural shift. It is acknowledging cultural change, and it is also acknowledging a different concept of culture. Classicist culture is normatively conceived, and consequently it is per se universal, and so on. It leads to the imposition of the same norms all over the church, and this inability to adapt.

Question: You said that intellectual conversion is escaping from a myth about knowledge. Inasmuch as you distinguish between the classical and modern culture in terms of science by the distinction between logic and method, would you say that that involves a shift, a breaking away from a myth about knowledge?

Lonergan: It is not quite a myth. That would be stretching the meaning of 'myth.' If we didn't have Aristotle and Plato, if they weren't endeavoring to distinguish philosophy and science, on the one hand, from commonsense knowledge, on the other, getting some distinction between the two, making some effort at saying what scientific knowledge would be, even though they

2 See above, p. 26, note 35.

are proceeding on an insufficient basis with what they got from geometry and arithmethic, it is very doubtful that we would have had a real development of science and a real basis for saying that science is something different. You really need the scientific development before you can say with precision and exactitude what a science is. What Plato and Aristotle do represent is the breakdown of myth, the triumph of *logos* over *mythos*. The myth is so powerful and so indubitable because it expresses something that is true in imaginative terms. Knowledge *is* a self-transcendence, and you can express that self-transcendence in the image of seeing something outside yourself. It becomes indubitable that this is what knowledge is. Follow out that principle, and you eliminate knowledge.

Question: Can you give another example of a spectacular intellectual conversion in the Church?

Lonergan: Either you have it or you don't. What happened at Nicea was that the council used a word that didn't occur in Scripture, 'homoousios.' Chalcedon used the word 'physis' in a sense that didn't occur in the Fathers, or in Basil or Gregory or Cyril of Alexandria.

Question: Can't this take place in the contemporary Church too?

Lonergan: The same sort of struggle is going on. What is going on at present is a different thing, it is a cultural change. It is more similar to the medieval shift. You have at the beginning of the thirteenth century the condemnations of Aristotle. At Oxford they started using Peter Lombard as the basis of theological teaching; it had been going on for a century in Paris. Thomas was condemned in Paris and in Canterbury. It was after the canonization of Aquinas that they were allowed to teach him in Paris. Of course, Aquinas would have been much more effective if all his work hadn't just been covered over with a cloud of these Aristotelian and Augustinian flare-ups: the corrections and the correction of the corrections – there was just an out-and-out battle in which anything refined just vanished.

Question: Regarding phase one and phase two, when you speak in your writings of the analogy of faith, say, for example, when you are arguing to the consubstantiality of the Spirit, you presuppose the consubstantiality of the Son, and you are using St John. Is this in phase one or phase two?

Lonergan: They are both phase two. In phase one, what are you doing? You are doing your research, interpreting your documents, you are using your interpreted documents to say what was going on, you discover that there are

a whole series of interpretations and a whole series of histories corresponding to people understanding Christianity differently. You line up all these
differences, and this gives you your dialectic, your elaborate *status quaes-
tionis*. You haven't made any decisions yet as to who is right. This is phase
one. But you are encountering the Christian fact, the religious fact. When
you start taking determinate positions, moving beyond phenomenology
and history and so on, that is where foundations comes in. What are the
foundations? They are the expression of religious conversion, and in later
stages of moral and intellectual conversion too. In terms of the foundations
you take sides with regard to the dialectic and the history and the interpretations. Then you do doctrines. Doctrines come out of your history and
your interpretations in the light that is made precise by the dialectic, in the
light of the foundations.

Question: In phase two, are intellectual, moral, and religious conversion
necessary before you proceed to your systematics?
Lonergan: Yes. In other words, intellectual conversion is very, very fundamental. We have seven centuries of disputed questions; there is no term
that has one definition, all terms have several definitions, according to the
different schools, the different periods, and so on. Catholic theologians
agree insofar as it is *de fide definita*. The critical problem is just as relevant to
theology as it is to philosophy, and more evidently relevant to theology.

Question: Where is the role of the moral theologian in the functional
specialties?
Lonergan: In doctrines, and systematics, depending on just how he is going
about it.

Question: Is there no movement to the more concrete?
Lonergan: Well, doctrines can be very concrete. The movement to the concrete is communications – how do you sell it? You have to talk to people
about it, and you talk differently to different people.

Question: Are you suggesting, then, that there is no real difference, that
there is no real specialty?
Lonergan: It is not a functional specialty, it is not a different functional
specialty. It is a different subject specialty. I'm suggesting that they both go
about their jobs the same way. And I would say the same too with regard to
the distinction as traditionally conceived as fundamental and dogmatic.

You will go about your *De Ecclesia* the same way you go about your *De Deo Trino*.

Question: But historically they haven't done that?
Lonergan: Oh, no. What corresponds to the eight traditionally, historically, are eight theologies, not one theology with eight functional specializations. When you divide up into the eight functional specialties that tie-in with one another, you are asking for one theology in place of all sorts of theologies. There is a demand for unity and coherence in the grand style. It cuts down on amateur contributions.

Question: Can you say something about the apprehension of values which precedes the judgments of value. Is this the fact that insight, the act of perception, grasps some kind of unity within data?
Lonergan: No, it isn't. There is an apprehension preceding it but what is perceived, or what is understood, or what is affirmed is revealed to be valuable by your feelings with regard to it. Feelings as revelatory, just as they reveal what you like and dislike, also reveal what is and is not valuable, what is and is not truly good.

Question: Isn't there a danger of subjectivism?
Lonergan: Yes, oh yes. That is why a criticism of feelings and of values, and so on, is very relevant, and an education of feelings, and a good milieu in which feelings can be educated and encouraged. They are very delicate plants that are very easily crushed. And you get the hard-boiled egoist.

Question: What is the relationship between chapter 3 and chapter 4, i.e., between 'the human good' and 'horizons and categories'?
Lonergan: I spoke of categories as derived from the transcendental basis and the different ways of derivation. One of the ways was: fill out the picture, instead of this highly schematic business of experiencing, understanding, judging, and deciding. And a main addition we've made to this is feelings, which give the push, the shove. I said that this experiencing, understanding, judging, deciding, can be paper thin. It is the directional side in many ways, but the power side is the feelings. Horizon is decision and feeling, values and decisions, mainly.

Question: Evaluation, then, would follow logically from the definition of horizon. That is, once horizon is defined in terms of being in love, the problem of evaluation is a logical consequence, although it's implicit in the horizon.

Lonergan: Love is a source that sees values but also sees the possibility of them.

Question: What about the difference between your use of feelings in *Insight* and your later use? In treating the notion of the good in *Insight* you say: '... it will not be amiss to assert emphatically that the identification of being and the good bypasses human feelings and sentiments to take its stand exclusively upon intelligible order and rational value.'[3] Is this a different use of the word?

Lonergan: There is a difference. It comes from Scheler and especially von Hildebrand. I am using feelings in *Insight* in the traditional Aristotelian-Thomist setup in which feelings are only sensitive. In von Hildebrand, feelings can be quite spiritual. They can reveal values right along the line.

Question: And you would accept that?
Lonergan: Yes. I'd accept that second one.

Question: You presented von Hildebrand's hierarchy of values in the chart as objective and normative, but, on the other hand, you said that the criterion or true judge of moral value is the self-transcending subject as authentic.
Lonergan: As fully developed too.

Question: How do these two fit together? Does the pattern of values come from the subject?
Lonergan: Take Scheler's theory of *ressentiment* in which a person's apprehension of values is distorted. To avoid that or correct it when it arises calls for a critique. So there is such a thing as the education of feelings and the refinement of feelings and development of feelings. Again, while the individual possesses the principles for making judgments of value insofar as he has the transcendental notion of value, while he has his feelings, and while he has his happy or unhappy conscience, and these are principles that will enable him to develop morally, still, it is the person who has developed morally whose judgment is going to be right. The person who is still developing will have points on which he is a less good judge, where he needs still to develop. The questions, of course, become more and more refined.

3 Lonergan, *Insight* 629.

Question: So the hierarchy of values is the objectification of the self-transcending subject?
Lonergan: Yes. And, then, a hierarchy is something very general.

Question: In your scheme of the human good are there dynamic as well as static relationships of these elements in the structure? Is there an inner dynamism from the pure potential of the individual all the way over to the terminal values?
Lonergan: That is implicit there. But the purpose of the scheme is to give a cross-section at any time. When you extend it over time you start getting these movements, the questions that can be asked at any time, at any stage of development of culture. There are, as you say, those implications of the dynamic, but I went on more explicitly to talk about the dynamic when I spoke of development of operations, development of feelings, progress and decline, and the developing moral subject or the developed moral subject as the one who makes the judgment of values.

Question: The question of terminal values often escapes people, and they work on the first two levels but not on the third. Is that true?
Lonergan: The third level means, Is it really good? Is it worthwhile? It is about the particular good and the [good of] order.

Question: So you would have a number of particular goods and a number of different orders, too, in any complex institution.
Lonergan: The good of order is endlessly complex, and it works in entirely different ways. For example, in economics it is interdependence; in politics it is more a matter of avoiding people taking the law into their own hands, and so on, preventing evils, protecting people, securing their liberties and rights.

Question: Can you add more relations to the scheme?
Lonergan: Yes. You can keep adding relations, but really one part is the individual, and the social is going from individual to individuals in a group, cooperating, belonging to institutions, being in personal relations with one another. That is also in the individuals as in a group and cooperating in the institutions with the personal relations. You have the continuous emergence of the particular goods when you consider the good as meeting each individual's requirements. You have the good of order insofar as there is this totality of particular goods brought about as recurrent, not just here and now by chance, but by good management. That good of order and the

particular goods are in each case true good, not merely apparent good, not the social illusion. And you have emerging on the bottom level a type of value, namely, the originating value, the ontic value, the value of the person, which is over and above the particular good and the good of order and the measure of a true human good of order.

Question: With regard to the analogy of Newton and the development of history, could you specify the scheme in terms of Newton's laws?

Lonergan: The only analogy is in the three steps. In each case the first step is quite preposterous. There are three steps in Newton. The first step is the law of inertia. The second step is the law of inverse squares applied to two bodies. The third step is inverse squares applied to several bodies. You get there the three-body problem, which they don't solve in the general case. When it is a two-body problem, one will move about the other in a conic section. But with the three-body problem there is no general solution.

Now in history the first approximation asks, what happens if everyone always is authentic, i.e., attentive, intelligent, reasonable, responsible? Second, what happens inasmuch they aren't? And you get the breakdown, in the individual case, the group case, and the general case. Secondly, this irrational behavior, this irresponsible behavior creates a non-intelligible, absurd situation, where everything is out of place; it is the motive that drives the revolutionaries to desperation.

1968

Discussion 4[1]

Question: At the beginning of your talk this morning, you contrasted belief and knowledge,[2] but from reading *Insight* it seems better to say that one gets knowledge not only through firsthand experience but also through belief. And yet this is not the way you were talking this morning. You were simply contrasting sharply belief and knowledge.

Lonergan: The contrast is between belief and immanently generated knowledge, out of one's experiencing, understanding, and judging.

Question: And so for all practical purposes the knowledge one gets from belief is just as good as what one has learned on one's own.

Lonergan: Usually, yes.

Question: What about belief and action as with the scientist, for example, in experiments. You spoke this morning more of belief that the slide rule is accurate, but isn't there belief in the sense that one believes that this experiment will work. It's not verifiable until you actually do it.

Lonergan: Wouldn't you call it hope, rather, or something like that?

Question: Well, yes, hope or belief. But it seems to me that this is an important notion of belief, especially when you start talking about belief in

1 Wednesday, 10 July 1968, Lauzon CD/MP3 490 (49000A0E060).
2 See above, pp. 513–15.

God. Belief in God is not belief in an object which is verifiable directly or indirectly but belief more in the sense of a commitment.

Lonergan: We will get on to belief and faith when we treat religion. I think it will be better to wait till then because it is quite a complicated business.

Question: Can you compare and contrast your definitions for intersubjectivity, art, symbols, and language?

Lonergan: Intersubjectivity: I was speaking of meaning in the intersubjective situation. It is meaning that is not expressed in language but in facial expression, in gestures, in attitudes, tone of voice, all this sort of thing. The meaning is conveyed; it lacks the univocity of language. I gave a series of contrasts with language: the univocity of language, language as always an objectified meaning unless it is in exclamations and tone of voice, and so on; then you move towards the intersubjective. It is a determinant in the interpersonal situation. The symbol: its proper function is internal communication between mind, heart, and body, between feelings, knowledge, decisions, the psyche, the neural underpinnings of all this that goes on. In art there is an objectification of a purely experiential pattern, where 'purely,' 'experiential,' and 'pattern' are described somewhat elaborately. The objectification involves insight grasping the dominant form and working out all its aspects; it is an idealization of the original artistic moment or inspiration. The artist really doesn't know his inspiration until he has it objectified, in a sense; it is incipient at the stage of the inspiration. In the art there is no distinction between meaning and meant; the distinction between meaning and meant does not yet arise. The art critic or the literary critic tries to pull it out of its artistic embodiment, and to communicate it conceptually and verbally.

Question: With symbols there is no distinction between meaning and meant?

Lonergan: No. They are of that elementary type of meaning. As Freud said, when you dream of lions you are not afraid of, you are not dreaming of lions.

Question: How would you specify the relationship between the symbolic and the artistic as vehicles or carriers of meaning?

Lonergan: They have different functions. As I said, the dragon or the monsters of symbolism are not artistic; they are equivalent symbols used to reinforce the expression of an affect.

Question: How about positively?

Lonergan: Oh well, the work of art can have a therapeutic effect – for example, the catharsis that Aristotle speaks of can be taken in that fashion. You feel fear and pity, and in that way you have an emotional release. But there is also to art a revelation of a fuller world, a fuller mode of living.

Question: How about the relationship between the purely experiential pattern and what you are calling internal communication?

Lonergan: The purely experiential pattern is something that of itself tends to and wants an objectification. The symbolic function needn't want that. The artist is impelled, driven to express himself; he can't rest until he gets it done.

Question: Is it his symbolic self that he is driven to express?

Lonergan: It may be that, but it needn't be that. There can be something terrifically detached about a work of art. Symbols function within the self according to the needs of integration, and so on. Perhaps the symbolic achievement of a high degree of integration, peak experiences, can be the basis of artistic expression.

Question: I can see the need for psychic distance.

Lonergan: That is in the expression.

Question: But besides the symbolic self what are the other possibilities that the artist would be trying to objectify?

Lonergan: Well, an apprehension of life, an apprehension of a mode of living, or a possibility of living, a realization of one's humanity. However, these are all further questions. I spoke about these things this morning to draw attention to the scope of the idea of meaning, the different types of it. This is preparatory to the later sections on hermeneutics, on interpretation, on communications, and things like that.

Question: What would you say the difference is between your theory of value and feeling as opposed to that of Max Scheler, whom you have alluded to, and of von Hildebrand?

Lonergan: In Scheler, and to a certain extent in von Hildebrand, there is an awful lot of intuitionism involved. They intuit essences, that sort of thing; they speak terrifically about the objectivity of these values. I put that objectivity in the fact that they promote self-transcendence and offer possibilities of self-transcendence. That is the fundamental shift: you are moving out of an intuitionist context and moving into what I have called transcendental method.

Question: So you would call for a criticism and an education of feelings in that sense?
Lonergan: Yes. I think they would too, insofar as they acknowledge that feelings can be distorted. Thus Scheler speaks of *ressentiment.*

Question: Their criterion for distortion wouldn't be the same, would it?
Lonergan: I suppose they would go into intuition again: you can *see* that this is distorted. It is a very powerful type of criticism. It leads to criticisms of whole cultures, and so on.

Question: What is the relationship in the work of art between the meaning and the value of the work?
Lonergan: The meaning is a carrier of value, isn't it? You are on a level of elemental meaning, where meaning and value aren't being distinguished. But there is the element of value insofar as it is contributing to self-transcendence, insofar as the work of art takes one out of oneself, as we say. You are stopped by beauty.

Question: Does the value depend upon the skills of the artist and the meaning depend upon his insights?
Lonergan: Sheer technique is dead, isn't it? That's why there are constantly new styles. And there have to be new styles, because the reproduction is just technique. Even when, say, painting reaches a climax or summit, they just don't keep doing the same thing; they can't. What this is is something that one participates in, tries out for oneself. As soon as you start trying to conceptualize it, you are moving outside art and into art criticism and art history. The point to that section this morning was to acknowledge that type of meaning and let it be, and know that it is there as a resource.

Question: I am intrigued by your threefold theory of language. What is the source of that theory, and how is symbol related to your theory of language? In what sense is symbol linguistic, a part of language, and in what sense is it not? Also, I'd be interested in knowing what you think of people who make a linguistic distinction between symbol and concept. Also at least some

theories put literary discourse as analogous to symbolic discourse and call literary discourse symbolic. Therefore your theory would be somewhat distinct.
Lonergan: I took symbol in a very precise sense, namely, an image of a real or imaginary object that evokes an affect or expresses an affect. That ties it down to the image. It may be visual or auditory, or motor, or anything like that, but it is that business of image. Consequently, by definition, I have separated it off from language. Now you move into symbolic narrative. For example, Northrop Frye conceives the myth as the story; that's what keeps you turning the pages; it's what vanishes when you give a summary to the play; it's what keeps you in your seat in the theatre, the way one thing leads on to the next, so it is a perfectly general notion of myth. The myth is the narrative that is concerned with symbolic materials, and you can take the symbols from the diurnal circle, the four seasons, and the growth, maturity, and decay of the organism. He more or less feels you can get all the symbolic narratives in those patterns. So myth would be distinct from symbol insofar as it is conceived as the story. Then I went on to literary language. Literary language really is language that is artistic; it is the objectification of the whole subject, and consequently not just on the logical level, but floating between the logical and the imaginative-affective, which is the level of the symbol. Now as to the sources, there are various sources. You get to putting things together eventually, being worked on from all sides. The distinction of ordinary, technical, and literary language I got from Alonso Schökel,[3] but I think he gets it from someone else.

Question: Could you comment again on your analogy between the artist and the mathematician as exploring fields of possibility?
Lonergan: Well, the mathematician doesn't verify, he constructs, and he constructs freely, he constructs without contradiction (he hopes). That is the case with the majority. Some are more exigent; they want the constructions to be intelligible, to have what we call positive intelligibility. Consequently, they will exclude constructions by excluded middle. There is talk of the non-Lebesgue integral; the Lebesgue integral is something with terrific generality, and no one has worked out what would be a non-Lebesgue integral, I am given to understand; I really don't know this stuff. But they don't want people going off into these negative things, and there is an awful lot of mathematics that is built up that way, on the basis of

---

3 A professor of theology at the Gregorian University when Lonergan was
   teaching there.

excluded middle. They are investigating mathematics as relevant to science. It is investigating possible ways in which data may be related. People in the nineteenth century who worked out the Riemannian geometry had no notion that it would ever be of any relevance to science. Einstein, when the possibility was pointed out to him, had to get to work and learn this mathematics; he didn't know it. But there had been developed in that fashion a possible way of organizing data.

Now what does the artist do? The artist pulls us out of our routine living, pulls us out of our sensitivity as an apparatus for fitting in as a ready-made non-trouble-maker into a ready-made world, perfectly integrated, responding in just the right way all the time. Or the artist frees our sensitivity from being dominated by the scientific life, being merely a function of the scientific life, so that all our sensitivity does is respond to the demands of intelligence, picking out the characteristics of a classification, and so on. Sensitivity can be thus molded by scientific desire. Or it can be molded in terms of some theory of physiology or physics or epistemology or psychology, not let to flow on its own. The purely experiential pattern is a liberation from alien forms, and consequently the possibility of enrichment, of sensitivity in its own spontaneous unfolding, along with the associations of the subject and its capacity for self-transcendence, and all the rest of it. Consequently, you can conceive it as an exploration of the possibilities of human living. In the traditional formation of the humanities, people come to appreciate poetry, they come to see something in it, and in that they are being educated. Something in them is being developed that wasn't there natively, so to speak. This is just a suggestion.

Question: With regard to the functional specialty 'systematics,' to what extent does the theologian have to use technical language?
Lonergan: The role of technical language in systematics is very large, because what he has to do is clarify the difference between a statement that is effective, that communicates, that is powerful, and, on the other hand, just what it means.

Question: Is this not the functional specialty 'interpretation'?
Lonergan: No, it is not interpretation of the text but of the doctrinal statement, the dogma. Does 'homoousios' mean anything at all? And if so, what? One person and two natures: does this mean something or does it not, and if so, what? And what follows? What is grace? Well, what isn't grace? Was God obliged to do anything at all? These were questions that tormented the

twelfth century, and they had no answers for them. They gave all sorts of answers that seem quite fantastic to us, because around 1230 an answer was found. Systematics is concerned with the fundamental meaningfulness of the doctrines of a religion. Communications is the further step of going from a technically exact, accurate account to the type of statement that is meaningful for different classes of people, different cultures, and so on.

Question: Do you envisage the possibility of different schools of theology developing different systematizations in which there are different technical languages?
Lonergan: I would not think of it that way myself. I'm not a pluralist to that extent. I think there will be one technically accurate account and if there are others they are wrong – or they may all be wrong. But I think that there are many modes of communication. To insist on one for all is to eliminate a large part of humanity, depending on the one you insist on. In communications you have the whole catechetical movement and the liturgy as a means of communication.

Question: What about placing the objectivity of values in the process of self-transcendence?
Lonergan: Insofar as the person who makes the evaluation is achieving self-transcendence, there is objectivity.

Question: What would that correspond to in Scholastic terms?
Lonergan: The *honestum*. That is what the value is in Scholastic terms, as opposed to and distinct from the *utile* and the *delectabile*. Except they thought of it purely in objective terms; they were much closer to Scheler. For me, objectivity is just the full realization of subjectivity. Be authentic in your subjectivity, and you are attaining objectivity, because man is self-transcending.

Question: You say that technical languages will be the same, but doesn't that presume that all languages are the same?
Lonergan: You distinguish between ordinary language, literary language, and technical language. Technical language is a language created ad hoc: you define all your terms. We have been building up a technical language insofar as we've been talking about transcendental method, and we have been giving the basis for that technical language. And we have been attempting to derive categories from the transcendental method. Now if you are going to get several languages out of that, either you are supposing that

I'm adding on levels to consciousness that don't exist, or someone else is knocking off ones that do, or I'm doing that. That is the only way you can get several languages there. Technical language is something extremely severe.

Question: But doesn't one's language change the whole framework by which you look at the world?
Lonergan: Oh, yes. That is why there is a world of theory.

Question: Doesn't it even change one's categories so that they are not transcultural?
Lonergan: The ways people talk about the subject, if they are not technical, will differ, and all the rest of it. There are very few instances of very sound objectifications of consciousness. You get something rather fine in the *Upanishads* on consciousness and its objectification. But there are not so many of them to say that there is going to be inevitable conflict.

Question: In your chapter on interpretation in *Insight* you say that you are dealing with a universal viewpoint but you are not interested in a universal language. Now if you change it over into this context, is it fair to say that when you talk about theological technical language you are talking about a universal language?
Lonergan: Yes. *Insight* is in a literary language, expressly. It is moving towards the technical, and so on, but the fundamental communication is literary, a moving viewpoint.

Question: To take your position and juxtapose it with Heidegger's, where he uses as technical terms things like 'non-objective thinking,' and so forth, it would seem that there is a great deal of possibility of conflict if not merely covertly at least overtly, and that people who do hold to these kinds of positions create the type of problem that was raised.
Lonergan: Oh, yes. You have to come to terms with Heidegger, and my talking about things like art and symbol and intersubjectivity is my covering of areas that Heidegger covers in a primary fashion; he is very largely concerned with language that is authentic, the type of language that molds the development of our consciousness. And that is very significant for communication.

Question: What is its significance for technical language?
Lonergan: There are certain invariants of things that don't change in experience. But, in general, the invariants lie more in the structures, and it is

to the structures that I'm attending, to arrive at my fundamental terms; it is not experiences at all.

Question: Is it true, then, that you are working towards a technical language?
Lonergan: Yes, fundamentally. I am concerned with it – as with the transcendental method. Secondly, the movement into theology: the introduction of infused charity as giving you the Christian subject to be self-appropriated and providing a special foundation for the special categories of theology. And I'm concerned with the critical problem as relevant to theological disputes and to clearing up theological ambiguities. I am not saying that I'm going to settle questions, but I want to be able to have a dialectic that presents all the alternatives, in a way that anyone who holds any of the alternatives would accept as a fair expression of his position. And I appeal to religious conversion as the way you move out of that impasse. In other words, take all this opposition between the Jesus of history and the Christ of faith: you have your variety of opinions in the dialectic, and you take your stand. Your faith comes in when you set up your foundations for a theology, and you are able to understand the other fellow's foundations too.

Question: You would say that this discourse is cast precisely in technical language?
Lonergan: Yes. In other words, the account of method aims at being technical. Becoming technical is always moving around the corner, turning the bend; it's what was not in science as long as non-sensible terms did not have currency. It is when you get to terms like mass, temperature, electromagnetic field, periodic table, evolution, that the thing becomes scientific in the strict sense, the narrow sense, and where things start moving. Prior to that – take botany and Linnaeus's classification, it is based on morphology, and so on. But it is just endless description, and you are never understanding any of the things any better. It is terrific erudition, but put into that an evolutionary theory, and understand how one plant comes from another, and you are moving on to the explanatory level.

Question: It seems to me that the basic problem of setting up a technical language is that it can very easily become a dead language in the sense that the Nicene Creed is a technical language and it didn't change. So really, a technical language must remain living, and that is very difficult – it seems to me.
Lonergan: Oh, no. Technical language is not a living language, it is not a language that communicates with everyone; it is a language with which

people who make the terrific effort of understanding it do their work. And the importance of it is that it is not open to misinterpretation; it is not confronted with a hermeneutical problem. There is no hermeneutic literature on Euclid's *Elements*, and it was written 2300 years ago. No one understands them without doing a lot of work. When one understands them, their meanings are the same, and the problems that can be raised about them are the same; they vary with the mathematical context. The Gospels have been the basis of different interpretations, different interpretative works, for centuries, and the interpretations have not yet dried up; we are still going on getting further commentaries.

Question: Euclid's language is a mathematical language; it is not a living language based on experience.
Lonergan: That's what I mean by technical language.

Question: But theology is not a matter of constructing a mathematical language, it is a matter of vital terms.
Lonergan: Oh, no. That's *Lebensphilosophie* imposed upon theology. That isn't what theology has meant in the Catholic tradition.

Question: Then we're back to the relation between theology and religion.
Lonergan: Yes.

Question: Do you envision the possibility of a technical language for what Dilthey calls the *Geisteswissenschaften*?
Lonergan: That's what we're aiming at. These eight functional specialties can be transposed to any subject in which an investigation of the past is consciously relevant to man's future action – in other words, the historian accepting the full responsibility of his writing a history, because when he writes a history he influences peoples' estimate of the past, and their estimate of the past influences their decisions with regard to the future. The historian can evade that responsibility, and then they generally settle down to editing texts, and so on. Or he can take that responsibility in carefree fashion.

Question: Is there the possibility of the development of a technical language?
Lonergan: Oh, yes, because this technical language that I'm thinking of is based upon the structure of the self-appropriated subject, and that

self-appropriation can keep on developing, and with it the meanings of the basic terms will keep on developing; you can keep on complicating, filling out those things that I spoke of. The account of metaphysics I gave in chapter 14 of *Insight* is continuity without rigidity. And that is what we want in theology too. That is what we want in developing religion, and that is what we want in developing dogma.

Question: When you talk about the metaphysical equivalents in *Insight* you say the metaphysician will be able to assign concrete potencies, forms, and acts in terms of what the scientists know.
Lonergan: He learns from the scientist what the forms are, but he says that there are forms.

Question: Would the technical language of theology be such that what one learns from the other functional specialties would be this same type of assigning?
Lonergan: Theology is a positive science; it isn't just a heuristic structure as metaphysics is. It is a structure that is being filled out by positive inquiry; that is why it starts from research.

Question: Developing continuity without rigidity could be a good definition of life, and so it would make a technical language a very living language.
Lonergan: Well, in that sense of 'living.' But when people talk about a living language, they mean something that turns you on.

Question: How would you correlate the experiential element in objectivity and the purely experiential pattern in aesthetics?
Lonergan: The artist is not concerned with objectivity. He is concerned with objectifying this purely experiential pattern, which he finds good or, rather, beautiful or fair. Karl Jaspers, in a discussion of art, says there is something radically irresponsible about the artistic thrust. In other words, those questions are not arising. The artist is caught up in something, in doing it. It is out of the materials of experiencing, but you can be considering the experiencing from the viewpoint of something that is going on in you, the perceiving, and you can consider the experiencing from the viewpoint of the perceived, the given. Experiential objectivity is on that side of the perceived. The purely experiential pattern is on the other side. At least that's where its significance lies. It is the *Gestalt*, the formation of the experience.

Question: I thought experiential objectivity was a more undifferentiated notion.

Lonergan: Experiential objectivity is, in another sense, a very refined and remote notion. The good scientific observer is not the average man using his eyes; it is the man who has been trained to have hawk's eyes in a certain direction, to see just what's there. He has to incarnate the scientific goal and aim, to be a really good observer. Otherwise, he is more an individual who is reacting to what is presented to him, in terms of his interests and tastes, and so on. The scientist observes, looks, for the sake of looking.

Question: We talk about four levels of consciousness. In talking about the aesthetic is this something that moves between the sensitive and the intellectual and yet is something of its own?

Lonergan: The way I distinguish them was in terms not of levels of consciousness but as patterns of experience. In chapter 6 of *Insight*, I distinguish the biological pattern of experience, an aesthetic pattern, a mystical pattern, an intellectual pattern, a dramatic pattern, a practical pattern.

1968

Discussion 5[1]

Question: Would you clarify the point that the terminating good is the universe?

Lonergan: When we spoke of the good and values before, we spoke simply in terms of man's being good, his self-transcending. We spoke of a cognitive self-transcendence in terms of knowledge, and a real self-transcendence in terms of benevolence and beneficence and love. We were setting up the human moral order, and we distinguished between originating value, namely, the existential subject that transcends himself, and the terminal value, i.e., the good that he does. When one goes on to the question of God and acknowledges God as good, God becomes originating value in a much more fundamental sense, and the scope of terminal value is enlarged; it goes beyond the human good to include the whole universe. There is an extension of both terms. It involves an inclusion of the human good within a far larger context of the good. For the person who is an atheist and does not acknowledge God, the only moral good he can speak about is human morality.

Question: Is it not a bit misleading to speak of the universe as terminal value?
Lonergan: Not if you draw the proper distinctions.

Question: On that same point, if a person let his desire for the true and the good become all-involving, what would this religious dimension really add?

1 Thursday, 11 July 1968, Lauzon CD/MP3 492 (49200A0E060).

Lonergan: Well, consider alienation. If this whole created process is just blind, if it is absurd, literally absurd, without rhyme or reason, without ultimate meaning, if the only possibility of true value lies in man alone, well, man can still be moral and be a tragic figure, or he can say, 'It is silly for me to bother my head about that.' Either he considers the universe absurd and he is a tragic figure, or he surrenders entirely the notion of the good. The acknowledgment of the universe as value, in the sense of truly good, comes only from an acknowledgment of God. There is no moral goodness to it without there being some person who is morally good at its source.

Question: You might think of him as a tragic figure, but Heidegger would think that what he is doing is sensible. He wouldn't think of himself as a tragic figure. He is not going to admit that he believes in God; it doesn't seem like his life is meaningless, either that he is tragic or that he has given into the silliness of the universe.

Lonergan: That is the type of conclusion that needn't be drawn in the first generation. Nineteenth-century Victorians said that morality gets along fine without religion, and they wouldn't in any way think of criticizing Christian marriage. Their grandchildren don't think about it the same way.

Question: Are you arguing historically, then?

Lonergan: No. I am just pointing out that these things don't seem to follow, and de facto they may not follow in any given individual immediately. But either there is a reason for saying that the universe is a value and something worth cooperating with and in, or there is no reason for saying so. This has certain philosophic suppositions, no doubt, but there is the fact of alienation; there are the existentialists that go on to talk about the absurd, and there are the individuals who experience that in their own lives.

Question: You said that there are many philosophies but they can't all be right. You conclude therefore that there is one right philosophy.

Lonergan: I said that they could all be wrong.

Question: How do such philosophies as St Thomas's, Kant's, Heidegger's, etc., compare with yours? Is it a question of adequacy, truth and falsity, true to experience?

Lonergan: I do it for myself; I ask others to do it for themselves; I explain transcendental method as how they go about it.

Question: If you do this type of method correctly will you come up with one philosophy?
Lonergan: Yes.

Question: Aren't there many world views? What about different emotional backgrounds?
Lonergan: This is not a matter of emotions.

Question: But can you get to the world without these emotions?
Lonergan: Well, what do you mean by getting to the world?

Question: Ending up with the same conclusions about reality.
Lonergan: Well, are conclusions a matter of emotion?

Question: But my emotions affect my notion of reality, and I can't disregard that. It's going to affect my philosophy.
Lonergan: I think that that affects your attitude towards the study of philosophy, and the way you will direct your efforts in philosophy, and the degree to which you would be willing to accept directives in doing philosophy. But learning philosophy is going around the corner; it is not a matter of seeing things the way you always saw them.

Question: But whose corner?
Lonergan: It will be your corner, and you'll do it.

Question: But can't there be a healthy and legitimate pluralism of complementary philosophies?
Lonergan: There is a sense in which there is pluralism. But philosophy is one of the points where that sort of thing is at a minimum, at least with regard to the fundamental philosophic questions. There are certain operations that occur in human knowing. Where in the history of philosophy do you see the negation that there are certain kinds of operations that occur in human knowing? I am not drawing any conclusions from the operations but simply asking you to attend to the operations. That is all that transcendental method is.

Question: Does everyone get these operations in the same way?
Lonergan: Some get them and some don't. I haven't been teaching that; I have taught it on occasions, and people after about the tenth lecture come

in and say: 'I've got it!' But you don't get it by an act of will. It is walking down a tunnel.

Question: What is the relationship between your analysis and Eastern thought? In Buddhism the striving for the formally unconditioned and the striving for ultimate value would be looked upon as a form of sickness in the West that would have to be overcome by the techniques of meditation.

Lonergan: Buddhist thought comes out of prayer and the experience of prayer. You will find a very, very close parallel between Poulain's account of the prayer of quiet[2] and Zen Buddhism, very, very close. According to Friedrich Heiler, I think, or maybe it is somebody else, Ernst Benz – anyway, it is in *The History of Religions*[3] – this apparent negation of any divinity to Buddhism is the sort of thing that occurs and is paralleled by the way they handle logic. There is a divergence there across the whole map of thinking. When I was teaching in Toronto, there was a Hungarian who was a scholastic and had done his regency in Japan, and he had the story of a missionary who was working in a village. And he chatted with the religious leader of the place for about six years and finally convinced him of the principle of contradiction, and the fellow immediately became a Catholic. Now, that is the same sort of thing that I was talking about when I was talking about the intellectual conversion in the Church that occurred at Nicea, that is, the shift of the criterion of reality to the judgment – not to the form as in Platonism, not to the experience as in Stoicism with Tertullian. I think that would be the line at which I would work further at the point that you are raising. It is also true, as Friedrich Heiler says, that all high religions recognize a transcendent being. The Buddhists' statements are statements that come out of their experience of prayer, and they are denying the sort of being that is not transcendent, something like that; it seems to be their way of handling that. There is a fundamental problem there; the epistemological problem enters in and linguistic problems, and the type of experience they are working from.

Question: Is there some analogy between the Buddhist overcoming of striving and what you are talking about with the person attaining religious conversion

---

2 Augustin François Poulain, *The Graces of Interior Prayer*, trans. Leonora L. Yorke Smith (St Louis: Herder, 1950).

3 See above, p. 465, note 13. In *Method in Theology*, Lonergan refers to both Benz and Heiler on this point. See p. 110, note 8, in the context of the remarks in the text.

and going beyond the restlessness of living in a possibly absurd universe and committing to the universe as meaningful?

Lonergan: Yes. There is to the West an interest in this world, and this is also in Christianity. This is not paralleled in every religion. There is more activism in the West; there always has been.

Question: Religious conversion commits one to the universe as meaningful.

Lonergan: Yes. They think of it more in terms of escaping from this world – but that is more Hindu.

Question: [There followed a long question that challenges the consistency of Lonergan's use of the word 'insight,' claiming that he has many meanings or uses the word 'insight' in different ways. The question betrays ignorance of Lonergan's writings.]

Lonergan: May I explain something? I always use 'insight' in exactly the same sense. I don't talk about commonsense insights; I talk about the commonsense way in which insights accumulate and the way insights accumulate in the sciences. And I don't talk about the meaning of insight; I speak of its occurrence and experiencing its occurrence.

Question: What about Tillich's method of correlation? He felt that the method presupposed the question, and the problem would be with not raising the question.

Lonergan: I think that by the method of correlation was meant that the questions come out of philosophy and the answers are theological. And I think that there are also specifically theological questions that come out insofar as theology is reflection on religion.

Question: Are there other attitudes that are simply closed to the question of God?

Lonergan: I think there are. There is a terrific openness to God in a great deal of existential writing that is just missed out in a logical positivist approach, where the question just doesn't arise and it has no sense. Now, it is one thing for a philosophic position to be closed; it is another thing for an individual to be closed. With regard to revising a position, this is something I've covered in previous discussions.

Question: Eliade told me that he would use the word 'sacred' for the supernatural and vice versa; they are interchangeable. Would the Scholastic understanding of supernatural allow for them to be used interchangeably in the way he does use them? Could there be an experience of the sacred that would not be supernatural in our sense?

Lonergan: The word 'supernatural' has a precise technical meaning that emerged about the year 1230 AD. This comes out in the writings of Lottin on the doctrine of liberty from Anselm to Thomas, and in Landgraf's articles on grace; he went through all the manuscripts from Anselm to Thomas.[4] During the twelfth century and the first part of the thirteenth, there were insoluble problems: What do you mean by grace? What do you mean by liberty? There were all sorts of answers and none of them would work. The breakthrough came when they set grace above nature, faith above reason, charity above friendship, love of God above human friendship, and merit before God above the good opinion of men. They called one order supernatural and the other order natural, with an entitative distinction between them. That is what is meant by the supernatural. It has nothing to do with ghosts or miracles, or anything like that.

Now, is the experience of the sacred, in this light, a matter of grace? I wouldn't say that it would always have to be, because you might get instances of the sacred that were more aesthetic than anything. But the fact is that God gives his grace to everyone.

Question: Your emphasis is on thematization, but is what you are trying to thematize something real?

Lonergan: If there is nothing behind it, people will start off their conversation and their questions explaining that in their life they never had any experience of sensing; if there was an appearance of doing so, it was pure appearance; they are somnambulists. Secondly, they will say that never in their life did they have any experience of any type of intellectual curiosity, they never asked a question; and if they seemed to, it was just appearance. And never in their life did they understand anything; they never had the experience of understanding; that just doesn't occur in them, and if there are any signs of intelligence, don't pay them any attention.

Question (same questioner): All we can talk about is words.

Lonergan: Yes, that's true. But the words happen to have a meaning. Do you want to make those statements?

---

4 See above, p. 158, note 4, and p. 159, note 5.

Question (same questioner): In that sense the unthematic means a hypothesis.

Lonergan: No, no. You don't want to acknowledge anything apart from words, is that right? You are a strict conceptualist, or strict verbalist.

Question (same questioner): All I'm doing is using words.

Lonergan: I'm not saying you are using anything else when you talk. Can you speak of yourself seeing and not seeing as the result of the experiment of opening and closing your eyes?

Question (same questioner): What I mean by seeing may be different from what you mean by seeing. You are talking about abstract seeing.

Lonergan: No. I am not. I'm asking you if you have ever experienced seeing, yourself seeing? Have you experienced that?

Question (same questioner): Yes.

Lonergan: Oh, there is something behind the word when you say, 'I see,' then; an experience in you?

Question (same questioner): But what I mean by seeing and what you mean by seeing may not be the same thing.

Lonergan: I'm not asking you to mean the same thing. I'm asking you to mean something that you experience, and that you know very well takes place.

Question (same questioner): What I mean by reason and what the Buddhist means by reason is not the same thing.

Lonergan: OK. We can go into that later, but the first thing to know is to know what you are doing when you are knowing, if you want to follow this method I'm talking about. You don't have to follow it; it is only an invitation. I'm not trying to persuade anyone; I'm telling people what they might like doing.

Question (new questioner): Your assumption is that there is only one alternative, one idea of reason, that is, if a word is going to have a meaning there must be something that that means.

Lonergan: No. I'm not making assumptions. I'm asking a question.

Question (same questioner): Your assertion is that there has to be something behind the words about mental acts.

Lonergan: That isn't what I'm saying. What did I do? I asked him a question; I asked him if he wanted to make this statement; that's what I did.

Question (same questioner): It seems to me that a word is a word and that it has a proper use, it has a criterion, and certain correct situations in which it is used.
Lonergan: That is a well-known procedure of linguistic analysis. But it isn't the necessary procedure or the one and only procedure in philosophy of religion or theology.

Question (same questioner): It seems to help.
Lonergan: Oh, it is as good as far as it goes.

Question (same questioner): To go beyond it seems to require a justification.
Lonergan: People get their justifications themselves.

Question (same questioner): But that doesn't make any sense.
Lonergan: It makes some sense to some people, and they are the ones I wish to speak to.

Question: Are you trying to present insight in a way that a teacher of psychology would try to explain projection?
Lonergan: I'll give you the simplest proof of the fact of insight. The first proposition in Euclid's *Elements* is how to construct an equilateral triangle on a given base in a given plane. [Lonergan gives his usual example at the board.] Between the sensible data and the formulations or concepts there occur acts of understanding. A modern mathematician is so rigorous in his logic simply because he doesn't want to have occurring in his work insights that are not acknowledged. The logical weakness of Euclid is that he is using insights regularly that he doesn't acknowledge and doesn't formulate in definitions or postulates. Euclid isn't wrong, and the people who believed him absolutely right for over two thousand years were not wrong, but they were mistaken if they thought it was logical deduction.

Question: So there is a pedagogical way of presenting insight?
Lonergan: That is the first step with regard to insight, and you go on to other instances and gradually become quite clear about exactly what happens when you have insights; and people are having them all the time; they

are a dime a dozen. There is nothing mysterious about them whatever. But they are preconceptual.

Question: You spoke of God as the ground of intelligibility, the ground of the virtually unconditioned, the ground of value. If I understand your position in *Insight*, the problem of evil comes out of the confrontation of the fact of evil and the affirmation of God as ground of intelligibility and of the virtually unconditioned. Is the point you made this morning about God as ground of value, and that this can only be affirmed by the existential subject –
Lonergan: It is fully accepted only on the level of the existential subject.

Question (same questioner)**:** Does this involve moral conversion to overcome the difficulties that evil presents?
Lonergan: It is more religious conversion. The problem of evil, the fact that evils exist, is something that raises the question about the goodness of God. There is an acceptance of God as good on the cognitional level; but it isn't acceptance in the full sense. Acceptance in the full sense is choice and decision.

Question (same questioner)**:** It also raises the question about his existence. When you say that people know God naturally but with grace, is it only the existential subject with God's grace that won't end up with the dilemma of accepting God as the ground of intelligibility but also acknowledging the fact of evil?
Lonergan: Usually, people don't end up on a dilemma, as if it is one thing or the other. These distinctions are rather difficult to draw. There is the problem of evil and, in general, it is God's grace that brings one beyond it. The statements in Vatican I about natural knowledge of God mean only that there is a valid argument that can be apprehended in an act that's not supernatural *quoad substantiam*. There was a phrase in it to the effect that there was no necessity of a religious tradition, a tradition about God, a traditional doctrine about God; they had that in there against the moderate traditionalists at one time, and it was removed from the canon. There was also the statement '*ab homine lapso certo cognosci potest,*' and the *ab homine lapso* was cut out. So that doesn't mean that people without grace get to knowledge of God but that the knowledge of God is not a supernatural act, an intrinsically supernatural act.

1968

Discussion 6[1]

Question: You say, 'God loves.' Is there any way that your transcendental method can arrive at the conclusion that God loves, or is it merely a conclusion of faith?

Lonergan: I believe that it is a conclusion that can be reached in the way it was reached in *Insight.* But that is not the further thing that comes with the gift of God's grace. What I said about being in relation to God as subject, and speaking about God as the subject as object, which is a matter of religion, of faith, infused charity, and so on – the point I was making there was that, when God is just object and you are in a subject to subject relationship with God through grace, and you can objectify that relationship, religious discourse about God consequently differs from merely philosophic discourse.

Question: Can you correlate the notions of belief and horizon, especially 'belief' as it was used in the last few sentences that you spoke?

Lonergan: Horizon is the range of one's interest and knowledge. One's knowledge is largely a matter of belief. Is that enough?

Question (same questioner): Can you interrelate the notions of successive higher viewpoints in *Insight* and the notion of the sublation of the three conversions that you brought out in the last part of the lecture?

Lonergan: 'Successive higher viewpoints' was simply in terms of insights. To take simple examples: you can get the context of rules and operations

---

1 Friday, 12 July 1968, Lauzon CD/MP3 494 (49400A0E060).

provided by elementary arithmetic and operate in that field and then discover the need of, for example, negative numbers; and go on from negative numbers to the real numbers; and feel the need to introduce the imaginary numbers to round off the system of the real numbers. Your definitions will be changing as you go along. Like the example of 0.9 repeating. If you consider this a number, well, you will have to change your meaning of equality from 'no difference in magnitude' to 'no assignable difference in magnitude.' In other words, it is replacing one set of concepts by a modification of that set, putting that set on an entirely different basis. It is purely on the level of understanding and conceptualization – a fuller understanding. This other is a fuller development, a fuller self-transcendence.

Question (same questioner)**:** When you spoke of emergent probability, you spoke of moving from coincidental aggregates at one level to higher levels that become systematized by a new integrator. Now, it would seem that the notions are very close in as much as you say that sublation retains everything of the lower and yet is integrated within a higher and on a new basis.
Lonergan: With regard to emergent probability, it also involves the emergence of new forms. And you can think of grace as the final stage in that process.

Question: You attach religious conversion to the highest level of responsibility. Are the other two types of conversion (intellectual and moral) anyway attached to being reasonable, being intelligent, being attentive?
Lonergan: Intellectual conversion is on the first three levels: experience, understanding, judging. Moral conversion is on the existential level. Religious conversion is with regard to that unrestricted element in the transcendental notions, fulfilment on that aspect of the unrestricted.

Question: I find it difficult to understand why you speak of a religionless Christianity as being excluded. It would seem that you would require that Christianity be religious in the specific sense of ecclesiastical and consequently, then, that theology also be religious in that sense of doctrinal.
Lonergan: My reason is that you can have it without the reflective component, and many people can live very happily that way, but it isn't the whole story. There is to man that need for giving specific expression and developing and clarifying.

Question (same questioner): Can that specific expression be on the level of Kingdom of God with transcultural reference to comparative religions rather than just to religions of the West?

Lonergan: Yes. But what I'm talking against is blotting out what is good in past developments. I'm not saying that everything in past developments has been perfect. I'm also talking against blotting out differences: ecumenism doesn't mean that. It means understanding other people.

Question (same questioner): Couldn't there then be the inclusion of doctrinal theology within a wider notion of theology that would be foundational and that need not be, and could hardly be, religious in the narrow sense?

Lonergan: What I am thinking of are theologies that are contradictorily opposed; there are those contradictions. And that is why I speak of dialectic, and an advance towards mutual understanding, and things like that.

Question (same questioner): Then you would allow for these other theologies that would be from other religions?

Lonergan: They exist, the other religions exist, and if they have a theology let it exist. And let it have its place in the dialectic, and so on.

Question (same questioner): Then how about a theology that would take that fact for granted and operate that way?

Lonergan: I would like all theologies to do that.

Question (same questioner): And they can and still be doctrinal?

Lonergan: Being doctrinal is in the second phase. People not only listen; they also speak. And when they speak they speak coherently and determinately.

Question (same questioner): What you are doing doesn't seem to be specially ecclesiastical or doctrinal.

Lonergan: I'm doing method; I'm not doing theology. I have done theology in other works that I'm not retracting.

Question: If one were to work out the implications of your method for a theory of social change, it seems to me that the implications are that it would suggest going beyond the present theories of revolution worked out by the student radicals, the white radicals, and the militants, and by the human sciences, and providing more structures to aim at religious and moral conversion, in which the direction of those structures would be not towards the institutions but towards the releasing of the full human potential: such things as Carl Rogers would be doing in encounter groups: the building of communities which are aimed not specifically at action but the release of human subjectivity. Is that a legitimate implication? I'm getting at this realization of the law of the cross and the use of art forms and media to release this deeper human potential.

Lonergan: All I've offered is a general analysis of human process in terms of progress, decline, redemption. Some analysis of the way it works out is in the section 'The Longer Cycle,' in chapter 7 of *Insight*, and 'Moral Impotence,' chapter 18. And carrying these notions on – I have more on it in my *De Verbo Incarnato*, the last thesis on the meaning of the Redemption, the significance of the redemption. Further implications are up to individuals on their own responsibilities to discover. You can use this, but if you are going to get down to practical business, it will be a matter of going forward. I've been content to try and make some changes in theology and the way theology works and the way people work at it. In general, I don't think in what I'm saying there is any basis for one person telling *others* just what they have to do. Especially this business of 'The Law of the Cross': it is invitation; it is counsel, not precept; you can reveal its meaningfulness; but it has to be the decision of individuals, I think. In other words, it is not to be changed into a law.

Question (same questioner): But don't you communicate that?
Lonergan: Yes. But don't communicate it in the form of a precept.

Question (same questioner): So you communicate the atmosphere in which people do experience the invitation?
Lonergan: Sure. That's why people make retreats; and they make resolutions. But *they* make them. They are not told what to do: 'you must do this.'

Question: What about communicating this method to other cultures? Would they be able to develop a sound philosophy and a sound Catholic theology in each of those cultures, which would appeal to the people in those cultures?
Lonergan: There are profound differences. The experience of the West with the medieval universities and all the subsequent developments have given Western culture a shape and an interest in intellectual techniques that have not been developed, for example, even in Russia, where the

language is supposed to be full of idioms. I think Edmund Wilson remarks on his surprise that a translator of a Russian novel did not get a Russian to read his translation and correct the obvious mistakes. And the Russian said to him that if he got six Russians and did that with six, he would have had six translations. In other words, there isn't the precision to the language. There has been a terrific influence of logic, and so on, on the languages of the Western tradition.

Answering a question the other day on Buddhism and its way of talking about the ultimate – it is either Ernst Benz or Friedrich Heiler, I forget which article it was in – it was said that there is there a difficulty which reappears in their logic. And there is a very definite stage in Western development. It started with the questioning of the Greeks, and the development of philosophy. It is paralleled exactly in these other cultures. So what's going to happen when they start doing theology? In comparative religions, at the present time, the aim is to so talk about Islam that a Muslim will agree that you are saying things truly; and similarly with regard to Buddhism and the other religions. There is that development going on. But just what way they would do theology is still a further question.

Again, when I speak of them, what I'm thinking of really is our understanding them. For one of us to go into one of those cultures and start working there, that is a further step. It is a matter of transposing Christianity into a new culture. The things that have been required in the past seem in many ways exaggerated. It is almost impossible to get a native clergy in cultures where you can't make the demands for the priesthood that you make in other countries. Native clergy should be something that we come to much more quickly. But that whole business of the transcultural and adapting to different cultures is a thing that we have to get on to; it is part of the movement from the classicist to the modern.

Question: Is De Nobili working on the same principles as you are?
Lonergan: I have a certain inspiration from De Nobili, in a vague sort of way.

Question: With regard to the Christian atheist, having ultimate concern and not being convinced by any philosophic proof for God, you admit the possibility and yet you say it is likely to be unstable. The only ways out that I can see are that either one find a truth that can satisfy him or otherwise decide to affirm God because otherwise life will go into trivialization.
Lonergan: Well, he can believe in God too.

Question: What is the difference between that and what I said.

Lonergan: Well, perhaps it is what you meant when you said he could affirm God. There is immanently generated knowledge and there is accepting something as true because someone you respect, someone you consider competent, has told you. That's belief. And that's 98% of most peoples' knowledge – perhaps 99%. Telling people to find things out for themselves and not to believe is a good way of emptying their minds of all possible convictions, if they apply it rigorously, if they really take you seriously – as they seem to be doing.

Question: Have you reflected much on the fact – what I consider a fact – of social insight, the insight of more than an individual, into an experience that is only had in a community, that is part of not self-appropriation but, say, community-appropriation?

Lonergan: I said something about it this morning when I said that being religious, being in love with God, is intimate and personal, but not solitary; there comes out of it the religious community, the religious group; the members of the group understand one another and further one another; the thing becomes not merely a group but over time, there is a succession of members; and it can become historical not only in the sense that it is over time but in the sense that it is a response to God, to a divine entry into human history.

Now, social insight: there is my notion of common sense, which is an accumulation of insights that are common to a group, or within the group they are complementary; and the individuals all understand one another, and as they move to the next village they find people there a little strange but not very much; but when they get into another country they find things really odd.

Question (same questioner)**:** I'm thinking just of the insight that is into an experience, the kind of practical insight that leads into decision, that's one of the steps in decision-making. When you're dealing with common sense and the cosmopolis of common sense, it's basically critical, just as in hermeneutics the canons of criticism are present. But I'm not thinking so much of cultural or social insight in terms of critical awareness or the role of the critic within the society but the creator within the society; can you say something on that?

Lonergan: That is Toynbee's 'Challenge and Response,' the creative minority. And there is the notion of progress in *Insight*, it is the practical insight, the policy, the decision, carrying it out, criticizing the results, further insight, further policy, that ongoing progress.

Question (same questioner): Is it some kind of creative leap?
Lonergan: Yes. It's a bright idea. And it catches on; everyone sees it at once. But it isn't social in the sense that it is located in some super-mind.

Question (same questioner): So many of my questions reach back into this area. I don't say I would expect you to have answered it. But it seems a primary area of research in terms of the social breakdown in which we're living.
Lonergan: Well, I can't do everything myself, you know! I'd like a lot of people to do some of these other things.

Question: At times there seems to be a certain unification to your topics, for example, functional specialization. But then, as you continued, there seemed to be a greater disparateness: you hit one thing and then another; and, as one person expressed it, 'Well, he seems to be saying a lot of commonsense things about religious experience, but he doesn't seem to be heading towards any kind of a synthesis.' And I was wondering whether in the later portion of your book you would be heading towards a greater unification such as you do head to in *Insight*?
Lonergan: I'm discussing method, and the rest of the book will be on the eight functional specializations: talking about what you do when you are doing theology. These four chapters: 'Horizons and Categories,' 'The Human Good, Values, Beliefs,' 'Meaning,' and 'Religion' are written to complement *Insight*, which was not orientated to strictly theological topics. They are tools for theological thought that would belong to more than one functional specialty. For example, 'Meaning' when you treat it in interpretation, when you treat it in Communications, or when you treat it in systematics – well, it is relevant to all of them. 'Horizons and Categories': well, it could be principally in foundations, but it is relevant to other things too. So what I've been doing here is, as you say, a collection of things that had best be treated at once, rather than a little in this or that later chapter. But I'm not presenting a doctrinal synthesis or a systematic synthesis; I'm discussing what one is doing in all the different aspects of doing theology and the general tools that may be used in doing theology, at least for a start; you may find better ones – well, then, drop these and take some other ones: notions on horizon, categories, transcultural categories, all that sort of thing.

Question: Would you say, then, that the scientific or the specifically explanatory nature of your work will be in the relationship of the functional specialties to one another and the relation of 'Horizons and Categories,' and so on, to each of the functional specialties?

Lonergan: Yes. It is separating out what has to be separated out if, on the one hand, you are to avoid totalitarian imperialisms, one part wanting to be the whole of theology; or, on the other hand, excessive demands preventing people from doing particular tasks well, and not demanding that they do absolutely everything.

Well, that seems to be it. I wish to thank you for your very kind attention during all these days and say how much pleasure I had from such a generous and intelligent and loving audience.

Appendix:
Hermeneutics[1]

1 Hermeneutics and exegesis are concerned with the meaning of texts. Hermeneutics is concerned with general principles, exegesis is concerned with their application to particular eases.

2 Hermeneutics is not a primary field of inquiry.
Per se the meaning of texts is plain and stands in no need of any exegesis. *Per accidens*, as a result of any of a number of blocks that may arise, the work of the interpreter becomes necessary,

The point can be demonstrated. If every text needed an exegesis, then the exegesis would need an exegesis, and so on to infinity. Similarly, the general theory, hermeneutics, would itself need an exegesis, and the need would be recurrent.

3 The primary field of inquiry is cognitional theory. It deals with knowing in all cases. One of these cases is knowing what an author meant in writing a given sentence, paragraph, chapter, book.

Hence, within the framework of a satisfactory theory of knowledge, hermeneutics is not a matter of special difficulty or interest. Such has been *classical* hermeneutics, expounded by Aristotle and refined down the centuries.

---

1 Based on the autograph of a document provided by Lonergan at the Regis College Institute of 1962. The autograph is found on the website www.bernardlonergan.com, at 85900DTE060. For what seems to be the distributed document itself, see the same site, at 60700DTEL60.

Contemporary hermeneutics, on the other hand, is a matter of considerable difficulty and interest, mainly for four reasons.

First, the issues have been placed within the context of historical consciousness. The classicist view that 'plus ça change, plus c'est le même chose' has given way to an attention to detail, to differences in detail, to an understanding of man and meaning that rises from the detailed differences to be noted in the course of human development.

Secondly, in the *Geisteswissenschaften* (as distinct from behavioral sciences) the basic category is meaning, and so hermeneutics, which deals with meaning, has a key role.

Thirdly, the lack of a commonly accepted cognitional theory has resulted:

(a) in the application of mistaken cognitional theories to the problems of hermeneutics;

(b) in efforts to employ hermeneutical problems as the springboard towards the solution of the philosophic issues;

(e) in the attitude of the 'plain' man who brushes aside such theoretical considerations, proceeds by what he names simple and honest common sense, and is usually guided by the more superficial and absurd catchphrases developed by applying mistaken cognitional theory to hermeneutical problems.

Fourthly, modern man has been busy creating a modern world, in freeing himself from reliance on tradition and authority, in working out his own world-view comparable in completeness to the Christian view that ruled in an earlier age. This has brought about a climate and an exigence for reinterpretation

– of Greek and Latin classical authors, removed from the context of Christian humanism, and revealed as pagans;

– of the scriptures, removed from the context of Christian doctrinal development, and restored to the pre-dogmatic context of the history of religions;

– of the Law, removed from the context of Christian philosophy and morality, and placed within the context of some contemporary philosophy or attitude toward life.

4 Accordingly, the problems of contemporary hermeneutics are to a great extent coincident with the problems of method in contemporary Catholic theology.

We do not propose to reject historical consciousness and human science because we reject 'modernity.' At the same time, we do not propose to slip into 'modernity' because we wish to accept historical consciousness and human science.

We wish, then, an integration of dogmatic theology with historical consciousness and human science, but without the aberrations of the Enlightenment, the Romantic movement, Idealism, Historicism, Dilthey's *Lebensphilosophie*, and existentialist *Transzendenz innerhalb der Immanenz*, or the naturalist 'Principle of the Empty Head, Postulate of the Commonplace, and Axiom of Familiarity.'

Plainly, such an integration cannot be conceived, much less achieved, without facing squarely the issues involved in the science of cognitional theory that underlies hermeneutics.

5 There are three basic exegetical operations: (1) understanding the text, (2) judging how correct one's understanding of the text is, and (3) stating what one judges to be the correct understanding of the text.

Understanding the text has four main aspects:

(a) one understands the thing or object that the text refers to;

(b) one understands the words employed in the text;

(c) one understands the author who employed the words;

(d) it is not 'one,' 'l'on,' 'Das Mann' that understands, but I do, as a result of a process of learning and at times as a result of a conversion.

Judging how correct one's understanding of the text is raises the problem of context, of the hermeneutic circle, of the relativity of the 'whole,' of limiting considerations on the possible relevance of more remote inquiries, and of limitations placed upon the scope of one's interpretation.

Stating what one judges to be the correct understanding of the text raises the issue of absolute context, of 'existential' categories, of the use of human sciences in exegesis, and of the problems of correct communication in their relativity to a given group of readers.

6 Understanding the thing or object

The Urphänomen is not *intelligere verba* but *intelligere rem per verba*.

Exegesis, at a first level, presupposes knowledge of things, objects, and of the language that names them.

Because we already have the universal potential knowledge of the thing dealt with in the text, we find *per se* that the meaning of the text is plain, that it simply applies to a particular the universal and potential knowledge we already have of the particular.

It is true, of course, that my understanding of the thing or object or the true understanding of the thing may not be the author's. But the point to 'understanding the thing' is not that it settles what the author means, but that without it there is no possibility of understanding the author.

A blind man is not going to understand a description of colors; a person that has never attended to his own acts of intelligence is not going to understand a description of intelligence; etc.

By understanding the thing or object is not meant understanding only the things or objects of the visible universe. The thing or object in question may be (a) in the visible universe, (b) in the world of theory, (c) in the world of interiority, or (d) in the world of the sacred, of religion.

The contention that the interpreter should have his own understanding of the object, know what that understanding is, and distinguish it from the author's understanding of the object amounts to a rejection of what may be called 'The Principle of the Empty Head.'

The 'Principle of the Empty Head' contends that if one is to be objective, if one is not to drag in one's own notions, if one is not to settle in an a priori fashion what the text must mean no matter what it says, if one is not to 'read into' the text what is not there, then one must drop all preconceptions of every kind, see just what is in the text and nothing more, let the author speak for himself, let the author interpret himself.

What I have named the 'Principle of the Empty Head,' clearly enough, is a widespread view of correct interpretation.

The 'Principle of the Empty Head' is a confusion of three distinct issues based upon an utterly inadequate account or presumption regarding the nature of human knowledge.

So far from tackling in series the three tasks of (a) understanding the thing, (b) understanding the author's meaning concerning the thing, and (c) judging whether one's understanding is correct, the 'Principle of the Empty Head' rests upon a naive intuitionism that, so far from judging the correctness of its understanding, has no need to judge because it sees what's there, and so far from bothering about understanding the thing, has no need of understanding anything but just looks at what's there.

In fact, what is there? There are printed signs in a given order. That is all that is there. Anything over and above a reissue of the same signs in the same order will be mediated by the experience, intelligence, and judgment of the interpreter.

To reject the 'Principle of the Empty Head' is to insist that the wider the interpreter's experience, the deeper and fuller his understanding, the profounder his judgment, then the better equipped he will be to approach the task of stating what the author means.

The basis for this contention is simple.

Interpretation is a matter of proceeding from habitual, potential, universal knowledge to a second act that regards the concrete and particular: what was meant by the author in this text.

The less that habitual knowledge, the less the likelihood that the interpreter will be able to think of what the author means. The greater that habitual knowledge, the greater the likelihood that the interpreter will be able to think of what the author means.

When a critic of an interpretation states, 'I do not see how Aristotle, St Paul, Aquinas, Kant, could have meant what the interpreter says he meant,' then the literal meaning of the critic's words is that he does not possess the habitual knowledge that would enable him to see how the author could have meant what the interpreter says he meant.

While the 'Principle of the Empty Head' is widespread in positivist and in Catholic circles, it is vigorously rejected elsewhere. See H.G. Gadamer, *Wahrheit und Methode* 254f. and R. Bultmann, 'Das Problem der Hermeneutik,' *ZfThK* 47, p. 64.[2]

7   Understanding the words

Understanding the thing accounts for the *per se* plain meaning of the text. This plain meaning is obvious and ultimate when the author and the interpreter understand the same thing in the same way.

However, as in conversation, so in reading, the author may be speaking of X' and the interpreter may be thinking of X". In that case, sooner or later, there arises a difficulty. Not everything true of X' will be true of X", so that the author will appear to the interpreter to be saying what is not true or even what is absurd.

At this point the controversialist has all he wants: on the basis of his mistaken assumption that the author is speaking of X", he sets about demonstrating the author's errors and absurdities.

---

2   See above, pp. 115, note 13, and 213, note 4. In *Method in Theology*, p. 158, note 2, Lonergan translates the reference from Bultmann and also indicates it was reprinted in *Glauben und Verstehen*, 2, at p. 230: 'Nothing is sillier than the requirement that an interpreter must silence his subjectivity, extinguish his individuality, if he is to attain objective knowledge. That requirement makes good sense only in so far as it is taken to mean that the interpreter has to silence his personal wishes with regard to the outcome of the interpretation … For the rest, unfortunately, the requirement overlooks the very essence of genuine understanding. Such understanding presupposes precisely the utmost liveliness of the understanding subject and the richest possible development of his individuality.'

The interpreter, however, considers the possibility that he himself is at fault. He rereads. He reads further. Eventually he makes the discovery that the text makes some sense when X' is substituted for X".

The process can occur any number of times with respect to any number of instances of X' and X". It is the process of learning, the self-correcting process of learning. It is the manner in which we acquire and develop common sense. It heads towards a limit in which we possess a habitual core of insights that enables us to deal with any situation, any text of any group, by adding one or two more insights relevant to the situation or text in hand.

Such understanding of the text must not be confused either with judgment on the truth of that understanding or with a statement on the meaning of the text in virtue of that understanding. One has to understand before one can pass judgment on that understanding; one has to have the understanding before one can express it. Understanding the text is such a prior understanding.

Such understanding matches the hermeneutical circle.

The meaning of the text is an intentional entity; it is a single intention that unfolds itself through parts, sections, chapters, paragraphs, sentences, words. We can grasp the unity, the whole, only through the parts. Yet at the same time the parts are determined in their meaning by the whole, which each partially reveals. It is by the self-correcting process of learning that we spiral into the meaning of the text, understanding the whole through the parts, and understanding parts in light of the whole.

Rules of hermeneutics or of exegesis list the points worth considering in one's efforts to arrive at an understanding of the text. Such are the analysis of the composition of the text, the determination of the author's purpose, of the people for whom he wrote, the characterization of the means he employed: linguistic, grammatical, stylistic, etc., etc.

The point to be made here is that one does not understand the text because one has observed the rules, but that one observes the rules in order to arrive at an understanding of the text. Observing the rules can be mere pedantry that leads to an understanding of nothing of any moment, to missing the point entirely. The essential observance is advertence to what I do not understand and the sustained rereading, search, inventiveness, that eliminates *my* lack of understanding.

8 Understanding the Author

When the meaning of a text is plain, then *with* the author and *by* his words we understand the thing.

When a simple misunderstanding arises (e.g., the author is thinking of X' and the reader of X", then its correction is a relatively simple process of rereading and inventiveness.

But when there is need of the long and arduous use of the self-correcting process of learning, when a first reading yields a little understanding and a host of puzzles, then the problem is not so much understanding the thing or the words as understanding the author himself, his nation, language, time, culture, way of life, and cast of mind.

The self-correcting process of learning is not only the way we acquire common sense in the first instance, but also the way in which we acquire an understanding of other peoples' common sense. Even with our contemporaries of the same culture, language, and station in life, we not only understand things with them, but also understand things in our own way and, as well, their different way of understanding the same things. We can remark that a phrase or an action is 'just like you': we mean that it fits into our understanding of the way you understand and so go about things. But just as we can come to an understanding of our fellows' understanding, a commonsense grasp of the ways in which we understand not with them but them, so this process can be pushed to a full development when the self-correcting process of learning brings us to an understanding of the common sense of another place, time, culture, cast of mind.

The phrase 'understanding one another's common sense' must not be misunderstood. Properly, it is not understanding what common sense is, a task of the cognitional theorist. Again, it is not making another's common sense one's own, so that one would go about speaking and acting like an Athenian of the 5th century BC. But just as common sense is understanding what is to be said and what is to be done in any of the situations that commonly arise, so understanding another's common sense is understanding what he would say and what he would do in any of the situations that commonly arose in his place and time.

This understanding another's common sense is very similar to what in Romantic hermeneutics is named *Einfühlen*, 'empathy.'

[Romantic hermeneutics was] derived from Winckelmann and developed by Schleiermacher and Dilthey to be attacked by contemporaries under the influence of Heidegger (*Being and Time*, §§72–77).

Romantic hermeneutics conceives the text as *Ausdruck*, the exegete's task as *Einfühlen*, and the criterion of the exegete's task as *Reproducieren*, an ability to say just why the author in each phrase expressed himself in the precise manner in which he did.

It singles out a valid task of the interpreter and it gives an approximate account of the way in which the task is performed; but it is incomplete as well as approximate, and so it has been subjected to a good deal of criticism (Bultmann, Gadamer).

Conceiving the text as *Ausdruck* correctly draws attention to the aesthetic, intersubjective, symbolic dimensions of meaning; but it overlooks or pre-scinds from or fails to insist on the aspect of linguistic meaning by which it is true or false, by which it pertains to an absolute domain, by which it can be transferred from one context to another.

Again, empathy is the simplest description of the way in which we grasp intersubjective, aesthetic, or symbolic meanings. But it contains more than a suggestion of an extrinsicism that overlooks the development of the inter-preter, his acquiring an understanding of another's mode of understanding, the widening of his horizon to include or fuse with the horizon of others. So far from raising and solving the problem of the transference of meaning from the context of an ancient writer to the context of the contemporary readers of the contemporary interpreters, it encourages a mythic elimination of the problem by suggesting that the interpreter feels his way into another's mind and heart, his thought and sensibility; and it leads to a falsification of issues inasmuch as it implies that there can be no legitimate transference from one context to another, that either one thinks with the mind of Paul or else one has no objective knowledge of Paul's meaning whatever.

Finally, the criterion of *Reproducieren* is excessive. It means that one not only understands the author but also can do what the author himself could not do, namely, explain why he wrote in just the way he did. Common sense understands what is to be said and what is to be done; but common sense does not understand itself and much less does it explain itself.

9 The Development of the Interpreter

The major texts, the classics in religion, letters, philosophy, theology, not only are beyond the original horizon of their interpreters, but also demand an intellectual, moral, religious conversion of the interpreter over and above the broadening of his horizon.

In this case the reader's original knowledge of the thing is just inadequate. He will come to know the thing only insofar as he pushes the self-correcting process of learning to a revolution of his own outlook. He can succeed in acquiring that habitual understanding of the author that spontaneously finds his wave-length and locks onto it only after he has effected a radical change in himself.

This is the existential dimension of the problem of hermeneutics.

Its existence is at the root of the perennial divisions of mankind in their views on morality, on philosophy, on religion.

Moreover, insofar as the radical conversion is only the basic step, insofar as there remains the further task of thinking out everything from the new and profounder viewpoint, there results the characteristic of the classic: 'A classic is a writing that is never fully understood. But those that are educated and educate themselves must always want to learn more from it.'[3]

From the existential dimension there follows another basic aspect of the task of hermeneutics.

The classics ground a tradition, an *Überlieferung*, a culture. They create the milieu in which they are studied and interpreted. They produce in the reader through the tradition the *Vorverständnis* that he will need when he comes to read, study, interpret.

Such a tradition may be genuine, authentic, a long accumulation of insights, adjustments, reinterpretations, that repeats the original message afresh for each age. In that case, the reader will exclaim as did the disciples on the way to Emmaus, 'Did not our hearts burn within us when he spoke on the way and opened to us the Scriptures?' (Luke 24.32).

On the other hand, the tradition may be inauthentic. It may consist in a watering-down of the original message, in recasting it into terms and meanings that fit into the assumptions and convictions of those that have dodged the issue of radical conversion. In that case, a genuine interpretation will be met with incredulity and ridicule, as was St Paul preaching in Rome and quoting Isaiah, 'You shall indeed hear but never understand' (Acts 28.26).

It is in this perspective that is to be understood Gadamer's attack on the *Aufklärung* and on *Historismus* as involving a bias against bias in general.

Inasmuch as these movements were concerned with creating a new world for man, a new tradition, a new culture, they were astute in laying down a principle that excluded the possibility of a tradition.

But inasmuch as the destruction of tradition implies a continuous return to primitive barbarism – which was not the aim of the Enlightenment or of *Historismus* – these movements were incoherent and shortsighted.

---

3 Quoted from Friedrich Schlegel by H.G. Gadamer, *Wahrheit und Methode* 274, note 2.

The ultimate issue here lies between Descartes's advocacy of a universal doubt and Newman's preference for universal belief.

10 Judging the Correctness of One's Understanding of the Text

Such a judgment has the same criterion as any judgment on the correctness of commonsense insight.

The decisive question is whether one's understanding of the text is invulnerable, whether it hits the bull's-eye, whether it meets all relevant further questions.

Here the key word is 'relevant.' It implies a reference to a determinate prospective judgment. Without such a judgment in view, one has no criterion, no reference point, for determining which further questions are relevant.

It follows that judgment on the correctness of one's understanding of the text is, not a general judgment on that understanding in all its aspects, but limited judgments with respect to determinate and restricted points. They will be of the type: At least the author means this, At least he does not mean that.

The same point comes to light from the hermeneutical circle. One understands the whole only through the parts, and nonetheless the meaning of the parts is dependent on the whole. Insofar as this circle is merely logical, it is surmounted by understanding. But it has a further and core fundamental aspect, namely, the relativity of the whole. With respect to a word, the sentence is the whole. With respect to a sentence, the paragraph is the whole. With respect to the paragraph, the chapter is the whole. With respect to the chapter, the book is the whole. But the book itself stands in a further, far more complex type of context that includes the *opera omnia* of the author, his background, his sources, his contemporaries, the state of the question in his day, the issues then predominant, the author's aim and scope, his prospective readers, etc. In brief, there is an ever-broadening hermeneutic context that ultimately finds itself in a historical context. Not only is the historical context to be known only through the hermeneutic contexts, but also it does not possess the type of intelligibility to be found in a hermeneutic context; the latter is like the general's plan; the former is like the course of the battle.

Now it is true that this relativity of the whole does not imply a complete fluidity, a *panta rhei* of meaning. The meaning of the parts is affected by the whole, but it is not affected in all respects. That Brutus killed Caesar can be placed in a context that praises Brutus and, equally well, in a context that damns him; but it does not fit into a context in which it is true that Caesar killed Brutus. The Gospel of St John has been read in a Hellenistic context and now is being read in a Palestinian context brought to light by the discoveries at Qumrân. The change in context involves a change in perspectives, a change in difficulties, a change in the questions that are raised and discussed. But still this change in context does not change much in a commentary that is based upon exact analyses of the text and that is content to make cautious and restricted judgments on meaning.

There is to be noted a relation between the two reasons given for the restricted judgments to be made by the exegete. Our understanding of the text is correct insofar as it enables us to meet all further relevant questions. But what are such questions? One can pin them down in two manners. One can assign the prospective judgment to which they would be relevant. One can assign the field from which relevant questions might come. Because the field has a measure of indeterminateness, one is driven to assigning the prospective judgment. Inasmuch as one assigns such judgment, one finds oneself assigning determinate and restricted assertions.

The issue can be put in a third manner. The exegete begins from his *Fragestellung*, his own viewpoint, interests, concerns, that lead him to question the text. As he learns from the text, his *Fragestellung* becomes transformed; he discovers the questions the author was asking and attempting to meet; he understands the author in terms of the author's own questions and answers. Such an understanding of an author defines a context, settles all that is relevant to it, and all that has no bearing on itself. If that understanding of the author is correct, then there are no further relevant questions. Still, to determine whether that understanding is correct is made difficult by the indeterminacy of the whole. And until that indeterminacy can be eliminated, the exegete has to have recourse to the device of making restricted and limited judgments instead of pronouncing just what is the sum and substance, the essence and the accidents, of all the meaning contained in the text.

11 Statement of the Meaning of the Text

In stating the meaning of the text the exegete employs concepts, but there are notable differences of opinion on the type of concepts he should employ.

(a) Albert Descamps, 'Réflexions sur la méthode en théologie biblique,' *Sacra Pagina*, 1, 132–57.[4]

---

4 See above, p. 74, note 16.

Passage cited from pp. 142–43:

Cette théologie sera aussi diverse que le sont, aux yeux de l'exégète averti, les innombrables auteurs bibliques; à la limite, il y aura d'autant des théologies bibliques qu'il y a d'auteurs inspirés, car on s'attachera avant tout à respecter l'originalité de chacun d'eux.

Le chercheur paraîtra se complaire aux cheminements lents, et prendra souvent le sentier des écoliers; sa description aura la saveur des choses anciennes; elle donnera au lecteur une impression de dépaysement, d'étrangeté, d'archaisme; le scrupule de l'authenticité se traduira dans le choix d'une langue aussi biblique que possible, dans le souci d'éviter la transposition hâtive en vocables plus récents, fussent-ils accrédités dans la tradition théologique. Il y a tout un problème de la discrétion dans la choix de la langue en théologie biblique.

Tout exposé d'ensemble devra se construire suivant les conclusions de la chronologie et de l'histoire littéraire des écrits bibliques; il sera la préférence génétique. C'est pourquoi les questions de la date et de l'authenticité des écrits inspirés, apparemment secondaires en théologie biblique, y ont en réalité une importance décisive.

Ces exposés d'ensemble resteront d'ailleurs assez particuliers; s'ils embrassent la totalité des livres bibliques, ils ne porteront que sur un point de doctrine bien délimité; s'ils ont un objet complexe, ils ne porteront que sur un écrit ou un group d'écrits. Quant à la théologie biblique qui voudrait embrasser l'ensemble ou du moins un vaste secteur de la littérature inspirée, elle ne le pourra qu'en restant intérieurement très diverse, un peu comme le restera, au plan profane, une histoire générale de l'Europe ou du monde.

Certains rêvent, il est vrai, d'une sorte de raccourci, c'est-à-dire d'un exposé du dessein général de Dieu à travers l'histoire des deux Testaments; ce serait même là, suivant plusieurs auteurs, une forme privilégiée de théologie biblique. En réalité, il nous semble que l'esquisse de ce dessein n'appartient à la théologie biblique que dans la mesure même où l'historien peut s'y réconnaître; le croyant lui-même n'atteint le plan divin qu'à travers les multiples intentions des hagiographes.

The foregoing view may be named 'commonsense communication of a commonsense understanding of the text.'

The exegete begins from contemporary common sense; he develops the common sense of another time; he speaks to his pupils by beginning from their common sense and leading them into the multiple modes of the common sense of the multiple scriptural authors; that goal is vast, complex, endlessly nuanced.

In turn, the pupils will be able to communicate their understanding in the same manner, uttering what initially gives an impression of *dépaysement, détrangeté, d'archaïsme*; but when they have reached understanding, it will become familiar to them.

(b) Besides the foregoing 'commonsense communication of a common-sense understanding of the text,' one may envisage a scientific communication of a commonsense understanding of the text.

Such scientific communication rises spontaneously from the foregoing commonsense communication, for the very effort to communicate involves *die Wendung zur Idee.*

This tendency and turn may be illustrated by the composition of grammars and lexicons, which are based upon familiar understanding of groups of texts, and summarize recurrent elements or features to be found in texts. Again, from the grammars and lexicons of different languages or dialects, there arise another tendency and turn to the idea in the form of comparative grammars and comparative language study. To take a different instance, place names in texts lead to studies that collect the lot of them on a map; time references in texts lead to studies that collect the lot of them in a chronology; personal names in texts lead to genealogies, biographical dictionaries, outlines of history, etc.

Now the exegete draws upon all such studies in his work of interpreting particular texts. From one viewpoint, his work is one of applying the results of investigations in a large number of specialized fields. But there is also another viewpoint that arises in the measure that the application recurs over long series of texts.

For stating the meaning of the text is a totally new and disparate task only on the first occasion. As the number of occasions mounts on which one states the meaning of texts, one finds oneself stating over and over again the same meanings or slightly different meanings, and so one begins to compare and classify, to find basic recurrent categories, their differentiations, their frequencies.

Genetic processes next come to one's attention, and from the fact one may proceed to the cause or the form or the end of the genesis.

So A. Descamps casually mentions both categories and genetic considerations in his reflections on the method of biblical theology.

So M. Peinador lays it down that everyone would consider biblical theology to be a theology expressed in the very categories of the biblical authors. *Sacra Pagina*, 1, p. 168.[5]

5 On Peinador, see above, p. 75, note 16.

(c) In the third place, one may ask about the foundations of a scientific communication of a commonsense understanding of the text.

This question appears in Descamps's discussion, first, when he begins by ruling out of court H.-I. Marrou's contentions expressed in *De la connaissance historique*, and secondly, when he discusses Duméry's demand for a 'critique radicale,' pp. 133–36, 154–57.[6]

It appears in Peinador's illustration of biblical categories by the 'images' of the people of God and the kingdom of God (p. 168), and as well in his requirement that biblical theology presupposes definite dogmas.

But it also appears in the use of Hegelian thought as the spine of historical development (as in the Tübingen school of 19th-century higher criticism) and in Bultmann's use of Heidegger's existentialism, particularly in his interpretation of St Paul. Cf. Macquarrie, *An Existentialist Theology* (London: SCM Press, 1955 and 1960).

Finally, the same question appears in *Insight*, chapter 17, section 3.

There are a number of factors that enter into this problem and we must begin first from an enumeration and a description.

First, the effort to attain a scientific communication of a commonsense understanding of texts takes the interpreter beyond the explicit context of the original authors. Comparisons, classifications, the listing of categories and their differentiations, the observation and explanation of genetic processes, begin from the context of the original authors but they thematize it, and by that very fact go beyond it to ask and answer questions that the original authors did not undertake to discuss.

Implicit in the foregoing shift of context is the shift from hermeneutics to history. In hermeneutics the question is, What did the author mean insofar as his meaning is conveyed by his text? In history the question becomes, What was going forward? The battle plan of the general answers questions of the hermeneutic type, for that plan tells what the general meant to do. The actual course of the battle differs not a little from the victorious general's plan, and a great deal from the defeated general's plan. To ask about the actual course of the battle is to ask a historical question, and its answer is normally not this or that man's intention or meaning, but what results from the interplay of numerous and conflicting intentions and meanings.

Now the original authors used categories, effected differentiations of categories, brought about developments, but they did not sit back and reflect on what they had done. It is precisely this that is done when the scientific

6 On Marrou and Duméry, see above, p. 245, note 16, and p. 342, note 2.

communication of a commonsense understanding of texts is attempted. It moves beyond the explicit context of any given author's meaning to construct a historical context that contains, analyzes, and relates successive explicit contexts.

Secondly, the commonsense understanding of texts begins from a contemporary brand of common sense, that of the interpreter, and moves to an understanding of the common sense of another place and time. For the interpreter, his own original common sense is a *Selbstverständlichkeit*; it is something too obvious to be explained, too certain to need justification, too closely correlated with dramatic-practical saying and doing to be submitted to analysis. Still, it is only one brand of common sense: each people, each culture, each language, each region, each generation, each social class has its own; and each finds the others' strange, something that in time one can come to understand, something that perhaps one will make one's own by sociocultural migration, but not something that is one and the same all over.

Now the contemporary differentiation of common sense, while it does not imply a relativism, does imply a relativity. When the interpreter interprets for someone, he bears in mind that person's horizon. He will speak differently at a congress of his colleagues, in his university lectures, and in a public address. He will be able to bring things home effectively precisely in the measure that he understands the common sense of his audience, i.e., understands what they will understand immediately and fully.

It follows that just as there is a *Wendung zur Idee* that goes beyond the context of the texts to be interpreted, so also there is a *Wendung zur Idee* that goes beyond the common sense of the interpreters, that determines their categories and the genetic process of the development of their science or field.

Thirdly, there exist human sciences. They are concerned with the order of human living in family and society, morals and education, state and law, economics and technics. They are concerned with the meaning of human living in intersubjectivity and symbol, in art and language, history and religion, literature, science, and philosophy.

Insofar as these fields of investigation get beyond the initial descriptive phase of observation, collection, comparison, classification, insofar as they attempt to explain, correlate, analyze process, they become systematic. Their ultimate categories and differentiation of categories are, or aim to be, not what happened to be the categories of this or that writer or group of writers, but what are demanded by the subject itself, what lie in the nature of man, what can fit all cases, what will bring out most effectively the nature and structure of each.

Now the results of such human science are an effective tool for the scientific communication of commonsense understanding of texts. They are such a tool, not only when employed on the original texts, but also when employed on the texts written by interpreters of the original texts. Just as the interpreter will not hesitate to employ grammars and lexicons, geographies and histories, in his interpretation of texts, so too he will avail himself of the tools of analysis and communication provided by the human sciences.

Fourthly, there exist philosophies and theologies. Already we have spoken of understanding the text as a development in the interpreter and indeed of a conversion of the interpreter. But such conversion and its opposite are thematized and objectified in philosophical and theological positions. In those fields they find scientific statement, and such scientific statement is the statement of the foundations of basic orientations and attitudes.

Now such basic orientations and attitudes find their unfolding, expression, concrete realization (1) in the original texts, (2) in the interpretations placed upon the original texts, and (3) in the manner in which the human sciences are conceived, grounded, directed, developed. The basic orientations and attitudes are the basic meanings of all texts, whether of authors, of interpreters, or of human scientists.

(d) Basic Context

Context is a remainder concept; it denotes the rest that is relevant to the interpretation of the text.

Material context is the rest of the documents or monuments relevant to the interpretation of the text.

Formal context is hermeneutic or historical.

Hermeneutic formal context is the dynamic mental and psychic background from which the author spoke or wrote; it is the set of habits of sensibility and skill, of intellect and will, that come to a second act in the text.

Historical formal context is the genetic-dialectical unity of a series of hermeneutic formal contexts.

The distinction between hermeneutic and historical is illustrated by the difference between the general's plan of battle and the actual course of the battle. The former has the unity conferred on it by a single mind (matched against other minds). The latter corresponds neither to the victorious nor to the defeated general's plan; it is what is realized through the conflicting plans and decisions and because of them; but it results not merely from plans and decisions but also from what they overlooked.

Basic context is a heuristic notion, partly determined and partly to be determined. It is what becomes determined in the totality of successful efforts at exegesis.

At a first approximation, the basic context is the pure desire to know, unfolding through experience, understanding, and judgment, and leading to the statements found in the texts of authors, interpreters, and critics.

Secondly, it is the pure desire as a reality with a real unfolding leading to actual statements in each of the relevant authors, interpreters, and critics.

Thirdly, it is a reality that develops, that proceeds from the undifferentiated through differentiation to an articulated integration. Such development is both individual (from infancy to senility) and historical (from primitives to contemporary culture).

Fourthly, it is a reality that undergoes conversion, intellectual, moral, and religious, and that is subject to aberration.

It is to be noted that basic context is (1) real, (2) one and many, (3) the ground of genetic relationships, and (4) the ground of dialectical relationships.

Further, it is at once factual and normative: the pure desire is both a fact and a norm; and observance of the norm and nonobservance are facts with a normative connotation.

Again, basic context is related to common sense and scientific statements of the commonsense understanding of texts, as the upper blade of scientific method to the lower blade. They are mutually determining, and they result in a philosophically or theologically grounded scientific statement of the commonsense understanding of the texts.

Cf. *Insight*, chapter 17, section 3 on 'The Truth of Interpretation'; chapter 15, section 7 on 'Genetic Method'; chapters 2–5 on empirical method; the epilogue on the addition of the dimension of faith to human development and dialectic.

(e) Logic of Basic Context

Basic context is a context of contexts; it is not on the level of the author's understanding, of what he means; it is not on the level of the interpreter's commonsense statement of a commonsense understanding of the author's meaning; it is not on the level of a scientific statement of a commonsense understanding of the author's meaning; it is the level on which genetic and dialectical relationships are found between the scientific accounts of successive authors' meanings.

Compare (1) reference frames, (2) the group of transformation equations defining the geometry of the reference frames, (3) the series of groups of transformations defining the series of geometries.

Because basic context places a series of authors within a genetic-dialectical unity, it goes beyond the intentions of the authors. It is historical, and the historical brings to light what was going forward through the authors' intentions and deeds but not merely because of their intentions and deeds but also because of what they overlooked or failed to do.

E.g., basic context relates the trinitarian doctrine of Tertullian, Origen, and Athanasius. But Tertullian did not do so; Origen did not do so; Athanasius did not do so.

This does not imply that basic context is only in the mind of the upper-blade historian. It is also in the minds of the authors, but there it is implicit, *vécu*, in the mode of *Verstehen*, etc. The genetic is in them as their dynamic openness or their stagnation; the dialectical is in them as their good or un-easy conscience.

Basic context differs from the scientific statement of a commonsense understanding of the text. Such scientific statement presupposes the commonsense understanding of the text and employs in stating that under-standing (1) the categories constructed from the text and (2) the categor-ies constructed by human science. Basic context is concerned with the genesis and dialectical aberrations of categories.

Basic context differs from commonsense understanding of the text; it is content to select in the light of its own principles (usually unknown to the author) significant if very brief points. E.g., to prove Tertullian had two distinct modes of thinking about the divinity of the Son. Such selection is not understanding Tertullian. Indeed, not even a scientific statement of a commonsense understanding of Tertullian does more than effect such se-lections, though it does so in a complete manner.

Cf. Ebeling, 'Die Bedeutung,' *LfThK* 47 33: 'Es hat die Einsicht an Boden gewonnen, dass eine reine objektivierende, nach dem Ideal der naturwis-senschaftlichen Methode arbeitende Gesichtsbetrachtung, die sich mit der Feststellung dessen benügt, wie es einmal gewesen ist, der Aufgabe des geschichtlichens Verstehens gar nicht gerecht wird und auch nur in gewis-sen Grenzen durchführbar ist, das dabei die Geschichte gerade stumm bleibt und es nur zu einer Aufhäufung toten Materials kommt statt zu einer lebendigen personalen Begegnung mit der Geschichte.'

Conversely, the questions arising from scientific statement and from basic context contribute nothing to commonsense understanding of the text or situation.

E.g., the Council of Ephesus defined Our Lady's divine maternity. The definition is a corollary to the explication of the Christian tradition and its sources: one and the same is God and man. But the naive are prone to ask, Did Our Lady know she was Mother of God? How did she know it? How did she conceive? How did she feel about it? How do you prove all this from scripture? Does St Luke write with your account of Our Lady's thoughts and feelings in mind?

Such questions arise solely from a total incomprehension of the nature and possibility of serious exegesis and serious history.

It is possible to arrive at a commonsense understanding of the texts, at a scientific statement of that commonsense understanding, at a basic context that relates in a genetic-dialectical series the scientific statements.

But this possibility does not amount to the possibility of giving reasonable answers to an imaginative curiosity. The answers have to be theological, and theological answers do not include an imaginative reconstruction of the text.

20 July 1962
Regis College, Toronto

Lexicon of Latin and Greek
Words and Phrases

---

actus, de se delimitatus: an act limited in itself

actus exercitus / actus signatus: the act as exercised / the act as (reflectively) signified

actus primus: first act

actus primus corporis organici: first act of an organic body

actus secundus: second act

anathema sit: let him be anathema

ancilla theologiae: handmaid of theology

anima est quodammodo omnia: the soul is in some way all things

anima humana naturaliter Christiana: the human soul (is) naturally Christian

an sit: is it? whether it is

ante omnem operationem mentis: before every operation of the mind

a parte rei: on the side of the thing

bonum et malum in rebus: good and evil (are) in things

caritas foras expellit timorem, et qui timet non est perfectus in caritate: love drives out fear, and whoever is afraid is not perfect in charity

causa cognoscendi / causa essendi: the cause of knowing / the cause of being

certa rerum cognitio per causas: certain knowledge of things through their causes

Christus ut Deus et Christus ut homo: Christ as God and Christ as man

compositio vel divisio: composition or division

compositio vel divisio per affirmationem vel negationem: composition or division through affirmation or negation

consensus Patrum: the consensus of the Fathers

consensus theologorum: the consensus of theologians

conversio ad phantasma: conversion to phantasm
cor ad cor loquitur: heart speaks to heart
credimus quia credimus: we believe because we believe

de fide definita: defined as a matter of faith
de fide divina et catholica: (a matter of) divine and Catholic faith
disputatio magistralis: an argument ordered to teaching
    (i.e., to understanding rather than to certitude)
distinctio formalis: formal distinction
distributive: distributively
doctrina catholica: Catholic doctrine

effusio ad exteriora: pouring [oneself] out on external things
eidos: form
emanatio intelligibilis: intelligible emanation
ens et bonum: being and the good
ens est id cui suo modo competit esse: being is that which has its own proper act
    of existence
ex analogia eorum quae naturaliter cognoscit: from an analogy with those things
    one knows naturally

facile mobilis per instinctus superioris motoris: easily movable by reason of the
    instigation of a higher mover
fides ex auditu: faith [comes] from hearing
fides humana / fides divina: human faith / divine faith
fides informis, fides formata: faith that is unformed, faith that is formed
fides per rationem adiuta: reason assisted by faith
formale quo / formale quod: the formality by which / the formality which (with
    reference to the supernatural, the 'formale quod' is that which is believed while
    the 'formale quo' is the motive for believing)

gratia gratis data: grace freely given
gratia sanans / gratia elevans: healing grace / elevating grace

habitus acquisitus: acquired habit
habitus naturalis: natural habit
homo non potest non peccare etiam damnabiliter: man is unable not to sin even to
    the incurring of damnation
homoousion: consubstantial

id quod est: that which is
imago Dei: image of God

immunis a necessitate: free of necessity

in facto esse: in (a state of) actual being (as opposed to becoming)

in fieri: in (a state of) becoming (as opposed to being)

in genere intelligibilium ut potentia: (of human intellect) potency in the genus of intelligible things

initium consiliandi: the beginning of taking counsel

in his quae sunt sine materia idem est intelligens et intellectum: in the immaterial order the one understanding and the thing understood are identical

in personis proprietas, in essentia unitas, in maiestate adoretur aequalitas: there is adored what is proper in the persons, the unity in essence, the equality (of the persons) in (divine) majesty

in rebus: in things

in rebus, non tantum in mente: in things, not just in the mind

in statu naturae purae: in the state of pure nature

intellectus in actu: intellect in act

intellectus agens: agent intellect

intellectus possibilis: possible intellect

intelligibile in sensibilibus: intelligible in the sensible

ipsum intelligere: the act of understanding itself (i.e., God)

intentio entis intendens: the intending intention of being

intentio intendens / intentio intenta: intending intention / intended intention

libertas errandi: the freedom to err

lumen fidei: the light of faith

lumen intellectus nostri est similitudo quaedam creata luminis increati: the light of our intellect is a created likeness of uncreated light

modus recipientis: mode of the receiver

morphē: form

motus intelligitur ex termino: movement is understood from the end

natum non factum: born not made

nihil scientiae vel intellectus acquiret et vacuus abscedet: he acquires nothing by way of knowledge or understanding and goes away empty

nobilissimum theologicum munus: the most noble task of theologians

non est caecus animae motus: it is not a blind movement of the soul

nonidentitas formalis a parte rei: formal nonidentity on the side of the thing

numerus et mensura motus secundum prius et posterius: the number and measure of motion in respect of before and after

omne ens est bonum: all being is good

omnia Deum appetunt ut finem: all things desire God as their end

per accidens: accidentally, not essentially

per affirmationem vel negationem: through (by way of) affirmation or negation

per quem omnia facta sunt / per quem nihil factum est: through whom all things were made / through whom nothing was made

potens omnia facere et fieri: able to do and become all things

praeambula fidei: the preambles to faith

praeter intentionem: beyond (one's) intention

primum quo vivimus, sentimus, intelligimus: the principle whereby we live, sense, understand

principiatum immediate / principiatum mediate: from a principle immediately / from a principle mediately

priora quoad nos / priora quoad se: first for us / first in itself

quae tractat de Deo et de aliis quae ad Deum referuntur: what treats of God and of other things that are referred to God

quibus auxiliis: with which means

quidditas: quiddity

quidditas sive natura in materia corporali existens: quiddity or nature existing in corporeal matter

quidquid movetur ab alio movetur: whatever is moved is moved by another

quidquid recipitur ad modum recipientis recipitur: whatever is received is received in the way proper to the receiver

quid sit: what is it?

quid sit Deus: what God is

quoad substantiam: in regard to the substance

quoad verum: in regard to the true

quod ubique, ab omnibus: what [is believed] everywhere and by all

ratio inferior / superior: lower and higher reason

rationes necessariae: necessary reasons

ratio per fidem illustrata: reason illumined by faith

ratio sub qua res attingitur: the formality under which the thing is attained

recta ratio agibilium: right reason as to what is to be done

reductio in principia: reduction to principles

reflexio ad phantasma: reflection to phantasms

reflexio supra phantasma: reflection on phantasms

res de qua agitur: the matter under consideration

sapientia iudicat de ente et non ente, et de iis quae per se sunt entis: wisdom judges concerning being and non-being, and about those matters that per se have to do with being

sapientis est ordinare: it is the property of the wise person to order (things)

secundum quid / simpliciter: under some aspect / absolutely

secundum rectam rationem: according to right reason

sensus ecclesiae: the sense of the church

sensus fidelium: the sense of the faithful

simplices fideles: the simple faithful

si quis dixerit, anathema sit: if anyone says ..., let him be anathema

species expressa: expressed species

species intelligibilis: intelligible species

splendor gloriae et figura substantiae eius: the splendor of God's glory and the exact imprint of God's very being (Hebrews 1.3)

substantia separata: separate substance

summa sapientia ordinat omnia: the highest wisdom orders everything

syllogismus faciens scire: a syllogism that enables one to know

terminus a quo / terminus ad quem: the term from which / the term to which

thaumazein: to wonder

theologice certa: theologically certain

to ti ēn einai: formal cause [approximately; Lonergan: 'the essence, what a thing was to be']

unicum esse: the only act of existing

unius substantiae: of one substance

unum multis commune: one common to many

unum multis commune in mente: one common to many in the mind

unum multis commune in re: one common to many in reality

unum multis commune reflexum: one common to many recognized reflexively

verbum: word

verbum complexum: compound word

verbum incomplexum: simple word

verbum spirans amorem: the word spirating love

verum et falsum sunt in mente / bonum et malum sunt in rebus: true and false are in the mind / good and evil are in things

verum est medium in quo ens cognoscitur: the true is the medium in which being is known

vetera novis augere et perficere: to augment and complete the old with the new

Index

Abelard, Peter, 68, 282, 285, 411, 474
Abstraction: and extrinsicism, 117–18; and formal object, 378; and Greek science, 378; and modern science, 590; and Scholasticism, 590; in Thomas, 388
Actus exercitus–actus signatus, see Implicit-explicit
Adam-Seth-Eve: and consubstantiality, 192–93
Adaptation: and assimilation and adjustment (Piaget), 5–6, 396, 500–501, 570
Adler, A., 526
Adler, M., 306, 324
Adoptionists, 187
Aeterni Patris, 274, 335
Affectivity: in Freud, 205; and human good, 500; and interpretation, 213; and linguistic discourse, 205–207; and Romantic hermeneutics, 177, 184, 218; and symbol, 204, 525
Agent intellect, 130–31
Age of reason, 14, 32, 104, 263, 289, 569
Alchemy, 312

Alexander of Alexandria, 26
Alexander IV, Pope, 45, 336
Alexandrian-Antiochene schemes, 165, 419, 458
Alfrink, B.J., 348
Alienation, 618
Altaner, B., 317 & n. 11, 385
Anachronism, 64, 165–66, 350–51, 403, 419; and fundamentalism, 348
Analogy: a. of being, 136; a. of faith, 21, 599; and ignorance, 197; a. of knowing and being, 134–35; and knowledge of God, 43, 136, 149; and natural/supernatural, 334; a. of proportion, and religious worlds, 60–61; psychological a., 131, 196–97, 413; and systematic theology (Vatican I), 151, 196 & n. 8, 411; and theological use of Aristotle, 475, 478; a. of truth, 331–32
Anathema sit, 126, 176–77, 344
Anselm, 159, 160, 285, 346, 411, 473, 586, 622
Apollinaris/Apollinarism, 160, 173, 187, 281, 378, 418
Apostles' Creed, 173, 416

A priori: and radical intending, 434; structure of subject is a.p. for group and history, 479, 487, 490

Archaism, 64, 166, 419

Archimedes, 291, 431

Arians/Arius, 26, 83, 161, 173, 174, 187, 278, 280, 291, 345, 357, 596, 597

Aristotelian-Augustinian controversy, 68–70, 599

Aristotle, 7, 10, 34, 51, 52, 54, 69, 70, 71, 72, 73, 74, 92, 94, 96, 102, 104, 106, 107 & n. 3, 110, 115, 116, 128, 135, 136, 137, 153, 158, 180, 190, 209, 235, 237, 248, 269, 283, 288, 289, 300, 301, 310, 325, 336, 377, 392, 396, 398, 414, 424, 432, 433, 445, 460, 468, 469, 470, 471, 475, 477, 478, 480, 488, 512, 531, 533, 538, 548, 571, 578, 584, 589, 592, 598, 599, 607, 635. *See also* Science: Aristotelian notion of

Arnou, R., 360 & n. 4

Art: and aesthetic meaning, 201–204, 380, 520–23; as carrier of meaning, 520–23; a. defined, 201, 520; and insight/understanding, 155, 522–23, 606; and objectivity, 615; and possibilities, 523, 607, 610; and representation, 520; and symbol, 524, 606–607; and transformation of objective world, 203, 522, 610; and transformation of subject, 522, 610

Assumption of Mary, 296, 339, 341, 418; and Immaculate Conception, 296, 341

Asveld, P., 48 & n. 19

Athanasius, 26, 83, 161, 173, 174, 188, 291, 345, 652

Atheism, 586; Christian a., 557

Augustine, 45, 46–47 & nn. 14–17, 69, 72, 109 & n. 5, 159, 174, 191, 192–93, 268, 278, 281, 287, 290, 291, 311, 355, 362, 385, 400, 412, 481, 483 & n. 3, 511 & n. 13, 540, 565, 584

Authenticity: a., horizon, and conversion, 32, 141, 253, 288, 291, 316–17, 360; in Bultmann, 231; and critique of subjects, 291, 400; and cultural development, 553–54; and dialectic, 32, 193; and differentiation, 595; and existentialism, 318; and history, 253, 255, 288, 360; human and Christian a., 32 n. 3, 486, 489, 492, 554, 582, 583, 584; and grace, 595; and human good, 500; and image of God, 550; and judgment of value, 510; and logic, 267; major and minor a., 15 n. 13; and method, 488; and moral conversion, 564; and normativity, 253; and orientation, 39, 499; and originating values, 492; and position-counterposition, 141; and progress, 482, 486; relative and absolute a., 15 & n. 13, 24; and science, 472; and self-transcendence, 482, 490; and truth and value, 490. *See also* Conversion; Horizon; Inauthenticity; Self-transcendence

Averroes, 104

Avicenna, 104

Axial period, 49, 592

Bachelard, G., 528

Baius, 278

Balthasar, H.U. von, 77 & n. 18

Barth, K., 296, 557

Basil of Caesarea, 161, 174, 369, 599

Baudouin, C., 526 & n. 3

Baur, F.C., 464

Bea, A. Cardinal, 309

Beatific vision: in Christ, 420; and divine wisdom, 105; formal object of,

19; in Galtier's Christology, 169; and
knowledge of God, 43, 150, 197,
360, 393, 414; in Scotus, 130; and
supernatural, 580
Becker, C., 386, 563
Begrifflichkeit, 69–70, 475, 477, 578
Being: b. is concrete, 30, 61, 509, 590;
concept of b., 131, 133; as everything
about everything, 131; as final object,
30, 31, 133; as formal object, 149,
152; and good, 30–31; idea of b.,
132; intention of b., 29; knowing and
b. in God, 117–18, 124; knowing and
b. isomorphic, 195; b. known in true
judgment, 118, 131–32; and meaning, 387; and metaphysics, 61;
notion of b., 104, 131; notion of b.
and basic context, 232, 252; notion,
concept, idea, and knowledge of b.,
131–32; notion of b. and wisdom,
103–104; real b., 536; spheres of b.,
536–37, 543, 585; transcendent b.,
543–44, 596; and unconditioned,
121; and unity of knowledge,
133–34, 139
Being in love, 48, 483, 506, 550; with
God, 484, 485, 486, 511, 517,
550–52, 555, 558, 566, 582, 631
Belief(s): act of b., 142–45, 515–17;
and act of will, 143, 144, 147, 148,
323, 327, 329, 333; and appropriation of heritage, 513; critique of b.,
517; and decline, 567; b. doubles
meaning of 'true,' 142; effects of b.,
142–43; elements of b., 143–45; and
existential history, 404; and extension of truth, 142; and horizon, 626;
human b. and divine faith, 145–47;
and immanently generated knowledge, 605; and judgment of value,
144, 324, 515; knowledge and b.,
141–50; motive of b., 143; object of

b., 143; possibility of b., 515;
preambles of b., 144–45, 328, 331;
process of b., 142–45, 515–17;
reflective understanding in b.,
144–45, 147, 328, 331; in science,
394, 514; b. and supernatural, 146,
147; b. and true, 142–43; universal b.
and universal doubt, 407, 515, 644.
See also Credibility and credendity;
Faith
Benz, E., 620 & n. 3, 630
Bernheim, E., 244 & n. 15
Bewusstsein, 571
Bias: and decline, 507; general b., 508;
group b., 507–508; individual b.,
507
Biblical: b. scholarship and systematics,
181, 285–86; b. theology, 75,
225–26, 245, 407; b. theology and
dogmatic theology, 336–37, 348–49,
352–53, 364–65, 386, 460; b.
theology and theory, 337–38
Bifurcation of nature, 459 & n. 11, 479,
586–87
Billot, L., 131
Binswanger, L., 18, 273 & n. 21, 529
& n. 13
Block: and conversion, 264; in grouping of operations, 42
Body of Christ: and first phase, 461,
463; and foundations, 341; and
interiority, 150; as medium of
theology, 150, 154, 361, 393; and
progress-decline, 40; and redemptive
order, 41–42, 298, 321; as theological problem, 67
Boethius, 75, 281, 385, 481
Bonaventure, 45, 311
Bossuet, J.-B., 385, 401
Bouillard, H., 189 & n. 4
Bourbaki school, 113
Boutroux, P., 23 & n. 24

Boyer, C., 386

Brahmanism, 64, 319

Break: in object and subject, 138–39

Breakdowns: and conversions, 562–68

Breton, S., 390 & n. 5

Brouwer, L.E.J., 113–14

Brunner, E., 382

Buber, M., 76

Buddhism, 596, 620, 630

Bultmann, R., 69, 80, 97 & n. 13, 213
    & n. 4, 231, 248, 269 & n. 13, 307–
    308, 330, 386, 413, 449–50, 584,
    588–89 & n. 5, 639 & n. 2, 642, 648

Buri, F., 589

Butterfield, H., 239 & n. 4, 409 & n. 4

Buytendijk, F.J.J., 379 & n. 5, 519 n. 2

Byzantine Scholasticism, 161, 459

Cajetan, 76, 281, 385

Cano, M., 391, 401, 476

Canon of scripture: 89, 175; and
    dogmatic element, 344, 349, 458

Capreolus, 76, 281, 385, 481

Carthage, Council of, 176–77

Cassirer, E., 58 & nn. 4 and 5, 230 &
    n. 13, 298, 320 & n. 13, 380

Castelli, E., 589

Categorial: and transcendental, 27,
    432–33, 477, 534, 537, 572

Categories: and anachronism and
    archaism, 166, 350; Aristotle's c.,
    531; base of general c., 486; base of
    special c., 486–87, 613; biblical c.,
    648–49; biblical c. and Arius, 345;
    and data, 487; c. as determinations,
    432–33; for early Jewish Christians,
    25; general c., 478–82; and human
    sciences, 231; c. of New Testament,
    281; and scientific communication of
    exegete, 228–29, 652; settled and
    unsettled c. in theology, 280–81,
    340–41; special c., 482–86; and

transcendentals, 27; transcultural c.,
    477–78, 482, 589; transformation of
    c., 346; transposition of c., 162–64,
    171, 184; undeveloped c., 280–81,
    340–41; use of c., 486–87; and
    Wendung zur Idee, 338. *See also*
    Categorial

Cato, 219

Causa cognoscendi and *causa essendi*,
    110–11, 281

Causality: for Aristotle, 445, 538; for
    Hume, 437; c. as intelligibility, 575;
    and mutual mediation, 392; primi-
    tive notion of c., 58

Causes: four c. and Greek science, 378,
    433, 445

Cerfaux, L., 49–50 & n. 21, 280

Certitude: and authorities, 152; and
    doctrines/systematics, 414; and
    Greek and modern notions of
    science, 95; and judgment, 100, 103,
    390

Chadwick, O., 401 & n. 8

Chalcedon, Council of: 64, 83–84, 161,
    173, 188, 291, 358, 410, 458–59, 599

Charity: and base of special categories,
    484; and being in love with God,
    484, 485, 511, 613; and Christian
    authenticity, 489; difficult to
    recognize, 484; and fear, 66, 320;
    and fulfilment of structure of
    consciousness, 583 (*see also* Self-
    transcendence: and religious love);
    and healing and elevating grace, 40,
    300; c. isomorphic with structure of
    intelligence and rationality, 289–90;
    c. not the same as being attentive,
    intelligent, reasonable, responsible,
    581; and supernatural, 335, 622; and
    wisdom, 290

Christ: beatific vision in, 419–20; body
    of, *see* Body of Christ; Christ-centered

theology, 304; and dogma, 334–35; knowing divinity of C., 79; knowledge and consciousness of C., 167–71, 196, 273, 412, 419; and meaning, 321, 380; names of, 402

Church: and juridicism, 410; and kingdom of God, 555–56, 557; and people of God, 410; as *signum levatum in gentibus*, 333; and sociology, 382, 392; theology of c. needs development, *see* Categories: undeveloped c. *See also* Body of Christ

Churchill, W., 247

Civilization: ancient high c., 22, 48, 59, 355–56, 530; and operations, 22; and religion, 257

Classical: c. consciousness, 164–65; c. culture: 73–74, 164, 381, 503, 542

Classicism, 74, 164–66, 209, 243, 301, 347, 381, 383, 384, 475, 492, 503, 542, 598, 630, 636

Classics: characteristic of c., 364, 374, 642, 643; in Renaissance, 74; and tradition, 220–21, 407, 419, 643

Clement of Alexandria, 345, 360, 418, 589

Cognitional theory: and hermeneutics, 209–10, 635–37; and method, 424, 443; c.t.-epistemology-metaphysics, 442, 446, 449, 578

Collaboration: in science, 94; of theology and other disciplines, 107

Collingwood, R.G., 238 & n. 2, 404

Commitment: and community, 541; and constitutive meaning, 383; existential c., 393; and judgment, 97–98, 292, 420; and personal relations, 498; in science, 269–70; in theology, 270

Common sense: and communication, 227; defined, 54, 136, 227, 337, 531; and exegesis, *see* Hermeneutics: and

exegesis; growing in c.s., 372–74, 640 (*see also* Learning); and hermeneutics, *see* Hermeneutics; and history, 247, 249, 250, 258; and horizon, 366; c.s. mediated by theory in human sciences, 54; and relations to us, 116, 532; and understanding others' c.s., 217–18, 219, 227, 229, 351, 356, 641, 649

Common sense and theory: 4, 12, 34, 42, 49–52, 56, 57, 64, 137, 155, 260, 314, 337, 489, 538; and Aristotle, 70; and critical exigence, 539; and general bias, 209–10, 508; and Greek councils, 141; and interiority, 60, 76, 77, 138–40, 592 (*see also* Critical exigence; Methodical exigence); and methodical exigence, 138–40; and movement from faith to theology, 156–58; and movement from scripture to theology, 166–70; and Plato, 70; and *priora quoad nos* and *quoad se*, 139; transpositions from c.s. to theory, 162–64, 184; and systematic exigence, 480, 538–39. *See also* Bifurcation of nature; Implicit-explicit; *Priora quoad nos*; *Priora quoad se*; Thematization

Communication: and meaning of text, *see* Stating the meaning of the text

Communications: as functional specialty, 449, 453, 455, 460, 462, 463, 487, 600, 607, 611, 632

Community: c. of faith, 559–61, 581, 631; and meaning, 383, 393, 541–42; mediated by interiority, 54, 67, 266; mediated by theology, 296; mediated by theory, 54, 266, 283; mediates religion, 54; mediates subject, 59; and narrative history, 237; and ordinary language, 531; in primitive mentality, 48; scientific c., 378,

472–73; and special categories, 485; world of c., *see* Common sense; Common sense and theory

Concept(s): c. of being, *see* Being: concept of; beyond elemental meaning, 204; in cognitional process, 129; and *esse*, 131; and hypothesis, 99; and judgment, 96, 131, 133, 256, 269; and notion, 131; in Scotist psychology, 12, 129–31; and technical language, 69; and understanding, 99, 100, 101, 112, 389, 471; and words, for Aquinas, 212

Conceptualism, 195

Concern: ultimate c., 553, 554, 557, 560, 565

Concrete: being is c., 30, 61, 509, 590; common sense deals with c., 54, 227, 231, 240, 250, 337, 508; and dialectic, 450, 525; and formal object, 19; good is c., 35, 37, 494; good of order is c., 37, 73, 496–97, 500; metaphysics and c., 615; methodological consideration c., 27; modern science concerned with c., 378; and syllogism, 11; transcendental notions c., 509; and universal, 89

Concrete universal: normative subject is c.u., 400

Condensation: and symbol, 205, 206, 207, 381, 525

Conflict(s): between concept and performance, 399, 442–43; c. material for dialectic, 450–51; c. resolved by foundations, 462; six possibilities of c. between science and theology, 489

Congar, Y., 3 & n. 2, 16–17 & nn. 15 and 16, 45 & n. 13, 68, 284

Consciousness: Augustine and Aquinas on c., 274, 290–91, 400; c. of Christ, *see* Christ: knowledge and consciousness of C.; classical c., 164–66; data of c. for cognitional theory/intentionality analysis/transcendental method, 129, 133, 430–31, 437, 490, 536, 574, 591; differentiated c., 44–45, 319, 381, 383, 416, 459, 480, 503, 537; differentiation of c. and exigences, 537–41; dynamism of c., and sacred/profane, 56, 60; and *existentiell*, 157; c. foundation of distinctions of sacred/profane, common sense/theory, inner/outer, 52–53; c. of freedom, 292; heightening of c., 435–37, 442, 487, 540, 569–71, 592; historical c., *see* Historical: h. consciousness; horizontal and vertical movements in c., 574–75; intentional c. and feelings, 504; intentional c. and question of God, 483–85, 543–49, 583, 584, 586, 617; and language, 530–31; levels of c., 133, 278–79, 292–93, 429–35, 437–38, 454–55; levels of c. and functional specialties, 454–55; mythic c., 122; patterns of c., *see* Patterns of experience; and presence, 46–47; rational c. and rational self-c., 293; and reference to God, 257; c. of scientist, 137; selectivity of c., 199; self-c. and self-knowledge, 132–33; specialization of c. and common sense/theory, 60, 158; structure of c. and common sense/theory, 50–51, 56, 314; structure of c. and subject/object, 56, 60, 314; symbolic c., 44–45, 164, 312; and Trinity, 273; undifferentiated c., 44–45, 58, 59, 312, 319, 417, 480; unity of c., 561–62; word as completion of c., 541

Consent: thematizing c., 292

Conservatism: true c., 255

Constantinople, First Council of, 93

Constantinople, Second Council of, 83

Constantinople, Third Council of, 83, 160

Consubstantial: context of, 173; and development of dogmatic–theologic-al context, 340; different meanings of c., 186; and degrees of thematiza-tion, 340; and having the same predi-cates, 26, 187, 308; and theoretic element, 83, 334–35. *See also* Homoousion; Nicea

Contagion: psychic c., 518

Context: absolute c., 637; always pre-supposed, 174; basic c., 232–33, 252, 650–53; dogmatic-theological c., *see* Dogmatic-theological context; ex-periential and systematic c., 162–63, 171; formal c., 232, 650; and her-meneutic circle, 644; historical for-mal c. and hermeneutic formal c., 223, 232, 360, 644, 648–49, 650; and horizon, 467–68; and interpreta-tion, 449, 461; judgment always in a c., 104, 417; and judgment of inter-pretation, 637; and judgment of value, 511–13; logical c. and method-ical c., 470–72, 473, 491, 492; ma-terial c., 232, 650; and method, 470–72, 473; c. a remainder concept, 20, 182, 232, 650; and Romantic her-meneutics, 177, 184, 219–20; c. of symbol, 526–28; and transposition/ transferring, 165, 171, 177, 178, 179, 180, 181, 184, 219, 335, 642; truth independent of c., 183–84, 335, 370–71, 406, 407, 644–45; truth and meaning depend on c., 470–71

Contingency: c. of courses of action, 332; and modern science, 382, 470; and necessity in Greek thought, 390, 470; and prudence, 107, 470; and relations of nature and grace, 90; and theology, 106–107; and virtually unconditioned, 536; c. of world, 391, 543, 545

Contingent predication, 414

Continuum: in Greek and modern science, 378

Contradiction: principle of, 93, 263, 355–56, 390, 571, 620; performative c., 399, 442

Controversialist: and interpreter, 214, 404, 471, 639

Conversion: and absolute horizon, 396; and basic context, 651; and block in development, 264; and breakdowns, 567–68; and Catholic faith, 15, 32, 262, 303; and dialectic, 27, 32, 141, 185, 193, 288, 291; differences of intellectual, moral, and religious c., 400; and foundations, 452, 455, 564, 588, 600; and hermeneutics/ interpretation, 211, 220, 230, 407, 642–43, 650; and horizon/authenti-city, 32, 39, 108, 141, 185, 193, 252, 253, 262, 264, 288, 291, 360; intellectual c., 14–15, 27, 33, 263, 294, 400, 463, 562–64, 598, 627; intellectual and moral c., 596–97 (*see also* Stoics/Stoicism); moral c., 14, 262–63, 303, 564–65, 627; moral and religious c., 303–304, 596–97; and normative element, 253; and orientation, 39, 396, 397, 497, 499; c. personal, communal, and histor-ical, 452, 463; relations of three conversions, 565–66, 596–97; religious c., 15, 32, 67, 262, 303, 560, 565, 621, 625, 627; religious c. and normative subject, 399; c. as reorganization/transformation of subject, 14–15, 262, 452; in science and in faith, 271; social, historical, and doctrinal dimensions of c., 463; and systematics, 600; three kinds of c., 14, 32; and tradition, 221

Coreth, E., 53 & n. 24, 279 & n. 29, 399

Correlation: method of, 621

Credibility and credendity: judgment of, 144, 147, 326, 328, 331

Critical exigence, 123, 124, 125, 138, 140, 149, 283, 284, 539

Critical problem, 391, 600, 613

Cullmann, O., 308 & n. 4

Culture: as blocking apprehension of theory, 51–52; classical c., see Classical: c. culture; see also Historical consciousness; classicist and empirical notions of c., 492–93, 598; classics and c., 220, 643; lower and higher c., 502–503; c. as meaning of a way of life, 493; modern c., 491, 542, 598; stages in c., 542

Cyril of Alexandria, 84, 161, 173–74, 187–88, 291, 308, 345, 359, 360, 409, 418, 599

Daniélou, J., 25 & n. 32, 415 & n. 3

Daseinsanalyse for theology, 485, 572, 584, 589

Data: and categories, 487; and cognitional process, 86, 93, 94, 99, 129, 130, 199, 411, 430–37, 574; d. of consciousness, 129, 133, 430–31, 437, 490, 536, 574, 591; and Kant, 121; in natural science, human science, theology, 251, 391–92, 592–93; and objectivity, 100, 389; and reflective understanding, 576; text as d. and as truth, 179–80, 391–92; theory increases d., 461, 570; and types of specialization, 446–48

Dawson, C., 313

Decline: progress and d., see Progress: and decline; and unauthenticity, 508

De Deo Trino, 25, 273, 279, 285, 382, 409, 413, 456, 457, 601

De Finance, J., 512 & n. 14, 549

Definition: explicit and implicit d., 427; heuristic d., 180–81, 348–49; implicit d. and human good, 495; implicit d. and operations, 578; implicit d. and system, 443; and priora quoad se, 51; and Socrates, 51, 136–37, 530, 537–38; as word, 11, 129, 148

De la Taille, M., 481

Deliberation: d. about d., 543–44

De Lubac, H., 382 & n. 18

Demythologization, 564, 589

De Nobili, R., 630

Denzingertheologie, 153, 293

Déodat de Basly, 168

Depression: economic d., 36, 283

Descamps, A., 74–75 & n. 16, 225–27, 231, 245, 337–38, 348, 352, 387, 407, 645, 647, 648

Descartes, R., 23, 145, 345, 385, 481, 515, 644

Description: and explanation, 57–58; and observation, 425

Desire: for finite and infinite, 43; for God, 43, 48, 60, 205, 257, 311; and moral conversion, 14, 32, 262; natural d. for vision of God, 43, 304, 394; and particular good, 36, 497; and sacred, 45; and transcendent exigence, 540. See also Desire to know

Desire to know: and basic context, 232, 651; and belief, 149, 152; and intellectual drive, 420; and mobility of worlds, 61; and molding of sensitivity, 610; and notion of being, 131; and questions, 566; and theoretic subject, 50

Deus Scientiarum Dominus, 84, 274, 379, 385

Development: and anachronism/ archaism, 64, 166; d. of child (Piaget), 5–8, 22, 23–24, 396; of civilizations, 22; classifying d., 22, 42–55; and common sense/theory, 42, 49–52, 57; and comparative method, 185–88; and contexts, 20–23; and dialectic, 27, 31, 32, 33, 192–94; and differentiation of consciousness, 44; as differentiation and integration, 42, 87, 313, 315, 319, 457, 466, 481, 556, 651; and differentiation of operations, 34 (*see also* Differentiation); of doctrine/dogma, *see* Dogma/doctrine, development of; of dogmatic-theological context, 20–23, 32, 172–74; of feelings, 504–506, 511, 524–25, 602, 603; and genetic method, 27, 467; and habits, 22–24; and heuristic procedures, 181; and historical investigation, 244; and horizon, 13–14, 396; and human good, 35, 494–500; in *Insight*, 24; d. of interpreter, 213, 220–21, 230, 404, 407, 642–44, 650; levels of d., 397; and limits, 56–60; and meaning, 40, 242; and mediation, 53–54, 59–60; mediates subject, 59–60; and operations, 1–24 passim, 31, 34, 42, 396, 500–504, 603; and sacred–profane, 42, 57, 433–46; and subject–object, 42, 46–49, 57; of theology, 19, 21, 75, 89, 112, 150, 172, 185, 194, 277, 361, 456–57, 466, 489; and truth, 90; understanding d., 71. *See also* Conversion

De Verbo Incarnato, 50, 259, 273, 280, 281, 420, 629

de Waelhens, A., 18 & n. 20, 264

Dialectic: Aristotelian d., 94; and basic context, 651–53; and categories, 487; and encounter, 455; and formal context, 650; and foundations, 452–53, 462, 464, 465, 600; as functional specialty, 449, 450–51, 461, 462, 560, 613; and normative, 284; and positive theology, 588; d. of sin, decline, redemption, 299, 302; and transcendental method, 443. *See also* Development: and dialectic; Dialectical

Dialectical: d. aspect to development, *see* Development: and dialectic; genetic and d. relations, 232, 467, 651–52; d. heuristic structures, 478; and horizons, 467, 473; meaning of word 'dialectical,' 31; d. method(s): 24, 27, 31, 32, 33, 192–94, 277, 360, 418, 528, 600

Differentiation: and Augustine-Bonaventure compared to Thomas, 45; of categories, 647, 648, 649; of consciousness, 44, 319, 416, 417, 459, 503, 537 (*see also* Consciousness: differentiated c.); and evolution of meanings, 381; and exigences of meaning, 537; of inner and outer, 56; and integration, 42, 87, 313, 315, 319, 457, 466, 481, 556, 651; and language, 200; and mediation, 59; of methods, 395–414 passim; modern d. of science, 72; of operations, 6, 13, 21, 31, 34, 42, 501; of religion and secular, 554, 558; of religion and theology, 459–60, 540; retreat from d., 518, 554; of sacred and profane, 44–46, 56; of theory/science and common sense, 51, 52–53, 137, 138–39, 314, 592; undeveloped d., 518; d. within theology, 460; of worlds, 52, 60

Dilthey, W., 41, 48 & n. 18, 77, 154,
218 & n. 8, 240, 243, 274, 284, 386,
391, 406, 614, 637, 641
Diodore of Tarsus, 187
Distinction: defined, 118; knowing d.,
and judgment, 118, 121; notional d.
defined, 117; and predicates, 562;
real d. defined, 117; Scotist formal
d., 117
Divino Afflante Spiritu, 274, 476
Docta ignorantia, 433
Doctrine: and dogma, *see* Dogma/doc-
trine; and historical consciousness,
75; history of d. and d. itself, 27, 33,
188–90, 277, 284, 465; and thematization, 184, 349–41; and theory, 66,
166, 184. *See also* Doctrines; Dogma/
doctrine: development of
Doctrines: as functional specialty, 449,
453, 455, 456–57, 462–65, 600
Dodd, C.H., 349, 407
Dogma/doctrine: development of, 27,
31, 85, 89, 93, 112, 161–62, 165,
172–74, 184, 185, 342, 359, 361–62,
385, 394, 409, 415–18, 476
Dogmatic element in Christianity, 344
Dogmatic-theological context: 19–23,
30, 31, 88, 154, 158, 168, 169, 170,
171, 172, 173, 174, 182, 185, 190,
307–308, 340, 357–58
Dogmatic theology: function/job of,
277, 295, 307, 364, 401, 403, 409,
410; and formal object, 19; and historical consciousness, 637; and judgment, 392, 409, 411; and method,
408–10; and positive theology, *see*
Positive theology; and scripture/bib-
lical theology/exegesis, 170, 175–81,
317, 336–37, 348–49, 357–58, 359,
364–65, 386, 418–20, 460; and systematic theology, *see* Systematic theology; uses heuristic definitions,

180–81, 348–53. *See also* Dogma/
doctrine: development of; Dogmatic-
theological context; Positive theolo-
gy; Systematic theology;
Thematization
Donatism, 262, 326
Donnelly, P., 401 & n. 46
Dreams: and consciousness, 570; exis-
tential inte4rpretation of, 529; and
Freud, 206; and Fromm, 527; of the
morning, 273 (*see also* Binswanger, L.)
Driesch, H., 393
Drifter, 398
Droysen, J.G., 240
Duméry, H., 78 & n. 20, 342–43 & nn.
2–4, 648
Durand, G., 65 & n. 12, 205–206, 380,
528
Dynamic: materially and formally d.,
435, 480, 572

Ebeling, G., 213, 243, 454, 652
Ecclesiasticus, 64
Eddington, A., 57 & n. 2, 81, 137,
383
Education: e. as transmission of
meaning, 298
Einstein, A., 91, 116, 142, 235, 253,
270, 271, 331, 402, 469, 610
Eliade, M., 44 & n. 12, 58, 230,
251–52, 275 & n. 24, 276, 312, 380
& n. 6, 528 & n. 9, 582, 587, 621
Emergent probability, 482, 627
Emotional identification, 518–19
Empathy (*Einfühlen*): in Romantic
hermeneutics, 177, 218, 641–42
Empedocles, 371
Empiricism, 126, 390, 397, 536–37,
546–47, 561, 563–64
Encounter: and dialectic, 455; and
meaning, 379; and recognition of
God's love, 560; theology as e., 454

Enlightenment, the: 221, 240, 352,
387, 403, 407, 447, 472, 637, 643
Ephesus, Council of, 93, 173, 174, 308,
358, 398, 418, 652
Epistemology: and dogma, 79; Gilso-
nian e., 263; and methodology, 122;
and positing absolute, 96–97; and
positive studies, 386; psychology/
cognitional theory, e., and metaphysics, 124–25, 138, 413, 442–43, 446,
449, 578
Esprit de finesse, 100–104, 371, 372
Esse naturale/ Esse intentionale: 41, 215,
235–36, 297, 320, 361; and imma-
nentism/ idealism, 274
Essentialism, 269, 398
Estius (Willem H. von Est), 69, 411,
460
Euclid, 9, 23, 85, 86, 103, 129, 130,
156, 381, 389, 390, 407, 589, 614,
624
Eunomius, 192, 369
Evil: and God, 625; sin and e., 66, 294,
319, 566; transformation of, 259,
300, 486, 508, 559
Exegesis/exegete: and biblical theology
(Descamps), 225, 352; and common
sense, 229, 338, 351, 645; and
communication, 229; and dogmatic
theology/theologian, 170, 180,
348–50, 352; and hermeneutics,
208–209, 635; and interpretation
(functional specialty), 447–48;
operations of, 637; and probable
opinion, 347; and rules, 216, 404,
640; and textual critic, 456, 461; and
theory, 228
Exigence, *see* Critical exigence;
Methodical exigence; Systematic
exigence; Transcendent exigence
Existentialism: 75, 401, 476, 546
Existential moment, 564

Existenz, 398
Existenziell-existenzial, 157–58. *See* also
Implicit-explicit
Experience-experiment, 157, 158, 172,
180. *See also* Implicit-explicit
Experiencing-understanding-judging:
15, 54, 150, 195–96, 279, 605; and
potency-form-act, 34, 135, 279
Experiencing-understanding-judging-
deciding: 46, 427, 432, 436, 478, 534,
591, 601; as applied to experiencing-
understanding-judging-deciding,
437–38
Expression (*Ausdruck*); modes of e. and
interpretation, 371; in Romantic
hermeneutics, 175, 178, 218, 219,
364; religious e., *see* Religious
expression
Extrinsicism: 108–22 passim, 126, 140,
141, 398, 642
Ezekiel, 565

Facts: historical f., 564
Faith: and absolute positing, 97; act of,
97, 143–44, 326–28, 330–34, 393;
analogy of, 21; assent of, 330, 392; f.
of authority and scientific f., 111–12,
398; as existential commitment, 393;
as eye of love, 560–61; and freedom,
326–27; and God's knowledge of
mysteries, 183; human and divine f.,
145–47; as knowledge born of religious love, 558; and levels of consciousness, 561; light of f., 147–50,
271–72, 286, 323; and natural
knowledge, 151–52, 322; and new
interiority, 150; object of, 334–35;
motive of, 148; preambles of, 144,
145, 328, 331; process of, 142; rationality of act of f., 293, 331; as recognition of God's love, 560; reflective
understanding in f., 147–48, 323; as

response, 560; as supernatural act/ truths, *see* Supernatural; and theology, 150–58 passim, 160, 322; transforms reason, 391–92, 393, 399; and worlds of community and theory, 159–60, 161, 166, 170, 173, 174. *See also* Belief(s)

Family: and being in love, 483; and good of order, 36, 37, 41, 73, 495

Fanaticism, 558

Fay, C.R., 264 & n. 7

Fear: and moral conversion, 14, 32, 262; and sin, 66; symbols of, 65, 319;

Feeling(s): aberrations of, 506; community of, 517–18; development of, 504–506; fellow f., 518; and human good, 498; intentional f., 504, 505; nonintentional f., 504; for Scheler, 305, 607–608; and symbols, 523; and value, 505, 510–11, 526

Fessard, G., 40 & n. 8, 302, 498

Fichte, J.G., 546

Fideism: and Barth, 557

Fides scientifica, 111–12, 398

Fifth Lateran Council, 117

Figures of speech, 533

Fire: 'What is fire?' as heuristic structure, 180, 480–81

First: f. for us and f. in itself, 50. See also *Priora quoad nos*; *Priora quoad se*

First Lateran Council, 83

First Vatican Council, 30, 84, 146, 150, 151, 152, 172, 183, 194, 196, 274, 286, 295, 322, 335, 349, 382, 388, 392, 401, 404, 411, 550, 625

Flavell, J.H., 396 & n. 3, 501

Formalism: and deviation of worlds, 62–63

Foundations: and Bultmann's hermeneutics, 248; and communication of meaning of text, 228–30, 648; and conversion, 455, 600; and dialectic,

464–65; and doctrines, 453; faith and f. of theology, 341–42, 613; as functional specialty, 452, 462; and fundamental theology, 395, 412, 452, 583; and interiority, 342

Fourteenth-century decadence, 109–10

Fourth Lateran Council, 149

Francis of Assisi, 276

Frankfort, H., 58 & n. 3, 380

Frankl, V., 529 & n. 13

Fraudes Apollinistarum, 173

Freedom: and act of faith, 326–27; f. *in causa*, 326–27; consciousness of f., 292; and human good, 35, 301–302; in medieval theology, 159–60

Freud, S., 39, 205, 206, 379, 381, 526–27, 529, 606

Fries, H., 86–87 & n. 7, 134 & n. 6, 381

Frings, M., 504 & n. 11

Frohschammer, J., 274

Fromm, E., 527 & n. 5

Frye, N., 528 & n. 10, 609

Functional specialties/specialization: 446–66 passim, 591, 592; as complication of basic structure, 478, 485; and horizon, 468; and human sciences, 614; and moral theology, 600; and one theology, 601

Fundamentalism, 348

Fundamentaltheologie (Rahner), 487, 584

Fundamental theology, 280, 413; and foundations, 395, 412, 452, 583

Gadamer, H.-G., 18, 115 & n. 13, 213, 221, 241, 332, 386, 403, 407, 425, 639, 642, 643 & n. 3

Galileo, 121, 469, 514

Galois, É., 57

Galtier, P., 167, 168 & n. 9, 169, 171

Gardiner, P., 241 & n. 11

Gargan, E., 257 & n. 21

Garrigou-Lagrange, R., 386

Genetic method, 191, 651

Geometry: for Aristotle, 424; and basic context, 651; Euclidean and non-Euclidean g., 23, 469; and *esprit de finesse*, 103; Riemannian g., 610

German Historical School, 41, 240, 246, 254

Gilbert de la Porrée, 68

Gilkey, L., 539

Gilson, É., 17 & nn. 16 and 17, 119, 120, 255, 263 & n. 6, 402

Gnostics/Gnosticism: 25, 26, 187, 318, 345, 415

God: in Aquinas, 34, 118, 135, 414; in Aristotle, 414; and contingent predication, 414; and desire, 43, 48, 60, 205, 257, 311, 394; formally unconditioned, 98, 586; 'God is,' 79, 125, 307; 'God loves,' 626; knowing and being are one in G., 124, 135; knowledge of G. analogous, 43, 149, 197; knowledge of G. mediated, 43, 60, 307, 311, 393; G. known in three ways, 360–61; natural knowledge of G., 625; and necessity, 382; as object, 134, 304–307, 545–47, 561–62; as objective, 4, 54, 257; in Old and New Testament, 281; as originating value, 549–50, 617; as perfect integration, 67; G. of philosophers and of religion, 548–49, 562–63; power and wisdom of, 105; as pure act, 34; question of, 483–85, 543–49, 554, 583, 584, 585, 586; and religious conversion, 15; G. a self-constituting existential subject, 413; as self-transcending, 550; and theology, 19, 150, 360, 361, 362, 411, 463; and verification, 548

Gödel, K., 390, 469

Gonseth, F., 114

Good: and being, 30, 32; always concrete, 35, 37, 494; evil into g., 300,

508; and holy, 596; human g., *see* Human good; as object of will, 31, 97, 294; g. of order, *see* Human good: and good of order; particular g., *see* Human good: and particular good; 'simply g.,' 39; and similitude of God, 43; supernatural g., 148; g. as terminal value, *see* Human good: and terminal values; in things, 34–35, 37, 301; true g. and merely apparent g., 497, 505, 509, 510, 544, 601. *See also* Value(s)

Grabmann, M., 284 & n. 3

Grace: actual g., 160; actual g. and vital act, 189–90; certainty about g., 580–81; and divine essence, 414; elevating g., 40, 329; and emergent probability, 627; g. given to everyone, 582; healing g., 40, 147, 329; in history, 299; and Immaculate Conception, 341; medieval problems concerning g., 158–60, 174, 277–78, 610–11, 622; nature and g., 90, 382; operative and cooperative g., 565 (see also *Gratia operans*); and reflective act of understanding in faith, 323, 328; sanctifying g. and formal effects, 368; and supernatural truth, 258; and theorem of supernatural, 335

Graham, Billy, 324

Gratia operans, 191, 208, 265. *See also* Grace: operative and cooperative g.

Gratian, 411

Gregory IX, Pope, 45

Gregory Nazianzen, 192, 193, 369

Gregory of Nyssa, 192, 193, 369

Grimm, H., 41, 240

Günther, A., 274

Gutwenger, E., 167–72 & n. 8

Habit(s): 5–8, 12–14, 19, 23, 24, 31, 32, 35, 37, 38, 51, 102, 135, 137,

159–60, 212, 278, 293, 300, 366, 396, 397, 398, 538, 650

Haughton, R., 498 & n. 5

Harnack, A. von, 29, 241 & n. 12, 244

Haute vulgarisation, 52, 164, 272, 276

Hearing: in New Testament, 344

Hegel, G.W.F., 40, 48, 53, 55, 64, 97, 104, 125, 209, 240, 242, 269, 302, 359, 390, 392, 426, 443, 498, 546, 565, 648

Heidegger, M., 17–18 & n. 19, 41, 69, 76, 97, 104, 125–26, 157, 219, 231, 243 & n. 13, 264–65, 274, 275, 305, 430, 433, 437, 449, 572, 612, 618, 641, 648

Heiler, F., 465 & n. 13, 582, 583, 596, 620, 630

Henry of Ghent, 290

Herder, J.G., 406

Heresy: and doctrinal development, 31, 141, 416

Hermeneutic circle, 215–16, 222, 370, 404, 407, 423, 637

Hermeneutics: and blocks, 403; and cognitional theory, 209–10, 563, 636, 637; and epistemology, 386; and exegesis, 208, 635; existential dimension of h., 643; and history, 229, 231, 359–60; not a primary field of inquiry, 208–209, 635; Romantic h., 177–79, 184, 218–20, 358–59, 364, 406, 408, 641; rules of, 216, 640. *See also* Exegesis; Meaning; Understanding the text

Hermes, G., 274

Heuristic: and basic context, 232, 650; h. definitions, and dogmatic theology, 180–81, 348–49; h. function of method, 444; metaphysics as h. structure, 478; h. notion, 75, 180–81, 232, 234, 480–81, 650; h. structures (classical, statistical, genetic, dialectical), 478

Heussi, K., 240–41 & n. 6, 244–46, 386

Higher viewpoints: and conversions, 626; and development, 482

Hippolytus, 75, 416

Historical: h. consciousness: 41, 73–76, 166, 209, 210, 241–42, 243, 297, 321, 384, 386, 403, 636, 637; h. essay, 250; h. method, 244–49; h. relativism, 242–44; h. studies: methodological classification of h. studies, 249–59; h. theology, 359

Historicism, 637

Historismus: 235, 240, 241, 243, 244, 246, 248–49, 384, 401, 643

History: and apologetics, 257–58; basic h., 450; and common sense, 54, 107; critical h., 238–40, 254; and doctrines, 464–65 (*see also* Doctrine: history of d. and d. itself); existential and narrative h., 236–38, 253–54, 332–33, 404; as functional specialty, 450, 454–55, 461–63, 560, 588, 591; general h., 450; and hermeneutics, *see* Hermeneutics: and history; and meaning, 297, 321, 542; norms found in study of h., 193; and perspectives, 247–48 (*see also* Perspectivism); and philosophy, 242, 252–53; and positive theology, 94, 357; as progress-decline-redemption, *see* Progress; and religion, 256–57; and science, 251–52; scientific h., 404; special h., 450; theological mediation of h., 258–59; and tradition, 253–56; h. written and h. written about, 345; and time, 235–36

Hoenen, P., 398 & n. 5

Holiness: h. as distinct, 566

Holy: the h. as a type of good, 596

Holy Ghost/Holy Spirit: gift(s) of, 288–90; procession of, 192–93

Homoousion, 26, 29, 83, 161, 165, 186, 280, 308, 408

Horizon(s): absolute h., 396, 398, 402, 405, 408; and belief, 626; broadening of h., 13–14, 220, 272, 642; complementary, genetic, and dialectical relations of h., 467; and conversion, 14–15, 32, 141, 193, 252–53, 264, 288, 290, 291, 316; h. defined, 13, 366, 395, 466–67; and foundations, 452–53, 462; and habits, 14; and horizontal and vertical liberty, 512, 549; and inauthenticity, 15–17, 24, 32, 141, 185, 193, 252–53, 264, 288, 290, 291, 316; and love, 559, 601–602; and method, 466, 468–72; and philosophies, 563–64; and pole-field, 395; and question of God, 545, 586; relative h., 396–98, 402; social h., 397; and worlds, 83

Horney, K., 506, 571

Hostie, R., 571

Hugo, V., 206, 374

Human good: based on nature, 40; formally constituted by meaning, 40, 41, 274, 297–98; and freedom, 301–302; and good of order, 36–38, 594–95; levels of, 297; as object of historical study, 274; and particular good, 35–36, 594–95; and progress and decline, 506; social mediation of, 35, 310–11; structure of, 35–40, 397, 495; summary statement of, 500; and supernatural, 259, 549–50; and terminal values, 38–40, 594–95. *See also* Good

Human sciences: and categories, 231, 487–88, 652; and church, 300; and communication of commonsense understanding, 230; h.s. empirical, 72–73, 347, 352, 354, 377; and

existential involvement, 323; and hermeneutics, 209; and history, 251–52; meaning is fundamental category in, 209, 230, 391, 592; and mediation of community by theory, 54; naturalist tendency in, 115; and theology, 72–73; and turn to theory, 184; and *Verstehen*, 155

Humani Generis, 31, 172, 183, 357, 364, 408

Hume, D., 195, 437, 442, 575

Hunt, J. McVicker, 396 & n. 2

Husserl, E., 41, 62 & n. 10, 63, 76, 87, 97, 125, 154, 219, 243, 267–68 & n. 12, 269, 274, 343, 382, 386, 387, 395, 400, 467, 572

Huyghe, R., 380 & n. 10

Hylomorphism, 70, 290

Hypothesis: and conception, 99; and experiments, 429, 451; in interpretation, 178; and judgment, 131, 482; and science, 158, 378, 548; in systematic theology, 411, 413; and truth, 564; and wisdom, 106

Idealism: absolute i., 133, 546; and empiricism, 563, 575; and *esse naturale*, 243, 274; and historical consciousness, 321; and immanentism, 97; and naive realism, 576; and Platonism, 413

Ideals: scientific i., 23

Ideas (Plato), 70

Ideology: and context of deviation, 512; and group bias, 508–9; and Marx, 79; and totalitarianism, 299

'If … then,' 114, 267

Ignatius of Antioch, 416, 464

Ignatius Loyola, 559

Illative sense, 100–4, 372

Immaculate Conception: and Assumption, 296; dogma of, 341

Immanentism: 97, 108, 122, 123–27, 140, 141, 274

Immediacy: world of, *see* World(s)

Implication: material and formal i., 114

Implicit-explicit, 27, 31, 154, 155, 156, 161, 176, 177, 190, 291, 297, 344, 410

Inauthenticity, 15–18, 39, 62, 252, 255, 261, 262, 264, 267, 277, 288, 290, 399, 400, 407, 508, 553, 557, 592, 643. *See also* Authenticity

Incarnate meaning, 380

Individualism, 48–49, 274–75, 276

Infallibility: minimum sense of, 335

Infallible: intelligence i. regarding image, 221–22

Insight: in Aquinas, 129; in art, 155, 522–23, 606; and common sense, 372, 402, 531–32, 538, 640; and conceptualism, 195; criterion of correctness of i., 222; and Euclid, 86, 389, 624; experiencing i., 429; and form, 61, 290; and formulation, 573–74; and hermeneutic circle, 215–16; in history, 253; and human science, 166; and intelligent consciousness, 278, 430, 437; and intersubjectivity, 199; and judgment, 221–22, 372, 431; Lonergan's meaning of word 'insight,' 577, 621; and mastery/familiarity, 38, 105, 215, 262, 291, 356, 372, 373, 391; and phantasm, 138; and phenomenology, 76, 85, 87, 381, 575–76; i. preconceptual, 625; and science, 157, 378, 426; social i., 631; and *Verstehen*, 430

Insight (the book), 12, 18, 24, 40, 99, 100, 131, 133, 141, 197, 215, 232, 252, 259, 261, 263, 264, 276, 279, 288, 298, 300, 316, 347, 368, 372, 382, 389, 394, 399, 404, 427, 429,

478, 479, 482, 507, 508, 543, 549, 570, 576, 577, 588, 596, 602, 605, 612, 615, 616, 625, 626, 629, 631, 632, 648, 651

Institutions: and good of order, 35, 37–38, 39, 397, 495–96, 497, 500; and habits, 35; and meaning, 41, 242, 297–98, 384, 542

Instrumentalization: of experience, 203, 521

Integration of worlds, 64–67, 70, 83, 315, 319, 320

Intellectual pattern of experience, 56, 139, 164, 314, 315, 416, 616

Intellectus possibilis, 129, 131

Intelligibility: necessary and de facto (empirical) i., 71–72, 90, 91–95, 101, 106–107, 126–27, 325, 378, 382, 468–70, 573

Intentio intendens: and *intentio intenta*, 131

Intentionality: and consciousness, 428–29; fulfilment of, 484–85, 551; and language, 530–31; levels of, 429–30; and names, 530; and objects of operations, 428–29, 561; and question of God, 543, 583, 586; and symbols, 526; and transcendental notions, 509

Interdisciplinary problems: and science and theology, 491; and transcendental method, 444

Interiority: and antithesis with external world, 46–49, 56, 76, 77, 300; and authenticity, 291; and being in love, 48; and conversion, 291; and critical exigence, 138, 284, 539–40; and existential subject, 399; faith and a new i., 150; and foundations, 342; and Hegel, 48, 55; and horizon, 291; and lay retreat movement, 54; mediates community, 54, 67, 266,

284; mediates theory, 54, 67, 266, 284; mediation of, 9, 257; and method, 284, 592; and methodical exigence, 138–40, 540; and presence, 47; and reason illumined by faith, 150; and subjectivity, 268, 287; and wisdom, 288–89; as world, 4, 9, 52, 57, 59, 60, 61, 64, 76, 82, 85, 136, 212, 252, 301, 366, 479, 480, 539, 540, 638

Interpretation: existential dimension of, 220; as functional specialty, 449, 452, 453, 454, 455, 461, 462, 487; three main points in, 211. *See also* Exegesis; Hermeneutics; Judging correctness of one's understanding; Stating what one judges the correct interpretation of the text; Understanding the text

Intersubjectivity: and meaning, 198–201, 230, 517–20, 535, 587, 606, 649

Introspection: meanings of, 292, 429; in Thomas, 400

Irenaeus, 258, 345

Islam, 321

'Isms,' 384

Isomorphism of knowing and known, 134–35, 195, 279

Jansenism, 401

Jansenius, 278

Jaspers, K., 15 & n. 14, 49 & n. 20, 124, 262 & n. 5, 264, 276, 380, 572, 592, 615

Jerome, 597

Jesuit education, 74

Jewish Christian theology, 25, 26, 187, 345

John (evangelist), 66, 181, 223–24, 348, 370, 403, 407, 420, 550, 645

John Damascene, 192, 193

John of St Thomas, 12, 267

Journet, C., 4 & n. 4

Judging correctness of one's interpretation, 221–25, 644–45

Judgment: as absolute positing, 96–97, 124, 132, 269, 324, 398; and Aristotelian-Thomist tradition, 96, 256, 269; and cognitive self-transcendence, 432, 563; and commitment, 97–98, 292; and community, 498; and context, 104; criteria of j., 510, 536, 585; and doctrines, 453, 455; experience, understanding, and j., *see* Experiencing-understanding-judging; and faith/belief, *see* Belief(s) and Faith; and immanentism, 133; and knowing, 132, 163; modal j., 97; and modern notion of science, 95; and morality of intellect, 97; more easily conscious of j. than of insight, 292; and phenomenology, 87, 575; and questions for reflection, 95; as rational, 98, 430, 432; and reflective understanding, 99, 327; and responsibility, 97–98; in science, 115; and self-correcting process, 215; and statements, 96; theological j., 106; j. of value, 133, 278, 292, 324, 363, 510–12, 594; j. of value and belief, 515; and virtually unconditioned, 98–100, 121, 124, 536, 585; and wisdom, 102

Jung, C.G., 44, 312, 379–80, 526–27, 571

Juridicism: and ecclesiology, 410. *See also* Law

Justin Martyr, 359, 476

Kabôd Yahweh, 308

Kant, I., 29 n. 38, 34, 39, 48, 96, 120, 121, 124, 125, 149, 240, 263, 271, 294, 317, 399, 434, 442, 545, 546, 547, 561

Keller, H., 530, 541
Keynes, J.M., 265
Kierkegaard, S., 64, 178, 546, 547
Kingdom of God, 484, 485, 555–57, 566
Klempt, A., 254 n. 20
Knowing: and believing, 141–50, 151–52, 514; as a compound of operations, 132, 134–36, 195, 434; k. knowing, 91; and levels of consciousness, 252, 279; and meaning, 541; and metaphysics, 134–36, 195, 279; structure of, 28–29, 99, 388–91; and taking a look, 117–22, 429, 564
Knowledge: of being, 132; in potency and act, 107; proper object of, 132; sociology of, 78–79; unity of human k., 126, 133–34

Ladrière, J., 390 & n. 3
Lake, F., 527 & n. 7
Landgraf, A.M., 158 n. 4, 159, 174, 277–78 & n. 28, 355, 622
Langer, S., 201 & n. 12, 203, 206, 292, 380 & n. 9, 381, 519, 520, 523
Langlois, C., 244 & n. 14, 245, 253, 386
Language: as carrier of meaning, 529–55; early l., 230; meaningfulness of (Wittgenstein), 577–79; and symbol, 608–9; technical l., 8, 480, 539, 592, 610–15; and world mediated by meaning, 8, 502. See also Meaning: linguistic m.
La Rochefoucauld, F. de, 97, 294
Lavoisier, A., 180, 481
Law: and theology, 382, 410, 585
Lawton, J.S., 79 & n. 26
Learning: self-correcting process of l., 38, 105, 140, 214–15, 216, 217, 220, 222, 351, 356, 404, 640, 641, 642
Lebreton, J., 588

Lee, T.D., 157 n. 2
Leibniz, G.W., 23
Leo XIII, Pope, 91
Leontius of Byzantium, 174
Lévi-Strauss, C., 432
Lewis, H.D., 125 & n. 23
Liberty: consciousness of, 293, 497; horizontal and vertical l., 512, 549; and orientation, 35, 39, 300, 397, 495, 497; and originating value, 35; and personal relations, 498–99; as self-determination, 497; Thomas on l., 191; vertical l., 559, 565
Lightfoot, J.B., 464
Limits: and development, 56–60, 136
Lindsay, Robert Bruce, 283 & n. 2
Linguistic analysis, 624
Logic: and authenticity/inauthenticity, 267; l. of basic context, 651–53; fundamental l., 267; in Greek and modern science, 378; and method, 100–102, 391, 426, 471, 488, 492; and oversight of intelligence, 110; and propositions, 101; symbolic l., 113–14, 198, 267, 531
Logos: in Gospel of John, 181, 348–49; and *mythos*, 164, 542, 599; and thematization, 344
Lombard, Peter, 68–69, 160, 286, 411, 412, 460, 474, 599. See also *Sentences, Books of*
Lonergan, B., 5 n. 6, 12 n. 11, 14 n. 12, 15 n. 13, 24 & n. 26, 25 & n. 30, 26 nn. 33 and 35, 32 n. 3, 35 n. 6, 52 n. 23, 55 n. 26, 63 n. 11, 65 n. 12, 79 n. 26, 86 nn. 4–5, 93 n. 10, 96 n. 12, 114 n. 11, 119 n. 22, 131 nn. 3–4, 153 n. 12, 189 & n. 3, 193 n. 6, 198 & n. 10, 208 & n. 2, 213 n. 4, 240 n. 5, 259 n. 22, 265 n. 9, 273 nn. 19–20, 320 nn. 13–14, 363 n. 5, 390 nn. 3 and 5, 392 n. 6, 399 & n. 6,

409 & n. 5, 413, 420, 457 & n. 8, 483
n. 2, 484 n. 4, 526 n. 3, 549 n. 5, 602
n. 3, 620 n. 3, 639 n. 2
Looking: conceiving knowing as l., 118,
120–22, 541, 564
Lottin, O., 159 & n. 5, 622
Love: and authenticity, 486; and
charity, 289; imitation of divine l.,
550; l. of neighbor and l. of God,
596; and redemption, 508; religious
l., 558–60; and self-transcendence,
483, 509; three kinds of l., 483. *See
also* Being in love
Löwith, K., 241 & nn. 7–8, 243

Macquarrie, J., 648
Magisterium: and theology, 194, 296,
317
Malinowski, B., 59 & n. 7, 311, 381
Mannheim, K., 78–79 & nn. 22–23
Marcel, G., 77 & n. 17, 78, 81
Maréchal, J., 382
Margenau, Henry, 283 & n. 2
Marrou, H.-I., 245 & n. 16, 246, 253,
386, 648
Marston, R., 69
Marx, K./Marxists, 79, 242, 261, 299,
397, 403, 507
Maslow, A., 499 & n. 7, 512, 528
Mathematics: and art, 609–10; consciousness in m., 50; foundations of,
113–14; necessity and modern m.,
469; and scientific ideals, 23; and
theory, 52
May, R., 529 & n. 13
Maximus the Confessor, 174
McGrath, F., 385 & n. 26
Meaning: 40–42; acts of m., 535; active
m., 535; aesthetic (artistic) m., 40,
198, 201–204, 380, 520–23; carriers
of m., 517–33 passim; cognitive function of m., 541; common m., 458 (*see
also* Community: and meaning);
communicative function of m., 541;
conceptual m., 200; m. as conscious
finality, 387; m. constitutive of human institutions/reality, 41, 297–98,
321, 381, 383, 384, 391, 393, 542;
and context, 470; control of m., 381,
592; m. develops/evolves, 41, 321,
381; and education, 298; effective
function of m., 542; elemental m.,
522–23, 526, 535, 606; elements of
m., 534–37; exigences of m., 537–41;
as *esse intentionale*, 41, 215, 242, 297,
361; formal acts of m., 535; m. as formal element of human good, 40–41,
297; formative function of m., 541;
full acts of m., 535; functions of m.,
541–42; and *Geisteswissenschaften*,
209–10, 636; and hermeneutics, *see*
Hermeneutics; and historical consciousness, *see* Historical: h. consciousness; and history, 242, 297,
321, 542; and human sciences, 377,
391; incarnate m., 380; instrumental
acts of m., 535; intersubjective m.,
40–41, 198–201, 379, 517–20, 606;
linguistic m., 40, 197–98, 204–207,
219, 379, 380, 519–20, 526, 529–33,
541, 642 (*see also* Language); literary
m., 381; performative m., 535; potential m., 535; and revelation, 41–
42, 321, 560; sources of m., 534;
symbolic m., 40, 44, 164, 198, 204–
207, 379, 523–29; technical m., 380–
81; terms of m., 536–37; m. of texts,
see Hermeneutics *and* Understanding
the text; world constituted by m.,
298, 384, 391; world mediated by m.,
8–9, 384, 391, 502–504, 562–63,
564
Mediation: and Aristotle, 54–55, 392;
and Christianity, 55, 361; and classi-

fying developments, 53–55; m. of common sense and theory by interiority, 67, 140, 266; m. of community by theory, 280, 283; fundamental meaning of m., 54, 59; general sense of m., 59, 311, 392; in Hegel, 55, 392; m. of immediacy, 60; m. of interiority by community and theory, 9, 13, 257; method and m., 67; mutual m., 392; mutual self-m., 393; Piaget and m., 8, 502; m. of sacred by community, theory, and interiority, 257; self-m., 393; social m. of human good, 35, 38, 42, 310–11; theological m. of history, 258–59; and theology, 150; m. of theory by interiority, 140; three types of, 8–9 (language, technical language, interiority); m. of tradition, 257–58

Meinecke, F., 240 & n. 5, 243

Memory: and levels of consciousness, 569, 574

Mendeleev, D., 71

Merton, R., 79 & n. 25

Metaphysics: Catholic m., 79; and cognitional theory, 124–25, 134–36, 195, 443, 446, 578; and concrete, 61; and development, 24; as integral heuristic structure, 478; and sciences, 138; and theology, 368

Method: and authenticity, 15–18; comparative m., 24, 27, 185–88, 190, 360, 451; and conversion, 14–15; m. defined, 425; and development of a science, 21–22; dialectical m., 24, 27, 192–94, 360; dogmatic m., 408–10; foundational m., 414; and foundations, 341; fundamental problem of m. in theology, 475; genetic m., 24, 27, 191, 360; historical m., 244–49; and horizon, 13–14, 24, 466–72; and interiority, 4, 140, 150, 284; and

logic, 100–102, 391, 426, 471, 488, 492; as mediation of world of theory and of community by interiority, 67; and objects, 19–24; and operations, 4–12, 24, 153, 266, 384, 472; positive m., 409; preliminary notion of m., 425–26; and rules, 426; and self-appropriation, 138; and subject, 4, 12–18, 24–29, 31–33, 266, 391; and systematics, 194–95; m. of theology and theology, 293; theology has not one m. but a set of methods, 446; three approaches to m., 423–24; transcendental m., *see* Transcendental method; and transcendental precepts, 442; and upper blade, 253, 651; and worlds, 316

Methodical exigence, 138–40, 540

Meyerhoff, H., 241 & n. 10

Middle Platonism, 345, 360

Missions: divine m. and Trinity in New Testament, 50

Modernism: and immanentism, 125; oath against, 21

Modernity, 210, 321, 636–37

Monophysites, 161, 174, 281, 291, 358

Monothelites, 174, 281, 413

Moral impotence, 347, 595, 629

Moreau, J., 343 & n. 7

Morel, G., 320 & n. 14, 380

'Most noble task' of theology, 84, 348, 408

Motive, 148, 328–30

Mowrer, O.H., 529 & n. 12

Mystical body: categories for, 280, 341, 382; and history, 341; and mediation/thematizaton in theology, 150, 399, 463

Mysticism: and transcendental notions, 547

Myth/mythic consciousness: and demythologization, 588–89; and imagining transcendence, 122; and symbolic consciousness, 58–59, 369, 609

Naive realism: and animal knowledge, 575; breakdown of, 391; and materialism, 304; and 'projection,' 312; as stage in doctrinal history, 345, 413; and visual Western, 564. *See also* Conversion: intellectual c.; Looking
Name/Naming: significance of, 530
Naturalist: n. tendency in human science, 115
Natural theology, 19, 111, 150, 360–61
Nature: n. at Chalcedon and before, 161; pure n., 106, 346–47; two kinds of n., 161
'Nature of …,' 82, 444
Necessity: absolute and contingent n., 90, 93, 101–102, 126–27, 222, 268, 469; and science, 378, 382, 390, 473, 573
Neill, S., 464 & n. 12
Neo-Chalcedonism, 83
Nestorius/Nestorians, 173–74, 187, 281, 291, 308, 345, 409, 418
Newman, J.H., 100, 101–102, 103, 145, 204, 262, 275, 326, 356, 372, 382, 383, 385, 407, 515, 560, 644
Newton, I., 51, 96, 116, 164, 235, 240, 266, 314, 331, 371, 383, 402, 506, 604
Nicea, Council of, 26, 29, 64, 83, 92, 93, 161, 173–74, 186, 187, 220, 308, 344, 357, 359, 400, 409, 410, 416, 418, 458, 596–97, 599, 620
Niebuhr, B., 240
Niel, H., 55 & n. 27, 392
Nietzsche, F., 247–48, 257, 297, 313, 461, 546
Nihilism, 297

Nisbet, R., 275 & n. 25
Notion (in Lonergan's strict sense): basic context as heuristic n., 232, 650; of being, 104, 131–32, 232, 252, 279, 304, 509, 575; and concept, 131; defined, 131; heuristic n., 181, 234; transcendental n., *see* Transcendental(s); of value, 39, 508–10, 512, 594, 602, 618
Nunc: and time/eternity, 235

Obiectum formale quod/quo, 328–30
Object(s): elementary and compounded o., 195–96, 434–35; final o., 30; formal o., 19–20, 21, 149–50, 152, 378; and functional specialties, *see* Functional specialties/specialization: and objects; God as o., *see* God: as object; immediate and mediate relation to o., 8, 13, 509, 546; and intentional feelings, *see* Feeling(s): intentional f.; material o., 19–20; and operations, 4–5, 6, 24, 28, 428, 443, 478, 501; proper o., 33, 132, 149–50, 152, 279, 290, 313; proportionate o., 28–29, 135, 196, 290; subject and o., and development, *see* Development: and subject-object; supernatural formal o., see *Obiectum formale quod/quo*; *see also* Supernatural: s. formal object; terminal o., 30; terminal o. in theology, 30; transcendental o., 152
Objectification: of conscious intentionality as applying operations as intentional to operations as conscious, 437; of purely experiential pattern, 201, 203, 364, 520, 606, 615
Objectivity: absolute o., 390; experiential o., 389, 401, 615–16; normative o., 389; as self-transcending subjectivity, 510, 546, 607–608, 611; three elements in o., 100

Obscurantism, 434

O'Connor, R. Eric, 13–14

O'Hara, C., 373

'One and the same' (Chalcedon), 174, 187, 652

Operation(s): applying o. as intentional to o. as conscious, 437; basic pattern of o., 11–12, 33, 426–35; as basic terms, 342, 427; block or limit in grouping of o., 42–55, 136; combining differentiated o., 6, 7, 31; and consciousness, 428–29; development of o., 500–503, 603; differentiation of, 6, 9, 13, 21, 31, 34: elementary and compounded o., 434–35; experiencing the o., 10–11; explanatory apprehension of o., 427; group of differentiated o., 6–7, 9–10, 19, 20, 21–22, 23, 31; and habits, 5–8, 31; logical and non-logical o., 267, 426; and method, 4–12, 67, 391, 425, 426–35; and objects, see Object(s): and operations; and Piaget, 5–8, 42, 314, 396; and subject, 12–18, 428; two dimensions of o., 429

Orientation: and act of freedom, 35; and authenticity; 39; and conversion, 39, 396, 397, 499; as direction of development, 499; and human good, 35, 497; and originating value, 35, 39; and personal relations, 35

Origen, 26 & n. 34, 75, 187, 277, 280, 360, 413, 418, 596–97, 652

Oscillation: and integration of worlds, 64–65, 315, 319

Parmenides, 104

Pascal, B., 100, 101–102, 103, 204, 558, 561

Patripassians, 187

Pattern(s): abstract and concrete p., 201–202, 520; experiential p. and art, 201–203, 364, 520–23, 606, 610, 615; p. of experience, 276–77, 383, 479, 616. See also Intellectual pattern of experience

Paul, 40, 49–50, 55, 165, 176, 207, 219, 221, 257–58, 280, 281, 306, 317, 357, 406, 420, 452, 456, 465, 483, 551, 588, 643

Pavlov, I., 527

Peckham, J., 412

Peinador, M., 74–75 & n. 16, 647–48

Pelagians, 174, 176, 191, 291

Penalty: and redemption, 259, 300

Perfections: pure p., 279

Person: development of notion of, 75–76, 281, 385, 481; and nature, 161; and object, 305–307, 545–47; 'What is a person?' as heuristic notion/structure, 75, 481

Personalism: 76–77, 476, 546, 547

Perspectivism, 247, 248, 378

Petavius, Dionysius (Denis Petau), 93, 95, 165, 476

Phases (in theology): two p. in theology, 277, 454–65, 478

Phenomenology: and eclipse of theory, 76–80, 85; and insight into data, 76, 85, 87, 575–76; and judgment, 87, 575–76

Philip the Chancellor, 186

Philologie, 460

Philosophy: Christian p., 345; and history, 252–53; mediates religion, 53; and method in theology, 293; modern p., 384 & n. 23, 390, 391; and pluralism, 619; and self-appropriation, 138; and theology, 230–32, 286–87, 341–43, 368, 413, 446, 572; and upper blade, 253

Philosophy of ..., 284, 413

Photius, 192, 193

Physis: *p. anhypostatos* and *p. enhypostatos*, 161

Piaget, J., 5–8 & nn. 6–7 and 9; 22, 23, 31, 42, 53, 271, 275, 311, 314, 391, 396, 397, 420, 500, 501, 502, 503, 570

Pius IX, Pope, 84, 183, 194

Pius XII, Pope, 84, 182, 194

Planck, M., 253, 270 & n. 16

Plato, 51, 70, 81, 96, 104, 135, 190, 248, 269, 371, 373, 381, 382, 537, 598, 599

Platonism, 26, 70, 187, 345, 360, 398, 413, 418, 596, 597, 620

Plotinus, 104, 343

Pluralism, 492–93, 619

Positing: and faith, 143; and judgment, 96–97, 124, 132, 269, 324, 398

Position and counterposition, 141, 341, 399, 418, 443, 479

Positive theology, 33, 82, 85, 94, 112, 182–94, 277, 357, 359, 361, 379, 382, 385, 386, 387, 392, 393, 401–404, 405, 406–408, 409, 411, 415, 418, 457, 460, 476, 588

Positivism: 401, 464, 546, 576; Christian p., 153

Potency-form-act, 33–34, 135, 196, 279, 283, 368

Poulain, A.F., 620 & n. 2

Practical theology, 363

Preconceptual: insights are p., 625; and Scotus, 130; and unity of classical and modern ideals of science, 127, 128–29

Preface of Trinity, 26, 186, 308, 369, 597–98

Prejudgment against prejudgment, 221, 332

Presence: and consciousness, 46–47, 133, 278, 292, 314, 399, 428–29, 430

Principle of the empty head, 212, 221, 637, 638, 639

Priora quoad nos: 49, 50, 51, 137, 279, 280, 281

Priora quoad se: 49, 51, 137, 139, 281, 538

Procession: and analogy in rational part, 196–97, 273; of Holy Spirit, 192–93

Progress: and creative minority, 631; and decline, 40, 62, 209, 244, 482, 486, 494, 499, 506–508, 550, 556, 565, 595, 603, 629; and religion, 551

Prudence: and wisdom, 107–108, 390, 470

Psychological analogy, 131, 197, 413

Quaestio: definition of, 68; as technique, 68–69, 454, 460, 474

Quantum physics: and change in notion of science, 469; and intellectual pattern, 139, 271, 391; and relations of things to one another, 402

Quasi-formal causality: and Scheeben, 63

Question(s): the q. *An sit/Utrum sit*, 95, 108 & n. 4, 126, 148, 152, 158, 286; for deliberation, 430, 483, 509, 566; q. of God, *see* God: question of; for intelligence, 92, 95, 96, 108 n. 4, 126, 278, 433, 482, 509, 566, 585; the q. *Quid sit*, 92, 94, 95, 96, 108 & n. 4, 110, 126, 148, 152, 158, 197, 286; for reflection, 95, 108 & n. 4, 126, 433, 482–83, 509, 566; relevant q., 222, 407, 644, 645; three fundamental q., 442, 446

Questioning questioning, 543–49, 554. *See also* God: question of; Question(s)

Qumrân, 223–24, 349–50, 645

Quoad nos and *quoad se*, see *Priora quoad nos*, *Priora quoad se*

Rahner, H., 277 & n. 27

Rahner, K., 296, 355, 413 & nn. 6–7, 476, 487 & n. 7, 559, 565 & n. 6, 584

Ranke, L. von, 41, 239, 240, 386

Rationalism: and light of faith, 149, 271–72

Rationalization: and obnubilation, 400–401

'Reading into,' 212–13, 351, 638

Realism: critical r., 413, 563, 597; discursive r., 121; dogmatic r., 413, 418, 597; and existentialism-phenomenology, 125–26; intuitive r., 119, 121, 122; naive r. breaks down, 391; naive historical r., 408; naive r. and materialism, 304; naive r. in Tertullian, 345, 413; naive r. and visual Westerners, 564; and 'object,' 546

Reason illumined by faith: 84 n. 2; and faith aided by reason, 151, 286, 293; and theology, 151, 194, 322, 346, 360–61, 392, 393, 411

Redemption: and Christology, 50, 280; r. contingent, 90, 382, 391; and history, 299–300; and human good, 258–59, 482, 629; and human sciences, 383; and love, 508

Redfield, R., 380 & n. 15

Reflection on reflection, 543–44

Reflexio ad phantasma: and *conversio ad phantasma*, 130

Relation(s): (inter)personal r. and human good, 35, 39–40, 300–301, 397, 497–99, 524, 603; r. not a distinct metaphysical element, 368; r. in Trinity and philosophy, 369

Relativism: and extrinsicism, 113; historical r., 242–44, 378; and perspectivism, 248, 378; and pluralism, 492; and transcendental method, 443

Relativity: and change in notion of science, 469

Religion and theology: differentiation of, 458–59, 540–41

Religious expression, 553–58

Reproduction (*Reproduzieren*): in Romantic hermeneutics, 218, 220

Research: common historical r., 249–50, 251–52, 255, 258, 290; as functional specialty, 449, 452, 454, 455, 461, 463, 487, 560, 588, 590, 615; general and special r., 449

Ressentiment, 506, 512, 602, 608

Revelation: and common sense, 295, 308; development of r., 89; and divine wisdom, 105–106; entrusted to church, 392; and formal and proper objects of intellect, 150; and historical consciousness, 321; and meaning, 41–42, 321, 560; sources of r. never exhausted, 31, 172, 183, 364

Revision: not subject to radical r., 288, 439, 443, 478, 571

Richard of St Victor, 75, 281, 385, 481

Richard, R., 555 & n. 2

Richardson, A., 386 & n. 28, 401, 409

Richardson, W., 430 & n. 4, 454, 485, 584

Ricoeur, P., 527 & n. 4

Rimini, Council of, 597

Rogers, C., 499 & n. 6, 506, 526, 527 & n. 6, 570, 629

Romantic hermeneutics, *see* Hermeneutics: Romantic h.

Romans 5.5, 483, 559

Romanticism, 32, 401

Rosmini, A., 400

Ross, D., 424 & n. 2

Rostovtzeff, M., 53 & n. 25, 239

Rothacker, E., 246, 255–56, 284 & n. 3

Rouët de Journel, M.J., 68 & n. 14, 474

Roure, M.L, 390 & n. 4

Rousselot, P., 148 & n. 10, 394
Russell, B., 23, 389

Sabellianism, 416
Sacraments: categories for s., 340–41
Sacred and profane, 34, 42, 43–46, 52,
    56, 57, 312, 314, 554
Sanctifying grace: formal effects of, 368
Savigny, F.C. von, 41, 240
Scheeben, M., 63 & n. 11
Scheler, M., 76, 78 & n. 21, 87, 133–34
    & n. 5, 198 & n. 11, 304–307, 379,
    504, 505, 506, 512, 517, 518, 547,
    602, 607, 608, 611
Schelling, F.W.J., 546
Schilpp, P.A., 270 & n. 14
Schlegel, F., 643 n. 2
Schleiermacher, F., 218 & n. 7, 406, 641
Schmaus, M., 367
Schökel, A., 609
Scholasticism: decadent S., 16, 82, 126,
    401; and world of theory, 82, 84, 335
Schopenhauer, A., 546
Science: Aristotelian notion of, 70–71,
    88–90, 103, 107, 377–79, 445, 460,
    469, 470, 573, 590; birth trauma of
    modern s., 488; and certitude, 95;
    conflict of s. and theology, 489; de-
    fined by operations, 21; human s., see
    Human sciences; and knowledge of
    singular, 89, 107, 325; and know-
    ledge of things in relation to each
    other, 116; modern notion of, 71–73,
    88–90, 377–79, 446, 468, 488; mod-
    ern notion of s. and theology, 90–92,
    94–95, 107, 385; and technical
    terms, 69–70; unity of ancient and
    modern ideals of s., 128–30, 315,
    325, 382
Scotus, John Duns, 76, 104, 117, 129,
    130, 131, 281, 284, 285, 290, 341,
    382, 385, 481

Scripture: argument from/according to
    s., 418–20; as founding a tradition,
    357; from s. to dogma/theology, 83,
    161, 165, 166–70, 418–20; as true,
    171, 175–81, 183, 348–49, 364;
    various approaches to s., 175–76,
    309–10, 365; as word of God, 176
Second Vatican Council, 556
Secular: and imitation of God's love,
    555–57
Secularism, 254, 255, 257, 313, 417,
    555
Secularization theology, 555–57
Seignobos, C., 244–45 & n. 14, 253,
    386
Self-appropriation, 138, 139, 252, 253,
    399, 427, 431
Self-consciousness: rational s-c., 292–93,
    363, 393; and self-knowledge, 132–33
Self-transcendence, 483 & n. 2, 490,
    499, 509, 510, 516, 547, 549, 581
Sentences, Books of, 68–69, 285, 460,
    474. See also Lombard, Peter
Serialization, 482, 590
Shakespeare, W., 206–207
Shintoism, 543
Simmel, G., 260 & n. 3, 458
Sin: and charity, 66, 319; dialectic of s.,
    299, 302; original s., 72, 347; as
    privation, 294; and surd corrupting
    human good, 40, 42, 258–59,
    298–99, 508
Sinfulness: s. distinct from moral evil, 566
Skinner, B.F., 490
Smile: phenomenology of, 199–201,
    379, 519–20
Snow, C.P., 383 & n. 20
Sociology of knowledge, 78–79; divine
    s. of k., 392
Socrates: 51, 57, 60, 81, 136–37,
    537–38
Soteriology: and New Testament, 49–50

Soul: for Aristotle, 116–17, 301, 310

Spanneut, M., 360 & n. 3, 418

Specialization: three types of s., 446–48. *See also* Functional specialties/specialization

Species expressa, 129

Species impressa, 129–30

Species intelligibilis, 11–12, 129–31, 135

Speculative theology, *see* Systematic theology

Spiritual Exercises, 399

Stark, W., 79 & n.24

Stating what one judges the correct interpretation of the text, 211, 225–33, 354, 637, 645–53

Stekel, W., 571

Stoics/Stoicism, 33, 294, 303, 360, 413, 417–18, 620

Structure: basic s., 478; and categories, 478–86; cognitional s., 12, 388–89, 441; complicate the s., 478–79, 485; concrete instances of basic s., 479, 485–86; differentiating basic s., 479–80, 486; filling out basic s., 479, 486; in historical facts, 244; of horizons, 467–68, 473; of human good, *see* Human good: structure of; isomorphic s., 135, 195, 279, 289; setting basic s. in motion, 480–82, 486; and worlds, 50–51, 52, 56, 60, 314

Suarez, F., 76, 281, 328, 385, 481

Subject: Aristotelian analysis of, 70; and authenticity/inauthenticity, 15, 31–33, 479; and conversion, 14–15, 31–33, 141, 262, 452; and differentiation of worlds, 60; dramatic and theoretical s., 158; existential s., 399, 471, 472, 473, 488, 490, 549, 558, 565, 566, 617, 625; forgetting the s., 70; and horizon, 13–14, 31–33, 395–96; s. in love, 566; mediated by

development (community, theory, religion), 59; and *mens* in Augustine, 47, 400; and method, *see* Method: and subject; neglected s., 398; normative s., 398–401; objectification of, 70, 163; and operations, 5, 279, 428; psychological s., 163, 168–69, 428; psychological s. in Christ, 163–71, 273; s. as s., 279; truncated s., 398; world of s. (interiority), 42, 46–49. *See also* Consciousness; Interiority

Sublation, 565, 626, 627

Subordinationism, 26, 418

Sufficient evidence, 98–100, 438, 510, 563

Summation and integration: and dogmatic-theological context, 171–75

Supernatural: and faith, 146–51, 152, 217, 286–87, 341; s. formal object, 328–30; and human good, 259 (*see also* Human good); and sacred, 621–22; theorem of, 82, 158, 160, 186, 622

Superstructure, 261, 402, 459

Surd: and sin, *see* Sin: and surd

Swinburne, A.G., 206, 381

Syllogism, 10–11, 98, 99, 110–11, 153, 470, 571, 576

Symbol(s): and affect/feeling, 204, 532–29; and art, 587; as carriers of meaning, 523–29, 587; and condensation, 205–207, 525; s. defined, 523; evocation of s., 523, 525; and internal communication, 526, 529, 535, 541, 606, 607; interpretative contexts for s., 526–29; transvaluation of s., 525

Symbolic animal: man as, 298, 320

Symbolic consciousness, 164

Symbolic logic, *see* Logic: symbolic l.

Systematic exigence, 136–37, 140, 154, 283, 480, 537–38, 539

Systematics: as functional specialty, 449, 453, 455, 456, 460, 462–63, 487, 588, 589, 600, 610–11, 632. *See also* Systematic theology

Systematic theology: 194–97, 277, 280, 361, 410–13, 418, 456–57. *See also* Systematics

Tarski, A., 114

Taylor, V., 308 & n. 4

Technical language: and theology, 475, 610–15; and theory, 8, 50, 81, 381, 480, 532, 539, 592. *See also* Science: and technical terms; Terms: technical t.

Teilhard de Chardin, P., 316

Teresa of Avila, 42, 60, 61, 276, 313

Terms: basic t. and relations, 51, 69, 137, 196, 443, 587; interiority (operations) and basic t., 342, 427; and implicit definition, 427, 443, 495; t. of meaning, 536–37; technical t., 8, 16, 58

Tertullian: 25, 26 & n. 34, 27, 32–33, 75, 174, 187, 258, 277, 279–80, 345, 357, 359, 360, 413, 418, 596, 597, 620, 652

Thales, 51, 57, 60, 81, 137, 314, 383, 443

Thematization: and Assumption, 339–40; and critical history, 254–55; degrees of t., 340–41; t. described, 154; development of dogma as t., 339; and discovering development of dogma, 161; and dogmatic theology, 175–81; and experience/experiment, 157–58; first t., 433; and implicit/explicit, 157–58, 190; instances of t., 162–64; and *logos*, 344; and narrative history, 237, 238,

253–54; t., summation, integration, 170–74; t. of transcendental method, 478; truth and t., 182–85

Theodore of Mopsuestia, 173, 187

Theodorus of Tarsus, 173

Theology: adding time to medieval t., 4, 22, 339; biblical t., *see* Biblical: biblical t.; and certitude, 95, 152; Christ and t., 304; and classification of development, 22; dogmatic t., 19, 175–81, 277, 296, 307, 361, 385, 386, 392, 401, 402, 409, 410, 411, 412, 418, 419, 454, 637; dogmatic t. and biblical t., 336–37, 348–49, 352–53, 364–65, 386; and faith, 152–55, 322–23; from faith to t., 153–55, 156–58; foundations of, 395–96, 452; and functional specialties, *see* Functional specialties/specialization; fundamental problem in t., 40, 66, 475; fundamental t., 280–81, 412, 413, 452, 453–54; God and t., 304, 362, 411; t. a habit, 31; and historical consciousness, 321, 350–51, 386, 475, 637; and interiority, 287; and judgment, 95–100, 392; and magisterium, 317; mediated by word of God and order of church, 150, 361, 393; mediated and mediating t., 463; mediates religion, 307; t. and method of t., 293; object(s) of t., 4, 19, 30, 304, 411, 445; pastoral t., 454; phases of t., 454–55; and philosophy, 286, 341–47, 368–69, 413, 415, 445–46; positive t., 33, 182–94, 277, 357, 359, 361, 382, 385, 386, 392, 393, 401–404, 405, 406–408, 409, 411, 412, 418, 460; practical t., 363; and questions *An sit* and *Quid sit*, 286; as *ratio per fidem illustrata* not *fides per rationem adiuta*, 151, 286, 322; and

religion, 458–59, 540–41; as science, 19, 392; and science Greek and modern, 88–92, 95, 487–92; starting point of t., 279–80; and supernatural, 159, 335; systematic t., 194–97, 277, 280, 361, 410–13, 418, 454, 456–57; thematization and dogmatic t., 175–81; theoretic/systematic element in t., 81–88; three types of t., 150; unity of t., 360–62, 457–66; and Vatican I, *see* First Vatican Council: and reason illumined by faith; and wisdom, 95, 102, 103–108; and worlds (common sense, theory, interiority, and transcendence), 54, 316–17, 362
Theoria: in Greek Fathers, 397
Theory: and common sense, *see* Common sense and theory; eclipse of t., 76–80, 82; as element in theology, 81–87; mediated by interiority, 54, 266, 284; mediates common sense, 54, 266, 280, 283, 284; mediates religion, 54; mediates subject, 59–60; and movement from faith to theology, 156–58; and Nicea, 308; and *priora quoad se*, see *Priora quoad se*; and systematic exigence, 136–37; and technical language, *see* Technical language: and theory; and things in relation to one another, 49; world of, *see* Common sense and theory *and* World(s)
Thing in itself: and metaphysical extrinsicism, 116–18
Thomas Aquinas, 4, 9, 12, 17, 28 & n. 37, 30, 31, 34, 43, 50, 52, 68 & n. 13, 69, 70, 75, 76, 79, 84, 89, 92, 94 & n. 11, 96, 104, 105, 107, 111, 112, 118 & n. 19, 126, 129, 130, 131, 133, 135, 141 & n. 8, 152, 153, 160 & n. 6, 189, 190, 191, 195 & n. 7, 196,

197, 198, 208, 212, 215, 235, 265, 267, 268, 269, 274, 279, 281, 284, 285, 288, 289, 290, 293, 294, 300, 303, 304, 306, 311, 315, 320, 328, 332, 334, 335, 336, 345, 346, 360, 362, 365, 382, 385, 388, 394, 396, 400, 401, 403, 412, 414, 430, 474, 475, 503, 504, 550, 578, 589, 599, 618, 622
Thomas à Kempis, 48, 287
Time: adding t. to medieval theology, 4, 22, 339; in Aquinas, 235; Aristotelian definition of t., 235; in Einstein, 235; and *esse reale, naturale, intentionale*, 235–36; and eternity, 235; and history, 235–36; in Newton, 235
Tiphanus, 76, 167, 168, 281, 481
Toynbee, A., 42 & n. 11, 64–65, 66, 256–57, 568, 631
Tradition: authentic and inauthentic t., 220, 221; and classics, 220; and history, 253–56
Traditionalism, 274, 625
Transcendence: in knowing, 121, 124; and truth, 183; within immanence, 126
Transcendental(s): and categorial, *see* Categorial; t. concepts, 433; t. *ens*, 152; in Kantian sense, 29 n. 38, 34 & n. 4; and meaning, 387; and mysticism, 547; and normative subject, 399; t. notions, 433, 434, 435, 441, 477, 503, 509, 510, 512, 596, 602, 627; t. object of intellect, 152; t. precepts, 442; and question of God, 545, 548; in Scholastic sense, 27–28
Transcendental method: 24–29, 33, 268, 435–40, 540; and basic terms and relations, 592; functions of t.m., 442–46; and human sciences, 490–91; and revision, 571–72 (*see also* Revision); and theology, 484–85;

as transcultural, 477, 478, 589 (*see also* Categories: transcultural c.)

Transcendent exigence, 540

Transcultural, *see* Transcendental method: as transcultural

Transformation: t. of evil into good, 300

Transposition: from common sense to dogma, 184, 277, 305, 406; and context, 181, 184, 219; and Romantic hermeneutics, 184, 220; t. from scripture to Nicea, 219–20; and symbols, 65; and worlds of community, interiority, and theory, 85

Trent, Council of, 64, 349, 420, 589

Trinity: in New Testament, 50; and philosophy, 369; in Thomas, 50, 300

Troeltsch, E., 77 & n. 19

Troisfontaines, R., 77 & n. 17

Trouillard, J., 343 & nn. 5–6, 390 n. 5

Truth: absolute, independent, public, unconditioned character of t., 177, 183, 271; and context, 183–84, 335, 470–71; text as datum and as t., 179; thematization of t. and dogma, 175

Unconditioned: formally u., 98; and immanentism, 124; and judgment, 124; and question of God, 543; and syllogism, 98, 111; and truth, 177, 183, 271. *See also* Virtually unconditioned

Understanding: and concepts, 112, 289; and conceptualism, 195; experiencing u., 10; and faith, 392; and form, 11, 12, 33, 34, 130, 131, 196, 290; in sensible data, 85, 94, 130; and systematics, 453; theological u., 89; and *verbum*, 11, 12. *See also* Understanding the text

Understanding the text: 211–21, 403–404, 406–407, 637; and

development/conversion of the interpreter, 220–21, 404, 407, 642–44; and understanding the author, 216–18, 404, 406, 640–42; and understanding the thing/object, 211–14, 404, 637–39; and understanding the words, 214–16, 403, 639–40

Universalization: and development of dogma, 415

Universal viewpoint: and development, 482, 612

Universe: as terminal value, 550, 617

Unknown: known u., 433–34

Upper blade, 253, 350, 487, 651

Vagaggini, C., 346 & n. 8

Value(s): apprehension of v. as loving and hating (Scheler), 134, 305; cultural v., 505; and feelings, 498, 505, 506, 510, 512, 526, 558; God as originating v., 549, 550; as *honestum*, 611; judgment of v., 133, 144, 278, 292, 324, 327, 363, 453, 509, 510–12, 515, 516, 559, 560, 567, 594, 601, 602, 603; notion of v., 39, 508–10, 512, 594, 602; originating v., 35, 39, 497–98, 499, 507, 565, 604, 617; personal v., 505, 510, 511, 549; religious v., 505, 549–52, 553, 596; and satisfactions, 498–99, 564; scale of v., 468, 498, 499, 505, 506, 512, 558, 559, 565; social v., 505, 510; terminal v., 35, 38–40, 300, 301, 397, 495, 497, 499, 549, 550, 594, 603, 617; vital v., 505, 510

Van Ackeren, G., 272 n. 18

Veatch, H.B., 267 n. 11

Vécu-thématique, see Implicit-explicit

Verstehen-Erklären, see Implicit-explicit

Vignaux, P., 110 & n. 6

Vincent of Lérins, 385 & n. 27, 402

Virgil, 275 & n. 23

Virtually unconditioned, 98, 99, 100, 111, 121, 138, 144, 327, 510, 536, 537, 543, 544, 585, 586, 625

Vital act: 189–90, 265–66

Voegelin, E., 58 & n. 6, 257 & n. 21, 380 & n. 14

Von Hildebrand, D., 504 & n. 10, 505, 602, 607

'We': prior 'we' of intersubjectivity, 517, 547, 561

Weber, M., 472

Wendung zur Idee, 85, 141, 227, 260, 310, 338, 458, 647, 649

Whitehead, A.N., 23, 459 & n. 11, 479, 488 & n. 8, 586

Wie es eigentlich gewesen, 239

Will: and intellectual operations, 293; and rational self-consciousness, 293

Williams, C., 555 & n. 3

Wilson, E., 630

Winckelmann, J.J., 175 & n. 11, 218, 219, 406, 641

Wisdom: in Aquinas, 104, 288; and beatific vision, 105; and charity, 289–90; and collaboration, 107; divine w., 105; divisions of w., 105; and dogmatic-theological context, 308; genesis of w., 105; as gift of the Holy Spirit, 288–89; and history, 289; and intellectual light, 104; and interiority, 288–90; and judgment, 102; as metaphysics, 288; must be acquired, 104; and notion of being, 104; and order, 289; participations of divine w., 105–106; particular w., 106; philosophic w., 106; and prudence, 107, 470; and

science and intellect, 103; and selection of terms, 104; and self-correcting process, 105; w. speculative, 107; w. of theologian, 105–106; theology and w., 103–108; w. ultimate, 103, 104; understanding, knowledge, and w. (Vatican I), 31, 172, 183

Wittgenstein, L., 577

Wolf, F., 460

Word: as completion of consciousness, 541; in New Testament, 344; preaching, teaching, hearing the w. and thematization, 344

Word of God: as datum, 391; as mediating theology, 150, 298, 361; as true, 176, 391, 596

Wordsworth, W., 44, 311, 522

World(s): common sense, theory, interiority as w., 4, 9, 48, 49–52, 76, 77, 82, 85, 136, 138, 252, 300, 315, 362, 366, 480, 539–40, 638; w. as concrete, 61; w. constituted by meaning, 298, 384, 391; development of w., 59–60; differentiation of w., 59–60; differentiation of w. and differentiation of subject, 60; as differentiations of basic structure, 480; as fields of possible objects, 60; general points on w., 60–64; w. of immediacy and w. mediated by image, symbol, meaning, 8–9, 384, 391, 502–504, 562–63, 564; integration of w., *see* Integration of worlds; and limits, 56–59; w. as mobile, 61, 66

Xiberta, B.F.M., 274 & n. 22, 385

Yang, C.N., 157 n. 2